T0180533

GRADUATE TEXTS IN COMPUTER SCIENCE

Editors
David Gries
Fred B. Schneider

ꞮꞮpringer

w York
rlin
idelberg
rcelona
dapest
ng Kong
idon
lan
is
ita Clara
gapore
kyo

GRADUATE TEXTS IN COMPUTER SCIENCE

Ralph-Johan Back   Joakim von Wright

REFINEMENT CALCULUS

A Systematic Introduction

With 27 Illustrations

Springer

Ralph-Johan Back
Joakim von Wright
Department of Computer Science
Åbo Akademi University
Lemminkäisenkatu 14
FIN-20520 Turku, Finland
backrj@abo.fi
jwright@abo.fi

Series Editors
David Gries
Fred B. Schneider

Department of Computer Science
Cornell University
Upson Hall
Ithaca, NY 14853-7501, USA

Library of Congress Cataloging-in-Publication Data
Back, Ralph-Johan.
    Refinement calculus : a systematic introduction / Ralph-Johan
Back, Joakim von Wright.
        p.   cm. — (Graduate texts in computer science)
    ISBN 0-387-98417-8 (alk. paper)
    1. Electronic digital computers—Programming.   2. Calculus.
3. Computer logic.   I. Wright, J. von (Joakim), 1955–
II. Title.   III. Series: Graduate texts in computer science
(Springer-Verlag New York Inc.)
QA76.6.B28   1998
005.1´4—dc21   97-47336

Printed on acid-free paper.

Production managed by Lesley Poliner; manufacturing supervised by Thomas King.
Photocomposed copy prepared from the authors' LATₑX files.
Printed and bound by Hamilton Printing Co., Rensselaer, NY.
Printed in the United States of America.

9 8 7 6 5 4 3 2 1

ISBN 0-387-98417-8 Springer-Verlag New York Berlin Heidelberg   SPIN 10658041

Preface

The refinement calculus is a framework for reasoning about correctness and refinement of programs. The primary application of the calculus is the derivation of traditional imperative programs, where programs are constructed by stepwise refinement. Each refinement step is required to preserve the correctness of the previous version of the program. We study the basic rules for this kind of program derivation in detail, looking at specification statements and their implementation, how to construct recursive and iterative program statements, and how to use procedures in program derivations. The refinement calculus is an extension of Dijkstra's weakest precondition calculus, where program statements are modeled as predicate transformers.

We extend the traditional interpretation of predicate transformers as executable program statements to that of contracts that regulate the behavior of competing agents and to games that are played between two players. The traditional interpretation of predicate transformers as programs falls out of this as a special case, where one of the two players has only a very rudimentary role to play. Our extension yields a number of new potential applications for the refinement calculus theory, like reasoning about correctness of interactive program statements and analyzing two-person games and their winning strategies.

Program refinement involves reasoning in many domains. We have to reason about properties of functions, predicates and sets, relations, and program statements described as predicate transformers. These different entities are in fact mathematically all very similar, and they form the refinement calculus hierarchy. In this book we examine the ways in which these different domains are related to each other and how one can move between them. Lattice theory forms a unifying conceptual basis that captures similarities between the domains, while higher-order logic serves a a common logic that we can use to reason about entities in these domains.

We present a new foundation for the refinement calculus based on lattice theory an higher-order logic, together with a simple theory of program variables. These topic are covered in the first part of the book. Higher-order logic is described in a new wa that is strongly influenced by lattice theory. This part also introduces notions neede for imperative programs, program variables, expressions, assignment statement blocks with local variables, and procedures. The second part of the book describe the predicate transformer approach to programming logic and program semantic as well as the notion of program refinement. We also study the operational semantic of contracts, games, and program statements, and show how it is related to th predicate transformer interpretation of these. The third part of the book shows ho to handle recursion and iteration in the refinement calculus and also describes ho to use the calculus to reason about games. It also presents case studies of progra refinement. The last part of the book studies more specific issues related to progra refinement, such as implementing specification statements, making refinements i context, and transforming iterative structures in a correctness-preserving way.

The refinement calculus has been a topic of investigation for nearly twenty yea now, and a great number of papers have been published in this area. However, a sy tematic introduction to the mathematical and logical basis for program refineme has been missing. The information required to study this field is scattered throug many journal and conference papers, and has never been presented as a cohere whole. This book addresses this problem by giving a systematic introduction t the field. The book partly summarizes work that has been published earlier, b ourselves and by other authors, but most of the material is new and has not bee published before.

The emphasis in this book is on the mathematical and logical basis of program r finement. Although we do give examples and case studies of program constructio this is not primarily a hands-on book on how to construct programs in practic For reasons of space we have been forced to omit a great deal of material that w wanted to include in the book. In particular, we decided not to include the importa topics of data refinement and parallel and reactive system refinement here (thoug a simple approach to data refinement is described in Chapter 17). We plan to tre these topics in a comprehensive way in a separate book.

The book is intended for graduate students and advanced undergraduates inte ested in the mathematics and logic needed for program derivations, as well as fc programmers and researchers interested in a deeper understanding of these issue The book provides new insight into the methods for program derivations, as we as new understanding of program semantics and of the logic for reasoning abo programs.

The book should be easy to use in teaching. We have tried to explain things quite carefully, and proofs are often given in reasonable detail. We have also included quite a number of examples and exercises. A previous understanding of logic and programming methodology is helpful but not necessary in order to understand the material in the book. The first, second, and third parts of the book can be given as successive courses, with suitable material added from the fourth part.

Acknowledgments

This book was inspired and influenced by a number of other researchers in the field. In particular, Edsger Dijkstra's work on predicate transformers and his systematic approach to constructing programs has been an important source of inspiration, as has the work of Tony Hoare on the logic of programming. Jaco de Bakker's work on programming language semantics has formed another strong influence, in particular the stringent way in which he has approached the topic. We very much appreciate Carroll Morgan's work on the refinement calculus, which has provided many ideas and a friendly competitive environment that has been much appreciated. Finally, Michael Gordon's work has shown the usefulness of higher-order logic as a framework for reasoning about both hardware and software and about formal theories in general.

Our close coworkers Reino Kurki-Suonio and Kaisa Sere deserve a special thanks for many years of fruitful and inspiring collaboration in the area of programming methodology and the logic for systematic program construction.

We are indebted to many other colleagues for numerous enlightening discussions on the topics treated in this book. Our thanks go to Sten Agerholm, Roland Backhouse, Eike Best, Michael Butler, Rutger Dijkstra, Wim Feijen, Nissim Francez, Marcel van de Goot, David Gries, Jim Grundy, John Harrison, Ian Hayes, Eric Hehner, Wim Hesselink, Peter Hofstee, Cliff Jones, Bengt Jonsson, He Jifeng, Joost Kok, Rustan Leino, Alain Martin, Tom Melham, David Nauman, Greg Nelson, John Tucker, Amir Pnueli, Xu Qiwen, Emil Sekerinski, Jan van de Snepscheut, Mark Staples, Reino Vainio, and Wolfgang Weck.

We also want to thank our students, who have provided an inspiring environment for discussing these topics and have read and given detailed comments on many previous versions of the book: Thomas Beijar, Martin Büchi, Eric Hedman, Philipp Heuberger, Linas Laibinis, Thomas Långbacka, Leonid Mikhajlov, Anna Mikhajlova, Lasse Nielsen, Rimvydas Rukšėnas, Mauno Rönkkö, and Marina Waldén.

The Department of Computer Science at Abo Akademi University and Turku Centre for Computer Science (TUCS) have provided a most stimulating working environment. The sabbaticals at the California Institute of Technology, Cambridge

University, and Utrecht University have also been very fruitful and are hereby gratefully acknowledged. The generous support of the Academy of Finland and the Ministry of Education of Finland for the research reported in this book is also much appreciated.

Last but not least, we want to thank our (sometimes more, sometimes less) patient wives and children, who have been long waiting for this book to be finished: Barbro Back, Pia, Rasmus, and Ida Back, Birgitta Snickars von Wright, Heidi, Minea, Elin and Julius von Wright.

Ralph-Johan Back
Joakim von Wright

Department of Computer Science
Åbo Akademi University
June 30, 1997

Contents

ntroduction

The *refinement calculus* is a logical framework for reasoning about programs. It is concerned with two main questions: is a program *correct* with respect to a given specification, and how can we improve, or *refine*, a program while preserving its correctness. Both programs and specifications can be seen as special cases of a more general notion, that of a *contract* between independent agents. Refinement is defined as a relation between contracts and turns out to be a lattice ordering. Correctness is a special case of refinement where a specification is refined by a program.

The refinement calculus is formalized within higher-order logic. This allows us to prove the correctness of programs and to calculate program refinements in a rigorous, mathematically precise manner. Lattice theory and higher-order logic together form the mathematical basis for the calculus.

We start with an informal introduction to some of the central concepts in the calculus: the notion of a contract as a generalization of programs and specifications, how program correctness is generalized to contracts, and how refinement of contracts is defined. We also show how these general concepts are related to more traditional notions used in programming and program correctness. We will elaborate on these issues in the rest of the book, along the way introducing and studying many other notions that we need for program correctness and refinement.

1 Contracts

Let us start from the most general notion used, that of a contract. Consider a collection of *agents*, where each agent has the capability to change the world in various ways through its *actions* and can *choose* between different courses of action. The behavior of agents and their cooperation is regulated by *contracts*.

Before going into this in more detail, a short remark on the notation that we use in order. We denote function application with an infix dot, writing $f.x$, rather than the more traditional $f(x)$. We write $A \to B$ for the set of all functions $f : A \to B$. Functions can be of *higher order*, so that the argument or value of a function can be a function itself. For instance, if f is a function in $A \to (B \to C)$ and a an element of A, then $f.a$ is a function in $B \to C$. If b is an element of B, then $(f.a).b$ is an element of C. Function application associates to the left, so $(f.a).b$ can be written as just $f.a.b$.

We will use standard set-theoretic and logical notation in our informal discussion in this and the next chapter. In particular, we write $\mathsf{T}, \mathsf{F}, \neg b, b \wedge c, b \vee c, b \Rightarrow c, b \equiv$ for, respectively, truth, falsity, negation, conjunction, disjunction, implication, and equivalence in logical formulas. We write universal quantification as $(\forall x \cdot b)$ and existential quantification as $(\exists x \cdot b)$. These notions will all be given precise definitions when higher-order logic is introduced, but for now, we rely on an informal understanding.

States and State Changes

We assume that the world is described as a *state* σ. The *state space* Σ is the set of all possible states (or worlds). An agent changes the state by applying a function to the present state, yielding a new state $f.\sigma$. An agent can have different functions for changing the world. We will write $\langle f \rangle$ for the action that changes the state from σ to $f.\sigma$, and refer to this as an *update action*.

A special case is the identity function $\mathsf{id} : \Sigma \to \Sigma$, which does not change the world at all, $\mathsf{id}.\sigma = \sigma$. We write $\mathsf{skip} = \langle \mathsf{id} \rangle$ for the action that applies the identity function to the present state.

We think of the state as having a number of *attributes* $x_1, \ldots, x_n$, each of which can be observed and changed independently of the others. Such attributes are usually called *program variables*. The *value* of an attribute x, $\mathsf{val}.x$, is a function that depends on the state: $\mathsf{val}.x.\sigma$ gives the value of attribute x in state σ. It models an observation of some property of the state. For each attribute x_i, there is also an *update function* $\mathsf{set}.x_i$ that we use to change the state so that attribute x_i gets a specific value: $\mathsf{set}.x.a.\sigma$ is the new state that we get by setting the value of attribute x to a without changing the values of any of the other attributes.

State changes are conveniently expressed as *assignments*. For instance, $x_i := x_i + x_j$ describes a function from state σ to the state $\mathsf{set}.x_i.a.\sigma$, where a = $\mathsf{val}.x_i.\sigma + \mathsf{val}.x_j.\sigma$ is the value of *expression* $x_i + x_j$ in state σ. The action that carries out this assignment is then $\langle x_i := x_i + x_j \rangle$. We drop the angular brackets around assignments in the examples below, as it will always be clear that an assignment action rather than just the assignment function is intended.

Contracts

A *contract* regulates the behavior of an agent. The contract can stipulate that the agent must carry out actions in a specific order. This is written as a *sequential action* $S_1 ; S_2 ; \ldots ; S_m$, where $S_1, \ldots, S_m$ are the individual actions that the agent has to carry out. For any initial state $\sigma = \sigma_0$, the agent has to produce a succession of states $\sigma_1, \ldots, \sigma_m$, where σ_i is the result of performing action S_i in state σ_{i-1}.

A contract may also require the agent to choose one of the alternative actions $S_1, \ldots, S_m$. The choice is written as the *alternative action* $S_1 \sqcup \cdots \sqcup S_m$. The choice between these alternatives is free; i.e., any alternative may be carried out by the agent, but the agent must choose one of the given alternatives.

These two constructs, together with the basic actions described above, give us a very simple language for contracts:

$$S \quad ::= \quad \langle f \rangle \mid S_1 ; S_2 \mid S_1 \sqcup S_2 .$$

Each *statement* in this language describes a contract for an agent. We have restricted ourselves to binary composition only. Arbitrary composition can be expressed in terms of binary composition, as sequential and alternative composition are both assumed to be associative: $S_1 ; (S_2 ; S_3) = (S_1 ; S_2) ; S_3$, and $S_1 \sqcup (S_2 \sqcup S_3) = (S_1 \sqcup S_2) \sqcup S_3$. We assume that semicolon binds more strongly than choice.

We can observe certain other properties that this language of contracts is expected to satisfy. For instance, we expect that

$$\text{skip} ; S = S \quad \text{and} \quad S = S ; \text{skip} ,$$

because continuing by not changing the world should not affect the meaning of a contract. The order in which the alternatives are presented should also not be important; only the *set* of alternatives matters, so that

$$S \sqcup S = S \quad \text{and} \quad S_1 \sqcup S_2 = S_2 \sqcup S_1 .$$

The following is an example of a contract statement:

$$x := 1 ; (x := x + y \sqcup \text{skip}) ; y := x - 1 .$$

This stipulates that the agent first has to set the attribute x to 1, then it must choose between either changing the state by assigning the value of $x + y$ to the attribute x or not changing the state, and finally it has to set attribute y to the value of $x - 1$. This assumes that the state space has the two attributes x and y (it may have more attributes, but the values of other attributes are not changed). The agent is said to *satisfy* (or *follow*) the contract if it behaves in accordance with it.

Cooperation Between Agents

Consider next two agents, a and b, that work on the same state independently
each other. Each agent has a will of its own and makes decisions for itself. If the
two agents want to cooperate, they need a contract that stipulates their respect
obligations. A typical situation is that one of the agents, say a, acts as a *client*, a
the other, b, as a *server*. Assume that agent a follows contract S,

$$S \ = \ x := 0 \, ; (T \, ; x := x + 1 \sqcup \text{skip}) \, ,$$

where T is the contract for agent b,

$$T \ = \ (y := 1 \sqcup y := 2) \, ; x := x + y \, .$$

The occurrence of T in the contract statement S signals that a asks agent b to ca
out its contract T.

We can combine the two statements S and T into a single contract statement t
regulates the behavior of both agents. Because this combined contract is carr
out by two different agents, we need to explicitly indicate for each choice whet
it is made by a or by b. The combined contract is described by

$$S \ = \ x := 0 \, ; ((y := 1 \sqcup_b y := 2) \, ; x := x + y \, ; x := x + 1 \sqcup_a \text{skip}) \, .$$

Thus, the combined contract is just the result of substituting the contract of T
the call on T in the contract of S and explicitly indicating for each choice wh
agent is responsible for it. For basic actions like skip and assignments, it does
matter which agent carries out the state change, because the effect will be the sa

Assertions

An *assertion* is a requirement that the agent must satisfy in a given state. We expr
an assertion as $\{g\}$, where g is a condition on the state. For instance, $\{x + y =$
expresses that the sum of (the values of attributes) x and y in the state must
zero. An example of a contract with an assertion is the following:

$$S \ = \ x := 1 \, ; (x := x + y \, ; \{x > 1\} \sqcup x := x + z) \, ; y := x - 1 \, .$$

Here we require that $x > 1$ must hold after the assignment in the first alternat
has been completed. If this assertion does in fact hold there when the agent carr
out the contract, then the state is unchanged, and the agent simply carries on w
the rest of the contract. If, however, the assertion does not hold, then the agent
breached the contract.

Analyzing this example, we can see that the agent will breach the contract if y
initially and the agent chooses the first alternative. The agent does not, howev
need to breach the contract, because he can choose the second alternative, wh
does not have any assertions, and then successfully complete the contract.

The assertion {true} is always satisfied, so adding this assertion anywhere in a contract has no effect; i.e., {true} = skip. The assertion {false} is an *impossible assertion*. It is never satisfied and will always result in the agent breaching the contract.

When looking at the combined contract of two agents, a and b, it is again very important to explicitly indicate which party breaches the contract. Thus, if we have

$$
\begin{aligned}
S &= x := 0 ; (T ; x := x + 1 \sqcup \{\text{false}\}) ; \{y = x\} , \\
T &= (y := 1 \sqcup y := 2 ; \{\text{false}\}) ,
\end{aligned}
$$

then the combined contract is

$$
\begin{aligned}
S = \ & x := 0; \\
& ((y := 1 \sqcup_b y := 2 ; \{\text{false}\}_b) ; x := x + 1 \sqcup_a \{\text{false}\}_a); \\
& \{y = x\}_a .
\end{aligned}
$$

Here the index indicates which agent has the obligation to satisfy the assertion.

Assumptions

Besides assertions, there is another notion that is important when making a contract between two parties. This is the *assumptions* that each of the parties makes, as their condition for engaging in the contract. We will express an assumption as $[g]$, where g is a condition on the state. Consider as an example the contract

$$
[x \geq 0] ; (x := x + y \sqcup x := x + z) ; y := x - 1 .
$$

Here the assumption of the agent carrying out this contract is that $x \geq 0$ holds initially. If this is not the case, then the agent is released of any obligation to carry out his part of the contract.

The assumption [true] is always satisfied, so we have that [true] = skip. The assumption [false] is never satisfied and will always release the agent from his obligation to continue with the contract. It is thus an *impossible assumption*.

As with assertions, we permit assumptions to occur at any place in the contract statement. For instance, consider the statement

$$
x := 1 ; (x := x + y ; [x > 1] \sqcup x := x + z) ; y := x - 1 .
$$

Here the agent assumes that $x > 1$ after carrying out the assignment of the first choice. If this is not the case, the agent is released from its contract. Again, we notice that the agent does not have to choose the first alternative; he can choose the second alternative and carry out the contract to the end.

Finally consider combining the contracts for two agents. As with assertions and choice, we also have to indicate explicitly for each assumption whether it is made by agent a or agent b.

1.2   Using Contracts

We use agents to achieve something, i.e., to establish some new, more desirab[le]
state. We describe the desired states by giving the condition that they have [to]
satisfy (the *postcondition*). The possibility of an agent achieving such a desir[ed]
state depends on the means it has available, i.e., on the functions that it can u[se]
to change the state. If the agent cannot achieve the required state for itself, then [it]
needs to involve other agents.

Taking Sides

We will assume that the contract is always made between an agent whose goals [we]
want to further (*our agent*) and another agent whose goals are not important to u[s.]
We denote our agent's choices by ⊔, and the choice of the other agent by ⊔°. In [a]
similar way, we distinguish between $\{g\}$ and $\{g\}°$ and between $[g]$ and $[g]°$. Th[is]
avoids the introduction of arbitrary names for agents when analyzing a contract[.]

We extend the language for describing contracts to include combined contracts wi[th]
two different agents interacting. The syntax is then as follows, with assumptio[ns]
and assertions added as new contract statements:

$$S \quad ::= \quad \langle f \rangle \mid \{g\} \mid \{g\}° \mid [g] \mid [g]° \mid S_1 \; ; \; S_2 \mid S_1 \sqcup S_2 \mid S_1 \sqcup° S_2 \; .$$

Combining the two contracts

$$S \;=\; x := 0 \, ; (T \, ; x := x + 1 \, ; \{x = y\} \sqcup \text{skip}) \, ,$$
$$T \;=\; [x \geq 0] \, ; (y := 1 \sqcup y := 2) \, ,$$

where contract S is for our agent and contract T is for the other agent, results [in]
the single contract

$$S \;=\; x := 0 \, ; ([x \geq 0]° \, ; (y := 1 \sqcup° y := 2) \, ; x := x + 1 \, ; \{x = y\} \sqcup \text{skip})$$

This is the contract statement from our agent's point of view.

Given a contract for a single agent and a desired postcondition, we can ask wheth[er]
the contract can establish the postcondition. This will again depend on the *initi[al]
state*, the state in which we start to carry out the contract. For instance, consid[er]
the contract

$$S \;=\; x := x + 1 \sqcup x := x + 2 \; .$$

The agent can establish postcondition $x = 2$ if $x = 1$ or $x = 0$ initially. Whe[n]
$x = 1$ initially, the agent should choose the first alternative; but when $x = 0$, t[he]
agent should choose the second alternative.

The agent can also establish postcondition $x = 1$ with this contract if the initi[al]
state satisfies $x = -1$ or $x = 0$. From initial state $x = 0$, the agent can th[us]
establish either $x = 1$ or $x = 2$, by suitable choice of alternatives.

The postcondition need not determine a unique final state. For instance, the agent may want to achieve either $x = 1$ or $x = 2$. The agent can establish this condition in an initial state where $x = -1$ or $x = 0$ or $x = 1$.

Satisfying a Contract

We need to be more precise about what it means for an agent to achieve some condition by satisfying a contract. Obviously, breaching the contract does not satisfy the contract. On the other hand, an agent cannot be required to follow a contract if the assumptions that it makes are violated. Violating the assumptions releases the agent from the contract. As the fault is not with the agent, it is considered to have satisfied the contract in this case.

We can illustrate these points by considering first the statement S that consists of a single assertion action, say $S = \{x \geq 0\}$. An agent can establish a condition q with this action only if $x \geq 0$ holds (so that the contract is not broken) and if in addition, q already holds (as the state is not changed if $x \geq 0$ holds).

Consider next $S = [x \geq 0]$. If $x \geq 0$ holds initially, then the effect of the action is just a skip. In this case q will be established provided that q already was true of the state before the action. If $x \geq 0$ does not hold, then the assumptions that the agent makes are violated, so the agent is considered to have satisfied its contract to establish q.

We will say that the agent *can satisfy contract S to establish postcondition q in initial state* σ if the agent either can achieve a final state that satisfies q without breaching the contract or is released from the contract by an assumption that is violated. Let us denote this by $\sigma \ \{\!| \ S \ |\!\} \ q$.

Two Agents

Consider now the situation where the agent is not alone in carrying out its contract but cooperates with another agent. Whether the contract can be used to establish a certain postcondition will then also depend on what the other agent does. In analyzing whether our agent can achieve a certain condition with S, we will assume that the other agent does not breach S with its actions. We will say that $\sigma \ \{\!| \ S \ |\!\} \ q$ holds if

(i) assuming that the assumptions that our agent makes are satisfied, and

(ii) assuming that the other agent does not breach the contract,

then from state σ, our agent can always establish a final state that satisfies condition q without itself breaching the contract. When there is another agent involved, our agent has to be able to satisfy the contract no matter how the other agent makes its choices. This means that the agent has to take into account all possible alternatives

that the other agent has and be able to establish the desired condition no ma
which alternatives are chosen by the other agent.

The above definition means that our agent satisfies the contract (for any condi
q) if the other agent breaches its contract. This relieves our agent from any fur
duties to follow the contract. It is considered to have satisfied the contract, as
fault was not with it.

In particular, this means that a total breach of contract by the other agent, {fals
has the same effect as if our agent had made the impossible assumption [fa
Thus {false}° = [false] when we consider only what it means to satisfy a contr
In both cases, our agent is considered to have satisfied the contract, no matter v
condition was to be established.

Many Agents

We have assumed above that there are at most two agents, our agent and the o
agent. Let us now complete the picture by considering the situation where there
more agents. Consider first the situation where we have three agents, a, b, an
Assume that a is our agent. Then it does not matter from our point of view whe
the two other agents b and c are really separate agents, each with its own free
or whether there is a single will that determines the choices made by both b an
Therefore, in analyzing what can be achieved with a contract, we will denote
by $\sqcup$, and $\sqcup_b$ and $\sqcup_c$ both by $\sqcup°$.

Similarly, if our agent a cooperates with agent b to achieve some common ge
but agent c has different goals, then we would use $\sqcup$ for $\sqcup_a$ and $\sqcup_b$, while we we
use $\sqcup°$ for $\sqcup_c$.

In general, situations with more than two agents can always be reduced to the
where we only need to consider two agents: our agent and its allies, considere
a single agent, and all the other agents together, also considered as a single ag

Contracts as Games

Our main concern with a contract is to determine whether we (our agent) can
the contract to achieve our stated goals. In this sense, our agent has to make
right choices in its cooperation with other agents, who are pursuing different g
that need not be in agreement with our goals. The other agents need not be hosti
our goals; they just have different priorities and are free to make their own cho
However, because we cannot influence the other agents in any way, we have t
prepared for the worst and consider the other agent as hostile if we want to ach
certainty of reaching a specific condition.

As far as analyzing what can be achieved with a contract, it is therefore justifi
consider the agents involved as the two opponents in a game. The actions tha

agents can take are the moves in the game. The rules of the game are expressed by the contract S: it states what moves the two opponents can take and when. Given an initial state σ, the goal for our agent is to establish a given postcondition q. The other agent tries to prevent our agent from establishing this postcondition. We will make this a little bit more dramatic and call our agent the *angel* and the other agent the *demon*. In the game, we talk about an *angelic choice* when the choice is made by our agent, and about *demonic choice* when the choice is made by the demon.

A player in a game is said to have a *winning strategy* in a certain initial state if the player can win (by doing the right moves) no matter what the opponent does. Satisfaction of a contract now corresponds to the existence of a winning strategy: $\sigma \,\{\!| \, S \,|\!\} \, q$ holds if and only if the angel has a winning strategy to reach the goal q when playing with the rules S, when the initial state of the game is σ.

If our agent is forced to breach an assertion, then it loses the game directly. If the other agent is forced to breach an assertion, it loses the game, and our agent then wins. In this way, the angel can win the game either by reaching a final state that satisfies the stated condition, by forcing the demon to breach an assertion, or by choosing an alternative where one of its own assumptions is false. In all other cases, the angel loses the game.

3   Computers as Agents

We have not yet said what agents are. They could be humans, they could be computers, or they could be processes in a computer system. They could be programmers building software systems. A central feature of these agents is that they can make free choices. This means that the behavior of agents is *nondeterministic*, in the sense that it cannot be predicted with certainty.

Explaining free will for humans is a well-known problem in philosophy. For computers, the fact that we need to postulate a free will might be even more confusing, but actually, it is not. Basically, nondeterminism in computer systems comes from *information hiding*. Certain information that determines the behavior of a computing agent is not revealed to other agents interacting with this agent. Therefore, behavior that is actually deterministic will appear nondeterministic to an outside agent because it cannot see the reasons for the choices made. It will appear as if the agent is making arbitrary choices, when in fact these choices may be completely determined by some hidden information. Typically there are some internal, hidden, state components that are not visible to outside viewers. A choice might also depend on some natural random phenomena, or it may depend on time-critical features that are unknown to the other agents.

Information hiding is the central principle in designing a large computer or software system as a collection of cooperating agents. The purpose is to restrict information

disclosed about an agent's behavior to a minimum, in order to keep as many option
open as possible for later changes and extensions of the behavior.

A common situation is that the user of a computer system is seen as our agen
(the angel), the other agent (the demon) being the computer system itself. Then
contract corresponds to the *protocol* by which the user interacts with the compute
The protocol lays down the alternatives that the user has available in his interactic
with the computing agent (menu choices, executable commands, etc). In a te
editor, these alternatives could include opening a new file for editing, typing som
text into the editor, and saving the file. There may also be certain restrictions th
have to be satisfied when using the operations of the system, such as that tl
user can only open a file that is registered in the file system. These restrictio
are assumptions from the point of view of the system. The response to violatir
restrictions can vary, from a polite warning or error message to a system crash «
the system being locked in an infinite loop. The restrictions are thus assertions f
the user, who must satisfy them if he wants to achieve his goals.

Another common situation is that both agents are components of a computer sy
tem. For example, one component/agent could be a *client*, and the other could be
server. The client issues requests to the server, who carries out the requests accor
ing to the specification that has been given for the possible requests. The serv
procedures that are invoked by the client's requests have conditions associated wi
them that restrict the input parameters and the global system state. These cond
tions are assertions for the client, who has to satisfy them when calling a serv
procedure. The same conditions are assumptions for the server, who may assum
that they hold when starting to comply with a request. The server has to achie
some final state (possibly returning some output values) when the assumptions a
satisfied. This constitutes the contract between the client and the server.

There is an interesting form of duality between the client and the server. Whe
we are programming the client, then any internal choices that the server can mak
increase our uncertainty about what can happen when a request is invoked. "
achieve some desired effect, we have to guard ourselves against any possible choi
that the server can make. Thus, the client is the angel and the server is the demo
On the other hand, when we are programming the server, then any choices th
the client makes, e.g., in choosing values for the input parameters, increases o
uncertainty about the initial state in which the request is made, and all possibiliti
need to be considered when complying with the request. Now the server is tl
angel and the client is the demon.

1.4   Algebra of Contracts

A contract statement regulates the means for achieving something. Since we a
only interested in our own agent, we see the contract as a tool for our agent

achieve some goals. If we compare two contract statements for our agent, say S and S', then we can say that the latter is at least as good as the former if any condition that we can establish with the first contract can also be established with the second contract. We then say that S is *refined by* S' and denote this by $S \sqsubseteq S'$. More formally, we can define $S \sqsubseteq S'$ to hold if

$$\sigma \{| S |\} q \implies \sigma \{| S' |\} q, \quad \text{for any } \sigma \text{ and } q.$$

Evidently $S \sqsubseteq S$ always holds, so refinement is *reflexive*. It is also easy to see that refinement is *transitive*: $S \sqsubseteq S'$ and $S' \sqsubseteq S''$ implies $S \sqsubseteq S''$. We will also postulate that two contracts are equal if each refines the other. This means that the two contracts are equally good for achieving any conditions that our agent might need to establish. This gives us *antisymmetry* for contracts: $S \sqsubseteq S'$ and $S' \sqsubseteq S$ implies $S = S'$. In terms of satisfying contracts, we then have that $S = S'$ if and only if

$$\sigma \{| S |\} q \equiv \sigma \{| S' |\} q, \quad \text{for any } \sigma \text{ and } q.$$

These properties imply that contracts form a *partial ordering*.

It is evident that $\{\text{false}\} \sqsubseteq S$ for any contract S, because we cannot satisfy the contract $\{\text{false}\}$ in any initial state, for any final condition. Hence, any contract is an improvement over this worst of all contracts. Also, it should be clear that $S \sqsubseteq [\text{false}]$: the assumptions of contract $[\text{false}]$ are never satisfied, so this contract is satisfied in any initial state for any final condition. Hence, this is the best of all contracts. This means that the partial order of contracts is in fact *bounded*: it has a *least* and a *greatest element*.

Consider next the contract $S = x := x + 1 \sqcup x := x + 2$. Then $\sigma \{| S |\} q$ holds if our agent, by choosing either $x := x + 1$ or $x := x + 2$, can establish q in initial state σ. Thus, we have that

$$\sigma \{| x := x + 1 \sqcup x := x + 2 |\} q \quad \text{iff}$$
$$\sigma \{| x := x + 1 |\} q \quad \text{or} \quad \sigma \{| x := x + 2 |\} q \, .$$

For instance, we have that

$$x = 0 \{| x := x + 1 \sqcup x := x + 2 |\} x = 1$$

holds, because

$$x = 0 \{| x := x + 1 |\} x = 1 \, .$$

(Here, $x = 0$ stands for the predicate that holds in exactly those states in which the value of x is 0, and similarly for $x = 1$.)

Consider then the contract $x := x + 1 \sqcup^{\circ} x := x + 2$. In this case, the other agent is making the choice. Hence, our agent can be certain to satisfy the contract to achieve a certain final condition q (in initial state σ) if and only if he can satisfy both $x := x + 1$ and $x := x + 2$ to achieve the required final conditions. In other words, we have that

$$\sigma \{\!|\, x := x + 1 \sqcup^\circ x := x + 2 \,|\!\} q \quad \text{iff}$$
$$\sigma \{\!|\, x := x + 1 \,|\!\} q \quad \text{and} \quad \sigma \{\!|\, x := x + 2 \,|\!\} q \ .$$

This reflects the fact that our agent cannot influence the choice of the other agent and hence must be able to satisfy whichever contract the other agent chooses.

The contracts will in fact form a *lattice* with the refinement ordering, where $\sqcup$ the *join* in the lattice and $\sqcup^\circ$ is the *meet*. Following standard lattice notation, we will, therefore, in what follows write $\sqcap$ for $\sqcup^\circ$. The impossible assertion {false} the bottom of the lattice of contracts, and the impossible assumption [false] is the top of the lattice.

We will generalize the notion of a contract to permit choices over an arbitrary set of contracts, $\sqcup\{S_i \mid i \in I\}$ and $\sqcap\{S_i \mid i \in I\}$. The set of contracts may be empty, it may be infinite. With this extension, the contracts will in fact form a *complete lattice*.

The sequential composition operation is also important here. It is easy to see that contracts form a *monoid* with respect to the composition operation, with skip the identity element. Contracts as we have described them above thus have a very simple algebraic structure; i.e., they form a complete lattice with respect to $\sqsubseteq$, and they form a monoid with respect to sequential composition.

A further generalization of contracts will permit the initial and final state spaces to be different. Thus, the contract may be initiated in a state σ in Σ, but we permit operations in the contract that change the state space, so that the final state may be in another state space Γ. The simple monoid structure of contracts is then not sufficient, and we need to consider the more general notion of a *category* contracts. The different state spaces will form the *objects* of the category, while the *morphisms* of the category are the contracts. The skip action will be the identity morphism, and composition of morphisms will be just the ordinary sequential composition of actions.

We will explain these algebraic concepts in more detail in the next chapter. Here we have only indicated the relevance of the lattice and category-theoretic concepts in order to motivate the reader to study and appreciate these notions.

1.5 Programming Constructs

We have above given a rather restricted set of statements for describing contracts. As we argued above, contracts can be used to describe the way in which program components interact with each other. Hence, we should be able to describe traditional programming constructs, such as conditional statements, iteration, and recursion, as contracts. This is what they essentially are: statements that oblige the computer system to carry out specific sequences of actions.

Conditional Contracts

Consider first a conditional statement such as

if $x \geq 0$ then $x := x + 1$ else $x := x + 2$ fi .

We can consider this a *conditional contract*, defined in terms of previous constructs, as follows:

if $x \geq 0$ then $x := x + 1$ else $x := x + 2$ fi $=$

$\{x \geq 0\} ; x := x + 1 \sqcup \{x < 0\} ; x := x + 2$.

Thus, the agent can choose between two alternatives. The agent will, however, always choose only one of these, the one for which the *guard* $x \geq 0$ is true, because choosing the alternative where the guard is false would breach the contract. Hence the agent does not have a real choice if he wants to satisfy the contract.

We could also define the conditional in terms of choices made by the other agent as follows:

if $x \geq 0$ then $x := x + 1$ else $x := x + 2$ fi $=$

$[x \geq 0] ; x := x + 1 \sqcap [x < 0] ; x := x + 2$.

These two definitions are equivalent. The choice made by the other agent is not controllable by our agent, so to achieve some desired condition, our agent has to be prepared for both alternatives, to carry out $x := x + 1$ assuming $x \geq 0$, and to carry out $x := x + 2$ assuming $x < 0$. If the other agent is to carry out the contract without violating our agent's assumptions, it has to choose the first alternative when $x \geq 0$ and the second alternative when $x \geq 0$ is false.

The *guarded conditional statement* introduced by Dijkstra [53], of the form if $g_1 \rightarrow S_1 [] \cdots [] g_m \rightarrow S_m$ fi, is a generalization of the traditional conditional statement. In this case, the guards $g_1, \ldots, g_m$ need not be mutually exclusive (as they are in the traditional conditional statement). The choice between executing S_i or S_j is done nondeterministically when the two guards g_i and g_j both hold. Dijkstra's interpretation of the nondeterminism is that it should not be controllable. In our framework, this means that the choice is demonic. This gives the following definition:

if $g_1 \rightarrow S_1 [] \cdots [] g_m \rightarrow S_m$ fi $=$

$\{g_1 \vee \cdots \vee g_m\} ; ([g_1] ; S_1 \sqcap \cdots \sqcap [g_m] ; S_m)$.

The first assert statement tests that at least one of the guards is true in the state. If not, then the result is an abortion of the execution, which amounts to our agent breaching the contract. If at least one of the guards holds in the state, then the other agent will choose which alternative to continue with. To avoid breaching the contract, the other agent chooses an alternative for which the guard is true.

If we take the first definition of the traditional conditional statement as the starting point, we get another generalized conditional statement, which has a very different interpretation. Here the nondeterminism is controllable by our agent; the choice angelic:

$$\text{if } g_1 :: S_1 \; [] \; \cdots \; [] \; g_m :: S_m \text{ fi } = \{g_1\}; S_1 \sqcup \cdots \sqcup \{g_m\}; S_m \; .$$

This statement will again cause a breach of the contract if none of the assertions holds in the state. If at least one of the assertions holds, then our agent gets to choose the alternative to continue with. This construct can be interpreted as context-sensitive *menu choice*: the alternatives from which our agent chooses are items on a menu, and the assertions determine which of these items are enabled in a particular state.

Recursive Contracts

We can make the language of contracts even more interesting from a programming point of view by permitting recursive statements of contracts. This can be defined by extending the syntax as follows:

$$S \; ::= \; \cdots \; | \; X \; | \; (\mu X \cdot S_1) \; .$$

Here X is a variable that ranges over contract statements, while $(\mu X \cdot S_1)$ is the contract statement S_1, where each occurrence of X in S_1 is interpreted as a recursive invocation of the contract S_1.

It is more customary to define a recursive contract by an equation of the form

$$X \; = \; S_1 \; ,$$

where S_1 usually contains some occurrences of X. This defines the recursive contract $(\mu X \cdot S_1)$.

An example of a recursive contract is

$$X \; = \; (x := x + 1 \; ; \; X \sqcup \text{skip}) \; .$$

Here the agent can choose between increasing x by one and repeating the process or finishing. In this way, the agent can set x to any value that is equal to or greater than the initial value of x.

We will later show that we can introduce recursive contracts in terms of infinite choices, so we do not actually need to postulate recursive contracts. Like the conditional contract, they can be introduced as convenient abbreviations defined in terms of more primitive contracts.

A recursive contract introduces the possibility of nontermination, so we have to decide what nontermination means in our framework. We will interpret nontermination as a breach of contract by our agent, making this something to be avoided. This corresponds to intuition: delaying a task indefinitely is not considered to be an acceptable way of satisfying a contract.

Iteration

Iteration is defined in terms of recursion. For example, the standard while loop is defined as follows:

$$\text{while } g \text{ do } S \text{ od} = (\mu X \cdot \text{ if } g \text{ then } S \,; X \text{ else skip fi}) .$$

An example is the following little contract, which applies the function f to an initial value $x = a$ until the value becomes larger than some fixed constant b:

$$x := a \,; \text{while } x \le b \text{ do } x := f.x \text{ od} .$$

The same contract can be defined as $x := a \,; X$ where X is defined by the recursive definition

$$X = \text{if } x \le b \text{ then } x := f.x \,; X \text{ else skip fi} .$$

Specification Constructs

A program is usually built as a collection of interacting components. When programming a specific component, we consider the other components to be controlled by other agents. We may need some of these components in order to carry out the task set for our component, but we cannot influence the choices made by the other agents. The situation is analogous to a contractor using subcontractors.

A *specification* of a program component is a contract that gives some constraints on how the component is to behave but leaves freedom for the other agent (the subcontractor or the implementer) to decide how the actual behavior of the component is to be realized. A specification therefore often involves uncontrollable choice between a number of alternatives.

For instance, if we want to specify that the variable x is to be set to some value between 0 and 9, then we can express this as the contract

$$x := 0 \sqcap x := 1 \sqcap \cdots \sqcap x := 9 .$$

Then our agent does not know precisely which alternative will be chosen by the other agent, so whatever it wants to achieve, it should achieve it no matter which alternative is chosen.

This contract can be improved from the point of view of our agent by getting of the uncertainty. We have, e.g., that

$$x := 0 \sqcap x := 1 \sqcap \cdots \sqcap x := 9 \sqsubseteq x := 3 .$$

This means that $x := 3$ is a correct *implementation* of the specification. A other statement $x := n, n = 0, \ldots, 9$, is also a refinement and thus a corr implementation of the specification. Moreover, any choice that cuts down on number of alternatives will also be a refinement of the specification. An examp is

$$x := 0 \sqcap x := 1 \sqcap \cdots \sqcap x := 9 \sqsubseteq x := 3 \sqcap x := 7 .$$

This explains the central importance of the notion of refinement in analyzi contracts: it captures and generalizes the notion of implementing a specificatio

In some situations we need to consider an infinite number of alternatives. I instance, to set x to any nonnegative value, we can use the following specificati

$$\sqcap \{x := n \mid n \geq 0\} .$$

Here one of the statements $x := n$ is chosen from the infinite set of possible sta ments. As an executable statement, this construct would be difficult to implem in its full generality (in the sense that any possibility could be chosen in practic However, when we look at it as a contract, it is perfectly acceptable. It just sta some constraint on what the other agent can choose, where the constraint happe to be such that it permits an infinite number of possible choices for the other age

Relational Assignments

We have assumed that an agent can change the state by applying a state-chang function f to the present state. More generally, we can assume that the agent change the state by applying a relation R to the present state. In a given state the agent is free to choose as next state any state σ' that satisfies $\sigma R \sigma'$. Let write $\{R\}$ for the action that changes the state in this way. We consider $\{R\}$ to a contract that shows the freedom that the agent has in choosing the next sta However, the agent must choose one of the states permitted by R. If there is state σ' such that $\sigma R \sigma'$ holds, then the agent is forced to breach the contra Thus the agent can satisfy the contract $\{R\}$ to establish condition q in initial st σ if and only if there is some state σ' such that $\sigma R \sigma'$ and $\sigma' \in q$.

The contract $\{R\}$ describes the freedom our agent has in choosing the next sta The contract $\{R\}^\circ$ is denoted by $[R]$. Here the choice of the next state is m by the other agent, and our agent has no influence on this choice. If there is state σ' such that $\sigma R \sigma'$, then the other agent is forced to breach the contra This means that our agent can satisfy the contract $[R]$ to establish condition q initial state σ if $\sigma' \in q$ for every σ' such that $\sigma R \sigma'$. In particular, our agent v satisfy the contract if there is no σ' such that $\sigma \ R \ \sigma'$. Keeping the game-theoretic interpretation of contracts in mind, we refer to $\{R\}$ as an *angelic update* and to $[R]$ as a *demonic update*.

We can generalize the assignment $x := e$ to a *relational assignment* $(x := a \mid b)$. An example is the relational assignment $(x := n \mid n > x)$. This relates the initial state σ to a final state σ' when $\sigma' = \text{set}.x.n.\sigma$ and $n > \text{val}.x.\sigma$ hold. In other words, the relational assignment nondeterministically chooses some value n that satisfies the condition $n > \text{val}.x.\sigma$ and assigns it to x. In general, $(x := a \mid b)$ relates states σ and σ' to each other when $\sigma' = \text{set}.x.a.\sigma$ and b holds in σ. We can now describe angelic updates like $\{x := n \mid n > x\}$ and demonic updates like $[x := n \mid n > x]$, where the relation between initial and final states is described by $(x := n \mid n > x)$.

We can use demonic updates as specifications. We have, e.g., that

$$[x := n \mid n > x] \ \sqsubseteq \ x := x + 2 \ ,$$

so $x := x + 2$ is a possible implementation of this specification, because the number of possible final states that the other agent can choose in a given initial state is restricted to just one. Another possible implementation is $x := x + 1 \sqcap x := x + 2$, which is less deterministic than the first, but still much more deterministic than the original specification.

The angelic update can also be used as a specification. In this case, the contract

$$\{x := n \mid n > x\}$$

expresses that we are free to choose a new value for x that is greater than the present value. A refinement in this case is a contract that gives our agent even more freedom to choose. For instance,

$$\{x := n \mid n > x\} \ \sqsubseteq \ \{x := n \mid n \geq x\} \ .$$

Here the refinement adds the possibility of not increasing the value of x, so there is at lest one more alternative to choose from. In general, a refinement decreases the number of choices for the other agent and increases the number of choices for our agent.

Pre–postcondition Specifications

A common way to specify a program statement is to give a *precondition p* and a *postcondition q* on the state that the implementation must satisfy, assuming that only certain program variables are changed. Consider as an example the specification with the precondition $x \geq 0$ and postcondition $x' > x$, where x' stands for the new value of the program variable. Assume further that only the program variable x may be changed. This pre-postcondition specification is expressed by the contract

$$\{x \geq 0\} ; [x := x' \mid x' > x] .$$

Thus, the contract is breached unless $x \geq 0$ holds in the state initially. If th condition is true, then x is assigned some value x' for which $x' > x$ holds in th initial state.

Contracts as Generalized Specifications

Consider the following example of a contract that uses both kinds of nondetermi ism:

$$\{x, e := x_0, e_0 \mid x_0 \geq 0 \land e_0 > 0\} ;$$
$$[x := x_1 \mid -e \leq x - x_1^2 \leq e] .$$

The purpose of this contract is to compute the square root of a number. Our age first chooses new values x_0 and e_0 for x and e such that the condition $x_0 \geq 0 \land e_0 >$ holds. Then the other agent chooses some new value x_1 for x such that the conditie $-e \leq x - x_1^2 \leq e$ holds. This contract requires that our agent first choose a val x_0 for which the square root should be computed and a precision e_0 with whie the square root should be computed. Then the other agent is given the task actually producing a new value x_1 as the required square root. The computed val is not uniquely determined by the specification, but is known only up to the giv precision.

The above contract describes a simple interaction between a user of a squar root package and the system that computes the square root. Contracts generali the traditional notion of a pre–postcondition specification to more intricate us interactions with a system (or client interactions with a server).

In general, the interaction may be much more involved and may require fu ther choices by the user of the system and the system itself during the course computation. For instance, the following describes a simple *event loop* interactic

$$(\mu X \bullet \text{if } g_1 :: S_1 [] \cdots [] g_m :: S_m \text{ fi} ; X \sqcup \text{skip}) .$$

Here the user of the system repeatedly executes one of the actions that is enabl until he decides to stop the repetition. The user will be forced to stop the repetitie if none of the actions is enabled but he may otherwise freely repeat the loop many times as he desires.

1.7 Correctness

Let S be a contract statement, and let p and q be two predicates (the *preconditi* and the *postcondition*). Then we say that S is *correct* with respect to p and denoted by $p \{\!| S |\!\} q$, if $\sigma \{\!| S |\!\} q$ holds for every σ that satisfies p. Program statements are special kinds of contract statements, so this also defines correctness for program statements. Thus $p \{\!| S |\!\} q$ expresses that for any initial state in p, our agent can choose an execution of S that either establishes q or leads to some of its assumptions being violated.

Let us compare this definition with the traditional notion of *total correctness* of programs. This requires that program S be guaranteed to terminate in a state that satisfies postcondition q whenever the initial state satisfies precondition p. Compared to a program, our statements are more powerful; they can describe behavior that is not usually associated with programs. Programs are assumed to have only demonic nondeterminism (or sometimes only angelic nondeterminism) but not both kinds of nondeterminism. Breaching the contract can be seen as a form of nontermination (abortion), but there is no counterpart to breaching an assumption for ordinary programs. Total correctness takes demonic nondeterminism into account by requiring that the program be guaranteed to terminate in some desired final state no matter what demonic choices are made. Our definition extends this by requiring that there be a way for our agent (the angel) to make its choices so that it can establish the required postcondition no matter what demonic choices are made. If there are no angelic choices or assumptions, then our definition coincides with the traditional notion of total correctness for nondeterministic programs.

Correctness Problems

Our general goal is to construct program statements (or more general contract statements) that are correct with respect to some given specification. This is the *programming problem*. Of course, programs are also required to satisfy other criteria, such as efficiency and portability, but we concentrate here on correctness. There are, however, different ways of approaching this problem.

(i) We may assume that precondition p and postcondition q are given and that statement S has already been constructed by some means. We are asked to prove that $p \{\!| S |\!\} q$ holds. This is the *correctness problem*, the traditional center of interest in programming logics.

(ii) The precondition p and postcondition q are given. Our task is to derive a suitable program statement S such that $p \{\!| S |\!\} q$ holds. This is the *program derivation problem*, which is one of the central topics of this book.

(iii) The program statement S is given. We want to find a suitable precondition p and postcondition q such that $p \{\!| S |\!\} q$ holds. This is the *program analysis problem*; we ask what the program does. This is sometimes referred to as *reverse engineering*. If the postcondition q is also given, then we need to find a suitable precondition p such that $p \{\!| S |\!\} q$ holds. This is *precondition analysis*: we want to determine the conditions under which the program behaves as required. Alternatively, the precondition p could be given, and we should find a suitable postcondition q such that $p \{ | S | \} q$ holds. This is *postconditic analysis*; we want to describe the effect of a program statement for certa initial states.

(iv) We want to find an interesting precondition p, postcondition q, and progra statements S such that $p \{ | S | \} q$ holds. This could be called *explorati programming*. We construct the program and its specification hand in han making the program and its specification more precise as part of the progra construction process. A variant of explorative programming arises when t postcondition q is given, and the task is to find an interesting statement S a a precondition p such that $p \{ | S | \} q$ holds. This leads to a form of *backwa program derivation*, where we try to derive from the postcondition a progra that will achieve this postcondition. Another variant is that the preconditic p is given, and we try to derive an interesting statement S and a postconditic q such that $p \{ | S | \} q$ holds. This kind of *forward program derivation* probably the least interesting of the problems to be considered, because t precondition usually does not contain much information and does not give much direction in searching for interesting programs.

The word *suitable* above is important, because for many problems there are tri ial solutions that are immediately available. For the program derivation proble [false] will satisfy any pre- and postcondition. For precondition analysis we c always choose the trivial precondition false, and for postcondition analysis we c often at least get true as a feasible postcondition (when the program statement guaranteed to terminate).

The refinement calculus is a framework for studying these different kinds of que tions. In what follows we will look at some of these paradigms in somewhat mo detail.

1.8 Refinement of Programs

A central application of the refinement calculus is the derivation of a program th satisfies a given specification. The method for program derivation that we w be particularly interested in is known as *stepwise refinement*. The basic idea is follows. We start with a high-level specification of what a program is required do. This specification is then *implemented* by a program statement that achiev what the specification says, but usually contains parts that are not implemented t only specified. These subspecifications are then implemented by other progra statements, possibly containing other unimplemented parts in turn. This proce continues until all specifications have been implemented by the program text, a we then have an executable program. Thus, this classic stepwise refinement meth proceeds in a *top-down* fashion.

Besides this top-down method for program development, another idea that was merged with the stepwise refinement method was that of *program transformation*. Here a program is changed by applying a transformation that changes it in a way that preserves the correctness of the original program. Transformations of source text, such as *loop folding* and *unfolding*, *data refinement*, and *program optimization*, are examples of this approach.

The refinement relation between contract statements is defined so that it preserves correctness: If $S \sqsubseteq S'$ and $p \ \{\!| \ S \ |\!\} \ q$ holds, then $p \ \{\!| \ S' \ |\!\} \ q$ will also hold. This is the case for any choice of precondition p and postcondition q.

The formalization of the stepwise refinement method in the refinement calculus is based on this observation. We start with an initial statement S_0 that satisfies some correctness criteria that we have been given; i.e., we assume that $p \ \{\!| \ S_0 \ |\!\} \ q$. Then we derive a sequence of successive refinements

$$S_0 \sqsubseteq S_1 \sqsubseteq \cdots \sqsubseteq S_n \ .$$

By transitivity, we have that $S_0 \sqsubseteq S_n$, and because refinement preserves correctness, we have that $p \ \{\!| \ S_n \ |\!\} \ q$ also holds. Thus, we have constructed a new statement S_n from the original statement S_0, where the new statement also satisfies our initial requirement.

An individual refinement step $S_i \sqsubseteq S_{i+1}$ can be established by, e.g., implementing some specification statement in S_i to get S_{i+1}, by applying some transformation rule to derive S_{i+1} from S_i, or by some other means. Sometimes, we need a whole subderivation to establish that the refinement step $S_i \sqsubseteq S_{i+1}$ is valid. The methods that we use for calculating or validating a refinement step form a collection of so-called *refinement laws*. These tell us how to find suitable refinement steps and under what conditions these steps are valid.

The purpose of the derivation is to find a program S_n that in some ways is better than the original program S_0. This program could be more space or time efficient, it could be implementable on a specific computer system or in a specific programming language (whereas the original one may not have been), or it could have other desirable properties that the original program was missing. The determination of these criteria and checking that the proposed refinements are indeed improvements over the original statements is considered to be outside the scope of this book. We focus on methods for proving that a refinement preserves correctness and on finding general rules that are known to preserve correctness.

Background

We give below a brief overview of the background of the refinement calculus, concentrating on earlier developments in this area. More recent work is described and referenced in the subsequent chapters.

The origins of the refinement calculus are in the *stepwise refinement method* for program construction that was put forward by Edsger W. Dijkstra [51] and Niklas Wirth [141]; the *transformational approach* to programming, put forward by Susan Gerhart [61] and by Rod Burstall and John Darlington [43]; and the early work program correctness and *data refinement* by C.A.R. Hoare [84, 87]. The purpose of the refinement calculus is to provide a solid logical foundation for these methods, based on the *weakest precondition* approach to total correctness of programs proposed by Dijkstra [53].

The refinement calculus is a further development of the weakest precondition theory; it was invented by Ralph-Johan Back in his Ph.D. thesis in 1978 [6] and shortly thereafter described in book form [7]. This work introduced the central notions of the calculus: the refinement relation between program statements, with the emphasis on preserving total correctness rather than partial correctness of programs; modeling program statements as predicate transformers; using specification statements as primitive program statements; the emphasis on monotonic program constructs to guarantee that component replacement preserves correctness; using assertion statements for refinement in context; and data refinement. The basic refinement rules for program statements were identified and proved to be sound, were the basic rules for data refinement of program statements.

A few journal papers describing the approach followed in the next few years. Specifications treated as executable statements were described by Back in a 1981 article [10]. The general notion of program refinement was also described that same year [9], and the denotational semantics of statements with unbounded nondeterminism (which was the result of adding arbitrary specification statements to a programming language) was described in yet another article in the same year [8]. However, the topic did not attract much interest from other researchers in the field at that time.

Interest in refinement calculus was revived around 1987–88. An overview and update of the refinement calculus approach was published by Back [11, 12], with better treatment of iteration and recursion, among other things. Back and Kaisa Sere applied the refinement calculus to stepwise construction of parallel and reactive programs and to the refinement of atomicity in parallel programs [15, 22, 24]. This work was based on the action system framework that had been developed earlier Back and Reino Kurki-Suonio [20]. This work uncovered a number of interesting foundational issues in the refinement calculus and also convinced the authors of the general usability of the approach in practice.

Carroll Morgan [102, 103, 104] and Joseph Morris [108] also started to publish papers on this topic around 1987–88. Both were essentially using the original refinement calculus framework, but they extended it with different specification statements and with miraculous statements (our assumptions), which were not allowed in the original calculus. Furthermore, Morris used a fixed-point approach handle recursion. Greg Nelson [113] also studied miraculous statements, although he had a slightly different approach to program refinement (requiring both total and partial correctness to be preserved). Wim Hesselink initiated the study of algebraic properties of program statements, based on the predicate transformer interpretation, but he concentrated on equivalence rather than refinement [77].

Morgan later published an influential book on program refinement [106]. This book incorporated his extensions to the refinement calculus and contained a number of case studies that described how to derive programs from specifications in the refinement calculus framework. This established the applicability of the calculus to practical programming problems. The book reformulates the original refinement calculus in a notation that is influenced by the Z specification style [133].

Another driving force for the further development of the calculus was the need to reengineer its mathematical basis. The lattice-theoretic study of refinement was initiated in a paper by Back and Joakim von Wright in 1989 [25, 27] on the duality in specification languages, where the fundamental program statements were identified and analyzed. In particular, this work introduced the central themes of angelic and demonic nondeterminism in the calculus. The use of lattice theory has led to a considerable simplification of the theory, as compared to earlier attempts, and made it much more streamlined. At the same time, the theory has also become much more general, and new applications for these generalizations have suggested themselves along the road.

The original formalization of the refinement calculus was done in infinitary logic [10]. The need for a logic stronger than first-order logic was evident already then, but the step to a full higher-order logic was taken only later by Back and von Wright [28, 30]. The higher-order logic formalization has since then been extended and reworked considerably, as documented in this book. A complete implementation of the refinement calculus has also been made by von Wright [144] using the HOL theorem-proving system [62]. The HOL system has influenced a number of design decisions in our formalization of the calculus. Many of the theorems presented in this book have been checked mechanically for correctness and now form the basis for a mechanized program-refinement environment that is being developed in a project led by von Wright [45, 97].

There are many other authors besides those mentioned above that have contributed to the development of the refinement calculus. Some of the work has aimed at extending the domain of applicability of the calculus to new areas, such as parallel programs [23], reactive programs [14, 31], and object-oriented programs [111, 129, 138]. Others have been looking at larger-scale applications of refinement methods [21, 117]. Theory development has also continued and has brought many new insights into this area [46, 58, 112]. A rather active research area is to build better computer-supported tools for program refinement [47, 67]. There has also been considerable work on transporting some of the techniques from the refinement calculus framework to other formalisms for program development, such as the CSP process algebra [44].

1.10   Overview of the Book

The previous sections have given an informal introduction to some of the ma concepts that we will study in this book. The first part of the book covers t foundations of the refinement calculus. As indicated above, lattices form the ma algebraic structures needed in the refinement calculus, so the book opens with overview of some basic notions of lattice theory. More lattice theory is introduc later on as needed. Higher-order logic, which we use as the logical framewo for reasoning about refinement, is presented next. We give an overview of high order logic, with a lattice-oriented axiomatization of this logic and introduce t derivational proof style that we are using throughout the book. We show how reason about functions, about truth values, sets, predicates, and relations. We al study the properties of states with attributes and show how to formalize the noti of program variables in higher-order logic.

Very simple contracts with no choices (deterministic programs) can be model as functions from states to states. More complicated contracts may be modeled relations on states, provided that all choices are made by only one agent. Gene contracts, where choices can be made by two or more agents, are modeled predicate transformers, i.e., functions that map postconditions to precondition This is the central notion to be studied in the second part of the book. We w describe the basic algebraic properties of predicate transformers. The notions correctness and refinement of predicate transformers will also be defined precise The lattice-theoretic interpretation of contracts is a direct extension of set theo so programs, specifications, and contracts in general share many properties w sets. This provides a familiar framework in which to reason about correctne and refinement of programs. We will show that contract statements in fact c be identified with the monotonic predicate transformers, and that more standa program statements correspond to subclasses of such predicate transformers. T notion of correctness is analyzed more carefully in this context, and we show h our formalization of correctness is related to standard ways of reasoning about to correctness of programs.

We will also look more carefully at alternative interpretations of contracts. As explained above, a contract can be seen as a game between an angel (our agent) a a demon (the other agent), where correctness corresponds to the existence of a w ning strategy for the angel. We define an operational *game semantics* for contra that formalizes this viewpoint. We also define the *choice semantics*, an alternati interpretation of contract statements that can be seen as a denotational semant for contracts. The predicate transformer semantics and the choice semantics equivalent, and both are abstractions of the game semantics.

The third part of the book introduces recursion and iteration of statements. Rec sion is explained in terms of fixed points of monotonic functions on lattices, a iteration is explained in terms of recursion, in the way we have described abo

Some of the material is based on ordinal arithmetic, so we give a short introduction to the concepts and results needed from this field. Iteration is studied in depth, because of its central status in reasoning about imperative programs. We illustrate the use of the refinement calculus framework by three case studies: one on deriving a nontrivial sorting algorithm, another on deriving a recursive search algorithm, and the third on determining the winning strategy for a classical game.

The fourth part of the book considers subclasses of contracts that are characterized by some homomorphism properties. These subclasses correspond to more standard models for sequential programs. For instance, Dijkstra's guarded commands fall into the subclass of conjunctive and continuous statements. We show how to describe traditional semantic models, like denotational semantics for deterministic and nondeterministic programs, in the refinement calculus framework. We also give normal forms for contracts in these different subclasses and show that the normal forms can be understood as specifications for the class of contracts in question.

We will in particular look at one very general subclass of contract statements, the *conjunctive statements*. This class is interesting because it corresponds to the standard model for program statements and specification statements. We will consider a collection of important refinement techniques in more detail for this class of statements. We analyze the notion of specification statements and study methods for refining specification statements into more concrete program statements. We show how the context of a program component can be taken into account and used in a refinement step. We also consider program transformation rules that change the control structure of programs, in particular rules for changing iteration statements.

Part I

Foundations

osets, Lattices, and Categories

This chapter introduces the central mathematical structures that are needed to formalize the refinement calculus: partially ordered sets (posets), lattices, and categories. We identify the basic properties of posets and lattices, and use them for a classification of lattices. We also show how to construct new lattices out of old ones as Cartesian products and function spaces. We study structure-preserving mappings (homomorphisms) on lattices. Finally, we show how to form a certain kind of category out of these lattices. The simple notions identified in this chapter underlie the formal reasoning about properties of programs, specifications, and contracts in general.

Partially Ordered Sets

Let A be a nonempty set and $\sqsubseteq$ a binary relation on A. We say that $\sqsubseteq$ is respectively *reflexive, transitive, symmetric,* and *antisymmetric* if

$$a \sqsubseteq a ,$$
(⊑ *reflexive*)
$$a \sqsubseteq b \wedge b \sqsubseteq c \Rightarrow a \sqsubseteq c ,$$
(⊑ *transitive*)
$$a \sqsubseteq b \Rightarrow b \sqsubseteq a ,$$
(⊑ *symmetric*)
$$a \sqsubseteq b \wedge b \sqsubseteq a \Rightarrow a = b ,$$
(⊑ *antisymmetric*)

for any choice of a, b, c in A (note that we assume that $\sqsubseteq$ binds more strongly than $\wedge$, which in turn binds more strongly than $\Rightarrow$; for a complete collection of precedence rules we refer to Appendix A).

Here a small note on notation is in order. We could write $a \sqsubseteq b \sqsubseteq c$ rather than $a \sqsubseteq b \wedge b \sqsubseteq c$ in the left-hand side of the transitivity rule. However, we will

restrict the use of such *continued relations* to a minimum; they will appear only
indicate ranges of numbers of the form $a \le x \le b$ and occasionally with contin
equalities of the form $a = b = c$.

The relation $\sqsubseteq$ is called a *preorder* if it is reflexive and transitive. The pair $(A,$
is then called a *preordered set*, or a *preset*. If the preorder $\sqsubseteq$ is also symmetric
is said to be an *equivalence relation*. If the preorder $\sqsubseteq$ is antisymmetric, it is s
to be a *partial order*, and $(A, \sqsubseteq)$ is then called a *partially ordered set*, or a *pos*

Generally, $a \sqsubset b$ stands for $a \sqsubseteq b \wedge \neg (b \sqsubseteq a)$. For posets, this means that $a \sqsubset$
stands for $a \sqsubseteq b \wedge a \ne b$. We also write $a \sqsupseteq b$ for $b \sqsubseteq a$ and $a \sqsupset b$ for $b \sqsubset$
The *dual* of the poset $(A, \sqsubseteq)$ is the poset $(A, \sqsupseteq)$.

A partial order is *linear* (or *total*) if

$$a \sqsubseteq b \vee b \sqsubseteq a \qquad\qquad (\sqsubseteq \textit{linea}$$

holds for every $a, b \in A$. A linear partial order is called a *linear order*, and $(A,$
is then a *linearly ordered set*.

In a *discrete order*, the only element that is comparable with an element a i
itself. This order is thus defined by $a \sqsubseteq b$ if and only if $a = b$ for any $a, b \in A$
discrete order is clearly both a partial order and an equivalence relation.

Let $B \subseteq A$, $B \ne \emptyset$. Evidently, the restriction $\sqsubseteq_B$ of $\sqsubseteq$ to B is reflexive (transiti
symmetric, antisymmetric, linear) on B if $\sqsubseteq$ is reflexive (transitive, symmetr
antisymmetric, linear) on A. Hence, $(B, \sqsubseteq_B)$ is a poset whenever $(A, \sqsubseteq)$ i
poset. We say that $(B, \sqsubseteq_B)$ is a *subposet* of $(A, \sqsubseteq)$.

Assume that $(A, \sqsubseteq)$ is a partially ordered set and that B is a subset of A.
element $a \in B$ is the *least element* of B if $a \sqsubseteq x$ for every element x in
Similarly, $b \in B$ is the *greatest element* of B if $x \sqsubseteq b$ for every element x in
The least and greatest elements are unique if they exist. The least element of
whole poset A is called the *bottom* of the poset and is denoted by $\bot$. The grea
element of the whole poset A is called the *top* of the poset and is denoted by $\top$
poset is said to be *bounded*, if it has a least and a greatest element. For such pos
we have

$$\bot \sqsubseteq a , \qquad\qquad (\bot \textit{ smalles}$$
$$a \sqsubseteq \top . \qquad\qquad (\top \textit{ greates}$$

A finite poset $(A, \sqsubseteq)$ is often pictured as a *Hasse diagram*. Each element in A
a node in the diagram. If there is an upward edge from a node a to a node b, t
$a \sqsubset b$. Relations $a \sqsubseteq b$ that can be inferred by reflexivity or transitivity are
indicated. Thus there is an edge from a to b in the Hasse diagram if and onl
$a \sqsubset b$ and there is no $c \ne a, b$ such that $a \sqsubset c \wedge c \sqsubset b$. We also use Ha
diagrams to describe parts of infinite posets. Figure 2.1 gives examples of Ha
diagrams.

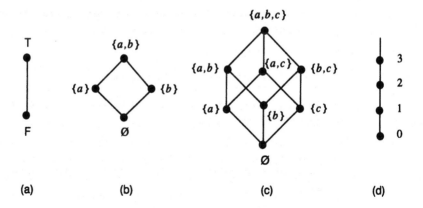

FIGURE 2.1. Poset examples

Truth-Value Poset

The set of truth values Bool = {F, T}, ordered by implication, is an important poset. We have that F ⇒ F and T ⇒ T, so implication is reflexive. If $b_1 \Rightarrow b_2$ and $b_2 \Rightarrow b_3$, then $b_1 \Rightarrow b_3$, so implication is transitive. Finally, if $b_1 \Rightarrow b_2$ and $b_2 \Rightarrow b_1$, then $b_1 = b_2$, so implication is also antisymmetric. Thus (Bool, ⇒) is a poset. In fact, implication is a linear ordering, because either $b_1 \Rightarrow b_2$ or $b_2 \Rightarrow b_1$, for any choice of truth values for b_1 and b_2. The truth-value poset is shown as a Hasse diagram in Figure 2.1a. The truth-value poset is evidently also bounded, with F as the least and T as the greatest element.

Power-Set Poset

The set of subsets $\mathcal{P}(A)$ of a given set A form another important poset. The pair $(\mathcal{P}(A), \subseteq)$ is a poset for any set A. This poset is described in Figure 2.1b for $A = \{a, b\}$ and in Figure 2.1c for $A = \{a, b, c\}$. Note that for $A = \{a\}$, we get a poset with the same structure as the truth-value poset in Figure 2.1a, if we make the correspondence $\emptyset = $ F and $\{a\} = $ T. Inclusion is linear only when $A = \emptyset$ or $A = \{a\}$; for $A = \{a, b\}$, neither $\{a\} \subseteq \{b\}$ nor $\{b\} \subseteq \{a\}$ holds. The power-set poset is also bounded, with $\emptyset$ as the least element and A as the greatest element.

Natural-Numbers Poset

The usual arithmetic ordering $\leq$ on natural numbers Nat = {0, 1, 2, ...} is also a partial order (Figure 2.1d). It is reflexive ($n \leq n$), transitive ($n \leq m \wedge m \leq k \Rightarrow n \leq k$), and antisymmetric ($n \leq m \wedge m \leq n \Rightarrow n = m$). Hence, (Nat, ≤) is a poset. In fact, it is a linearly ordered set, as $m \leq n$ or $n \leq m$ holds for any two natural numbers n and m. Another example is the linearly ordered set of (positive and negative) integers (Int, ≤), with the usual ordering. The natural numbers have a least element, 0, but do not have a greatest element. The integers have neither least nor a greatest element.

Congruence and Monotonicity

Let $(A, \sqsubseteq_A)$ and $(B, \sqsubseteq_B)$ be preorders. The function $f : A \rightarrow B$ is then said be *order-preserving* if

$$a \sqsubseteq_A a' \;\Rightarrow\; f.a \sqsubseteq_B f.a' \qquad\qquad (f \text{ order-preserving})$$

holds for all a and a' in A. The function f is said to be *order-embedding* if converse also holds, i.e., if

$$a \sqsubseteq_A a' \;\equiv\; f.a \sqsubseteq_B f.a' \;. \qquad\qquad (f \text{ order-embedding})$$

Assume that $f : A \rightarrow B$ is order-preserving. If the preorders $\sqsubseteq_A$ and $\sqsubseteq_B$ equivalence relations, then f is called a *congruence*. If they are partial orders, then f is said to be *monotonic*.

A binary function is said to be congruent (monotonic) if it is congruent (monotonic) in each of its arguments separately. For $f : A \times B \rightarrow C$, this is the case if only if the following holds:

$$a \sqsubseteq_A a' \,\wedge\, b \sqsubseteq_B b' \;\Rightarrow\; f.(a, b) \sqsubseteq_C f.(a', b') \;. \qquad\qquad (f \text{ monotonic})$$

A function f is said to be *antimonotonic* if

$$a \sqsubseteq_A a' \;\Rightarrow\; f.a \sqsupseteq_B f.a' \;. \qquad\qquad (f \text{ antimonotonic})$$

Antimonotonicity is really a monotonicity property: f as a function from poset $(A, \sqsubseteq_A)$ to poset $(B, \sqsubseteq_B)$ is antimonotonic if and only if f as a function from poset $(A, \sqsubseteq_A)$ to the *dual poset* $(B, \sqsupseteq_B)$ is monotonic.

Squaring is an example of a monotonic function on the natural numbers: $n \leq$ implies that $n^2 \leq m^2$. Squaring is antimonotonic on the negative numbers: natural numbers n and m, we have that $-n \leq -m$ implies that $n \geq m$, which turn implies that $(-n)^2 \geq (-m)^2$.

Addition and multiplication of natural numbers are examples of functions that monotonic in both arguments: if $n \leq n'$ and $m \leq m'$, then $n + m \leq n' + m'$ $n \cdot m \leq n' \cdot m'$.

Meet and Join

Let B be a subset of poset A. An element $a \in A$ is a *lower bound* of B if $a \sqsubseteq b$ every $b \in B$. Dually, an element $a \in A$ is an *upper bound* of B if $b \sqsubseteq a$ for every $b \in B$. The least element of a set is thus always a lower bound of the set, but converse need not hold, as a lower bound need not be an element of the set B.

The element a is the *greatest lower bound* (or *infimum*, or *meet*) of $B \subseteq A$ if a is the greatest element of the set of lower bounds of B. We write $\sqcap B$ for the greatest lower bound of a set B. When $B = \{b_1, b_2\}$, we write $b_1 \sqcap b_2$ for $\sqcap B$. A set of elements B need not have a greatest lower bound. However, if there is a greatest lower bound, then it is unique.

The greatest lower bound of an arbitrary set B is characterized by the following two properties:

$$b \in B \;\Rightarrow\; \sqcap B \sqsubseteq b \;, \qquad \qquad \text{(\textit{general} $\sqcap$ \textit{elimination})}$$
$$(\forall b \in B \cdot a \sqsubseteq b) \;\Rightarrow\; a \sqsubseteq \sqcap B \;, \qquad \text{(\textit{general} $\sqcap$ \textit{introduction})}$$

The first property states that $\sqcap B$ is a lower bound, and the second that it is the greatest of all lower bounds. The names for these properties reflect their intended use. The first property is used when we need to go from the meet to an element greater than the meet. The second is used when we want to go from some element to the meet of a set.

When the set B is given as an indexed set, $B = \{b_i \mid i \in I\}$, then we write $(\sqcap i \in I \cdot b_i)$ for the greatest lower bound $\sqcap B$ (the set I, which is used to index the elements, can be any set).

For two elements, the properties of the meet are as follows:

$$b_1 \sqcap b_2 \sqsubseteq b_1 \quad \text{and} \quad b_1 \sqcap b_2 \sqsubseteq b_2 \;, \qquad \text{(\textit{$\sqcap$ elimination})}$$
$$a \sqsubseteq b_1 \wedge a \sqsubseteq b_2 \;\Rightarrow\; a \sqsubseteq b_1 \sqcap b_2 \;. \qquad \text{(\textit{$\sqcap$ introduction})}$$

The dual definition is as follows. The element a is the *least upper bound* (or *supremum*, or *join*) of B if a is the least element of the set of upper bounds of B. We denote the least upper bound of B by $\sqcup B$. We write $b_1 \sqcup b_2$ for $\sqcup \{b_1, b_2\}$. The least upper bound of a set B is unique if it exists.

The supremum of an arbitrary set B is characterized by the following two properties:

$$b \in B \;\Rightarrow\; b \sqsubseteq \sqcup B \;, \qquad \qquad \text{(\textit{general} $\sqcup$ \textit{introduction})}$$
$$(\forall b \in B \cdot b \sqsubseteq a) \;\Rightarrow\; \sqcup B \sqsubseteq a \;. \qquad \text{(\textit{general} $\sqcup$ \textit{elimination})}$$

The first property states that $\sqcup B$ is an upper bound, and the second that it is the least of all upper bounds. The names for these properties again reflect their intended use. The first property shows how to go from an element to the join, which is a greater element. The second property shows how to go from the join to an element greater than the join.

Again, when the set B is given as an indexed set, $B = \{b_i \mid i \in I\}$, we write $(\sqcup i \in I \cdot b_i)$ for the greatest lower bound $\sqcup B$.

For binary joins (i.e., joins of two elements), we have that

$$b_1 \sqsubseteq b_1 \sqcup b_2 \quad \text{and} \quad b_2 \sqsubseteq b_1 \sqcup b_2 \;, \qquad \text{(\textit{$\sqcup$ introduction})}$$
$$b_1 \sqsubseteq a \wedge b_2 \sqsubseteq a \;\Rightarrow\; b_1 \sqcup b_2 \sqsubseteq a \;. \qquad \text{(\textit{$\sqcup$ elimination})}$$

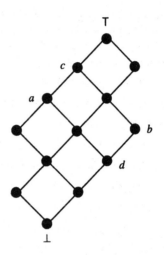

FIGURE 2.2. Poset with meets and joins

Figure 2.2 illustrates meets and joins in a poset. We have that $c = a \sqcup b$ a $d = a \sqcap b$ in the poset. The top $\top$ and bottom $\bot$ of the poset are also indicated the figure.

We have the following basic *correspondence* between the partial ordering, the lea upper bound, and the greatest lower bound.

Lemma 2.1   *The following properties hold for any a, b in a poset:*

$$a \sqcap b = a \;\equiv\; a \sqsubseteq b \, ,$$
$$a \sqcup b = b \;\equiv\; a \sqsubseteq b \, ,$$

(correspondence

whenever the meet and join in question exist.

Proof   We prove the required property for infimum. The proof for supremum analogous. We prove the equivalence by showing implication in both direction We first prove that $a \sqcap b = a \Rightarrow a \sqsubseteq b$:

$a = a \sqcap b$

$\Rightarrow$ {reflexivity of $\sqsubseteq$}

   $a \sqsubseteq a \sqcap b$

$\Rightarrow$ {$\sqcap$ elimination and transitivity of $\sqsubseteq$}

   $a \sqsubseteq b$

We then prove that $a \sqsubseteq b \Rightarrow a = a \sqcap b$:

$a \sqsubseteq b$

$\Rightarrow$ {reflexivity of $\sqsubseteq$}

$a \sqsubseteq a \land a \sqsubseteq b$

$\Rightarrow \{\sqcap \text{ introduction}\}$

$a \sqsubseteq a \sqcap b$

$\Rightarrow \{a \sqcap b \sqsubseteq a \text{ holds by } \sqcap \text{ elimination}\}$

$a \sqsubseteq a \sqcap b \land a \sqcap b \sqsubseteq a$

$\Rightarrow \{\text{antisymmetry of } \sqsubseteq\}$

$a = a \sqcap b$

□

We have here written the (informal) proofs as *linear derivations*, where each implication is written and justified on a line of its own. In Chapter 4 we will introduce a formal way of writing proofs that includes linear derivations such as these.

Because $\bot \sqsubseteq a$ and $a \sqsubseteq \top$ hold in any poset that has a top and a bottom, we have as special cases of this lemma that

$$a \sqcap \bot = \bot \qquad a \sqcup \bot = a , \qquad\qquad (\bot \text{ properties})$$
$$a \sqcap \top = a \qquad a \sqcup \top = \top , \qquad\qquad (\top \text{ properties})$$

for arbitrary a in a poset with top and bottom.

The conjunction $a \land b$ of truth values a and b satisfies the conditions for finite meet: (i) $a \land b \Rightarrow a$ and $a \land b \Rightarrow b$, so $a \land b$ is a lower bound of $\{a, b\}$; and (ii) if $c \Rightarrow a$ and $c \Rightarrow b$, then $c \Rightarrow a \land b$, so $a \land b$ is the greatest lower bound of $\{a, b\}$. Similarly, disjunction satisfies the properties of finite join. Thus, conjunction is the meet and disjunction the join in Bool.

In the power-set poset, we have again that $A \sqcap B = A \cap B$ for subsets A and B of D: (i) $A \cap B \subseteq A$ and $A \cap B \subseteq B$, so $A \cap B$ is a lower bound of $\{A, B\}$; (ii) if $C \subseteq A$ and $C \subseteq B$, then $C \subseteq A \cap B$, so $A \cap B$ is the greatest lower bound of $\{A, B\}$. Similarly, we have that $A \sqcup B = A \cup B$. We also have that $\bot = \emptyset$ and $\top = D$ in $(\mathcal{P}(D), \subseteq)$. For an arbitrary family K of sets in $\mathcal{P}(D)$, we have that $\sqcup K = \cup K$ and $\sqcap K = \cap K$.

For the natural numbers (with ordering $\leq$), it is easy to see that $m \sqcap n = m \min n$, while $m \sqcup n = m \max n$, where min gives the smaller and max the larger of the two elements. If K is an arbitrary nonempty set of natural numbers, then $\sqcap K$ always exists, but $\sqcup K$ exists only if K is finite. If we extend the natural numbers with the first infinite ordinal ω (ordinals are treated in detail in Chapter 18) to get Nat $\cup \{\omega\}$, then $\sqcup K$ also exists for arbitrary sets of natural numbers (and is always ω when K is infinite).

2.2   Lattices

A poset $(A, \sqsubseteq)$ (or, for simplicity, just A) is called a *lattice* if the meet $a \sqcap b$ a join $a \sqcup b$ exist in A for all pairs a, b of elements of A. A direct consequence this is that a poset $(A, \sqsubseteq)$ is a lattice if and only if $\sqcap B$ and $\sqcup B$ exist for all *fin nonempty subsets B* of A. The poset $(\mathsf{Bool}, \Rightarrow)$ is a lattice, as are $(\mathsf{Nat}, \leq)$, $(\mathsf{Int}, \leq$ and $(\mathcal{P}(D), \subseteq)$ for any D. The posets in Figure 2.1 are thus lattices, as is the pos in Figure 2.2.

The poset $(A, \sqsubseteq)$ is called a *meet semilattice* if $a \sqcap b$ exists in A for all pairs a a b of elements of A. A *join semilattice* is defined analogously.

If the partial order $(A, \sqsubseteq)$ is a lattice, then meet and join are defined for any pair elements in A, so lattice meet and join can be seen as binary operations on A. Th thus form an algebra on A. These operations can be shown to have the followi properties:

$$
\begin{array}{lll}
a \sqcap a = a & a \sqcup a = a , & \text{(idempotenc}e \\
a \sqcap b = b \sqcap a & a \sqcup b = b \sqcup a , & \text{(commutativit}y \\
a \sqcap (b \sqcap c) = (a \sqcap b) \sqcap c & a \sqcup (b \sqcup c) = (a \sqcup b) \sqcup c , & \text{(associativit}y \\
a \sqcap (a \sqcup b) = a & a \sqcup (a \sqcap b) = a . & \text{(absorptio}n
\end{array}
$$

Conversely, assume that we have an algebra A where the operations $\sqcap$ and $\sqcup$ satis the above properties. Define $a \sqsubseteq b$ to hold if and only if $a = a \sqcap b$ (or $a \sqcup b = $ i.e., assume that the correspondence between meet (or join) and ordering hol Then we can show that $(A, \sqsubseteq)$ is a lattice and that the operations $\sqcap$ and $\sqcup$ correspo to meet and join in this lattice. Hence, lattices can be introduced either as a spec kind of algebra or as a special kind of poset. We have above chosen the lat approach.

Meet and join, seen as operations, are easily shown to be monotonic with resp to the lattice ordering:

$$
\begin{array}{ll}
a \sqsubseteq a' \wedge b \sqsubseteq b' \;\Rightarrow\; a \sqcap b \sqsubseteq a' \sqcap b' , & \text{(}\sqcap \text{ monotoni}c \\
a \sqsubseteq a' \wedge b \sqsubseteq b' \;\Rightarrow\; a \sqcup b \sqsubseteq a' \sqcup b' . & \text{(}\sqcup \text{ monotoni}c
\end{array}
$$

We next define a number of additional properties that lattices may have and giv classification of lattices based on these properties. These additional properties tu out to be very important and will occur in different disguises over and over aga

Complete Lattices

A lattice A is *complete* if $\sqcap B$ and $\sqcup B$ exist in A for all subsets $B \subseteq A$. In particul greatest lower bounds and least upper bounds also must exist for empty B as w as for any infinite B.

Every complete lattice has a top and a bottom, so a complete lattice is always bounded. The bottom can be characterized either as the greatest lower bound of the whole lattice or as the least upper bound of the empty set. A dual characterization holds for the top. We thus have that

$$\bot = \sqcap A \quad \text{and} \quad \bot = \sqcup \emptyset \, , \qquad \textit{(bottom characterization)}$$
$$\top = \sqcup A \quad \text{and} \quad \top = \sqcap \emptyset \, . \qquad \textit{(top characterization)}$$

The truth-value lattice is a complete lattice, because any finite lattice is complete. Consider a set $B = \{b_i \mid i \in I\}$ of truth values. The set B must be either $\emptyset$, $\{F\}$, $\{T\}$, or $\{F, T\}$. For $B = \emptyset$, we already know that $\sqcap B = T$ and $\sqcup B = F$, by the above characterization. For $B \neq \emptyset$, we have that

$$(\sqcap i \in I \cdot b_i) \;=\; T \qquad \text{iff } b_i = T \text{ for all } i \in I,$$
$$(\sqcup i \in I \cdot b_i) \;=\; T \qquad \text{iff } b_i = T \text{ for some } i \in I.$$

The meet and join of indexed sets of truth values thus model universal and existential quantification, as we will show later.

The intersection and union of an arbitrary set of subsets of A is also a subset of A. Hence, the subset lattice is also a complete lattice.

The natural numbers form a *complete meet semilattice*, i.e., a poset where every nonempty subset has a meet. However, they do not form a complete lattice, because the join of an infinite set of natural numbers does not exist. The extended natural numbers Nat $\cup \{\omega\}$ do form a complete lattice.

Distributive Lattices

A lattice A is *distributive* if for any elements a, b, and c of A the following two properties hold, referred to as *meet distributivity* and *join distributivity*, respectively:

$$a \sqcup (b \sqcap c) \;=\; (a \sqcup b) \sqcap (a \sqcup c) \, , \qquad (\sqcap \textit{ distributivity})$$
$$a \sqcap (b \sqcup c) \;=\; (a \sqcap b) \sqcup (a \sqcap c) \, . \qquad (\sqcup \textit{ distributivity})$$

The distributivity properties do not necessarily generalize to infinite meets and joins in a lattice. We call the corresponding properties for infinite meets and joins the *infinite meet distributivity* condition and the *infinite join distributivity* condition. These conditions are

$$a \sqcup (\sqcap i \in I \cdot b_i) \;=\; (\sqcap i \in I \cdot a \sqcup b_i) \, , \qquad (\textit{infinite } \sqcap \textit{ distributivity})$$
$$a \sqcap (\sqcup i \in I \cdot b_i) \;=\; (\sqcup i \in I \cdot a \sqcap b_i) \, , \qquad (\textit{infinite } \sqcup \textit{ distributivity})$$

where a and b_i are elements of the lattice A, and I is any index set.

The property $a \wedge (b \vee c) = (a \wedge b) \vee (a \wedge c)$ holds for truth values, as does $a \vee (b \wedge c) = (a \vee b) \wedge (a \vee c)$. Thus, conjunction and disjunction satisfy the distributivity laws, so the truth-value lattice is in fact a distributive lattice. The infinite distributive conditions are trivially satisfied in any finite distributive lattice.

The subset lattice also satisfies the distributivity laws: $A \cap (B \cup C) = (A \cap B)$ $(A \cap C)$ and $A \cup (B \cap C) = (A \cup B) \cap (A \cup C)$. In fact, the subset lattice satisfies the infinite distributivity laws:

$$
\begin{aligned}
A \cup (\cap i \in I \cdot B_i) &= (\cap i \in I \cdot A \cup B_i) , \\
A \cap (\cup i \in I \cdot B_i) &= (\cup i \in I \cdot A \cap B_i) .
\end{aligned}
$$

The natural numbers also satisfy the distributivity laws:

$$
\begin{aligned}
m \text{ min } (n \text{ max } k) &= (m \text{ min } n) \text{ max } (m \text{ min } k) , \\
m \text{ max } (n \text{ min } k) &= (m \text{ max } n) \text{ min } (m \text{ max } k) .
\end{aligned}
$$

In addition, the infinite meet distributivity condition holds for natural numbers but not the corresponding join condition, as max is not defined for infinite sets natural numbers.

Boolean Lattices

A complete distributive lattice A is called a *complete Boolean lattice* if every element a in A has a unique *complement* $\neg a$ in A satisfying the conditions

$$
\begin{aligned}
a \cap \neg a &= \bot , & (\neg\ contradictio. \\
a \cup \neg a &= \top . & (\neg\ exhaustivenes
\end{aligned}
$$

Every complete Boolean lattice satisfies both infinite distributivity conditions. I a proof of this fact, we refer to standard texts on lattice theory.

The following *de Morgan* rules also hold in any complete Boolean lattice:

$$
\begin{aligned}
\neg (\cap i \in I \cdot a_i) &= (\cup i \in I \cdot \neg a_i) , & (de\ Morga. \\
\neg (\cup i \in I \cdot a_i) &= (\cap i \in I \cdot \neg a_i) ,
\end{aligned}
$$

where a_i are elements of the lattice and I is any index set.

We also note that complement is an *involution*:

$$
\neg (\neg a) = a . \qquad (\neg\ involutio.
$$

A direct consequence of this is that complement is a bijective function from complete Boolean lattice onto itself:

$$
a = b \equiv \neg a = \neg b . \qquad (\neg\ bijectiv
$$

Lattice complement is also antimonotonic with respect to the lattice ordering:

$$
a \sqsubseteq b \equiv \neg a \sqsupseteq \neg b . \qquad (\neg\ antimonotoni
$$

The truth values form a Boolean lattice, where $\neg$ is negation of truth values: We have that $a \wedge \neg a = \mathsf{F}$ and $a \vee \neg a = \mathsf{T}$. The following theorem summarizes the properties of the truth-value lattice that we have noted above.

Theorem 2.2   *The truth values with the implication ordering form a complete, Boolean, and linearly ordered lattice.*

In fact, it can be shown that any partially ordered set with at least two elements that satisfies the conditions of Theorem 2.2 is isomorphic to the truth-value lattice. Thus the truth-value lattice is completely characterized by the fact that it is a complete, Boolean, and linearly ordered lattice.

The subset lattice is also a Boolean lattice. It is bounded and distributed, as we have shown above. The complement of a subset A of D is the set $\neg A = D - A$. It is easy to see that $A \cup \neg A = D$ and $A \cap \neg A = \emptyset$, so the requirements on the complement are met.

The natural numbers do not form a Boolean lattice. Even if we add the limit ordinal ω to Nat, so that we get a complete distributive lattice, we still do not have a Boolean lattice.

Atomic Lattices

Let A be a lattice with a least element. The element $a \in A$ (where $a \neq \bot$) is called an *atom* if the following condition holds for each $b \in A$:

$$b \sqsubseteq a \;\;\Rightarrow\;\; b = \bot \vee b = a \ .$$

Thus, an atom is an element that is one step above the bottom element in a Hasse diagram.

A lattice A is said to be *atomic* if for each element x in A, we have that

$$x \;=\; \sqcup \{a \in A \mid a \text{ is an atom} \wedge a \sqsubseteq x\} \ .$$

The truth-value lattice is atomic. In fact, any finite complete Boolean lattice is atomic. The *representation theorem* states that any atomic complete Boolean lattice is isomorphic to the subset lattice of its atoms.

The subsets of a set also form an atomic lattice, where the atoms are the singleton sets. The definition of atomicity then states that any set in the subset lattice is the join (union) of its singleton subsets:

$$B \;=\; (\cup b \in B \cdot \{b\}) \ .$$

The following theorem summarizes the properties of the subset lattice that we have noted and proved above.

Theorem 2.3   *The subsets of a set D with the inclusion ordering form a complete, Boolean, and atomic lattice.*

Dual Lattice and Duality

The *dual* of a lattice $A = (A, \sqsubseteq)$ is the lattice $A^\circ = (A, \sqsupseteq)$. The dual lattice complete (distributive, Boolean) if and only if the lattice is complete (distributive Boolean). Meet in the dual lattice is join in the original lattice, and similarly, join in the dual lattice is meet in the original lattice. Complement is the same in both lattices.

Lattices satisfy the following *duality principle*. Let ϕ be a universal statement about lattices $(A, \sqsubseteq)$. The *dual statement* ϕ° is then constructed by interchanging $\sqsubseteq$ and $\sqsupseteq$, $\sqcap$ and $\sqcup$, $\perp$ and $\top$ in ϕ, while leaving $\neg$ unchanged. The dual statement true of all lattices if and only if the original statement is true of all lattices. The Morgan laws above provide an example of how this duality principle works.

We have shown earlier that the complement operation is antimonotonic rather than monotonic. This means that the complement operation is monotonic onto the dual of the lattice. If we consider complement as a function $\neg : A \to A^\circ$, then it is fact monotonic.

2.3   Product and Function Spaces

We now show how to construct new posets and lattices out of given posets lattices as product and function spaces.

Product Spaces

Let us first look at the Cartesian product. Let $(A, \sqsubseteq_A)$ and $(B, \sqsubseteq_B)$ be two posets We define a partial ordering on the Cartesian product $A \times B$ componentwise, by

$$(a, b) \sqsubseteq_{A \times B} (a', b') \quad \equiv \quad a \sqsubseteq_A a' \wedge b \sqsubseteq_B b' .   \qquad (\sqsubseteq \text{ of pairs}$$

The ordering thus holds between two pairs if and only if it holds for each component separately.

The Cartesian product of two posets is a poset itself, as the following lemma shows. In addition, the property of being a lattice is also inherited in a Cartesian product as are completeness, boundedness, (infinite) distributivity, and being a Boolean lattice.

Lemma 2.4   *Let $(A, \sqsubseteq)$ and $(B, \sqsubseteq)$ be posets. Then $(A \times B, \sqsubseteq)$ is also a poset when the ordering $\sqsubseteq$ on $A \times B$ is defined componentwise. This poset is a lattice (complete bounded, distributive, Boolean lattice) if A and B are lattices (complete, bounded distributive, Boolean lattices).*

The "if" in this lemma can be strengthened to "if and only if" when A and B are nonempty.

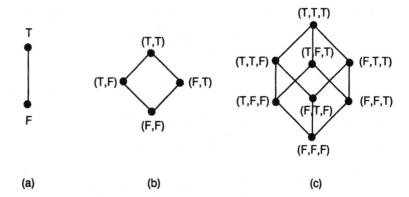

FIGURE 2.3. Products of the truth-value lattice

Assume that A and B are (bounded, Boolean) lattices. Bottom, top, complement, meet, and join in the product lattice are then componentwise extensions of the corresponding operations of the component lattices:

$$\begin{aligned}
\bot_{A \times B} &= (\bot_A, \bot_B) \,, & & (\bot \; of \; pairs) \\
\top_{A \times B} &= (\top_A, \top_B) \,, & & (\top \; of \; pairs) \\
\neg (a, b) &= (\neg a, \neg b) \,, & & (\neg \; of \; pairs) \\
(a, b) \sqcap (a', b') &= (a \sqcap a', b \sqcap b') \,, & & (\sqcap \; of \; pairs) \\
(a, b) \sqcup (a', b') &= (a \sqcup a', b \sqcup b') \,. & & (\sqcup \; of \; pairs)
\end{aligned}$$

These definitions are extended in the obvious way to the Cartesian product of an arbitrary number of posets.

The lattice (b) in Figure 2.1 has the same structure as the product lattice Bool $\times$ Bool, while lattice (c) in the same figure has the structure of the product lattice Bool $\times$ Bool $\times$ Bool. These product lattices are shown in Figure 2.3.

Function Spaces

Let A be a set and B a poset. Recall that $A \rightarrow B$ stands for the set of all functions $f : A \rightarrow B$. Two functions f and g in $A \rightarrow B$ are equal if they give the same values for each argument in A (this is known as the *extensionality principle*):

$$f = g \;\equiv\; (\forall x \in A \cdot f.x = g.x) \,.$$

We use this same idea to define a partial order on $A \rightarrow B$ as the extension of the partial order on B:

$$f \sqsubseteq_{A \rightarrow B} g \;\equiv\; (\forall x \in A \cdot f.x \sqsubseteq_B g.x) \qquad\qquad (\sqsubseteq \; of \; functions)$$

for any functions $f, g \in A \rightarrow B$. This is the extensionality principle for functions generalized to partial orderings. We say that the poset $A \rightarrow B$ is a *pointwise extension* of the poset B. The notion of pointwise extension is illustrated in Figure 2.4.

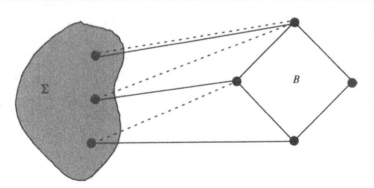

FIGURE 2.4. Pointwise extension ordering

The function indicated by the dashed arrows is here greater than the functi•
indicated by solid lines.

We have the same result for the pointwise extension to function spaces as f
Cartesian products.

Lemma 2.5 *Let B be a poset and A any set. Then the pointwise extension of B to $A \to B$*
also a poset. Furthermore, this poset is a lattice (complete, bounded, distributiv
Boolean lattice) if B is a lattice (complete, bounded, distributive, Boolean lattic•

Note that atomicity is a property that is not inherited by this extension (Exerci•
2.6).

The lattice operations in $A \to B$ are defined in terms of the correspondi•
operations on B, when B is a (bounded, Boolean) lattice. For any $x \in A$, •
define

$$
\begin{aligned}
\bot_{A \to B}.x &= \bot_B , &&(\bot \text{ of function}•\\
\top_{A \to B}.x &= \top_B , &&(\top \text{ of function}•\\
(\neg f).x &= \neg (f.x) , &&(\neg \text{ of function}•\\
(f \sqcap g).x &= f.x \sqcap g.x , &&(\sqcap \text{ of function}•\\
(f \sqcup g).x &= f.x \sqcup g.x . &&(\sqcup \text{ of function}•
\end{aligned}
$$

When B is a complete lattice, we define

$$
\begin{aligned}
(\sqcap i \in I \cdot f_i).x &= (\sqcap i \in I \cdot f_i.x) , &&(\text{general} \sqcap \text{ of function}•\\
(\sqcup i \in I \cdot f_i).x &= (\sqcup i \in I \cdot f_i.x) . &&(\text{general} \sqcup \text{ of function}•
\end{aligned}
$$

Subsets form a prime example of a pointwise extension construction. A sub•
$A \subseteq D$ can be described by a function $p_A : D \to$ Bool, which we define
$p_A.x = \top$ if and only if $x \in A$. Functions of this kind are known as *predicat•*
The predicates inherit lattice properties from the truth-value lattice. The pointw•
extension of the truth-value lattice to $D \to$ Bool is in fact a lattice that has exac•
the same structure as the subset lattice $\mathcal{P}(D)$.

Relations provide another example of pointwise extension. Set-theoretically, a relation is seen as a subset $r \subseteq A \times B$, but it can also be modeled as a function $R_r : A \to \mathcal{P}(B)$ by defining $R_r.a = \{b \in B \mid (a, b) \in r\}$. The relations $R : A \to \mathcal{P}(B)$ form a pointwise extension of the subset lattice, and this inherits the lattice properties of this simpler lattice. We will study both predicates and relations of this form in more detail later on.

Lattice Homomorphisms

Given a function from one lattice to another, we are interested in whether the function preserves some or all of the lattice structure of its domain. For instance, whether the bottom in the domain is mapped to the bottom in the range, whether meets are preserved, and so on. Functions that preserve this kind of lattice properties are generally known as *homomorphisms*.

Let A and B be lattices and $h : A \to B$. The following are special homomorphism properties that h may satisfy:

$$
\begin{aligned}
h.\bot_A &= \bot_B , & \text{(bottom homomorphism)} \\
h.\top_A &= \top_B , & \text{(top homomorphism)} \\
h.(a \sqcap_A a') &= h.a \sqcap_B h.a' , & \text{(meet homomorphism)} \\
h.(a \sqcup_A a') &= h.a \sqcup_B h.a' , & \text{(join homomorphism)} \\
h.(\neg_A a) &= \neg_B(h.a) . & \text{(complement homomorphism)}
\end{aligned}
$$

Thus, a bottom homomorphism maps the bottom of A to the bottom of B, while a top homomorphism maps the top of A to the top of B. Complement, meet, and join homomorphisms preserve complements, meets, and joins, respectively. A function on lattices can be homomorphic for only some of the lattice operations, or it can be homomorphic for all lattice operations. We say that the function h is a *lattice homomorphism* if it preserves meets and joins, and that it is a *Boolean lattice homomorphism* if it also preserves negation.

Figure 2.5 gives an example of a function from one lattice to another. The mapping indicated is a bottom and top homomorphism, and it is also a join homomorphism, but it is not a meet homomorphism, as is easily seen ($a \sqcap b = \bot$, but $f.a \sqcap f.b = c$ and $f.\bot \neq c$).

A (Boolean) lattice homomorphism $h : A \to B$ is said to be an *embedding* of A in B if h is injective (one-to-one). It is said to be an *epimorphism* (and B is an *image* of A) if h is surjective (onto). If h is both injective and surjective, i.e., a bijection, then we call it a (Boolean) *lattice isomorphism* and say that A and B are *isomorphic*.

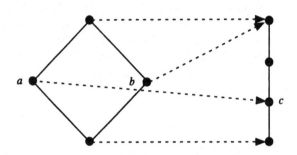

FIGURE 2.5. Homomorphic function

Binary Lattice Operations as Homomorphisms

The lattice operations themselves provide simple examples of homomorphis.
The property $a \sqcap (b \sqcap c) = (a \sqcap b) \sqcap (a \sqcap c)$ holds in any lattice. This prop
states that the function $f.x = a \sqcap x$ is meet homomorphic; we have that $f.(b \sqcap c$
$a \sqcap (b \sqcap c) = (a \sqcap b) \sqcap (a \sqcap c) = f.b \sqcap f.c$. Thus, the meet operation itsel
meet homomorphic in its right argument. By commutativity, meet is also a m
homomorphism in its left argument. Meet is also bottom homomorphic ($a \sqcap \bot =$
but usually not top homomorphic ($a \sqcap \top \neq \top$) in a complete lattice.

Similarly, join is join homomorphic and top homomorphic ($a \sqcup \top = \top$) but
usually bottom homomorphic ($a \sqcup \bot \neq \bot$) in a complete lattice.

Distributivity is also a homomorphism property. For instance, $a \sqcup (b \sqcap c) = ($
$b) \sqcap (a \sqcup c)$ states that the function $f.x = a \sqcup x$ is meet homomorphic, i.e., that
is meet homomorphic in its right argument (and hence in its left argument also
commutativity). Similarly, $a \sqcap (b \sqcup c) = (a \sqcap b) \sqcup (a \sqcap c)$ states that meet is
homomorphic in its right argument. Thus, lattice join is meet homomorphic
lattice meet is join homomorphic in a distributive lattice. Combining this with
previous result, we note that meet and join are both meet and join homomorphi
in a distributive lattice.

If we consider complement as a function $\neg : A \to A^\circ$, then it is a Boolean lat
isomorphism: $\neg \bot = \top$, $\neg (a \sqcup b) = (\neg a) \sqcap (\neg b)$, and so on.

Universal Meets and Joins

We extend the notion of a homomorphism to arbitrary sets of elements in a latt
as follows. We say that $h : A \to B$ is a *universal meet homomorphism* if
condition

$$h.(\sqcap i \in I \cdot a_i) = (\sqcap i \in I \cdot h.a_i) \qquad \textit{(universal } \sqcap \textit{ homomorphis}$$

holds for any set of elements $\{a_i \mid i \in I\}$ in A. We say that h is a *positive meet homomorphism* if this condition holds for any *nonempty* set of elements $\{a_i \mid i \in I\}$.

Dually, we say that h is a *universal join homomorphism* if the condition

$$h.(\sqcup i \in I \cdot a_i) \;=\; (\sqcup i \in I \cdot h.a_i) \qquad \text{(universal $\sqcup$ homomorphism)}$$

holds for any set $\{a_i \mid i \in I\}$ and that it is a *positive join homomorphism* if the condition holds for any nonempty set $\{a_i \mid i \in I\}$.

It is easy to see that lattice meet is a positive meet homomorphism: For $I \neq \emptyset$, we have $a \sqcap (\sqcap i \in I \cdot a_i) = (\sqcap i \in I \cdot a \sqcap a_i)$. However, lattice meet is usually not a universal meet homomorphism: We have $a \sqcap (\sqcap i \in \emptyset \cdot a_i) = a \sqcap \top = a$, but on the other hand, $(\sqcap i \in \emptyset \cdot a \sqcap a_i) = \top$.

Lattice meet is a positive join homomorphism if the lattice is infinitely join distributive. In fact, in this case it is even a universal join homomorphism, because $a \sqcap (\sqcup i \in \emptyset \cdot a_i) = a \sqcap \bot = \bot = (\sqcup i \in \emptyset \cdot a \sqcap a_i)$. The dual results hold for lattice joins.

Homomorphism Inclusions

The homomorphisms on a lattice are not independent of each other, as shown by the following lemma.

Lemma 2.6   *Let $h : A \to B$ be a function from lattice A to lattice B. Then*

    (a) *h is a universal meet (universal join) homomorphism if and only if h is a top (bottom) homomorphism and a positive meet (positive join) homomorphism;*

    (b) *if h is a positive meet (positive join) homomorphism, then h is a meet (join) homomorphism; and*

    (c) *if h is a meet or join homomorphism, then h is monotonic.*

Proof   We show the proof of (iii). The other properties follow directly from the definitions. Assume that h is a meet homomorphism. Then

    $a \sqsubseteq b$
  $\equiv$ {correspondence}
    $a = a \sqcap b$
  $\Rightarrow$ {functionality}
    $h.a = h.(a \sqcap b)$
  $\equiv$ {h is $\sqcap$-homomorphism}

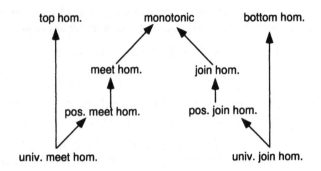

FIGURE 2.6. Homomorphism properties

$$h.a = h.a \sqcap h.b$$
$$\equiv \{\text{correspondence}\}$$
$$h.a \sqsubseteq h.b$$

The proof for join homomorphism is similar. $\square$

The implications between the different homomorphisms are shown in Figure 2 In this hierarchy, monotonicity and top and bottom homomorphisms are the wea est properties, while universal meet and join homomorphisms are the strong properties.

Tabular Representation

Because there are many lattices and operations on lattices that we consider in t book and there are also many homomorphism properties of interest, it becom cumbersome to list and memorize all the properties. On the other hand, the l momorphism properties are extremely useful when reasoning about lattices, so is worth identifying them all. We therefore introduce a concise tabular represe tation for describing monotonicity and homomorphism properties of functions lattices.

The homomorphism properties of the binary lattice operations were discuss above and are summarized in Table 2.1. The operations that we test for monoton ity and homomorphism are listed on the left. The monotonicity property is lis first on top of the table, in the column denoted $\sqsubseteq$. The homomorphism propert are then listed, with $\bot$ standing for bottom homomorphism, $\top$ for top homom phism, $\sqcap$ for positive meet homomorphism, $\sqcup$ for positive join homomorphism, a $\neg$ for complement homomorphism. We do not treat finite meet (or join) homom phism separately, because in most cases the same results hold for finite meet (jo homomorphism and positive meet (join) homomorphism. If needed, we explicitly indicate when a result holds only for finite meets or joins. Also, we do not have a separate entry for universal meet homomorphism, because that is equivalent to top and positive meet homomorphism both holding (and similarly for universal join homomorphism).

We write the label **is** in the top left corner to indicate that each table entry states whether the following assertion is true:

The function f (on the left) **is** *homomorphic* with respect to the operation g (on the top)

(for the relation $\sqsubseteq$, the assertion is that f **is** *monotonic* with respect to $\sqsubseteq$).

The table entry can be "yes" (meaning that this is always the case) or "no" (meaning that this need not be the case), or it can be a qualified "yes," with an indication of the condition under which the assertion holds. We write yes° for the case when the function is a homomorphism (or is monotonic) onto the dual lattice.

Pointwise Extension as Homomorphism

The pointwise extension theorem shows that if A is a partial order, then $B \to A$ is also a partial order, with the pointwise extension of $\sqsubseteq_A$ as the ordering, and that in fact the properties of being a lattice, complete lattice, distributive lattice, or Boolean lattice are all preserved by pointwise extension. Consider the function extend defined by extend.$f = f.x$, where x is a fixed element in A. This function maps elements in the lattice $(B \to A, \sqsubseteq_{B \to A})$ to elements in the lattice $(A, \sqsubseteq_A)$. Thus, we can ask whether it is a monotonic function, and to what extent it is a homomorphism. The results above answer all these questions affirmatively: pointwise extension is monotonic, and it is homomorphic for all lattice operations. Pointwise extension is thus a Boolean lattice homomorphism. Table 2.2 shows the relevant entries. We have, e.g., that

$$\text{extend}.(g \sqcap h) = \text{extend}.g \sqcap \text{extend}.h$$

in the case of meet homomorphism (see Exercise 2.3).

is	$\sqsubseteq$	$\bot$	$\top$	$\sqcap$	$\sqcup$	$\neg$
$f.x = x \sqcap a$	yes	yes	no	yes	yes[1]	no
$f.x = x \sqcup a$	yes	no	yes	yes[2]	yes	no
$f.x = \neg x$	yes°	yes°	yes°	yes°	yes°	yes

[1]when the lattice is infinitely join distributive
[2]when the lattice is infinitely meet distributive

TABLE 2.1. Homomorphic properties of lattice operations

is	⊑	⊥	⊤	⊓	⊔	¬
extend	yes	yes	yes	yes	yes	yes
fst	yes	yes	yes	yes	yes	yes
snd	yes	yes	yes	yes	yes	yes

TABLE 2.2. Homomorphic properties of pointwise extension

For the extension of lattices to a product of lattices, the corresponding result sta that projection onto the first or the second component preserves monotonicity is a lattice homomorphism. We have, e.g., that $\text{fst}(\bot_{A \times B}) = \bot_A$, that $\text{fst}.(a \sqcap b)$ $\text{fst}.a \sqcap \text{fst}.b$, and so on, as also shown in Table 2.2.

Lattice Operations as Homomorphisms

Consider finally the homomorphism properties of meet and join on lattices. Assu that A is a complete lattice. Then meet is a function from sets of elements in A elements in A, i.e., $\sqcap : \mathcal{P}A \to A$, and similarly for join. As we have shown abo $\mathcal{P}A$ is also a complete lattice ordered by inclusion. The characterization of top bottom shows that join is both bottom and top homomorphic:

$$\sqcup \emptyset = \bot \quad \text{and} \quad \sqcup A = \top .$$

Join is also monotonic,

$$B \subseteq B' \implies \sqcup B \sqsubseteq \sqcup B' ,$$

and it is join homomorphic,

$$\sqcup (B \cup B') = (\sqcup B) \sqcup (\sqcup B') .$$

However, join is neither meet homomorphic nor negation homomorphic.

In a similar way, it is easy to see that meet is bottom and top homomorphic to dual lattice A°:

$$\sqcap \emptyset = \top \quad \text{and} \quad \sqcap A = \bot .$$

Meet is antimonotonic,

$$B \subseteq B' \implies \sqcap B \sqsupseteq \sqcap B' ,$$

and it is join homomorphic onto the dual lattice

$$\sqcap (B \cup B') = (\sqcap B) \sqcap (\sqcap B') .$$

Table 2.3 summarizes these properties.

is	$\sqsubseteq$	$\bot$	$\top$	$\sqcap$	$\sqcup$	$\neg$
$\sqcap$	yes°	yes°	yes°	no	yes°	no
$\sqcup$	yes	yes	yes	no	yes	no

TABLE 2.3. Homomorphic properties of meet and join

5   Categories

Consider a collection of lattices and the possible homomorphisms between them. Take for instance all meet homomorphisms. We can see that the collection of meet homomorphisms is closed with respect to composition: if $h : A \rightarrow B$ is a meet homomorphism and $k : B \rightarrow C$ is a meet homomorphism, then $k \circ h : A \rightarrow C$ is also a meet homomorphism, as is easily checked:

$$(k \circ h).(a \sqcap b)$$
= {definition of functional composition}
$$k.(h.(a \sqcap b))$$
= {h is a meet homomorphism}
$$k.(h.a \sqcap h.b)$$
= {k is a meet homomorphism}
$$k.(h.a) \sqcap k.(h.b)$$
= {definition of functional composition}
$$(k \circ h).a \sqcap (k \circ h).b$$

The identity function id : $A \rightarrow A$ is a homomorphism for any operations or constants we choose to preserve. In particular, it is a meet homomorphism. A collection of lattices together with all meet homomorphisms between these lattices is an example of a *concrete category*; i.e., a category in which the objects are sets and the morphisms are structure-preserving functions from objects to objects.

In general, any collection of sets with a certain structure together with all the structure-preserving functions (homomorphisms) between these sets forms a concrete category. The collection of all posets together with all monotonic functions between the posets is another example of a concrete category. We can even consider the collection of all sets with a certain structure. This need not be a set itself, so the notion of a concrete category goes outside ordinary set theory. However, this notion provides a very useful abstraction, because it permits us to study all possible homomorphisms in a general way.

Abstract Categories

We can generalize the notion of a concrete category to an *(abstract) category.*
category C consists of a collection of *objects* Obj(C) and a collection of *morphism*
Mor(C). Each morphism has a *source* and a *target*, both of which are objects.
write $A \xrightarrow{f} B$ to indicate that f is a morphism with source A and target
Furthermore, there is a *composition* operator that takes a morphism $A \xrightarrow{f} B$ a
a morphism $B \xrightarrow{g} C$ to the morphism $A \xrightarrow{f;g} B$. Composition $f \; ; g$ is defin
only if the target of f is the source of g. Composition is required to be unique
defined and associative. Finally, for every object A there is a special morphism 1
the *identity morphism* on A, which is an identity element for composition. If the
is no danger of confusion, we usually drop the index and simply write 1 for 1_A.

Summarizing, the following always hold in a category:

$$f \; ; (g \; ; h) = (f \; ; g) \; ; h \; , \qquad \qquad \text{(; associative}$$
$$1 \; ; f = f \quad \text{and} \quad f \; ; 1 = f \; . \qquad \qquad \text{(1 uni}$$

We write $C(A, B)$ for the collection of all morphisms $A \xrightarrow{f} B$ in C. In catego
theory, we do not need to assume that the morphisms form a set. If they do, th
the category is said to be *small*.

Figure 2.7 illustrates these notions. The objects are A, B, C, and D; the morphism
are $A \xrightarrow{f} B$, $B \xrightarrow{g} C$, $B \xrightarrow{h} D$, $C \xrightarrow{j} D$, $D \xrightarrow{k} B$, the identi
morphisms for each object, and all morphisms that can be constructed from t
explicitly indicated morphisms by composition.

Any concrete category will be an abstract category, where the sets with structu
are the objects and the structure-preserving functions are the morphisms of

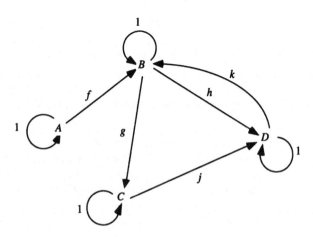

FIGURE 2.7. Objects and morphisms

category. In particular, the concrete category of sets with functions forms a category. The sets $A, B, \ldots$ are the objects and the functions $f : A \to B, \ldots$ are the morphisms $A \xrightarrow{f} B$. Composition in this category is forward functional composition, defined by $(f \bullet g).x = g(f(x))$, and the identity functions id : $A \to A$ are the unit morphisms 1_A in the category. Functional composition is associative, so the category properties hold.

We could also choose the functions $f : B \to A$ (the reverse direction) as the morphisms $A \xrightarrow{f} B$. In this case, composition is backward functional composition, defined by $(f \circ g).x = f(g(x))$, while the identity function id : $A \to A$ still serves as the unit morphism 1_A.

The collection of all relations also forms a category. Each object is a set, and as morphisms $A \xrightarrow{R} B$ we choose relations $R \subseteq A \times B$. The identity relation serves as the unit element, and composition is ordinary relational composition $R \bullet Q$, where $(x, z) \in R \bullet Q$ iff $(x, y) \in R$ and $(y, z) \in Q$, for some y. This is an example of a category that is not a concrete category.

A preorder can be seen as a special kind of category. The objects of the category are the elements of the preorder. There is a morphism $a \xrightarrow{f} b$ between two elements a and b if and only if $a \sqsubseteq b$. Reflexivity guarantees that there is an identity morphism, and transitivity guarantees that the composition of two morphisms is a morphism in the poset category.

Functors and Homomorphisms

The analogue to a lattice homomorphism in a category is a *functor*. Given two categories C and D, a functor F maps objects of C to objects of D and morphisms of C to morphisms of D in such a way that sources, targets, composition, and identities are preserved. This means that F maps every morphism $A \xrightarrow{f} B$ to a morphism $F.f$ with source $F.A$ and target $F.B$; i.e., $F.A \xrightarrow{F.f} F.B$ and the following holds:

$$F(f \,;\, g) = (F.f)\,;(F.g) \,, \qquad \text{(functor properties)}$$
$$F.1_A = 1_{(F.A)} \,.$$

A trivial example of a functor is the identity functor, which maps a category to itself. The functor F reduces to a homomorphism in the special case when it does not change the objects; i.e., $F.A = A$ for each object A.

Order-Enriched Categories

The function space construction gives us new lattices where partial order and the lattice operations are defined by pointwise extension. Since the elements are functions, we can also compose them, and there is an identity element for function composition. Relations have a similar structure. The function space constructio thus have both a lattice structure and a category structure. Most of the basic stru tures that are needed for the refinement calculus turn out to be categories of th kind.

Consider a category C where for arbitrary objects A and B the morphisms $C(A, $ are ordered by a relation $\sqsubseteq_{A,B}$. We say that C is an *order-enriched category* composition is *monotonic* in both arguments:

$$f \sqsubseteq_{A,B} f' \wedge g \sqsubseteq_{B,C} g' \;\Rightarrow\; f;g \sqsubseteq_{A,C} f';g'$$

(any category can in fact be viewed as such an order-enriched category if we choo the discrete partial order as the ordering). If composition is monotonic only in left argument,

$$f \sqsubseteq f' \;\Rightarrow\; f;g \sqsubseteq f';g \,,$$

then we call the category a *left order-enriched category*. A *right* order-enrich category is defined analogously. A category is obviously order-enriched if and on if it is both left and right order-enriched. If the ordering relation is a preorder, pos lattice, etc., we call the category a *preorder-enriched category*, a *poset-enrich category*, a *lattice-enriched category*, and so on.

The interaction between the order and category structures gives rise to numero distributivity possibilities. For example, we may want to know whether compositi distributes over lattice operations from the left or from the right. For instance, do $c;(a \sqcap b) = c;a \sqcap c;b$ (left distributivity over meet) hold, or does $(a \sqcap b);c = a;c \sqcap b$ (right distributivity over meet) hold? If the morphisms for a given source and targ form a complete lattice, we may ask whether $(\sqcap i \in I \cdot a_i);b = (\sqcap i \in I \cdot a_i ;$ Similarly, we may ask whether meet and join distribute over composition. F instance, is $(a;b) \sqcap c = (a \sqcap c);(b \sqcap c)$? In this case we need not distinguish l from right distributivity, since meet and join are commutative.

Example: Pointwise Extension

Assume that C is a category where the objects are posets $(A, \sqsubseteq_A), (B, \sqsubseteq_B), \ldots$ a the morphisms are functions $f : A \to B, \ldots$, ordered by the pointwise extensi of the ordering relation. Composition is backward functional composition. We c see that this category is left poset-enriched, as follows. Assume that $f \sqsubseteq g$. Th

$$(f;h).x$$
$$= \{\text{definition of composition}\}$$
$$f.(h.x)$$
$$\sqsubseteq \{\text{assumption}\}$$
$$g.(h.x)$$

= {definition of composition}

$(g ; h).x$

so $f \sqsubseteq g \Rightarrow f ; h \sqsubseteq g ; h$ follows by pointwise extension (a dual argument shows that if composition is forward function composition, then the category is right poset-enriched).

If we choose the monotonic functions $f : A \rightarrow B$ as the morphisms in this category, rather than all functions, then we get a (proper) poset-enriched category. Assume that $f \sqsubseteq g$ and h is monotonic. Then

$(h ; f).x$

= {definition of composition}

$h.(f.x)$

$\sqsubseteq$ {assumptions; pointwise extension}

$h.(g.x)$

= {definition of composition}

$(h ; g).x$

Next we consider distributivity of composition over lattice operators in either one of these categories. The following derivations show that composition distributes from the right over meet:

$((f \sqcap g) ; h).x$

= {definition of composition}

$(f \sqcap g).(h.x)$

= {pointwise extended meet}

$f.(h.x) \sqcap g.(h.x)$

= {definition of composition}

$(f ; h).x \sqcap (g ; h).x$

= {pointwise extended meet}

$(f ; h \sqcap g ; h).x$

so $(f \sqcap g) ; h = f ; h \sqcap g ; h$.

Right distributivity also holds for join, bottom, top, and complement. However, left distributivity does not in general hold for any of the lattice operations. Forward function composition again dually distributes from the left over lattice operations.

2.6   Summary and Discussion

We have given an overview of the basic notions of partial orders, of monotonicity
posets, and of meets and joins in posets. We have defined what it means for a po
to be a lattice and have identified a number of subclasses of lattices. We have a
shown how to build new posets and lattices from old ones using product and functi
spaces, and shown to what extent the lattice properties are inherited by the
constructions. We have looked at structure-preserving mappings (homomorphisn
between lattices and shown how collections of lattices form categories.

The category theory that we need in this book will be quite elementary. We mai
use it as an organizational concept for the different kinds of algebraic structu
that we need for the refinement calculus. It also allows us to treat different ki
of compositions in a uniform manner, in the same way as lattice theory allows
to treat ordering in a uniform manner across many different kinds of structures

The material on lattices presented here is rather standard and can be found in ma
classical references such as Birkhoff [40] and George Grätzer [63]. In particu
these references contain proofs of the theorems of infinite distributivity for cc
plete Boolean lattices and the representation theorem for atomic lattices. A mod
textbook is Davey and Priestley [50]. Good introductions to category theory a
its use in computer science have been written by Benjamin Pierce [116] and
Barr and Wells [38].

We have chosen to start our exposition of the refinement calculus with an overvi
of basic lattice-theoretic notions. The reason is that these simple ideas form
basis for the formalization of higher-order logic that we will consider next. T
large extent, reasoning about truth values, sets, relations, and program stateme
can be seen as different instantiations of the same basic lattice-theoretic conce
that we have described above. This has also motivated us to present the materia
somewhat more detail than what might be strictly needed, because it is import
to have a good intuitive grasp of the concepts involved.

2.7   Exercises

2.1   Let the set $A = \{1, 2, 3, 6, 8, 12\}$ be ordered such that $m \sqsubseteq n$ means that n
divisible by n. Find two numbers in A that do not have a least upper bound in A
it possible to find two numbers in A that do not have a greatest lower bound in

2.2   Show that the composition of two monotonic functions is a monotonic functio

2.3   Assume that B is a lattice and A is an arbitrary set. Show that pointwise extens
to the function space $A \to B$ is a lattice homomorphism.

2.4   Let L be the set of all cofinite sets of natural numbers (i.e., all sets that have a finite complement), ordered by set inclusion. Show that L is a lattice but not a complete lattice. Does it have a top or a bottom element?

2.5   Prove that the structure (Bool × Nat, $\sqsubseteq$) is a lattice, where $\sqsubseteq$ is the following ordering:

$$(b, n) \sqsubseteq (b', n') \equiv b \Rightarrow b' \wedge n \leq n' .$$

What are the least upper bounds and greatest lower bounds in this lattice? Is the lattice bounded, distributed, complete, Boolean? Show that f : Bool × Nat → Nat, where $f.(\text{F}, n) = 2n$ and $f.(\text{T}, n) = 2n + 1$ is monotonic but not an order embedding of (Bool × Nat, $\sqsubseteq$) into (Nat, $\leq$).

2.6   Let A be any infinite set. Then (A → Bool, $\subseteq$) is an atomic complete Boolean lattice. Show that (A → Bool) → (A → Bool) ordered by pointwise-extended set inclusion is not atomic.

2.7   Assume that f and g are bijective monotonic functions with $f \sqsubseteq g$. Show that $g^{-1} \sqsubseteq f^{-1}$.

2.8   Show that the implications in Figure 2.6 are all valid.

2.9   The function $f : \mathcal{P}(\text{Bool}) \rightarrow \mathcal{P}(\text{Nat})$ is defined such that

$$
\begin{aligned}
f.\emptyset &= \emptyset , \\
f.\{\text{F}\} &= \{0\} , \\
f.\{\text{T}\} &= \{x \mid x \neq 0\} , \\
f.\text{Bool} &= \text{Nat} .
\end{aligned}
$$

Show that f is a homomorphic embedding.

2.10 Let A be an arbitrary set and $\bot$ and $\top$ two elements not in A. Show that the set $A \cup \{\bot, \top\}$, ordered by

$$a \sqsubseteq b \equiv a = b \vee a = \bot \vee b = \top ,$$

is a complete lattice.

2.11 Show that the meet operation in a complete lattice has the following property:

$$x = \sqcap A \equiv (\forall y \cdot y \sqsubseteq x \equiv (\forall a \in A \cdot y \sqsubseteq a)) .$$

Since the definition characterizes meet using two properties (that it is a lower bound and that is greater than all lower bounds), this characterization can make proofs about meets shorter. What is the dual characterization of join?

igher-Order Logic

We now introduce the logical basis for program refinement, *higher-order logic*. This is an extension of the *simply typed lambda calculus* with logical connectives and quantifiers, permitting logical reasoning about functions in a very general way. In particular, it allows quantification over higher-order entities such as predicates and relations, a feature that we will find very useful in our formalization. The power of higher-order logic is similar to that of set theory. It is sufficient for expressing most ordinary mathematical theories and has a simple set-theoretic semantics.

We describe the basic framework of higher-order logic in this chapter: the syntactic entities of the logic, the semantic meaning of these entities, the notions of deduction and proof, and the notion of a theory. In the next chapter we then give the specific axioms and inference rules that are needed to reason about functions. These are the usual rules of the simply typed lambda calculus. The axioms and inference rules needed for reasoning about logical propositions in general are postponed to Chapter 6.

Types and Terms

In informal mathematics, functions have to be introduced with an explicit name before they can be used in mathematical expressions. Lambda calculus provides a mechanism for building expressions that denote functions (so-called *lambda expressions*), so that functions can be used without explicit definitions and naming.

Functions are constructed by λ-*abstraction*. The function that maps each na**t**
number n to its successor $n + 1$ is written as the lambda abstraction

$$(\lambda n : \text{Nat} \cdot n + 1) \ .$$

Here Nat is a *type* that denotes the set of natural numbers. The part λn :
expresses that the argument of the function is denoted by n and ranges over th**e**
of natural numbers Nat. The value of the function for argument n is given by
expression $n + 1$. The parentheses delineate the scope of the *bound variable* **n**

Lambda abstraction permits us to be precise about the variables and constant**s**
an expression. For instance, we can make a distinction between the functions

$$(\lambda n : \text{Nat} \cdot n - m) \quad \text{and} \quad (\lambda m : \text{Nat} \cdot n - m) \ .$$

In the first case, n is the argument of the function and m is a constant th**at**
assumed to have some fixed value (determined by the context). In the second lam**bda**
expression, it is the other way around. We can also nest lambda abstraction**s**
that, e.g.,

$$(\lambda m : \text{Nat} \cdot (\lambda n : \text{Nat} \cdot n - m))$$

is the function that maps each natural number m to the function $(\lambda n : \text{Nat} \cdot n -$

Applying a function to an argument is called *application*. Application is an o**per**
ation that takes two terms, t denoting a function and s denoting an argument,
gives as result the value of function t at argument s. The application of t to
written $t.s$. For example, we have that

$$
\begin{aligned}
(\lambda n : \text{Nat} \cdot n - m).(a + 3) &= (a + 3) - m \ , \\
(\lambda m : \text{Nat} \cdot (\lambda n : \text{Nat} \cdot n - m)).(a + 3) &= (\lambda n : \text{Nat} \cdot n - (a + 3)) \ .
\end{aligned}
$$

The exact rules for computing with abstractions and applications will be m**ade**
precise later. But before that, we need to be more precise about the syntax
semantics of lambda calculus types and expressions.

Types

The *types* of higher-order logic are expressions that denote sets. Let AT be a
structure, i.e., a set of type operators each having a name and an arity (an arity
natural number). *Types* over AT are defined by the following context-free gram**mar**

$$\Sigma \ ::= \ C \mid \Sigma_1 \to \Sigma_2 \mid Op(\Sigma_1, \ldots, \Sigma_n) \ . \tag{typ}$$

Here C is a nullary type operator (also called an *atomic type*) in AT, while $\Sigma_1, \ldots$
are types (we generally use Σ, Γ, and Δ as metavariables for types). The
operator $\to$ associates to the right, so that, e.g., $\Sigma_1 \to \Sigma_2 \to \Sigma_3$ abbrev**iates**
$\Sigma_1 \to (\Sigma_2 \to \Sigma_3)$. In the last alternative, Op is an n-ary type operator in AT
constructs a new type out of the types $\Sigma_1, \ldots, \Sigma_n$.

Each type denotes some *nonempty* set. The atomic types denote designated sets in the universe of all sets (this will be made more precise below). Higher-order logic postulates two atomic types: Bool, which denotes the two-element set of *truth values*, and Ind, which denotes an infinite set of *individuals*.

The *function type* $\Sigma_1 \rightarrow \Sigma_2$ stands for the set of all (total) functions from the set denoted by Σ_1 to the set denoted by Σ_2. Thus, e.g., Ind $\rightarrow$ Bool denotes the set of functions from individuals to truth values. Similarly, each type operator denotes a set-forming operation, and $Op(\Sigma_1, \ldots, \Sigma_n)$ stands for the result of applying that operation to the sets denoted by $\Sigma_1, \ldots, \Sigma_n$. In fact, we can view $\rightarrow$ as a binary type operator, mapping sets Σ_1 and Σ_2 to the set $\Sigma_1 \rightarrow \Sigma_2$. However, we prefer to give it special status, since it is so fundamental. It is possible to add new type operators (including atomic types) to the logic. This is illustrated in Chapter 4 and described in more detail in Chapter 10.

Part of the power of higher-order logic comes from the fact that we can iterate type construction to ever higher levels of functionality. For instance, (Ind $\rightarrow$ Bool) $\rightarrow$ Bool denotes the set of functions that take functions from individuals to truth values as arguments and return truth values as results. This is a set of *higher-order functions*.

Terms

The terms of higher-order logic are expressions that denote elements of types. Each term t in higher-order logic is associated with a unique type.

We assume that two disjoint infinite sets of *names* are given, *constant names* and *variable names*. A *constant* is a pair (c, Σ), written c_Σ, where c is a constant name and Σ is a type. Similarly, a *variable* is a pair (v, Σ), written v_Σ, where v is a variable name and Σ is a type.

Just as the definition of types is relative to a particular type structure AT, the definition of terms is relative to a given set SG of constants, called a *signature*, where each constant has a type over AT. The *terms* of higher-order logic are defined by the following context-free grammar:

$$
\begin{array}{llll}
t & ::= & v_\Sigma\ , & \textit{(variable)} \\
  & | & c_\Sigma\ , & \textit{(constant)} \\
  & | & t_1.t_2\ , & \textit{(application)} \\
  & | & (\lambda v_\Sigma \cdot t_1) & \textit{(abstraction)}
\end{array}
$$

(we use s and t as metavariables for terms; c, f, and g as metavariables for constants; and u, v, and w as metavariables for variables).

We associate a type with each term using the following rules:

(i) Each variable v_Σ is a term of type Σ.

(ii) Each constant c_Σ in SG is a term of type Σ.

(iii) If t is a term of type $\Sigma_1 \to \Sigma_2$ and t_1 a term of type Σ_1, then the *applicati* $t.t_1$ is a term of type Σ_2.

(iv) If v_{Σ_1} is a variable and t_2 a term of type Σ_2, then the *abstraction* $(\lambda v_{\Sigma_1} \cdot$ is a term of type $\Sigma_1 \to \Sigma_2$.

A term t is *well-typed* if it has a type Σ according to the above rules. The ty of each well-typed term is uniquely determined by the syntax. We write $t : \Sigma$ express that t has type Σ. A well-typed term $t : \Sigma$ denotes some element in set denoted by Σ, in the way described intuitively above. From now on, we alwa take 'term' to mean 'well-typed term'.

Type indications are usually omitted from constants and variables when this inf mation can be deduced from the structure of the term or from the context in wh the term is used. When needed, it is often sufficient to indicate the types of so variables in lambda abstractions. In this case, we prefer to write $(\lambda v : \Sigma \cdot t_1)$ $(\lambda v_\Sigma \cdot t_1)$, particularly if the type expression Σ is more complex.

Two different variables can have the same name, if they have different types. T different constants can also have the same name, provided that they have diffe types. Both kinds of *overloading* are quite convenient, provided that one adds ex type information or explanations whenever necessary to avoid ambiguity.

Precedence and Association

Application associates to the left, so that $t.t'.t''$ stands for $(t.t').t''$. In some ca we use a constant $f : \Sigma \to \Gamma \to \Delta$ as an *infix operator*, writing $x \ f \ y$ ra than $f.x.y$. Typical examples are addition and subtraction; we prefer to write x rather than $+.x.y$. Infix operators have lower precedence than ordinary funct application, and they always associate to the right. The precedences of diffe infix operators are listed in Appendix A. Parentheses can always be used to over (or emphasize) the precedences.

For some constants we use a *prefix* format, writing $f \ x$ for $f.x$, with the sa precedence. In particular, we write negation and complement as prefix consta and similarly for meets and joins over sets. Prefix operators have lower precede than function application, but higher precedence than infix operators.

A small number of constants are written as *postfix* operators. Most postfix opera are written as superscripts (e.g., S° is the duality operator $\circ$ applied to S). Pos operators have higher precedence than ordinary function application.

Abstraction is written as a *mixfix*, with delimiters (the parentheses) indicating scope of the abstraction. Abstraction has lower precedence than application. simplify nested applications, we can write $(\lambda v \cdot (\lambda v' \cdot t))$ as $(\lambda v \ v' \cdot t)$.

Substitution and Replacement

We make a distinction between free and bound occurrences of variables in a term. An occurrence of the variable v in term t is *bound* if it is within a subterm of t of the form $(\lambda v \cdot t')$; otherwise it is *free*. A variable is free in t if it occurs free in t, and it is bound in t if it occurs bound in t. A term in which all occurrences of variables are bound is called *closed*. Consider as an example the term

$$(\lambda n \cdot n - m).(a + 1) \ .$$

The variable n is here bound, while m and a are free. A variable can occur both free and bound in the same term. For example, the variable n occurs both free and bound in the term $n + (\lambda n \cdot n + 1).m$.

The term $t[v := t']$ stands for the result of substituting the term t' for all free occurrences of variable v in term t. If no free variable of t' becomes bound in $t[v := t']$, then we say that t' *is free for v in t*. Thus,

$$(\lambda n \cdot n - m).(a + 1)[m := (a - 1)]$$

is the same term as

$$(\lambda n \cdot n - (a - 1)).(a + 1) \ .$$

The term $(a - 1)$ is free for m in $(\lambda n \cdot n - m).(a + 1)$, because a does not become bound in the substitution. The term $(n - 1)$ would not be free for m in this term. We write $t[v_1, \ldots, v_m := t_1, \ldots, t_m]$ for the *simultaneous* substitution of terms $t_1, \ldots, t_m$ for variables $v_1, \ldots, v_m$ in t.

Substitution is sometimes used to indicate a term with specific occurrences of some subterm singled out; $t[v := s]$ is a term where the variable v is used in term t to indicate the positions of the interesting occurrences of subterm s.

Standard Types and Constants

It is necessary to impose some additional structure on the framework introduced so far. For now, we assume only a minimal structure that is needed to reason about functions. In Chapter 6, we introduce further structure for reasoning about truth and falsity.

We assume that every type structure contains the *standard type* Bool. Furthermore, we assume that every constant signature contains a *standard constant* called *equality*,

$$= \ : \ \Sigma \to \Sigma \to \text{Bool} \qquad\qquad\qquad (equality)$$

for each type Σ.

The intended (*standard*) interpretation is that Bool denotes a distinguished two-element set of truth values and that $=$ denotes equality on the set denoted by Σ.

3.2   Semantics

We give a brief description of the meaning (*semantics*) of types and terms in high-order logic. The semantics is set-theoretic; a type Σ denotes a set in a universe sets, and a term $t : \Sigma$ denotes an element in the set denoted by Σ.

We assume a universe (family) $\mathcal{U}$ of nonempty sets, which is closed under following operations: nonempty subset, Cartesian product, power set, and functi space. This means that, e.g., if X is in $\mathcal{U}$, and Y is a nonempty subset of X, then a Y is in $\mathcal{U}$. Furthermore, we assume that $\mathcal{U}$ contains a distinguished infinite set $\mathbf{I}$ elements are called *individuals*) and a distinguished two-element set $\mathbf{2} = \{\text{ff, tt}\}$ elements are called *truth values*). Finally, we assume that there is a choice functi called choice on $\mathcal{U}$ that chooses some (arbitrary) element from every nonempty s i.e., choice.$X \in X$ for all $X \in \mathcal{U}$, $X \neq \emptyset$. Not all these assumptions are needed this chapter, but we find it convenient to make all assumptions about the unive explicit from the start.

Semantics of Types

A *model* for a type structure AT is given by associating every n-ary type opera *op* in AT with some function $f : \mathcal{U}^n \to \mathcal{U}$ (the *meaning* of the operation).

We require that the type Bool be given a *standard meaning* as the set $\mathbf{2}$ and that function type constructor $\to$ be given a standard meaning as the function in $\mathcal{U}^2$ $\mathcal{U}$ that maps the pair (X, Y) to the set of all (set-theoretic) total functions from X Y. Given a model for AT, every type Σ denotes a set $\mathcal{M}.\Sigma$ (the *meaning of* Σ) in In a *standard model*, $\mathcal{M}.\text{Bool} = \mathbf{2}$ and $\mathcal{M}.(\Sigma \to \Gamma) = \{f \mid f : \mathcal{M}.\Sigma \to \mathcal{M}.$

For example, if $\times$ denotes Cartesian product, then (Bool $\times$ Bool) $\to$ Bool den the set of all functions $f : \mathbf{2} \times \mathbf{2} \to \mathbf{2}$, i.e., functions that map pairs of truth val to truth values.

Semantics of Terms

Now assume that type structure AT is given and that SG is a signature over AT *model* for SG determines (1) a model for AT and (2) for every constant $c : \Sigma$ in an element $\mathcal{M}.c \in \mathcal{M}.\Sigma$ (the *meaning of* c). In a *standard model* we require $= \ : \Sigma \to \Sigma \to$ Bool be given its *standard meaning* as equality on the set deno by Σ.

Consider a term t. An *environment* E for the term is a set of variable-value p $\{(x_1, a_1), \ldots, (x_n, a_n)\}$ that assigns a value a_i in $\mathcal{M}.\Sigma$ to every free variable x_i that occurs in t. The meaning of a term with free variables is determined rela to such an environment.

The meaning $\mathcal{M}_E.t$ of a term t in environment E is defined inductively, as follows. The model gives the meanings of constants,

$$\mathcal{M}_E.c \;=\; \mathcal{M}.c \;,$$

and the environment gives the meanings of variables,

$$\mathcal{M}_E.x \;=\; a, \quad \text{when } (x, a) \in E.$$

For application, we define

$$\mathcal{M}_E.t.t' \;=\; (\mathcal{M}_E.t).(\mathcal{M}_E.t') \;.$$

Thus, if t denotes a function f and t' denotes an element x, then $t.t'$ denotes the element $f.x$. Finally, the denotation $\mathcal{M}_E.(\lambda v : \Sigma \cdot t)$ of lambda abstraction is the function f, defined by

$$f.a \;=\; \mathcal{M}_{E'}.t \;,$$

that maps any $a \in \mathcal{M}.\Sigma$ to $\mathcal{M}_{E'}.t$, where E' is the same environment as E except that v is mapped to a. In this way, the meanings assigned to the constants determine the meanings of all terms that can be built out of these constants in a given environment.

For a closed term t, the the meaning is independent of the environment (since there are no free variables), and we can define $\mathcal{M}.t = \mathcal{M}_\emptyset.t$.

Deductive Systems

The syntax of higher-order logic is next extended with a deductive system in which we can prove properties of elements denoted by terms. We assume below that a standard type structure AT and a standard signature SG are given.

A *formula* is a term of type Bool. Given a specific assignment of values to the free variables in a formula (an environment), a formula thus always denotes a truth value.

A *sequent* is a pair (Φ, t), written

$$\Phi \vdash t \;, \tag{sequent}$$

where Φ is a finite set of formulas over SG (the *assumptions* of the sequent) and t is a single formula over SG (the *consequent* of the sequent). A sequent $\Phi \vdash t$ is *satisfied* in a model of the types in AT and constants in SG if any environment (with assignment of values to the free variables in Φ and t) that makes every formula in Φ true also makes t true. A sequent is *valid* if it is satisfied in every standard model.

An *inference* is a tuple of sequents $(\Phi_1 \vdash t_1, \ldots, \Phi_m \vdash t_m, \Phi \vdash t)$, $m \geq 0$. inference is usually written as

$$\frac{\Phi_1 \vdash t_1 \quad \cdots \quad \Phi_m \vdash t_m}{\Phi \vdash t} \, .$$ *(inferenc*

The sequents $\Phi_1 \vdash t_1, \ldots, \Phi_m \vdash t_m$ are called the *hypotheses* and $\Phi \vdash t$ is ca the *conclusion* of the inference.

An inference of higher-order logic is said to be *valid* if any standard model satisfies all the hypotheses also satisfies the conclusion.

A *deductive system* DS is a set of inferences. We usually define the inference a deductive system DS with a small collection of *inference rules*. These have same form as inferences but may contain metavariables that stand for arbitr terms and sets of formulas. As before, we use s and t as metavariables for ter c, f, and g for constants; and u, v, and w for variables. In addition, we use Φ finite sets of formulas. Any instantiation of these metavariables that satisfies associated *side condition* is then a permitted inference of the deductive system

An inference rule is written as

$$\frac{\Phi_1 \vdash t_1 \quad \cdots \quad \Phi_m \vdash t_m}{\Phi \vdash t} \quad \{R\}$$ *(inference ru*

• side condition.

The name of the inference rule is R. Here $\Phi_1, \ldots, \Phi_m$, Φ and $t_1, \ldots, t_m$, t may tain metavariables. The side condition states the requirements that an instantia of the metavariables with actual terms has to satisfy.

An inference with no hypotheses ($m = 0$) is called an *axiom*. An inference with no hypotheses is called an *axiom scheme* of DS. The line that separates (empty) set of hypotheses from the conclusion is usually omitted in axioms usually not in axiom schemes).

Deductions

We can construct new inferences from old ones by composition. If

$$\frac{\Phi_1 \vdash t_1 \quad \cdots \quad \Phi_i \vdash t_i \quad \cdots \quad \Phi_n \vdash t_n}{\Phi \vdash t}$$

is an instance of inference rule R (and thus satisfies the side condition if the one) and

$$\frac{\Phi_{i,1} \vdash t_{i,1} \quad \cdots \quad \Phi_{i,n} \vdash t_{i,n}}{\Phi_i \vdash t_i}$$

is an instance of inference rule R' with a conclusion that is the same as the ith hypothesis of the first inference, then their composition is the inference

$$\frac{\Phi_1 \vdash t_1 \ \cdots \ \Phi_{i,1} \vdash t_{i,1} \ \cdots \ \Phi_{i,n} \vdash t_{i,n} \ \cdots \ \Phi_n \vdash t_n}{\Phi \vdash t},$$

which we get from the first inference by replacing the hypothesis $\Phi_i \vdash t_i$ with the hypotheses $\Phi_{i,1} \vdash t_{i,1}, \ldots, \Phi_{i,n} \vdash t_{i,n}$.

A *deduction* in DS records the intermediate steps and the inference rules of DS that we have used to construct an inference. The deduction for the above inference is

$$\frac{\Phi_1 \vdash t_1 \ \cdots \ \dfrac{\Phi_{i,1} \vdash t_{i,1} \cdots \Phi_{i,n} \vdash t_{i,n} \ \{R'\}}{\Phi_i \vdash t_i} \ \cdots \ \Phi_n \vdash t_n \ \{R\}}{\Phi \vdash t}.$$

For each inference, we indicate the inference rule that determines it. The hypotheses of this deduction are the sequents that are not conclusions of inferences, and the conclusion of the whole derivation is $\Phi \vdash t$. By composing inferences, we can build deductions of arbitrary complexity.

A sequent $\Phi \vdash t$ is a *theorem* if there exists a *proof* of it, i.e., a deduction without any hypotheses and with the sequent as its conclusion.

Deductions can also be built by composing inference rules rather than inferences. In this case, we are building *deduction schemes*. One then has to be careful that the side conditions of all rules that are used in the deduction are satisfied. Each such deduction scheme gives us an inference rule where the conclusion is the final conclusion of the whole deduction scheme, the hypotheses are the topmost hypotheses of the deduction scheme, and the side condition consists of the accumulated side conditions of the rules used in the deduction. An inference rule arrived at in this way is called a *derived inference rule*.

A derived inference rule without any hypotheses is called a *theorem scheme*. A theorem scheme may thus have side conditions, and it may contain metavariables that stand for arbitrary terms or sets of formulas (a theorem cannot contain any metavariables).

Theories

A *theory* is determined by a type structure AT, a set of constants SG over AT (the signature), and a set of inference rules DS (the *primitive rules of inference*). The first determines the types that can be formed in the theory, the first and second together determine the terms and formulas that can be expressed in the theory, and all three together determine the proofs (and thus also the theorems and derived inference rules) in the theory.

A theory is *consistent* if there exists some sequent (over the signature of the theory) that cannot be derived. Once we have introduced the notion of falsity F, we can formulate this in a more familiar way; a theory is consistent if F cannot be proved as a theorem within the theory.

A theory is *sound* (with respect to a given model) if every sequent that can be proved in it is valid in the model. It is *complete* (with respect to a model) if a valid theorem can be proved using the deductive system of the theory.

A theory is *extended* by adding new types, new constants, and new inference rules. A theory extension thus makes the language more expressive and may permit more theorems to be proved. Anything provable in the original theory is, however, also provable in the extended theory.

An extension of a consistent theory need not be consistent. That is why it is desirable to extend the theory in a conservative way. An extension is said to be *conservative* if it does not extend the set of theorems over the old signature. This means that a sequent of the original theory can be proved in the extension if and only if it can be proved in the original theory. The advantage of a conservative extension is that it has a standard model whenever the original theory has one. This means that a conservative extension can never introduce inconsistency.

3.5 Summary and Discussion

This chapter has introduced the basic ingredients of higher-order logic: the syntax and semantics of types and terms, the notion of a deductive system, and the notion of a proof in higher-order logic. The basic notions of soundness and completeness of a deductive system have also been defined, as well as the notion of conservative theory extensions. For more details and two slightly different formulations of higher-order logic, we refer to the books by Peter Andrews [3] and by Michael Gordon and Tom Melham [62].

Higher-order logic is based on Alonzo Church's work on a simple theory of types [48], originally invented as a tool for studying the foundations of mathematics. The central notion of types was first proposed by Bertrand Russell and Alfred North Whitehead [140] in an attempt to avoid the paradoxes in naive set theory discovered by Russell.

There are also stronger and more expressive type theories, such as the Martin-Löf type theory [99] and the calculus of constructions [49]. These permit subtypes and dependent types to be expressed quite elegantly. However, typing may then not be decidable, so correct typing needs to be proved for an expression at the same time that the properties expressed by the formulas are proved. Thus, the price to be paid for the added expressiveness is that proofs become more complex. The semantics of the more expressive type theories are also more complex, and lose the simple set-theoretic interpretation that higher-order logic has. Overall, our feeling is that classical higher-order logic closely matches the intuition of a working mathematician, and that the loss of expressive power is not a serious drawback in practice. The lack of subtypes is perhaps the biggest disadvantage of higher-order logic, but we will show that there are some rather simple ways of getting around this restriction.

Exercises

3.1 Assume that Σ and Γ are types and that $c : \Sigma$ and $g : \Gamma \to$ Bool are constants. Deduce the types of all subterms of the following term:

$$(\lambda x : \text{Bool} \cdot \lambda y \cdot f.x.c = g.y) .$$

3.2 Show that the typing rules of higher-order logic rule out self-application of the form $t.t$; i.e., show that a term can never be applied to itself.

3.3 We want to create a theory over a single type T with the following constants:

$$P : T \to T \to \text{Bool} ,$$
$$A : T \to T \to \text{Bool} ,$$

and with the following two inference rules:

$$\frac{}{\vdash A.t.t} \; , \qquad \frac{\vdash A.t.t' \qquad \vdash P.t'.t''}{\vdash A.t.t''} \; .$$

(a) Write a deduction of $\vdash A.x.z$ from $\vdash P.x.y$ and $P.y.z$.

(b) Show that if there are deductions of $\vdash A.t.t'$ and $\vdash A.t'.t''$ using only the two inference rules above, then there is also a deduction of $\vdash A.t.t''$.

unctions

We start our overview of the basic axioms and inference of higher-order logic by studying the rules for reasoning about functions. These are essentially the rules of *simply typed lambda calculus*. A method of extending the logic by defining new constants is described. In association with this we also describe two ways of introducing new notation without extending the logic: abbreviations (syntactic sugaring) and local definitions. Furthermore, we consider an important practical issue: how to present proofs in a simple and readable way. The *natural deduction style* is the traditional way of presenting proofs and is the one that we have described in Chapter 3. However, we prefer an alternative *derivational proof style*, because we find it more readable and it scales up better to large proofs. The natural deduction style and the derivational proof style are just two different ways of writing proofs; the underlying notion of a proof is the same in both styles. Finally, we postulate a new type constructor that denotes a Cartesian product and investigate its basic properties.

Properties of Functions

There are basically three classes of rules that we use to reason about functions in higher-order logic: (1) rules that determine the basic properties of equality, (2) substitution and congruence rules for terms, and (3) conversion rules for abstraction and application. We look at all these rules in more detail below.

Equality

Equality is the most basic constant of higher-order logic. The following th**
inference rules establish that equality is an *equivalence relation*.

$$\frac{}{\vdash t = t} \text{ ,}$$

(= reflexiv**

$$\frac{\Phi \vdash t = t' \quad \Phi' \vdash t' = t''}{\Phi \cup \Phi' \vdash t = t''} \text{ ,}$$

(= transitiv**

$$\frac{\Phi \vdash t = t'}{\Phi \vdash t' = t} \text{ .}$$

(= symmetri**

There are no side conditions associated with these inference rules. The metava**
ables t, t', and t'' stand for arbitrary terms of arbitrary type. In particular, this me**
that the rules are also valid for terms of new types that are added to the logic la**

The transitivity rule is easily seen to hold for an arbitrary number of intermedi**
terms:

$$\frac{\Phi_1 \vdash t_1 = t_2 \quad \Phi_2 \vdash t_2 = t_3 \quad \cdots \quad \Phi_{n-1} \vdash t_{n-1} = t_n}{\Phi_1 \cup \cdots \cup \Phi_{n-1} \vdash t_1 = t_n} \text{ .}$$

The following is a deduction of this (derived) inference rule for $n = 4$:

$$\frac{\Phi_1 \vdash t_1 = t_2 \quad \dfrac{\Phi_2 \vdash t_2 = t_3 \quad \Phi_3 \vdash t_3 = t_4 \ \{= \text{trans.}\}}{\Phi_2 \cup \Phi_3 \vdash t_2 = t_4}}{\Phi_1 \cup \Phi_2 \cup \Phi_3 \vdash t_1 = t_4} \ \{= \text{trans.}\} \text{ .}$$

Substitution and Congruence

The *principle of substitution* is the general inference rule for equality. It states **
replacing subterms with equal terms preserves truth:

$$\frac{\Phi' \vdash t_1 = t_1' \quad \Phi \vdash t[v := t_1]}{\Phi \cup \Phi' \vdash t[v := t_1']}$$

(substitutio**

- t_1 and t_1' are free for v in t.

From this inference rule we can derive a rule that says that replacing equals **
equals preserves equality:

$$\frac{\Phi \vdash t_1 = t_1'}{\Phi \vdash t[v := t_1] = t[v := t_1']}$$

(substitute equals for equa**

- t_1 and t_1' are free for v in t.

The derivation of this rule uses reflexivity:

$$\frac{\Phi \vdash t_1 = t_1' \quad \dfrac{}{\vdash t[v := t_1] = t[v := \text{``} t_1 \text{''}]} \,\{= \text{refl.}\}}{\Phi \vdash t[v := t_1] = t[v := t_1']} \quad \{\text{subst.}\} \ .$$

We have here indicated the subterm that is replaced in the substitution within quotation marks ("t_1"). The quotation marks have no other significance; they serve only to emphasize the part of the term that is being changed.

A function associates a unique value with each argument: if the arguments are equal, then the values of the function on these arguments must also be equal. This is expressed by the following inference rule:

$$\frac{\Phi \vdash t' = t''}{\Phi \vdash t.t' = t.t''} \ . \hspace{3cm} (operand\ congruence)$$

In higher-order logic, there is also another possibility: we can have two different terms that describe the same function. If these two terms are applied to the same argument, the values should again be equal:

$$\frac{\Phi \vdash t' = t''}{\Phi \vdash t'.t = t''.t} \ . \hspace{3cm} (operator\ congruence)$$

Operator and operand congruence are both easily derived from the rule for replacing equals for equals.

Abstraction also preserves equality, as stated by the following rule of inference:

$$\frac{\Phi \vdash t = t'}{\Phi \vdash (\lambda v \cdot t) = (\lambda v \cdot t')} \hspace{2.5cm} (abstraction)$$
● v is not free in Φ.

The side condition states that this rule may be used only with sequents where the variable v does not occur free in any formula in Φ. That the side condition is necessary is seen from the sequent $x = 0 \vdash x + 1 = 1$. This is obviously true, but it does not follow that the function $(\lambda x \cdot x + 1)$ is the same as the function $(\lambda x \cdot 1)$, because the equality of the function values is established only in the special case when $x = 0$.

Symmetry and transitivity of equality can be proved from the other rules that we have given. Symmetry is proved using reflexivity and substitution:

$$\frac{\Phi \vdash t = t' \quad \dfrac{}{\Phi \vdash \text{``} t \text{''} = t} \,\{= \text{reflexive}\}}{\Phi \vdash t' = t} \quad \{\text{substitution}\} \ .$$

In a similar way, transitivity is proved using only substitution (Exercise 4.3).

Conversion Rules

The lambda calculus *conversion rules* provide the basic mechanism for manipul‌ing terms that denote functions. Two terms are considered equivalent if they di‌only with respect to the naming of bound variables. In other words, the names‌the bound variables are not significant. This property is expressed by the *rule o‌conversion*:

$$\vdash (\lambda v \cdot t) = (\lambda w \cdot t[v := w])$$

(α *conversio*

- w does not occur free in t.

An example of this rule is that $(\lambda x \cdot x + y) = (\lambda z \cdot z + y)$. However, $(\lambda x \cdot x + y)‌(\lambda y \cdot y + y)$ does not follow by this rule (and indeed, is not true), because y occ‌free in $(x + y)$. Remember that $t[v := w]$ stands for the substitution of variable‌for all free occurrences of v in t. The side condition guarantees that no free varia‌w in t becomes bound when we replace v with w.

The β *conversion rule* gives the basic property of function application:

$$\vdash (\lambda v \cdot t).t' = t[v := t']$$

(β *conversio*

- t' is free for v in t.

An example of this rule is that $(\lambda x \cdot x + y).(y + 1) = (y + 1) + y$.

Ignoring the side condition for β conversion is a common error in manipulat‌lambda terms. Consider as an example the term $(\lambda x \cdot (\lambda y \cdot x)).y$. If we carry‌the β conversion without considering the side condition, we get $(\lambda x \cdot (\lambda y \cdot x)).y$‌$(\lambda y \cdot y)$, i.e., the identity function, which is obviously wrong (we should get‌function that returns y for any argument). The free variable y has become bou‌in the resulting expression. Thus, we cannot apply the β-conversion rule direc‌to simplify this term.

The correct method is first to use α conversion to replace the bound variabl‌with another variable z that does not occur elsewhere in the formula, and t‌use β conversion and transitivity to establish the required result. In practice‌conversion is a basic step that is usually applied directly to a subterm, with‌further explanation.

The η *conversion rule* expresses that any term $t : \Sigma \to \Gamma$ can be written as‌abstraction of an application:

$$\vdash (\lambda v \cdot t.v) = t$$

(η *conversio*

- v is not free in t.

An example of this rule is that $(\lambda x \cdot (\lambda z \cdot z + y).x) = (\lambda z \cdot z + y)$. We‌understand the η conversion rule as essentially stating that abstraction is the inve‌

of application: application followed by abstraction is the identity transformation. The β conversion rule describes the converse situation, i.e., abstraction followed by application.

Finally, we have the principle of *extensionality*: two functions are equal if they give the same value for each argument in the domain:

$$\frac{\Phi \vdash t.v = t'.v}{\Phi \vdash t = t'} \qquad\qquad (extensionality)$$

- v not free in Φ, t or t'.

The requirement that v not be free in Φ means that v is not restricted by the assumptions in Φ; i.e., Φ is satisfied by any value for v. The extensionality principle and the rule of operand congruence together state that two functions are equal *if and only if* they give the same value for each argument in the domain.

We can prove extensionality from the more basic rules. Assume that v is not free in Φ, t, or t'. Figure 4.1 shows the deduction for the extensionality inference rule. The left subderivation uses η conversion and symmetry, the middle subderivation uses abstraction, and the right subderivation again uses η conversion. The conclusion follows by transitivity. The assumptions guarantee that the side conditions for abstraction and η conversion are satisfied in this deduction.

Derivations

The format for deductions that we have given above shows the structure of the argument quite clearly but is not suitable for writing larger deductions (either deductions with many inference steps or deductions where the terms are large), as should be evident from the proof of extensionality given here. We therefore introduce an alternative format for writing deductions that scales up better and that we choose as the main format for writing proofs throughout the rest of the book. This format is based on a few simple notational conventions: writing inference rules and deductions *sideways* with indentation to show hypothesis and subproofs, using assumptions with *scope* to avoid repeating the same assumption over and over again in a deduction, and identifying the special role that transitivity and substitution play in deductions. We refer to deductions in the format we propose

$$\frac{\vdash (\lambda v \cdot t.v) = t}{\vdash t = (\lambda v \cdot t.v)} \qquad \frac{\Phi \vdash t.v = t'.v}{\Phi \vdash (\lambda v \cdot t.v) = (\lambda v \cdot t'.v)} \qquad \frac{}{\vdash (\lambda v \cdot t'.v) = t'}$$
$$\frac{}{\Phi \vdash t = t'}$$

FIGURE 4.1. Deduction of extensionality inference rule

here as *derivations* or *calculational proofs*. We emphasize that a derivation is j⬤ an alternative way of writing deductions; the basic notion of a deduction is ⬤ changed.

Consider a deduction of the form

$$\frac{D_1 \quad D_2 \quad \cdots \quad D_m}{\Phi \vdash t = t'} \quad \{\text{rule name}\} .$$

We can write this deduction *sideways*, as follows:

$$\Phi$$

$$\vdash t$$

$$= \{\text{rule name}\}$$

- D_1
- D_2
$$\vdots$$
- D_m
- t'

where we assume that the subdeductions $D_1, D_2, \ldots, D_m$ are also written sidewa⬤ in the same way. Thus, rather than presenting the deduction as an upward-growi⬤ tree, we present it as a nested outline structure, with subdeductions shown ⬤ indented deductions.

This format contains exactly the same information as the usual format, but ⬤ information is arranged in a different way. Each part of the conclusion (the ⬤ sumption, the first term, the equality symbol, and the second term) is written o⬤ line of its own. The equality symbol is decorated with the name of the rule. T⬤ subdeductions are written indented one step to the right (each one marked wit⬤ bullet ⬤). We add a small dot in front of the second term when necessary to sh⬤ the nesting more clearly. This dot has no semantic meaning.

In most cases the hypotheses have the same assumptions as the conclusion in ⬤ inference. In such cases, the assumptions in the hypotheses are omitted, to ma⬤ the proof more concise. If a hypothesis adds some formulas to the assumptio⬤ of the conclusion, then only the added assumptions are shown for the hypothe⬤ within square brackets (examples of this will be shown in later chapters). In b⬤ cases, the turnstile symbol $\vdash$ is omitted. The turnstile symbol is used only wh⬤ we want to list the exact set of assumptions that are made for a hypothesis (th⬤ overriding the present scoping assumption).

On the abstract level of an inference rule, where a single symbol Φ is used for ⬤ assumptions, this may seem like a small gain. However, in real proofs the assum⬤ tions may be very large formulas, and the gain is considerable. Most repetitions ⬤ assumptions are implicit with this convention, and the proof is compressed co⬤ siderably. The convention is quite intuitive in the sideways format, where we c⬤

think of the assumption as having a *scope* that covers all nested subderivations (unless the implied assumptions are explicitly replaced by a new set of assumptions, marked by the turnstile symbol). An assumption in square brackets adds a new assumption to the assumptions already in force, so it is a *local* assumption.

The real advantage of the notational conventions above come when we also permit inference steps to be strung together by transitivity. Consider the following proof:

$$\frac{\dfrac{DD_1 \quad \{R_1\}}{\Phi \vdash t_0 = t_1} \quad \dfrac{DD_2 \quad \{R_2\}}{\Phi \vdash t_1 = t_2} \quad \cdots \quad \dfrac{DD_m \quad \{R_m\}}{\Phi \vdash t_{m-1} = t_m}}{\Phi \vdash t_0 = t_m} \; \{T\} \; ,$$

where $DD_1, DD_2, \ldots, DD_m$ are the subdeductions for each inference step (so each DD_i is a list of subdeductions $D_{i,1}, \ldots, D_{i,n_i}$). Note that the assumptions Φ are the same in each hypothesis. We write this proof in the sideways format as follows:

$$\Phi$$
$$\vdash t_0$$
$$= \{R_1\}$$
$$\qquad DD_1$$
$$\bullet \; t_1$$
$$= \{R_2\}$$
$$\qquad DD_2$$
$$\bullet \; t_2$$
$$\vdots$$
$$\bullet \; t_{m-1}$$
$$= \{R_m\}$$
$$\qquad DD_m$$
$$\bullet \; t_m$$

Transitivity is used implicitly in this derivation. We interpret the whole derivation as a proof of the statement $\Phi \vdash t_0 = t_m$. The inference step that explicitly states $\Phi \vdash t_0 = t_m$ (by transitivity) is omitted. This format is more economical than the original proof format, because the intermediate terms t_i are written out only once, while there are two occurrences of these terms in the original format. This again becomes important when the terms are large. Besides transitivity, we also use reflexivity and symmetry implicitly in derivations, as illustrated in the example below.

Example: Extensionality

The proof of extensionality is as follows when written as a derivation. The hypo[thesis] esis is $\Phi \vdash t.v = t'.v$ (recall that we assumed that v is not free in Φ, t, or t'). [We] have that

$$\Phi$$

$$\vdash t$$

$= \{\eta \text{ conversion; side condition satisfied by assumption}\}$

$\quad (\lambda v \cdot t.v)$

$= \{\text{abstraction, } v \text{ not free in } \Phi\}$

- $\quad t.v$
- $= \{\text{hypothesis}\}$
- $\quad t'.v$

· $(\lambda v \cdot t'.v)$

$= \{\eta \text{ conversion; side condition satisfied by assumption}\}$

$\quad t'$

We also use symmetry of equality implicitly: η conversion states that $(\lambda v \cdot t.v) =$ [t] but our derivation uses equality in the opposite direction in the first step. Note a[lso] that the assumptions Φ are available in the subderivation, so the hypothesis is rea[lly] $\Phi \vdash t.v = t'.v$.

The nested derivation in the example is typical of this proof technique. In prov[ing] that $(\lambda v \cdot t.v) = (\lambda v \cdot t'.v)$, we *focus* on the subcomponent $t.v$ of the first te[rm] and show that $t.v = t'.v$. This establishes the outer-level equality by abstracti[on]. In this example, the nested derivation is the hypothesis of the whole proof, bu[t in] general, we could have a longer proof here. If a nested derivation is obvious (e.[g.] using reflexivity), we may omit it and simply state its conclusion as a comme[nt]. The nested subderivation here is actually too short and obvious to be indica[ted] explicitly. In such cases, it is sufficient to indicate the subterm being replaced a[nd] explain the subderivation in the justification. The derivation is then as follows:

$$\Phi$$

$$\vdash t$$

$= \{\eta \text{ conversion; side condition satisfied by assumption}\}$

$\quad (\lambda v \cdot \text{``} t.v \text{''})$

$= \{\text{abstraction, } v \text{ not free in } \Phi, \text{ hypothesis}\}$

$\quad (\lambda v \cdot t'.v)$

$= \{\eta \text{ conversion; side condition satisfied by assumption}\}$

$\quad t'$

The derivational proof format shows the proofs of hypotheses in-line, indented one step to the right. This works as long as the indented proof is short. Deeply nested or long subproofs make the derivation difficult to follow. It is then better to make the proof of the hypothesis into a separate lemma that is proved either before or after the main proof. Alternatively, one can use a word processor with an outliner to construct the derivations. The outliner permits nested derivations to be hidden and shown as required and thus allows a better overall view of the whole derivation. An even better alternative is to have a proof editor with outlining capabilities, so that the correctness of the inference steps can also be checked mechanically.

Definitions

The most secure way of extending a theory is to define new constants explicitly. This is a conservative extension, so the consistency of the extended theory is guaranteed. We describe this method of extending a theory below, together with another simple mechanism, the use of local definitions.

Constant Definition

A new constant can be added to a theory by giving an (*explicit*) *constant definition* of the form

$$c \stackrel{\wedge}{=} t \, , \qquad\qquad\qquad \text{(constant definition)}$$

where t is a closed term. The definition adds the new constant c to the signature, and the new axiom

$$\vdash c = t$$

to the inference rules. Explicit constant definition is a conservative extension, since the added constant c has the same denotation as the term t. This means that any proof that uses the constant c can be rewritten as an equally valid proof that uses t instead of c.

An example of an explicitly defined constant is the *function composition* operator ∘ (written infix). It is typed as

$$\circ : (\Gamma \to \Delta) \to (\Sigma \to \Gamma) \to (\Sigma \to \Delta) \, ,$$

and its definition is

$$\circ \stackrel{\wedge}{=} (\lambda f \, g \, x \cdot f.(g.x)) \, . \qquad \text{(backward function composition)}$$

The following variation on β conversion can be used to *unfold* an explicit constant definition:

$$\frac{\Phi \vdash t = (\lambda v_1 \cdots v_n \bullet t')}{\Phi \vdash t.t_1. \cdots .t_n = t'[v_1, \ldots, v_n := t_1, \ldots, t_n]} \qquad \textit{(use of definition}$$
• none of the terms t_i contain any of the v_i free.

We derive this inference rule for the special case $n = 1$. Let the hypothesis be tl
$\Phi \vdash t = (\lambda v \bullet t')$ and assume that v is not free in t_1. We then have the followi
derivation of the inference rule:

Φ

$\vdash t.t_1$

$= \{$substitute equals for equals, hypothesis$\}$

$\quad (\lambda v \bullet t').t_1$

$= \{\beta$ conversion$\}$

$\quad t'[v := t_1]$

An explicit definition of a function constant is often more readable if we write
arguments on the left-hand side, writing $c.v \stackrel{\triangle}{=} t$ rather than $c \stackrel{\triangle}{=} (\lambda v \bullet t)$. Th
two ways of writing definitions are equivalent, in the sense that either one can
derived from the other.

As an example, we define the *identity function* and *forward composition* (writ
infix) of functions and give an alternative definition for backward composition
functions:

$$\begin{aligned}
\mathrm{id}.x &\stackrel{\triangle}{=} x \;, &\textit{(identit}\\
(f \bullet g).x &\stackrel{\triangle}{=} g.(f.x) \;, &\textit{(forward compositio}\\
(g \circ f).x &\stackrel{\triangle}{=} g.(f.x) \;. &\textit{(backward compositio}
\end{aligned}$$

Here typing requires that f and g be functions, where the result type of f is
same as the domain type of g.

Abbreviations

An alternative way of introducing new constructs into the logic is by using *syntae
sugaring*, or *abbreviations*. The syntax of higher-order logic is very terse; t
makes the logic conceptually simple, but terms can be difficult to read. We
increase readability by introducing conventions that allow us to write terms
a new way. This does not extend the signature; it merely adds a layer of "pret
printing" on top of the logic. This layer is very shallow; it is always possible to s
it away and work with the underlying pure terms if one wants to do that. Howe
by also stating inference rules in the sugared syntax, we can actually work on
abbreviation level all the time, forgetting completely about the pure syntax. We

abbreviations quite frequently in the subsequent chapters, in order to get a readable syntax for program constructs. We have already seen some example of syntactic sugar, e.g., the infix notation used for equality and function composition.

Local Definitions

A very useful example of syntactic sugaring is *local definitions*. We define the following abbreviation:

$$(\text{let } v = t' \text{ in } t) \quad \hat{=} \quad (\lambda v \cdot t).t' \;.$$

This gives us a way of writing terms with a kind of local context. A (sub)term of the form $(\text{let } v = t' \text{ in } t)$ can always be rewritten as $(\lambda v \cdot t).t'$ (and then β-converted). However, by using the let syntax we indicate that the term is going to be used in a specific way; we do not intend to rewrite it using β conversion.

An example of a local definition is

$$(\text{let } f = (\lambda x \cdot x + 1) \text{ in } f \circ f) \;.$$

We have by the definition that

$$(\text{let } f = (\lambda x \cdot x + 1) \text{ in } f \circ f).0$$
$$= \{\text{local definition}\}$$
$$(\lambda f \cdot f \circ f).(\lambda x \cdot x + 1).0$$
$$= \{\beta \text{ conversion}\}$$
$$((\lambda x \cdot x + 1) \circ (\lambda x \cdot x + 1)).0$$
$$= \{\text{functional composition}\}$$
$$(\lambda x \cdot x + 1).(\text{``} (\lambda x \cdot x + 1).0 \text{ ''})$$
$$= \{\beta \text{ conversion and simplification } 0 + 1 = 1\}$$
$$(\lambda x \cdot x + 1).1$$
$$= \{\beta \text{ conversion and simplification } 1 + 1 = 2\}$$
$$2$$

A typical useful property that can be expressed nicely in this syntax is the following:

$$\frac{\vdash (\text{let } v = t' \text{ in } t) = t}{}$$ (*vacuous* let)

• v not free in t.

Local definitions also distribute into applications:

$$\frac{\vdash (\text{let } v = t' \text{ in } t_1.t_2) = (\text{let } v = t' \text{ in } t_1).(\text{let } v = t' \text{ in } t_2)}{} \;,$$

and they distribute into lambda abstractions under certain conditions:

$$\frac{}{\vdash (\text{let } v = t' \text{ in } (\lambda y \cdot t)) = (\lambda y \cdot \text{let } v = t' \text{ in } t)}$$

- y not free in t'.

The let construct is useful for introducing temporary (local) names for subte[r] inside a term. This makes it possible to structure terms in a way that makes th[e] easier to read.

4.4 Product Type

Lambda abstraction permits us to describe functions over one variable. In pract[ice] we very often need functions over two or more variables. There are essentially [two] different ways of describing such functions. Either we define functions over tu[ples] directly, where tuples are elements of a product type, or we use *currying*. In [the] first case, a function for summing two natural numbers is written as

$$f.(x, y) \;=\; x + y \;.$$

Here (x, y) is an element of the *Cartesian product type* Nat $\times$ Nat, and f i[tself] is of the type Nat $\times$ Nat $\to$ Nat. In the second approach (currying), we write [the] function as

$$f.x.y \;=\; x + y \;.$$

In this case, f is of the type Nat $\to$ Nat $\to$ Nat. This approach uses higher-o[rder] functions in an essential way: $f.x$ is a function of type Nat $\to$ Nat. The advan[tage] of currying is that we can also talk about functions for which only part of [the] arguments are given; e.g., $f.x$ stands for the function $(\lambda y \cdot x + y)$: Nat $\to$ [Nat.] This is useful in many situations, as we will notice, so we will in general pr[efer] currying for functions with many arguments. However, the other approach also [has] its merits, as will also become evident later on.

We extend the type structure of higher-order logic with *product types*, which s[tand] for Cartesian products of types. Product types are added to higher-order logi[c in] the form of a binary type operator $\times$ (written infix). The operator $\times$ associate[s to] the right, so $\Sigma_1 \times \Sigma_2 \times \Sigma_3$ abbreviates $\Sigma_1 \times (\Sigma_2 \times \Sigma_3)$ (so a triple is real[ly a] nested pair). We also assume that the product constructor binds more strongly [than] the function constructor, so $\Sigma \to \Gamma \times \Delta$ stands for $\Sigma \to (\Gamma \times \Delta)$. The pro[duct] type $\Sigma_1 \times \Sigma_2$ stands for the Cartesian product of the sets denoted by Σ_1 and[Σ_2.] Thus Nat $\times$ Nat $\to$ Nat $\times$ Nat denotes functions on pairs of natural numbers.

In order to make use of products, we extend the logic with three new const[ants.] Elements of the product $\Sigma \times \Gamma$ are constructed using the *pairing* function (

$\Sigma \to \Gamma \to \Sigma \times \Gamma$). In addition, we introduce *projections* (fst : $\Sigma \times \Gamma \to \Sigma$ and snd : $\Sigma \times \Gamma \to \Gamma$). We use an infix comma for pairing, writing t, t' for pair.$t.t'$. We postulate the following properties for the product operations:

$$\vdash (\text{fst}.x, \text{snd}.x) = x \ , \qquad\qquad\qquad\qquad (pairing)$$
$$\vdash \text{fst}.(x, y) = x \ , \qquad\qquad\qquad\qquad\quad (projection\ 1)$$
$$\vdash \text{snd}.(x, y) = y \ , \qquad\qquad\qquad\qquad\quad (projection\ 2)$$
$$\vdash (x, y) = (x', y') \ \equiv\ x = x' \wedge y = y' \ . \qquad (congruence)$$

The first three axioms state that pairing and projections are inverses of each other. The last one states that pairing is a congruence and that equality on pairs is uniquely determined by equality on its components. We assume that pairing associates to the right, so that (t, t', t'') stands for $(t, (t', t''))$.

We introduce a special *paired abstraction* for products:

$$(\lambda u : \Sigma, v : \Gamma \cdot t) \stackrel{\triangle}{=} \qquad\qquad\qquad (paired\ abstraction)$$
$$(\lambda w : \Sigma \times \Gamma \cdot t[u, v := \text{fst}.w, \text{snd}.w]) \ ,$$

where w is an arbitrary variable that does not occur free in t. Since the syntax of higher-order logic does not allow paired abstraction, this is syntactic sugar; we can write terms with paired abstraction, but such a term always stands for a corresponding term in the basic syntax. The definition may not seem to be unique, but the α-conversion rule shows that it does not matter how we choose w.

The paired abstraction $(\lambda u, v \cdot t)$ introduces names for the components of the product, which can then be used inside the term, thus considerably simplifying the term. An example of paired abstraction is the function

$$(\lambda n : \text{Nat}, n' : \text{Nat} \cdot n + n') \ ,$$

which maps pairs (n, n') of numbers to the number $n + n'$. It is convenient to write this expression as $(\lambda n, n' : \text{Nat} \cdot n + n')$; i.e., the type indication is given only once for the preceding list of bound variables. Without paired abstraction we would have to write this term as $(\lambda x : \text{Nat} \times \text{Nat} \cdot \text{fst}.x + \text{snd}.x)$.

The conversion rules (α, β, and η conversion) can be generalized to paired abstractions. Thus, we have the following:

$$\overline{\Phi \vdash (\lambda u, v \cdot t) = (\lambda u', v' \cdot t[u, v := u', v'])}$$
• u' and v' do not occur in t,

$(\alpha\ conversio$

$$\overline{\Phi \vdash (\lambda u, v \cdot t).(t_1, t_2) = t[u, v := t_1, t_2]}$$
• t_1 is free for u and t_2 for v in t,

$(\beta\ conversio$

$$\overline{\Phi \vdash (\lambda u, v \cdot t.(u, v)) = t}$$
• u and v not free in t.

$(\eta\ conversio$

Note that these rules work directly on the syntactically sugared terms. Exactly for infix operators, this shows that we do not need to rewrite sugared terms in the basic syntax in order to do manipulations.

The rules above are easily justified using the basic conversion rules. For examp paired β conversion is justified as follows:

Φ

$\vdash (\lambda u, v \cdot t).(t_1, t_2)$

$= \{$definition of paired abstraction syntax$\}$

$(\lambda w \cdot t[u, v := \mathsf{fst}.w, \mathsf{snd}.w]).(t_1, t_2)$

$= \{\beta\text{-conversion}\}$

$t[u, v := \mathsf{fst}.w, \mathsf{snd}.w][w := (t_1, t_2)]$

$= \{$properties of substitution; w not free in $t\}$

$t[u, v := \mathsf{fst}.(t_1, t_2), \mathsf{snd}.(t_1, t_2)]$

$= \{$properties of projections$\}$

$t[u, v := t_1, t_2]$

4.5 Summary and Discussion

We have presented the fundamental rules that are needed for proving propert about functions. The rules for equality formalize the fact that equality is an equ alence relation. The substitution and abstraction rules formalize the principle substituting equals for equals. Finally, the α, β, and η conversion rules formal the basic notions of abstraction and application, and show how they are inter pendent. These rules for functions are not specific to higher-order logic; they the general rules of the simply typed lambda calculus, also due to Church [48]. An overview of various lambda calculi is given by Henk Barendregt [37].

We have introduced derivations as an alternative format for writing proofs. This format is based on a few simple observations that permit a one-to-one correspondence to be established between proofs in the style of natural deduction and derivational proofs. This derivational style is used for proofs throughout the rest of the book.

Derivations as described here are inspired by the *calculational proof format* introduced by van Gasteren, Dijkstra, and Wim Feijen and advocated by many computer scientists [54, 66, 60]. Although similar in spirit to their proof style, our approach differs in some important aspects from theirs. The basic underlying framework that we use is a sequent formulation of natural deduction for higher-order logic, while their proof style is based on Hilbert-style proofs. They combine the proof steps with a pointwise extended ordering relation, whereas we permit only simple ordering relations between proof steps. We also allow nested derivations in the proof. Nested calculational proofs have been proposed by, e.g., Jan van de Snepscheut, who suggested embedding calculational proofs within the comment brackets [131]. The approach taken here is more direct, in that the derivations are directly given in a nested (outline) format.

The use of nested derivations is a big advantage when the terms become larger. This is the case with program derivations, where the terms are program statements. The proof style developed here also lends itself quite nicely to machine-supported presentation, browsing, and construction of proofs. Work in this direction has been done by Jim Grundy and Thomas Långbacka [70].

Exercises

4.1 Write the proof of the rule "Substitute equals for equals" as a linear derivation.

4.2 Derive the rules of operator and operand congruence from the rule for replacing equals for equals.

4.3 Derive the transitivity rule for equality using only the substitution rule.

4.4 Derive the rule of η-conversion using other rules given in this chapter.

4.5 Show that the function composition operation ∘ is associative.

4.6 Derive the inference rules given for the let construct.

4.7 We define the constant twice by

$$\text{twice} \stackrel{\wedge}{=} (\lambda f \; x \cdot f.(f.x)) \; .$$

(a) What is the type of twice?

(b) Simplify (twice o twice).$(\lambda x \cdot x + 2).3$ (note that this is not a case of se application).

4.8 Define three constants (known as *combinators*) as follows:

$$
\begin{aligned}
I.x &= x \,, \\
S.f.g.x &= f.x.(g.x) \,, \\
K.x.y &= x \,.
\end{aligned}
$$

(a) What are the types of I, S and K?

(b) Prove that $I = S.K.K$.

4.9 Assume that T is a type and that $e : T$, inv $: T \to T$, and $+ : T \to T \to T$ (in are constants satisfying the following rules:

$$
\frac{}{\vdash s + (t + u) = (s + t) + u} \,,
$$

$$
\frac{}{\vdash s + e = s} \,,
$$

$$
\frac{}{\vdash s + \text{inv}.s = e} \,,
$$

$$
\frac{\Phi \vdash s + t = e}{\Phi \vdash t = \text{inv}.s} \,.
$$

Prove $\vdash$ inv.$(s + t) = $ inv.$t + $ inv.s by a derivation.

Imperative programs work by making successive changes to a state. In the introduction we assumed that an agent has available a collection of functions that it can apply to a state in order to change the state in some desired way. By composing such state functions we can describe more complicated state changes. This gives us a first, very simple model of programs, where a program is seen as a total function from a set of initial states to a set of final states.

The state in imperative programs is really an abstraction of the computer memory, where values can be stored in locations and subsequently read from these locations. A program variable is essentially an abstract location. We will show in this chapter how to formalize the notion of program variables in higher-order logic and give some basic properties of program variables. At the same time, this chapter serves as an illustration of how to use the axioms and inference rules for functions that we developed in Chapter 4 to reason about states and state changes.

State Transformers

A function from states to states describes a state change. In principle, any type in higher-order logic can be used as a state space. The types that we have introduced thus far are, however, rather poor at modeling the often very complicated aspects of states that we meet in practice. We therefore prefer to use states with program variables as described in the next section to model more complicated states and computations.

A state change may be within a single state space or from one state space to another. Let Σ and Γ be two state spaces. A function $f : \Sigma \rightarrow \Gamma$ is then called a *state transformer* from Σ to Γ (a function $f : \Sigma \rightarrow \Gamma$ where Σ is a considered a state space but Γ is not is called a *state function*). A *state transformer catege* is a category where the objects are state spaces and the morphisms are functi between these state spaces. The identity function is the identity morphism, a forward functional composition is the composition of morphisms:

$$1 \mathrel{\hat{=}} \mathsf{id} , \qquad\qquad\qquad (1\ of\ state\ transformer$$
$$f \mathbin{;} g \mathrel{\hat{=}} f \bullet g . \qquad\qquad\qquad (;\ of\ state\ transformer$$

Composition and identity satisfy the category requirements:

$$(f \bullet g) \bullet h = f \bullet (g \bullet h) \qquad\qquad (;\ associativ$$
$$\mathsf{id} \bullet f = f \quad \text{and} \quad f \bullet \mathsf{id} = f . \qquad (\mathsf{id}\ un$$

A morphism thus maps states to states. In this case, the two arrow notations $\Sigma \rightarrow \Gamma$ (function) and $\Sigma \xrightarrow{f} \Gamma$ (morphism) stand for the same thing.

A state transformer category is determined by a collection of types (state spaces) a a collection of state transformers that includes the identity state transformers on state spaces. In addition, we require that the composition of two state transform in the category be again a state transformer in the category.

In particular, let Tran_X be the state transformer category where the collectio of types forms the objects (state spaces) in the category and the morphisms defined by

$$\mathsf{Tran}_X(\Sigma, \Gamma) \mathrel{\hat{=}} \Sigma \rightarrow \Gamma , \qquad\qquad (state\ transforme$$

where Σ and Γ are state spaces in X. Thus, the morphisms from Σ to Γ are functions $f : \Sigma \rightarrow \Gamma$. In what follows, we will simply write Tran for Tran_X w the specific collection X of types is not important.

5.2 State Attributes and Program Variables

A program state will usually need to record a number of different aspects or tributes of the computation domain, which are then manipulated in the progr An *attribute of type* Γ *over state space* Σ is a pair (g, h) of functions, wl $g : \Sigma \rightarrow \Gamma$ is an *access function* and $h : \Gamma \rightarrow \Sigma \rightarrow \Sigma$ is an *update funct* Given a state σ, $g.\sigma$ gives the value of the attribute in this state (the value is of Γ), while $h.\gamma.\sigma$ is a new state that we get by setting the value of the attribute to value γ. The access and update functions of an attribute are accessed by the projection functions fst and snd. However, to make it easier to remember whic which, we will define two new functions, $\mathsf{val} = \mathsf{fst}$ and $\mathsf{set} = \mathsf{snd}$, as alterna names for the projection functions, so that $\mathsf{val}.(g, h) = g$ and $\mathsf{set}.(g, h) = h$.

A sequence of updates to a state σ, with x_1 first set to a_1, then x_2 set to a_2, ..., x_m set to a_m, is described in terms of forward composition as $((\text{set}.x_1.a_1) \bullet \cdots \bullet (\text{set}.x_m.a_m)).\sigma$. In the category of state transformers, this is written as $(\text{set}.x_1.a_1 ; \cdots ; \text{set}.x_m.a_m).\sigma$. We prefer the latter notation for composing state transformers.

Consider an attribute x. Setting this attribute to a specific value and then accessing the attribute should yield the same value; i.e.,

$$\text{val}.x.(\text{set}.x.a.\sigma) = a . \tag{a}$$

We also expect that the attributes can be set independently of each other. In particular, this means that setting the value of an attribute x does not change the value of attribute y when $x \neq y$:

$$\text{val}.y.(\text{set}.x.a.\sigma) = \text{val}.y.\sigma . \tag{b}$$

Next, an attribute can record only one value, so if we set the value of the attribute twice in succession, then only the last value is stored. This can be captured by the requirement

$$\text{set}.x.a ; \text{set}.x.b = \text{set}.x.b . \tag{c}$$

Also, the order in which two different attributes are set should not matter, so we require that

$$\text{set}.x.a ; \text{set}.y.b = \text{set}.y.b ; \text{set}.x.a . \tag{d}$$

Finally, we expect that setting an attribute to the value it already has does not change the state:

$$\text{set}.x.(\text{val}.x.\sigma).\sigma = \sigma . \tag{e}$$

Distinct attributes $x_1, \ldots, x_n$ are called *program variables* if they satisfy these *independence requirements* for any choice of x and y as two different attributes x_i and x_j in this list. The independence requirements essentially state the properties of an abstract memory with independent locations for storing values, where each location is associated with a specific type.

We often use a single name for a list of distinct state attributes, $x = x_1, \ldots, x_m$. Property (d) shows that it makes sense to write $\text{set}.x.a.\sigma$ if a is a corresponding list of values. Similarly, $\text{val}.x.\sigma$ can be used to stand for the list of values $\text{val}.x_1.\sigma, \ldots, \text{val}.x_m.\sigma$.

We can use these properties to determine the value of a program variable in a given state. For instance, assume that we first set x_1 to 3, then x_2 to 5, and then finally set

x_1 to 0. What is the value of program variable x_2 in the resulting state? We hav

$\text{val}.x_2.((\text{set}.x_1.3 \; ; \; \text{" set}.x_2.5 \; ; \; \text{set}.x_1.0 \text{ ").}\sigma)$

$= \{\text{property (d), associativity of functional composition}\}$

$\text{val}.x_2.(\text{" (set}.x_1.3 \; ; \; \text{set}.x_1.0 \; ; \; \text{set}.x_2.5).\sigma \text{ ")}$

$= \{\text{definition of forward composition}\}$

$\text{val}.x_2.(\text{set}.x_2.5.((\text{set}.x_1.3 \; ; \; \text{set}.x_1.0).\sigma))$

$= \{\text{property (a)}\}$

5

Since we have postulated properties for state attributes, we need to show that th
have a model. To show that the properties for a collection $x_1 : \Sigma_1, \ldots, x_m :$
of attributes is consistent, it is sufficient to consider the model where $\Sigma = \Sigma_1$
$\cdots \times \Sigma_m$ is the state space and x_i is the ith projection function on Σ. Furthermo
it is possible to show that the properties are complete with respect to this mod
in the sense that any state change in Σ can be described as a sequence of st
changes using update functions $\text{set}.x_i$ (in fact, in a normal form where no attrib
is updated more than once), and any state function $f : \Sigma \to \Delta$ can be descril
as a function over the access functions.

Expressions

A central use of program variables is in assignment statements like $x := x +$
Intuitively, this says that (the value of) program variable x is changed to the s
of (the values of) program variables x and y. In terms of attributes, this me
that the state σ is changed by setting the attribute x to a new value a, wh
$a = \text{val}.x.\sigma + \text{val}.y.\sigma$. The value a depends on the state σ, so the expression x ·
is a function from states to values.

An *expression* e on state space Σ is determined by the following grammar:

$$e \; ::= \; g \mid \dot{y} \mid \dot{f}.e_1.\cdots.e_m \; .$$

Here g is an access function, $g : \Sigma \to \Gamma$, y is a variable (*not* a program variab
and f is some (function) constant. We denote the pointwise extension of y
state function on Σ by $\dot{y}$, where $\dot{y} = (\lambda\sigma : \Sigma \cdot y)$. The pointwise extension o
is denoted by $\dot{f}$ and is defined for $m \geq 0$ by

$$\dot{f}.f_1.\cdots.f_m.\sigma \;\; = \;\; f.(f_1.\sigma).\cdots.(f_m.\sigma) \; .$$

A *Boolean expression* is an expression of type $\Sigma \to \text{Bool}$, a *natural num*
expression is an expression of type $\Sigma \to \text{Nat}$, and so on. An expression is
simply a term of higher-order logic that is built in a special way.

The pointwise-extended variable $\dot{y}$ permits us to have free variables that are not attributes in expressions. This will be needed later on, when we consider quantification of Boolean expressions.

An expression is thus constructed out of access functions, pointwise-extended variables, and pointwise-extended operations. We have earlier used pointwise-extended operations in connection with pointwise extension of lattices. Our definition of $\dot{f}$ generalizes this to operations with any number of arguments. For instance, we can define the pointwise extension of arithmetic operations by

$$
\begin{aligned}
\dot{0}.\sigma &= 0 \\
\dot{1}.\sigma &= 1 \\
&\;\;\vdots \\
(\dot{-}f_1).\sigma &= -(f_1.\sigma) \\
(f_1 \mathbin{\dot{+}} f_2).\sigma &= (f_1.\sigma) + (f_2.\sigma) \\
&\;\;\vdots
\end{aligned}
$$

An example of an expression written in infix notation is

$$(g_1 \mathbin{\dot{-}} \dot{1}) \mathbin{\dot{+}} (g_2 \mathbin{\dot{+}} \dot{z}) \ .$$

This expression contains two access functions, g_1 and g_2; the pointwise-extended variable $\dot{z}$; the pointwise-extended constant $\dot{1}$; and two pointwise-extended binary operations, $\dot{+}$ and $\dot{-}$.

Simpler Notation for Expressions

Explicit indication of pointwise extension becomes quite cumbersome in practice. Remember that a constant is determined by its name and its type. Hence, we are free to use the same name for both the function constant c and its pointwise extension $\dot{c}$, because these two constants have different types. Thus, we can define $\dot{0}.\sigma = 0$, $\dot{1}.\sigma = 1$, $(\dot{-}f_1).\sigma = -(f_1.\sigma)$, $(f_1 \dot{+} f_2).\sigma = (f_1.\sigma) + (f_2.\sigma)$, and so on, just as we did when extending lattice operations. We drop the explicit indication of pointwise extension when the type information is sufficient to determine that the operations must be pointwise extended. Thus, we can write the above expression in a more standard way as

$$(g_1 - 1) + (g_2 + z) \ .$$

The access functions that we use in an expression on Σ are the access functions of the attributes that we assume for the state space Σ. Thus, if we assume that Σ has attributes $x_1, \ldots, x_m$, then the access functions for Σ are $\mathsf{val}.x_1, \ldots, \mathsf{val}.x_m$. The expression would then be written as

$$(\mathsf{val}.x_1 - 1) + (\mathsf{val}.x_2 + z) \ ,$$

assuming that g_1 and g_2 are the access functions of attributes x_1 and x_2. In practice is cumbersome to indicate the access of each attribute explicitly. Most programmi languages therefore have the convention that the attribute name also stands for access function of the attribute. We follow this convention by postulating that any attribute x we also have an access function with the same name x (both w usually be assumed to be variables) such that

$$x \ = \ \text{val}.x \ .$$

Note that on the left-hand side we have $x : \Sigma \to \Gamma$ and on the right-hand si $x : (\Sigma \to \Gamma) \times (\Gamma \to \Sigma \to \Sigma)$, so the two variables have the same name different types; hence they are two different variables. We will choose this as last assumption about program variables.

With assumption (f), we can finally write the expression in a standard form, a would be written in most imperative programming languages:

$$(x_1 - 1) + (x_2 + z) \ .$$

We will assume that expressions are written in this way, using access function directly, rather than going via the attributes $(\text{val}.x)$.

As expressions are just ordinary terms of higher-order logic, we can prove pr erties of expressions in the usual way. As an example, consider proving th $(x + y) - y = x$. We have that

$$(x + y) - y$$
$$= \{\eta\text{-conversion}\}$$
$$(\lambda\sigma \cdot ((x + y) - y).\sigma)$$
$$= \{\text{pointwise extension}\}$$
$$(\lambda\sigma \cdot (x.\sigma + y.\sigma) - y.\sigma)$$
$$= \{\text{arithmetic}\}$$
$$(\lambda\sigma \cdot x.\sigma)$$
$$= \{\eta\text{-conversion}\}$$
$$x$$

Note that the justification "arithmetic" is used for an equality of the form $(a b) - b = a$, on the level of natural numbers, while the equality that we prove the same form but on the level of expressions. In Chapter 8 we will show how t kind of proof is generally done in a single step.

Assignment

The update operation is a simple form of assignment, where an explicit valu assigned to an attribute (used as a program variable). More generally, we wan permit an attribute to be assigned the value of an expression. Let e be an expression and let x be an attribute. We define the *assignment* $(x := e) : \Sigma \to \Sigma$ to be the following function:

$$(x := e).\sigma \;\overset{\wedge}{=}\; \mathsf{set}.x.(e.\sigma).\sigma \;. \qquad\qquad (assignment)$$

An example is the assignment $x := x + y - 3$, which maps an initial state σ to a final state $\sigma' = \mathsf{set}.x.a.\sigma$, where $a = (x + y - 3).\sigma = (x.\sigma + y.\sigma - 3) = (\mathsf{val}.x.\sigma + \mathsf{val}.y.\sigma - 3)$. For attributes $z \neq x$, we have $\mathsf{val}.z.\sigma' = \mathsf{val}.z.\sigma$ if the independence properties are assumed to hold.

The assignment permits us to express independence property (e) more nicely as

$$(x := x) \;=\; \mathsf{id} \;.$$

Properties (a)–(d) allow us to prove a result like $(x := a) ; (x := x) = (x := a)$, showing that an assignment of the value of an attribute to the same attribute is the identity function if the component has been assigned a value at least once. However, we cannot deduce $(x := x) = \mathsf{id}$ from the other properties, i.e., that the same assignment is an identity also when it is the first assignment to the component (Exercise 5.2).

The assignment is easily generalized to permit an assignment to a list of attributes, so called *multiple assignment*:

$$(x_1, \ldots, x_m := e_1, \ldots, e_m).\sigma \;\overset{\wedge}{=}$$
$$(\mathsf{set}.x_1.(e_1.\sigma) ; \mathsf{set}.x_2.(e_2.\sigma) ; \; \ldots \; ; \mathsf{set}.x_m.(e_m.\sigma)).\sigma \;,$$

where the attributes $x_1, \ldots, x_m$ must be distinct. The distinctness requirement implies, by independence property (d), that the order in a multiple assignment does not matter (Exercise 5.4):

$$(x_1, x_2 := e_1, e_2) \;=\; (x_2, x_1 := e_2, e_1) \;.$$

The assignment statement is built out of an attribute x and an expression e. Hence, we can apply the principle of operand congruence to assignment statements to determine when two assignment statements are equal. This gives us the rule

$$\frac{\Phi \vdash e = e'}{\Phi \vdash (x := e) = (x := e')} \;.$$

In fact, we can say something even stronger about the equality of two assignment statements, as will be shown in Section 8.4.

Reasoning with Program Variables

Let us next consider how to establish properties of expressions and state transformers that are described in terms of program variables. Let $P_a.x$ stand for assumption

(a) for attribute x, $P_b.x.y$ for assumption (b) for x and y, and so on. We write

$$\text{var } x_1 : \Gamma_1, \ldots, x_m : \Gamma_m$$

for the set of properties assumed to hold for program variables $x_1, \ldots, x_m$. M●
precisely, this set consists of the assumptions

$$P_a.x_i, \quad P_c.x_i, \quad P_e.x_i, \quad x_i = \text{val}.x_i, \quad i = 1, \ldots, m \ ,$$

that hold for each attribute x_i, and the assumptions

$$P_b.x_i.x_j, \quad P_d.x_i.x_j, \quad i = 1, \ldots, m, j = 1, \ldots, m, i \neq j \ ,$$

that hold for any pair x_i, x_j of attributes.

These assumptions arise from independence assumptions (a)–(e) together w●
assumption (f), by choosing x and y in all possible ways as two distinct attribu●
x_i and x_j.

We establish a property like $t = t'$, where t and t' are two expressions or two st●
transformers in program variables $x_1, \ldots, x_m$, by proving that

$$\text{var } x_1, \ldots, x_m \vdash t = t' \ .$$

Thus, in proving the equality of the two terms, we may assume that the indep●
dence assumptions hold for attributes $x_1, \ldots, x_m$ that occur in the terms.

Higher-order logic is *monotonic*, in the sense that adding assumptions to a theor●
(sequent) produces a new theorem. This is reflected in the inference rule

$$\frac{\Phi \vdash t}{\Phi, t' \vdash t} \ .$$

In the context of program variables, this means that if we have proved a prope●
like $t = t'$ for program variables $x_1, \ldots, x_m$, then this property will hold als●
we assume that there are more program variables on the state. In other words, ●
have

$$\frac{\text{var } x_1, \ldots, x_m \vdash t = t'}{\text{var } x_1, \ldots, x_m, x_{m+1}, \ldots, x_n \vdash t = t'} \ .$$

Another simple inference rule that we need when reasoning about program v●
ables is the following:

$$\frac{\text{var } x_1, \ldots, x_m \vdash t}{\text{var } x_1', \ldots, x_m' \vdash t[x_1, \ldots, x_m := x_1', \ldots, x_m']} \ .$$

We assume here that the new attributes $x_1', \ldots, x_m'$ are all distinct and are free ●
$x_1, \ldots, x_m$ in t. This means that we are free to replace the program variables ●
new program variables: the corresponding properties will still hold for the ●
program variables. This inference rule is also an easy consequence of the infere●
rules that are introduced in the next chapter.

Substitution Property

The following result (the *substitution lemma*) turns out to be of central importance to reasoning about programs with attributes and expressions.

Theorem 5.1 *Assume that x and y are state attributes. Furthermore, assume that e and f are expressions over x, y, both of the same type as x. Then*

$$\text{var } x, y \vdash e.((x := f).\sigma) = e[x := f].\sigma \ .$$

Note that on the left-hand side we have the assignment operation $x := f$, defined by $(x := f).\sigma = \text{set}.x.(f.\sigma).\sigma$, while on the right-hand side we have a substitution, where the term (expression) f is substituted for variable x in the term (expression) e. We can use substitution on the right-hand side, because x is an access function, i.e., a variable (of function type).

Proof The proof is by structural induction. First, assume that e is just an attribute. If e is access function x, then we have

$$x.(\text{set}.x.(f.\sigma).\sigma)$$
$$= \{\text{attribute properties (a), (f)}\}$$
$$f.\sigma$$
$$= \{\text{property of substitution}\}$$
$$x[x := f].\sigma$$

If e is an attribute y that is different from x, then we have

$$y.(\text{set}.x.(f.\sigma).\sigma)$$
$$= \{\text{attribute properties (b), (f)}\}$$
$$y.\sigma$$
$$= \{\text{property of substitution}\}$$
$$y[x := f].\sigma$$

If e is a pointwise extended variable $\dot{y}$, then we have

$$\dot{y}.((x := f).\sigma)$$
$$= \{\text{definition of } \dot{y}\}$$
$$y$$
$$= \{\text{definition of } \dot{y}\}$$
$$\dot{y}.\sigma$$
$$= \{\dot{y} \text{ has no subterms}\}$$
$$\dot{y}[x := f].\sigma$$

Finally, assume that e is an expression of the form $\dot{g}.e_1.\cdots.e_m$, $m \geq 0$, where $e_1, \ldots, e_m$ are expressions, and that the theorem holds for $e_1, \ldots, e_m$ (the induction hypothesis). Then we have that

$$(\dot{g}.e_1.\cdots.e_m).(\text{set}.x.(f.\sigma).\sigma)$$
$$= \{\text{definition of pointwise extension}, \sigma' = \text{set}.x.(f.\sigma).\sigma\}$$
$$g.(e_1.\sigma')\cdots.(e_m.\sigma')$$
$$= \{\text{induction assumption}\}$$
$$g.(e_1[x := f].\sigma).\cdots.(e_m[x := f].\sigma)$$
$$= \{\text{definition of pointwise extension}\}$$
$$(\dot{g}.e_1[x := f].\cdots.e_m[x := f]).\sigma$$
$$= \{\text{property of substitution}\}$$
$$(\dot{g}.e_1.\cdots.e_m)[x := f].\sigma$$

This last case covers also the case when e is a constant, by choosing $m = 0$. □

Note that the assumptions in var x, y form a subset of var $x, y, z_1, \ldots, z_m$, any collection of additional attributes $z_1, \ldots, z_m$. Therefore, the proof will in 1 establish

$$\text{var } x_1, \ldots, x_n \vdash e.((x := f).\sigma) = e[x := f].\sigma$$

for any collection of program variables that includes x, y. This is the monotonic principle that we already referred to above.

The following is a simple example of the use of this lemma:

$$\text{var } x, y : \text{Nat} \vdash (x \cdot y).((x := x + y).\sigma) = ((x + y) \cdot y).\sigma .$$

The substitution lemma is immediately generalized to multiple assignment, as lows. Assume that $x_1, \ldots, x_m$ are attributes of Σ, e is an expression, and $f_1, \ldots,$ are other expressions, where f_i is of the same type as x_1, for $i = 1, \ldots, m$. Th

$$\text{var } x_1, \ldots, x_m \vdash e.((x_1, \ldots, x_m := f_1, \ldots, f_m).\sigma) =$$
$$e[x_1, \ldots, x_m := f_1, \ldots, f_m].\sigma .$$

In fact, we can see the substitution lemma as stated in this form by consider $x := f$ as a multiple assignment, with $x = x_1, \ldots, x_m$ and $f = f_1, \ldots, f_m$. F now on, we let $x := e$ stand for a multiple assignment, unless we explicitly st that x is a single attribute.

An immediate consequence of the substitution lemma is the following.

Corollary 5.2   *Let e be an expression not involving attribute (list) x. Then*

$$\text{var } x \vdash e.((x := f).\sigma) = e.\sigma .$$

Assignments as State Transformers

State transformers form a category, with the identity function as the identity morphism and forward sequential composition as composition. An assignment is one way of describing state transformers that in practice is very useful. Let us therefore consider what the category operations are on assignments. For identity, we have already shown that $x := x$ is the same as id for any list of program variables x. The following theorem shows how to compose two successive assignments to the same variable x.

Theorem 5.3   *Let x be a list of attributes and f a list of expressions. Then*

$$\text{var } x \vdash \ (x := e) ; (x := f) = (x := f[x := e]) \ .$$

Proof   We prove the result for the case when x is a single attribute; the general case is proved in the same way.

$$((x := e) ; (x := f)).\sigma$$
$$= \{\text{definition of function composition}\}$$
$$(x := f).((x := e).\sigma)$$
$$= \{\text{definition of assignment}\}$$
$$\text{set.}x.(f.((x := e).\sigma)).((x := e).\sigma)$$
$$= \{\text{definition of assignment}\}$$
$$\text{set.}x.(f.((x := e).\sigma)).(\text{set.}x.(e.\sigma).\sigma)$$
$$= \{\text{attribute property (c)}\}$$
$$\text{set.}x.(f.((x := e).\sigma)).\sigma$$
$$= \{\text{substitution lemma}\}$$
$$\text{set.}x.(f[x := e].\sigma).\sigma$$
$$= \{\text{definition of assignment}\}$$
$$(x := f[x := e]).\sigma$$

□

Theorem 5.3 really only restates the definition of function composition, $f ; g = (\lambda x \cdot g.(f.x))$, but using the assignment notation with attributes and expressions. However, it is useful as a basic rule for merging two assignment statements into one or (reading it from right to left) splitting an assignment statement into two parts.

Theorem 5.3 requires that the two assignments be compatible, in the sense that they update exactly the same variables. The following lemma shows how we can make two assignments compatible.

Lemma 5.4   *Assume that x and y are disjoint lists of attributes. Then*

$$\text{var } x, y \vdash (x := e) = (y, x := y, e) .$$

Proof We have that

$$(y, x := y, e).\sigma$$
$$= \{\text{definition of multiple assignment}\}$$
$$(\text{set.}y.(y.\sigma) \, ; \, \text{set.}x.(e.\sigma)).\sigma$$
$$= \{\text{definition of sequential composition}\}$$
$$\text{set.}x.(e.\sigma).(\text{set.}y.(y.\sigma).\sigma)$$
$$= \{\text{attribute property (e)}\}$$
$$\text{set.}x.(e.\sigma).\sigma$$
$$= \{\text{definition of assignment}\}$$
$$x := e$$

$\square$

Theorem 5.3 together with Lemma 5.4 can now be used to compute the sequen
composition of two arbitrary assignments. Assume, for example, that x, y, an
are distinct attributes. Then

$$(x, y := e, f) \, ; \, (y, z := g, h)$$
$$= \{\text{add superfluous variables}\}$$
$$(x, y, z := e, f, z) \, ; \, (x, y, z := x, g, h)$$
$$= \{\text{merge assignments}\}$$
$$(x, y, z := x[x, y, z := e, f, z], g[x, y, z := e, f, z], h[x, y, z := e, f,$$
$$= \{\text{simplify}\}$$
$$(x, y, z := e, g[x, y := e, f], h[x, y := e, f])$$

Immediate consequences of Theorem 5.3 are the following rules for independ
assignments:

Corollary 5.5   (a) *Assume that x and y are disjoint (lists of) attributes. Then*

$$\text{var } x, y \vdash (x := e) \, ; \, (y := f) = (x, y := e, f[x := e]) .$$

(b) *Furthermore, if x is not free in f and y is not free in e, then*

$$\text{var } x, y \vdash (x := e) \, ; \, (y := f) = (y := f) \, ; \, (x := e) .$$

Proof We first prove (a):

$$((x := e) ; (y := f)).\sigma$$

$= \{\text{Lemma 5.4}\}$

$$((x, y := e, y) ; (x, y := x, f)).\sigma$$

$= \{\text{Theorem 5.3}\}$

$$(x, y := x[x, y := e, y], f[x, y := e, y])$$

$= \{\text{simplify substitutions}\}$

$$(x, y := e, f[x := e])$$

Now (b) follows by applying (a) twice. $\square$

Straight-Line Programs

We can use the framework built thus far to model *straight-line programs*, i.e., programs that perform only a sequence of successive changes to a state. These can be defined by the following very simple grammar:

$$f ::= \text{id} \mid x := e \mid f_1 ; f_2 .$$

Here x is a state attribute, e an expression, and f, f_1, and f_2 straight-line programs. Note that this definition does not introduce a new syntactic category. Instead, it identifies a specific subclass of state transformers: those that can be constructed in the manner described by the production rules.

Consider a simple straight-line program like

$$S = (x := x + y) ; (y := x - y) ; (x := x - y) . \tag{$*$}$$

The attributes here are (at least) x and y. The type of these attributes determines the state space of S. If x is an attribute on Σ, then $S : \Sigma \to \Sigma$; if x is an attribute on Γ, then $S : \Gamma \to \Gamma$. The straight-line program itself is of exactly the same form in both cases. We will in such cases say that $S : \Sigma \to \Sigma$ and $S : \Gamma \to \Gamma$ are *similar*. Similarity captures the notion that two state transformers expressed in terms of program variables are syntactically the same but may operate on different underlying state spaces. Properties of S that are expressed in terms of attributes of the state do not depend on whether the underlying state space is Σ or Γ. This is the main advantage of using state attributes with expressions and the assignment notation: we can prove properties that hold for the whole family of similar statements, rather than establishing a property only for a specific statement on a specific state space.

Alternatively, we can think of straight-line programs as being *polymorphic*. This means that we consider the underlying type Σ as a type variable that can be

instantiated to different concrete types. We have avoided using a polymorp[ic]
version of higher-order logic, for simplicity, but adding polymorphic terms do[es]
not present any difficulties and is, e.g., used in the underlying logic of the H[OL]
system [62].

Only very small parts of programs are straight-line programs. However, straig[ht-]
line programs form the building blocks of ordinary programs, because most i[m-]
perative programs are built up from such small pieces. It is therefore important[to]
be able to reason about these simple program fragments.

Let us give an example of how to use the assignment rules to reason about a straig[ht-]
line program. The following derivation shows that the state transformer (∗) abo[ve]
has the effect of swapping the values of the two attributes without using an ex[tra]
variable as temporary storage:

$$\text{var } x, y : \text{Nat}$$
$$\vdash \text{ “ } (x := x + y) ; (y := x - y) \text{ ” } ; (x := x - y)$$
$$= \{\text{merge assignments}\}$$
$$(x, y := x + y, \text{ “ } (x + y) - y \text{ ” }) ; (x := x - y)$$
$$= \{\text{simplify expression (derivation in Section 5.2)} \}$$
$$(x, y := x + y, x) ; (x := x - y)$$
$$= \{\text{merge assignments}\}$$
$$(x, y := \text{ “ } (x + y) - x \text{ ”}, x)$$
$$= \{\text{simplify expression}\}$$
$$(x, y := y, x)$$

We can compress any sequence of assignments to a single multiple assignment [by]
successive applications of the split/merge theorem. In some situations, this w[ill]
simplify the program, but in other cases it will make the resulting program lon[ger]
and more difficult to understand. Hence, there are situations where a sequence [of]
assignments is to be preferred and situations where a single multiple assignmen[t is]
better. Therefore, we need different ways of describing the same state transfor[mer]
and ways of moving between different equivalent descriptions.

5.5 Procedures

Let us now also show how to extend the simple straight-line programs wit[h a]
procedure mechanism. This mechanism is quite simple and will be used as s[uch]
also for the more complicated program models that we will describe later on.

Let us write the state transformer for swapping the values of program variable[s x]
and y in the previous section in full, without the abbreviations for assignments [and]

expressions. Then $(x := x + y) ; (y := x - y) ; (x := x - y)$ becomes

$(\lambda\sigma \cdot \text{set}.x.(\text{val}.x.\sigma + \text{val}.y.\sigma).\sigma)$;

$(\lambda\sigma \cdot \text{set}.y.(\text{val}.x.\sigma - \text{val}.y.\sigma).\sigma)$;

$(\lambda\sigma \cdot \text{set}.x.(\text{val}.x.\sigma - \text{val}.y.\sigma).\sigma)$.

The attributes x and y are thus the (only) free variables of this state transformer.

This state transformer will only swap the values of the program variables x and y. We could define a function of more general use by defining a constant *swap* that does what we want for any two attributes:

$$swap \stackrel{\wedge}{=} (\lambda x \; y \cdot x := x + y ; y := x - y ; x := x - y) \; .$$

Then the application of this function to some other attributes a and b, of the same type as x and y, is just

$$swap.a.b \; .$$

A simple calculation shows that

$$swap.a.b \;=\; (a := a + b ; b := a - b ; a := a - b) \; .$$

Lambda abstraction and application are thus available for program variables just as they are available for any other variables.

Let us compare this with the standard terminology used in programming languages. The *swap* function is actually a *procedure* that can be used in straight-line programs. The constant name *swap* is the *procedure name*, the attributes x and y that we have used to define the constant are the *formal parameters*, and the term that we use to define the constant is the *procedure body*. An application of the constant to other variables, like *swap.a.b*, is known as a *procedure call*, where a and b are the *actual parameters*. The specific method for parameter passing that we get by the above conventions is usually referred to as *call by reference*. Thus, the basic mechanisms of higher-order logic already contain all the features that we need for defining a procedure mechanism for straight-line programs. This same mechanism is also applicable as such to define procedures in the more expressive program models that we will study later on.

We will prove properties of straight-line programs only under the assumption that the attributes involved satisfy the independence assumptions, i.e., are in fact program variables. Thus, we can prove that

$$\text{var}\; x, y \vdash (x := x + y ; y := x - y ; x := x - y) =$$
$$(x, y := y, x) \; ,$$

although $x := x + y ; y := x - y ; x := x - y$ in general is not equal to $x, y := y, x$ (as this requires equality of the two state transformers for any attributes x and y, not only for independent attributes).

Using the definition of the *swap* procedure, we can deduce that

$$\text{var } x, y \vdash swap.x.y \;=\; (x, y := y, x) \,, \qquad ($$

and we can also deduce that

$$\text{var } a, b \vdash swap.a.b \;=\; (a, b := b, a)$$

using the rules for changing program variables described above.

Aliasing

Assuming that we have shown property (∗) for *swap.x.y*, what do we know ab
the properties of, say, *swap.a.a*. In other words, what happens if we give the sa
program variable *a* as actual parameter for both *x* and *y*? In programming lo₉
this is known as *aliasing*: two formal parameters are identified in the proced
call.

The problem with aliasing is that the independence assumptions actually imply
the program variables must be different attributes (provided that there is a s
attribute that can take two distinct values). To see this, assume that var x, y h
and that in addition, val.$x =$ val.y. Consider a state σ, a state $\sigma' = $ set.$x.1.\sigma$,
a state $\sigma'' = $ set.$x.2.\sigma'$. Then

$$2$$

$= \{\text{assumption (a)}\}$

val.$x.\sigma''$

$= \{\text{assumption val.}x = \text{val.}y\}$

val.$y.\sigma''$

$= \{\text{assumption (b)}\}$

val.$y.\sigma'$

$= \{\text{assumptions val.}x = \text{val.}y \text{ and (a)}\}$

$$1$$

which is a contradiction. Therefore, x and y must be different attributes. In a sim
way, we can show that the assumption set.$x = $ set.y also leads to a contradicti

The property (∗) thus implies that *swap.x.y* $= (x, y := y, x)$ holds for any
different attributes x and y that satisfy var x, y. This means that we know noth
about *swap.x.y* when x and y are the same variable: the proof has establis
property (∗) only for the case when x and y are different.

Aliasing as such is not illegal or wrong. On the contrary, the procedure call *swap.*
is a well-formed term that denotes a specific state transformer. We can even sh
that var $a \vdash swap.a.a = (a := 0)$ holds, but this requires a new proof; it canno
deduced from (∗).

This means that we always have to apply a procedure with two or more formal arguments to different program variables. This is known as the *nonaliasing* requirement for passing parameters by reference. In our context, it is a direct consequence of the way we have formalized procedures with parameters.

Blocks and Value Parameters

A state transformer $f : \Sigma \to \Gamma$ models a state change, starting in an initial state $\sigma : \Sigma$ and terminating in some final state $f.\sigma : \Gamma$. State transformers that are expressed using the program variable notation stay within the same state space. We shall now show how to define a *block*, which temporarily moves to a different state space. This construct permits us to embed state transformers on a "larger" state space into a state transformer on a "smaller" state space.

The definition of the block construct rests on the notion of state extension functions. The state transformers begin : $\Sigma \to \Gamma$ and end : $\Gamma \to \Sigma$ form a *state extension pair* if they satisfy

$$\text{begin ; end} \ = \ \text{id} , \tag{g}$$

i.e., if end is a left inverse of begin (the reason for calling end a *left inverse* of begin becomes clear if we write the condition as end ∘ begin = id). A state extension pair establishes a correspondence between elements of the two state spaces, so that every $\sigma \in \Sigma$ has a copy begin.σ in Γ and every $\gamma \in \Gamma$ has an original end.γ in Σ. A similar idea will be used to extend the logic with new types (see Chapter 10).

For given state spaces Σ and Γ there may exist many state extension pairs. In fact, one can show that any injective function can be used as the function begin (Exercise 5.7). However, the idea is that begin maps Σ to a copy of Σ inside Γ in a particular way that will be made clear below.

Given a state extension pair and a state transformer $f : \Gamma \to \Gamma$, we define a *block* to be a state transformer of the form

$$\text{begin ; } f \text{ ; end} . \tag{block}$$

The block maps state space Σ into the state space Γ and then performs the state change f before moving back to the original state space. The *extended state space* Γ is 'larger' than Σ, because begin is injective. This construct is illustrated as a *commuting diagram* in Figure 5.1.

Local Variables

Now assume that the state space Σ has program variables $x_1, \ldots, x_m$ satisfying the independence assumptions. Also assume that Γ is another state space with program variables $x_1, \ldots, x_m, y_1, \ldots, y_n$ satisfying the independence assumptions.

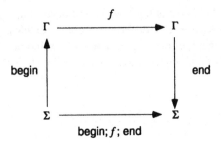

FIGURE 5.1. Blocks as state extensions

Furthermore, assume that a state extension pair between Σ and Γ satisfies following properties:

$$
\begin{aligned}
(x_i := a)\,;\,\text{begin} &= \text{begin}\,;\,(x_i := a)\,, \\
(x_i := a)\,;\,\text{end} &= \text{end}\,;\,(x_i := a)\,, \\
\text{val}.x_i &= \text{end}\,;\,\text{val}.x_i\,, \\
(y_j := b)\,;\,\text{end} &= \text{end}\,.
\end{aligned}
$$

Conditions (h), (j), and (k) state that there is a correspondence between the progr variable $x_1, \ldots, x_m$ on the two state spaces. Condition (l) states that a change y_j does not cause a change in the underlying global state, so the program variab $y_1, \ldots, y_n$ are local to Γ. These conditions are illustrated as commuting diagra in Figure 5.2. They generalize in a straightforward way to multiple assignmer For reference, we write all the state attribute properties in the same format collect them in Table 5.1.

$$
\begin{aligned}
\text{val}.x.(\text{set}.x.a.\sigma) &= a & \text{(a)} \\
\text{val}.y.(\text{set}.x.a.\sigma) &= \text{val}.y.\sigma & \text{(b)} \\
\text{set}.x.a\,;\,\text{set}.x.b &= \text{set}.x.b & \text{(c)} \\
\text{set}.x.a\,;\,\text{set}.y.b &= \text{set}.y.b\,;\,\text{set}.x.a & \text{(d)} \\
\text{set}.x.(\text{val}.x.\sigma).\sigma &= \sigma & \text{(e)} \\
x &= \text{val}.x & \text{(f)} \\
\text{begin}\,;\,\text{end} &= \text{id} & \text{(g)} \\
\text{set}.x.a\,;\,\text{begin} &= \text{begin}\,;\,\text{set}.x.a & \text{(h)} \\
\text{set}.x.a\,;\,\text{end} &= \text{end}\,;\,\text{set}.x.a & \text{(j)} \\
\text{val}.x.(\text{end}.\gamma) &= \text{val}.x.\gamma & \text{(k)} \\
\text{set}.y.b\,;\,\text{end} &= \text{end} & \text{(l)}
\end{aligned}
$$

TABLE 5.1. Independence requirements for attributes

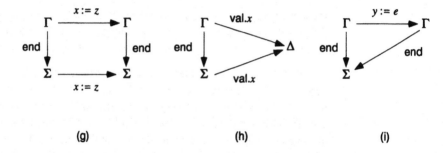

$$(g) \qquad\qquad (h) \qquad\qquad (i)$$

FIGURE 5.2. Block function properties

Let us introduce a special syntax for a block where these assumptions are satisfied:

begin var $y_1, \ldots, y_n := e_1, \ldots, e_n$; f end $\stackrel{\wedge}{=}$
    begin ; $(y_1, \ldots, y_n := e_1 \circ$ end, $\ldots, e_n \circ$ end) ; f ; end ,

where $e_1, \ldots, e_m$ are expressions over the global state space Σ (i.e., expressed in terms of program variables $x_1, \ldots, x_m$). The initialization $y_j := e_j \circ$ end makes the initial value of y_j the value of expression e_j in the global state. The variables $y_1, \ldots, y_n$ are called *local variables* in the block.

One may wonder whether it is possible to define state attributes in such a way that conditions (g)–(l) are satisfied. To see that this is indeed possible, assume that state space Σ is given, with program variables $x_1, \ldots, x_m$. By letting Γ be of the form $\Delta \times \Sigma$, where Δ has program variables $y_1, \ldots, y_n$, we can define the attributes over Γ in terms of the attributes over Σ and Δ as follows:

$$x_i \stackrel{\wedge}{=} x_i \circ \text{snd} ,$$
$$y_j \stackrel{\wedge}{=} y_j \circ \text{fst} .$$

The conditions (g)–(l) are then satisfied when begin.$\sigma = (\gamma', \sigma)$ and end.$\gamma =$ snd.γ, for some arbitrary γ' in Γ.

We permit local program variables to have the same name as global program variables. In this case, the corresponding access and update functions inside the block always refer to the local rather than the global attribute. This corresponds to a *redeclaration* of a variable that hides the corresponding attribute of the global state, making it inaccessible to the statement inside the block (except to the initialization). This attribute is, of course, available as usual outside the block.

As an example consider the following state transformer:

begin var $y, z := x + y, x - y$; $x := y + z$; $v := x + v$ end ;
$v := x + v$.

Here the initial state space Σ has program variables v, x, and y (it may have other program variables as well). The state transformer $(x := y + z)$; $(v := x + v)$

operates on a state space Γ that has program variables v, x, y, z, where v and x global and y and z are local. The local program variables y and z are initialize the values $x + y$ and $x - y$, where x and y access the global program variable

Note that the state transformer $v := x + v$ inside the block is similar to but not same as the state transformer $v := x + v$ outside the block. The state transfor inside the block works on the extended state space of the block body, while state transformer outside the block works on the global state space. The s attributes involved have the same names, but they have different domains. The of expressions and assignment notation allows us to ignore this difference w writing programs. In most cases, this is a good convention, because the distincti between the two statements are not important. However, when reasoning at general properties of statements in the refinement calculus, we need to keep distinction in mind. The distinction can always be made explicit by indicating types of the state attributes involved, so there is no confusion on the logical le where typing makes the two state transformer terms distinct.

The expression e that is used to initialize the value of the local program vari may depend on the values of the global variables at block entry. A traditional bl initializes the local program variables to some fixed value, which may or may be known. For instance, if y is of type Nat, then we may choose e to be s arbitrary natural number, or we may choose e to be 0. In either case, once convention is known, we do not need to indicate e explicitly in the syntax of block and can write the block simply as begin var y ; f end.

Working with Blocks

The basic properties of state extension pairs and program variables permit u prove properties about blocks, as the following example shows. The aim is to s two program variables using only single-variable assignments:

$$x, y := y, x$$
$= $ {characterization of state extension pair, local variable z}
  begin ; " end " ; $x, y := y, x$
$= $ {block property (j)}
  begin ; $z := x$; " end ; $x, y := y, x$ "
$= $ {properties (g) and (h)}
  begin ; " $z := x$; $x, y := y, x$ " ; end
$= $ {assignment reasoning (Exercise 5.6)}
  begin ; $z := x$; $x := y$; $y := z$; end
$= $ {definition of block syntax}
  begin var $z := x$; $x := y$; $y := z$ end

Here the first three steps accomplish an instance of what can be seen as a general principle of *block introduction*:

$$f \;=\; \text{begin var } y := e \,;\, f' \text{ end} \,, \qquad\qquad (block\ introduction)$$

where f is a state transformer written using only assignment notation (with no occurrence of local variable z) and f' and f are similar (in fact, we can allow f' to contain additional assignments to the local variable). Reading the block introduction from right to left, we see that at the same time we are given a principle of *block elimination*.

In fact, block introduction and elimination can be seen as special cases of *introduction and elimination of local variables*. The rule for this has the following form:

$$\begin{aligned} &\text{begin var } z := e' \,;\, f \text{ end} \;= \qquad\qquad (local\ variable\ introduction)\\ &\quad \text{begin var } y, z := e, e' \,;\, f' \text{ end} \end{aligned}$$

when f and f' are similar. The proof is a similar derivation as for the special case of block introduction. In this more general case, we can add or remove one or more local variables to or from a block.

Value Parameters

Recall the definition of procedures in Section 5.5. In principle, we can get along with just call by reference for procedures. In practice, other parameter-passing mechanisms are also useful for procedures, and the block construct gives us a way of handling these. The most important other mechanism is *call by value*. A procedure declaration usually indicates for each parameter whether it should be called by reference or called by value (or in some other way). Assume that we have a procedure declaration of the form

$$\text{proc } f(\text{var } x, \text{val } y) = s \,.$$

Here we use standard notation, with var x indicating that parameter x is to be passed by reference and val y indicating that y is to be passed by value. This procedure declaration is seen as syntactic sugaring for the following definition of constant f:

$$f.x.y \;\stackrel{\wedge}{=}\; s \,.$$

A call on the procedure f is assumed to be of the form $f(u, e)$, where u is some attribute and e an expression. This call is again seen as syntactic sugaring:

$$f(u, e) \;\stackrel{\wedge}{=}\; \text{begin var } y' := e \,;\, f.u.y' \text{ end} \,.$$

Thus, the call $f(u, e)$ is actually a block that introduces a local variable y' for the value parameter, with y' distinct from u, and assigns the actual value expression e

to this variable. We need to assume that no recursive calls on f are made wit the body of f, because straight-line programs are not expressive enough to me recursive procedures. Recursive procedures will be treated in detail in Chapter

Locally Defined Procedures

Recall that the let construct allows us to name a term locally. When we focus the body t in let $x = s$ in t, we get $x = s$ as a local assumption. The same idea be used to define procedures locally and to have the procedure definition availa as an assumption when reasoning about statements that contain procedure ca We define

$$\text{proc } f(\text{var } x, \text{val } y) = s \text{ in} \qquad\qquad (local\ procedu$$
$$\cdots f(u, e) \cdots$$
$$\stackrel{\wedge}{=}$$
$$\text{let } f = (\lambda x\ y \bullet s) \text{ in}$$
$$\cdots \text{begin var } y' := e\ ;\ f.u.y' \text{ end} \cdots$$

Here the dots $(\cdots)$ surrounding the procedure call indicate that the call is of a state transformer. We choose y' such that there is no name clash with The difference, compared with global procedures, is that f is now not a cons but a variable that has a local meaning inside the body of the let construct. definition shows a body with only a single procedure call, but statements multiple procedure calls work in exactly the same way.

As an example consider the following state transformer:

$$\text{proc Incr(var } x, \text{val } y) = (x := x + y) \text{ in}$$
$$\text{Incr}(a, a + b)\ ;\ b := 0$$

The following derivation shows what statement this is

$$\text{proc Incr(var } x, \text{val } y) = (x := x + y) \text{ in}$$
$$\text{Incr}(a, a \cdot b)\ ;\ b := 0$$
$$= \{\text{definition of procedure}\}$$
$$\text{let Incr} = (\lambda x\ y \bullet x := x + y) \text{ in}$$
$$\text{begin var } y := a \cdot b\ ;\ \text{Incr}(a, y) \text{ end}\ ;\ b := 0$$
$$= \{\text{definition of let }\}$$
$$(\lambda \text{Incr} \bullet \text{begin var } y := a \cdot b\ ;\ \text{Incr}(a, y) \text{ end}\ ;\ b := 0).(\lambda x\ y \bullet x := x$$
$$= \{\beta\text{-conversion}\}$$
$$\text{begin var } y := a \cdot b\ ;\ (\lambda x\ y \bullet x := x + y).(a, y) \text{ end}\ ;\ b := 0$$
$$= \{\beta\text{-conversion}\}$$
$$\text{begin var } y := a \cdot b\ ;\ a := a + y \text{ end}\ ;\ b := 0$$

Note that this is exactly what the meaning of $\mathsf{Incr}(a, a + b) ; b := 0$ would have been if Incr had been defined as a global procedure (constant).

One advantage of local procedures is that we can focus on the body of a procedure definition and rewrite it, since it is part of the term that we are transforming. For example, we can use the results of earlier derivations as follows:

$\quad$ proc $\mathsf{Swap}(\mathsf{var}\; x, y) =$ " $(x, y := y, x)$ " in

$\qquad \mathsf{Swap}(a, b) ; \mathsf{Swap}(c, d)$

$= \{$replace according to earlier derivation$\}$

$\qquad$ proc $\mathsf{Swap}(\mathsf{var}\; x, y) = \mathsf{begin}\; \mathsf{var}\; z := x ; x := y ; y := z\; \mathsf{end}$ in

$\qquad \mathsf{Swap}(a, b) ; \mathsf{Swap}(c, d)$

Summary and Discussion

In this chapter we have shown how to model program variables as independent attributes in higher-order logic, investigated the basic properties of attributes, and shown how to define expressions and assignments in terms of attributes. A number of basic properties of expressions and assignments were identified. As a result, we have a small and convenient theory of state transformers, which we can use to show equivalence of terms in this domain. We have also shown how to model blocks with local variables and procedures in this little equational theory of program variables.

The notion of a state with independent attributes is central to the imperative programming paradigm. We have tried to be precise about the notion of a program variable, an expression, and an assignment, because so much in what follows depends on a precise understanding of these issues.

States in programming logics are usually fixed to a specific model. For instance, one can model states as functions that map a set of program variable names to values. A detailed treatment of this approach is given by Jaco de Bakker [36]. This approach either requires all values to be of the same type, or it needs a logic with dependent types (or an untyped logic). Another approach is to define states as tuples, as done by, e.g., Back and von Wright [30]. Yet another popular model is to treat states as records. Higher-order logic can be extended with records (as is, e.g., done in the programming language Standard ML [100]). Dijkstra and Carel Scholten [54] also consider program variables as functions of a hidden state, but their treatment of program variables is otherwise quite different from ours.

We have chosen to state only the minimal assumptions that we need about states and their attributes in order to reason about programs with expressions and assignments. Models that consider states as functions, tuples or records will all satisfy the assumptions that we have given for states. In this way, we avoid choosing one specific model in favor of others.

5.8 Exercises

5.1 Show that the following property follows from the independence assumptions:

$$\text{set}.x.e.\sigma = \text{set}.x.e'.\sigma \;\Rightarrow\; e.\sigma = e'.\sigma \;.$$

5.2 Show that the following property follows from the independence assumption (a)–(d):

$$(x := a)\,;(x := x) \;=\; (x := a) \;.$$

Verify informally that it is still not possible to prove $(x := x) = $ id from the sa assumptions.

5.3 Assume a state space Nat where the two program variables b : Bool and x : are encoded as follows. For given state σ : Nat we let val.$b.\sigma$ = even.σ val.$x.\sigma = \sigma$ div 2. Describe the operations set.b and set.x.

5.4 Prove the following property:

$$(x, y := e_1, e_2) \;=\; (y, x := e_2, e_1) \;.$$

5.5 Verify the following using Corollary 5.2:

$$\begin{aligned}(x * y).((x, y := x + y, y + 1).\sigma) &= ((x + y) * (y + 1)).\sigma \;, \\ (x * y).((z := x + y).\sigma) &= (x * y).\sigma \;.\end{aligned}$$

5.6 Use the properties of assignments to show the following equality:

$$(z := x)\,;(x, y := y, x) = (z := x)\,;(x := y)\,;(y := z) \;.$$

5.7 Assume that a function $f : \Sigma \rightarrow \Gamma$ is given. Show that f has a left (right) inve if and only if f is injective (surjective).

5.8 When computing a sum, a local variable can be used to collect intermediate su Show the following equality:

$$\begin{aligned}&\text{var } x, y, z, s \vdash \\ &\quad y := x + y + z = \\ &\qquad \text{begin var } s := 0\,;\, s := s + x\,;\, s := s + y\,;\, s := s + z\,;\, y := s \text{ end}\end{aligned}$$

5.9 Assume the following procedure definition:

$$\begin{aligned}\text{Max(var } x, \text{val } y, z) &= x := \text{max}.y.z \;, \\ \text{Min(var } x, \text{val } y, z) &= x := \text{min}.y.z \;.\end{aligned}$$

where the operator max returns the greater of its two arguments and min retu the smaller. Prove in full formal detail the following:

$$\text{Max}(u, e, e')\,;\, u := e + e' - u \;=\; \text{Min}(u, e, e') \;.$$

Truth Values

In previous chapters we have introduced higher-order logic and described the constants and inference rules that are used for reasoning about functions. In this chapter we present the constants and inference rules that are needed for reasoning about logical formulas. We have shown earlier that the truth values form a complete Boolean lattice. Here we describe the general inference rules that are available for reasoning about Boolean lattices. The basic inference rules for truth values are then special cases of these general rules. Furthermore, inference rules for quantification follow from the fact the truth values form a complete lattice.

We also show how the derivation style works for reasoning about formulas with logical connectives. In particular, we show how subderivations that focus on a subterm of the term being transformed can use context-dependent local assumptions. We also give some inference rules for assumptions and show how to manipulate assumptions in proofs.

Inference Rules for Boolean Lattices

Assume that the type Σ denotes the set A. Then $\sqsubseteq : \Sigma \rightarrow \Sigma \rightarrow$ Bool denotes a relation on A. If $t_1 : \Sigma$ and $t_2 : \Sigma$ are two terms, then $t_1 \sqsubseteq t_2$ is a formula that is true if the relation denoted by $\sqsubseteq$ holds between the element denoted by t_1 and the element denoted by t_2.

The inference rule

$$\frac{}{\vdash t \sqsubseteq t} \qquad\qquad (\sqsubseteq \textit{reflexiv}$$

now states that $\sqsubseteq$ is reflexive. This inference rule may be taken as an axiom we want to postulate that the relation $\sqsubseteq$ is reflexive. Alternatively, it may also possible to derive it from other axioms and inference rules for the relation $\sqsubseteq$.

Similarly, the inference rule

$$\frac{\Phi \vdash t \sqsubseteq t' \quad \Phi' \vdash t' \sqsubseteq t''}{\Phi \cup \Phi' \vdash t \sqsubseteq t''} \qquad\qquad (\sqsubseteq \textit{transitiv}$$

is valid if the relation $\sqsubseteq$ is transitive. Writing the transitivity property as an inferer rule avoids the explicit use of an implication when expressing this property. Eit inference rules such as these may be postulated for the relation $\sqsubseteq$, or they may derivable by using other axioms and inference rules for the relation $\sqsubseteq$.

The collection of inference rules that hold for Boolean lattices are summarize Table 6.1. These inference rules are really schemes, where any concrete choice the constants $\sqsubseteq, \bot, \top, \sqcap, \sqcup$, and $\neg$ gives a collection of inference rules stating these constants form a Boolean lattice.

$$\frac{}{\vdash t \sqsubseteq t} \qquad\qquad \frac{\Phi \vdash t \sqsubseteq t' \quad \Phi' \vdash t' \sqsubseteq t''}{\Phi \cup \Phi' \vdash t \sqsubseteq t''} \qquad (\sqsubseteq \textit{reflexive})$$

$$\qquad\qquad\qquad\qquad\qquad (\sqsubseteq\textit{transitive})$$

$$\frac{\Phi \vdash t \sqsubseteq t' \quad \Phi' \vdash t' \sqsubseteq t}{\Phi \cup \Phi' \vdash t' = t} \qquad\qquad\qquad\qquad (\sqsubseteq \textit{antisymmetric})$$

$$\qquad\qquad\qquad\qquad\qquad (\bot \textit{ least})$$

$$\frac{}{\vdash \bot \sqsubseteq t} \qquad\qquad\qquad \frac{}{\vdash t \sqsubseteq \top} \qquad (\top \textit{ greatest})$$

$$\frac{\Phi \vdash s \sqsubseteq t \quad \Phi' \vdash s \sqsubseteq t'}{\Phi \cup \Phi' \vdash s \sqsubseteq t \sqcap t'} \qquad \frac{\Phi \vdash t \sqsubseteq s \quad \Phi' \vdash t' \sqsubseteq s}{\Phi \cup \Phi' \vdash t \sqcup t' \sqsubseteq s} \qquad (\sqcap \textit{ introduction})$$

$$\qquad\qquad\qquad\qquad\qquad (\sqcup \textit{ elimination})$$

$$\qquad\qquad\qquad\qquad\qquad (\sqcap \textit{ elimination})$$

$$\frac{}{\vdash t \sqcap t' \sqsubseteq t} \qquad\qquad \frac{}{\vdash t \sqcap t' \sqsubseteq t'}$$

$$\qquad\qquad\qquad\qquad\qquad (\sqcup \textit{ introduction})$$

$$\frac{}{\vdash t \sqsubseteq t \sqcup t'} \qquad\qquad \frac{}{\vdash t' \sqsubseteq t \sqcup t'}$$

$$\qquad\qquad\qquad\qquad\qquad (\sqcap \textit{ distributivity})$$

$$\frac{}{\vdash t \sqcup (t' \sqcap t'') = (t \sqcup t') \sqcap (t \sqcup t'')}$$

$$\qquad\qquad\qquad\qquad\qquad (\sqcup \textit{ distributivity})$$

$$\frac{}{\vdash t \sqcap (t' \sqcup t'') = (t \sqcap t') \sqcup (t \sqcap t'')}$$

$$\qquad\qquad\qquad\qquad\qquad (\neg \textit{ contradiction})$$

$$\frac{}{\vdash t \sqcap \neg t = \bot} \qquad\qquad \frac{}{\vdash t \sqcup \neg t = \top}$$

$$\qquad\qquad\qquad\qquad\qquad (\neg \textit{ exhaustion})$$

TABLE 6.1. Inference rules for Boolean lattices

Truth Values

Traditionally, the properties of truth values are given by picking out a few of the operations as basic, giving the axioms that determine their properties, and then defining the other logical constants explicitly in terms of these postulated constants. This approach works well if we want to do metamathematical reasoning about the higher-order logic itself, but it is unnecessarily cumbersome when we are interested only in using the logic.

Lattice theory provides a nicer way of characterizing the properties of truth values. We have already noted that the truth values form a Boolean and linearly ordered lattice. Any poset of this kind with at least two elements must be isomorphic to the standard model for truth values. Hence, we can take this collection of lattice properties as the axioms that characterize truth values.

The type Bool of truth values was postulated as a standard type in higher-order logic. We now further postulate the following constants:

$$\begin{aligned}
\mathsf{T} &: \mathsf{Bool} \,, & (true)\\
\mathsf{F} &: \mathsf{Bool} \,, & (false)\\
\neg &: \mathsf{Bool} \rightarrow \mathsf{Bool} \,, & (not)\\
\Rightarrow &: \mathsf{Bool} \rightarrow \mathsf{Bool} \rightarrow \mathsf{Bool} \,, & (implies)\\
\wedge &: \mathsf{Bool} \rightarrow \mathsf{Bool} \rightarrow \mathsf{Bool} \,, & (and)\\
\vee &: \mathsf{Bool} \rightarrow \mathsf{Bool} \rightarrow \mathsf{Bool} \,. & (or)
\end{aligned}$$

We prefer to use the symbol $\equiv$ (rather than $=$) for equality on Bool. We consider $t \Leftarrow t'$ as an alternative way of writing $t' \Rightarrow t$. The constants $\Rightarrow$, $\wedge$, and $\vee$ are (exactly like $=$ and $\equiv$) written infix and associate to the right. These constants are all intended to have their traditional meanings.

The infix logical connectives have lower precedence than other infixes (e.g., arithmetic operators and equality). Conjunction $\wedge$ has highest precedence, followed by the operations $\vee$, $\Rightarrow$, and $\equiv$, in that order. The precedence is overridden when necessary by explicit parenthesis. Note that $\equiv$ and $=$ are actually the same operation on Bool, but they have different precedences. For a complete list of infix precedences, see Appendix A.

Negation is a prefix operator. It has higher precedence than all infix operators except for the function application dot.

Inference Rules

We postulate that the truth values form a Boolean lattice with implication $\Rightarrow$ as the ordering relation. Falsity F is the bottom, truth T is the top, conjunction $\wedge$ is meet, disjunction $\vee$ is join, and negation $\neg$ is complement. This means that the above-listed inference rules for Boolean lattices hold for the truth values. This

$$\vdash t \Rightarrow t$$

$$\dfrac{\Phi \vdash t \Rightarrow t' \quad \Phi' \vdash t' \Rightarrow t''}{\Phi \cup \Phi' \vdash t \Rightarrow t''}$$

$$\dfrac{\Phi \vdash t \Rightarrow t' \quad \Phi' \vdash t' \Rightarrow t}{\Phi \cup \Phi' \vdash t' \equiv t}$$

$$\vdash F \Rightarrow t \qquad\qquad \vdash t \Rightarrow T$$

$$\dfrac{\Phi \vdash s \Rightarrow t \quad \Phi' \vdash s \Rightarrow t'}{\Phi \cup \Phi' \vdash s \Rightarrow t \wedge t'} \qquad \dfrac{\Phi \vdash t \Rightarrow s \quad \Phi' \vdash t' \Rightarrow s}{\Phi \cup \Phi' \vdash t \vee t' \Rightarrow s}$$

$$\vdash t \wedge t' \Rightarrow t \qquad \vdash t \wedge t' \Rightarrow t'$$

$$\vdash t \Rightarrow t \vee t' \qquad \vdash t' \Rightarrow t \vee t'$$

$$\vdash t \vee (t' \wedge t'') \equiv (t \vee t') \wedge (t \vee t'')$$

$$\vdash t \wedge (t' \vee t'') \equiv (t \wedge t') \vee (t \wedge t'')$$

$$\vdash t \wedge \neg t \equiv F \qquad\qquad \vdash t \vee \neg t \equiv T$$

(⇒ *reflexive*)

(⇒ *transitive*)

(⇒ *antisymmetric*)

(F *least*)

(T *greatest*)

(∧ *introduction*)

(∨ *elimination*)

(∧ *elimination*)

(∨ *introduction*)

(∧ *distributivity*)

(∨ *distributivity*)

(¬ *contradiction*)

(¬ *exhaustion*)

TABLE 6.2. Inference rules for truth values

gives us the inference rules for truth values shown in Table 6.2.

The truth-value lattice has two additional properties that are special to it. The property is that it is linearly ordered. This is expressed by the following axiom

$$\overline{\vdash (t \Rightarrow t') \vee (t' \Rightarrow t)} \; \cdot$$

(⇒ *line*

The second property is that we identify truth with theoremhood. This is expre by the following axiom:

$$\overline{\vdash T} \; \cdot$$

(*tr*

This axiom thus states that T is a theorem.

6.3 Derivations with Logical Connectives

The notion of a proof is not changed when we add the new rules (like truth linearity of implication above); it is only the underlying theory that is exten The rules have been expressed as inference rules, in the format used for na deduction. However, we prefer to use derivations rather than deductions also for reasoning about logical formulas in general. There is then one small problem. The format requires that each proof step must be of the form $t \sqsubseteq t'$, where $\sqsubseteq$ is a preorder. Only equality and implication are of this form. How should we give a derivational proof for sequents of the form $\Phi \vdash t_1 \wedge t_2$ or $\Phi \vdash t_1 \vee t_2$?

The following inference rule shows the way out of this dilemma. It essentially says that stating a proposition is the same as stating that it is equivalent to the constant T (which stands for truth):

$$\frac{}{\vdash t \equiv (t \equiv \mathsf{T})} \cdot \qquad\qquad (\equiv \mathsf{T}\ rule)$$

Similarly, we have a rule that says that stating the negation of a proposition is the same as stating that it is equivalent to the constant F (which thus stands for *falsity*):

$$\frac{}{\vdash \neg t \equiv (t \equiv \mathsf{F})} \cdot \qquad\qquad (\equiv \mathsf{F}\ rule)$$

The proofs of these rules are left as exercises to the reader (Exercise 6.1). The proofs are rather long, involving antisymmetry of $\equiv$, substitution, and properties of T and F.

In fact, the following variations of these rules are also valid

$$\frac{}{\vdash t \equiv (\mathsf{T} \Rightarrow t)} , \qquad\qquad (\mathsf{T} \Rightarrow rule)$$

$$\frac{}{\vdash \neg t \equiv (t \Rightarrow \mathsf{F})} , \qquad\qquad (\Rightarrow \mathsf{F}\ rule)$$

since the implications in the opposite direction are trivially true.

The solution to the problem posed above is now simple. To prove a theorem $\Phi \vdash t$, where t is not of the form required for a derivation, it is sufficient to give a derivation for $\Phi \vdash t \equiv \mathsf{T}$, as shown by the following deduction:

$$\frac{\Phi \vdash t \equiv \mathsf{T} \qquad \dfrac{}{\vdash t \equiv (t \equiv \mathsf{T})}\ \{\equiv \mathsf{T}\ rule\}}{\Phi \vdash t}\ \{substitution\} \ .$$

The $\mathsf{T} \Rightarrow$ rule shows that it is in fact sufficient to give a derivation for $\Phi \vdash \mathsf{T} \Rightarrow t$. Similarly, if we want to prove $\Phi \vdash \neg t$, then it is sufficient to give a derivation for $\Phi \vdash t \equiv \mathsf{F}$ or for $\Phi \vdash t \Rightarrow \mathsf{F}$ (the latter amounts to a *proof by contradiction*).

We illustrate derivations with logical connectives below by looking at a selection of standard propositional inference rules. There are many such rules, but space does not permit us to present them all. They can in most cases be easily derived from existing rules.

Properties of Truth and Falsity

For truth and falsity, we have the following useful rules (in fact, the correspond
rules hold in every complete lattice):

$$\frac{}{\vdash \mathsf{T} \land t \equiv t} \quad ,$$

(T∧ *ru*

$$\frac{}{\vdash \mathsf{T} \lor t \equiv \mathsf{T}} \quad ,$$

(T∨ *ru*

$$\frac{}{\vdash \mathsf{F} \land t \equiv \mathsf{F}} \quad ,$$

(F∧ *ru*

$$\frac{}{\vdash \mathsf{F} \lor t \equiv t} \quad .$$

(F∨ *ru*

Let us consider the first one of these, as an example of a simple derivational pr
in logic.

$$\vdash t$$
$$\Rightarrow \{\land \text{ introduction}\}$$
$$\bullet \quad t$$
$$\Rightarrow \quad \{\mathsf{T} \text{ greatest}\}$$
$$\mathsf{T}$$
$$\bullet \quad t$$
$$\Rightarrow \quad \{\text{reflexivity}\}$$
$$t$$
$$\cdot \quad \mathsf{T} \land t$$

This establishes that $\vdash t \Rightarrow \mathsf{T} \land t$. The opposite implication ($\mathsf{T} \land t \Rightarrow t$) is
instance of $\land$ elimination, so $\mathsf{T} \land t \equiv t$ follows by antisymmetry.

Two-Valued Logic

Another important property is that there are exactly two truth values. This is sta
by the following inference rule:

$$\frac{}{\vdash (t \equiv \mathsf{T}) \lor (t \equiv \mathsf{F})} \quad .$$

(*Boolean cas*

Higher-order logic is thus a *two-valued logic*. We prove this rule with a derivati
rewriting the goal in the form $\vdash \mathsf{T} \equiv (t \equiv \mathsf{T}) \lor (t \equiv \mathsf{F})$. The following derivat
establishes the theorem:

$$\vdash (t \equiv \mathsf{T}) \lor (\text{``} t \equiv \mathsf{F} \text{''})$$

$\equiv$ {substitution; $\equiv$ F rule}

$\quad (t \equiv \mathsf{T}) \vee \neg t$

$\equiv$ {substitution; $\equiv$ T rule}

$\quad (t \equiv \mathsf{T}) \vee \neg (t \equiv \mathsf{T})$

$\equiv$ {exhaustiveness}

$\quad \mathsf{T}$

Modus Ponens

The *modus ponens* rule is the following:

$$\frac{\Phi \vdash t \quad \Phi' \vdash t \Rightarrow t'}{\Phi \cup \Phi' \vdash t'} \ . \qquad\qquad (modus\ ponens)$$

The proof is as follows, with hypotheses $\Phi \vdash t$ and $\Phi' \vdash t \Rightarrow t'$:

$\quad \Phi \cup \Phi'$

$\vdash \mathsf{T}$

$\Rightarrow$ {$\mathsf{T} \Rightarrow$ rule; first hypothesis}

$\quad t$

$\Rightarrow$ {second hypothesis}

$\quad t'$

The derivation establishes $\Phi \cup \Phi' \vdash \mathsf{T} \Rightarrow t'$, from which the required result follows by the $\mathsf{T} \Rightarrow$ rule.

Quantification

The inference rules postulated above formalize propositional logic, but for quantification we need additional constants and inference rules. We introduce the following operations for quantification:

$\forall : (\Sigma \rightarrow \mathsf{Bool}) \rightarrow \mathsf{Bool}$,   *(for all)*

$\exists : (\Sigma \rightarrow \mathsf{Bool}) \rightarrow \mathsf{Bool}$.   *(exists)*

The *quantifiers* $\forall$ and $\exists$ thus take predicates as their arguments.

Quantification provides an example of the advantage of higher-order logic over first-order logic. In first-order logic, we have to build universal quantification into the syntax of formulas. In higher-order logic, universal and existential quantification are constants.

Following standard practice, we use *binder notation* for quantifiers, writing $(\forall v$
for $\forall.(\lambda v \cdot t)$ and $(\exists v \cdot t)$ for $\exists.(\lambda v \cdot t)$. This notation has the same (low) precede
as λ-abstraction.

Let A be a predicate of some type Σ; i.e., $A : \Sigma \to \mathsf{Bool}$. Then the intentio
that $\forall.A \equiv \mathsf{T}$ if and only if $A.x \equiv \mathsf{T}$ *for all* x in Σ. Also, we want that $\exists.A \equiv$
and only if $A.x \equiv \mathsf{T}$ *for some* x in Σ. Because Σ is assumed to be nonempty,
latter is equivalent to $A.x \equiv \mathsf{F}$ not holding for every x in Σ.

Rules for Universal Quantification

What rules can we postulate for universal quantification? Consider the set B
$\{A.x \mid x \in \Sigma\}$, i.e., the range of A. This set cannot be empty, because $\Sigma \neq \emptyset$
it must be either $\{\mathsf{F}\}$, $\{\mathsf{T}\}$, or $\{\mathsf{F}, \mathsf{T}\}$. We have that $\wedge B = \mathsf{T}$ if and only if $B =$
which again can hold only when $A.x = \mathsf{T}$ for each x in Σ. Thus, we see
$\wedge B \equiv \forall.A$. This suggests that we should use the properties of general meets as
inference rules for universal quantification.

Let t be a Boolean term with a possible free occurrence of variable v. Then
$(\lambda v : \Sigma \cdot t)$ is of type $\Sigma \to \mathsf{Bool}$, i.e., a predicate. Using binder notation, $\forall.$
written as $(\forall v \cdot t)$. We have that $B = \{A.x \mid x \in \Sigma\} = \{(\lambda v \cdot t).x \mid x \in B$
$\{t[v := x] \mid x \in B\}$, so any element of B must be of the form $t[v := t']$ for se
t'. Because $\forall.A$ is also $\wedge B$, we can use the rules for general meets. General n
introduction again gives us the introduction rule for universal quantification:

$$\frac{\Phi \vdash s \Rightarrow t}{\Phi \vdash s \Rightarrow (\forall v \cdot t)} \qquad (\forall \text{ introductio}$$
- v not free in s or Φ.

General meet elimination gives us the elimination rule for universal quantifica

$$\frac{}{\vdash (\forall v \cdot t) \Rightarrow t[v := t']} \qquad (\forall \text{ eliminati}$$
- t' is free for v in t.

The $\forall$ introduction rule is also known as *generalization*, the $\forall$ elimination rul
specialization. Intuitively, the introduction rule says that if we can prove that s
holds for an arbitrary v, i.e., $(\forall v \cdot s \Rightarrow t)$, then we have that $s \Rightarrow (\forall v \cdot t)$.
elimination rule is also straightforward: if we have proved that a property hold:
all v, then it must hold for any specific element (denoted by some term t') tha
choose to consider.

Rule for Existential Quantification

For existential quantification we can reason similarly. If $B = \{A.x \mid x \in \Sigma\}$, then $\vee B = \mathsf{T}$ if and only if $B \neq \{\mathsf{F}\}$, which is again equivalent to $A.x = \mathsf{T}$ for some x in Σ. Thus, $\vee B \equiv \exists.A$. General join introduction gives us the introduction rule

$$\frac{}{\vdash t[v := t'] \Rightarrow (\exists v \cdot t)}$$

(∃ *introduction*)

- t' is free for v in t.

General join elimination gives us the elimination rule:

$$\frac{\Phi \vdash t \Rightarrow s}{\Phi \vdash (\exists v \cdot t) \Rightarrow s}$$

(∃ *elimination*)

- v not free in s or Φ.

Again, the hypothesis in the elimination rule states that $t \Rightarrow s$ holds for every value of v in Σ (because v is not free in s or in Φ).

The introduction rule simply states that if we have proved a property for some element (denoted by a term t'), then there exists a v such that the property holds. The elimination rule again says that if we are able to prove that s follows from t without making any assumptions about which value is chosen for v, then the mere existence of some value v that makes t true implies s.

The lattice-theoretic arguments for the introduction and elimination rules should be seen as arguments for the validity of these rules. Formally, we need to postulate the quantifier introduction and elimination rules above for the truth values Bool, because they cannot be derived from the other rules that have been postulated for truth values. Table 6.3 shows some other useful inference rules for reasoning about quantified formulas, which are derivable from the basic introduction and elimination rules that we have presented here.

We also define the *exists-unique quantifier* ∃! by

$$\frac{}{\vdash (\exists! v \cdot t) \equiv (\exists v \cdot t \wedge (\forall v' \cdot t[v := v'] \Rightarrow v' = v))}$$

Thus $(\exists! x \cdot t)$ means that there exists a unique value x that makes t true.

Bounded Quantification

The scope of the bound variable in a universal or existential quantification can be restricted to satisfy some additional condition b. The *bounded* universal and existential quantification is defined by

$$(\forall v \mid b \cdot t) \stackrel{\wedge}{=} (\forall v \cdot b \Rightarrow t),$$
$$(\exists v \mid b \cdot t) \stackrel{\wedge}{=} (\exists v \cdot b \wedge t).$$

$\vdash (\forall v \bullet v = t \;\Rightarrow\; t') \equiv t'[v := t]$ $\vdash (\exists v \bullet v = t \wedge t') \equiv t'[v := t])$ $(\forall, \exists\; one\text{-}point)$
• v not free in t • v not free in t

$\vdash (\forall v \bullet t) \equiv t$ $\vdash (\exists v \bullet t) \equiv t$ $(\forall, \exists\; vacuous)$
• v not free in t • v not free in t

$\vdash \neg (\forall v \bullet t) \equiv (\exists v \bullet \neg t)$ $\vdash \neg (\exists v \bullet t) \equiv (\forall v \bullet \neg t)$ $(de\; Morgan)$

$\vdash (\forall v \bullet t \wedge t') \equiv (\forall v \bullet t) \wedge (\forall v \bullet t')$ $(distribute\; \wedge)$

$\vdash (\exists v \bullet t \vee t') \equiv (\exists v \bullet t) \vee (\exists v \bullet t')$ $(distribute\; \vee)$

$\vdash (\forall v \bullet t \Rightarrow t') \equiv ((\exists v \bullet t) \Rightarrow t')$ $\vdash (\forall v \bullet t \Rightarrow t') \equiv (t \Rightarrow (\forall v \bullet t'))$ $(distribute\; \forall\; over \Rightarrow)$
• v not free in t' • v not free in t

$\vdash (\exists v \bullet t \Rightarrow t') \equiv ((\forall v \bullet t) \Rightarrow t')$ $\vdash (\exists v \bullet t \Rightarrow t') \equiv (t \Rightarrow (\exists v \bullet t'))$
• v not free in t' • v not free in t $(distribute\; \exists\; over \Rightarrow)$

TABLE 6.3. Inference rules for quantified formulas

For instance, we have

$$(\forall x \mid x > 0 \bullet x/x = 1) \;\;\equiv\;\; (\forall x \bullet x > 0 \Rightarrow x/x = 1) \;.$$

Note that functions in higher-order logic are always total, so $0/0$ is well-defin
but the properties of division may not allow us to conclude anything about
value of $0/0$.

The inference rules for bounded quantification are generalizations of the b
quantifier rules given earlier and can be derived from these.

6.5 Assumptions

A sequent $\Phi \vdash t$ states that t follows from Φ. Hence, assumptions and implica
are closely related. In fact, we can consider assumptions as just a convenient de
for working with implications.

The two basic rules for handling assumptions show how we can move the left-h
side of an implication into the assumption and vice versa:

$$\frac{\Phi, t \vdash t'}{\Phi \vdash t \Rightarrow t'} \;,$$ $(dischar$

$$\frac{\Phi \vdash t \Rightarrow t'}{\Phi, t \vdash t'} \;.$$ $(undischar$

The first rule is also known as the *deduction theorem* (following standard practice, we write Φ, t for $\Phi \cup \{t\}$ in inference rules). Together these two rules show that assumptions and sequents are just a variant of implication, and that we can move between these two representations quite freely. However, it is important to note the difference between an inference and an implication. For example, the rule of generalization allows us to infer $\vdash (\forall x \cdot t)$ from $\vdash t$, but the implication $t \Rightarrow (\forall x \cdot t)$ is generally not a theorem.

Derived Rules

We exemplify the above rules of inference by using them in the derivation of some further rules that are useful in practice.

The first inference rule says that we may always conclude a formula that is taken as an assumption:

$$\frac{}{\Phi, t \vdash t} \cdot \qquad\qquad\qquad (assume)$$

This rule is a direct consequence of the reflexivity of implication and undischarging:

$$\frac{\dfrac{\{\Rightarrow \text{reflexivity}\}}{\Phi \vdash t \Rightarrow t}}{\Phi, t \vdash t} \{\text{undischarge}\} \ .$$

The following inference rule formalizes the basic method of splitting up a proof of a theorem t' into a subproof where a lemma t is proved first and then later used to prove the main theorem:

$$\frac{\Phi \vdash t \quad \Phi', t \vdash t'}{\Phi \cup \Phi' \vdash t'} \cdot \qquad\qquad (use\ of\ lemma)$$

This inference rule is also known as the *cut rule*. It is variant of the modus ponens inference rule. The proof is a simple application of modus ponens and discharging.

We finally give a convenient rule for case analysis:

$$\frac{\Phi, t \vdash t' \quad \Phi', \neg t \vdash t'}{\Phi \cup \Phi' \vdash t'} \cdot \qquad\qquad (case\ analysis)$$

The proof for this is as follows, with hypotheses $\Phi, t \vdash t'$, and $\Phi', \neg t \vdash t'$.

$$\Phi \cup \Phi'$$
$$\vdash \top$$
$$\equiv \{\neg \text{ exhaustion}\}$$
$$t \vee \neg t$$
$$\Rightarrow \{\vee \text{ elimination}\}$$

$$\bullet \quad t$$
$$\Rightarrow \quad \{\text{undischarge in hypothesis } \Phi, t \vdash t'\}$$
$$\quad t'$$
$$\bullet \quad \neg t$$
$$\Rightarrow \quad \{\text{undischarge in hypothesis } \Phi', \neg t \vdash t'\}$$
$$\quad t'$$
$$\bullet \quad t'$$

Here we have a derivation with a mix of $\equiv$ and $\Rightarrow$, and the conclusion is then $\mathsf{T} \Rightarrow t'$. In general, we can mix relations in a derivation, and the overall conclus then states that the initial and the final terms are related by the composition of relations involved. Composition of relations will be treated formally in Chapte Here it is sufficient to note that a composition of $\Rightarrow$ and $\equiv$ is $\Rightarrow$.

As we already mentioned in the previous chapter, higher-order logic is *monoto* in the sense that adding assumptions to a sequent cannot make it false:

$$\frac{\Phi \vdash t}{\Phi, t' \vdash t} \quad .$$

(*add assumptie*)

This rule can be derived using rules of substitution, $\equiv \mathsf{T}$, and discharging.

Another inference rule that we referred to in the previous chapter allowed u change the free variables in a sequent:

$$\frac{\Phi, s \vdash t}{\Phi, s[x := x'] \vdash t[x := x']}$$

(*change free variabl*)

$\bullet$ x is not free in Φ, x' free for x in s and t.

This follows from the inference rules for assumption discharging and undisch. ing, together with the rules for introduction and elimination of universal quan cation.

6.6   Derivations with Local Assumptions

The substitution rule tells us that we can always start a subderivation by focu on a subterm if the relation that we are working on is equality. There are spe situations in which focusing allows us to make local assumptions that depend the context.

Focusing Rules for Connectives

The following inference rule is easily derived from the rules that have been given earlier (Exercise 6.6):

$$\frac{\Phi, t \vdash t_1 \equiv t_2}{\Phi \vdash t \wedge t_1 \equiv t \wedge t_2} \; .$$

This rule shows that when we focus on one conjunct t_1 of a Boolean term $t \wedge t_1$, we may use t as an additional assumption in the subderivation. A dual rule shows that when focusing on a disjunct we may assume the negation of the other disjunct:

$$\frac{\Phi, \neg t \vdash t_1 \equiv t_2}{\Phi \vdash t \vee t_1 \equiv t \vee t_2} \; .$$

Using the fact that implication can be rewritten using negation and disjunction, we immediately get rules for focusing on the subterms of an implication:

$$\frac{\Phi, t \vdash t_1 \equiv t_2}{\Phi \vdash t \Rightarrow t_1 \equiv t \Rightarrow t_2} \; , \qquad \frac{\Phi, \neg t \vdash t_1 \equiv t_2}{\Phi \vdash t_1 \Rightarrow t \equiv t_2 \Rightarrow t} \; .$$

The following small example shows how local assumptions are used in proofs. We prove the *tautology*

$$\vdash \; p \Rightarrow ((p \Rightarrow q) \Rightarrow q) \; .$$

The derivation illustrates the rule for focusing on the consequent of an implication.

$$p \Rightarrow (\text{``} (p \Rightarrow q) \Rightarrow q \text{''})$$
$\equiv$ {replace subterm, use local assumption}
- $[p]$
  $(p \Rightarrow q) \Rightarrow q$
  $\equiv$ {local assumption says $p \equiv \mathsf{T}$}
  $(\mathsf{T} \Rightarrow q) \Rightarrow q$
  $\equiv$ {$\mathsf{T} \Rightarrow$ rule}
  $q \Rightarrow q$
  $\equiv$ {reflexivity}
  T
- $p \Rightarrow \mathsf{T}$
$\equiv$ {T greatest}
T

Here the main derivation has no assumptions. In the subderivation, p is added as a local assumption and used when rewriting.

Focusing and Monotonicity

Assume that f is a monotonic function. Then the following inference rule ho
for f:

$$\frac{\Phi \vdash t \sqsubseteq t'}{\Phi \vdash f.t \sqsubseteq f.t'} \; .$$

Thus, we can focus on the subterm t in $f.t$ and work with the partial order in
subderivation. Here the partial order can be arbitrary (including $\Rightarrow$ and $\Leftarrow$ on tr
values). Furthermore, it can be shown that the rules for local assumptions are v
also when working with $\Rightarrow$ or $\Leftarrow$ rather than $\equiv$ (Exercise 6.7).

Since the quantifiers are monotonic with respect to implication (and reverse im
cation), it is possible to focus inside quantifiers. However, it should be noted
if we focus on t in an expression $(Qv \cdot t)$ (where Q is a quantifier or a bind
then *no assumptions involving the variable v are available*, since the subterm
not within the scope of that variable v. This problem can always be avoided
α-converting the expression so that v is replaced by a fresh variable (by a *fr*
variable we mean a variable that does not appear free in any of the terms that
are currently considering).

Note that in the case of antimonotonic functions (such as negation on truth val
the subderivation works with the ordering in the opposite direction to the n
derivation.

As an example, we prove one-half of the *one-point rule* for the existential quanti

$$\vdash (\exists v \cdot v = t \wedge t') \Rightarrow t'[v := t]$$

- v not free in t.

The derivation is as follows, assuming that v is not free in t:

$$(\exists v \cdot v = t \wedge \text{``} t' \text{''})$$
$$\equiv \{\text{substitute using local assumption } v = t\}$$
$$(\exists v \cdot \text{``} v = t \wedge t'[v := t] \text{''})$$
$$\Rightarrow \{\wedge \text{ elimination in monotonic context}\}$$
$$(\exists v \cdot t'[v := t])$$
$$\equiv \{\text{drop vacuous quantifier; } v \text{ not free in } t'[v := t]\}$$
$$t'[v := t]$$

(in the last step we use another quantifier rule, see Exercise 6.8).

Here we have skipped the details of the subderivation, where we focus both in
a quantifier and inside a conjunction. Since the conjunction is within the scop
the bound variable v, we may use the assumption $v = t$ in the subderivation.

This derivation also illustrates (in the step justified by $\wedge$ elimination) how we do a replacement in a single step, rather than starting a subderivation that would make the proof unnecessarily long.

Focusing and Local Definitions

We end this chapter by showing how the idea of focusing allows us to use local definitions as assumptions. The following inference rule shows that if we focus on the body t' of a term let $v = t$ in t', then $v = t$ becomes a local assumption:

$$\frac{\Phi, v = t \vdash t_1 \sim t'_1}{\Phi \vdash (\text{let } v = t \text{ in } t_1) \sim (\text{let } v = t \text{ in } t'_1)} \ ,$$

where $\sim$ is an arbitrary relation (Exercise 6.10).

The rules for working with the let construct can be used to introduce (and eliminate) local procedures and procedure calls in the middle of a derivation. The following derivation shows how a procedure can be introduced by identifying a state transformer and naming it.

$$(a, b := b, a) \,;\, (c, d := d, c)$$

$=$ {introduce vacuous procedure definition}

   $\text{proc Swap} = (\lambda x. y \cdot x, y := y, x) \text{ in}$

   $(a, b := b, a) \,;\, (c, d := d, c)$

$=$ {use local assumption to rewrite body of let construct}

   $\text{proc Swap} = (\lambda x \ y \cdot x, y := y, x) \text{ in}$

   $\text{Swap}.a.b \,;\, \text{Swap}.c.d$

$=$ {switch to procedure syntax}

   $\text{proc Swap(var } x, y) = (x, y := y, x) \text{ in}$

   $\text{Swap}(a, b) \,;\, \text{Swap}(c, d)$

In practice, we can omit some of the intermediate steps of a derivation like this and simply introduce the procedure in one step and the calls to it in another step.

Summary and Discussion

We have presented the axioms and inference rules for reasoning about truth values. These rules allow us to reason about the standard logical connectives and about quantification. We have also given rules for manipulating assumptions in proofs. We showed how to prove arbitrary formulas with a derivation, using the fact that asserting a formula is the same as asserting that the formula is equivalent to truth. This device allows us to retain the one-to-one correspondence between derivational

proofs and proofs in the style of natural deduction. The derivations that we g
here generalize the traditional calculational style in that they permit manipulat
of assumptions inside proofs and permit nested derivations.

Andrews' textbook [3] gives a comprehensive overview of type theory and high
order logic. The version of higher-order logic that we describe in this book is clc
to the version underlying the interactive theorem-proving system HOL [62].
main difference is that we do not have polymorphic types and that we have cho
a different set of basic axioms and inference rules for the logical operations.
more detailed description and analysis of the semantics of higher-order logic,
refer to these same authors.

Both Andrews and Gordon and Melham attempt to formalize higher-order lc
with as few constants and inference rules as possible and define most of the log
constants explicitly in terms of the few postulated constants. Gordon and Melh
choose as primitive inference rules (variants of) assume, reflexivity of equal
α and β conversion, substitution, abstraction, discharge, and modus ponens
a rule of type instantiation. In addition, they have five axioms: Boolean ca
antisymmetry of implication, η conversion, ϵ introduction, and infinity (we
meet the last two of these in the next chapter). Andrews has a slightly differ
collection of axioms and inference rules for higher-order logic.

We have here presented an alternative, lattice-based formalization of higher-or
logic. The correspondence between lattice theory and logic is well known
old, dating back to George Boole in the nineteenth century. The advantage
formalizing higher-order logic in this way is that we can build a single collect
of inference rules that are applicable across a large range of different domains, fr
reasoning about logical terms and sets to refinement of program statements
large modular systems. This cuts down on the conceptual overhead that is nee
in program construction and clearly identifies the common patterns of reason
in the different domains of discourse.

The idea of using focusing and subderivations in posets (and generally in structu
other than Bool) builds on the refinement diagrams of Back [16], the hierarch
reasoning method of Robinson and John Staples [122] (window inference),
Grundy's extension to this method [68, 69].

6.8 Exercises

6.1   Prove the $\equiv$ T and $\equiv$ F rules using only the general rules of higher-order logic
the basic inference rules for truth values.

6.2   Prove that meet and join in a lattice are commutative, using only antisymmetry
the introduction, elimination, and distributivity rules for meet and join.

6.3   Prove the correspondence rule for meet:

$$\vdash t \sqsubseteq t' \equiv t \sqcap t' = t$$

using only the basic inference rules for lattices.

6.4   Prove the classical principle of double negation

$$\vdash \neg\neg t \equiv t$$

using only rules given in this chapter (hint: use case analysis; first prove $\vdash \neg T \equiv F$ and $\vdash \neg F \equiv T$).

6.5   Prove that implication can be expressed with negation and disjunction:

$$\vdash t \Rightarrow t' \equiv \neg t \vee t' \ .$$

6.6   Prove the rule for focusing on a conjunct:

$$\frac{\Phi, t \vdash t_1 \equiv t_2}{\Phi \vdash t \wedge t_1 \equiv t \wedge t_2}$$

(hint: do case analysis on t).

6.7   Prove the rule for focusing on a conjunct under implication:

$$\frac{\Phi, t \vdash t_1 \Rightarrow t_2}{\Phi \vdash t \wedge t_1 \Rightarrow t \wedge t_2} \ .$$

Then formulate and prove the corresponding rules for disjunction and implication.

6.8   Derive the rules for *dropping vacuous quantifications*:

$$\vdash (\forall v \cdot t) \equiv t \qquad\qquad \vdash (\exists v \cdot t) \equiv t$$
- v not free in t,   • v not free in t.

6.9   Derive the one-point rule for universal quantification:

$$\vdash (\forall v \cdot v = t \ \Rightarrow \ t') \equiv t'[v := t]$$
- v not free in t.

6.10   Derive the rules for focusing inside let expressions.

redicates and Sets

In this chapter we show how to formalize predicates in higher-order logic and how to reason about their properties in a general way. Sets are identified with predicates, so the formalization of predicates also gives us a formalization of set theory in higher-order logic. The inference rules for predicates and sets are also special cases of the inference rules for Boolean lattices. These structures are in fact complete lattices, so the general rules for meets and joins are also available. We complete our formalization of higher-order logic by giving the final constants and inference rules that need to be postulated: an axiom of infinity and an axiom of choice.

Predicates and Sets

Let Σ be some type in higher-order logic. A *predicate* on Σ is a function $p : \Sigma \to$ Bool. The predicates over Σ thus form a function space. We write $\mathcal{P}(\Sigma)$ for this space:

$$\mathcal{P}(\Sigma) \;\triangleq\; \Sigma \to \text{Bool} . \qquad\qquad (\textit{predicate space})$$

A predicate $p : \Sigma \to$ Bool determines a subset $A_p \subseteq \Sigma$, defined by $A_p = \{\sigma \in \Sigma \mid p.\sigma \equiv \mathsf{T}\}$. Conversely, any subset $A \subseteq \Sigma$ determines a predicate $p_A : \Sigma \to$ Bool satisfying $p_A.\sigma \equiv \mathsf{T}$ if and only if $\sigma \in A$. Thus, we have two ways of describing sets, either using the traditional set-theoretic framework or using functions that range over truth values.

The pointwise extension of the implication ordering on Bool gives us an ordering of predicates:

$$p \subseteq q \;\; \hat{=} \;\; (\forall \sigma : \Sigma \cdot p.\sigma \Rightarrow q.\sigma) \;. \qquad\qquad (\subseteq \textit{of predicate}$$

Because Bool is a complete Boolean lattice, the predicates over Σ also form complete Boolean lattice.

Corollary 7.1 $(\mathcal{P}(\Sigma), \subseteq)$ *is a complete Boolean and atomic lattice.*

The operations on predicates are defined by pointwise extension of the operati on truth values:

$$\begin{aligned}
\text{false}.\sigma &\;\hat{=}\; \mathsf{F} \;, & (\bot \textit{ of predicate} \\
\text{true}.\sigma &\;\hat{=}\; \mathsf{T} \;, & (\top \textit{ of predicate} \\
(p \cap q).\sigma &\;\hat{=}\; p.\sigma \wedge q.\sigma \;, & (\cap \textit{ of predicate} \\
(p \cup q).\sigma &\;\hat{=}\; p.\sigma \vee q.\sigma \;, & (\cup \textit{ of predicate} \\
(\neg p).\sigma &\;\hat{=}\; \neg p.\sigma \;. & (\neg \textit{ of predicate}
\end{aligned}$$

The operations on predicates are inherited from the operations on truth values, so is the naming of these operations: false is the *identically false* predicate and the *identically true* predicate. Predicate meet is referred to as *conjunction* of pre cates, predicate join is called *disjunction* of predicates, and predicate complem is called *negation* of a predicate.

Implication and equivalence on predicates are also defined pointwise, by

$$\begin{aligned}
(p \Rightarrow q).\sigma &\;\hat{=}\; p.\sigma \Rightarrow q.\sigma \;, & (\Rightarrow \textit{ of predicate} \\
(p \equiv q).\sigma &\;\hat{=}\; p.\sigma \equiv q.\sigma \;. & (\equiv \textit{ of predicate}
\end{aligned}$$

Implication $(p \Rightarrow q)$ and ordering $(p \subseteq q)$ are related by

$$p \subseteq q \;\equiv\; (\forall \sigma \cdot (p \Rightarrow q).\sigma) \;.$$

A similar relationship holds between equality $=$ and equivalence $\equiv$, namely

$$p = q \;\equiv\; (\forall \sigma \cdot (p \equiv q).\sigma) \;.$$

Sets as Predicates

The predicate ordering coincides with subset inclusion: $A \subseteq B$ if and onl $p_A \subseteq p_B$. Predicate false corresponds to the empty set, $p_\emptyset = $ false, and predi true corresponds to the universal set, $p_\Sigma = $ true. Meet (or conjunction) of predic is intersection: $\sigma \in A \cap B$ if and only if $(p_A \cap p_B).\sigma \equiv \mathsf{T}$, and similarly, join disjunction) of predicates is union, and complement (negation) of predicates i complement.

The traditional set-theoretic notation is introduced as an abbreviation in hig order logic:

$$\{\sigma : \Sigma \mid t\} \overset{\triangle}{=} (\lambda\sigma : \Sigma \cdot t) \ . \qquad\qquad (set\ comprehension)$$

Thus, $\{\sigma : \Sigma \mid A.\sigma\}$ is just syntactic sugar for $(\lambda\sigma : \Sigma \cdot A.\sigma)$, which in turn is the same as A (by η-conversion). Similarly, $\sigma \in A$ is just syntactic sugar for $A.\sigma$. We often write just Σ for the universal set U_Σ when there is no danger of confusion.

Any set in higher-order logic must be a subset of some type Σ. Hence, each type is a *universal set* for its subsets, so there is an infinite number of universal sets (and an infinite number of empty sets).

Properties of Predicates

The general properties for Boolean lattices hold for predicates. For instance, $\subseteq$ is a partial ordering, so the transitivity rule holds,

$$\frac{\Phi \vdash t \subseteq t' \quad \Phi' \vdash t' \subseteq t''}{\Phi \cup \Phi' \vdash t \subseteq t''} \ . \qquad\qquad (\subseteq\ transitive)$$

Similarly, the rule of meet introduction is

$$\frac{\Phi \vdash s \subseteq t \quad \Phi' \vdash s \subseteq t'}{\Phi \cup \Phi' \vdash s \subseteq t \cap t'} \ . \qquad\qquad (\cap\ introduction)$$

These properties can be derived in higher-order logic from the corresponding properties for truth values, using the definitions of the operations on predicates. Hence, we need not postulate these properties; they can be proved from the postulates that we have introduced earlier. The difference with truth values is that neither linearity nor theoremhood holds for the predicate lattice.

We show how to derive two of the Boolean lattice rules for predicates and sets: reflexivity and transitivity of set inclusion $\subseteq$. Reflexivity is proved as follows:

$$A \subseteq A$$
$\equiv$ {definition of inclusion}
$$(\forall a \cdot A.a \Rightarrow A.a)$$
$\equiv$ {reflexivity of $\Rightarrow$}
$$(\forall a \cdot \mathsf{T})$$
$\equiv$ {drop vacuous quantification}
$$\mathsf{T}$$

This establishes that $A \subseteq A$.

For transitivity, we reason as follows:

$$A \subseteq B \wedge B \subseteq C$$

$\equiv$ {definition of inclusion}

$$(\forall a \cdot A.a \Rightarrow B.a) \wedge (\forall a \cdot B.a \Rightarrow C.a)$$

$\equiv$ {quantifier rule}

$$(\forall a \cdot (A.a \Rightarrow B.a) \wedge (B.a \Rightarrow C.a))$$

$\Rightarrow$ {transitivity of implication; monotonic context}

$$(\forall a \cdot A.a \Rightarrow C.a)$$

$\equiv$ {definition of inclusion}

$$A \subseteq C$$

7.2   Images and Indexed Sets

Let $f : \Sigma \rightarrow \Gamma$ be a function. Then we define the *image* of set $A \subseteq \Sigma$ un function f by

$$\text{im.} f.A \;\hat{=}\; \{y : \Gamma \mid (\exists x \cdot x \in A \wedge y = f.x)\} \;. \qquad (imag$$

The image is thus a subset of Γ. We follow ordinary mathematical practice write $f.A$ for im. $f.A$ when this cannot cause confusion. The *range* of a functio then the image of its domain:

$$\text{ran.} f \;\hat{=}\; f.\Sigma \;. \qquad (rang$$

Note that $f.\{x\} = \{f.x\}$ for $x \in \Sigma$, so function application and set format commute for singletons.

The extension of a function $f : \Sigma \rightarrow \Gamma$ to im. $f \in \mathcal{P}(\Sigma) \rightarrow \mathcal{P}(\Gamma)$ always has inverse preim. $f : \mathcal{P}(\Gamma) \rightarrow \mathcal{P}(\Sigma)$, defined by

$$\text{preim.} f.B \;\hat{=}\; \{x \mid f.x \in B\} \qquad (preimag$$

for arbitrary $B \subseteq \Gamma$. Again, we follow ordinary mathematical practice and w the preimage as $f^{-1}.B$ when this cannot cause confusion. The set preim. $f.E$ called the *preimage* (or *inverse image*) of B under f.

For a fixed f, the image im. $f : \mathcal{P}(\Sigma) \rightarrow \mathcal{P}(\Gamma)$ is a function from one lattice another. Hence, we may ask about the homomorphism properties of this functi These are easily established: the image is monotonic,

$$A \subseteq A' \;\Rightarrow\; \text{im.} f.A \subseteq \text{im.} f.A' \;,$$

and it is bottom and join homomorphic,

is	$\sqsubseteq$	$\bot$	$\top$	$\sqcap$	$\sqcup$	$\neg$
im. f	yes	yes	no	no	yes	no
preim. f	yes	yes	yes	yes	yes	yes
$(\lambda a \cdot (\sqcap i \in I \cdot a.i))$	yes	yes [1]	yes	yes	no	no
$(\lambda a \cdot (\sqcup i \in I \cdot a.i))$	yes	yes	yes [1]	no	yes	no
$(\lambda I \cdot (\sqcap i \in I \cdot a.i))$	yes°	yes°	yes°	no	yes°	no
$(\lambda I \cdot (\sqcup i \in I \cdot a.i))$	yes	yes	yes	no	yes	no

[1] when index set I is nonempty

TABLE 7.1. Homomorphic properties of images

$$\text{im}.f.\emptyset \;=\; \emptyset \;,$$
$$\text{im}.f.(A \cup A') \;=\; \text{im}.f.A \cup \text{im}.f.A' \;.$$

For the preimage preim. $f : \mathcal{P}(\Gamma) \to \mathcal{P}(\Sigma)$, we have even stronger homomorphism properties. The preimage is both bottom and top homomorphic, it is monotonic, and it is meet and join homomorphic. It is even negation homomorphic. The homomorphism properties of the image and preimage operation are summarized in Table 7.1.

We have used the indexed set notation earlier in an informal way, in connection with meets and joins of arbitrary sets in a poset. Let us now define it formally in terms of images. The *indexed set* $\{a.i \mid i \in I\}$ is really a set image. For $a : \Sigma \to \Gamma$ and $I \subseteq \Sigma$, we define

$$\{a.i \mid i \in I\} \;\stackrel{\wedge}{=}\; \text{im}.a.I \;.$$

In general, we define

$$\{t \mid i \in I\} \;\stackrel{\wedge}{=}\; \text{im}.(\lambda i \cdot t).I$$

for t a term of type Γ. The indexed set is thus determined by an *index function* $(\lambda i \cdot t)$ and an *index range I*. The index i itself is a bound variable. The traditional notation $\{a_i \mid i \in I\}$ is also used as an alternative for $\{a.i \mid i \in I\}$.

Inference Rules for Complete Lattices

We gave the inference rules for binary meets and joins in lattices in the preceding chapter. Let us now consider complete lattices where meets and joins are defined for arbitrary sets of elements. A meet takes a set of elements as an argument and returns the greatest lower bound of the elements in the set. It is thus a set operation,

similar to quantification, whereas binary meet and binary join are operations
pairs of elements.

If the set is given as an index set $\{t \mid i \in I\}$, then we can use the *indexed nota*
for its meet and join. We define

$$(\sqcap i \in I \cdot t) \;\hat{=}\; \sqcap\{t \mid i \in I\} \;,$$ (*indexed me*

$$(\sqcup i \in I \cdot t) \;\hat{=}\; \sqcup\{t \mid i \in I\} \;.$$ (*indexed jo*

If I is of the form $\{i \mid b\}$, then we use the notation $(\sqcap i \mid b \cdot t)$ as a shorthand
$(\sqcap i \in \{i \mid b\} \cdot t)$, and similarly for joins.

The characterizations of meet and join then justify the following inference r
for indexed meets and joins:

$$\frac{\Phi, i \in I \vdash s \sqsubseteq t}{\Phi \vdash s \sqsubseteq (\sqcap i \in I \cdot t)}$$ (*general ⊓ introductic*
- i not free in s, Φ, or I,

$$\frac{}{t' \in I \vdash (\sqcap i \in I \cdot t) \sqsubseteq t[i := t']}$$ (*general ⊓ eliminati*
- t' is free for i in t,

$$\frac{}{t' \in I \vdash t[i := t'] \sqsubseteq (\sqcup i \in I \cdot t)}$$ (*general ⊔ introductic*
- t' is free for i in t,

$$\frac{\Phi, i \in I \vdash t \sqsubseteq s}{\Phi \vdash (\sqcup i \in I \cdot t) \sqsubseteq s}$$ (*general ⊔ eliminati*
- i not free in s, Φ, or I.

Index Range Homomorphisms

The indexed meet is a function of the form $\sqcap(\text{im}.a.I)$. For a fixed a, we have
$(\lambda I \cdot \sqcap (\text{im}.a.I)) : \mathcal{P}(\Sigma) \to \Gamma$, where Γ is a complete lattice. Hence, we can
about the homomorphism properties of this function from the power-set lattic
the lattice Γ. We first notice that the indexed meet is antimonotonic and the inde
join is monotonic in the index range:

$$I \subseteq J \;\Rightarrow\; (\sqcap i \in I \cdot a.i) \sqsupseteq (\sqcap i \in J \cdot a.i) \;,$$ (*range monotonic*

$$I \subseteq J \;\Rightarrow\; (\sqcup i \in I \cdot a.i) \sqsubseteq (\sqcup i \in J \cdot a.i) \;.$$

For the empty range, we have that

$$(\sqcap i \in \emptyset \cdot a.i) \;=\; \top \;,$$ (*empty ran*

$$(\sqcup i \in \emptyset \cdot a.i) \;=\; \bot \;.$$

We can split up an index range into smaller sets using the following *range split property*:

$$(\sqcap i \in I \cup J \cdot a.i) \;=\; (\sqcap i \in I \cdot a.i) \sqcap (\sqcap i \in J \cdot a.i) \;, \qquad \text{(range split)}$$
$$(\sqcup i \in I \cup J \cdot a.i) \;=\; (\sqcup i \in I \cdot a.i) \sqcup (\sqcup i \in J \cdot a.i) \;.$$

These properties follow directly from the homomorphism properties of the meet, join, and range operators. Thus, indexed joins are bottom and join homomorphic onto Γ, while indexed meets are bottom and join homomorphism onto the dual lattice Γ°. These properties are summarized in Table 7.1.

Index Function Homomorphims

We can also consider the homomorphism properties of the indexed meet $\sqcap \, (im.a.I)$ when we fix I instead. The function $(\lambda a \cdot \sqcap (im.a.I))$ maps functions in $\Sigma \to \Gamma$ to elements in Γ. Because Γ is a complete lattice, we may assume that the functions are pointwise ordered. Then $(\lambda a \cdot \sqcap (im.a.I))$ is a function from the complete lattice $\Sigma \to \Gamma$ to the complete lattice Γ, so we can again ask about its the homomorphic properties. These will be generalizations of the homomorphic properties for binary meet and join that we have described earlier.

For binary meet, we have that $b \sqsubseteq b'$ and $c \sqsubseteq c'$ implies that $b \sqcap c \sqsubseteq b' \sqcap c'$ and $b \sqcup c \sqsubseteq b' \sqcup c'$; i.e, binary meet is monotonic in both arguments. For an indexed meet and join, this generalizes to

$$a \sqsubseteq b \;\Rightarrow\; (\sqcap i \in I \cdot a.i) \sqsubseteq (\sqcap i \in I \cdot b.i) \;, \qquad \text{(image monotonicity)}$$
$$a \sqsubseteq b \;\Rightarrow\; (\sqcup i \in I \cdot a.i) \sqsubseteq (\sqcup i \in I \cdot b.i) \;.$$

Furthermore, indexed meets and joins are both bottom and top homomorphic:

$$(\sqcap i \in I \cdot \perp.i) \;=\; \perp \quad \text{when } I \neq \emptyset \;,$$
$$(\sqcup i \in I \cdot \perp.i) \;=\; \perp \;,$$
$$(\sqcap i \in I \cdot \top.i) \;=\; \top \;,$$
$$(\sqcup i \in I \cdot \top.i) \;=\; \top \quad \text{when } I \neq \emptyset \;.$$

Indexed meet is also meet homomorphic (so it is in fact universally meet homomorphic), and indexed join is also join homomorphic (universally join homomorphic):

$$(\sqcap i \in I \cdot (a \sqcap b).i) \;=\; (\sqcap i \in I \cdot a.i) \sqcap (\sqcap i \in I \cdot b.i) \;,$$
$$(\sqcup i \in I \cdot (a \sqcup b).i) \;=\; (\sqcup i \in I \cdot a.i) \sqcup (\sqcup i \in I \cdot b.i) \;.$$

These results are summarized in Table 7.1.

Bounded Quantification

Let us write $(\forall i \in I \cdot t)$ for $(\forall i \mid i \in I \cdot t)$ and $(\exists i \in I \cdot t)$ for $(\exists i \mid i \in I \cdot t)$. Then it is easily seen that $(\forall i \in I \cdot t) = (\wedge i \in I \cdot t)$ and that $(\exists i \in I \cdot t) = (\vee i \in$

$I \cdot t$). Thus, bounded quantification is a special case of indexed meet and j
and has properties that follow directly from the general properties by specializi
In particular, the rules for introduction and elimination of bounded quantificat
given in the previous chapter are instances of the general rules for indexed me
and joins, as is easily shown.

The homomorphism properties for indexed meets and joins also hold for boun
quantification. For example, universal quantification is antimonotonic, and e
tential quantification is monotonic in the index range:

$$I \subseteq J \;\Rightarrow\; ((\forall i \in I \cdot t) \Leftarrow (\forall i \in J \cdot t)) , \qquad (\textit{range monotonici}$$
$$I \subseteq J \;\Rightarrow\; ((\exists i \in I \cdot t) \Rightarrow (\exists i \in J \cdot t)) .$$

If the range is empty, the universal quantification is trivially true and existen
quantification is trivially false:

$$(\forall i \in \emptyset \cdot t) \;=\; \mathsf{T} , \qquad\qquad (\textit{empty rang}$$
$$(\exists i \in \emptyset \cdot t) \;=\; \mathsf{F} .$$

The technique for range splitting is also very useful:

$$(\forall i \in I \cup J \cdot t) \;=\; (\forall i \in I \cdot t) \wedge (\forall i \in J \cdot t) , \qquad (\textit{range sp}$$
$$(\exists i \in I \cup J \cdot t) \;=\; (\exists i \in I \cdot t) \vee (\exists i \in J \cdot t) .$$

The range-splitting and empty-range properties become particularly useful
reasoning about properties of arrays in programs. These properties are all dire
derivable in higher-order logic by using the definition of bounded quantifica
and the quantifier rules.

The index function homomorphisms also give us useful rules for reasoning ab
bounded quantification. The formulation and proof of these are given as an exer
(Exercise 7.4).

General Conjunction and Disjunction

The predicate lattice is a complete lattice, so indexed meets and joins are
available for predicates. We write $(\sqcap i \in I \cdot p_i)$ for the indexed meet of a
$\{p_i \mid i \in I\}$ of predicates and define $(\sqcup i \in I \cdot p_i)$ analogously. In set theory
talk about the *intersection* and *union* of a family of sets. Indexed meet and joi
predicates can be seen as pointwise extensions of bounded quantification:

$$(\sqcap i \in I \cdot p_i).\sigma \;\equiv\; (\forall i \in I \cdot p_i.\sigma) , \qquad (\textit{general conjuncti}$$
$$(\sqcup i \in I \cdot p_i).\sigma \;\equiv\; (\exists i \in I \cdot p_i.\sigma) . \qquad (\textit{general disjuncti}$$

The inference rules for these are the ones for general meets and joins, speciali
to predicates. The general $\sqcap$ introduction rule is, e.g.,

$$\frac{\Phi, i \in I \vdash p \subseteq q_i}{\Phi \vdash p \subseteq (\cap i \in I \cdot q_i)} \qquad\qquad (general \cap introduction)$$
- i not free in p, Φ, or I.

Selection and Individuals

Higher-order logic needs two more postulates in order to allow a proper formalization of arithmetic. These are specific properties that we need for the type structure: we need at least one type with an infinite number of elements, and we need to be able to choose one element from any set of elements in a type. These two requirements correspond to the set-theoretic axioms of infinity and choice.

Selection

We need to postulate one more constant to get the full power of higher-order logic. This is the *selection operator* ϵ of type

$$\epsilon : (\Sigma \to \text{Bool}) \to \Sigma \; . \qquad\qquad (select)$$

This operator takes a set (predicate) A of elements in Σ as its argument and returns an element $\epsilon.A$ in A if A is not empty. If A is empty, then $\epsilon.A$ is some (unknown) element in the universal set Σ. We use binder notation for selection and write $(\epsilon v \cdot t)$ for $\epsilon.(\lambda v \cdot t)$.

The selection operation embodies the *axiom of choice*, since it allows us to choose an element from any set. The rules for introducing and eliminating selection reflect the idea that $\epsilon.A$ denotes an arbitrary element selected from the set A.

$$\frac{}{\Phi \vdash (\exists v \cdot t) \Rightarrow t[v := (\epsilon v \cdot t)]} \; , \qquad\qquad (\epsilon \; introduction)$$

$$\frac{\Phi \vdash t \Rightarrow s}{\Phi \vdash t[v := (\epsilon v \cdot t)] \Rightarrow s} \qquad\qquad (\epsilon \; elimination)$$
- v is not free in Φ or s.

The first rule states that if there is an element that makes t true, then $(\epsilon v \cdot t)$ denotes such an element. The second rule is justified in the same way as the $\exists$ elimination rule.

The selection operator allows us introduce a constant denoting an *arbitrary element* for any type:

$$\text{arb} \; \hat{=} \; (\epsilon x : \Sigma \cdot F) \; . \qquad\qquad (arbitrary \; element)$$

Since the selection operation is always defined, arb always returns some val
However, we have no information about arb : Σ other than it is of type Σ.

The Type of Individuals

In addition to the type Bool, which denotes the truth values, higher-order logic a
postulates a standard type Ind, which denotes a set of *individuals*. The only th
we know about the individuals is that there are infinitely many of them. The *axi*
of infinity (one of the basic axioms of higher-order logic) is formulated as follo

$$\vdash (\exists f : \text{Ind} \to \text{Ind} \cdot \text{oneone}.f \wedge \neg \text{onto}.f) .$$ *(infinity axio*

This states that there exists a function f on Ind that is injective but not surjecti
This implies that Ind can be mapped injectively onto a proper subset of its
which is possible only if Ind is infinite. The notion of a function being *injective*
one-to-one) and *surjective* (or *onto*) is defined as follows:

$$\text{oneone}.f \;\;\overset{\wedge}{=}\;\; (\forall x\, x' \cdot f.x = f.x' \Rightarrow x = x') ,$$ *(injectivi*
$$\text{onto}.f \;\;\overset{\wedge}{=}\;\; (\forall y \cdot \exists x \cdot y = f.x) .$$ *(surjectivi*

A function that is both injective and surjective is said to be *bijective*:

$$\text{bijective}.f \;\;\overset{\wedge}{=}\;\; \text{oneone}.f \wedge \text{onto}.f .$$ *(bijectiv*

Figure 7.1 illustrates the way in which this requirement forces the interpretatio
Ind to be infinite. For the finite set $\{0, 1, 2, 3\}$, it is easy to see that there is no v
in which we can define a function on this set that is injective but not surject
However, for an infinite set $\{0, 1, 2, 3, \ldots\}$, the figure on the right-hand side gi
an example of a function that is injective but not surjective (0 is not in the ra
of this function). In this case, the function illustrated is the successor function
the natural numbers. Later we show how this idea can be used to define the nat
numbers as a set that is isomorphic to a subset of the individuals.

7.6 Summary and Discussion

This chapter has shown how to formalize reasoning about predicates and set
higher-order logic. The notions of indexed meets and joins were formally defir
and general inference rules for a complete Boolean lattice were given in te
of indexed meets and joins. In particular, we considered bounded quantificati
which arises as a special case of indexed meets and joins. To our knowledge,
homomorphism properties of indexed meets and joins have not been investiga
in detail before.

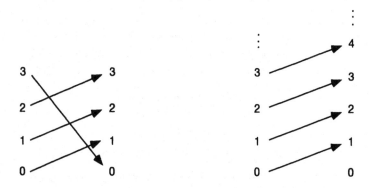

FIGURE 7.1. Injective functions on finite and infinite sets

The remaining axioms and inference rules of higher-order logic were also presented. These axioms postulate that there exists an infinite set, and that we can choose some element from any set. Individuals were introduced as a new standard type, in addition to Bool. In this respect, we give the same foundation for higher-order logic as Andrews [3] and Gordon and Melham [62]. Church's original formulation had an operator for *definite description* rather than the selection operator [48].

Exercises

7.1 A set B over a type Σ is really a function $B : \Sigma \to$ Bool. This means that we can talk about the image im.$B.A$ of another set A under B. This image is a set of truth values. Show the following:

(a) im.$B.B = \{$T$\}$, if $B \neq \emptyset$.

(b) im.$B.\emptyset = \emptyset$.

Under what condition is im.$B.A = \{$F$\}$? Under what condition is im.$B.A = \{$F, T$\}$?

7.2 Show that images and inverse images are related as follows:

$$\text{im.}f.(f^{-1}.Y) \subseteq Y \quad \text{and} \quad X \subseteq f^{-1}.(\text{im.}f.X) .$$

7.3 Show that the complement $\neg$ in a complete Boolean lattice is a bijective function.

7.4 The index-function homomorphism properties for lattices have counterparts for bounded quantification. For example, image monotonicity for meets corresponds to the following rule:

$$(\forall i \cdot p.i \Rightarrow q.i) \;\Rightarrow\; (\forall i \in I \cdot p.i) \Rightarrow (\forall i \in I \cdot q.i) .$$

Prove this rule and formulate other similar rules.

7.5   In first-order logic it is common to introduce a *Skolem function* when one proved a theorem of the form $(\forall v \cdot \exists w \cdot t)$. Such a function f is assumed to sati the property $(\forall v \cdot t[w := f.v])$. In higher-order logic, the introduction of a Skol function can be based on a derived inference rule:

$$\frac{\Phi \vdash (\forall v \cdot \exists w \cdot t.w)}{\Phi \vdash (\exists f \cdot \forall v \cdot t.(f.v))} \qquad\qquad \textit{(skolemizatio}$$

- w not free in t.

Derive this inference rule using only the rules given in the text.

7.6   Prove the following theorem (the axiom of choice):

$$(\exists f : \mathcal{P}(\Sigma) \to \Sigma \cdot \forall A \in \mathcal{P}(\Sigma) \mid A \neq \emptyset \cdot f.A \in A) .$$

7.7   Prove the following theorems:

(a) injective. $f \equiv (\exists g \cdot g \circ f = \text{id})$.

(b) surjective. $f \equiv (\exists g \cdot f \circ g = \text{id})$.

(c) bijective. $f \equiv (\exists g \cdot g \circ f = \text{id} \land f \circ g = \text{id})$.

Note that (c) is not a trivial consequence of (a) and (b).

7.8   Try to formulate an intuitively appealing definition of the constant finite, wh finite. A means that the set A is finite.

In the previous chapter we showed how to reason about predicates and sets in general. In programming, predicates arise in two different disguises. First, they are used to describe control structures with branching, like conditional statements and loops. Second, they are used to express correctness conditions for programs. In both cases, the predicates are expressed in terms of program variables, so they are really Boolean expressions. In this chapter, we will look more closely at Boolean expressions and at how to reason about their properties.

Boolean Expressions

A *Boolean expression* is an expression of type $\Sigma \to \text{Bool}$; i.e., it is a predicate on Σ. We usually prefer to use the (pointwise extended) truth-value operations for Boolean expressions, writing $b_1 \wedge b_2 \wedge \text{T} \Rightarrow b_3 \vee b_4 \vee \text{F}$ rather than the predicate/set notation $b_1 \cap b_2 \cap \text{true} \Rightarrow b_3 \cup b_4 \cup \text{false}$. We are usually interested in the value of a Boolean expression b in a specific state σ, and the correspondence between the Boolean expression and its value in the state is then very direct:

$$(b_1 \wedge b_2 \wedge \text{T} \Rightarrow b_3 \vee b_4 \vee \text{F}).\sigma =$$
$$b_1.\sigma \wedge b_2.\sigma \wedge \text{T} \Rightarrow b_3.\sigma \vee b_4.\sigma \vee \text{F} .$$

We can also have quantified Boolean expressions, such as $(\forall i \in I \cdot b) = (\cap i \in I \cdot b)$ and $(\exists i \in I \cdot b) = (\cup i \in I \cdot b)$. Then $(\forall i \in I \cdot b).\sigma \equiv (\forall i \in I \cdot b.\sigma)$ and $(\exists i \in I \cdot b).\sigma \equiv (\exists i \in I \cdot b.\sigma)$. For example, the Boolean expression $(\exists z : \text{Nat} \cdot x = y \cdot z)$ states that the value of attribute x is divisible by the value of attribute y. We use the same abbreviations for quantified Boolean expressions as we have for quantified truth-value formulas. The Boolean expression $\neg\,(\exists y\,z\,|\,$ $2 \wedge z \geq 2 \cdot x = y \cdot z)$ contains a bounded quantification and is equivalent $\neg\,(\exists y\,z \cdot y \geq 2 \wedge z \geq 2 \wedge x = y \cdot z)$. It states that the value of attribute x is pri

Let e be an expression. We define the *base term* $\bar{e}$ associated with the express e as follows:

$$
\begin{aligned}
\overline{x_{\Sigma \to \Gamma}} &= x_\Gamma \;, \\
\overline{\dot{y}} &= y \;, \\
\overline{\dot{f} \cdot g_1 \cdots \cdot g_m} &= f \cdot \overline{g_1} \cdots \cdot \overline{g_m} \;.
\end{aligned}
$$

For Boolean expressions, we also define

$$
\begin{aligned}
\overline{(\forall i \in I \cdot b)} &= (\forall i \in I \cdot \bar{b}) \;, \\
\overline{(\exists i \in I \cdot b)} &= (\exists i \in I \cdot \bar{b}) \;.
\end{aligned}
$$

For each expression e of type $\Sigma \to \Gamma$, this determines a term $\bar{e}$ of type Γ. instance, repeated rewriting using the definitions above gives

$$
\overline{(x_{\Sigma \to \mathsf{Nat}} - 1) + (y_{\Sigma \to \mathsf{Nat}} + z)} = (x_{\mathsf{Nat}} - 1) + (y_{\mathsf{Nat}} + z) \;.
$$

The value of an expression e in a state σ can be determined using the base term as shown by the following lemma. Note that in the lemma, the substitution repl a variable x_Γ by the term $x_{\Sigma \to \Gamma}.\sigma$ (the value of the access function of attribu in state σ).

Lemma 8.1 *Let $x_1, \ldots, x_m$ be the attributes of expression e. Then*

$$
e.\sigma = \bar{e}[x_1, \ldots, x_m := x_1.\sigma, \ldots, x_m.\sigma] \;.
$$

Proof Assume that the substitution $x_1, \ldots, x_m := x_1.\sigma, \ldots, x_m.\sigma$ is writte $x := x.\sigma$. We prove this theorem scheme by induction over the structure of expression e. When e is the access function of attribute x, then we have that $x.$ $x[x := x.\sigma]$. When e is $\dot{y}$, we have that $\dot{y}.\sigma = (\lambda\sigma \cdot y).\sigma = y = y[x := x.\sigma$

Consider next the case when e is an application $\dot{f} \cdot e_1 \cdots \cdot e_m$. We then have th

$$
\dot{f} \cdot e_1 \cdots \cdot e_m . \sigma
$$
$= \{$definition of pointwise extension$\}$
$$
f \cdot (e_1.\sigma) \cdots \cdot (e_m.\sigma)
$$
$= \{$induction hypothesis$\}$
$$
f \cdot (e_1[x := x.\sigma]) \cdots \cdot (e_m[x := x.\sigma])
$$
$= \{$property of substitution, f is a constant$\}$
$$
(f \cdot e_1 \cdots \cdot e_m)[x := x.\sigma]
$$

The case when e is a quantified Boolean expression is proved in a similar wa

Note that Lemma 8.1 states that a certain property holds for all expressions. Since the property of being an expression is not defined inside higher-order logic, the proof is necessary informal, in the sense that it is outside the logic. The rule in Lemma 8.1 is a theorem scheme, and e is a metavariable that can be instantiated to any expression (but not to an arbitrary term of higher-order logic).

Reasoning About Boolean Expressions

The properties that we want to prove about programs can often be reduced to proving inclusion $b \subseteq c$ or equality $b = c$ between two Boolean expressions. Here we will show how to reduce such inclusions and equalities to properties for the corresponding base terms $\bar{b}$ and $\bar{c}$.

orollary 8.2   *Let $x_1, \ldots, x_m$ be the attributes of the Boolean expression b. Then*

$$b.\sigma \;\equiv\; (\exists x_1 \cdots x_m \bullet x_1 = x_1.\sigma \wedge \cdots \wedge x_m = x_m.\sigma \wedge \bar{b}) \;.$$

This corollary to Lemma 8.1 allows us to reduce inclusion between Boolean expressions to implication between the corresponding base terms. Consider as an example how to establish that $(x \leq y) \subseteq (x < y + 2)$. Intuitively, this says that whenever condition $x \leq y$ holds (in a state), condition $x < y + 2$ also holds (in this same state). We have that

$$x \leq y$$
$$= \{\text{set theory}\}$$
$$\{\sigma \mid (x \leq y).\sigma\}$$
$$= \{\text{Corollary 8.2}\}$$
$$\{\sigma \mid \exists x\, y \bullet x = x.\sigma \wedge y = y.\sigma \wedge \text{“}x \leq y\text{”}\}$$
$$\subseteq \{\text{focus on Boolean term}\}$$

$$\qquad \bullet \quad x \leq y$$
$$\qquad \Rightarrow \quad \{\text{arithmetic}\}$$
$$\qquad \quad x < y + 2$$
$$\bullet \; \{\sigma \mid \exists x\, y \bullet x = x.\sigma \wedge y = y.\sigma \wedge x < y + 2\}$$
$$= \{\text{Corollary 8.2}\}$$
$$x < y + 2$$

Notice how the corollary allows us to focus on proving an implication between Boolean terms in order to establish inclusion between the Boolean expressions. In the same way, we can establish equality of two Boolean expressions by proving equivalence for their corresponding base terms. We refer to this way of establishing inclusion or equality of a Boolean expression as *reduction*.

In practice, this level of detail in a proof is unnecessary. We will omit the de
of the reduction in subsequent proofs. The above derivation is then

$$x \leq y$$
$$\subseteq \{\text{reduction}\}$$
$$\bullet \quad x \leq y$$
$$\Rightarrow \quad \{\text{arithmetic}\}$$
$$x < y + 2$$
$$\bullet \ x < y + 2$$

The fact that the step is justified as a reduction signals that the inner derivati
done on Boolean formulas and not on Boolean expressions. In simple cases
this one, we will usually omit the nested derivation altogether and make imp
use of reduction:

$$x \leq y$$
$$\subseteq \{\text{arithmetic}\}$$
$$x < y + 2$$

Here the use of $\subseteq$ (rather than $\Rightarrow$) shows that we are relating two Boo
expressions rather than two Boolean terms.

Alternative Reduction

We can also reduce $b \subseteq c$ directly to an implication between base terms, as sh
by the following lemma.

Lemma 8.3   *Let b and c be Boolean expressions, and let $x = x_1, \ldots, x_m$ be the attributes
occur in these. Then*

(a) $\vdash (\forall x_1 \cdots x_m \bullet \overline{b} \Rightarrow \overline{c}) \Rightarrow b \subseteq c$,

(b) $\text{var } x_1, \ldots, x_m \vdash (\forall x_1 \cdots x_m \bullet \overline{b} \Rightarrow \overline{c}) \equiv b \subseteq c$.

Proof Let $x := x.\sigma$ stand for $x_1 := x_1.\sigma, \ldots, x_m := x_m.\sigma$. We have for (a)

$$\vdash (\forall x_1 \ldots x_m \bullet \overline{b} \Rightarrow \overline{c})$$
$$\Rightarrow \{\text{specialization; } \sigma \text{ a fresh variable}\}$$
$$\overline{b}[x := x.\sigma] \Rightarrow \overline{c}[x := x.\sigma]$$
$$\equiv \{\text{substitution property}\}$$
$$b.\sigma \Rightarrow c.\sigma$$

and the result then follows by generalization.

For (b), we also have to prove the reverse implication:

$$\text{var } x_1, \ldots, x_m$$
$$\vdash b \subseteq c$$
$$\equiv \{\text{definition of inclusion}\}$$
$$(\forall \sigma \cdot b.\sigma \Rightarrow c.\sigma)$$
$$\equiv \{\text{substitution property}\}$$
$$(\forall \sigma \cdot \overline{b}[x := x.\sigma] \Rightarrow \overline{c}[x := x.\sigma])$$
$$\Rightarrow \{\text{specialize, } \sigma' := (\text{set}.x_1.x_1 ; \cdots ; \text{set}.x_m.x_m).\sigma\}$$
$$\overline{b}[x := x.\sigma'] \Rightarrow \overline{c}[x := x.\sigma']$$
$$\equiv \{\text{property of state attributes: } x_i.\sigma' = x_i\}$$
$$\overline{b} \Rightarrow \overline{c}$$

The result then follows by generalization, as the variables $x_1, \ldots, x_m$ are not free in b and c, nor in var $x_1, \ldots, x_m$. $\square$

As an example, consider again establishing $(x \leq y) \subseteq (x < y + 2)$. We have that

$$\text{var } x, y$$
$$\vdash (x \leq y) \subseteq (x < y + 2)$$
$$\equiv \{\text{reduction}\}$$
$$(\forall x \ y \cdot x \leq y \Rightarrow x < y + 2)$$
$$\equiv \{\text{arithmetic}\}$$
$$\top$$

This form of reduction is simpler to use when we want to establish as inclusion like $(x \leq y) \subseteq (x < y + 2)$ as a single formula, whereas the first form of reduction is more convenient when we want to derive a superset $(x < y + 2)$ from a subset $(x \leq y)$ or vice versa.

Conditional Expressions

The conditional construct, usually denoted by if ... then ... else ... fi, is of central importance in mathematics as well as in programming languages. In mathematics, it allows us to define functions by cases. In programs, it permits us to choose between alternative computation paths depending on the present state of the computation.

In this section, we define a conditional construct that allows us to define functions by cases in general. Then we show how to extend this to conditional expressions and conditional state transformers.

Conditionals

Let us define a new constant, the *conditional* cond : Bool $\to \Sigma \to \Sigma \to \Sigma$. [^]
intended meaning is that cond.$t.t_1.t_2$ is t_1 if $t \equiv$ T and t_2 otherwise:

$$\text{cond}.t.t_1.t_2 \;\stackrel{\wedge}{=}\; \qquad\qquad\qquad\qquad\qquad\qquad (condition\ldots$$
$$(\epsilon x \cdot ((t \equiv \text{T}) \Rightarrow x = t_1) \wedge ((t \equiv \text{F}) \Rightarrow x = t_2)) \; .$$

We can make the conditional operator more palatable by adding some synta[x]
sugar:

$$\text{if } t \text{ then } t_1 \text{ else } t_2 \text{ fi } \stackrel{\wedge}{=} \text{ cond}.t.t_1.t_2 \; .$$

The if $\ldots$ fi construct makes conditionals easier to read and manipulate. For [it]
to work, we need inference rules for the new construct. Three basic inference r[ules]
are the following (Exercise 8.2):

$$\frac{\Phi \vdash t}{\Phi \vdash \text{if } t \text{ then } t_1 \text{ else } t_2 \text{ fi } = t_1} \; ,$$

$$\frac{\Phi \vdash \neg t}{\Phi \vdash \text{if } t \text{ then } t_1 \text{ else } t_2 \text{ fi } = t_2} \; ,$$

$$\frac{}{\vdash \text{if } t \text{ then } t' \text{ else } t' \text{ fi } = t'} \; .$$

The conditional operator is needed to define functions by cases. For instance[, we]
can define the maximum function on natural numbers as follows:

$$\text{max}.x.y \;\stackrel{\wedge}{=}\; \text{if } x \leq y \text{ then } y \text{ else } x \text{ fi } .$$

The rules above then allow us to deduce, e.g., that

$$\text{max}.x.(x + 2)$$
$$= \{\text{definition of max}\}$$
$$\text{if ``} x \leq x + 2 \text{ '' then } x + 2 \text{ else } x \text{ fi}$$
$$= \{\text{arithmetic}\}$$
$$\text{if T then } x + 2 \text{ else } x \text{ fi}$$
$$= \{\text{conditional rule}\}$$
$$x + 2$$

Similarly as for let terms, the condition (or its negation) becomes a local assump[tion]
when focusing on either branch of a conditional. This is justified by the follow[ing]
rules:

$$\frac{\Phi, t \vdash t_1 \sim t_1'}{\Phi \vdash (\text{if } t \text{ then } t_1 \text{ else } t_2 \text{ fi}) \sim (\text{if } t \text{ then } t_1' \text{ else } t_2 \text{ fi})}$$

and

$$\frac{\Phi, \neg t \vdash t_2 \sim t_2'}{\Phi \vdash (\text{if } t \text{ then } t_1 \text{ else } t_2 \text{ fi}) \sim (\text{if } t \text{ then } t_1 \text{ else } t_2' \text{ fi})} \; ,$$

where $\sim$ is an arbitrary relation.

Conditional Expressions and State Transformers

The conditional operator is extended pointwise as follows. Let b be a predicate on Σ, and let $f : \Sigma \rightarrow \Gamma$ and $g : \Sigma \rightarrow \Gamma$ be two state functions. Then we define the *conditional state function* if b then f else g fi $: \Sigma \rightarrow \Gamma$ by

$$(\text{if } b \text{ then } f \text{ else } g \text{ fi}).\sigma \; \hat{=} \; \text{if } b.\sigma \text{ then } f.\sigma \text{ else } g.\sigma \text{ fi} \; .$$

When b, f, and g are expressions, then we refer to this construct as a *conditional expression*. When f and g are state transformers, then we call this a *conditional state transformer*.

The following state transformer sets attribute x to the maximum of attributes x and y:

if $x \leq y$ then $x := y$ else id fi .

An example of a conditional expression is, e.g.,

if $x \leq y$ then y else x fi ,

which gives the maximum of attributes x and y directly.

The following result shows how to establish equality of two conditional state transformers with the same condition:

Theorem 8.4 *Let f, f', g, and g' be state transformers and b a predicate. Then*

(if b then f else g fi) $=$ (if b then f' else g' fi) $\equiv$
$$b \subseteq (f = f') \wedge \neg b \subseteq (g = g') \; .$$

This follows directly from the definitions and the inference rules for conditionals. The condition $b \subseteq (f = f')$ is a kind of *conditional equality*. It says that the functions f and f' have to have the same values in a state whenever the state satisfies b.

We can identify a number of other useful equality rules for working with conditional expressions and conditional state transformers.

Theorem 8.5 *The following rules hold for conditional state functions:*

(a) if b then f else f fi $= f$,

(b) if b then f else g fi $=$ if $\neg b$ then g else f fi ,

(c) if b then f else g fi ; h = if b then f ; h else g ; h fi ,

(d) h ; if b then f else g fi = if h ; b then h ; f else h ; g fi .

We leave the proof of these equalities as exercises (Exercise 8.4).

In the last rule we use the fact that h ; b is a predicate (but not a Boolean expressi▮ if h is a state transformer and b is a predicate. By noting that $(x := e)$; $b = b[x▮ e]$ (Exercise 8.5), we get a special case of the last rule that uses only Bool▮ expressions:

$$x := e \text{ ; if } b \text{ then } f \text{ else } g \text{ fi } =$$
$$\text{if } b[x := e] \text{ then } x := e \text{ ; } f \text{ else } x := e \text{ ; } g \text{ fi .}$$

8.4 Proving Properties About Conditional State Transformers

Let us add conditional state transformers to the straight-line programs that we h▮ described earlier. The language is thus defined by the following syntax:

$$f \quad ::= \quad \text{id} \mid x := e \mid f_1 ; f_2 \mid \text{if } b \text{ then } f_1 \text{ else } f_2 \text{ fi .}$$

Here x is a list of distinct state attributes, e a corresponding list of expressions, b a Boolean expression.

An obvious property that we want to prove of a straight-line program is that equal to another one. As an example, consider the simple program $x := x+1$;▮ $x - 1$. Let us prove that it is really the identity state transformer. We have tha▮

  var x : Nat

$\vdash (x := x + 1) ; (x := x - 1)$
$= \{\text{merge assignments (Theorem 5.3)}\}$
  $(x := \text{“} (x + 1) - 1 \text{”})$
$= \{\text{functionality of assignment, arithmetic}\}$
  $(x := x)$
$= \{\text{property (e)}\}$
  id

The second step uses the functionality of assignment, i.e., that $e = e' \Rightarrow (x := e) = (x := e')$.

Pointwise Functionality

Any function f is a congruence with respect to equality; $a = b$ implies $f.a = f.b$. In many cases, functionality is not sufficient, and we need a stro▮ property. Let us say that a function f is *pointwise functional* if

$$(\forall \sigma \cdot e.\sigma = e'.\sigma \;\Rightarrow\; f.e.\sigma = f.e'.\sigma) \;. \qquad (pointwise\ functionality)$$

This condition can be written as

$$(e = e') \;\subseteq\; (f.e = f.e') \;.$$

The equalities that occur in these expressions are pointwise extended operations (the typing would not be correct otherwise).

Pointwise extended functions $\dot{f}$ are always pointwise functional: if $e.\sigma = e'.\sigma$, then

$$\dot{f}.e.\sigma = f.(e.\sigma) = f.(e'.\sigma) = \dot{f}.e'.\sigma \;.$$

This means that expressions in general are pointwise functional. We generalize this to arbitrary components of expressions.

Lemma 8.6 *Let e and e' be two expressions and let h be another expression. Then*

$$(e = e') \;\subseteq\; (h[x := e] = h[x := e']) \;.$$

The proof is by induction on the structure of expressions. As an example, we have that

$$(x + y = z) \;\subseteq\; ((x + y) * z = z * z) \;.$$

The assignment function $x := e$ is not a pointwise extended function, but it is pointwise functional:

$$(e = e') \;\subseteq\; (x := e = x := e') \;.$$

This follows directly from the definition of assignment.

We can use this property to reason about equivalence of assignments on certain states. For instance, we have that

$$x \le y$$
$$\subseteq \{\text{reduction: } (\forall x\ y \cdot x \le y \Rightarrow x \text{ max } y = y)\}$$
$$x \text{ max } y = y$$
$$\subseteq \{\text{pointwise functionality of assignment}\}$$
$$(x := x \text{ max } y) = (x := y)$$

so the state transformers $x := x \text{ max } y$ and $x := y$ are equal in those states where $x \le y$.

Sequential composition is pointwise functional in its first argument:

$$(f = f') \;\subseteq\; (f\,;g = f'\,;g) \;.$$

However, sequential composition is not pointwise functional in its second argument. Instead, we have that

$$(g = g').(f.\sigma) \implies (f ; g = f ; g').\sigma .$$

As we compare the functions in two different states, pointwise functionality does not hold.

Conditional state functions (expressions and state transformers) are pointwise extended operations, so they are also pointwise functional in all arguments:

$$(b = b' \wedge f = f' \wedge g = g') \subseteq$$
$$\text{if } b \text{ then } f \text{ else } g \text{ fi} = \text{if } b' \text{ then } f' \text{ else } g' \text{ fi} .$$

Example Proof

Let us illustrate these proof rules by showing that the little straight-line program for computing the maximum of two program variables that we have given above is correct, i.e., that it is the same state transformer as $(x := x \text{ max } y)$:

$(x := x \text{ max } y)$

= {conditional expression rule}

  if $x \leq y$ then $(x := x \text{ max } y)$ else $(x := x \text{ max } y)$ fi

= {equality of conditionals, generalization}

- $x \leq y$
$\subseteq$ {derivation above}
  $(x := x \text{ max } y) = (x := y)$
- $x > y$
$\subseteq$ {reduction and assignment property}
  $(x := x \text{ max } y) = (x := x)$

· if $x \leq y$ then $x := y$ else " $x := x$ " fi

= {property (e) of attributes}

  if $x \leq y$ then $x := y$ else id fi

8.5 Summary and Discussion

We have shown how to reason about Boolean expressions and conditional straight-line programs. We have shown how to reduce properties about Boolean expressions to properties about ordinary Boolean terms.

An alternative way of handling predicates is taken by Dijkstra and Scholten in [.]. They build a theory of Boolean expressions ab initio, by defining the syntax for them directly and postulating a collection of properties that Boolean expressions satisfy.

They take pointwise functionality (which they call *punctuality*) as the basic rule, in combination with the *everywhere* operator $[b]$, which corresponds to universal quantification in our framework: $[b] \equiv (\forall \sigma \cdot b.\sigma)$. With these correspondences, the laws for predicate expressions derived by Dijkstra and Scholten can be derived in our framework too. The approach that we have chosen here is closer to traditional logic, in that we compare Boolean expressions directly for inclusion or equality and use the reduction theorem to move between reasoning on the predicate level and reasoning on the truth-value level.

Exercises

8.1 Show that if t_1 and t_2 are Boolean terms, then

$$\text{if } t \text{ then } t_1 \text{ else } t_2 \text{ fi} \equiv (t \wedge t_1) \vee (\neg t \wedge t_2) .$$

8.2 Derive the three inference rules for the if ... fi construct given in the text.

8.3 Derive the two focusing rules for the if ... fi construct given in the text.

8.4 Prove the rules for conditional state transformers given in Theorem 8.5.

8.5 Show that if b is a Boolean expression, then $(x := e) ; b = b[x := e]$.

8.6 Show that conditionals on two levels are related as follows:

$$\text{if } b \text{ then } x := e_1 \text{ else } x := e_2 \text{ fi} = (x := \text{if } b \text{ then } e_1 \text{ else } e_2 \text{ fi}) .$$

8.7 Generalize Theorem 8.4 to permit the conditions to be different.

Let us next look at how relations are handled in higher-order logic. Relations, like predicates, form a complete Boolean lattice and thus have essentially the same set of inference rules as predicates. We can define new operations on relations, giving additional properties. In particular, relations combine a lattice and a category structure. Relations also provide us with a more expressive way of describing state changes, where the effect can be nondeterministic in some states and undefined in other states.

Relation Spaces

We define the *relation space* from Σ to Γ, denoted by $\Sigma \leftrightarrow \Gamma$, by

$$\Sigma \leftrightarrow \Gamma \ \overset{\wedge}{=} \ \Sigma \to \mathcal{P}(\Gamma) \ . \qquad\qquad \textit{(relation space)}$$

A relation between Σ and Γ is in set theory seen as a subset $r \subseteq \Sigma \times \Gamma$. The set-theoretic view and the function view taken here are linked in a simple way. The set r determines a function $P_r : \Sigma \to \mathcal{P}(\Gamma)$, defined by $P_r.a.b = \top$ if and only if $(a, b) \in r$. Conversely, the function $P : \Sigma \to \mathcal{P}(\Gamma)$ determines the set $r_P \subseteq \Sigma \times \Gamma$, by $r_P = \{(a, b) \mid P.a.b = \top\}$.

Lattice of Relations

The relation space arises as a pointwise extension of the predicate space. For two relations $P, Q \in \Sigma \leftrightarrow \Gamma$, the partial ordering is defined by

$$P \subseteq Q \ \hat{=} \ (\forall \sigma : \Sigma \cdot P.\sigma \subseteq Q.\sigma) \ . \qquad (\subseteq \text{ of relation}$$

It is easy to see that $P \subseteq Q$ is equivalent to $(\forall \sigma \ \gamma \cdot P.\sigma.\gamma \Rightarrow Q.\sigma.\gamma)$.

By the pointwise extension theorem, the relation space inherits the property
being a complete Boolean lattice from the predicate lattice. The relation spac
also atomic.

Theorem 9.1 $(\Sigma \leftrightarrow \Gamma, \subseteq)$ *is a complete, Boolean, and atomic lattice.*
The lattice operations on relations are also the pointwise extensions of the co
sponding operations on predicates. We define these as follows, for $\sigma : \Sigma$:

$$\text{False.}\sigma \ \hat{=} \ \text{false} \ , \qquad \qquad (\perp \text{ of relation}$$
$$\text{True.}\sigma \ \hat{=} \ \text{true} \ , \qquad \qquad (\top \text{ of relation}$$
$$(P \cap Q).\sigma \ \hat{=} \ P.\sigma \cap Q.\sigma \ , \qquad \qquad (\cap \text{ of relation}$$
$$(P \cup Q).\sigma \ \hat{=} \ P.\sigma \cup Q.\sigma \ , \qquad \qquad (\cup \text{ of relation}$$
$$(\neg P).\sigma \ \hat{=} \ \neg P.\sigma \ . \qquad \qquad (\neg \text{ of relation}$$

The naming here is similar to that for predicates: False is the *identically false* r
tion, True the identically true relation, and we talk about the conjunction, disjunc
and negation of relations.

The inference rules for Boolean lattices are valid for relations. Similarly as
predicates, we can derive these inference rules from the corresponding rules
predicates and truth values, so we do not need to postulate them.

In a set-theoretic interpretation, False is the empty relation, and True is the unive
relation that relates any two elements to each other. Relation $\neg P$ is the complen
of the relation P, while $P \cap Q$ is the intersection of two relations P and Q,
$P \cup Q$ is the union of these two relations, as would be expected.

Since relations form a complete lattice, indexed meets and joins are also availa
for relations. We write $(\cap i \in I \cdot R_i)$ for the indexed meet of a set $\{R_i \mid i \in$
of relations, and $(\cup i \in I \cdot R_i)$ for the indexed join. The indexed meet and joi
relations are pointwise extensions of the corresponding constructs for predica

$$(\cap i \in I \cdot R_i).\sigma \ = \ (\cap i \in I \cdot R_i.\sigma) \ , \qquad \textit{(general conjunctic}$$
$$(\cup i \in I \cdot R_i).\sigma \ = \ (\cup i \in I \cdot R_i.\sigma) \ . \qquad \textit{(general disjunctic}$$

The inference rules for these are again the rules for general meets and jo
specialized to relations.

Other Operations on Relations

Relations form a rather rich domain, and there are a number of other us
operations that we can define on them. We consider here the most important o

The *identity relation* and *composition* of relations are defined as follows:

$$\mathsf{Id}.\sigma.\gamma \;\; \overset{\wedge}{=} \;\; \sigma = \gamma \; , \tag{\textit{identity}}$$

$$(P \bullet Q).\sigma.\delta \;\; \overset{\wedge}{=} \;\; (\exists \gamma \cdot P.\sigma.\gamma \wedge Q.\gamma.\delta) \; . \tag{\textit{composition}}$$

As with functional composition, the range type of P must be the same as the domain type of Q for the typing to be correct.

The *inverse* of relation R is R^{-1}, defined by

$$R^{-1}.\sigma.\gamma \;\; \overset{\wedge}{=} \;\; R.\gamma.\sigma \; . \tag{\textit{inverse relation}}$$

State Relation Category

A *state relation category* has state spaces as objects and state relations as morphisms. Thus, $\Sigma \overset{P}{\longrightarrow} \Gamma$ means that P is a relation of type $\Sigma \leftrightarrow \Gamma$. The identity relations are identity morphisms, and composition is *forward* relational composition:

$$1 \;\; \overset{\wedge}{=} \;\; \mathsf{Id} \; , \tag{1 \textit{for state relations}}$$

$$P \,;\, Q \;\; \overset{\wedge}{=} \;\; P \bullet Q \; . \tag{; \textit{for state relations}}$$

A special kind of state relation category is Rel_X, which has all types in X as objects and all relations between two objects as morphisms; i.e.,

$$\mathsf{Rel}_X(\Sigma, \Gamma) \;\; \overset{\wedge}{=} \;\; \Sigma \leftrightarrow \Gamma \; .$$

We write Rel for Rel_X when the collection X of state spaces is not important. We leave it to the reader to verify that Rel is indeed a category (Exercise 9.5), i.e., that

$$(P \,;\, Q) \,;\, R = P \,;\, (Q \,;\, R) \; , \tag{; \textit{associative}}$$

$$\mathsf{Id} \,;\, R = R \quad \text{and} \quad R \,;\, \mathsf{Id} = R \; . \tag{\mathsf{Id} \textit{unit}}$$

It is easy to see that composition is monotonic with respect to relation ordering:

$$P \subseteq P' \wedge Q \subseteq Q' \;\; \Rightarrow \;\; P \,;\, Q \subseteq P' \,;\, Q' \; . \tag{; \textit{monotonic}}$$

We summarize the results about relations in the following theorem.

Theorem 9.2 Rel_X *forms a complete atomic Boolean lattice-enriched category.*

Furthermore, composition distributes over bottom and join, both from left and right:

$$P \,;\, \mathsf{False} \; = \; \mathsf{False} \; , \tag{\mathsf{False} \textit{distributivity}}$$

$$\mathsf{False} \,;\, P \; = \; \mathsf{False} \; ,$$

$$P \,;\, (Q \cup R) \; = \; P \,;\, Q \; \cup \; P \,;\, R \; , \tag{\cup \textit{distributivity}}$$

$$(P \cup Q) \,;\, R \; = \; P \,;\, R \; \cup \; Q \,;\, R \; .$$

Composition does not, however, distribute over meets and not over top (Exerc 9.6).

9.3   Coercion Operators

We can construct relations from predicates and functions using *coercion operatio* Let $p : \Sigma \to$ Bool and $f : \Sigma \to \Gamma$. We define the *test* relation $|p| : \Sigma \leftrightarrow \Sigma$ the *mapping* relation $|f| : \Sigma \leftrightarrow \Gamma$, by

$$|p|.\sigma.\gamma \; \hat{=} \; \sigma = \gamma \wedge p.\sigma \; , \qquad\qquad (te$$
$$|f|.\sigma.\gamma \; \hat{=} \; f.\sigma = \gamma \; . \qquad\qquad (mappir$$

Thus, $|p|$ is a subset of the identity relation and holds where p is satisfied, w $|f|$ is the relation that describes the function f.

These operations are useful when we want to express conditions involving p icates, functions, and relations. Using the $| \cdot |$ operators, we can often write conditions on the relational level. For example, the expression $p.\sigma \wedge R.\sigma.\gamma$ be written as $(|p| ; R).\sigma.\gamma$, as shown by the following derivation:

$$(|p| ; R).\sigma.\gamma$$
$$\equiv \{\text{definition of composition}\}$$
$$(\exists \sigma' \cdot |p|.\sigma.\sigma' \wedge R.\sigma'.\gamma)$$
$$\equiv \{\text{definition of test relation}\}$$
$$(\exists \sigma' \cdot \sigma = \sigma' \wedge p.\sigma \wedge R.\sigma'.\gamma)$$
$$\equiv \{\text{one-point rule}\}$$
$$p.\sigma \wedge R.\sigma.\gamma$$

The test constructor $| \cdot | : \mathcal{P}(\Sigma) \to \text{Rel}(\Sigma, \Sigma)$ is easily seen to be monotoni addition, it preserves bottom, positive meets and universal joins. However, it not preserve top or negation. Furthermore, we have the following properties:

$$|\text{true}| \; = \; \text{Id} \; ,$$
$$|p \cap q| \; = \; |p| ; |q| \; .$$

It is also easily checked that the mapping relation operator preserves identity sequential composition:

$$|\text{id}| \; = \; \text{Id} \; ,$$
$$|f ; g| \; = \; |f| ; |g| \; .$$

The *domain* and *range* of a relation are defined as follows:

is	$\sqsubseteq$	$\bot$	$\top$	$\sqcap$	$\sqcup$	$\neg$	1	;
$(\lambda p \cdot \lvert p \rvert)$	yes	yes	no	yes	yes	no	yes	yes
$(\lambda f \cdot \lvert f \rvert)$	yes	-	-	-	-	-	yes	yes
$(\lambda R \cdot \text{dom}.R)$	yes	yes	yes	no	yes	no	yes	no
$(\lambda R \cdot \text{ran}.R)$	yes	yes	yes	no	yes	no	yes	no

TABLE 9.1. Homomorphic properties of coercion operations

$$\text{dom}.R.\sigma \;\overset{\triangle}{=}\; (\exists \gamma \cdot R.\sigma.\gamma) \,, \qquad\qquad (domain)$$

$$\text{ran}.R.\gamma \;\overset{\triangle}{=}\; (\exists \sigma \cdot R.\sigma.\gamma) \,. \qquad\qquad (range)$$

The operations dom.R and ran.R, which give the domain and range of a relation R, are both monotonic with respect to the relation ordering, and they are bottom, top, and join homomorphic (but not meet homomorphic). These homomorphism properties are summarized in Table 9.1.

Partial Functions

A relation $R : \Sigma \leftrightarrow \Gamma$ is said to be *deterministic* (or *functional*) if every $\sigma \in \Sigma$ is related to at most one $\gamma \in \Gamma$, i.e., if

$$(\forall \sigma\, \gamma\, \gamma' \cdot R.\sigma.\gamma \wedge R.\sigma.\gamma' \Rightarrow \gamma' = \gamma) \,. \qquad (deterministic\ relation)$$

Deterministic relations model *partial functions*, which thus form a subset of relations. The empty relation False is a partial function, as are the test $\lvert p \rvert$ and map $\lvert f \rvert$. Composition of relations preserves determinism, and so does intersection. Relations described in terms of these constants and operations are therefore always deterministic.

Relational Assignment

The assignment notation is very convenient for describing functions that change the values of attributes of a state. We can extend the assignment notation in a rather straightforward way to relations between states with attributes.

Assume that $x : \Sigma \rightarrow \Gamma$ is an attribute and b a Boolean expression of type Γ with possible free occurrences of a fresh variable $x' : \Gamma$. We define the *relational assignment* $(x := x' \mid b)$ as the following state relation:

$$(x := x' \mid b).\sigma \;\overset{\triangle}{=}\; \{\text{set}.x.x'.\sigma \mid b.\sigma\} \,. \qquad (relational\ assignment)$$

An example of a relational assignment is

$$(x := x' \mid x' \geq x + y) \ .$$

This assignment relates states σ and $\sigma' = \text{set}.x.x'.\sigma$ whenever x' satisfies x val.$x.\sigma$ + val.$y.\sigma$. Note that we could as well write this assignment as $(x := z \mid x + y)$. The use of primed variables in relational assignments is merely a traditio way of indicating new values for program variables.

The above definition of the relational assignment is slightly awkward to us proofs, so we often use the following alternative characterization:

Lemma 9.3 *The relational assignment has the following property:*

$$(x := x' \mid b).\sigma.\sigma' \ \equiv \ (\exists x' \bullet \sigma' = \text{set}.x.x'.\sigma \wedge b.\sigma) \ .$$

Proof The proof is a simple derivation:

$$(x := x' \mid b).\sigma.\sigma'$$
$$\equiv \{\text{definition of relational assignment}\}$$
$$\sigma' \in \{\text{set}.x.x'.\sigma \mid b.\sigma\}$$
$$\equiv \{\text{set membership}\}$$
$$(\exists x' \bullet \sigma' = \text{set}.x.x'.\sigma \wedge b.\sigma\}$$

$\square$

The relational assignment is also easily generalized to *multiple relational ass* *ment*, which permits two or more state components to be changed simultaneou

$$(x_1, \ldots, x_m := x_1', \ldots, x_m' \mid b).\sigma \ \stackrel{\wedge}{=}$$
$$\{(\text{set}.x_1.x_1' \ ; \cdots ; \text{set}.x_m.x_m').\sigma \mid b.\sigma\} \ ,$$

where we assume that $x_1, \ldots, x_m$ are distinct attributes.

Basic Properties of Relational Assignment

The relational assignment gives us a convenient way of expressing relatior terms of program variables. When working with relational assignments, we use properties of relations, but in order to make this work smoothly, we properties stated explicitly in terms of assignment statements.

We start with a number of lattice-oriented homomorphism properties that re concepts from the level of relations to the level of Boolean expressions in relational assignments:

Theorem 9.4 *Assume that x is a list of program variables and that b and c are Boo expressions. Then*

(a) var $x \vdash (x := x' \mid F) = \mathsf{False}$.

(b) var $x \vdash (x := x' \mid b \wedge c) = (x := x' \mid b) \cap (x := x' \mid c)$.

(c) var $x \vdash (x := x' \mid b \vee c) = (x := x' \mid b) \cup (x := x' \mid c)$.

(d) var $x \vdash (x := x' \mid b) \subseteq (x := x' \mid c) \equiv (\forall x' \cdot b \subseteq c)$.

Proof We show the proof of case (d), for the case when x is a single state attribute. The generalization to the case when x is a list of variables is straightforward.

$$(x := x' \mid b) \subseteq (x := x' \mid c)$$

$\equiv \{\text{definition of } \subseteq, \text{Lemma 9.3}\}$

$\quad (\forall \sigma\, \gamma \cdot (\exists x' \cdot \gamma = \mathrm{set}.x.x'.\sigma \wedge b.\sigma) \Rightarrow (\exists x' \cdot \gamma = \mathrm{set}.x.x'.\sigma \wedge c.\sigma))$

$\equiv \{\text{quantifier rules}\}$

$\quad (\forall \sigma\, \gamma\, x' \cdot \gamma = \mathrm{set}.x.x'.\sigma \wedge b.\sigma \Rightarrow (\exists x' \cdot \gamma = \mathrm{set}.x.x'.\sigma \wedge c.\sigma))$

$\equiv \{\text{one-point rule (rename captured variable)}\}$

$\quad (\forall \sigma\, x' \cdot b.\sigma \Rightarrow (\exists x'' \cdot \mathrm{set}.x.x'.\sigma = \mathrm{set}.x.x''.\sigma \wedge c[x' := x''].\sigma))$

$\equiv \{\text{state attribute properties say } \mathrm{set}.x.x'.\sigma = \mathrm{set}.x.x''.\sigma \equiv x' = x''\}$

$\quad (\forall \sigma\, x' \cdot b.\sigma \Rightarrow (\exists x'' \cdot x' = x'' \wedge c[x' := x''].\sigma))$

$\equiv \{\text{one-point rule}\}$

$\quad (\forall \sigma\, x' \cdot b.\sigma \Rightarrow c.\sigma)$

$\equiv \{\text{pointwise extension}\}$

$\quad (\forall x' \cdot b \subseteq c)$

Cases (a)–(c) are proved in a similar style. $\square$

The rules for meet and join are easily extended to arbitrary meets and joins:

$$\text{var } x \vdash (x := x' \mid (\forall i \cdot b_i)) = (\cap i \in I \cdot (x := x' \mid b_i)) ,$$
$$\text{var } x \vdash (x := x' \mid (\exists i \cdot b_i)) = (\cup i \in I \cdot (x := x' \mid b_i)) .$$

However, there are no similar results for negation or top.

The rules in Theorem 9.4 require that the relational assignments involved all update exactly the same variables. When reasoning about assignments that work on different collections of variables, we can use the following rule to make the assignments compatible:

Lemma 9.5   *Assume that x and y are lists of program variables and that b is a Boolean expression in which y' does not occur free. Then*

$$\text{var } x, y \vdash (x := x' \mid b) = (x, y := x', y' \mid b \wedge y' = y) .$$

Proof   The proof follows the idea of the proof of Theorem 9.4, rewriting w
definitions and using state attribute properties. □

Next consider properties of sequential composition and identity:

Theorem 9.6   *Assume that x is a list of attributes. Then*

(a) var $x \vdash (x := x' \mid x' = x) = \text{Id}$.

(b) var $x \vdash (x := x' \mid b) ; (x := x' \mid c) =$
$$(x := x' \mid (\exists x'' \cdot b[x' := x''] \wedge c[x := x''])) .$$

The proof is again a straightforward application of definitions and state attrib
properties, so we omit it.

Finally, we show how the coercions between predicates and functions on the
hand and relations on the other hand are reflected in the assignment notation.
omit the proof, since it is done the same way as in the previous lemmas.

Theorem 9.7   *Assume that x is a list of program variables, e is an expression, and b and c*
Boolean expressions. Furthermore, assume that x' does not occur free in b o
Then

(a) var $x \vdash |b| = (x := x' \mid b \wedge x' = x)$.

(b) var $x \vdash |x := e| = (x := x' \mid x' = e)$.

(c) var $x \vdash \text{dom}.(x := x' \mid c) = (\exists x' \cdot c)$.

Derived Properties of Relational Assignments

From Theorem 9.6 follow two rules for independent relational assignment.

Corollary 9.8   *Assume that x and y are disjoint (lists of) attributes.*

(a) *If y' does not occur free in b, and x' does not occur free in c, then*

var $x, y \vdash (x := x' \mid b) ; (y := y' \mid c) =$
$$(x, y := x', y' \mid b \wedge c[x := x']) .$$

(b) *If x and x' do not occur free in c, and y and y' do not occur free in b,*

var $x, y \vdash (x := x' \mid b) ; (y := y' \mid c) = (y := y' \mid c) ; (x := x' \mid b)$.

Two other special cases of Theorem 9.6 (b) are the following rules for ad
leading and trailing assignments:

Corollary 9.9   (a) *If x' and y' are not free in e, then*

var $x, y \vdash (x, y := x', y' \mid b[x := e]) = |x := e| ; (x, y := x', y' \mid b)$

(b) *If x' is not free in b and y is not free in e, then*

$$\text{var } x, y \vdash (x, y := x', y' \mid b \wedge x' = e) = (y := y' \mid b) \, ; \, |x := e[y' := y]| \; .$$

Example: Dividing a Problem into Subproblems

The rule in Theorem 9.6 (b) can be used to divide a problem into two (smaller) subproblems. The following simple example illustrates this:

$$(x, y := x', y' \mid \mathsf{factor}.x'.x \wedge \mathsf{factor}.x'.y \wedge m \leq (x' \cdot y') \leq n) =$$
$$(x, y := x', y' \mid \mathsf{factor}.x'.x \wedge \mathsf{factor}.x'.y) \, ; \, (y := y' \mid m \leq (x \cdot y') \leq n) \; .$$

The original assignment requires us to set x and y to new values x' and y' such that x' is a factor in both x and y and the product $x' \cdot y'$ is within certain bounds. This can be done by first finding a suitable value for x (and allowing y to change arbitrarily) and then finding a suitable value for y. The following derivation justifies the equality:

$$(x, y := x', y' \mid \mathsf{factor}.x'.x \wedge \mathsf{factor}.x'.y) \, ; \, (y := y' \mid m \leq (x \cdot y') \leq n)$$

$= \{\text{make assignments compatible}\}$

$$(x, y := x', y' \mid \mathsf{factor}.x'.x \wedge \mathsf{factor}.x'.y) \, ;$$
$$(x, y := x', y' \mid x' = x \wedge m \leq (x \cdot y') \leq n)$$

$= \{\text{composition of relational assignments}\}$

$$(x, y := x', y' \mid$$
$$(\exists x'' \, y'' \cdot \mathsf{factor}.x''.x \wedge \mathsf{factor}.x''.y \wedge x' = x'' \wedge m \leq (x'' \cdot y') \leq n))$$

$= \{\text{one-point rule, vacuous quantification}\}$

$$(x, y := x', y' \mid \mathsf{factor}.x'.x \wedge \mathsf{factor}.x'.y \wedge m \leq (x' \cdot y') \leq n)$$

Relations as Programs

Relations are more expressive than (total) functions and are therefore better suited to model programs. The simplest program model (apart from a total function) is that of a partial function, which permits us to say that a program is defined only for certain initial states. For instance, we might want to say that the assignment $x := x/y$ is defined only in an initial state where $y \neq 0$. Similarly, we can model nontermination of a program with undefinedness. This is a rather classical approach to modeling programs.

With relations we can also model *nondeterminism*. In this case, a program may have two or more possible final states, but we do not know which one is going to be chosen (demonic nondeterminism), or we can ourselves choose the final state (angelic nondeterminism).

We can also make the syntax of relations more program-like by adding co
tional state relations, in the same way as we defined conditional state transform
Consider first the relation $|p|$; R,where p is a predicate. The intuition is that
relation maps initial states in p as R does, but initial states outside p are maj
to the empty set. We then define the *conditional state relation* if p then P else
by using this as a building block:

$$\text{if } p \text{ then } P \text{ else } Q \text{ fi} \quad \stackrel{\triangle}{=} \quad |p|\,; P \cup |\neg p|\,; Q \ .$$

Note that conditional relations preserve determinism (Exercise 9.4). We can
a *guarded relation* to define a conditional relation with an arbitrary numbe
alternatives that need not be mutually exclusive:

$$|p_1|\,; R_1 \cup \cdots \cup |p_m|\,; R_m \ .$$

Here p_i and p_j may both hold for some state, and thus both relations are applic
in that state.

We can also define iteration with relations. We define the *reflexive transitive clo*
of a relation R, denoted by R^*, by

$$R^* \quad \stackrel{\triangle}{=} \quad (\cup i \mid i \geq 0 \cdot R^i) \ ,$$

where

$$R^0 \quad \stackrel{\triangle}{=} \quad \text{Id} \ ,$$
$$R^{i+1} \quad \stackrel{\triangle}{=} \quad R\,; R^i, \quad i = 0, 1, 2 \ldots \ .$$

We can then define an *iterated relation* of the form while p do R od by

$$\text{while } p \text{ do } R \text{ od} \quad \stackrel{\triangle}{=} \quad (|p|\,; R)^*\,; |\neg p| \ .$$

It is easy to see that (while p do R od).$\sigma.\sigma'$ holds if and only if there exi
sequence of states $\sigma = \sigma_0, \sigma_1, \ldots, \sigma_n = \sigma'$ such that $p.\sigma_i \wedge R.\sigma_i.\sigma_{i+1}$ hold
$i = 0, 1, \ldots, n-1$ and $\neg p.\sigma_n$ holds (i.e., if σ' can be reached from σ by iter
R as long as condition p holds). If condition p always holds for states reac
by R from some initial state σ, then (while p do R od).σ will be empty. Thu
model nontermination with partiality.

Let us collect the above constructs into a language in which to express
relations. We define this as follows:

$$R \quad ::= \quad \text{Id} \mid |b| \mid (x := x' \mid b) \mid R_1\,; R_2 \mid R_1 \cup R_2 \mid R_1^* \ .$$

Here b is a expression, while x is a list of state attributes.

This language permits nondeterministic choice in the assignment, the union, an
iteration. By replacing these with functional assignment, deterministic conditi
and while loops, we have a standard deterministic programming language v
the constructs are interpreted as partial functions. The syntax for this is as fol

$$R \quad ::= \quad \mathsf{Id} \mid |b| \mid |x := e| \mid R_1 \, ; \, R_2 \mid \text{if } b \text{ then } R_1 \text{ else } R_2 \text{ fi} \mid \text{while } b \text{ do } R \text{ od } .$$

Here the test relation and the iteration introduce partiality into the language.

Blocks and procedures were defined for state transformers and can obviously also be defined for relations in a similar manner. Thus, we can introduce a relational block with local variables (see Exercise 9.12). Similarly, we can define a relational procedure, i.e., a name for a relation that can be called using reference and value parameters. However, we will not make use of these constructs on the the relational level. We return to blocks and procedures on the program statement level in later chapters.

Correctness and Refinement

Let us go back to our original goal: to model the behavior of agents whose interaction is bound by contracts. Relations allow us to model contracts where only one agent is permitted to make choices. Consider first the situation where only our agent can make choices. We assume that the contract statement is expressed as a state relation in the language above, where we interpret $R_1 \cup R_2$ as $R_1 \sqcup R_2$. It is then clear that our agent can establish the postcondition q in initial state σ with relation R if

$$(\exists \sigma' \cdot R.\sigma.\sigma' \wedge q.\sigma') .$$

This therefore defines $\sigma \, \{\!| \, R \, |\!\} \, q$ when all choices are angelic. To achieve the postcondition, it is sufficient that some state σ' that satisfies q can be reached from σ with R. If there is no σ' such that $R.\sigma.\sigma'$, then our agent clearly cannot establish the postcondition and has to breach the contract.

Consider then the situation where only the other agent can make any choices. In this case, we interpret $R_1 \cup R_2$ as $R_1 \sqcap R_2$. Our agent can then be sure that condition q is established in initial state σ with R only if

$$(\forall \sigma' \cdot R.\sigma.\sigma' \Rightarrow q.\sigma') .$$

If this holds, the other agent cannot avoid establishing the postcondition q, because every state reachable from σ will establish this postcondition. If there is no σ' such that $R.\sigma.\sigma'$, then the other agent has to breach the contract, so our agent trivially satisfies the contract.

Thus, there is an angelic and a demonic interpretation of relations in our language for state relations. We can choose to let $\cup$ model either kind of nondeterminism. However, we have to fix either interpretation for $\cup$, so we cannot model both kinds of nondeterminism at the same time with relations.

We obviously also get two different notions of correctness for state relations. say that R is *angelically correct* with respect to precondition p and postcondit q if

$$p.\sigma \;\Rightarrow\; (\exists \sigma' \cdot R.\sigma.\sigma' \wedge q.\sigma')$$

holds for each σ. This is the same as requiring $(\forall \sigma \cdot p.\sigma \Rightarrow (R.\sigma \cap q \neq \emptyset))$ ran.$(|p|\,; R) \cap q \neq \emptyset$.

Dually, we say that R is *demonically correct* with respect to p and q if

$$p.\sigma \;\Rightarrow\; (\forall \sigma' \cdot R.\sigma.\sigma' \Rightarrow q.\sigma') \;.$$

This is again the same as requiring that $(\forall \sigma \cdot p.\sigma \Rightarrow (R.\sigma \subseteq q))$ or ran.$(|p|; R)$ q.

Deterministic Programs

If the relation R is deterministic, then we have a partial function. A choice betw two or more alternatives is then not possible, but there is still the possibility that not defined for some initial states. In this case the angelic correctness requirem states that for any initial state σ that satisfies p there must exist a final state reachable from σ such that $q.\sigma'$ holds. In other words, the execution must termin in a final state that satisfies q. Angelic nondeterminism for deterministic relati thus amounts to what is more commonly known as *total correctness.*

On the other hand, demonic correctness states that for any initial state σ satisfies p, if there exists a final state σ' reachable from σ, then $q.\sigma'$ must h Demonic nondeterminism for deterministic relations thus captures the notio *partial correctness.*

The difference between these two notions of correctness for deterministic progr is whether we consider the situation in which there is no final state as good or b If we have an angelic interpretation, then our agent is supposed to carry out execution, so a missing final state is a breach of contract and is thus bad. In demonic interpretation the other agent is making the choices, so a missing f state is good for our agent.

Refinement

Since we have two notions of correctness, there are also two different kind refinement for state relations, depending on whether we assume that the nonde minism expressed by the relation is angelic or demonic. If it is angelic, then can define refinement by

$$R \sqsubseteq R' \;\equiv\; R \subseteq R' \;. \qquad \textit{(angelic refineme}$$

The definition of refinement says that $R \sqsubseteq R'$ holds iff $\sigma \mathrel{\{\!\!|} R \mathrel{|\!\!\}} q \Rightarrow \sigma \mathrel{\{\!\!|} R' \mathrel{|\!\!\}} q$ holds for every σ and every q. With an angelic interpretation this is the case if and only if $R \subseteq R'$ (Exercise 9.10). Intuitively, this means that a refinement can only increase the set of final states among which our agent can choose and hence makes it easier for it to satisfy the contract.

In a similar way a demonic interpretation of the nondeterminism in relations implies that refinement is defined by

$$R \sqsubseteq R' \;\equiv\; R \supseteq R' \,. \qquad\qquad \textit{(demonic refinement)}$$

In this case the refinement decreases the set of final states among which the other agent can choose, and hence it can only make it easier for our agent to satisfy the contract.

Relations as Specifications

Relations are very useful for describing the intended effect of programs, i.e., to give specifications. The nondeterminism is then interpreted as a *don't care* nondeterminism: the implementer is given freedom to choose any of the permitted outcomes. This is demonic nondeterminism, where the user is prepared for any choice that the system makes. Consider our example specification from the introduction, computing the square root of x with precision e. This can be expressed by the relational assignment

$$(x := y \mid -e < x - y^2 < e) \,.$$

Any program that yields a final result that satisfies this relation is then acceptable.

We might be more specific and request the square root to be computed only if $x \geq 0$ and $e > 0$ initially. This is captured by the following relation:

if $x \geq 0 \wedge e > 0$ then $(x := y \mid -e < x - y^2 < e)$ else True fi .

We do not require anything of the final state when $x < 0$ or $e \leq 0$. We can also be more specific if we want, and state that in this case nothing should be done. This would correspond to the specification

if $x \geq 0 \wedge e > 0$ then $(x := y \mid -e < x - y^2 < e)$ else Id fi .

Looking at a relation as a specification, a correct implementation is the same as a (demonic) refinement of the relation. Any relation that is more deterministic than the specification is a correct implementation. In particular, we would have that

if $x \geq 0 \wedge e > 0$ then $(x := y \mid -e < x - y^2 < e)$ else True fi $\sqsubseteq$
        if $x \geq 0 \wedge e > 0$ then $|x := \sqrt{x}|$ else Id fi .

9.7   Summary

This chapter introduced state relations and described their lattice- and catego
theoretic properties. We showed how relations can be used to model progra
where there is only one kind of nondeterminism, either angelic or demonic. We a
looked at the notions of correctness and refinement for both these interpretati
of state relations. For deterministic programs, angelic correctness is the same
total correctness, and demonic correctness is the same as partial correctness. Th
is a long tradition of modeling programs as relations. An early textbook where t
approach is described was written by de Bakker [36]. A relational view is also
the heart of formalisms such as VDM [94] and Z [133]. The origin of the relatio
view is in the relation calculus of Alfred Tarski [135].

Relational assignments are useful for specifying the required behavior of progra
without overspecification. We described a simple programming language based
relations that is more expressive than the straight-line programs and discussed
notions of correctness and refinement for programs described in this langua
The notion of a relational assignment is based on the nondeterministic assignm
statement originally proposed by Back [6] and further studied in [12].

The relational model is restricted in that we cannot have both angelic and demo
nondeterminism at the same time in a program. Neither does it permit us to exp
either kind of nondeterminism together with nontermination. This shows that
relational model has its limitations, and that there are situations in which we n
to choose a more general model for programs, such as the predicate transfor
model that we will describe shortly. However, for many purposes, the relatio
model is quite sufficient.

9.8   Exercises

9.1   Show that any relation space is an atomic lattice.

9.2   Show that the identity relation is deterministic and that composition of two de
ministic relations is deterministic.

9.3   Prove Theorem 9.4 (a). Then explain why there is no rule of the form $(x := x' \mid T$
True.

9.4   Show that the conditional relation preserves determinism; i.e., if relations Q an
are deterministic, then any relation of the form if p then Q else R fi is determinis

9.5   Verify that Rel is a category.

9.6   Show that in the category of state relations, composition distributes over bott
and join both from the left and from the right. Give a counterexample showing
composition does not distribute over meet or over top.

9.7   Show that if R is a state relation, then the following properties hold:

$$|\text{dom}.R| \subseteq R ; R^{-1} \, ,$$
$$|\text{ran}.R| \subseteq R^{-1} ; R \, .$$

9.8   Prove Corollary 9.9.

9.9   Prove the following:

$$R^* ; R^* = R^* \, ,$$
$$(R^*)^* = R^* \, .$$

9.10   Show that relations R and R' satisfy

$$(\forall q \ \sigma \cdot \{R\}.q.\sigma \Rightarrow \{R'\}.q.\sigma)$$

if and only if $R \subseteq R'$.

9.11   Carry out the detailed proof of Corollary 9.8.

9.12   Define a relational block with local variable y a follows:

begin var $y \mid b$; R end $\;\;\stackrel{\wedge}{=}\;\;$ $|$begin$|$; $(y := y' \mid b[y := y'])$; $|$end$|$,

where the *initialization predicate* b is a predicate over the global variables and y.
Show that begin var $y \mid b$; Id end = Id.

ypes and Data Structures

So far, we have assumed a fixed collection of types, type operators, constants and axioms in the logic. We next consider how to extend our theories to model new domains of discourse by defining new types with associated constants and inference rules. Either we can postulate a new type by giving a collection of axioms and inference rules that determine the properties of the type, or we can construct a new type as being isomorphic to a subset of some existing type. We describe both these methods below. We use the axiomatic approach to introduce the important type of *natural numbers*. As another example, we show how to define *lists* and *disjoint sums*. The latter can be seen as the category-theoretic dual to Cartesian products. The constructive approach is illustrated by showing an alternative definition of natural numbers.

We then look at how to define the standard data structures commonly used in programming languages: *records*, *arrays* and *pointers*. We show how to formalize their properties as rather straightforward extensions of the way we formalized program variables. We also show how to reason about such structures.

1 Postulating a New Type

We postulate a new type by introducing a new atomic type or type operator, extending the signature of the logic with the operations needed for the type and extending the deductive system with new axioms and inference rules that postulate the properties of these operations. We have already shown how to postulate a product type. Here we show how to define natural numbers, lists, and disjoint sums. The first is an example of an atomic type; the two others are type constructors like the product.

Natural Numbers

The type Nat of *natural numbers* is an atomic type. It has constants 0 : Nat
suc : Nat → Nat (the successor function). We introduce the type Nat by addin
and suc to the signature and postulating Peano's axioms:

$$\vdash (\forall n \cdot \neg (suc.n = 0)) \ ,$$
$$\vdash (\forall m \ n \cdot suc.m = suc.n \Rightarrow m = n) \ ,$$
$$\vdash (\forall p \cdot p.0 \wedge (\forall n \cdot p.n \Rightarrow p.(suc.n)) \Rightarrow (\forall n \cdot p.n))$$

(from now on, we will generally write axioms and theorems without outermost
versal quantifiers and without leading turnstile if there are no assumptions).
first axioms states that 0 is not a successor. The second axiom states that the s
cessor function is injective. The last axiom is the induction axiom. Peano's axi
are sufficient for developing arithmetic in higher-order logic, because addition
multiplication (and other operations on naturals) can be defined as new consta
Note that the induction principle is stated as a single theorem in higher-order lo
using quantification over all predicates p. In a first-order logic, we would nee
use an axiom scheme to define induction.

The numerals $1, 2, \ldots$ can be seen as a (potentially) infinite collection of
constants, each with its own definition $(1 = suc.0, 2 = suc.1,$ etc.$)$.

Sequences

A *sequence* is a finite ordered collection of elements that are all of the same ty
We shall here introduce sequences by postulating a number of axioms, much in
same way as we introduced the natural numbers. There are two basic constants
sequences: the empty sequence $\langle \rangle$: Seq of Σ and the (infix) sequence constru
& : (Seq of Σ) → Σ → (Seq of Σ), which extends a sequence with an elem
The postulates are the following:

$$s\&x \neq \langle \rangle \ ,$$
$$s\&x = s'\&x' \Rightarrow s = s' \wedge x = x' \ ,$$
$$p.\langle \rangle \wedge (\forall s \ x \cdot p.s \Rightarrow p.(s\&x)) \Rightarrow (\forall s \cdot p.s) \ .$$

Note how these axioms resemble the axioms for the natural numbers. In addi
to the two basic constants, we introduce two other constants, last : Seq of Σ −
and butlast : Seq of Σ → Seq of Σ, with axioms

$$last.(s\&x) = x \ ,$$
$$butlast.(s\&x) = s \ .$$

Since all functions are total, last applied to $\langle \rangle$ will return some value, about wl
we know nothing.

In practice, we use angle bracket notation for concrete sequences, so $\langle 1, 2, 3 \rangle$ st
for $((\langle \rangle \& 1)\&2)\&3$.

Sum Type

Dually to products, we extend the type structure of higher-order logic with *sum types*, standing for disjoint unions. Sums are added through a binary type operator +, written infix. Exactly as for products, we assume that + associates to the right, so $\Sigma + \Gamma + \Delta$ stands for $\Sigma + (\Gamma + \Delta)$. Furthermore, we assume that + has higher precedence than $\rightarrow$ but lower than $\times$.

Elements of the sum are constructed from elements of Σ and Γ using the *injection functions* inl : $\Sigma \rightarrow \Sigma + \Gamma$ and inr : $\Gamma \rightarrow \Sigma + \Gamma$. In addition to the injection functions, we introduce four other new constants for handling sums. The *test functions* isl : $\Sigma + \Gamma \rightarrow$ Bool and isr : $\Sigma + \Gamma \rightarrow$ Bool tell us where an element in the sum originates, and the *projection functions* outl : $\Sigma + \Gamma \rightarrow \Sigma$ and outr : $\Sigma + \Gamma \rightarrow \Gamma$ project an element from the sum back into the component where it originates.

Thus the sum type is characterized by the following property, for an arbitrary $\delta : \Sigma + \Gamma$:

$$(\exists \sigma : \Sigma \cdot \delta = \mathsf{inl}.\sigma) \vee (\exists \gamma : \Gamma \cdot \delta = \mathsf{inr}.\gamma) \ . \qquad \textit{(sum characterization)}$$

Furthermore, we have the following properties for isl and isr:

$$\begin{aligned}
\mathsf{isl}.(\mathsf{inl}.\sigma) &\equiv \mathsf{T} & \mathsf{isl}.(\mathsf{inr}.\gamma) &\equiv \mathsf{F} \ , & \textit{(left test)} \\
\mathsf{isr}.(\mathsf{inl}.\sigma) &\equiv \mathsf{F} & \mathsf{isr}.(\mathsf{inr}.\gamma) &\equiv \mathsf{T} \ , & \textit{(right test)}
\end{aligned}$$

and the following properties for outl and outr:

$$\begin{aligned}
\mathsf{outl}.(\mathsf{inl}.\sigma) &= \sigma \ , & \textit{(left project)} \\
\mathsf{outr}.(\mathsf{inr}.\gamma) &= \gamma \ . & \textit{(right project)}
\end{aligned}$$

Note that outl : $\Sigma + \Gamma \rightarrow \Sigma$ and outr : $\Sigma + \Gamma \rightarrow \Gamma$ are not uniquely defined by these equations; we do not say anything about the value of $\mathsf{outl}.(\mathsf{inr}.\gamma)$ or $\mathsf{outr}.(\mathsf{inl}.\sigma)$.

Equality on sums is as follows:

$$\begin{aligned}
\mathsf{inl}.\sigma = \mathsf{inl}.\sigma' &\equiv \sigma = \sigma' \ , & \textit{(sum equality)} \\
\mathsf{inl}.\sigma = \mathsf{inr}.\gamma &\equiv \mathsf{F} \ , \\
\mathsf{inr}.\gamma = \mathsf{inr}.\gamma' &\equiv \gamma = \gamma' \ .
\end{aligned}$$

If Σ and Γ each is equipped with an ordering, then we assume that the sum $\Sigma + \Gamma$ is ordered as follows:

$$\begin{aligned}
\mathsf{inl}.\sigma \sqsubseteq \mathsf{inl}.\sigma' &\equiv \sigma \sqsubseteq \sigma' \ , & \textit{(sum ordering)} \\
\mathsf{inl}.\sigma \sqsubseteq \mathsf{inr}.\gamma &\equiv \mathsf{T} \ , \\
\mathsf{inr}.\gamma \sqsubseteq \mathsf{inl}.\sigma &\equiv \mathsf{F} \ , \\
\mathsf{inr}.\gamma \sqsubseteq \mathsf{inr}.\gamma' &\equiv \gamma \sqsubseteq \gamma' \ .
\end{aligned}$$

Thus the orderings within Σ and Γ are preserved, but every element of Σ is smaller than every element of Γ.

10.2 Constructing a New Type

Another way of extending a theory with a new type is to construct the new ty
in terms of existing types. We extend higher-order logic with a new type T
asserting that this type is isomorphic to a nonempty subset A of some existing t
Σ. The new type T is not a subset of Σ, because all types in higher-order lo
must be disjoint. Rather, there is a bijection between the elements of T and
elements in A. Using the bijection, we can then define operations over the n
type in terms of already existing operations over the old type.

The *principle of extension by type definition* in higher-order logic allows us
introduce a new type in this way. The resulting extension of the logic is conservati
so this approach also guarantees consistency of the extension. The steps requi
are the following:

(i) Specify a subset A of some existing type.

(ii) Prove that the set A is nonempty.

(iii) Assert that the new type is in one-to-one correspondence with A.

Formally, the logic is extended with a new type by a definition

$$T \cong A \; .$$ (*type definitio*

where T is the name of the new type and $A : \Sigma \to$ Bool is a closed term such
$(\exists x \cdot A.x)$ is a theorem (so A denotes a nonempty set). This extends the the
with a new type T, the new constants abs : $\Sigma \to T$ and rep : $T \to \Sigma$, and
following theorem:

$$\vdash (\forall x : T \cdot \text{abs}.(\text{rep}.x) = x) \land (\forall y \mid y \in A \cdot \text{rep}.(\text{abs}.y) = y) \; .$$

This theorem states that correspondence between the type T and the represent
set A is given by the *abstraction function* abs and the *representation function*
This construction is illustrated in Figure 10.1.

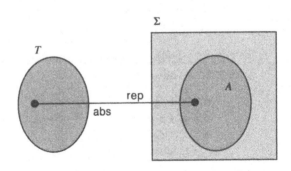

FIGURE 10.1. Defining a new type T

The type Σ can contain uninstantiated types $\Sigma_1, \ldots, \Sigma_n$; in this case T becomes an n-ary *type operator*.

Unit Type

As a first simple example, we introduce the *type* Unit, which contains exactly one element. This can be done by choosing the value T : Bool to represent the unique element of Unit. We have that $\{T\} = (\lambda x : \text{Bool} \cdot x)$, so we define the type by

$$\text{Unit} \;\cong\; (\lambda x : \text{Bool} \cdot x) \; . \qquad\qquad\qquad\qquad \textit{(unit type)}$$

There is at least one value in the representation set; i.e., $\vdash (\exists x \cdot (\lambda x : \text{Bool} \cdot x).x)$ holds, because

$$(\exists x \cdot (\lambda x : \text{Bool} \cdot x).x)$$
$$\equiv \{\beta \text{ conversion}\}$$
$$(\exists x \cdot x)$$
$$\Leftarrow \{\exists \text{ introduction with witness T}\}$$
$$\text{T}$$

Now we can define unit to be the single element of Unit, using an ordinary constant definition:

$$\text{unit} \;\stackrel{\wedge}{=}\; (\epsilon x : \text{Unit} \cdot \text{T}) \; .$$

Natural Numbers

As a more elaborate example, we show how the natural numbers themselves can be defined in terms of the individuals. Here we make use of the infinity axiom; we assume that the function $f : \text{Ind} \rightarrow \text{Ind}$ is injective but not surjective (see Chapter 7). We will not go through all the details of the construction, since we only want to illustrate how the type-definition mechanism works.

The natural numbers can be built so that 0 is represented by an arbitrary element outside the range of f (such an element exists since f is not surjective), i.e., $(\epsilon x \cdot x \notin \text{ran}. f)$. Furthermore, the successor function is represented by f. The subset of Ind that we then choose to represent the natural numbers is the smallest subset that contains $(\epsilon x \cdot x \notin \text{ran}. f)$ and is closed under f. This set N is characterized as

$$N \;=\; \cap\{A \mid (\epsilon x \cdot x \notin \text{ran}. f) \in A \wedge (\forall x \cdot x \in A \Rightarrow f.x \in A)\} \; .$$

The proof that N is nonempty is trivial. We can thus give the type definition:

$$\text{Nat} \;\cong\; N \; . \qquad\qquad\qquad\qquad\qquad \textit{(natural numbers)}$$

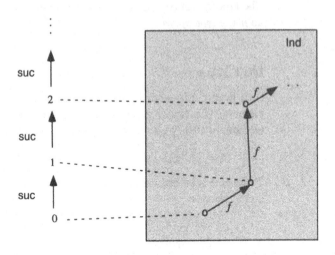

FIGURE 10.2. Constructing the natural numbers Nat

Now we can define 0 and the successor function using the abstraction and rep sentation functions that the type definition has added:

$$0 \triangleq \text{abs.}(\epsilon x \cdot x \notin \text{ran.} f) ,$$
$$\text{suc.} n \triangleq \text{abs.}(f.(\text{rep.} n)) .$$

This definition is illustrated in Figure 10.2.

The Peano postulates can now be proved as theorems rather than asserted as axior The first two postulates follow directly from the fact that f is injective (this ensu that the successor function is injective) and not surjective (this ensures that 0 is a successor). The proof of the induction postulate is more complicated, so we or it here.

10.3 Record Types

The previous section introduced a number of types that are useful for expressi mathematical properties in general. In programming languages we use types structure data that are stored in the state. Below we consider such *data types data structures*) in more detail. We will look at record types in this section a consider array types and pointer types in the following sections.

We have earlier assumed that a state space is a type with attributes that can be r and changed, and that we describe state-changing functions (state transforme by giving their effect on the attributes of the state. These attributes are progr variables when they satisfy the independence assumptions.

We can also define a type with specific attributes directly, as a *record type*. Let us define a new m-ary type operator record for each $m \geq 1$. Let us write

$$\Gamma \;=\; \text{record } k_1 : \Gamma_1 \; ; \cdots ; k_m : \Gamma_m \text{ end}$$

for the definition $\Gamma = \text{record}(\Gamma_1, \ldots, \Gamma_m)$ together with the definition of the attributes $k_1, \ldots, k_m$ on Γ, where attribute k_i has type $(\Gamma \rightarrow \Gamma_i) \times (\Gamma_i \rightarrow \Gamma \rightarrow \Gamma)$. An element of a record type is called a *record*. Note that we here assume that the attributes are constants, whereas program variables are modeled as variables.

The definition of the access and update operations is as before. We require that the constants $k_1, \ldots, k_m$ satisfy the independence assumptions (a)–(f), i.e., that

$$\text{var } k_1 : \Gamma_1, \ldots, k_m : \Gamma_m$$

holds. The explicit definition of Γ as a record type means that it is a completely new type, of which we know nothing except that it has the constants $k_1, \ldots, k_m$. These constants satisfy the independence assumptions, now taken as axioms. A state space may have attributes other than those explicitly declared, but for record types we assume that it has only the declared attributes.

We introduce a shorthand for the access and update operations on records, writing

$$\gamma[k] \;\stackrel{\wedge}{=}\; \text{val}.k.\gamma \;,$$
$$\gamma(k \leftarrow a) \;\stackrel{\wedge}{=}\; \text{set}.k.a.\gamma \;.$$

In addition to the independence axioms, we assume one more property of records that we do not assume for states with attributes in general:

$$\gamma = \gamma' \;\equiv\; k_1.\gamma = k_1.\gamma' \wedge \ldots \wedge k_m.\gamma = k_m.\gamma' \;. \qquad\qquad (identification)$$

This states that two records are equal if and only if they have the same values for all attributes. In other words, a record is identified by its attributes. This is essentially the same property that we assumed for the product type (that a pair is identified by its projections) and is a form of extensionality.

This property is not assumed for states with attributes in general, because it would invalidate the monotonicity property for state transformers defined in terms of attributes. The monotonicity property states that if we have proved a property assuming a specific collection of state attributes, then the same property still holds if we assume that the state also has other attributes. It is not obvious that we actually want to have the identification axiom for record types. This depends on whether or not we want to compare two records for equality. The *object-oriented programming paradigm* assumes that records are extendable by adding new attributes and that the monotonicity property holds for records. If we follow this paradigm, then we would not assume the identification property. In traditional Pascal-like languages the identification property is assumed to hold, as there is no mechanism for record type extension.

Record Expressions and Record Assignment

Let us now consider expressions that have records as values. The most cen●
record operation is one that computes a new record value from a given rec●
value by changing some specific attribute.

Assume that R is a state attribute (i.e., a program variable) of record type Γ, k is●
attribute of the record, and e is an expression. We define a *record update*, deno●
by $R(k \leftarrow e)$, as follows:

$$(R(k \leftarrow e)).\sigma \; \stackrel{\wedge}{=} \; (R.\sigma)(k \leftarrow e.\sigma) \; . \qquad \text{(record updat●}$$

In a given state σ, this expression returns a new record γ' that we get by changing●
attribute k of the record $\gamma = R.\sigma$ to the value $e.\sigma$. Thus, both the record and the n●
value for the attribute are given as expressions on the state. The record update is ●
pointwise extension of the set.k operation: $(R.\sigma)(k \leftarrow e.\sigma) = \text{set}.k.(e.\sigma).(R.●$

Let us also define a record attribute expression by

$$R[k].\sigma \; \stackrel{\wedge}{=} \; (R.\sigma)[k] \; . \qquad \text{(record attribute expressio●}$$

Thus, the record $R.\sigma$ is first computed, and then the attribute k is determi●
from the computed record value. This is again the pointwise extension of the ●
operation on record values.

We finally define record assignment by

$$R[k] := e \; \stackrel{\wedge}{=} \; R := R(k \leftarrow e) \; . \qquad \text{(record assignme●}$$

Record assignment is thus written as if it were an assignment to the attribute k●
the record. In reality, a record assignment is an assignment of a new updated rec●
value to the record variable.

The notation for record attributes varies. In Pascal, the standard notation is R●
whereas we write this here as $R[k]$, in conformance with the array indexing ●
eration that we will introduce below. The Pascal dot notation cannot be used h●
because application is the wrong way around; we think of k as the function tha●
applied to R. The record assignment notation is in conformance with establis●
notation in Pascal and many other languages.

A simple example of a record type is an account, which we can define by

    Account =   record name : String ; amount : Nat end .

If we have two record variables A, B : Account, then

    A[amount] := A[amount] + B[amount] ;
    B[amount] := 0

describes the transfer of all the money in B to A.

Records as Constructed Types

We have here defined record types by postulating a collection of constants (the attributes or fields) and postulating that these satisfy the independence assumptions. We could also define records as constructed types. The type record $k_1 : \Gamma_1; \cdots; k_m : \Gamma_m$ end could be represented by the product type $\Gamma_1 \times \cdots \times \Gamma_m$. We would then define, for $i = 1, \ldots, m$,

$$
\begin{aligned}
\mathsf{val}.k_i.\gamma &= \pi_i^m.(\mathsf{rep}.\gamma) \ , \\
\mathsf{set}.k_i.a.\gamma &= \mathsf{abs}.(\mathsf{update}_i^m.a.(\mathsf{rep}.\gamma)) \ .
\end{aligned}
$$

Here π_i^m denotes the ith component in the tuple with m components, and $\mathsf{update}_i^m.a$ denotes the operation that changes the ith component of a tuple to the value a, without changing the other components. These operations are straightforward to define for any particular values of m and i.

With these definitions, it is easy to show that the record type satisfies the independence axioms that we have postulated for it above (Exercise 10.9).

.4 Array Types

An *array* is used to store a collection of data items of the same type, to be accessed by indices (which usually are natural numbers). We can define a binary type operator array that constructs arrays from given types. Let us write

$$
\Gamma \stackrel{\wedge}{=} \mathsf{array} \ \Delta \ \mathsf{of} \ \Phi
$$

for $\Gamma = \mathsf{array}(\Delta, \Phi)$. Here Δ is the *index type*, and Φ is the *component type*.

Let us postulate two operations, $\mathsf{val} : \Delta \to \Gamma \to \Phi$ for retrieving the value of an array, and $\mathsf{set} : \Delta \to \Phi \to \Gamma \to \Gamma$ for updating a specific array element. Thus $\mathsf{val}.x.\gamma$ stands for the value of array γ at index x, while $\mathsf{set}.x.\phi.\gamma$ stands for the new array that we get from γ by setting the element indexed by x to the value ϕ. Note the difference here as compared to records and program variables, for which the access functions returned the first or second component of an attribute. Here the access and update functions are really functions on the index set. We use the same abbreviations for arrays as for records:

$$
\begin{aligned}
\gamma[x] &\stackrel{\wedge}{=} \mathsf{val}.x.\gamma \ , \\
\gamma(x \leftarrow a) &\stackrel{\wedge}{=} \mathsf{set}.x.a.\gamma \ .
\end{aligned}
$$

We will assume that $\mathsf{val}.x$ and $\mathsf{set}.x$ satisfy the independence axioms for all possible values of $x \in \Delta$. In other words, we postulate the axioms in Figure 10.1 (x and y are indices and a, b array element values). We also assume extensionality for arrays:

$$
\begin{aligned}
\gamma(x \leftarrow a)[x] &= a & \text{(a)} \\
x \neq y \Rightarrow \gamma(x \leftarrow a)[y] &= \gamma[y] & \text{(b)} \\
\gamma(x \leftarrow a)(x \leftarrow b) &= \gamma(x \rightarrow b) & \text{(c)} \\
x \neq y \Rightarrow \gamma(x \leftarrow a)(y \rightarrow b) &= \gamma(y \leftarrow b)(x \leftarrow a) & \text{(d)} \\
\gamma(x \leftarrow \gamma[x]) &= \gamma & \text{(e)}
\end{aligned}
$$

TABLE 10.1. Independence requirements for array elements

$$
\gamma = \gamma' \;\equiv\; (\forall x \in \Delta \cdot \gamma[x] = \gamma'[x]) \;. \qquad \textit{(identificatio}
$$

Array Expressions and Array Assignment

Assume that A is an expression of array type and i an expression of index ty
We define an *array access* operation as follows:

$$
A[i].\sigma \;\stackrel{\wedge}{=}\; (A.\sigma)[i.\sigma] \;. \qquad \textit{(array acce}
$$

This is really the pointwise extension of the val operation:

$$
\mathrm{val}.(i.\sigma).(A.\sigma) = (A.\sigma)[i.\sigma] = A[i].\sigma \;.
$$

We define *array update* by

$$
(A(i \leftarrow e)).\sigma \;\stackrel{\wedge}{=}\; (A.\sigma)(i.\sigma \leftarrow e.\sigma) \;. \qquad \textit{(array upda}
$$

Thus, a difference between arrays and records is that for arrays the index may a
depend on the state, whereas for records, the index (attribute) is always fixed
this way arrays permit indirect addressing of data elements, which is not poss
with records or global variables. The array update is again the pointwise extens
of the set operation.

Finally, we define array assignment in the same way as for records:

$$
A[i] := e \;\stackrel{\wedge}{=}\; A := A(i \leftarrow e) \;. \qquad \textit{(array assignme}
$$

The above formalization of arrays assumes that a type is given as the index ty
Thus, array Nat of Bool is an array that permits any natural number to be use
an index, so the array itself is an infinite data structure. Programming langua
usually constrain the indices to some subset of the index type: we would de
something like array $10 \ldots 120$ of Nat to indicate that only indices in the ra
$10 \le x \le 120$ are permitted. An array specified in this way is defined by adding
index constraint to the index axioms. As an example, if the index range is m .
then the second axiom becomes

$$m \leq x \leq n \wedge m \leq y \leq n \wedge x \neq y \;\Rightarrow\; \gamma[x \leftarrow a][y] = \gamma[y] \;.$$

The identification axiom would then state that two arrays are the same if they have the same values for all indices in the permitted range.

Arrays as Constructed Types

We can also define $\Gamma = $ array Δ of Φ as a constructed type. We choose $\Delta \rightarrow \Phi$ as the representation type. Then we define

$$\begin{aligned} \mathsf{val}.x.\gamma &= \mathsf{rep}.\gamma.x \;, \\ \mathsf{set}.x.\phi.\gamma &= \mathsf{abs}.(\mathsf{update}.x.\phi.(\mathsf{rep}.\gamma)) \;, \end{aligned}$$

where we define the update operation for functions by

$$\mathsf{update}.x.a.f \;=\; (\lambda y \cdot \mathsf{if}\ x = y\ \mathsf{then}\ a\ \mathsf{else}\ f.y\ \mathsf{fi}) \;.$$

It is easy to show that the independence axioms above are satisfied with these definitions (Exercise 10.9).

This shows that we could in fact consider functions $\Delta \rightarrow \Phi$ directly as arrays. This is, however, only the simplest form of arrays. As soon as we put more restrictions on the array, such as restricting the indices to some range, the representation becomes more involved, and the advantages of defining an array as a type of its own become more substantial. For instance, we could choose to represent a bounded array array $m \ldots n$ of Γ by the type (Nat $\rightarrow \Gamma$) $\times$ Nat $\times$ Nat, where the first component determined the value of the array at different indices, the second component records the lower bound, and the last component records the upper bound. We could also add operations min and max for the arrays that return the lower and upper limit for the permitted indices.

This construction of arrays would also permit us to define *dynamic arrays*. In this case, we would in addition to the usual array operations also have operations that could change the index range of the array. For instance, we could define an operation incmax that extends the maximum index of the array by one, and an operation decmax that decreases the maximum permitted index by one, and similarly for changing the minimum permitted index.

Defining Constants over Arrays

When reasoning about arrays and about programs that handle arrays, we need more than just the basic array concepts. For example, we will use the notion of *swapping two elements* in an array. We define the constant swap such that swap$.x.y.\gamma$ stands for the result of swapping elements x and y in array γ:

$$(\text{swap}.x.y.\gamma)[z] \;=\; \begin{cases} \gamma[y] & \text{if } z = x, \\ \gamma[x] & \text{if } z = y, \\ \gamma[z] & \text{otherwise.} \end{cases}$$

All constants over arrays (and records) are automatically also available as pointw extended constants. Thus, e.g., we have that

$$(\text{swap}.i.j.A).\sigma \;=\; \text{swap}.(i.\sigma).(j.\sigma).(A.\sigma) \;.$$

This means that we can always apply reduction to expression with arrays a records.

As another example, we define what it means for the restriction of an array t certain index set to be *sorted* (here, and in what follows, we take Nat as the defa index set for arrays):

$$\text{sorted}.\gamma.X \;\overset{\wedge}{=}\; (\forall x\, y \mid x \in X \wedge y \in X \cdot x \le y \Rightarrow \gamma[x] \le \gamma[y]) \;.$$

We can then use the explicit definition to derive properties for sorted. For examp we have that

$$\text{sorted}.\gamma.\emptyset$$

$\equiv$ {definition}

$$(\forall x\, y \mid x \in \emptyset \wedge y \in \emptyset \cdot x \le y \Rightarrow \gamma[x] \le \gamma[y])$$

$\equiv$ {quantification over empty range}

$$\mathsf{T}$$

Thus $\text{sorted}.\gamma.\emptyset$ always holds.

Another property that we will find useful later on is the following:

$$(\forall x\, y \mid x \in X \wedge y \in Y \cdot x < y \wedge \gamma[x] \le \gamma[y]) \Rightarrow$$
$$(\text{sorted}.\gamma.X \wedge \text{sorted}.\gamma.Y \equiv \text{sorted}.\gamma.(X \cup Y)) \;.$$

The proof of this theorem illustrates the way in which we reason about arrays us bounded quantification and range splitting:

$$(\forall x\, y \mid x \in X \wedge y \in Y \cdot x < y \wedge \gamma[x] \le \gamma[y])$$

$\vdash \text{sorted}.\gamma.(X \cup Y)$

$\equiv$ {definition}

$$(\forall x\, y \mid x \in X \cup Y \wedge y \in X \cup Y \cdot x \le y \Rightarrow \gamma[x] \le \gamma[y])$$

$\equiv$ {range split}

$$(\forall x\, y \mid x \in X \wedge y \in X \cdot x \le y \Rightarrow \gamma[x] \le \gamma[y]) \wedge$$
$$(\forall x\, y \mid x \in Y \wedge y \in Y \cdot x \le y \Rightarrow \gamma[x] \le \gamma[y]) \wedge$$

$$(\forall x\ y \mid x \in X \land y \in Y \cdot x \leq y \Rightarrow \gamma[x] \leq \gamma[y]) \land$$
$$(\forall x\ y \mid x \in Y \land y \in X \cdot x \leq y \Rightarrow \gamma[x] \leq \gamma[y])$$

$\equiv$ {definition of sorted}

sorted.γ.$X \land$ sorted.γ.$Y \land$
$$(\forall x\ y \mid x \in X \land y \in Y \cdot x \leq y \Rightarrow \gamma[x] \leq \gamma[y]) \land$$
$$(\forall x\ y \mid x \in Y \land y \in X \cdot x \leq y \Rightarrow \gamma[x] \leq \gamma[y])$$

$\equiv$ {assumption}

sorted.γ.$X \land$ sorted.γ.$Y \land$
$$(\forall x\ y \mid x \in X \land y \in Y \cdot (x \leq y \Rightarrow \gamma[x] \leq \gamma[y]) \land x < y) \land$$
$$(\forall x\ y \mid x \in Y \land y \in X \cdot (x \leq y \Rightarrow \gamma[x] \leq \gamma[y]) \land y < x)$$

$\equiv$ {properties of predicates}

sorted.γ.$X \land$ sorted.γ.$Y \land$
$$(\forall x\ y \mid x \in X \land y \in Y \cdot x < y \land \gamma[x] \leq \gamma[y]) \land$$
$$(\forall x\ y \mid x \in Y \land y \in X \cdot y < x)$$

$\equiv$ {assumption, last two conjuncts simplify to T}

sorted.γ.$X \land$ sorted.γ.Y

In fact, these two properties characterize sorted for finite index sets, so we could also introduce the constant sorted by postulating them as axioms.

We will in our examples use the notion of a *permutation* of an array. For this we need the number of occurrences of an element a in array γ restricted to index set X:

$$\text{occurrence}.a.\gamma.X \;\stackrel{\wedge}{=}\; (\#x \in X \cdot \gamma[x] = a) ,$$

where $\#$ is the "number of" quantifier (for a definition, see Exercise 10.10). We define permutation.γ.X.δ.Y to mean that the restriction of array γ to index set X is a permutation of the restriction of δ to index set Y:

$$\text{permutation}.\gamma.X.\delta.Y \;\stackrel{\wedge}{=}\; (\forall a \cdot \text{occurrence}.a.\gamma.X = \text{occurrence}.a.\delta.Y) .$$

For some properties of permutation, see Exercise 10.11.

5 Dynamic Data Structures

Dynamic data structures are often identified with pointer structures. The machinery that we already have introduced is sufficient to define such structures. Assume that we want to define a data type that consists of nodes with specific fields. Some of these fields are basic data, while others are pointers to other nodes. Say that we want to define nodes that have two fields, d and q, where d stores the data in the

node while q is a pointer to another node. We then define the whole dynamic d
structure as a type of the form

$$\Gamma \;=\; \text{array } I \text{ of record } d : T ; q : I \text{ end} .$$

Here the index set I is the set of pointer values, while the nodes in the struct
are records, with $d : T$ as the basic data field and q the pointer field.

We can declare a program variable $D : \Gamma$ to contain the whole (dynamic) d
structure, usually referred to as the *heap*. In the spirit of Pascal, most programm
languages do not declare the heap explicitly. Declaring the heap as a state attrib
makes the fact that dynamic data structures are just (infinite) arrays explicit.
cessing a node determined by pointer p is then simply expressed as $D[p]$; i
it is an array expression. Similarly, updating a node determined by p in the d
structure is expressed as $D[p] := D[p](d \leftarrow e)$ or $D[p] := D[p](q \leftarrow$
depending on which field we want to change in the node. We can write this e
more concisely as $D[p][d] := e$ or $D[p][q] := e$.

Dynamic data structures differ from ordinary arrays in that we have a way
generating new pointer (index) values that have not been used before. A sim
way is to use Nat as the index set for the heap D and keep a separate counter
for the heap to give the next unused index, with $\{1, 2, \ldots, new.\sigma - 1\}$ being
indices that already have been used in state σ. This permits us to generate
indices dynamically whenever needed and to use index value 0 (called nil) fo
pointer that is never used.

Summarizing the above, a declaration of the form

    type T = record ... end ;

    var p : pointer to T

can be seen as a shorthand for the following declaration:

    type T = record ... end ;

    var D : array Nat of T ;

    var new : Nat := 1 ;

    var p : Nat

Here D is the heap variable associated with the record type T, and new is
variable that records the least unused index in D.

We then write $p\uparrow$ for $D[p]$ so that the heap is kept implicit, $p\uparrow x$ for the
cess $D[p][x]$ and $p\uparrow x := e$ for the update operation $D[p][x] := e$. The s
transformer new p is define by

$$\text{new } p \;\overset{\wedge}{=}\; p, new := new, new + 1 .$$

The compiler enforces the restriction that p can be used only in these three cont
and in particular, that no arithmetic operations are performed on p.

This approach to modeling pointers is very simple, but it shows the basic ideas involved. In particular, it shows that dynamic data structures with pointers in essence are nothing but (infinite) arrays. We can forbid pointer arithmetic by choosing, e.g., Ind rather than Nat as the pointer type, and arb$_{\text{Ind}}$ as the value nil. We then have to explicitly record the set of all pointer values that have been generated this far. More elaborate pointer types can easily be defined, where we can have two or more heaps, each with its own pointer type. A more detailed discussion of dynamic data structures with examples is, however, outside the scope of this book.

.6 Summary and Discussion

We have shown above how to build theories in higher-order logic by extending a given theory with new types, constants, and inference rules. Theories are extended either axiomatically, by postulating new types, constants, and inference rules, or constructively, by defining new types and constants in terms of existing constructs and deriving their properties. The big advantage of the latter approach is that the resulting theory extension is conservative and hence known to be consistent. We have illustrated these two methods with a number of examples. The type-definition mechanism that we use has been described in detail (both for basic types and type operators) by Gordon and Melham [62]. The way in which the product and sum theories are postulated is quite standard, see, e.g., Larry Paulson's book [115].

This chapter illustrates how theories are built in higher-order logic. One theory is built on top of another theory, as an extension. Different extensions of a basic theory can be combined by just joining all the extensions together. As long as the types and constants introduced are syntactically different in all these extensions and the extensions are conservative, the resulting combined extension is also a conservative extension of the original theory.

Data types as they are used in programming languages are defined just as other types. Either we can postulate new data types, or we can introduce them as constructed types. We have here chosen the first approach, because the basic data types that we are interested in, records, arrays, and pointers, come as quite straightforward generalizations of the notion of independent state attributes. However, we have also indicated for these data types how they would be defined explicitly as constructed types, as a way of demonstrating the consistency of extending higher-order logic with theories about records, arrays, and pointer structures.

7 Exercises

10.1 Construct a type tri with three elements A, B, and C and then define a function of type tri $\rightarrow$ Bool that maps A and B to T and C to F.

10.2 Construct product types using $\Sigma \to \Gamma \to$ Bool as the type representing $\Sigma \times$ What is the predicate that characterizes the appropriate subset of $\Sigma \to \Gamma$ Bool? How are pair, fst, and snd defined? Prove that the characteristic properties products are in fact theorems under your definitions.

10.3 The sum type operator can be defined explicitly as follows:

$$\Sigma + \Gamma \;\cong\; \{(b, \sigma, \gamma) : \text{Bool} \times \Sigma \times \Gamma \mid (b \wedge \gamma = \text{arb}) \vee (\neg b \wedge \sigma = \text{arb})\}$$

Define the injection, test, and projection functions (inl, inr, isl, isr, outl, outr) ε prove that they have the properties given in Section 10.1.

10.4 Use the axioms and definitions for sequences given in the text to derive the followi properties:

$$s \neq \langle\rangle \Rightarrow (\text{butlast}.s)\&(\text{last}.s) = s \;,$$
$$s = \langle\rangle \vee (\exists s' \; x \cdot s = s' \& x) \;.$$

10.5 We have seen how the higher-order capabilities of higher-order logic allow ι induction principle to be stated as a theorem. Another important feature of ι natural numbers that can also be derived within the logic is the principle of functi definition by primitive recursion. In fact, it is possible to derive the followi theorem from the Peano axioms:

$$(\forall e \; f \cdot \exists! g \cdot g.0 = e \wedge (\forall n \cdot g.(\text{suc}.n) = f.(g.n).n)) \;.$$

We can then define (see exercises below) a new constant natrec that has following properties:

$$\text{natrec}.e.\,f.0 = e \;,$$
$$\text{natrec}.e.\,f.(\text{suc}.n) = f.(\text{natrec}.e.\,f.n).n \;.$$

This constant can be used as a tool for defining recursive functions. For examp we define

$$\text{even} \;\stackrel{\wedge}{=}\; \text{natrec}.\text{T}.(\lambda b \; n \cdot \neg b) \;.$$

Show that even has the following property:

$$(\text{even}.0 \equiv \text{T}) \wedge (\forall n \cdot \text{even}.(\text{suc}.n) \equiv \neg (\text{even}.n)) \;.$$

10.6 Define the constant $+$, standing for addition of natural numbers, as follows:

$$+ \;\stackrel{\wedge}{=}\; \text{natrec}.(\lambda x \cdot x).(\lambda f \; m \; n \cdot \text{suc}.(f.n)) \;.$$

Show that addition has the following property:

$$(\forall n \cdot + .0.n = n) \wedge (\forall m \; n \cdot + .(\text{suc } m).n = \text{suc}.(+.m.n)) \;.$$

Then use the induction principle to prove that

$$(\forall n \cdot + .n.0 = n) \;.$$

10.7   Derive the following theorem from the Peano axioms:

$$(\forall e\ f \cdot \exists g \cdot (g.0 = e) \wedge (\forall n \cdot g.(\text{suc } n) = f.(g.n).n))\ .$$

10.8   Use the theorem proved in Exercise 10.7 to find a suitable definition of the constant natrec. Verify that natrec satisfies the property

$$(\forall e\ f \cdot \text{natrec}.e.f.0 = e\ \wedge$$
$$(\forall n \cdot \text{natrec}.e.f.(\text{suc } n) = f.(\text{natrec}.e.f.n).n))\ .$$

10.9   Show that both records and arrays satisfy the independence axioms.

10.10   Assume that the constant cardrel satisfies the following:

$$(\text{cardrel}.A.0 \equiv A = \emptyset)\ \wedge$$
$$(\forall n \cdot \text{cardrel}.A.(n+1) \equiv (\exists x \in A \cdot \text{cardrel}.(\lambda y \in A \cdot y \neq x).n)$$

(such a constant can be defined using primitive recursion, see previous exercises). Then define

$$\text{card}.A \ \stackrel{\wedge}{=} \ (\varepsilon n \cdot \text{cardrel}.A.n)$$

and convince yourself that card.A denotes the number of elements in A if A is finite. Now we can define the "number of" quantifier as the binder version of card:

$$(\#x \in A \cdot p.x) \ \stackrel{\wedge}{=} \ \text{card}.(\lambda x \in A \cdot p.x)\ .$$

10.11   Show that permutation satisfies the following properties:

permutation.$A.I.A.I$,

permutation.$A.I.B.J \Rightarrow$ permutation.$B.J.A.I$,

permutation.$A.I.B.J \wedge$ permutation.$B.J.C.K \Rightarrow$ permutation.$A.I.C.K$,

$i \in I \wedge j \in I \Rightarrow$ permutation.$A.I.(\text{swap}.i.j.A).I$.

Part II

Statements

redicate Transformers

We described the basic notion of a contract between independent agents in the introduction and showed a number of properties that it would be reasonable to expect contracts to have. We did not, however, say what kind of mathematical entities contracts are. The interpretation of contracts depends on what features are considered essential and what are inessential. We now make the assumption that the essential feature of a contract is what can be achieved with it. From this point of view, contracts can be interpreted as *predicate transformers*, functions from predicates to predicates. We will explore this approach below in detail, concentrating first on basic mathematical properties of predicate transformers and on how contracts are interpreted as predicate transformers.

1 Satisfying Contracts

We have defined $\sigma \,\{\!| \, S \,|\!\}\, q$ to mean that our agent can satisfy the contract S to establish condition q when the initial state is σ. We want to define this notion precisely for contracts. We could do this by first defining how an agent carries out a contract and, based on this, then define what it means for the agent to satisfy a contract. We will also do this, but later on. Here we will follow a simpler path, where we define $\sigma \,\{\!| \, S \,|\!\}\, q$ directly, by induction on the structure of contracts, using our intuitive understanding of how contracts are satisfied.

Let us look at the language of contract statements introduced in the first chapter:

$$ S \ ::= \ \langle f \rangle \,|\, \{g\} \,|\, [g] \,|\, S_1 \,;\, S_2 \,|\, S_1 \sqcap S_2 \,|\, S_1 \sqcup S_2 \ . $$

Consider first the update $\langle f \rangle$. It has the effect of changing the present state σ **to** new state $f.\sigma$. There is no choice involved here, neither for our agent or the ot**her** agent, since there is only one possible next state. In this case, we obviously h**ave** that $\sigma \mathrel{\{\!|} \langle f \rangle \mathrel{|\!\}} q$ holds if and only if $f.\sigma \in q$.

The assertion $\{g\}$ has no effect on the state if g holds, but otherwise it will bre**ak** the contract. Hence, $\sigma \mathrel{\{\!|} \{g\} \mathrel{|\!\}} q$ holds if and only if $\sigma \in g \cap q$. Condition g m**ust** hold initially in order to avoid breaching the contract, and condition q must h**old** initially if it is to hold for the final state, because the state is not changed.

The assumption $[g]$ also has no effect on the state if g holds, but if g does not h**old** then the assumption is false and the contract is satisfied trivially. Thus, $\sigma \mathrel{\{\!|} [g] \mathrel{|\!\}} q$ holds iff either $\sigma \in \neg g$ or $\sigma \in q$, i.e., iff $\sigma \in \neg g \cup q$.

Consider next the angelic choice $S_1 \sqcup S_2$. Our agent gets to choose the alternative**, so** it is sufficient that either one of the two contracts can be satisfied. Thus $\sigma \mathrel{\{\!|} S_1 \sqcup S_2 \mathrel{|\!\}} q$ holds iff either $\sigma \mathrel{\{\!|} S_1 \mathrel{|\!\}} q$ or $\sigma \mathrel{\{\!|} S_2 \mathrel{|\!\}} q$ holds.

For the demonic choice $S_1 \sqcap S_2$, we have that $\sigma \mathrel{\{\!|} S_1 \sqcap S_2 \mathrel{|\!\}} q$ holds iff both $\sigma \mathrel{\{\!|} S_1 \mathrel{|\!\}} q$ and $\sigma \mathrel{\{\!|} S_2 \mathrel{|\!\}} q$ hold. Because the other agent gets to choose the alternative, **our** agent must be able to satisfy both contracts in order to satisfy the whole contr**act.**

Let us finally consider satisfaction of a sequential composition $S_1 ; S_2$ of contra**cts.** Our agent can satisfy this contract to establish q from σ if he can satisfy **S_1** to establish some intermediate condition from which he then can satisfy S**2 to** establish q. Thus, $\sigma \mathrel{\{\!|} S_1 ; S_2 \mathrel{|\!\}} q$ holds if and only if $\sigma \mathrel{\{\!|} S_1 \mathrel{|\!\}} q'$, where q' is a **set** of states σ' for which $\sigma' \mathrel{\{\!|} S_2 \mathrel{|\!\}} q$ holds.

Weakest Preconditions

For any contract S and any condition q to be established, we define wp.$S.q$ as **the** set of all initial states from which S can be satisfied to establish q:

$$\text{wp}.S.q \;\stackrel{\wedge}{=}\; \{\sigma \mid \sigma \mathrel{\{\!|} S \mathrel{|\!\}} q\}\ .$$

We refer to wp.$S.q$ as the *weakest precondition* for satisfying S to establish q**.**

We can use this definition to give an alternative definition of satisfaction for **se-** quential composition: $\sigma \mathrel{\{\!|} S_1 ; S_2 \mathrel{|\!\}} q$ holds iff $\sigma \mathrel{\{\!|} S_1 \mathrel{|\!\}} (\text{wp}.S_2.q)$. Strictly speak**ing,** this is equivalent to the previous definition only if we assume that if a con**tract** establishes a condition q, then it will also establish any weaker condition q'. **The** *monotonicity property* of weakest preconditions for contracts will be shown to **hold** in Chapter 13.

We can look at wp as a function that assigns to each contract statement S a fu**nc-** tion from predicates to predicates; i.e., wp.$S : \mathcal{P}(\Sigma) \to \mathcal{P}(\Sigma)$, when Σ is **the** state space. Thus, wp.S is a *predicate transformer*. From the definitions of satisfaction above, we can immediately determine wp.S for the statements of our simple language for contracts:

$$
\begin{aligned}
\text{wp.}\langle f\rangle.q &= f^{-1}.q \ , \\
\text{wp.}\{g\}.q &= g \cap q \ , \\
\text{wp.}[g].q &= \neg g \cup q \ , \\
\text{wp.}(S_1 \, ; \, S_2).q &= \text{wp.}S_1.(\text{wp.}S_2.q) \ , \\
\text{wp.}(S_1 \sqcup S_2).q &= \text{wp.}S_1.q \cup \text{wp.}S_2.q \ , \\
\text{wp.}(S_1 \sqcap S_2).q &= \text{wp.}S_1.q \cap \text{wp.}S_2.q \ .
\end{aligned}
$$

Let us check the first equation. We have that

wp.$\langle f\rangle.q$

$=$ {definition of weakest preconditions}

$\{\sigma \mid \sigma \, \{\!\!\{ \, \langle f\rangle \, \}\!\!\} \, q\}$

$=$ {satisfaction of the update statement}

$\{\sigma \mid f.\sigma \in q\}$

$=$ {definition of inverse image}

$f^{-1}.q$

The other equalities are also easily checked. These definitions permit us to compute the weakest precondition for any contract to establish any postcondition.

The satisfaction of contracts is captured very directly by the notion of weakest precondition:

$$\sigma \, \{\!\!\{ \, S \, \}\!\!\} \, q \ \equiv \ \text{wp.}S.q.\sigma \ .$$

There are, however, definite advantages in formalizing the notion of satisfaction in terms of predicate transformers rather that in terms of a ternary relation. This will become obvious as the theory is further developed.

.2   Predicate Transformers

The preceding section justifies studying the mathematical properties of predicate transformers in more detail. The *set of predicate transformers from Σ to Γ*, denoted by $\Sigma \mapsto \Gamma$, is defined by

$$\Sigma \mapsto \Gamma \ \overset{\triangle}{=} \ \mathcal{P}(\Gamma) \to \mathcal{P}(\Sigma) \ . \qquad\qquad \textit{(predicate transformers)}$$

A predicate transformer is thus a function that maps postconditions to preconditions. By using the notation $\Sigma \mapsto \Gamma$, we uniformly treat the first argument (Σ) as the *initial state space* and the second (Γ) as the *final state space* for state transformers, state relations, and predicate transformers.

Predicate Transformer Lattice

We define the *refinement ordering* on predicate transformers as the pointw[e]
extension of the subset ordering on $\mathcal{P}(\Sigma)$: for $S, T \in \Sigma \mapsto \Gamma$, we have

$$S \sqsubseteq T \;\;\hat{=}\;\; (\forall q \in \mathcal{P}(\Gamma) \cdot S.q \subseteq T.q) \; . \quad (\sqsubseteq \textit{for predicate transformer})$$

Hence, $(\Sigma \mapsto \Gamma, \sqsubseteq)$ is again a complete Boolean lattice, by the pointwise exten[sion]
property.

The lattice operations on predicate transformers are pointwise extensions of
corresponding operations on predicates:

$$
\begin{aligned}
\textsf{abort}.q &\;\hat{=}\; \textsf{false} \; , & (\bot \textit{ of predicate transformer}) \\
\textsf{magic}.q &\;\hat{=}\; \textsf{true} \; , & (\top \textit{ of predicate transformer}) \\
(\neg S).q &\;\hat{=}\; \neg S.q \; , & (\neg \textit{ of predicate transformer}) \\
(S \sqcap T).q &\;\hat{=}\; S.q \sqcap T.q \; , & (\sqcap \textit{ of predicate transformer}) \\
(S \sqcup T).q &\;\hat{=}\; S.q \sqcup T.q \; . & (\sqcup \textit{ of predicate transformer})
\end{aligned}
$$

The names for the bottom and top of the predicate transformer lattice, abort [and]
magic, are by now traditional, and we have chosen not to change them. We comm[ent]
on their interpretation below.

Implication and equivalence on predicate transformers can also be defined [by]
pointwise extension:

$$
\begin{aligned}
(S \Rightarrow T).q &\;\hat{=}\; S.q \Rightarrow T.q \; , & (\Rightarrow \textit{ of predicate transformer}) \\
(S \equiv T).q &\;\hat{=}\; S.q \equiv T.q \; . & (\equiv \textit{ of predicate transformer})
\end{aligned}
$$

Thus, these two operations satisfy the usual laws: $(S \Rightarrow T) = (\neg S \sqcup T)$ [and]
$(S \equiv T) = (S \Rightarrow T) \sqcap (T \Rightarrow S)$.

Meet and join are also defined on arbitrary sets of predicate transformers:

$$
\begin{aligned}
(\sqcap i \in I \cdot S_i).q &\;\hat{=}\; (\sqcap i \in I \cdot S_i.q) \; , & (\textit{general}) \\
(\sqcup i \in I \cdot S_i).q &\;\hat{=}\; (\sqcup i \in I \cdot S_i.q) \; . & (\textit{general})
\end{aligned}
$$

Predicate Transformer Category

A *predicate transformer category* has types as objects and predicate transform[er]
as morphisms.

We have that

$$
\begin{aligned}
1 &\;\hat{=}\; \textsf{skip} \; , & (1 \textit{ of predicate transformer}) \\
S ; T &\;\hat{=}\; S \circ T \; . & (; \textit{ of predicate transformer})
\end{aligned}
$$

Composition of predicate transformers $S; T$ is thus *backward* function composition $S \circ T$, while the identity morphism is

$$\text{skip} = (\lambda q \cdot q) .$$

These operations satisfy the category requirements:

$$(S \circ T) \circ U = S \circ (T \circ U) , \qquad\qquad (\circ \textit{ associative})$$
$$\text{skip} \circ S = S \quad \text{and} \quad S \circ \text{skip} = S . \qquad\qquad (\text{skip } \textit{unit})$$

The reader should notice that we use forward composition in state transformer categories and in state relation categories, while composition in predicate transformer categories is backward.

Since the morphisms in a predicate transformer category are functions ordered by pointwise extension and the composition operator is backward function composition, we have the monotonicity property from Section 2.5:

$$S \sqsubseteq S' \;\Rightarrow\; S; T \sqsubseteq S'; T .$$

However, composition is not monotonic in its second argument (this is because predicate transformers are not necessarily monotonic).

The predicate transformer category Ptran_X has the collection of state spaces X as objects and all predicate transformers between two state spaces as its morphisms:

$$\text{Ptran}_X(\Sigma, \Gamma) \;\triangleq\; \Sigma \mapsto \Gamma .$$

We summarize the results about predicate transformers in this category in the following theorem.

Theorem 11.1 Ptran_X *is a left complete Boolean lattice-enriched category.*

As also noted in Section 2.5, we get a proper (both a left and a right) complete lattice-enriched category if we restrict ourselves to monotonic predicate transformers. Monotonic predicate transformers are studied in more detail in Chapter 13.

The same asymmetry between left and right also holds for the distributivity properties of composition. We have distributivity from the right for all lattice operations:

$$
\begin{aligned}
\text{magic}; T &= \text{magic} , \\
\text{abort}; T &= \text{abort} , \\
(\neg S); T &= \neg S; T , \\
(S_1 \sqcap S_2); T &= S_1; T \sqcap S_2; T , \\
(S_1 \sqcup S_2); T &= S_1; T \sqcup S_2; T .
\end{aligned}
$$

The last properties generalize to meets and joins for arbitrary statements; i.e.,

$$
\begin{aligned}
(\sqcap i \in I \cdot S); T &= (\sqcap i \in I \cdot S; T) , \\
(\sqcup i \in I \cdot S); T &= (\sqcup i \in I \cdot S; T) .
\end{aligned}
$$

However, none of the corresponding left distributivity properties hold in gene
(not even if we assume monotonicity).

11.3   Basic Predicate Transformers

Let us now return to the weakest precondition predicate transformers. From the
initions above, we see that the three basic ways of composing contracts – sequen
composition and angelic and demonic choice – all correspond to operations in
lattice-enriched category of predicate transformers.

We can underline this close correspondence between contract statements and pr
icate transformers by introducing specific predicate transformers that directly
respond to weakest preconditions of the basic contract statements. Let us de
the *functional update*, the *assertion*, and the *assumption predicate transformer*
follows:

$$\langle f \rangle.q \; \hat{=} \; f^{-1}.q \; , \qquad\qquad\qquad (functional\ upda$$
$$\{g\}.q \; \hat{=} \; g \cap q \; , \qquad\qquad\qquad\qquad (asserti$$
$$[g].q \; \hat{=} \; \neg g \cup q \; . \qquad\qquad\qquad\qquad (assumptio$$

The definitions of weakest preconditions for basic contract statements then simp
to

$$\mathsf{wp}.\langle f \rangle \; = \; \langle f \rangle \; ,$$
$$\mathsf{wp}.\{g\} \; = \; \{g\} \; ,$$
$$\mathsf{wp}.[g] \; = \; [g] \; .$$

On the left-hand side we have a wp applied to a contract statement; on the right-h
side we have a predicate transformer.

We can express the main constants of the predicate transformer category in te
of the functional update, assertion, and assumption predicate transformers:

$$\mathsf{abort} \; = \; \{false\} \; ,$$
$$\mathsf{skip} \; = \; \langle id \rangle \; = \; \{true\} \; = \; [true] \; ,$$
$$\mathsf{magic} \; = \; [false] \; .$$

In particular, we then have that

$$\mathsf{wp}.\{false\} \; = \; \mathsf{abort} \; ,$$
$$\mathsf{wp}.[false] \; = \; \mathsf{magic} \; ,$$

which shows how to interpret the impossible assertion and the impossible assu
tion. The impossible assertion is the bottom of the predicate transformer lat
while the impossible assumption is the top of this lattice. For the contract that
not change anything, we have

$$\text{wp.skip} \;=\; \text{skip} \;.$$

Any contract statement S defined by the language above can thus be directly expressed as a weakest-precondition predicate transformer. The function wp is really a homomorphism from the syntactic algebra of contract statements to the semantic algebra of predicate transformers. For instance, we have that

$$\text{wp.}(\langle f \rangle \,;\, (\langle h \rangle \,;\, \{\text{false}\} \sqcup \text{skip}) \,;\, \langle k \rangle) \;=\; \langle f \rangle \,;\, (\langle h \rangle \,;\, \text{abort} \sqcup \text{skip}) \,;\, \langle k \rangle \;.$$

Again, on the left-hand side we have the weakest precondition of a contract statement, on the right-hand side a predicate transformer. This permits us to consider contracts directly as predicate transformers. The context will usually tell whether we have a contract statement or a predicate transformer.

The names for the bottom and top of the predicate-transformer lattice are by now traditional. They arise from interpreting predicate transformers as describing the execution of program statements. Then abort is seen as a failure: the computation has to be *aborted* because something went wrong. The execution may have gone into an infinite loop, there may have been a run-time error, or something else bad might have happened. The essential thing is that we lose control of the execution and do not know what happens after an abort. Our interpretation of contracts interprets abort as the assertion that is impossible to satisfy and thus always leads to a contract violation, preventing our agent from satisfying the contract, no matter what condition was supposed to be achieved.

In the program execution interpretation magic is a statement that immediately achieves whatever condition our program was supposed to, as if a *miracle* had occurred. This does not have any direct counterpart in existing programming languages, as this statement is not implementable. However, it serves as a convenient abstraction when manipulating program statements. In this respect, it is similar to the use of imaginary numbers: these simplify calculations even though they strictly speaking do not have any counterpart in reality. In our interpretation of contracts, magic is the assumption that is impossible to satisfy and thus will always discharge our agent from any obligation to follow the contract. Interpreting the statements we have introduced as talking about contracts in general, rather than just about program execution, allows us to give simple and intuitive interpretations to both abort and magic. As we have already shown, program statements can then be seen as a special kind of contract.

Expressions and Assignment Statements

In practice we use expressions with program variables to describe assert and assumption statements. For instance, the assert statement $\{x \geq y + 2\}$ has no effect in a state σ where $x.\sigma \geq y.\sigma + 2$ but leads to a breach of the contract in state where this condition is not satisfied. Using the definition of assert statements, can, e.g., determine that

$$\{x \geq y + 2\}.(x \leq 10) \;=\; (x \geq y + 2 \wedge x \leq 10)$$

because $\{p\}.q = p \cap q$ (written $p \wedge q$ when p and q are Boolean expression For the corresponding assumption, we get

$$[x \geq y + 2].(x \leq 10) \;=\; (x \geq y + 2 \Rightarrow x \leq 10)$$

because $[p].q = (p \Rightarrow q)$.

The *assignment statement* $\langle x := e \rangle$ is a particularly useful functional update. H x is a program variable and e an expression, as usual. By the definition, we have $\langle x := e \rangle.q.\sigma = q((x := e).\sigma)$. This can be further simplified by the substitut lemma for assignments to $q[x := e].\sigma$. This gives us the following important re (usually referred to as the *assignment axiom*, although here it is not an axiom a theorem):

Theorem 11.2 *Let x be an attribute (or a list of attributes), e an expression (or a list of expressio and q a Boolean expression. Then*

$$\text{var } x \vdash \langle x := e \rangle.q = q[x := e] \;.$$

We usually omit the explicit angular brackets for assignment statements when context makes it is clear that an assignment statement rather than an assignme intended.

As an example, we can use this rule to calculate the weakest precondition $x := x + y \,;\, y := y + 1$ establishing condition $x \geq y$. We have that

> var x, y : Nat
> $\vdash ((\langle x := x + y \rangle \,;\, \langle y := y + 1 \rangle).(x \geq y)$
> $= \{$definition of sequential composition$\}$
> $\quad \langle x := x + y \rangle.(\langle y := y + 1 \rangle.(x \geq y))$
> $= \{$assignment rule$\}$
> $\quad \langle x := x + y \rangle.(x \geq y + 1)$
> $= \{$assignment rule$\}$
> $\quad x + y \geq y + 1$
> $= \{$arithmetic$\}$
> $\quad x \geq 1$

This shows how the calculation of weakest preconditions is kept simple using assignment rule.

4 Relational Updates

Let us now look at the angelic update $\{R\}$ and the demonic update $[R]$. Satisfying the angelic update $\{R\}$ in initial state σ to establish q requires that there be a state γ such that $R.\sigma.\gamma$ holds and $\gamma \in q$. Our agent can then satisfy the contract by choosing such a next state γ. If there is no state γ such that $R.\sigma.\gamma$, then the contract is breached.

Satisfying the demonic update $[R]$ in initial state σ to establish q again requires that for every state γ such that $R.\sigma.\gamma$, the condition $\gamma \in q$ must hold. Then no matter how the other agent chooses the next state, condition q will be established. If there is no final state γ such that $R.\sigma.\gamma$ holds, then the other agent has to breach the contract, and our agent is discharged of its obligations. The functional update and the two relational updates are illustrated in Figure 11.1.

The argument above justifies defining predicate transformers corresponding to the two updates: the *angelic update* $\{R\} : \Sigma \mapsto \Gamma$ and the *demonic update* $[R] : \Sigma \mapsto \Gamma$, defined as follows:

$$\{R\}.q.\sigma \;\;\hat{=}\;\; (\exists \gamma \in \Gamma \cdot R.\sigma.\gamma \wedge q.\gamma) \;, \qquad \textit{(angelic update)}$$
$$[R].q.\sigma \;\;\hat{=}\;\; (\forall \gamma \in \Gamma \cdot R.\sigma.\gamma \Rightarrow q.\gamma) \;. \qquad \textit{(demonic update)}$$

Since these predicate transformers capture the behaviors of the update contract statements, we simply define

$$\mathsf{wp}.\{R\} \equiv \{R\} \quad \text{and} \quad \mathsf{wp}.[R] \equiv [R] \;.$$

In set notation the two updates are as follows:

$$\{R\}.q.\sigma \equiv R.\sigma \cap q \neq \emptyset \quad \text{and} \quad [R].q.\sigma \equiv R.\sigma \subseteq q \;.$$

As special cases, we have

$$\{\mathsf{False}\} = \mathsf{abort} \quad \text{and} \quad [\mathsf{False}] = \mathsf{magic} \;.$$

This characterization of abort and magic is more general than the one we can achieve with asserts and guards, because the relation False can go from one state space Σ to a different state space Γ, and hence we can define abort : $\Sigma \mapsto \Gamma$ and magic : $\Sigma \mapsto \Gamma$, whereas with asserts and guards, we can only define abort : $\Sigma \mapsto \Sigma$ and magic : $\Sigma \mapsto \Sigma$ on a single state space Σ.

Special cases of the relational updates are

$$\mathsf{choose} \;\;\hat{=}\;\; \{\mathsf{True}\} \;, \qquad \textit{(arbitrary choice)}$$
$$\mathsf{chaos} \;\;\hat{=}\;\; [\mathsf{True}] \;. \qquad \textit{(chaotic choice)}$$

The first stands for an arbitrary angelic choice and the second for an arbitrary demonic choice.

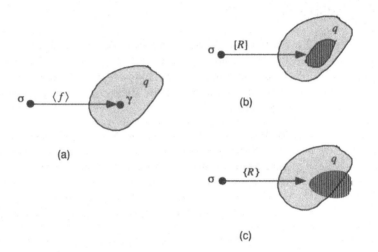

FIGURE 11.1. (a) Functional update, (b) demonic update, (c) angelic update

Commutativity of Updates with Test and Map

The injection of predicates (or functions) into relations, and the subsequent construction of demonic and angelic updates from these commutes with forming guards and asserts (or functional updates) directly; i.e.,

$$\{ \, |p| \, \} \;=\; \{p\} \,, \qquad [\, |p| \,] \;=\; [p] \,,$$
$$\{ \, |f| \, \} \;=\; \langle f \rangle \,, \qquad [\, |f| \,] \;=\; \langle f \rangle \,.$$

The proofs of these properties are left as an exercise (Exercise 11.3).

Relational Assignment Statements

A *demonic assignment statement* is a demonic update $[R]$, where R is a relation. It is thus a statement of the form $[(x := x' \mid b)]$. We omit the inner parentheses, writing the demonic assignment as $[x := x' \mid b]$. Similarly, an *angelic assignment statement* is a angelic update $\{R\}$, where R is a relational assignment. Again the inner parentheses are usually omitted, so we write an angelic assignment $\{x := x' \mid b\}$. This is generalized to simultaneous updates of two or more program variables in the obvious way.

For instance, the statement

$$\{x, e := x', e' \mid x' \ge 0 \wedge e' > 0\} \,;$$
$$[x := y \mid -e \le x - y^2 \le e]$$

first updates both the x and e components of the state (angelically) so that new value of x is nonnegative and the new value of e is positive. After this

x component is changed so that the square of its new value differs by less than the value of e from its old value.

We can also derive substitution rules for the relational assignment statements. These rules make use of the pointwise extension of the existential and universal quantifiers that we have defined above, in connection with meets and joins over arbitrary sets of predicates.

Theorem 11.3 *Assume that x is a list of program variables and b and q are Boolean expressions in which x' does not occur free in q. Then*

(a) var $x \vdash \{x := x' \mid b\}.q = (\exists x' \cdot b \wedge q[x := x'])$.

(b) var $x \vdash [x := x' \mid b].q = (\forall x' \cdot b \Rightarrow q[x := x'])$.

Proof We prove the first case here; the second one is established by analogous reasoning.

$$\{x := x' \mid b\}.q.\sigma$$
$\equiv$ {definition of angelic update}
$$(\exists \gamma \cdot (x := x' \mid b).\sigma.\gamma \wedge q.\gamma)$$
$\equiv$ {characterization of relational assignment}
$$(\exists \gamma \cdot (\exists x' \cdot \gamma = \text{set}.x.x'.\sigma \wedge b.\sigma) \wedge q.\gamma)$$
$\equiv$ {properties of existential quantification}
$$(\exists \gamma\, x' \cdot \gamma = \text{set}.x.x'.\sigma \wedge b.\sigma \wedge q.\gamma)$$
$\equiv$ {one-point rule}
$$(\exists x' \cdot b.\sigma \wedge q.(\text{set}.x.x'.\sigma))$$
$\equiv$ {substitution property}
$$(\exists x' \cdot b.\sigma \wedge q[x := x'].\sigma)$$
$\equiv$ {pointwise extension}
$$(\exists x' \cdot b \wedge q[x := x']).\sigma$$

□

From now on, we will omit the assumption var x from theorems and rules unless there is some special reason to state it.

Consider as an example the demonic assignment statement $[x := x' \mid x' > x + y]$. We have by the above rule that

$$[x := x' \mid x' > x + y].(x > y)$$
$=$ {rule for demonic assignment}
$$(\forall x' \cdot x' > x + y \Rightarrow x' > y)$$

= {reduction, arithmetic}

$x \geq 0$

Note that the result of the simplification is a Boolean expression.

11.5 Duality

The *dual* $S^\circ : \Sigma \mapsto \Gamma$ of a predicate transformer $S : \Sigma \mapsto \Gamma$ is defined by

$$S^\circ.q \;\; \hat{=} \;\; \neg\, S.(\neg q) \;. \qquad\qquad (dual\ predicate\ transform$$

A consequence of the definition is that $(S^\circ)^\circ = S$, so dualization is an involu
(Exercise 11.5).

Theorem 11.4 *The following dualities hold between predicate transformers:*

$$\begin{array}{llll}
\langle f \rangle^\circ &=& \langle f \rangle \;, & \qquad (S_1 ; S_2)^\circ &=& S_1^\circ ; S_2^\circ \;, \\
\{p\}^\circ &=& [p] \;, & \qquad (\sqcup i \in I \cdot S_i)^\circ &=& (\sqcap i \in I \cdot S_i^\circ) \;, \\
\{R\}^\circ &=& [R] \;.
\end{array}$$

Proof For assertions, we have

$\quad \{p\}^\circ.q$

$= $ {definitions of assert and duals}

$\quad \neg\,(p \cap \neg q)$

$= $ {lattice properties}

$\quad \neg p \cup q$

$= $ {definition of guard}

$\quad [p].q$

The proofs of the other parts are similar (Exercise 11.6). □

Thus, the basic operations for constructing predicate transformers come in
each one with its dual. Functional update and sequential composition are their
duals. The characterization of the constant predicate transformers also implies

$\quad$ magic$^\circ$ = abort ,$\qquad\qquad$ skip$^\circ$ = skip .

Since $(S^\circ)^\circ = S$, all the duality properties listed above can be read in rev
Thus, for example, $[p]^\circ = \{p\}$ and abort$^\circ$ = magic.

.6 Preconditions and Guards

Let $S : \Sigma \mapsto \Gamma$ be a predicate transformer. Let us define the following operations in $(\Sigma \mapsto \Gamma) \to \mathcal{P}(\Sigma)$:

$$\mathsf{m}.S \;\stackrel{\wedge}{=}\; (\cap q : \mathcal{P}(\Gamma) \cdot S.q) , \qquad \textit{(miracle precondition)}$$
$$\mathsf{t}.S \;\stackrel{\wedge}{=}\; (\cup q : \mathcal{P}(\Gamma) \cdot S.q) . \qquad \textit{(abortion guard)}$$

Thus, $\mathsf{m}.S$ holds in an initial state if S is guaranteed to establish every postcondition in this state, while $\mathsf{t}.S$ holds in an initial state if S is guaranteed to establish some postcondition.

In addition, we introduce special notation for the negations of these operations as well.

$$\mathsf{a}.S \;\stackrel{\wedge}{=}\; \neg \mathsf{t}.S , \qquad \textit{(abortion precondition)}$$
$$\mathsf{g}.S \;\stackrel{\wedge}{=}\; \neg \mathsf{m}.S . \qquad \textit{(miracle guard)}$$

Intuitively, the abortion precondition characterizes those initial states in which our agent cannot avoid breaching the contract (abortion will occur). The abortion guard is the complement of this and characterizes those initial states in which a breach can be avoided (it *guards against* abortion). Similarly, the miracle precondition characterizes those initial states in which our agent can choose to discharge the obligations of the contract (a miracle can occur), while a miracle guard characterizes the complement of this, i.e., the initial states in which this is not possible (it guards against miracles). In practice, the abortion guard $\mathsf{t}.S$ and the miracle guard $\mathsf{g}.S$ are more useful than the other two.

It is easily seen that $\mathsf{m}.S \subseteq \mathsf{t}.S$. Hence, the abortion and the miracle guards partition the initial state space into three disjoint sets:

(i) The states in $\mathsf{m}.S$ from which any postcondition can be established. These are the initial states in which our agent can choose to be discharged from its obligations to satisfy the contract.

(ii) The states in $\mathsf{a}.S$ from which no postcondition can be established. These are the states in which our agent cannot avoid breaching the contract.

(iii) The states in $\mathsf{t}.S \cap \mathsf{g}.S$ from which some postconditions can be established and some cannot. These are the states in which a discharge of obligation is impossible for our agent, and a breach of contract can be avoided, so some postcondition will be established.

This trichotomy turns out to be a fundamental aspect of the predicate transformer approach to program semantics, and we will meet it again and again in different disguises in the subsequent discussion (Figure 11.2).

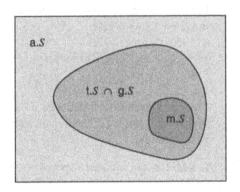

FIGURE 11.2. Partitioning of state space

11.7   Summary and Discussion

This chapter has introduced the fundamental notion for modeling program sta
ments in higher-order logic, the predicate transformer. We have shown that
predicate transformers form a special kind of lattice-enriched category, wh
determines the basic algebraic properties of predicate transformers.

Predicate transformers were introduced by Dijkstra [52, 53] to give a seman
to a language with nondeterminism. They were used to represent a variety of
mantic functions for programs: the most commonly used are weakest preconditi
weakest liberal precondition, and strongest postcondition. An older overview
the semantic treatment of predicate transformers can be found in the work of
Bakker [36]. Dijkstra and Scholten [54] give a treatment of predicate transform
with an attempt to derive their mathematical and logical treatment directly fr
first principles. Most semantic treatments of predicate transformers have conc
trated on more restricted classes, in the style of traditional denotational seman
[119, 130]. The fact that the set of all predicate transformers forms a compl
Boolean lattice was first explicitly used by Morris [108], Hesselink [79], and B
and von Wright [26].

In addition to introducing the algebraic structure of predicate transformers,
also identified a particular set of basic predicate transformers. These form
main vehicle for subsequent investigations on how to use predicate transform
to model program constructs and programming. Dijkstra's original language
guarded commands [52, 53] identified skip, abort, assignments (generalized h
to arbitrary functional updates), and sequential composition as basic constru
and additionally introduced a (finitely demonic) nondeterministic conditional at
loop construct. Back [6] introduced a nondeterministic assignment (modeled h

as the demonic update), and de Bakker [36] used a meet (choice) operation on predicate transformers. Miracles (guard and magic) were added by Morgan [104], Morris [108], and Nelson [113] for basic sequential statements, and by Back [15] to model enabledness of statements executed in a parallel context. Angelic nondeterminism was added (as an angelic assignment) by Back [13] and by Gardiner and Morgan [59] (as a "conjunction operation"). The full collection of basic predicate transformers as described here were first identified by Back and von Wright [25].

Duality was used in reasoning about predicate transformers already by Pedro Guerreiro in [71]. The specification language of Back and von Wright [26, 27] is based on the fundamental dualities between demonic and angelic nondeterminism and between nontermination and miracles. Dijkstra and Scholten [54] introduce a notion of converse predicate transformers that is closely related to duals.

The original formalization of the refinement calculus [7] was based on infinitary logic [95, 127], in order to permit a simple characterization of iteration. First-order predicate calculus is not very suitable as a basis for the refinement calculus, because the very definition of refinement involves a quantification over functions (all possible postconditions), which cannot be expressed directly in the syntax of first-order logic. Higher-order logic permits quantification over functions, so it is a good framework for the formalization of refinement calculus. The first systematic investigation of higher-order logic as a basis for the refinement calculus was undertaken by Back and von Wright [30].

The notion of angelic nondeterminism goes back to the theory of nondeterministic automata and the nondeterministic programs of Robert Floyd [56]. Angelic versions of weakest preconditions were investigated by Dean Jacobs and Gries [92], but this work did not include angelically nondeterministic statements. Manfred Broy [42] discusses the use of demonic and angelic nondeterminism, in particular with respect to concurrency. The basic duality between angelic and demonic statements was identified and studied in detail by Back and von Wright [25, 27, 29]. Some applications of angelic nondeterminism are shown by Nigel Ward and Ian Hayes [139] based on this work. Angelic nondeterminism is also used in a theory of program inversion by von Wright [142]. A binary join operator, but interpreted as parallel independent execution, was studied by Eike Best [39].

Category-theoretic studies of program refinement have been pioneered by Claire Martin, David Nauman, Paul Gardiner, and Oege de Moer [57, 58, 98, 112]. It is not our intention to go very deep into category theory. We mainly use it as a framework for unifying the treatment of the different domains of discourse in the refinement calculus.

The assignment rule derived here is exactly the definition of the weakest-precondition semantics for assignments of Dijkstra [53], which in turn is based on the assignment axiom of Hoare [84]. Thus we can recover Dijkstra's syntactic characterization of weakest preconditions as theorems in our more general framework.

11.8 Exercises

11.1 Show that $\{p\} \sqsubseteq [p]$ holds for an arbitrary predicate p.

11.2 Relation R is said to be *total* if $(\forall \sigma \cdot \exists y \cdot R.\sigma.y)$ holds. Show that $[R] \sqsubseteq$ holds if and only if the relation R is total.

11.3 Prove the following properties of the test and map relations for an arbitrary predicate p and arbitrary function f:

$$\{|p|\} = \{p\} , \qquad\qquad [|p|] = [p] ,$$
$$\{|f|\} = \langle f \rangle , \qquad\qquad [|f|] = \langle f \rangle .$$

11.4 Prove the following:

$$\text{chaos} \sqsubseteq \text{skip} , \qquad\qquad \text{skip} \sqsubseteq \text{choose} .$$

Furthermore, show that equality holds if and only if the state space is a single

11.5 Show that $(S^\circ)^\circ = S$ holds for an arbitrary predicate transformer S.

11.6 Complete the proof of Theorem 11.4.

11.7 Use the assignment rules to compute the following:

(a) $(x, y := x + z, y - z).(x + y = w)$.

(b) $(x, y := x + z, y - z).(x = y)$.

11.8 Complete the proof of Theorem 11.3.

2

The Refinement Calculus Hierarchy

The predicate transformers that we use to model contracts are constructed from other predicate transformers or from simpler elements, like state predicates, state transformers, or state relations. The predicate transformer constructors can thus be seen as functions that map elements in one domain to the domain itself or to another domain. The basic question that we investigate in this chapter is to what extent the lattice and category structure is preserved by these constructors, i.e., to what extent the constructors are monotonic and homomorphic.

The use of monotonicity and homomorphism is particularly relevant in programming, because we may view programs as different kinds of entities, depending on what features we need. For instance, a straight-line program is best viewed as just a state transformer, and its properties are easiest to analyze in this simple framework. However, if a straight-line program occurs as a component of a larger program, with relational assignments, then we need to use state relations as our program model. In this case, we can embed the straight-line program f into the relational program as a mapping $|f|$. Or if we need the even more powerful framework of contracts and predicate transformers, then we can embed the straight-line program as an update statement $\langle f \rangle$ in a larger predicate transformer context.

1   State Categories

We have shown earlier that state transformers, state relations, and predicate transformers form categories of a certain kind, where the objects are state spaces (or types) and the morphisms are either functions, relations, or predicate transformers between the state spaces. In general, we will refer to these categories as *st* *categories*.

Essentially, all the state categories are order-enriched categories. Relations form complete Boolean lattice-enriched category, while predicate transformers form left complete Boolean lattice-enriched category. State transformers form a discr order-enriched category (we assume only the discrete ordering for state spaces, $f \sqsubseteq g \equiv f = g$).

State Predicate Category

We can also model predicates as categories with types as objects. A *state predic category* has state spaces as objects and predicates as morphisms. Each predic p in $\mathcal{P}(\Sigma)$ is a morphism with source Σ and target Σ. There are no morphis between two different state spaces. The composition operator is meet ($\cap$), and identity on Σ is the predicate true:

$$1 \;\hat{=}\; \text{true} \,, \qquad\qquad\qquad (1 \text{ for state predicate}$$
$$p \,;q \;\hat{=}\; p \cap q \,. \qquad\qquad\qquad (; \text{ for state predicate}$$

The reader may verify that the defining properties for a category are satisf (Exercise 12.6):

$$p \cap (q \cap r) = (p \cap q) \cap r \,, \qquad\qquad (\cap \text{ associativ}$$
$$\text{true} \cap p = p \quad\text{and}\quad p \cap \text{true} = p \,. \qquad\qquad (\text{true un}$$

To avoid confusion, we consistently use $\cap$ as the symbol for the composit operator on predicates. Similarly, we always write true rather than 1 for the un

It is easy to see that composition is monotonic with respect to the predicate orderi

$$p \subseteq p' \wedge q \subseteq q' \;\Rightarrow\; p \cap q \subseteq p' \cap q' \,. \qquad\qquad (\cap \text{ monoton}$$

We let Pred_X denote the state predicate category with objects X and all predic on Σ as morphisms $\text{Pred}_X(\Sigma, \Sigma)$.

Theorem 12.1 Pred_X *is a complete atomic Boolean lattice-enriched category.*

Composition is easily seen to distribute over bottom, meet, and join in this catege both from the left and from the right. For example, distribution from the left o bottom means that $p \cap \text{false} = \text{false}$ (to see that this is a distributivity prope recall that false is the empty join).

Since composition is also a lattice operation, we will not make much direct us the fact that Pred is a category.

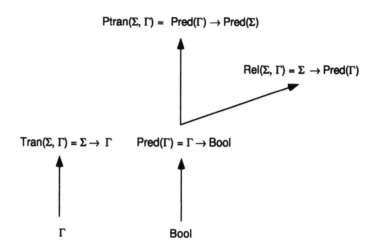

FIGURE 12.1. Pointwise extended poset and lattice categories

The refinement calculus hierarchy

All the basic entities of the refinement calculus are built by (iterated) pointwise extension from the lattice of truth values Bool and an arbitrary collection X of *state spaces* $\Sigma, \Gamma, \Delta, \ldots$ The latter can be any collection of types, as we have noted earlier. For imperative programs, we would usually choose types that define states with attributes as state spaces. The pointwise extension hierarchy of categories that we have constructed is shown pictorially in Figure 12.1.

All the basic domains of the refinement calculus are order-enriched categories, in most cases different kinds of lattice-enriched categories. Thus they have many properties in common, which simplifies reasoning in these domains. Rather than having one set of inference rules for predicates, one for state transformers, one for relations, and one for predicate transformers, we have a single collection of inference rules based on the general lattice and categorical properties of order-enriched categories. Classifying each of the basic domains as forming a specific kind of order-enriched category, as we have done above, determines what inference rules are available for reasoning about entities in this particular domain.

The basic categories and the operations that link them are shown in Figure 12.2. We refer to this collection of domains and operations as the *refinement calculus hierarchy*. It provides the basic framework within which we reason about properties of programs, specifications, and contracts in general.

Due to pointwise extension, the basic domains of the refinement calculus hierarchy share the same algebraic structure. Furthermore, a term at one level of the hierarchy can be expressed in terms of elements at a lower level of the hierarchy by using a homomorphism property or the definition of pointwise extension directly. This

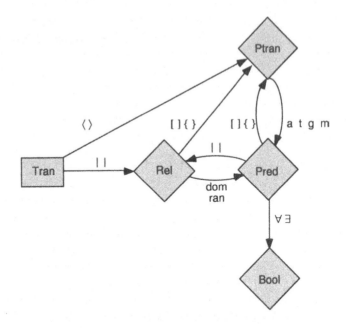

FIGURE 12.2. Operations in the refinement calculus hierarchy

means that we can often choose the level in the refinement calculus hierarch
which to carry out an argument. It is usually preferable to argue at as high a l
as possible. The notation is then more concise, and the proof is more algeb
and shows the structure of the argument more clearly. However, if an argun
at one level becomes too involved, we can reduce the level by writing out
pointwise extension explicitly. This movement between levels in the refiner
calculus hierarchy is typical of arguments in the calculus.

12.2 Homomorphisms

We will here be particularly interested in the monotonicity and homomorp
properties of predicate transformer constructors. We are interested in quest
such as whether the structure of predicates is preserved by the guard and a
constructors, and whether the structure of functions and relations is prese
by the updates. Knowing the basic algebraic properties of the basic constru
allows us to easily determine the algebraic properties of program statements
are defined in terms of these.

Sequential Composition

All the basic predicate transformers, considered as mappings from elements of other domains to predicate transformers, preserve sequential composition and identities. Thus they are homomorphisms. Duality is also a homomorphism on predicate transformers.

Theorem 12.2   *The following homomorphism properties hold for the basic predicate transformers:*

$$
\begin{array}{llll}
\text{(a)} & \{p \cap q\} = \{p\} ; \{q\} , & \{\text{true}\} = \text{skip} , \\
\text{(b)} & [p \cap q] = [p] ; [q] , & [\text{true}] = \text{skip} , \\
\text{(c)} & \langle f ; g \rangle = \langle f \rangle ; \langle g \rangle , & \langle \text{id} \rangle = \text{skip} , \\
\text{(d)} & \{P ; Q\} = \{P\} ; \{Q\} , & \{\text{Id}\} = \text{skip} , \\
\text{(e)} & [P ; Q] = [P] ; [Q] , & [\text{Id}] = \text{skip} , \\
\text{(f)} & (S_1 ; S_2)^\circ = S_1^\circ ; S_2^\circ , & \text{skip}^\circ = \text{skip} .
\end{array}
$$

Proof The proofs are straightforward. For example, we have

$$\{p \cap q\}.r$$
$= \{\text{definition}\}$
$$p \cap q \cap r$$
$= \{\text{definition of assert}\}$
$$\{p\}.(q \cap r)$$
$= \{\text{definition of assert}\}$
$$\{p\}.(\{q\}.r)$$
$= \{\text{definition of sequential composition}\}$
$$(\{p\} ; \{q\}).r$$

□

The homomorphism properties for sequential composition and identity are summarized in Table 12.1.

Guards and Asserts

For asserts and guards we have the following lattice homomorphism properties, in addition to the functor properties listed above.

Theorem 12.3   *The assert and guard constructors satisfy the following properties:*

(a) $p \subseteq q \equiv \{p\} \sqsubseteq \{q\}$,
       $p \subseteq q \equiv [p] \sqsupseteq [q]$;
(b) $\{false\} = abort$,
       $[false] = magic$;
(c) $\{\sqcup i \in I \cdot p_i\} = (\sqcup i \in I \cdot \{p_i\})$,
       $[\sqcup i \in I \cdot p_i] = (\sqcap i \in I \cdot [p_i])$;
(d) $\{\sqcap i \in I \cdot p_i\} = (\sqcap i \in I \cdot \{p_i\})$,   *when* $I \neq \emptyset$,
       $[\sqcap i \in I \cdot p_i] = (\sqcup i \in I \cdot [p_i])$,   *when* $I \neq \emptyset$.

Proof The proofs are straightforward. $\square$

The assert constructor $(\lambda p \cdot \{p\}) : \mathcal{P}(\Sigma) \to (\Sigma \mapsto \Sigma)$ is thus monotonic, it preserves bottom, positive meets, and universal joins. The guard constructor $(\lambda p \cdot [p]) : \mathcal{P}(\Sigma) \to (\Sigma \mapsto \Sigma)$, being the dual of assert, is antimonotonic, preserves bottom, positive meets, and universal joins onto the dual lattice $(\Sigma \mapsto \Sigma)^\circ$.

In fact, the equivalences in Theorem 12.3 show that the assert constructor *homomorphically embeds* the predicates $\mathcal{P}(\Sigma)$ in $\Sigma \mapsto \Sigma$. This means that reasoning about asserts can be reduced to reasoning about predicates. Similarly, the guard constructor homomorphically embeds the predicates into the dual of the predicate transformer lattice.

Updates

We have the following results for the homomorphic properties of functional relational updates.

is	$\sqsubseteq$	$\perp$	$\top$	$\sqcap$	$\sqcup$	$\neg$	1	;
$(\lambda p \cdot \{p\})$	yes	yes	no	yes [1]	yes	no	yes	yes
$(\lambda p \cdot [p])$	yes$^\circ$	yes$^\circ$	no	yes$^{\circ 1}$	yes$^\circ$	no	yes	yes
$(\lambda f \cdot \langle f \rangle)$	yes	-	-	-	-	-	yes	yes
$(\lambda R \cdot \{R\})$	yes	yes	no	no	yes	no	yes	yes
$(\lambda R \cdot [R])$	yes$^\circ$	yes$^\circ$	no	no	yes$^\circ$	no	yes	yes

[1] when the meet is taken over nonempty sets

TABLE 12.1. Homomorphic properties of basic predicate transformers

heorem 12.4 *The update constructs satisfy the following lattice-theoretic properties:*

(a) $\quad f = g \;\equiv\; \langle f \rangle = \langle g \rangle$;

(b) $\quad P \subseteq Q \;\equiv\; \{P\} \sqsubseteq \{Q\}$,

$\qquad\quad P \subseteq Q \;\equiv\; [P] \sqsupseteq [Q]$;

(c) $\quad \{False\} \;=\; abort$,

$\qquad\quad [False] \;=\; magic$;

(d) $\{\sqcup i \in I \cdot R_i\} \;=\; (\sqcup i \in I \cdot \{R_i\})$,

$\quad [\sqcup i \in I \cdot R_i] \;=\; (\sqcap i \in I \cdot [R_i])$.

Proof The proofs are again straightforward. □

The angelic update construction $(\lambda R \cdot \{R\}) : \mathsf{Rel}(\Sigma, \Gamma) \to (\Sigma \mapsto \Gamma)$ is thus monotonic, and it preserves bottom and universal joins. Dually, the demonic update construction $(\lambda R \cdot [R]) : \mathsf{Rel}(\Sigma, \Gamma) \to (\Sigma \mapsto \Gamma)$ is antimonotonic, and it preserves bottom and universal joins onto the dual lattice $(\Sigma \mapsto \Gamma)^\circ$. These properties are also listed in Table 12.1. Note further that the function space $\mathsf{Tran}(\Sigma, \Gamma)$ is homomorphically embedded in $\Sigma \mapsto \Gamma$ through the functional update constructor. Similarly, angelic update embeds $\mathsf{Rel}(\Sigma, \Gamma)$ into $\Sigma \mapsto \Gamma$, and demonic update embeds $\mathsf{Rel}(\Sigma, \Gamma)$ into the dual of $\Sigma \mapsto \Gamma$.

Compound Predicate Transformers

The monotonicity and homomorphism properties of compound predicate transformers follow directly from the general lattice and category properties, e.g.,

$$(S_1 \sqcap S_2) ; T \;=\; S_1 ; T \sqcap S_2 ; T$$

We repeat these properties in Table 12.2 for reference, together with the properties for the dualization construct.

Preconditions and Guards of Statements

We finally consider the projection of predicate transformers onto predicates by the precondition and guard constructors, and to what extent these functions preserve the structure of predicate transformers.

is	$\sqsubseteq$	$\perp$	$\top$	$\sqcap$	$\sqcup$	$\neg$	1	;
$(\lambda S \cdot S ; T)$	yes	yes	yes	yes	yes	yes	no	no
$(\lambda S \cdot S \sqcap T)$	yes	yes	no	yes	yes	no	no	no
$(\lambda S \cdot S \sqcup T)$	yes	no	yes	yes	yes	no	no	no
$(\lambda S \cdot \neg S)$	yes°	yes°	yes°	yes°	yes°	yes	no	no
$(\lambda S \cdot S^\circ)$	yes°	yes°	yes°	yes°	yes°	yes	yes	yes

TABLE 12.2. Homomorphic properties of compound predicate transformers

Theorem 12.5   *Let S and T be predicate transformers. Then the following properties hold.*

(a) $$S \sqsubseteq T \implies \text{m}.S \subseteq \text{m}.T \ ,$$
$$S \sqsubseteq T \implies \text{t}.S \subseteq \text{t}.T \ ;$$

(b) $$\text{m.abort} = \text{false} \ ,$$
$$\text{t.abort} = \text{false} \ ;$$

(c) $$\text{m.magic} = \text{true} \ ,$$
$$\text{t.magic} = \text{true} \ ;$$

(d) $$\text{m}.(\sqcap i \in I \cdot S_i) = (\cap i \in I \cdot \text{m}.S_i) \ ,$$
$$\text{t}.(\sqcup i \in I \cdot S_i) = (\cup i \in I \cdot \text{t}.S_i) \ .$$

Proof The proofs are straightforward. □

Thus, the miracle precondition constructor $\text{m} : (\Sigma \mapsto \Gamma) \to \mathcal{P}(\Sigma)$ is monotonic and it preserves bottom, top, and universal meets. The abortion guard construct $\text{t}(\Sigma \mapsto \Gamma) \to \mathcal{P}(\Sigma)$ is also monotonic and it preserves bottom, top, and universal joins. These properties are listed in Table 12.3. We also show their corresponding properties for the two other domain constructors, $\text{g}.S$ and $\text{a}.S$.

Example

As an example of using homomorphisms in proofs, we show that the property $\langle f \rangle ; [f^{-1}] \sqsubseteq \text{skip}$ holds for an arbitrary state transformer f:

$$\langle f \rangle ; [f^{-1}]$$
= {properties of mapping relation construct}
$$[\, |f| \,] ; [f^{-1}]$$
= {homomorphism}
$$[\, |f| ; f^{-1} \,]$$
$\sqsubseteq$ {$|\text{dom}.R| \subseteq R ; R^{-1}$ by Exercise 9.7}
$$[\, |\text{dom}.|f|| \,]$$
= {all functions are total}
$$[\, |\text{true}| \,]$$

is	$\sqsubseteq$	$\perp$	$\top$	$\sqcap$	$\sqcup$	$\neg$
$(\lambda S \cdot \text{m}.S)$	yes	yes	yes	no	yes	no
$(\lambda S \cdot \text{t}.S)$	yes	yes	yes	yes	no	no
$(\lambda S \cdot \text{a}.S)$	yes°	yes°	yes°	no	yes°	no
$(\lambda S \cdot \text{g}.S)$	yes°	yes°	yes°	yes°	no	no

TABLE 12.3. Homomorphic properties of preconditions and guards

$$= \{|\text{true}| = \text{Id, demonic update is functor}\}$$
skip

Note how the derivation uses homomorphism properties to move between different levels in the refinement calculus hierarchy. A similar derivation proves the dual property skip $\sqsubseteq \{f^{-1}\}$; $\langle f \rangle$ (Exercise 12.5).

.3 Summary and Discussion

We have here identified the basic algebraic structure that underlies the refinement calculus: the refinement calculus hierarchy. This structure is formed by the state categories, all constructed by pointwise extensions from the state spaces and the truth-value lattice. All state categories share the same basic algebraic structure of order-enriched categories, in most cases combining a lattice with a category structure. It forms a rich *(many-sorted) algebra*, where refinement arguments can be carried out on many levels in the hierarchy. The refinement calculus hierarchy and the fundamental role that pointwise extension plays in it were identified in [26].

We have looked here at the operations within this structure and in particular studied to what extent these operations preserve the lattice and category structures of their domains. Homomorphic properties of predicate transformers have, to our knowledge, not been investigated in this way systematically before, although many of the homomorphism properties that we have listed above are well known from the literature. Algebraic collections of laws for programs in a relational setting have been given by Hoare et al. in [90]. Hesselink uses algebraic properties to define his notion of command algebras, for which positive meet-homomorphic predicate transformers provide models [80]. The homomorphism properties are important in practical reasoning, because they form the main method by which an argument on one level of the refinement calculus hierarchy can be reduced to a simpler argument on another (in most cases lower) level of the hierarchy.

Another important aspect of the refinement calculus hierarchy that we have identified above is that it clearly demonstrates the different semantic models for programming languages that are available. Methods for program derivations based on these different models (partial functions, relations, and predicate transformers) need not be seen as competing but rather as complementary. A theory of functional programming is in fact embedded as a subtheory in the theory of predicate transformers. Similarly, relational programming and the denotational semantics of deterministic programs form subtheories of the predicate transformer theory. The homomorphism properties show how results in one theory can be carried over to another theory. It also shows that mixed program derivations are quite feasible. For instance, a functional program derivation might well start with a relational or

(demonically) nondeterministic program statement. This aspect will become e
clearer later on, when we study iteration and recursion, and when we show how
relate different semantics of programming languages.

The tabular representation of homomorphisms that we introduced in this chap
is expanded with new operations later on, and also with new operations that
may wish to be preserved by homomorphisms. We are in fact building one la
table describing the homomorphism properties of useful predicate transform
constructors. This table will be revealed piece by piece as we go along, whene
a new constructor is introduced. The whole table is given in Appendix B.

12.4   Exercises

12.1   Use suitable rules to simplify the following in a detailed derivation:

(a) $\langle x := x + y \rangle \,;\, \langle y := x - y \rangle$.

(b) $\langle x := x + 1 \rangle \,;\, [x := x' \mid x < x' < x + 3]$.

12.2   Prove the following parts of Theorem 12.2:

$$\{P \,;\, Q\} = \{P\} \,;\, \{Q\} \qquad \text{and} \qquad [P \,;\, Q] = [P] \,;\, [Q]$$

for arbitrary relations P and Q.

12.3   Prove the following homomorphism properties over relations:

$$\{P \cup Q\} = \{P\} \sqcup \{Q\} \qquad \text{and} \qquad [P \cup Q] = [P] \sqcap [Q] \,.$$

12.4   Give an example of predicate transformers S, T, and U such that $S \sqsubseteq T$
$U \,;\, S \not\sqsubseteq U \,;\, T$.

12.5   Use homomorphism properties to prove the following for an arbitrary state tra
former f:

$$\mathsf{skip} \sqsubseteq \{f^{-1}\} \,;\, \langle f \rangle \,.$$

12.6   Show that Pred is a category, with $\cap$ as the composition operator.

12.7   Prove that composition is monotonic with respect to the ordering in the categ
of state predicates and in the category of state relations.

12.8   Show that the following homomorphism properties hold for arbitrary state pr
cates p and q:

$$\begin{aligned}
|p| \subseteq |q| &\equiv p \subseteq q \,, & |p| \,;\, |q| &= |p \cap q| \,, \\
|p| \cap |q| &= |p \cap q| \,, & |p| \cup |q| &= |p \cup q| \,.
\end{aligned}$$

tatements

In this chapter we show that the basic predicate transformers that we have introduced to model contracts (asserts, guards, functional updates, demonic and angelic updates) are all monotonic. In addition, composition, meet, and join preserve monotonicity. Conversely, any monotonic predicate transformer can be described in terms of these constructs, in a sense to be made more precise below. In fact, it is possible to write any monotonic predicate transformer in a normal form.

There are also other reasons for considering the monotonic predicate transformers in more detail. By restricting our attention to monotonic predicate transformers, we get that sequential composition is monotonic in both arguments. This means that we have a complete lattice-enriched category. Without monotonicity, we have only a left Boolean lattice-enriched category. Although we now lose the Boolean lattice property, we gain a simpler category structure.

1   Subtyping, Sublattices and Subcategories

We are interested in the sublattice of monotonic predicate transformers. Before we can study this particular sublattice in more detail, we need to be more precise about the terminology and define the notions of subtypes, subposets, sublattices, and subcategories generally.

Subtyping

We have until now assumed that a poset is a pair $(\Sigma, \sqsubseteq)$, where Σ is a type and $\sqsubseteq: \Sigma \to \Sigma \to$ Bool is a relation on Σ. In practice, this is too restrictive; we also

need to consider posets $(A, \sqsubseteq_A)$, where A is a subset of Σ. In set theory, we wo
then choose $\sqsubseteq_A$ to be the restriction of $\sqsubseteq$ to A, so that $\sqsubseteq_A \subseteq A \times A$. In higher-or
logic, we would like to define $\sqsubseteq_A: A \rightarrow A \rightarrow$ Bool. This is not, however, possil
because A is not a type, except when $A = \Sigma$.

Instead, we choose to *relativize* the notions needed for posets and lattices. We
that the relation $\sqsubseteq: \Sigma \rightarrow \Sigma \rightarrow$ Bool is *reflexive on* A if $a \sqsubseteq a$ holds for ev
$a \in A$, that it is *transitive on* A if $a \sqsubseteq b \wedge b \sqsubseteq c \Rightarrow a \sqsubseteq c$ for any $a, b, c \in$
and so on. In fact, the definitions that we have given for posets and lattice:
the introductory chapter are already relativized, because we were careful in e
definition to point out that the requirement expressed need hold only for eleme
in the set A. Thus, we can talk about the bottom of A, the top of A, the meet ir
the join in A, the negation in A, and so on. We say that $(A, \sqsubseteq)$ is a poset if $\sqsubseteq$
reflexive, transitive, and antisymmetric on A. The lattice definitions are relativi
in a similar way.

We also have to relativize the notion of functions from one poset to another.
$(A, \sqsubseteq_1)$ and $(B, \sqsubseteq_2)$ be two posets, where $A \subseteq \Sigma$, $B \subseteq \Gamma$, $\sqsubseteq_1: \Sigma \rightarrow \Sigma \rightarrow B$
and $\sqsubseteq_2: \Gamma \rightarrow \Gamma \rightarrow$ Bool. The function $f : \Sigma \rightarrow \Gamma$ is said to be *monotonic o*
if $a \sqsubseteq_1 a' \Rightarrow f.a \sqsubseteq_2 f.a'$ holds for any $a, a' \in A$. Order-preserving functions
congruences are relativized in the same way.

Consider next the function space construction. For $A \subseteq \Sigma$ and $B \subseteq \Gamma$, we we
like to say that f is a function from A to B; i.e., $f : A \rightarrow B$. However, again
have the problem that $A \rightarrow B$ is not a type. We solve this problem by defining
set

$$A \rightarrow B \;\hat{=}\; \{f : \Sigma \rightarrow \Gamma \mid (\forall a \in A \cdot f.a \in B)\} . \qquad \text{(function spa}$$

In other words, $A \rightarrow B$ is the set of all functions of type $\Sigma \rightarrow \Gamma$ that i
elements in A to elements in B. Instead of writing $f : A \rightarrow B$, we can
express essentially the same thing by stating that $f \in A \rightarrow B$. By definition,
have that $A \rightarrow B \subseteq \Sigma \rightarrow \Gamma$. Hence, we can consider $A \rightarrow B$ as a *subtyp*
$\Sigma \rightarrow \Gamma$.

We can consider any set $A \subseteq \Sigma$ as a subtype of Σ (permitting also empty
types). The type constructor $\rightarrow$ applied to subtypes then generates a subtyp
the corresponding type. We have that

$$A' \subseteq A \wedge B \subseteq B' \;\Rightarrow\; A \rightarrow B \subseteq A' \rightarrow B' .$$

Thus, the function space constructor is antimonotonic in its first argument
monotonic in its second.

Now consider the pointwise extensions $A \rightarrow \Gamma$, where the domain is a su
and the range is a type. We have that $A \rightarrow \Gamma = A' \rightarrow \Gamma$, for any A, A
Σ. In particular, this means that $\mathcal{P}(A) = A \rightarrow$ Bool is the same collectio
Boolean functions as $\mathcal{P}(\Sigma) = \Sigma \rightarrow$ Bool. Continuing from here, we also find

$A \leftrightarrow B = A \to B \to$ Bool is the same as $\Sigma \leftrightarrow \Gamma$, and $A \mapsto B = \mathcal{P}(B) \to \mathcal{P}(A)$ is the same as $\Sigma \mapsto \Gamma$. Thus, predicates, relations and predicate transformers can be subtyped in an arbitrary fashion. A *subtyping assertion* $f \in A \to B$ is then trivially true when B is some type Γ, but otherwise we need to check that $f.a \in B$ really holds for every $a \in A$.

Pointwise Extension, Antisymmetry

We also need to check whether the pointwise extension theorem holds for subtypes. We define the ordering on $A \to B$ by $f \sqsubseteq_{A \to B} g$ if and only if $(\forall a \in A \cdot f.a \sqsubseteq_B g.a)$. Assume that B is a poset. Then $f \sqsubseteq_{A \to B} f$ holds, and $f \sqsubseteq_{A \to B} g$ and $g \sqsubseteq_{A \to B} h$ implies that $f \sqsubseteq_{A \to B} h$; so $\sqsubseteq_{A \to B}$ is reflexive and transitive. However, it is not antisymmetric: $f \sqsubseteq_{A \to B} g$ and $g \sqsubseteq_{A \to B} f$ implies that $f.a = g.a$ for every $a \in A$, but it does not imply that this holds for every a in Σ. In other words, equality would also need to be relativized. Writing $f =_C g$ for $(\forall c \in C \cdot f.c = g.c)$, which says that $f = g$ on C, we have that $f \sqsubseteq_{A \to B} g$ and $g \sqsubseteq_{A \to B} f$ implies $f =_A g$.

Antisymmetry does hold in $\Sigma \to B$, i.e., when the domain is chosen to be a type, because $f =_\Sigma g$ is the same as $f = g$. Generally, the pointwise extension theorem holds for any extension of B to $\Sigma \to B$.

We could fix the pointwise extension theorem by making a small adjustment in our definition of the function space. Defining $A \to B$ instead as $\{f : \Sigma \to \Gamma \mid (\forall x \in A \cdot f.x \in B) \land (\forall x \notin A \cdot f.x = \text{arb})\}$, we would also get antisymmetry, and the pointwise extension theorem would be in full force. This trick implies that all functions $f \in A \to B$ have the same value outside domain A, so they are equal if and only if they have the same value for each element in A. We do not choose this approach here, because for our purposes it will be sufficient to consider only pointwise extensions of the form $\Sigma \to B$.

Sublattices and Subcategories

Let $(A, \sqsubseteq)$ be a poset, where A is a set in Σ and $\sqsubseteq$ is a relation on Σ. Let B be a nonempty subset of A. Then $(B, \sqsubseteq)$ is also a poset, said to be a *subposet* of $(A, \sqsubseteq)$.

The ordering relation $\sqsubseteq: \Sigma \leftrightarrow \Sigma$ is thus the same in both the poset A and in its subposet B. However, the supremum and infimum in these posets may depend on the elements that are included in the poset, and hence need not be the same. This is illustrated in Figure 13.1. Let A consist of all the elements in this lattice, and let B consist of the elements that are marked black. Then the supremum of the set $\{a, b\}$ is d in the poset A and c in the poset B. Hence, we may need to indicate explicitly in which poset the supremum and the infimum are taken, writing $a \sqcup_A b = d$ and $a \sqcup_B b = c$.

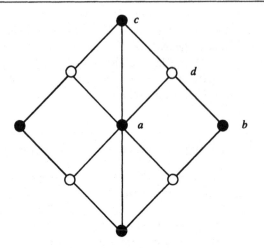

FIGURE 13.1. Sublattice

A subset B of a lattice $(A, \sqsubseteq)$ is a *sublattice* of A if $(B, \sqsubseteq)$ is a lattice and $a \sqcap_B$ $a \sqcap_A b$ and $a \sqcup_B b = a \sqcup_A b$ for any a, b in B. A subset B of the lattice A is a *comp* *sublattice* of A if B is a complete lattice and $\sqcap_B C = \sqcap_A C$ and $\sqcup_B C = \sqcup_A C$ any subset C of B. In particular, this implies that $\perp_B = \perp_A$ and $\top_B = \top_A$. N that the subset B of the lattice A in Figure 13.1 is a lattice, but it is *not* a sublat of A, since $a \sqcup_A b \neq a \sqcup_B b$.

If we view a lattice A as an algebra $(A, \sqcap_A, \sqcup_A)$, then the sublattice definition b down to requiring that the subset B of A must be a *subalgebra*; i.e., the operati $\sqcap_B$ and $\sqcup_B$ must be defined for any a, b in B (with values in B), and they n give the same result as $\sqcap_A$ and $\sqcup_A$ for any two elements a, b in B: $a \sqcap_B b = a \sqcap$ and $a \sqcup_B b = a \sqcup_A b$.

This notion of a subalgebra leads to the notion of a subcategory, as follows. C be a category, with objects *Obj* and morphisms *Mor*, and C' a category w objects *Obj'* and morphisms *Mor'*. Then C' is a subcategory of C if *Obj'* $\subseteq$ C *Mor'* $\subseteq$ *Mor*, and if units and composition are the same in C' as in C.

Monotonicity

Assume that posets A and B are given. We write $A \to_m B$ for the set of monoto functions from A to B:

$$A \to_m B \ \hat{=} \ \{ f \in A \to B \mid (\forall x \ y \in A \cdot x \sqsubseteq y \ \Rightarrow \ f.x \sqsubseteq f.y) \} \ .$$

Thus $f \in A \to_m B$ if and only if f maps A into B and f is monotonic o We refer to $A \to_m B$ as the set of *monotonic functions from poset A to pose* If A is a type Σ, then $\Sigma \to_m B$ forms a sublattice of the lattice $\Sigma \to B$ w the ordering is determined by pointwise extension of a lattice. This is stated more generally in the following theorem.

Theorem 13.1 *Let $(\Sigma, \sqsubseteq)$ and $(B, \sqsubseteq)$ be posets. Then the pointwise extension of these posets to $(\Sigma \to_m B, \sqsubseteq)$ is also a poset. This poset is a (complete, distributive) sublattice of $(\Sigma \to B, \sqsubseteq)$ if B is a (complete, distributive) lattice.*

Proof The proof is straightforward. For example, $(\Sigma \to_m B, \sqsubseteq)$ is sublattice of $(\Sigma \to B, \sqsubseteq)$, since meets and joins preserve monotonicity. $\square$

Note that the property of being a Boolean lattice is not preserved, because the pointwise extension of a complement is not a complement in the lattice of monotonic functions. If f is monotonic and $a \sqsubseteq b$, then

$$a \sqsubseteq b$$
$$\Rightarrow \{\text{functionality}\}$$
$$f.a \sqsubseteq f.b$$
$$\equiv \{\text{negation is antimonotonic}\}$$
$$\neg(f.a) \sqsupseteq \neg(f.b)$$
$$\equiv \{\text{pointwise extension}\}$$
$$(\neg f).a \sqsupseteq (\neg f).b$$

so $\neg f$ is antimonotonic and not monotonic.

13.2 Monotonic Predicate Transformers

Since a predicate transformer is a function between partial orders, it makes sense to consider monotonic predicate transformers. Let us use the notation $\Sigma \mapsto_m \Gamma$ for the *monotonic predicate transformers* for given state spaces Σ and Γ:

$$\Sigma \mapsto_m \Gamma \triangleq \mathcal{P}(\Gamma) \to_m \mathcal{P}(\Sigma) .$$

The pointwise extension theorem (Theorem 13.1) gives us the following result.

Corollary 13.2 $(\Sigma \mapsto_m \Gamma, \sqsubseteq)$ *is a complete sublattice of* $(\Sigma \mapsto \Gamma, \sqsubseteq)$.

We let Mtran$_X$ denote the category in which the objects are types in X and the morphisms are the monotonic predicate transformers, Mtran$_X(\Sigma, \Gamma) = \Sigma \mapsto_m \Gamma$. This is easily seen to be a subcategory of Ptran$_X$: the identity predicate transformer on a given state space Σ is monotonic, and the composition of two monotonic predicate transformers is always monotonic.

Corollary 13.3 Mtran$_X$ *is a subcategory of* Ptran$_X$.

Sequential Composition

In Section 12.2 we described those monotonicity and homomorphism prope[...]
that hold in general for the basic predicate transformer constructors. We get m[...]
homomorphism properties when we restrict our attention to monotonic predi[...]
transformers only. Sequential composition in particular is monotonic only w[...]
respect to the refinement ordering in its first argument, as shown in Section 1[...]
However, it is monotonic also in its second argument if the first argument [...]
monotonic predicate transformer (Table 13.1).

Lemma 13.4   *Let T_1 and T_2 be arbitrary predicate transformers and S a monotonic predi[...]
transformer. Then*

$$T_1 \sqsubseteq T_2 \;\Rightarrow\; S; T_1 \sqsubseteq S; T_2 \;.$$

Proof

$$S \text{ monotonic}, \; T_1 \sqsubseteq T_2$$
$$\vdash (S; T_1).q$$
$$= \{\text{definition of composition}\}$$
$$S.(T_1.q)$$
$$\sqsubseteq \{\text{monotonicity of } S, \text{ assumption } T_1.q \subseteq T_2.q\}$$
$$S.(T_2.q)$$
$$= \{\text{definition of composition}\}$$
$$(S; T_2).q$$

□

Lemma 13.4 is in fact a special case of the more general fact that a function [...]
monotonic if and only if $g_1 \sqsubseteq g_2 \;\Rightarrow\; f \circ g_1 \sqsubseteq f \circ g_2$ (Exercise 13.1).

Combining Lemma 13.4 with the fact that sequential composition is always m[...]
tonic in its left argument, we have the following central result.

Corollary 13.5   *Let S_1, S_2, T_1, and T_2 be monotonic predicate transformers. Then*

$$S_1 \sqsubseteq S_2 \wedge T_1 \sqsubseteq T_2 \;\Rightarrow\; S_1; T_1 \sqsubseteq S_2; T_2 \;.$$

Thus we can characterize the monotonic predicate transformers as follows:

Theorem 13.6   Mtran$_X$ *is a complete lattice-enriched category.*

Preconditions and Guards

The guards and preconditions have simple characterizations and more prop[...]
when the predicate transformers involved are monotonic.

is	$\sqsubseteq$
$(\lambda T \cdot S ; T)$	yes [1]

[1] when S is monotonic

TABLE 13.1. Monotonicity of sequential composition

Lemma 13.7 *If S, S_1, and S_2 are monotonic predicate transformers, then*

$$
\begin{array}{rcl}
t.S & = & S.\text{true} , \\
m.S & = & S.\text{false} , \\
t.(S_1 ; S_2) & = & S_1.(t.S_2) , \\
m.(S_1 ; S_2) & = & S_1.(m.S_2) ,
\end{array}
\qquad
\begin{array}{rcl}
a.S & = & \neg S.\text{true} , \\
g.S & = & \neg S.\text{false} , \\
a.(S_1 ; S_2) & = & S_1^\circ.(a.S_2) , \\
g.(S_1 ; S_2) & = & S_1^\circ.(g.S_2) .
\end{array}
$$

Proof The proofs are straightforward (Exercise 13.4). □

3 Statements and Monotonic Predicate Transformers

From now on, we use the word *(predicate transformer) statement* to denote a predicate transformer built using only the five basic predicate transformers (assert, guard, functional update, angelic update, and demonic update) and the three basic predicate transformer constructors (sequential composition, meet, and join). We emphasize that a statement is a higher-order logic term of a special form that denotes a predicate transformer. Statements do not form a new syntactic category, but rather a subset of an existing syntactic category (that of all predicate transformer terms). The *basic statements* are constructed out of predicates, functions, and relations: $\{p\}$, $[p]$, $\langle f \rangle$, $\{R\}$, and $[R]$. By combining basic statements with sequential composition, meet, and join, we get *compound statements*.

Our first result establishes that all basic statements are monotonic and that the operations for constructing compound statements also preserve monotonicity.

Lemma 13.8 *The predicate transformers $\langle f \rangle$, $\{p\}$, $[p]$, $\{R\}$, and $[R]$ are all monotonic, for an arbitrary function f, predicate p, and relation R. Furthermore, composition, meet, and join of predicate transformers preserve monotonicity.*

Proof We prove that $\{p\}$ is monotonic. Let q and q' be arbitrary. Then

$$q \subseteq q'$$
$$\vdash \{p\}.q$$
$$= \{\text{definition of assert}\}$$
$$p \cap q$$
$$\subseteq \{\text{monotonicity of meet, assumption } q \subseteq q'\}$$
$$p \cap q'$$

$= \{$ definition of assert$\}$

$\{p\}.q'$

The proofs for $[p]$, $\langle f \rangle$, $\{R\}$, and $[R]$ are similar.

For sequential composition, the derivation is as follows:

S monotonic, S' monotonic, $q \subseteq q'$

$\vdash (S ; S').q$

$= \{$ definition of composition$\}$

$S.(S'.q)$

$\subseteq \{$ monotonicity of S and $S'\}$

$S.(S'.q')$

$= \{$ definition of composition$\}$

$(S ; S').q'$

The results for meets and joins follow from Theorem 13.1. $\square$

Lemma 13.8 is illustrated in Table 13.2. This table shows for each operation the left whether it *preserves* the homomorphism property indicated on the top. a direct consequence of this lemma, we get the following important result.

Theorem 13.9 *All statements are monotonic.*

Normal Form

We do not usually distinguish between a statement as a term in higher-order lc (syntax) and the monotonic predicate transformer that it denotes (semantics). can make the distinction if we need to, by talking about the *statement term* the *statement denotation*, respectively. We shall now show that any monotc predicate transformer term can in fact be written as a statement term.

Theorem 13.10 *Let S be an arbitrary monotonic predicate transformer term. Then there exist s relation terms P and Q such that $S = \{P\} ; [Q]$.*

is	$\sqsubseteq$
$\{p\}$	yes
$[p]$	yes
$\langle f \rangle$	yes
$\{R\}$	yes
$[R]$	yes

preserves	$\sqsubseteq$
;	yes
$\sqcap$	yes
$\sqcup$	yes

TABLE 13.2. Monotonicity of basic and compound statements

Proof Assume that $S : \Sigma \rightarrow \Gamma$ is a monotonic predicate transformer. Define relations $P : \Sigma \leftrightarrow \mathcal{P}(\Gamma)$ and $Q : \mathcal{P}(\Gamma) \leftrightarrow \Gamma$ as follows:

$$P.\sigma.\delta \equiv S.\delta.\sigma ,$$
$$Q.\delta.\gamma \equiv \delta.\gamma .$$

Thus P holds for initial state σ and final state δ if the predicate $S.\delta$ holds in the state σ, and Q holds for initial state δ and final state γ if the predicate δ holds in the state γ (note that the intermediate state space has the type of predicates over the final state space).

Then, for an arbitrary predicate q and arbitrary state σ_0 we have

$$(\{P\} ; [Q]).q.\sigma_0$$

$\equiv$ {definitions}

$$(\exists \delta \cdot S.\delta.\sigma_0 \wedge (\forall \gamma \cdot \delta.\gamma \Rightarrow q.\gamma))$$

$\equiv$ {definitions}

$$(\exists \delta \cdot S.\delta.\sigma_0 \wedge \delta \subseteq q)$$

$\equiv$ {mutual implication}

  - $(\exists \delta \cdot S.\delta.\sigma_0 \wedge \delta \subseteq q)$
  $\Rightarrow$ {S is monotonic, context says $\delta \subseteq q$}
     $(\exists \delta \cdot S.q.\sigma_0 \wedge \delta \subseteq q)$
  $\Rightarrow$ {$\wedge$ elimination}
     $(\exists \delta \cdot S.q.\sigma_0)$
  $\Rightarrow$ {quantifier rule}
     $S.q.\sigma_0$

  - $(\exists \delta \cdot S.\delta.\sigma_0 \wedge \delta \subseteq q)$
  $\Leftarrow$ {$\exists$ introduction; witness $\delta := q$}
     $S.q.\sigma_0 \wedge q \subseteq q$
  $\equiv$ {reflexivity}
     $S.q.\sigma_0$

  $\cdot$ $S.q.\sigma_0$

which shows that $S = \{P\} ; [Q]$. $\square$

This result has the following important corollary.

Corollary 13.11 *Any term that denotes a monotonic predicate transformer can be expressed as a statement term.*

In other words, if S is a term that denotes a monotonic predicate transformer, then there is a statement term S' such that $S = S'$. This follows directly from the theorem above by choosing $S' = \{P\} ; [Q]$, where P and Q are terms that are constructed from S in the way shown in the proof of the theorem.

Note that this result does not mean that every monotonic predicate transformer can be expressed as a statement. That this is impossible is shown by a simple cardinality argument. There are uncountably many monotonic predicate transformers (beca the type Ind is infinite), but there can only be countably many terms that den monotonic predicate transformers, because there is only a countable number terms altogether in higher-order logic. What the corollary says is that if a monoto predicate transformer can be described by a term in higher-order logic, then it also be described as a statement.

The decomposition used in the proof of Theorem 13.10 is interesting in its Intuitively, it splits execution of S into two parts. The intermediate state spac the predicate space over Γ, so its elements correspond to subsets of Γ. Given ini state σ, the angelic update $\{P\}$ chooses a predicate δ such that S is guaranteed establish δ. Then the demonic update $[Q]$ chooses an arbitrary state γ in δ. kind of two-stage update forms a very simple game between the angel and demon, with one move for each.

The normal form theorem shows that if we wanted to be economical, we wo need to use only $\{R\}$, $[R]$, and sequential composition to describe all monoto predicate transformers. The other constructs would be definable in terms of th However, we have introduced a larger number of constructs because they co spond to important abstractions that we meet over and over again in the subseq development.

We have shown earlier that the basic statements can all be expressed as angeli demonic update: $\langle f \rangle = \{|f|\} = [|f|]$, $\{p\} = \{|p|\}$ and $[p] = [|p|]$. In reason about statements, we usually take advantage of this fact. We may thus without of generality assume that a statement S is built as follows:

$$S ::= \{Q\} \mid [Q] \mid S_1 ; S_2 \mid (\sqcap i \in I \cdot S_i) \mid (\sqcup i \in I \cdot S_i) .$$

The use of the arbitrary meet and join in a syntax definition needs a little bi explanation. An indexed meet $(\sqcap i \in I \cdot S_i)$ can always be written more explic as

$$(\sqcap i \in I \cdot S_i) \;=\; \sqcap(\mathrm{im}.S.I) ,$$

where S is a function that assigns to each index i a statement $S.i$, and I is s subset of all possible indices. A similar argument holds for indexed joins. As bef the statement syntax does not define a new syntactic category, but merely se to identify a specific subclass of predicate transformers.

Shunting Rules

The duality between assert and guard predicate transformers gives rise to following useful *shunting rules*.

Lemma 13.12   *Let p be an arbitrary predicate and S and S' arbitrary monotonic predi transformers. Then*

(a) $\{p\} ; S \sqsubseteq S' \equiv S \sqsubseteq [p] ; S'$.

(b) $S \sqsubseteq S' ; \{p\} \equiv S ; [p] \sqsubseteq S'$.

Proof Part (a) follows directly from the definitions and from the shunting rule for predicates (i.e., $p \cap q \sqsubseteq r \equiv p \sqsubseteq \neg q \cup r$). For part (b), we have

$\qquad S \sqsubseteq S' ; \{p\}$

$\equiv$ {definition}

$\qquad (\forall q \cdot S.q \subseteq S'.(p \cap q))$

$\Rightarrow$ {specialization $q := \neg p \cup q$}

$\qquad S.(\neg p \cup q) \subseteq S'.(p \cap (\neg p \cup q))$

$\equiv$ {lattice properties of predicates}

$\qquad S.(\neg p \cup q) \subseteq S'.(p \cap q)$

$\Rightarrow$ {S' monotonic}

$\qquad S.(\neg p \cup q) \subseteq S'.q$

$\equiv$ {definition of guard}

$\qquad (S ; [p]).q \subseteq S'.q$

so the forward implication half of (b) follows by generalization. The reverse implication is proved in the same way. □

4 Derived Statements

The statements that we have introduced above are sufficient to express all monotonic predicate transformer terms, as we just have shown. However, the notation is quite terse and somewhat removed from traditional programming language constructs. We therefore introduce a number of *derived statements*, i.e., statements that really are abbreviations for other statements but that have a useful operational interpretation. We have seen how abort, chaos, skip, choose, and magic can be expressed in terms of basic predicate transformers, so we can view them as derived statements. We can think of them merely as abbreviations that can be removed whenever needed.

Let us next consider two other important derived statements: conditional statements and blocks with local variables. We have met these constructs before, as state transformers and state relations. Now we show how to define these as predicate transformers. Other important derived statements, such as recursion and iteration, will be introduced later on, in Chapters 20 and 21.

Conditional Statements

As we already showed in the introduction, we can define the *deterministic co*
tional statement by

$$\text{if } g \text{ then } S_1 \text{ else } S_2 \text{ fi } \stackrel{\wedge}{=} [g] ; S_1 \sqcap [\neg g] ; S_2 . \qquad\qquad (condition$$

From the definition it follows that this determines the following predicate tr
former:

$$(\text{if } g \text{ then } S_1 \text{ else } S_2 \text{ fi}).q = (\neg g \cup S_1.q) \cap (g \cup S_2.q)$$

or, equivalently,

$$(\text{if } g \text{ then } S_1 \text{ else } S_2 \text{ fi}).q = (g \cap S_1.q) \cup (\neg g \cap S_2.q) .$$

Intuitively, if g then S_1 else S_2 fi is a deterministic choice. If g holds, then S_1 is
cuted; otherwise S_2 is executed. Thus the meet in the definition does not intro
any real nondeterminism. In fact, from the above it follows that the determin
conditional can also be written using asserts and a join:

$$\text{if } g \text{ then } S_1 \text{ else } S_2 \text{ fi } = \{g\} ; S_1 \sqcup \{\neg g\} ; S_2 .$$

We can also define the nondeterministic *guarded conditional statement* in term
the more basic constructs:

$$\text{if } g_1 \rightarrow S_1 \; [] \; \cdots \; [] \; g_m \rightarrow S_m \text{ fi } =$$
$$\{g_1 \vee \cdots \vee g_m\} ; ([g_1] ; S_1 \sqcap \cdots \sqcap [g_m] ; S_m) .$$

The assert statement tests that at least one of the guards is true in the state. If
then we have abortion; otherwise one of the alternatives for which the guard is
is chosen demonically and executed. In contrast with the deterministic conditi
this statement may be genuinely (demonically) nondeterministic. This hap
when two or more guards are satisfied in a given state, and the effect of execu
the corresponding statements is different.

Because we have an explicit definition of the conditional statement, we can
rive its homomorphism properties from the corresponding properties of its b
constituents. For instance, the deterministic conditional constructor is (joi
monotonic in its predicate transformer arguments:

$$S_1 \sqsubseteq S_1' \wedge S_2 \sqsubseteq S_2' \;\Rightarrow\; \text{if } g \text{ then } S_1 \text{ else } S_2 \text{ fi } \sqsubseteq \text{ if } g \text{ then } S_1' \text{ else } S_2' \text{ fi}$$

The deterministic conditional is (jointly) bottom and top homomorphic in its p
icate transformer arguments. This means that if $S_1 = $ abort and $S_2 = $ abort,
the conditional is also abort, and similarly for magic. However, the condition
neither jointly meet homomorphic nor jointly join homomorphic in its predi
transformer arguments. Furthermore, it is neither monotonic nor homomorph
its predicate argument. Choosing the deterministic conditional as a basic predi

transformer constructor would therefore not be very wise algebraically, because there are so few homomorphism properties that hold in general.

The properties for the guarded conditional statement are essentially the same as for the deterministic conditional statement. In other words, the guarded conditional statement is monotonic in its statement arguments and jointly top and bottom homomorphic in all its statement arguments, but no other homomorphism properties hold in general. The monotonicity and homomorphism properties of the conditionals are summarized in Table 13.3.

Blocks

The block construct for state transformers allows us to model a situation where the state space is temporarily extended. In exactly the same way, we can define a block construct for predicate transformers that permits us to embed statements on a "larger" state space into a statement on a "smaller" state space.

The block construct for predicate transformers is defined in analogy with the state transformer block:

$$\langle\text{begin}\rangle ; S ; \langle\text{end}\rangle .\qquad\qquad\text{(\textit{block statement})}$$

Given state extension pair $\text{begin} : \Sigma \to \Gamma$ and $\text{end} : \Gamma \to \Sigma$ and statement $S : \Gamma \mapsto \Gamma$ (the *body* of the block), the block has functionality $\Sigma \mapsto \Sigma$. Intuitively, the block maps state space Σ into Γ and then executes S before moving back to the original state space.

In practice, the block construct is used with program variable notation, under the same assumptions as for state transformer blocks (Chapter 5). Thus,

$$\text{begin var } y := e ; S \text{ end} \;\overset{\wedge}{=}\; \langle\text{begin}\rangle ; \langle y := e \circ \text{end}\rangle ; S ; \langle\text{end}\rangle ,$$

and similarly for a block with multiple local variables.

Let us compute the predicate transformer that the block defines.

Lemma 13.13   *Assume that* begin var $y := e$; S end *is a block statement where the expression e does not mention variable y and the body S is written using only program variable notation, and that q is a Boolean expression over the global variables. Then*

$$(\text{begin var } y := e ; S \text{ end}).q \;=\; (S.q)[y := e] .$$

Proof   We have

$$(\text{begin var } y := e ; S \text{ end}).q$$
$$= \{\text{definitions of block and sequential composition}\}$$
$$\langle\text{begin}\rangle.((y := e \circ \text{end}).(S.((\text{end}).q)))$$

≡ {assignment axiom, e does not mention y}

⟨begin⟩.$(S.($⟨end⟩$.q))[y := e]$

The fact that S is using only program variable notation guarantees that the assi‐
ment axiom can be applied in the second step of the derivation. We leave it to
reader to show that ⟨end⟩.$q = q$. Similarly, we leave it to the reader to show
⟨begin⟩.$q = q$ if q does not mention the local variable. □

The block constructor $(\lambda S \cdot \text{begin var } y := e ; S \text{ end})$ is very regular, as it satis
all basic homomorphism properties that can be expected of statements. Th
properties are summarized in Table 13.3.

Theorem 13.14   *The block constructor is monotonic:*

$$S \sqsubseteq S' \;\Rightarrow\; \text{begin var } y := e ; S \text{ end} \sqsubseteq \text{begin var } y := e ; S' \text{ end} .$$

*Furthermore, the block constructor is ⊥-, ⊤-, ⊓- and ⊔-homomorphic, an
preserves* skip.

Proof The proof is left to the reader as an exercise (Exercise 13.12). □

As an example, consider the following statement:

begin var $z := x ; x := y ; y := z$ end ,

where the global variables are x and y. This is the swapping example of Chapt
lifted to the level of statements. In fact, it is possible to prove (Exercise 13.13)
following homomorphism property for blocks:

⟨begin var $y := e ; f$ end⟩ $=$ begin var $y := e ; ⟨f⟩$ end .

Thus we immediately have

begin var $z := x ; x := y ; y := z$ end $=$ $⟨x, y := y, x⟩$

by the example in Section 5.6.

Blocks with Nondeterministic Initialization

We generalize the block statement by allowing a (demonically) nondetermin
initialization of the local variables. We define

is	⊑	⊥	⊤	⊓	⊔	¬	1	;
$(\lambda S, T \cdot \text{if } g \text{ then } S \text{ else } T \text{ fi})$	yes	yes	yes	no	no	no	yes	no
$(\lambda S_1, \ldots, S_n \cdot \text{if } g_1 \rightarrow S_1 \text{ [] } \cdots \text{ [] } g_n \rightarrow S_n \text{ fi})$	yes	yes	yes	no	no	no	yes	no
$(\lambda S \cdot \text{begin var } y := e ; S \text{ end})$	yes	yes	yes	yes	yes	no	yes	no

TABLE 13.3. Homomorphic properties of derived statements

$$\text{begin var } y \mid b \text{ ; } S \text{ end} \;\; \hat{=} \;\; \langle\text{begin}\rangle \text{ ; } [y := y' \mid b[y := y']] \text{ ; } S \text{ ; } \langle\text{end}\rangle \text{ ,}$$

where b is a Boolean expression that can mention both global and local variables. A derivation like the one in the proof of Lemma 13.13 shows which predicate transformer this block is:

$$(\text{begin var } y \mid b \text{ ; } S \text{ end}).q \;\; = \;\; (\forall y \cdot b \Rightarrow S.q) \text{ ,}$$

where q is a Boolean expression in which y does not occur free.

Exactly as for state transformer blocks, we can also permit implicit initialization conventions. Thus,

$$\text{begin var } y \text{ ; } S \text{ end}$$

can by convention mean a totally nondeterministic initialization (with initialization predicate true). Alternatively, it can mean a standard initialization, e.g., initialization to 0 for a variable of type Nat.

.5   Procedures

The notion of procedures can be lifted directly from the state transformer level (Section 5.6) to the predicate transformer level. Thus, a definition of the form

$$\text{proc } N(\text{var } x, \text{val } y) = S$$

is syntactic sugaring for the definition $N.x.y \hat{=} S$. Furthermore, a procedure call of the form $N(z, e)$, where z is a variable and e an expression, is to be interpreted as follows:

$$N(z, e) \;\; \hat{=} \;\; \text{begin var } y' := e \text{ ; } N.z.y' \text{ end .}$$

As an example, consider the following procedure, which stores the smaller of the values m and n in the variable x:

$$\text{proc Min}(\text{var } x, \text{val } m, n) \;\; =$$
$$\text{if } m \le n \rightarrow x := m \text{ [] } m \ge n \rightarrow x := n \text{ fi .}$$

A typical call to this procedure could look as follows, where y and z are program variables:

$$\text{Min}(y, z + 1, y) \text{ .}$$

According to the definition, this call really stands for

> begin var $m, n := z + 1, y$;
>   if $m \leq n \rightarrow y := m \ [] \ m \geq n \rightarrow y := n$ fi
> end

Local procedures on the statement level are handled exactly as on the state tra
former level. We define a *statement with local procedure* as follows:

> proc $N(\text{var } x, \text{val } y) = S$ in   (*local procedu*
> $\cdots N(u, e) \cdots$
>
> $\overset{\wedge}{=}$
>
> let $N = (\lambda x \ y \cdot S)$ in
> $\cdots$ begin var $y' := e$; $N.u.y'$ end $\cdots$

Procedures and calls to them can be introduced and eliminated on the statem
level in exactly the same way as for state transformers.

The following example illustrates the use of a local procedure:

> proc Min(var x, val m, n) =
>   if $m \leq n \rightarrow x := m \ [] \ m \geq n \rightarrow x := n$ fi
> in
> Min(y, y, z) ; Min(x, x, y) .

13.6 Summary and Discussion

In this chapter we have shown how contract statements can be interpreted as mo
tonic predicate transformers. The monotonic predicate transformers form a sub
tice and subcategory of predicate transformers, so we can reason about monoto
predicate transformers in the larger context of all predicate transformers. We h
defined predicate transformer statements as predicate transformer terms that
built in terms of the basic predicate transformers and three algebraic composi
operators: sequential composition, meet, and join. We have shown that any s
statement is a monotonic predicate transformer. Conversely, we have also sh
that predicate transformer statements can be taken as a normal form for monot
predicate transformers: any monotonic predicate transformer that can be expres
as a higher-order logic term can also be expressed as such a statement. We also
fined three standard programming constructs (conditional statements, blocks
local variables, and procedures) in terms of more basic constructs.

We use a two-phase approach to defining the language of contracts, specificati
and programs. First, we introduce basic predicate transformers and predicate tra
former constructors, which have been chosen so that they have simple and reg

algebraic properties. Then we define more traditional constructs in terms of these. This approach allows us to derive the algebraic properties of the traditional constructs in a simple way, and also shows more clearly the underlying mathematical notions. The (less attractive) alternative would be to postulate the more traditional program constructs such as conditionals and blocks directly as predicate transformers, and then derive their monotonicity and homomorphism properties directly from these definitions.

Hesselink develops a similar but more restricted algebra in which statements are conjunctive predicate transformers (i.e., predicate transformers that preserve nonempty meets). He takes assert, guard, meet, and sequential composition as basic (and later includes a join operator also), additionally assuming a collection of procedure names [80, 81, 82].

We use the same constructs for both contract statements and predicate transformer statements. This allows us to identify these two whenever convenient and reason about contract statements as if they were predicate transformers. This way of identifying contract statements with their associated predicate transformers is an important device, because it allows a purely algebraic treatment of contract, specification, and program statements, where the specific syntax chosen for expressing statements is irrelevant.

Another consequence of this is that we do not need to make the distinction between syntax, semantics, and proof theory that is traditional in programming logics. The syntax for predicate transformer statements is just the syntax of higher-order logic, with a little bit of syntactic sugaring here and there. The semantics is the semantics of higher-order logic. This is a simple set-theoretic semantics, as we have shown. The special properties that these statements have are a consequence of the operations that we have introduced by explicit constant definitions in higher-order logic. The proof theory that we use is also the proof theory of higher-order logic. The refinement calculus is a theory within higher-order logic, and as such, it uses exactly the same set of basic axioms and inference rules as any other theory in higher-order logic. What is new in the refinement calculus is expressed as theorems and derived rules of inference, which are proved (not postulated) in higher-order logic.

A consequence of choosing higher-order logic as the underlying logic for the refinement calculus is that the calculus is consistent by construction. This is because higher-order logic has been shown to be consistent, and the refinement calculus is a conservative extension of this logic. The theorems are also sound in the standard semantics of higher-order logic, where statements are interpreted as higher-order functions, because the basic axioms and inference rules of higher-order logic are sound.

Of course, this alone does not prove that the theorems are also correct in the sense that they are true in an *operational* interpretation of contract statements, which

explains a contract in terms of the possible behaviors that it permits for the age
involved. That this is also the case will be demonstrated in the next chapter, wh
the operational semantics of contract statements is defined.

This is also the reason why we need to distinguish between contract statem
and predicate transformer statements. The predicate transformer interpretation
though extremely useful for reasoning about properties of contracts, is still just
possible interpretation of contracts. The operational interpretation gives ano
semantics for contracts. A third interpretation of contract statements will also
presented, where we show how to interpret contracts as special kinds of functi
on the initial state.

A notation where every monotonic predicate transformer term is expressibl
a statement was originally introduced by Back and von Wright [26, 27],
an original normal form theorem. The normal form theorem presented here
proved by von Wright [143]. The guarded conditional was originally introdu
by Dijkstra [53]. Blocks and procedures have been handled formally by Hoare
and Gries and Levin [65], among others.

13.7 Exercises

13.1   Prove that if Γ and Δ are partially ordered, then

$$f \text{ monotonic} \equiv$$
$$(\forall g_1 : \Gamma \to \Delta \cdot \forall g_2 : \Gamma \to \Delta \cdot g_1 \sqsubseteq g_2 \Rightarrow f ; g_1 \sqsubseteq f ; g_2)$$

for an arbitrary function $f : \Sigma \to \Gamma$.

13.2   Show that if S is a monotonic predicate transformer, then the following *sub
tributivity* property holds:

$$S_1 ; (S_2 \sqcap S_3) \sqsubseteq S_1 ; S_2 \sqcap S_1 ; S_3 .$$

13.3   Fill in the missing parts of the proof of Lemma 13.8.

13.4   Prove Lemma 13.7.

13.5   By the duality principle, there is a dual normal form $[P] ; \{Q\}$ in addition t
normal form $\{P\} ; [Q]$ for monotonic statements given in this chapter. Derive
normal form and interpret it intuitively.

13.6   Show that if S is a monotonic predicate transformer, then the following prope
hold for arbitrary predicates p and q:

$$S.(p \cap q) \subseteq S.p \cap S.q ,$$
$$S.p \cup S.q \subseteq S.(p \cup q) .$$

13.7   Show that the following holds for arbitrary state relation R:

$$[R] \; = \; [\lambda\sigma \cdot \exists\gamma \cdot R.\sigma.\gamma]\,;\, \sqcap\{\langle f\rangle \mid (\forall\sigma \cdot R.\sigma \neq \emptyset \Rightarrow R.\sigma.(f.\sigma))\} \; .$$

Interpret this equality intuitively.

13.8 Show that the deterministic conditional is monotonic with respect to substatement replacement:

$$S_1 \sqsubseteq S_1' \wedge S_2 \sqsubseteq S_2' \Rightarrow$$

if g then S_1 else S_2 fi $\sqsubseteq$ if g then S_1' else S_2' fi .

13.9 Prove the following rule:

if g then $S_1 \sqcap S_2$ else S fi $=$

if g then S_1 else S fi $\sqcap$ if g then S_2 else S fi .

13.10 Recall the definitions of the chaos and choose statements:

chaos $\stackrel{\wedge}{=}$ [True] , $\qquad$ choose $\stackrel{\wedge}{=}$ {True} .

Show that the following refinements hold for an arbitrary monotonic predicate transformer S:

S ; chaos	$\sqsubseteq$	chaos ; S ,	abort ; S	$\sqsubseteq$	S ; abort ,
S ; skip	$\sqsubseteq$	skip ; S ,	skip ; S	$\sqsubseteq$	S ; skip ,
S ; magic	$\sqsubseteq$	magic ; S ,	choose ; S	$\sqsubseteq$	S ; choose .

13.11 Find instantiations for the monotonic predicate transformer S to show the following:

S ; abort	$\not\sqsubseteq$	abort ; S ,
S ; choose	$\not\sqsubseteq$	choose ; S ,

chaos ; S	$\not\sqsubseteq$	S ; chaos ,
magic ; S	$\not\sqsubseteq$	S ; magic .

13.12 Prove that the block construct begin var $y := e$; S end is $\perp$-, $\top$-, $\sqcap$-, and $\sqcup$-homomorphic in its statement argument S.

13.13 Prove the following rule:

⟨begin var $y := e$; f end⟩ $=$ begin var $y := e$; ⟨f⟩ end .

atements as Games

In the previous chapter we showed that contract statements can be interpreted as (monotonic) predicate transformers. But predicate transformers are pure mathematical entities, functions from predicates (sets) to predicates, and as such have no direct computational interpretation. The way in which statements are assumed to be executed as programs has only been explained informally. Because both angelic and demonic nondeterminism is involved in statement execution, it is not obvious how statement execution should be defined formally. In this chapter, we therefore proceed to give an operational interpretation of contract statements as *games*. We show that the predicate transformer semantics is an abstraction of the game semantics, in the sense that we can compute the former from the latter. Both correctness of statements and refinement can be explained operationally in terms of winning strategies in games.

Game Interpretation

We will assume that contract statements have the following syntax:

$$S ::= \{Q\} \mid [Q] \mid S_1 ; S_2 \mid (\sqcap i \in I \cdot S_i) \mid (\sqcup i \in I \cdot S_i) .$$

Here Q is a relation term and I a set term of higher-order logic. We assume that there is a rule that associates a contract statement S_i with each index $i \in I$ in a meet $(\sqcap i \in I \cdot S_i)$ (and similarly for a join).

We will interpret contract statements in terms of a game that is played between two opponents, called the *angel* and the *demon*. The *game semantics* describes how a contract statement S encodes the *rules* of a game. For a *play* (or *execution*) of the *game* (statement) S, we also need to give the *initial position* (initial state) σ of the game and a *goal* (a postcondition) $q \subseteq \Gamma$ that describes the set of final s that are winning positions.

For a given postcondition q, the angel tries to reach a final state that satisfi starting from the initial state σ. The demon tries to prevent this. Both follow rules of the game, as described by the statement S. The statement determine turns of the game, as well as the moves that are permitted for each player. The proceeds by a sequence of moves, where each move either leads to a new sta forces the player that is to make the move to quit (and hence lose the game). move is carried out by either the angel or the demon.

There are two basic moves, described by the demonic and the angelic up statements. The angelic update statement $\{Q\}$ is executed by the angel in st by choosing some state γ such that $Q.\sigma.\gamma$ holds. If no such state exists, the angel cannot carry out this move and quits (loses). The demonic update state $[Q]$ is similar, except that it is carried out by the demon. It chooses some st such that $Q.\sigma.\gamma$ holds. If no such state exists, then the demon cannot carry o move and quits.

The sequential composition $S_1 ; S_2$ is executed in initial state σ by first playin game S_1 in initial state σ. If this game leads to a final state γ, then the game played from this state. The final state of this game is the final state of the game $S_1 ; S_2$.

A demonic choice $(\sqcap i \in I \cdot S_i)$ is executed in initial state σ by the demon cho some game $S_i, i \in I$, to be played in initial state σ. If $I = \emptyset$, then there is no that can be played in initial state σ, and the demon has to quit. The angelic c $(\sqcup i \in I \cdot S_i)$ is executed similarly, but by the angel.

Skip, abort, and magic statements, as well as guards, asserts, and functiona dates, can all be seen as special cases of demonic and angelic updates. Thu do not need to define the meaning of these constructs in the operational sema Similarly, the operational semantics also explains the execution of derived ments (like the conditional statement) that are built out of the constructs, for we give an explicit interpretation.

Operational Semantics

We define the game interpretation of statements using structured operation mantics. The basic notion in such a semantics is that of a *transition relati* between pairs *(configurations)* (S, σ) where S is a contract statement and σ a The relation $(S, \sigma) \rightarrow (S', \sigma')$ holds (and we say that a *transition* from confi tion (S, σ) to configuration (S', σ') is possible) if one execution step of stat S in state σ can lead to state σ', with statement S' remaining to be execute ecution terminates when a configuration (Λ, σ) is reached, where Λ is the *empty statement* symbol.

In our operational semantics, a configuration is a pair (S, σ), where

- S is either an ordinary statement in $\Sigma \mapsto \Gamma$ or the empty statement symbol Λ, and
- σ is either a state in Σ, the special symbol $\top$ standing for *success*, or the special symbol $\bot$ standing for *failure*.

We take the point of view of the angel with regard to the notions of failure and success. Thus, success means that the angel has won while failure means that the angel has lost. From the demon's point of view, success is something to avoid.

The transition relation (i.e., the permitted moves) is inductively defined by a collection of axioms and inference rules. The relation $\rightarrow$ is defined to be the smallest relation that satisfies the following:

- *Angelic update*

$$\frac{R.\sigma.\gamma}{(\{R\}, \sigma) \rightarrow (\Lambda, \gamma)} \, , \qquad \frac{R.\sigma = \emptyset}{(\{R\}, \sigma) \rightarrow (\Lambda, \bot)} \, ,$$

$$\frac{}{(\{R\}, \bot) \rightarrow (\Lambda, \bot)} \, , \qquad \frac{}{(\{R\}, \top) \rightarrow (\Lambda, \top)} \, ;$$

- *Demonic update*

$$\frac{R.\sigma.\gamma}{([R], \sigma) \rightarrow (\Lambda, \gamma)} \, , \qquad \frac{R.\sigma = \emptyset}{([R], \sigma) \rightarrow (\Lambda, \top)} \, ,$$

$$\frac{}{([R], \bot) \rightarrow (\Lambda, \bot)} \, , \qquad \frac{}{([R], \top) \rightarrow (\Lambda, \top)} \, ;$$

- *Sequential composition*

$$\frac{(S_1, \sigma) \rightarrow (S_1', \gamma), \quad S_1' \neq \Lambda}{(S_1 \,;\, S_2, \sigma) \rightarrow (S_1' \,;\, S_2, \gamma)} \, , \qquad \frac{(S_1, \sigma) \rightarrow (\Lambda, \gamma)}{(S_1 \,;\, S_2, \sigma) \rightarrow (S_2, \gamma)} \, ;$$

- *Angelic choice*

$$\frac{k \in I}{((\sqcup i \in I \cdot S_i), \sigma) \rightarrow (S_k, \sigma)} \, , \qquad \frac{I = \emptyset}{((\sqcup i \in I \cdot S_i), \sigma) \rightarrow (\Lambda, \bot)} \, ;$$

- *Demonic choice*

$$\frac{k \in I}{((\sqcap i \in I \cdot S_i), \sigma) \rightarrow (S_k, \sigma)} \, , \qquad \frac{I = \emptyset}{((\sqcap i \in I \cdot S_i), \sigma) \rightarrow (\Lambda, \top)} \, .$$

These axioms and inference rules formalize the informal description given above of the moves in the game.

Classification of Configurations

Since there are no rules for *empty configurations* of the form (Λ, σ), moves possible only in configurations (S, σ) where S is a proper statement. Furtherm by inspecting the rules, we notice that for any given configuration (S, σ), at m one of the axioms and inference rules is applicable. If S is an angelic update an angelic choice (join) of statements, then only the angel can make a move this case we say that the configuration (S, σ) is *angelic*. Dually, if S is a demo update or a demonic choice of statements, then only the demon can make a m and the configuration is called *demonic*. Finally, if S is a sequential composit $S = S_1 ; S_2$, then the possible transitions are given by the possible transition S_1. In this case, we say that the configuration is angelic if (S_1, σ) is angelic demonic if (S_1, σ) is demonic. This means that every configuration is either em demonic, or angelic.

Plays

A *play* of the game S in initial state σ is a sequence of configurations

$$C_0 \to C_1 \to C_2 \to \cdots$$

where

(i) $C_0 = (S, \sigma)$,

(ii) each move $C_i \to C_{i+1}$ is permitted by the axiomatization above, and

(iii) if the sequence is finite with last configuration C_n, then $C_n = (\Lambda, \gamma)$, some $\gamma \in \Gamma \cup \{\top, \bot\}$.

Intuitively, a play shows us, step by step, what choices the demon and the a have made in a sequence of moves. A finite play cannot be extended, sinc moves are possible from an empty configuration (in fact, infinite plays are n possible; see Lemma 14.1 below).

The *game interpretation* of contract statement S, denoted by gm.S, is a func that maps each initial state σ to the set of plays of S in initial state σ. The g interpretation of S thus describes for each initial state σ the possible behavio the angel and the demon when following contract S.

For a given goal q, we say that the angel wins a play of a game (or the play *win*) if the final configuration (Λ, σ) satisfies $\sigma \in q \cup \{\top\}$.

Example Game

Let us illustrate the concepts introduced above with the following simple gam state of the game is given by an integer x. Let inc.$x.x' \equiv (0 \le x < x' \le 2)$

dec.x.$x' \equiv (0 \geq x > x' \geq -2)$, where x ranges over the integers. The rules of the game are given by the statement

$$S = [\text{inc}] \,;\, (\{\text{dec}\} \sqcup [\text{inc}]) \sqcap (\{\text{dec}\} \sqcup [\text{inc}]) \,;\, \{\text{dec}\} \,.$$

We consider a play where the initial state is $x = 0$ and the goal (postcondition) q is $x = -2 \vee x = 2$.

The following is a possible sequence of moves:

$([\text{inc}] \,;\, (\{\text{dec}\} \sqcup [\text{inc}]) \sqcap (\{\text{dec}\} \sqcup [\text{inc}]) \,;\, \{\text{dec}\}, 0)$

$\rightarrow$ {demon chooses first alternative}

$([\text{inc}] \,;\, (\{\text{dec}\} \sqcup [\text{inc}]), 0)$

$\rightarrow$ {demon increases state value; inc.0.1 holds}

$(\{\text{dec}\} \sqcup [\text{inc}], 1)$

$\rightarrow$ {angel chooses second alternative}

$([\text{inc}], 1)$

$\rightarrow$ {demon increases state value; inc.1.2 holds}

$(\Lambda, 2)$

Note that the initial configuration is demonic. After the demon chooses the first substatement of the meet, the second configuration is also demonic: a sequential composition with a leading demonic update. After the demon has executed the update, the result is an angelic configuration, and the angel chooses the second alternative, which again gives a demonic configuration. Finally, the demon executes this update, and the empty configuration is reached.

Another possible sequence of moves is the following:

$([\text{inc}] \,;\, (\{\text{dec}\} \sqcup [\text{inc}]) \sqcap (\{\text{dec}\} \sqcup [\text{inc}]) \,;\, \{\text{dec}\}, 0)$

$\rightarrow$ {demon chooses second alternative}

$((\{\text{dec}\} \sqcup [\text{inc}]) \,;\, \{\text{dec}\}, 0)$

$\rightarrow$ {angel chooses first component in leading statement}

$(\{\text{dec}\} \,;\, \{\text{dec}\}, 0)$

$\rightarrow$ {angel decreases state value; dec.0.(-1) holds}

$(\{\text{dec}\}, -1)$

$\rightarrow$ {angel decreases state value; dec.(-1).(-2) holds}

$(\Lambda, -2)$

In both these cases the angel wins the play, since the state component of the final (empty) configuration is in both cases in the set $q = \{-2, 2\}$.

Finally, the following is a play where the angel loses:

$$([\text{inc}] ; (\{\text{dec}\} \sqcup [\text{inc}]) \sqcap (\{\text{dec}\} \sqcup [\text{inc}]) ; \{\text{dec}\}, 0)$$

→ {demon chooses second alternative}

$$((\{\text{dec}\} \sqcup [\text{inc}]) ; \{\text{dec}\}, 0)$$

→ {angel chooses second component in leading statement}

$$([\text{inc}] ; \{\text{dec}\}, 0)$$

→ {demon increases state value; inc.0.1 holds}

$$(\{\text{dec}\}, 1)$$

→ {angel has no legal move; dec.1 = ∅}

$$(\Lambda, \perp)$$

Figure 14.1 shows all possible sequences of moves of the game described ab᷂
when the initial state is $x = 0$ (in this figure, we have decorated the transiᴛ
arrows with A and D to indicate whether the angel or the demon makes the moᵛ

As this example shows, a given initial configuration can permit a variety of plᵃ
with very diverse outcomes (final configurations). In accordance with our gaᵐ
theoretic point of view, we are interested in what sets of outcomes the angel ᵃ
force the game to reach, regardless of how the demon makes its moves. We sᵃ
consider this in the next section, but first we show that all plays are necessaᵃ
finite.

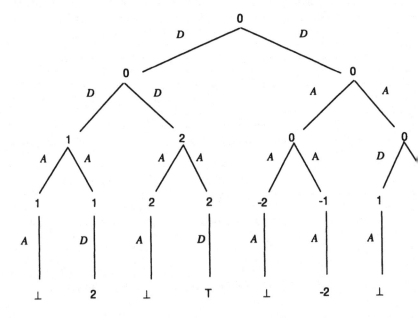

FIGURE 14.1. All sequences of moves from initial state 0

Termination

A game always ends with either the demon or the angel winning. This is because all plays of a game S are finite. Intuitively, we can justify this by noting that every move decreases the size of the game that remains to be played. The formal argument requires us to be explicit about what we mean by the size of a game. This again requires us to use ordinals. Readers who are not familiar with these may at this point choose to first read Chapter 18 on well-founded sets and ordinals, before going through the proof of the lemma.

Lemma 14.1   *All plays of a game are finite.*

Proof Define the following inductive ordinal measure on statement terms (including the empty statement):

$$
\begin{aligned}
M.\Lambda &= 0 , \\
M.\{R\} &= 1 , \\
M.[R] &= 1 , \\
M.(S_1 ; S_2) &= M.S_2 + M.S_1 , \\
M.(\sqcap i \in I \cdot S_i) &= (\lim i \in I \cdot M.S_i) + 1 , \\
M.(\sqcup i \in I \cdot S_i) &= (\lim i \in I \cdot M.S_i) + 1 .
\end{aligned}
$$

This measure is well-defined, since I is always a set (this guarantees that the measure of every statement is an ordinal). By induction on the structure of the statement S, one can show that any move according to the transition relation $\rightarrow$ decreases this measure in the statement part of a given configuration (S, σ). Since the ordinals are well-founded, this guarantees that no configuration can permit more than a finite number of moves. □

Even though every play is finite, it is possible to devise games in which there is no upper bound on the number of moves needed to play the game. The following example shows this. Let R be an arbitrary relation and define statements S_n for each natural number n by $S_0 = [R]$ and $S_{n+1} = [R] ; S_n$. Then consider the statement $(\sqcup n \in \text{Nat} \cdot S_n)$ in any initial state σ. If we are given some purported bound m on the number of moves, then the angel can start by making the move

$$((\sqcup n \in \text{Nat} \cdot S_n), \sigma) \;\rightarrow\; (S_m, \sigma) .$$

After this, the demon makes exactly $m + 1$ moves, so the total number of moves will be greater than m.

Winning Strategies

We shall now use the operational semantics to define what a strategy is and what it means for the angel to have a winning strategy for game S in initial state σ with

respect to goal (postcondition) q. The idea is that a strategy (for the angel) tells
angel what to do in each angelic configuration and that a strategy is winning if
angel can win a game by always moving according to the strategy.

A *strategy* (for the angel) is a function f that maps configurations to configurati
in such a way that $C \to f.C$ holds for all angelic configurations C. Thus, gi
an arbitrary angelic configuration C, a strategy f determines a transition (a m
for the angel) $C \to f.C$.

Now assume that we are given statement S and initial state σ. A strategy f *ad*
a play $C_0 \to C_1 \to \cdots \to C_n$ if $C_0 = (S, \sigma)$ and if $C_{i+1} = f.C_i$ when
configuration C_i is angelic.

The strategy f is a *winning strategy* for game S in initial state σ with respec
goal q if for every play $(S, \sigma) \to \cdots \to (\Lambda, \gamma)$ admitted by f, the condi
$\gamma \in q \cup \{\top\}$ holds. Thus, f is a winning strategy if the angel is guaranteed to
when it makes its moves according to f.

Obviously, we can define the notion of a strategy for the demon dually. Howe
since the notion of winning is connected to the angel, we concentrate on strate
for the angel.

The Winning Strategy Theorem

We shall now show that the existence of winning strategies is closely related to
predicate transformer semantics. In fact, we show that there is a winning strat
for game S in initial state σ with respect to postcondition q if and only if wp.S.
holds. Since the notion of winning strategy was derived from the operational
mantics, this shows how the predicate transformer semantics can be derived f
the operational semantics.

Theorem 14.2   *Assume that contract statement S, state σ, and predicate q are given. Then t
is a winning strategy for game S in initial state σ with respect to postconditi
if and only if wp.S.q.σ holds.*

Proof   The proof is by induction over the structure of the statement S. In
proof, we need a few additional notions about strategies. To simplify the reason
we assume that strategies can be "undefined" for configurations that we are
interested in (this undefinedness can be accomplished by augmenting the collec
of all configurations with an extra "undefined" element). The *domain* Dom.
a strategy f is the set of configurations for which f is defined. We further de
the *domain of interest* for a strategy f with respect to configuration (S, σ) (wr
IDom(f, S, σ)) to be the set of all angelic configurations in all plays of $(S$
admitted by f. Obviously, f's restriction to IDom(f, S, σ) determines whe
f is a winning strategy or not, since configurations outside IDom(f, S, σ) ca
occur while the game is being played.

We now consider the five cases of the inductive proof. Cases 1 and 2 are the base cases (the two relational updates), while cases 3, 4, and 5 are step cases (meet, join, and sequential composition).

(i) For the demonic update $[R]$, the domain of interest of any winning strategy is empty, since the angel never makes any moves. Thus,

> winning strategy exists for $[R]$ in σ with respect to q
>
> $\equiv$ {definitions}
>
> > for every transition $([R], \sigma) \rightarrow (\Lambda, \gamma)$ we must have $\gamma \in q \cup \{\top\}$
>
> $\equiv$ {operational semantics}
>
> > $R.\sigma \subseteq q$
>
> $\equiv$ {definition of update}
>
> > $\mathrm{wp}.[R].q.\sigma$

(ii) For the angelic update $\{R\}$, the reasoning is similar. In this case, the domain of interest contains the single configuration $(\{R\}, \sigma)$, and a winning strategy is one that maps this configuration to some (Λ, γ) where $\gamma \in q \cup \{\top\}$. Thus,

> winning strategy exists for $\{R\}$ in σ with respect to q
>
> $\equiv$ {definitions}
>
> > there is a transition $(\{R\}, \sigma) \rightarrow (\Lambda, \gamma)$ such that $\gamma \in q \cup \{\top\}$
>
> $\equiv$ {operational semantics}
>
> > $R.\sigma \cap q \neq \emptyset$
>
> $\equiv$ {definition of update}
>
> > $\mathrm{wp}.\{R\}.q.\sigma$

(iii) Next, we consider meets. For this part of the proof, we need to define a *merge* of strategies. Assume that a set of strategies $\{f_i \mid i \in I\}$ is given. A strategy f is a merge of this set if the following holds for all configurations (S, σ):

$$(\exists i \in I \cdot (S, \sigma) \in \mathrm{Dom}.f_i) \Rightarrow$$
$$(\exists i \in I \cdot (S, \sigma) \in \mathrm{Dom}.f_i \wedge f.(S, \sigma) = f_i.(S, \sigma)) \ .$$

In other words, we require that if a configuration is in the domain of one or more of the strategies f_i, then f agrees with one of them. Using the axiom of choice, it is easily shown that a merge always exists for any collection of strategies.

The following observation is now crucial. Assume that f is a winning strategy for game S in initial state σ with respect to goal q and that f is undefined outside $\mathrm{IDom}(f, S, \sigma)$. Similarly, assume that f' is a winning strategy for game S' in initial state σ' with respect to the same goal q and that f' is undefined outside $\mathrm{IDom}(f', S', \sigma')$. Then *any merge of f and f' is also a winning strategy for both S in σ and S' in σ' with respect to q*. This is true, because if f and f' disagree on some configuration that is in the domain of interest of both (f, S, σ) and $(f', S', \cdot$ then both strategies must lead to a win from this configuration.

The induction assumption for the meet is now that for all $i \in I$ there is a winn strategy for game S_i in initial state σ with respect to postcondition q if and on $\text{wp}.S_i.q.\sigma$ holds. Then we have

$\qquad$ f is winning strategy for $(\sqcap i \in I \cdot S_i)$ in σ with respect to q

$\Rightarrow$ {operational semantics, definition of winning strategy}

$\qquad$ f is winning strategy for each S_i in σ with respect to q

$\equiv$ {induction assumption}

$\qquad$ $(\forall i \in I \cdot \text{wp}.S_i.q.\sigma)$

$\equiv$ {definition of meet}

$\qquad$ $\text{wp}.(\sqcap i \in I \cdot S_i).q.\sigma$

so the existence of a winning strategy for the meet implies $\text{wp}.(\sqcap i \in I \cdot S_i).q$ For the reverse implication, the induction assumption tells us that for each $i \in$ there exists a winning strategy f_i for S_i in σ with respect to goal q. Let f_i' the result of restricting strategy f_i to the domain of interest of (f_i, S_i, σ). observation above then guarantees that any merge of the strategies f_i' is a winn strategy for $(\sqcap i \in I \cdot S_i)$.

(iv) Now consider join. First,

$\qquad$ f is winning strategy for $(\sqcup i \in I \cdot S_i)$ in σ with respect to q

$\Rightarrow$ {operational semantics, definition of winning strategy}

$\qquad$ f is winning strategy for S_i in σ with respect to q, for some $i \in I$

$\equiv$ {induction assumption}

$\qquad$ $(\exists i \in I \cdot \text{wp}.S_i.q.\sigma)$

$\equiv$ {definition of join}

$\qquad$ $\text{wp}.(\sqcup i \in I \cdot S_i).q.\sigma$

so the existence of a winning strategy for the join implies $(\sqcup i \in I \cdot S_i).q.\sigma$. the opposite implication here, we note that if f is a winning strategy for S_i with respect to q, then we can adjust f so that $f.((\sqcup i \in I \cdot S_i), \sigma) = (S_i, \sigma$ get a winning strategy for $(\sqcup i \in I \cdot S_i)$. This works because $((\sqcup i \in I \cdot S_i), \sigma$ necessarily outside $\text{IDom}(f, S_i, \sigma)$.

(v) Finally, we consider sequential composition. First, we note from the defini of the operational semantics that a play of the game $S_1 ; S_2$ is of the form

$$(S_1 ; S_2, \sigma_0) \rightarrow \cdots (S_2, \sigma_m) \rightarrow \cdots (\Lambda, \sigma_n) ,$$

and furthermore,

(a) $(S_1, \sigma_0) \rightarrow \cdots \rightarrow (\Lambda, \sigma_m)$ is a play of the game S_1 in initial state σ_0, an

(b) $(S_2, \sigma_m) \rightarrow \cdots \rightarrow (\Lambda, \sigma_n)$ is a play of the game S_2 in initial state σ_m.

The induction assumption is that the statement of the theorem is true for S_1 and S_2. Assume that f is a winning strategy for S_1 ; S_2 in initial state σ with respect to q and let p be the set containing all second (state) components of the final configurations of plays of (S_1, σ) admitted by f. Then define a strategy f' by $f'.(S, \gamma) = f.(S ; S_2, \gamma)$ so that f' is a winning strategy for S_1 in σ with respect to p. The induction assumption then tells us that wp.$S_1.p.\sigma$ holds. Furthermore, we know that f is a winning strategy for S_2 in any initial state $\gamma \in p$ with respect to q, so the induction assumption tells us that $(\forall \gamma \in p \cdot \mathsf{wp}.S_2.q.\gamma)$. Then

$$\mathsf{wp}.S_1.p.\sigma \wedge (\forall \gamma \in p \cdot \mathsf{wp}.S_2.q.\gamma)$$

$\equiv$ {definition of bounded quantification}

$$\mathsf{wp}.S_1.p.\sigma \wedge (\forall \gamma \cdot p.\gamma \Rightarrow \mathsf{wp}.S_2.q.\gamma)$$

$\equiv$ {pointwise extension}

$$\mathsf{wp}.S_1.p.\sigma \wedge p \subseteq \mathsf{wp}.S_2.q$$

$\Rightarrow$ {monotonicity of wp.S_1}

$$\mathsf{wp}.S_1.(\mathsf{wp}.S_2.q).\sigma$$

$\Rightarrow$ {definition of sequential composition}

$$\mathsf{wp}.(S_1 ; S_2).q.\sigma$$

For the opposite direction, we assume that wp.$(S_1 ; S_2).q.\sigma$. Again, this means that we have, with $p = \mathsf{wp}.S_2.q$,

$$\mathsf{wp}.S_1.p.\sigma \wedge (\forall \gamma \in p \cdot \mathsf{wp}.S_2.q.\gamma) \ .$$

The induction assumption then tells us that there is a winning strategy f for S_1 in initial state σ with respect to p and that for every $\gamma \in p$ there is a winning strategy g_γ for S_2 in initial state γ with respect to q. Now define f' such that $f'.(S ; S_2, \delta) = (T ; S_2, \gamma)$ whenever $f.(S, \delta) = (T, \gamma)$ for all S and all δ, and f is undefined everywhere else. Next let g'_γ be the result of restricting g_γ to $\mathsf{IDom}(g_\gamma, S_2, \gamma)$ for all $\gamma \in p$, and let g be a merge of f' and all the strategies in $\{g'_\gamma \mid \gamma \in p\}$. This makes g a winning strategy for S_1 ; S_2 in initial state σ with respect to q, and the proof is finished. $\square$

Theorem 14.2 shows that the operational semantics uniquely defines the predicate transformer semantics. Since the operational semantics contains information not only about input–output behavior, but also about intermediate states, it is obviously not possible in general to go the other way.

14.3 Correctness and Refinement

The notion of correctness can now also be explained operationally. Recall t
contract statement S is correct with respect to precondition p and postcondi
q, denoted by $p \{\!| S |\!\} q$, if $p \subseteq$ wp.$S.q$. The postcondition plays the role c
goal, while the precondition plays the role of permitted initial states. Correctr
operationally means that the angel has a winning strategy for goal q in any ini
state that satisfies predicate p.

Consider again the game described by the statement

$$S \;=\; [\text{inc}]\,;\,(\{\text{dec}\} \sqcup [\text{inc}]) \sqcap (\{\text{dec}\} \sqcup [\text{inc}])\,;\,\{\text{dec}\}\,,$$

where inc.$x.x' = (0 \le x < x' \le 2)$ and dec.$x.x' = (0 \ge x > x' \ge -$
Figure 14.1 shows all possible sequences of moves of this game when the ini
state is $x = 0$. Consider the goal $x = -2 \lor x = 2$. From Figure 14.1 it is e
to see that the angel always can win the game with this goal: no matter what
demon does, the angel can choose his moves so that either the demon has to
(symbolized by $\top$) or the game terminates in a final state where $x = 2$ or $x =$
Hence, the angel has a winning strategy for this goal in initial state 0, so

$$x = 0 \{\!| S |\!\} x = -2 \lor x = 2$$

holds operationally.

On the other hand, one can see that the angel does not have a winning strategy
the goal $x = -1 \lor x = 1$ from the same initial state 0.

Let us compute the weakest precondition for S to establish the postcondition
$(x = -2 \lor x = 2)$. We have that

$$([\text{inc}]\,;\,(\{\text{dec}\} \sqcup [\text{inc}]) \sqcap (\{\text{dec}\} \sqcup [\text{inc}])\,;\,\{\text{dec}\}).q$$

$= \{\text{definition of meet}\}$

$$([\text{inc}]\,;\,(\{\text{dec}\} \sqcup [\text{inc}])).q \land (((\{\text{dec}\} \sqcup [\text{inc}])\,;\,\{\text{dec}\})).q$$

$= \{\text{definition of sequential composition}\}$

$$[\text{inc}].(((\{\text{dec}\} \sqcup [\text{inc}]).q) \land (\{\text{dec}\} \sqcup [\text{inc}]).(\{\text{dec}\}.q)$$

$= \{\text{definition of join}\}$

$$[\text{inc}].(\{\text{dec}\}.q \lor [\text{inc}].q) \land (\{\text{dec}\}.(\{\text{dec}\}.q) \lor [\text{inc}].(\{\text{dec}\}.q))$$

$= \{\text{use }[\text{inc}].q = (x \ne 0) \text{ and } \{\text{dec}\}.q = (x = 0 \lor x = -1)\}$

$$[\text{inc}].(x = 0 \lor x = -1 \lor x \ne 0) \land$$
$$(\{\text{dec}\}.(x = 0 \lor x = -1) \lor [\text{inc}].(x = 0 \lor x = -1))$$

$= \{\text{simplify}\}$

$$([\text{inc}].\top \land (\{\text{dec}\}.(x = 0 \lor x = -1) \lor [\text{inc}].(x = 0 \lor x = -1))$$

$= \{\text{definitions of updates}\}$

$$\top \land (x = 0 \lor \text{F})$$

= {simplify}

$x = 0$

Thus, the angel has a winning strategy only for $x = 0$.

Let us then look more closely at refinement of contract statements. In the predicate transformer semantics, the refinement $S \sqsubseteq S'$ is valid if and only if $(\forall q\, \sigma \cdot S.q.\sigma \Rightarrow S'.q.\sigma)$ holds. With the game interpretation, this means that for any choice of goal q and any choice of initial state σ, if the angel has a winning strategy in S, then it must also have a winning strategy in S'. Thus, a refinement has to increase the angel's possibilities of winning, or at least keep them the same.

The angel's possibilities of winning can be increased in two ways, either by adding some choices for the angel or by removing some choices for the demon. Figure 14.2 shows a refinement of the previous game, where we have added two new choices for the angel and removed two choices for the demon (the latter shown as dashed lines). Note that when we remove the demon's only choice, then the result is an empty choice for the demon, i.e., a miracle. As a result, the angel now also has a winning strategy for establishing $x = -1 \lor x = 1$ in initial state 0, besides also being able to establish $x = -2 \lor x = 2$ as before.

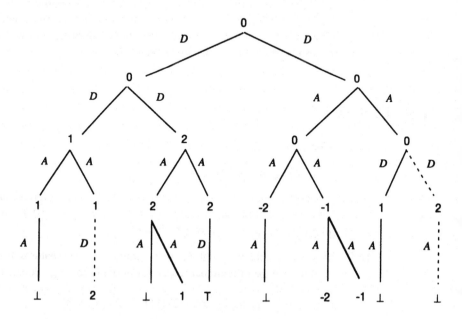

FIGURE 14.2. Refinement of game

14.4 Summary and Discussion

We have described an operational semantics for statements, based on the notion
a game that is played between an angel and a demon. Correctness has been sho
to amount to the angel having a winning strategy for the game. We defined
game semantics using structured operational semantics. This semantic definit
method was originally introduced in Gordon Plotkin's lecture notes [120].

A game-theoretic interpretation of logical formulas was proposed by Jaakko I
tikka [83]. Disjunction and existential quantification are there resolved as mo
by Player (∃loise or angel) and conjunction and universal quantification as mo
by Opponent (∀belard or demon). This has been developed further by Yan
Moschovakis [109] and Peter Aczel [2].

David Harel [72] introduced the idea of developing programs using AND/OR-tr
These are quite similar to the games that we have presented here. The notion
game semantics is a suitable operational interpretation for monotonic predi
transformers was originally put forward by Back and von Wright [25].

The idea of viewing the interaction between a system and its environment as a g
has also been considered by Martin Abadi, Leslie Lamport and Pierre Wolper
and by Moschovakis [110]. A different, operationally flavored, semantics using
notion of games is given for a language similar to ours by Hesselink [82]. T
are also a number of similarities with the process algebras developed by H
[88] and Robin Milner [101], in particular with the notions of internal and exte
nondeterminism. Process algebras do not, however, consider state-based progra
The notion of total correctness is also not used there; instead, correctness is s
as a simulation relation between automata.

14.5 Exercises

14.1 Consider the game

$$\{dim\} \; ; \; [dim] \; ; \; \{dim\} \; ; \; [dim]$$

where $dim = (x := x' \mid 1 < x \wedge x - 2 \leq x' < x)$ under declaration var x :
Assume an initial state where $x = 6$ and goal $q = (x = 0)$. Compute two differ
plays for this game, one of which is a win.

14.2 Assume that the program variable x ranges over the natural numbers. Draw
to illustrate the operational semantics of the following two statements:

(a) $S_1 : \quad (x := 1 \sqcup x := 2) \sqcap (x := 1 \sqcup x := 3)$.

(b) $S_2 : \quad x := 1 \sqcup (x := 2 \sqcap x := 3)$.

Although S_1 and S_2 denote the same predicate transformer (prove this!), the trees are different. Is it possible to define an equivalence relation on this kind of tree such that the trees representing two statements S and S' are equivalent if and only if S and S' denote the same predicate transformer?

14.3   Consider the game

$$[x := x' \mid \mathsf{T}] \; ; \{y := y' \mid \mathsf{T}\}$$

under declaration var x, y : Nat. Assume an arbitrary initial state and goal $q = (x = y)$. Describe a winning strategy. Compare this problem with proving that $(\forall x \cdot \exists y \cdot x = y)$ is a theorem.

14.4   Consider the game S defined as

$$(x := 1 \sqcup x := 2) \sqcap (x := 2 \sqcup x := 3) \sqcap (x := 3 \sqcup x := 1)$$

under declaration var x : Nat. Assume an arbitrary initial state σ_0 and goal $q = (x \neq 2)$.

(a) Show $\sigma_0 \, \{\!\mid S \mid\!\} \, q$.

(b) Describe a winning strategy.

14.5   Consider the game S defined as

$$(x := 1 \sqcap x := 2) \sqcup (x := 2 \sqcap x := 3) \sqcup (x := 3 \sqcap x := 1)$$

under declaration var x : Nat.

(a) Show that this game denotes the same predicate transformer as the game given in the preceding exercise.

(b) Assume an arbitrary initial state and goal $q = (x \neq 2)$. Describe a winning strategy for S.

Choice Semantics

We now introduce a third semantic interpretation of statements, the *choice semantics*. Statements are here interpreted as functions that map each initial state to a set of predicates over the final state space. This means that we have altogether three different semantics for statements: an (operational) game semantics, a (backward) predicate transformer semantics, and a (forward) choice semantics. We show that these semantics are consistent with each other (we have already seen that this holds for the predicate transformer semantics and the game semantics). The predicate transformer semantics and the choice semantics are equivalent in the sense that either of them determines the other. The set of predicates that the choice semantics gives for an initial state is in fact the set of postconditions that the statement is guaranteed to establish from this initial state. Thus both choice semantics and predicate transformer semantics are abstractions of the game semantics in the sense that they can be determined from the game semantics for a statement. The converse does not hold, so the game semantics is more detailed than either of the other two. The choice semantics can be interpreted as describing a simple two-step game, so it is also directly connected to the view of statements as games.

Forward and Backward Semantics

The choice semantics describes any contract statement S as a function that maps initial states to sets of predicates on final states, with the intuition that if initial state σ is mapped to a set containing predicate q, then our agent can satisfy S in initial state σ to establish postcondition q. Note that we think of the postcondition as

being specified before the execution, so it is perfectly acceptable that a statem
S establishes two postconditions q_1 and q_2 that contradict each other.

First we introduce an auxiliary function that is useful in discussing the ch
semantics. Let $S : \Sigma \mapsto \Gamma$ be a predicate transformer. This means that S
function with the following type:

$$S : (\Gamma \to \text{Bool}) \to (\Sigma \to \text{Bool}) .$$

Now let $\overline{S}$ be the function of type

$$\overline{S} : \Sigma \to (\Gamma \to \text{Bool}) \to \text{Bool}$$

defined by

$$\overline{S}.\sigma.q \stackrel{\wedge}{=} S.q.\sigma .$$

In other words, $\overline{S}$ is almost the same function as S, except for the ordering of
arguments σ and q. Obviously, $\overline{S}.\sigma$ is a set of predicates, i.e., a set of sets, so
defining condition can be written equivalently as

$$q \in \overline{S}.\sigma \equiv S.q.\sigma .$$

Thus, $\overline{S}$ is a function from initial states to sets of sets of final states.

We have defined $\overline{S}$ above for an arbitrary predicate transformer S. However, st
ments always denote monotonic predicate transformers, so it is of interest to k
what property of $\overline{S}$ corresponds to monotonicity of S.

Lemma 15.1   *Let S be a monotonic predicate transformer and σ an arbitrary state. Then $\overline{S}$
upward closed; i.e.,*

$$p \in \overline{S}.\sigma \wedge p \subseteq q \implies q \in \overline{S}.\sigma$$

holds for all predicates p and q.

Proof   The proof is straightforward, by the definition of $\overline{S}$. $\square$

The converse of Lemma 15.1 also holds, in the following sense:

Lemma 15.2   *Given an upward closed family of sets of states $A_\sigma \subseteq \mathcal{P}(\Gamma)$ for every state σ, t
is a unique monotonic predicate transformer S such that $\overline{S}.\sigma = A_\sigma$ for all σ.*

Proof   We construct S according to the intuition of the normal form provide
Theorem 13.10. Its operational interpretation is that given initial state σ, the a
first chooses a set γ in A_σ, and the demon then chooses one of the elements of
the final state. Hence, we set $S = \{\lambda\sigma \; \gamma \cdot \gamma \in A_\sigma\} ; [\lambda\gamma \; \delta \cdot \delta \in \gamma]$. The follow
calculation verifies that this is the desired statement:

$q \in \bar{S}.\sigma$

$\equiv$ {definition of $\bar{S}$ and of S}

$(\{\lambda\sigma\ \gamma \cdot \gamma \in A_\sigma\} ; [\lambda\gamma\ \delta \cdot \delta \in \gamma]).q.\sigma$

$\equiv$ {statement definitions}

$(\exists\gamma \cdot \gamma \in A_\sigma \wedge (\forall\delta \cdot \delta \in \gamma \Rightarrow \delta \in q))$

$\equiv$ {subset inclusion is pointwise extension}

$(\exists\gamma \cdot \gamma \in A_\sigma \wedge \gamma \subseteq q)$

$\equiv$ {A_σ was assumed to be upward closed}

$q \in A_\sigma$

The proof of uniqueness is straightforward. $\square$

Choice Semantics

We now define the *choice semantics* ch.S of a contract statement S inductively, so that ch.S is a function that maps every initial state to a set of predicates over the final state space. The contract statement S (viewed through the game semantics) is equivalent to the simple game in which the angel chooses a predicate $q \in$ ch.$S.\sigma$, and the demon then chooses a final state $\gamma \in q$. If ch.$S.\sigma$ is empty, then the angel loses, since it cannot choose any predicate. Similarly, if the angel chooses the empty predicate false, then it wins, since the demon cannot choose any state in false.

The choice semantics is defined inductively by the following rules, for arbitrary contract statement S:

$$
\begin{aligned}
\text{ch.}\{R\}.\sigma &= \{q \mid R.\sigma \cap q \neq \emptyset\} \ , \\
\text{ch.}[R].\sigma &= \{q \mid R.\sigma \subseteq q\} \ , \\
\text{ch.}(S_1 ; S_2).\sigma &= (\cup\, p \in \text{ch.}S_1.\sigma \cdot (\cap\sigma' \in p \cdot \text{ch.}S_2.\sigma')) \ , \\
\text{ch.}(\sqcap i \in I \cdot S_i).\sigma &= (\cap i \in I \cdot \text{ch.}S_i.\sigma) \ , \\
\text{ch.}(\sqcup i \in I \cdot S_i).\sigma &= (\cup i \in I \cdot \text{ch.}S_i.\sigma) \ .
\end{aligned}
$$

The intuition behind the definitions for the updates, meet, and join should be clear. For sequential composition, the intuition requires some explanation. For each set p that the angel offers the demon according to S_1, the demon chooses some state $\sigma' \in p$. Thus, the angel can guarantee only what is common to all such states (hence the intersection over σ').

15.2 Comparing Semantics for Contract Statements

We have now introduced three different semantics for statements: the backw
predicate transformer semantics, the forward choice semantics, and the operatic
game semantics. In the previous chapter, we described the relationship betw
predicate transformer semantics and game semantics. Here we look at the
lationship between choice semantics and predicate transformer semantics.
relationship between choice semantics and the game semantics follows from t

Theorem 15.3   *For an arbitrary contract statement S, the choice semantics satisfies* $\mathrm{ch}.S = \overline{\mathrm{w}}$

Proof The proof is by induction on the structure of statement S. First consider
angelic update:

$$q \in \overline{\mathrm{wp}.\{R\}.\sigma}$$
$$\equiv \{\text{definition of } \overline{S}\}$$
$$\mathrm{wp}.\{R\}.q.\sigma$$
$$\equiv \{\text{definition of wp for } \{R\}\}$$
$$R.\sigma \cap q \neq \emptyset$$

The derivation for the other base case (demonic update) is similar.

Next we consider the three step cases. First we have sequential composition,
the induction assumption that $\mathrm{ch}.S_1 = \overline{\mathrm{wp}.S_1}$ and $\mathrm{ch}.S_2 = \overline{\mathrm{wp}.S_2}$:

$$\mathrm{wp}.(S_1 ; S_2).q.\sigma$$
$$\equiv \{\text{definition of sequential composition}\}$$
$$\mathrm{wp}.S_1.(\mathrm{wp}.S_2.q).\sigma$$
$$\equiv \{\text{induction assumption for } S_1\}$$
$$(\mathrm{wp}.S_2.q) \in (\mathrm{ch}.S_1.\sigma)$$
$$\equiv \{\text{induction assumption for } S_2\}$$
$$\{\sigma' \mid q \in \mathrm{ch}.S_2.\sigma'\} \in \mathrm{ch}.S_1.\sigma$$
$$\equiv \left\{ \begin{array}{l} \Rightarrow: \text{ choose } p := \{\sigma' \mid q \in \mathrm{ch}.S_2.\sigma'\} \\ \Leftarrow: \ p \subseteq \{\sigma' \mid q \in \mathrm{ch}.S_2.\sigma'\} \text{ and upward closure} \end{array} \right.$$
$$(\exists p \in \mathrm{ch}.S_1.\sigma \cdot (\forall \sigma' \in p \cdot q \in \mathrm{ch}.S_2.\sigma'))$$
$$\equiv \{\text{set theory}\}$$
$$q \in (\cup \, p \in \mathrm{ch}.S_1.\sigma \cdot (\cap \sigma' \in p \cdot \mathrm{ch}.S_2.\sigma'))$$

For meet (the second step case) we have the following derivation, with the induc
assumption that $\mathrm{ch}.S_i = \overline{\mathrm{wp}.S_i}$ for all $i \in I$:

$$\mathrm{wp}.(\sqcap i \in I \cdot S_i).q.\sigma$$
$$\equiv \{\text{definition of meet}\}$$
$$(\forall i \in I \cdot \mathrm{wp}.S_i.q.\sigma)$$

$\equiv$ {induction assumption}

$\quad (\forall i \in I \cdot q \in \text{ch}.S_i.\sigma)$

$\equiv$ {set theory}

$\quad q \in (\cap i \in I \cdot \text{ch}.S_i.\sigma)$

The derivation for the third step case, $(\sqcup i \in I \cdot S_i)$, is similar. $\square$

Computing $\text{ch}.S.\sigma$ for a given statement S and initial state σ can be very tedious, since the inductive definition for sequential composition is complicated. Thus Theorem 15.3 is an important help; it shows that we can compute the choice semantics directly from the predicate transformer semantics.

Using the definitions of derived statements, we also get the following equations for assertions, guards, and functional updates (Exercise 15.1):

$$\begin{aligned}
\text{ch}.\{p\}.\sigma &= \{q \mid \sigma \in p \cap q\}, \\
\text{ch}.[p].\sigma &= \{q \mid \sigma \in \neg p \cup q\}, \\
\text{ch}.\langle f \rangle.\sigma &= \{q \mid f.\sigma \in q\}.
\end{aligned}$$

In particular,

$$\begin{aligned}
\text{ch}.\text{abort}.\sigma &= \emptyset, \\
\text{ch}.\text{magic}.\sigma &= \mathcal{P}(\Gamma), \\
\text{ch}.\text{skip}.\sigma &= \{q \mid \sigma \in q\}.
\end{aligned}$$

Relating the Three Semantics

The game semantics $\text{gm}.S$ describes S as a function from initial states to the set of plays from that initial state. The predicate transformer semantics $\text{wp}.S$ describes S as a predicate transformer. Finally, the choice semantics $\text{ch}.S$ describes S as a function from initial states to sets of sets of final states. These three semantics are illustrated in Figure 15.1.

Let us define a function ws such that $\text{ws}.G.q.\sigma$ holds if there is a winning strategy for the set of plays $G.\sigma$ to establish q. The result that we proved about weakest preconditions and winning strategies then states that

$$\text{wp}.S = \text{ws}.(\text{gm}.S).$$

The result that we proved about choice semantics and weakest precondition semantics states that

$$\text{ch}.S = \overline{\text{wp}.S}.$$

Let us further define $\text{ws}'.G.\sigma.q = \text{ws}.G.q.\sigma$. Then

$$\text{ws}'.G = \overline{\text{ws}.G}.$$

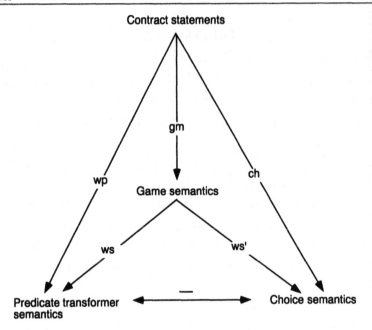

FIGURE 15.1. Semantics of statements

Then it follows from these equalities that

$$ch.S = ws'.(gm.S) .$$

Thus, the diagram in Figure 15.1 is really a commuting diagram. It shows all th
semantic interpretations and the way these interpretations are related to each ot

As the figure shows, the game semantics is the most detailed one, while the
other semantics are abstractions of the game semantics and derivable from e
other.

15.3   Refinement in the Choice Semantics

The choice semantics introduces two new domains into the refinement calcv
hierarchy: sets of predicates and functions from states to sets of predicates.
introduce the name Res(Γ) for the upward closed sets of predicates over Γ and
name Stran(Σ, Γ) for the functions that map states in Σ to upward closed set
predicates over Γ:

$$Res(\Gamma) \triangleq \{Q : \mathcal{P}(\mathcal{P}(\Gamma)) \mid Q \text{ upward closed}\} ,$$
$$Stran(\Sigma, \Gamma) \triangleq \Sigma \rightarrow Res(\Gamma) .$$

Then Res(Γ) is a complete lattice when ordered by subset inclusion $\subseteq$. It follows directly that Stran(Σ, Γ) is a complete lattice when ordered by the pointwise extension of subset inclusion. As usual, we let Res$_X$ and Stran$_X$ denote the collections of all upward-closed sets of predicates and all sets of functions from states to (upward-closed) sets of predicates, respectively, for a given collection X of state spaces. Both Res$_X$ and Stran$_X$ can be seen as categories (see Exercise 15.3).

Using the relationships between the different semantics, we can easily characterize refinement in the choice semantics.

rollary 15.4   *The refinement relation on predicate transformers corresponds to pointwise set inclusion for choice semantics; for all contract statements S, we have*

$$\text{wp.}S \sqsubseteq \text{wp.}S' \equiv (\forall \sigma \cdot \text{ch.}S.\sigma \subseteq \text{ch.}S'.\sigma) .$$

Proof

$$\text{wp.}S \sqsubseteq \text{wp.}S'$$

$\equiv$ {definition of refinement}

$$(\forall q\ \sigma \cdot \text{wp.}S.q.\sigma \Rightarrow \text{wp.}S'.q.\sigma)$$

$\equiv$ {definition of $\overline{S}$}

$$(\forall q\ \sigma \cdot \overline{\text{wp.}S}.\sigma.q \Rightarrow \overline{\text{wp.}S'}.\sigma.q)$$

$\equiv$ {pointwise extension}

$$(\forall \sigma \cdot \overline{\text{wp.}S}.\sigma \subseteq \overline{\text{wp.}S'}.\sigma)$$

$\equiv$ {Theorem 15.3}

$$(\forall \sigma \cdot \text{ch.}S.\sigma \subseteq \text{ch.}S'.\sigma)$$

$\square$

Thus, refinement means adding sets of possible final states for the angel to choose between. In terms of the game-theoretic interpretation, this implies that refinement increases the choices of the angel. By duality, it is obvious that decreasing the demon's choices is also refinement. Because the set ch.$S.\sigma$ is upward closed, removing elements from a set of states that the angel can choose implies adding new sets for the angel to choose between (a smaller set has more supersets).

The extended hierarchy of poset- and lattice-enriched categories is illustrated in Figure 15.2.

Summary and Discussion

We have shown in this chapter how to define a forward semantics for statements that is equivalent to the predicate transformer semantics. It models a two-step game.

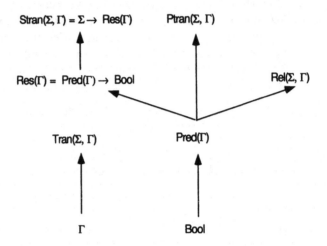

FIGURE 15.2. Extended refinement calculus hierarchy

The choice semantics is a generalization of traditional relational semantics, w
a program statement is described by a function that maps every initial state t
set of all possible final states. This kind of semantics has been studied extensi
for an overview see, e.g., [5]. We will return to it in more detail in Chapter 26.
choice semantics is clearly more expressive than functional semantics or relati
semantics, and thus predicate transformer semantics is also more expressive
these more traditional semantic frameworks. The essential power that the ch
semantics and predicate semantics bring is that we can model both angelic
demonic nondeterminism in a single statement. With relational semantics, we
to choose whether to interpret relations angelically or demonically, but we ca
have both interpretations in the same program.

15.5 Exercises

15.1   Derive the choice semantics for the assert, guard, and functional update:

$$\text{ch.}\{p\}.\sigma = \{q \mid \sigma \in p \cap q\} \, ,$$
$$\text{ch.}[p].\sigma = \{q \mid \sigma \in \neg p \cup q\} \, ,$$
$$\text{ch.}\langle f\rangle.\sigma = \{q \mid f.\sigma \in q\} \, .$$

15.2   Recall that a set $\mathcal{A}$ of sets is upward closed if the following holds:

$$(\forall A \, B \cdot A \in \mathcal{A} \wedge A \subseteq B \Rightarrow B \in \mathcal{A}) \, .$$

Show that if $\mathcal{A}$ and $\mathcal{B}$ are upward closed sets, then $\mathcal{A} \cap \mathcal{B}$ is also upward clo

15.3   Recall the definitions of Res and Stran:

$$\mathsf{Res}(\Gamma) \;\triangleq\; \{Q : \mathcal{P}(\mathcal{P}(\Gamma)) \mid Q \text{ upward closed}\} \;,$$
$$\mathsf{Stran}(\Sigma, \Gamma) \;\triangleq\; \Sigma \to \mathsf{Res}(\Gamma) \;.$$

(a) Show that $\mathsf{Res}(\Gamma)$ is a complete lattice.

(b) Show that both Res and Stran are categories when composition in Res is set intersection and composition in Stran is defined as follows:

$$(f\,;g).\sigma \;=\; (\cup\, p \in f.\sigma \cdot (\cap\, \sigma' \in p \cdot g.\sigma'))$$

for $f : \mathsf{Stran}(\Sigma, \Gamma)$ and $g : \mathsf{Stran}(\Gamma, \Delta)$.

15.4 Use the inductive definition to compute the choice semantics for statement

$$\{\mathsf{dim}\}\,;\,[\mathsf{dim}]\,;\,\{\mathsf{dim}\}\;,$$

where $\mathsf{dim} = (x := x' \mid 1 < x \wedge x - 2 \le x' < x)$. Assume a state space Nat (so $x.\sigma = \sigma$) and initial state $x = 5$.

15.5 Derive the choice semantics for if g then S_1 else S_2 fi.

ubclasses of Statements

Not only monotonicity, but also other homomorphism properties of predicate transformers turn out to be important in modeling programming constructs. In this chapter we study homomorphic predicate transformers, i.e., predicate transformers that preserve some of the predicate lattice structure. We consider the four basic homomorphism properties — bottom, top, meet, and join homomorphism — to see to what extent the constructs in our statement language preserve these properties. These homomorphism properties are closely linked to distributivity properties of statements.

If a collection of basic statements has a certain homomorphism property and the statement constructors preserve this property, then we get a subalgebra of statements generated by these constructs, where every statement has the homomorphism property in question. We use this to identify a number of important subclasses of statements. Programming language semantics has to a large extent concentrated on studying such subclasses of statements. Partly this is because the subclasses are closer to actual implementable programming languages, and partly because their mathematical models are simpler.

1 Homomorphic Predicate Transformers

We introduce specific (and by now traditional) names for the basic homomorphism properties of predicate transformers. A predicate transformer S is said to be *strict* (or *nonmiraculous*) if it preserves bottom, and *terminating* (or *nonaborting*) if it preserves top. Furthermore, S is *conjunctive* if it preserves nonempty meets of pred-

icates, and *disjunctive* if it preserves nonempty joins of predicates. Summarizi
the properties are:

$$S.\text{false} = \text{false} ,$$ (S stri◄
$$S.\text{true} = \text{true} ,$$ (S terminatir◄
$$S.(\cap i \in I \cdot q_i) = (\cap i \in I \cdot S.q_i), \quad I \neq \emptyset ,$$ (S conjunctiv◄
$$S.(\cup i \in I \cdot q_i) = (\cup i \in I \cdot S.q_i), \quad I \neq \emptyset .$$ (S disjunctiv◄

Furthermore, a predicate transformer is *universally conjunctive* if it preserves
bitrary meets of predicates (i.e., it is both terminating and conjunctive). Dual◄
is *universally disjunctive* if it preserves arbitrary joins of predicates (i.e., it is b◄
strict and disjunctive).

In addition to the above four properties, we will comment on negation ho◄
morphism (the property $S.(\neg q) = \neg S.q$), whenever it holds. However, negat◄
homomorphism is not a very common property, so we will not have much to
about it.

The four homomorphism properties stated above are independent of each ot◄
Thus, a predicate transformer can be strict without being conjunctive, it can◄
conjunctive without being terminating, etc. However, conjunctivity and disjunc◄
ity both imply monotonicity, as was shown for lattice homomorphisms in gen◄
(Lemma 2.6).

Homomorphism Properties

The homomorphism properties of basic statements are given in the follow◄
theorems.

Theorem 16.1   *Let state transformer f, state predicate p, and state relation R be arbitrary. T*

(a) $\{p\}$ *is conjunctive and universally disjunctive.*

(b) $[p]$ *is disjunctive and universally conjunctive.*

(c) $\langle f \rangle$ *is universally conjunctive, universally disjunctive, and negation ho◄
morphic.*

(d) $\{R\}$ *is universally disjunctive.*

(e) $[R]$ *is universally conjunctive.*

Proof   We show the proof for conjunctivity of assert; the other proofs are sim◄

$$I \text{ nonempty}$$
$$\vdash \{p\}.(\cap i \in I \cdot q_i)$$
$$= \{\text{definition of assert}\}$$

$$p \cap (\cap i \in I \cdot q_i)$$
$$= \{\text{infinite distributivity, } I \text{ nonempty}\}$$
$$(\cap i \in I \cdot p \cap q_i)$$
$$= \{\text{definition of assert}\}$$
$$(\cap i \in I \cdot \{p\}.q_i)$$

□

Table 16.1 shows the homomorphism properties of the basic statements. In this table, as in others, $\cap$ and $\sqcup$ stand for arbitrary *nonempty* meets and joins. We see that the functional update $\langle f \rangle$ has all possible homomorphism properties as a predicate transformer: it even preserves negations. The assert $\{p\}$ is nearly as well behaved, but it does not necessarily preserve top or negation. Dually, the guard $[p]$ does not in general preserve bottom or negation. The relational updates have even fewer homomorphism properties.

Since the basic statement constructors (sequential composition, meet, and join) can have two or more statement arguments, we consider *joint* preservation of homomorphism properties. For example, joint strictness preservation of sequential composition means that $S_1 ; S_2$ is strict whenever S_1 and S_2 are both strict.

Theorem 16.2 *The statement constructors have the following properties:*

(a) *Sequential composition preserves joint strictness and joint termination, joint conjunctivity and joint disjunctivity, and joint negation homomorphism.*

(b) *Meets preserve joint termination and joint conjunctivity.*

(c) *Joins preserve joint strictness and joint disjunctivity.*

Proof We show that sequential composition preserves conjunctivity; the other proofs are similar.

$$S_1 \text{ conjunctive, } S_2 \text{ conjunctive}$$
$$\vdash (S_1 ; S_2).(\cap i \in I \cdot q_i)$$
$$= \{\text{definition of composition}\}$$

is	$\perp$	$\top$	$\cap$	$\sqcup$	$\neg$
$\{p\}$	yes	no	yes	yes	no
$[p]$	no	yes	yes	yes	no
$\langle f \rangle$	yes	yes	yes	yes	yes
$\{R\}$	yes	no	no	yes	no
$[R]$	no	yes	yes	no	no

TABLE 16.1. Homomorphic properties of basic predicate transformers

$$S_1.(S_2.(\cap i \in I \cdot q_i))$$
$$= \{S_2 \text{ conjunctive}\}$$
$$S_1.(\cap i \in I \cdot S_2.q_i)$$
$$= \{S_1 \text{ conjunctive}\}$$
$$(\cap i \in I \cdot S_1.(S_2.q_i))$$
$$= \{\text{definition of composition}\}$$
$$(\cap i \in I \cdot (S_1 ; S_2).q_i)$$

□

Table 16.2 shows for each statement constructor (composition, meet, and jo which homomorphism properties it preserves. Thus, we have that sequential co position is the most well behaved, preserving all homomorphism properties. other operations are less well behaved. For instance, meets do not preserve j homomorphisms or negation homomorphisms, while joins do not preserve m homomorphisms or negation homomorphisms. These results generalize direct indexed meets and joins.

As a direct consequence of the above theorems, we find that skip has all ho morphism properties, abort is conjunctive and universally disjunctive, and mag disjunctive and universally conjunctive. For the other derived statements we h the following result.

Theorem 16.3   *The derived statement constructors preserve homomorphism properties in t statement arguments as follows:*

(a) *The deterministic conditional preserves (joint) strictness, termination, c junctivity, and disjunctivity.*

(b) *The guarded conditional preserves (joint) strictness, termination, and c junctivity.*

(c) *The block preserves strictness, termination, conjunctivity, and disjunctiv*

Proof The proof is left as an exercise to the reader (Exercise 16.3). □

preserves	$\perp$	$\top$	$\cap$	$\sqcup$	$\neg$
;	yes	yes	yes	yes	yes
$\cap$	no	yes	yes	no	no
$\sqcup$	yes	no	no	yes	no

TABLE 16.2. Homomorphic properties preserved by statement constructors

preserves	$\bot$	$\top$	$\sqcap$	$\sqcup$	$\neg$
$(\lambda S, T \cdot \text{if } g \text{ then } S \text{ else } T \text{ fi})$	yes	yes	yes	yes	yes
$(\lambda S_1, \ldots, S_n \cdot \text{if } g_1 \to S_1 \;[]\; \cdots \;[]\; g_n \to S_n \text{ fi})$	yes	yes	yes	no	no
$(\lambda S \cdot \text{begin var } y := e \; ; \; S \text{ end})$	yes	yes	yes	yes	no

TABLE 16.3. Homomorphic properties preserved by derived constructors

The homomorphism preservation of derived statements is summarized in Table 16.3.

Left Distributivity

Sequential composition always distributes from the right over lattice operations (see Section 12.2) but does not in general distribute from the left over these operations. To get distributivity from the left, we need additional homomorphism assumptions on the components of the sequential composition, in the same way as we needed additional assumptions for monotonicity of sequential composition.

Theorem 16.4 *Let S and S_i be predicate transformers, for i in some nonempty index set I. Then*

$$
\begin{aligned}
S \; ; \; \text{abort} &= \text{abort} && \text{if } S \text{ is strict,} \\
S \; ; \; \text{magic} &= \text{magic} && \text{if } S \text{ is terminating,} \\
S \; ; \; (\sqcap i \in I \cdot S_i) &= (\sqcap i \in I \cdot S \; ; \; S_i) && \text{if } S \text{ is conjunctive,} \\
S \; ; \; (\sqcup i \in I \cdot S_i) &= (\sqcup i \in I \cdot S \; ; \; S_i) && \text{if } S \text{ is disjunctive,} \\
S \; ; \; (\neg T) &= \neg (S \; ; \; T) && \text{if } S \text{ is } \neg\text{-homomorphic.}
\end{aligned}
$$

Table 16.4 summarizes these distributivity properties of sequential composition (they follow directly from the definition of sequential composition).

Homomorphism Properties of Procedure Calls

Recall that a procedure is a (named) predicate transformer that is referred to using procedure calls. Since a procedure call itself is a predicate transformer, we can ask what homomorphism properties it has. A procedure call executes the body of the procedure, with suitable instantiations, so we would expect a procedure call to have the same homomorphism properties as the procedure body. In fact, this is the case, both for global and local procedures.

is	$\bot$	$\top$	$\sqcap$	$\sqcup$	$\neg$
$(\lambda T \cdot S \; ; \; T)$	yes [1]	yes [2]	yes [3]	yes [4]	yes [5]

[1] if S is strict   [2] if S is terminating   [3] if S is conjunctive
[4] if S is disjunctive   [5] if S is $\neg$-homomorphic

TABLE 16.4. Homomorphic properties of composition

Theorem 16.5   *Assume that procedure N (var x, val y) is defined as statement S, either globally*
locally. Then any call N (u, e) is strict (terminating, conjunctive, disjunctive)
is strict (terminating, conjunctive, disjunctive).

Proof By the definition, a procedure call $N(u, e)$ is equal to a statement of the f
begin var $y' := e$; $N.u.y'$ end. The result now follows, since $N.u.y$ is the sa
as S, except for a change in variable names, and since deterministically initiali
blocks preserve the four basic homomorphism properties. □

16.2   Subcategories of Statements

Predicate transformers are very general and expressive. By restricting oursel
to subcollections of predicate transformers that satisfy different homomorph
properties, we lose some of this expressiveness. On the other hand, there are
more properties that can be used in reasoning about computations.

When identifying such restricted collections of predicate transformers, we c
sider the four basic homomorphism properties: strictness ($\perp$-homomorphism),
mination ($\top$-homomorphism), conjunctivity ($\sqcap$-homomorphism) and disjuncti
($\sqcup$-homomorphism). Since these four homomorphism properties are indepene
of each other, there are 16 different ways of combining them. We consider s
of these, but not all, in more detail below.

We first show that any homomorphism characterizes a subcategory of the predi
transformers.

Lemma 16.6   *Assume that ϕ is an n-ary operation on predicates. Let X be a collection of s*
spaces, and let $\text{Ptran}'_X (\Sigma, \Gamma)$ consist of all those predicate transformers in Σ H
that are ϕ-homomorphic. Then Ptran'_X is a category, and it is a subcategor
Ptran_X.

Proof Obviously, it is sufficient to show that skip is ϕ-homomorphic and
composition in Ptran preserves ϕ-homomorphism for an arbitrary operation ϕ.
have, for an n-ary operation ϕ,

$$\text{skip}.(\phi.p_1. \cdots .p_n)$$
$$= \{\text{skip is identity}\}$$
$$\phi.p_1. \cdots .p_n$$
$$= \{\text{skip is identity}\}$$
$$\phi.(\text{skip}.p_1). \cdots .(\text{skip}.p_n)$$

which shows that skip is ϕ-homomorphic. Similarly, assuming that S and S'
ϕ-homomorphic, we have

$$(S \,;\, S').(\phi.p_1.\,\cdots\,.p_n)$$
$$= \{\text{definition of composition}\}$$
$$S.(S'.(\phi.p_1.\,\cdots\,.p_n))$$
$$= \{S' \text{ homomorphic}\}$$
$$S.(\phi.(S'.p_1).\,\cdots\,.(S'.p_n))$$
$$= \{S \text{ homomorphic}\}$$
$$\phi.(S.(S'.p_1)).\,\cdots\,.(S.(S'.p_n))$$
$$= \{\text{definition of composition}\}$$
$$\phi.(((S \,;\, S').p_1).\,\cdots\,.((S \,;\, S').p_n))$$

$\square$

A similar argument can be used if ϕ is an operation on sets of predicate transformers (such as meet or join).

In particular, Lemma 16.6 shows that we have subcategories of Ptran when we restrict ourselves to conjunctive or to disjunctive predicate transformers. Furthermore, the conjunction of two homomorphism properties is also a homomorphism property, so the *functional* (i.e., conjunctive and disjunctive) predicate transformers are also a subcategory of Ptran. To make it easier to talk about these major subcategories, we introduce the following names:

- Ctran$_X$ is the category of conjunctive predicate transformers on X.
- Dtran$_X$ is the category of disjunctive predicate transformers on X.
- Ftran$_X$ is the category of functional predicate transformers on X.

Since both conjunctivity and disjunctivity imply monotonicity, we find that Ctran and Dtran are both subcategories of Mtran. Similarly, Ftran is a subcategory of both Ctran and Dtran (see Figure 16.1).

Lemma 16.6 also shows that we get subcategories of Ptran when we use strictness and termination as restricting properties. We consider these as giving a *secondary classification* and use superscripts ($\perp$ and $\top$) on the names to indicate these additional restrictions. Thus, for example,

- Dtran$_X^\perp$ is the category of universally disjunctive (disjunctive and strict) predicate transformers on X.
- Ftran$_X^\perp$ is the category of partial function (strict functional) predicate transformers on X.

Every category C constructed in this way is a subcategory of all categories that we get by dropping one or more of the properties used to restrict C. For example, Ctran$^{\perp\top}$ is a subcategory both of Ctran$^\top$ and of Mtran$^\perp$.

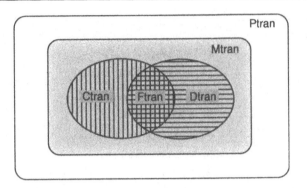

FIGURE 16.1. Main predicate transformer subcategories

The reader should be warned that not all homomorphism properties are vis
from a name; if $S \in$ Ctran, then S is not only conjunctive but also monotonic (si
conjunctivity implies monotonicity).

Some of the subcategories of Ptran that we have identified come in dual pairs.
example, $\mathrm{Ctran}^\top$ and $\mathrm{Dtran}^\perp$ are dual. Because of the general duality princi
every property of a class immediately implies a dual property for the dual cla₅

16.3   Summary and Discussion

Dijkstra's original weakest precondition semantics [53] assumed that every p₅
cate transformer determined by a program statement satisfies a number of "he₅
iness conditions". In our terminology these conditions are essentially strictn
conjunctivity, and continuity (continuity is treated in Chapter 22).

The original healthiness restrictions were later weakened one by one, in orde
enlarge the range of applications and to achieve algebraic simplicity. Continuity
first dropped by Back [6] with the introduction of the nondeterministic assignn
statement. Strictness was dropped by Morgan [104], Morris [108], and Ne
[113] with the introduction of miracles (although de Bakker [36] and Eric He₅
[75] earlier had indirectly introduced nonstrict constructs). Finally, conjuncti
was weakened to monotonicity with the angelic abstraction statement of Back [
the lattice-based specification language of Back and von Wright [26, 27], and
conjunction operator of Gardiner and Morgan [59].

The argument for dropping these restrictions is quite simple. From a proof-theo
point of view, there is no reason to insist on a more restricted classes of stateme
unless properties of these restricted classes are really needed to carry throug₅
proof. Otherwise, a derivation can as well be carried out in the general pred₅
transformer framework, where no restrictions are made on the predicate tr
formers. If a refinement between two statements can be derived in this ge₅

framework, it is also valid when the statements belong to some subclasses of statements. The fact that some intermediate steps in the derivation might not be executable on a real computer has no consequences for the derivation, since the intermediate stages were not intended to be implemented anyway.

.4 Exercises

16.1   Show that the assert $\{p\}$ is universally disjunctive but not terminating.

16.2   Show that the demonic update $[R]$ is universally conjunctive.

16.3   Prove Theorem 16.3.

16.4   In Dijkstra's original formulation of the "healthiness conditions" for predicate transformers, finite conjunctivity was required, rather than the (positive) conjunctivity used here. A predicate transformer S is *finitely conjunctive* if

$$S.(p \cap q) \;=\; S.p \cap S.q$$

for arbitrary predicates p and q. Give an example of a predicate transformer S that is finitely conjunctive but not positively conjunctive. Hint: A counterexample with Nat as the underlying state space can be found by considering cofinite predicates, i.e., predicates p such that $\neg p$ is finite.

16.5   Show that if S is finitely conjunctive then

$$S.(\neg p \cup q) \;\subseteq\; \neg S.p \cup S.q$$

for arbitrary predicates p and q. Under what condition(s) does equality hold.

16.6   Find a counterexample to show that the guarded conditional does not preserve disjunctivity.

16.7   Let $R : \Sigma \leftrightarrow \Gamma$ be a state relation.

(a) Show that $\{R\}$ is conjunctive if R is a deterministic relation.

(b) Show that $[R]$ is strict if R is a total relation, i.e., if $\mathrm{dom}.R = \Sigma$.

7

Correctness and Refinement of Statements

Previous chapters have introduced monotonic predicate transformers as the basic model for contract statements. These can be used to describe programs, program specifications, games, and, of course, contracts and agreements. The predicate transformer semantics was originally designed for reasoning about the correctness of program statements. We will show below how to use predicate transformers to reason about correctness-preserving program refinements.

We define the notion of correctness for predicate transformer statements and show how to establish the correctness of statements. The relationship between correctness and refinement is analyzed. We then show how to derive correct programs from given specifications, using the stepwise refinement paradigm. Finally, we show how the properties of predicate transformers that we have derived in previous chapters permit us to find and justify individual refinement steps.

1 Correctness

Recall the definition of correctness for contract statements: S is correct with respect to precondition p and postcondition q, written $p \lbrace\!\lbrace S \rbrace\!\rbrace q$, if $(\forall \sigma \mid \sigma \in p \cdot \sigma \lbrace\!\lbrace S \rbrace\!\rbrace q)$. Hence, we have that

$$p \lbrace\!\lbrace S \rbrace\!\rbrace q \;\equiv\; p \subseteq \text{wp}.S.q \; .$$

This motivates us to define the notion of correctness also directly for predicate transformers: The predicate transformer S is *correct* with respect to precondition p and postcondition q, denoted by $p \lbrace\!\lbrace S \rbrace\!\rbrace q$, if $p \subseteq S.q$ holds.

The traditional method for proving correctness of programs is known as *Ho* *logic*. This is a collection of inference rules that permit us to reduce the correctn of a program statement to the correctness of its components. Dijkstra's predic transformer method provides an alternative approach, which can be used in the sa way to reduce the correctness of any statement to the correctness of its constituer We give below the rules for reasoning about correctness of statements and illustr their use with a simple example.

Correctness Rules

For basic statements, correctness is reduced to properties of predicates, functio and relations.

Theorem 17.1   *For an arbitrary relation R and predicates p, r, and q:*

(a) $p \{\!| \{r\} |\!\} q \equiv p \subseteq r \cap q$,

(b) $p \{\!| [r] |\!\} q \equiv p \cap r \subseteq q$,

(c) $p \{\!| \langle f \rangle |\!\} q \equiv p \subseteq f^{-1}.q$,

(d) $p \{\!| \{R\} |\!\} q \equiv \text{ran.}(|p| ; R) \cap q \neq \text{false}$,

(e) $p \{\!| [R] |\!\} q \equiv \text{ran.}(|p| ; R) \subseteq q$.

Proof   The results follow directly from the statement definitions and the definit of correctness. □

The last two correctness rules of this theorem can be written equivalently as follo

$$p \{\!| \{R\} |\!\} q \;\equiv\; (\forall \sigma \cdot p.\sigma \Rightarrow (\exists \gamma \cdot R.\sigma.\gamma \wedge q.\gamma)) ,$$
$$p \{\!| [R] |\!\} q \;\equiv\; (\forall \sigma \cdot p.\sigma \Rightarrow (\forall \gamma \cdot R.\sigma.\gamma \Rightarrow q.\gamma)) .$$

As special cases, we have

$$p \{\!| \text{abort} |\!\} q \;\equiv\; p = \text{false} ,$$
$$p \{\!| \text{skip} |\!\} q \;\equiv\; p \subseteq q ,$$
$$p \{\!| \text{magic} |\!\} q \;\equiv\; \top .$$

For the compound statements, we have the following rules. These rules all us to reduce the correctness of a compound statement to the correctness of constituents.

Theorem 17.2   *For arbitrary statements S_i and predicates p, r, and q:*

(a) $p \{\!| S_1 ; S_2 |\!\} q \;\equiv\; (\exists r \cdot p \{\!| S_1 |\!\} r \wedge r \{\!| S_2 |\!\} q)$.

(b) $p \{| (\sqcap i \in I \cdot S_i) |\} q \equiv (\forall i \in I \cdot p \{| S_i |\} q)$.

(c) $p \{| (\sqcup i \in I \cdot S_i) |\} q \equiv (\forall \sigma \mid p.\sigma \cdot \exists i \in I \cdot \{\sigma\} \{| S_i |\} q)$.

Proof We show the first result here. We have that

$$p \subseteq S_1.r, r \subseteq S_2.q$$
$$\vdash p$$
$$\subseteq \{\text{first assumption}\}$$
$$S_1.r$$
$$\subseteq \{\text{second assumption, } S \text{ monotonic}\}$$
$$S_1.(S_2.q)$$
$$= \{\text{definition of composition}\}$$
$$(S_1 ; S_2).q$$

Hence the implication from right to left follows by the rule for eliminating existential quantification. Implication in the other direction follows directly by choosing $r = S_1.q$. $\square$

Note that the correctness rule for angelic choice (join) permits the alternative S_i that is chosen to depend on the present state σ.

From the rules for update statements we can derive rules for assignment statements when the precondition and the postcondition are Boolean expressions:

$$p \{| x := e |\} q \equiv p \subseteq q[x := e] \ ,$$
$$p \{| [x := x'|b] |\} q \equiv p \subseteq (\forall x' \cdot b \Rightarrow q[x := x']) \ ,$$
$$p \{| \{x := x'|b\} |\} q \equiv p \subseteq (\exists x' \cdot b \wedge q[x := x']) \ .$$

Rules for the correctness of derived statements are easily derived from the basic rules. For the conditional statements, we have

$$p \{| \text{if } g \text{ then } S_1 \text{ else } S_2 \text{ fi} |\} q \equiv (p \cap g \{| S_1 |\} q) \wedge (p \cap \neg g \{| S_2 |\} q)$$

for the deterministic conditional and

$$p \{| \text{if } g_1 \rightarrow S_1 [] \ldots [] g_n \rightarrow S_n \text{ fi} |\} q \equiv$$
$$(p \subseteq (\exists i \mid i \leq n \cdot g_i)) \wedge (\forall i \mid i \leq n \cdot p \cap g_i \{| S_i |\} q)$$

for the guarded conditional.

Finally, for the block we have the following rule:

$$p \{| \text{begin var } y \mid b; S \text{ end} |\} q \equiv (\forall y \cdot p \cap b \{| S |\} q) \ ,$$

provided that y is not free in p or q. The justification for this rule is as follows:

$$p \ \{\!\!|\ \text{begin var } y \mid b \ ; \ S \ \text{end} \ |\!\!\}\ q$$

$\equiv$ {definition of correctness}

$$p \subseteq (\text{begin var } y \mid b \ ; \ S \ \text{end}).q$$

$\equiv$ {block semantics, rewrite $p \subseteq q$ as true $\subseteq (p \Rightarrow q)$}

$$\text{true} \subseteq (p \Rightarrow (\forall y \cdot b \Rightarrow S.q))$$

$\equiv$ {y not free in p, rewrite}

$$\text{true} \subseteq (\forall y \cdot p \wedge b \Rightarrow S.q)$$

$\equiv$ {pointwise extension, $\mathsf{T} \Rightarrow$ rule}

$$(\forall y \cdot p \cap b \subseteq S.q)$$

$\equiv$ {definition of correctness}

$$(\forall y \cdot p \cap b \ \{\!\!|\ S \ |\!\!\}\ q)$$

We can use these rules from left to right (top-down) to reduce the correctness
a larger program statement to a smaller one. This is the method that we use
determine whether a given program statement is correct with respect to given p
and postconditions. The application of the rules in this direction is straightforwa
except for the sequential composition rule, which requires us to invent an int
mediate condition. The situation will be similar later on, when we consider h
to establish the correctness of loops. There we also have to invent an intermedi
condition, known as the loop invariant.

We can also use the rules from right to left (bottom-up), to gradually build up mo
and more complex program statements. This could be one way to do explorati
programming.

There is an important difference between the Hoare-like axioms and inference ru
for establishing correctness, and the use of the predicate transformer semantics
originally proposed by Dijkstra for the same purpose (aside from the fact t
Hoare's axiomatization is concerned with partial correctness and Dijkstra's w
total correctness). The former permits us to prove that a program is correct
indeed it is, but does not allow us to say anything about an incorrect program.
the predicate transformer approach, the correctness assertion $p \ \{\!\!|\ S \ |\!\!\}\ q$ is jus
formula like any other, so we can try to prove it correct, or we can try to pro
it incorrect, or we can prove other desirable properties of statements. Hence,
predicate transformer approach is more flexible than Hoare-like axiomatizatio
In addition, the predicate transformer formulation of correctness is done with
introducing any new axioms or inference rules, being essentially just an applicat
of higher-order logic. Hoare logic, on the other hand, requires a completely n
axiom system to be built, with its own notion of terms and formulas and its o
axioms and inference rules, usually built on top of a standard first-order logic.

Example

The following simple derivation illustrates the way in which these rules are used to establish correctness of a statement. We show that

$$\text{true } \{\!| \, x := n \,; [y := y' \mid y' > x] \, |\!\} \, y > n \; .$$

Here x and y are program variables, and n can be either a constant, a free variable, or a program variable (the derivation looks the same regardless of which alternative is chosen). We have that

$\quad \text{true } \{\!| \, x := n \,; [y := y' \mid y' > x] \, |\!\} \, y > n$

$\Leftarrow$ {sequential rule, $x = n$ as intermediate predicate}

$\quad (\text{“ true } \{\!| \, x := n \, |\!\} \, x = n \text{ ”}) \wedge (x = n \, \{\!| \, [y := y' \mid y' > x] \, |\!\} \, y > n)$

$\equiv$ {assignment rule}

$\quad \text{“ true } \subseteq (n = n) \text{ ”} \wedge (x = n \, \{\!| \, [y := y' \mid y' > x] \, |\!\} \, y > n)$

$\equiv$ {reduction}

$\quad \mathsf{T} \wedge (x = n \, \{\!| \, [y := y' \mid y' > x] \, |\!\} \, y > n)$

$\equiv$ {T greatest, demonic assignment rule}

$\quad (x = n) \subseteq (\forall y' \cdot y' > x \Rightarrow y' > n)$

$\equiv$ {reduction: $(\forall x \, n \cdot x = n \Rightarrow (\forall y' \cdot y' > x \Rightarrow y' > n))$}

$\quad \mathsf{T}$

2   Stepwise Refinement

Let us next study in more detail how the notion of refinement of statements is used in program construction. In particular, we are interested in the *stepwise refinement method* for program construction. This method emphasizes systematic program construction, starting from given program requirements and working stepwise towards a final program that satisfies these requirements.

The following lemma shows that refinement of a statement is the same as *preserving correctness* of the statement.

Lemma 17.3   *Let S and S' be two predicate transformers. Then*

$$S \sqsubseteq S' \;\equiv\; (\forall p \, q \cdot p \, \{\!| \, S \, |\!\} \, q \Rightarrow p \, \{\!| \, S' \, |\!\} \, q) \;.$$

Proof

$\quad S \sqsubseteq S'$

$\equiv$ {definition of refinement}

$\quad (\forall q \cdot \text{“ } S.q \subseteq S'.q \text{ ”})$

$\equiv$ {mutual implication}

- $S.q \subseteq S'.q$
$\Rightarrow$ {transitivity of inclusion}
$(\forall p \cdot p \subseteq S.q \Rightarrow p \subseteq S'.q)$

- $S.q \subseteq S'.q$
$\equiv$ {reflexivity, $\mathsf{T} \Rightarrow$ rule}
$S.q \subseteq S.q \Rightarrow S.q \subseteq S'.q$
$\Leftarrow$ {specialization, $p := S.q$}
$(\forall p \cdot p \subseteq S.q \Rightarrow p \subseteq S'.q)$

$\cdot \ (\forall p\, q \cdot p \subseteq S.q \Rightarrow p \subseteq S'.q)$
$\equiv$ {definition of correctness}
$(\forall p\, q \cdot p \,\{\!| S |\!\}\, q \Rightarrow p \,\{\!| S' |\!\}\, q)$

$\square$

Note that the proof uses only the reflexivity and transitivity of the refinem
ordering, so it would hold even if refinement were only a preorder.

Thus refinement is a relation that preserves the correctness of a statement: If $S \sqsubseteq$
then S' satisfies any correctness condition that S satisfies. The result also shows
refinement is the *weakest relation* that preserves correctness (the strongest re
tion is equality). Thus, refinement exactly characterizes the property of preserv
correctness of statements.

The stepwise refinement method is based on this observation. We start with
initial statement S_0 that satisfies some correctness criteria that we have given;
we assume that $p \,\{\!| S_0 |\!\}\, q$. Then we derive a sequence of successive refineme
$S_0 \sqsubseteq S_1 \sqsubseteq \cdots \sqsubseteq S_n$. By transitivity, we have that $S_0 \sqsubseteq S_n$, and because refinem
preserves correctness, we have that $p \,\{\!| S_n |\!\}\, q$. We have constructed a new statem
S_n from the original statement S_0, where the new statement also satisfies our ini
requirement.

Even if our aim is to derive a program statement from a program specificat
we may move within the full predicate transformer category when carrying
a program derivation. Only the final program that we derive has to fall int
subclass of predicate transformers that are considered executable. This is illustra
in Figure 17.1, where we indicate that Pascal-like programs form a subclass of
functional statements.

On the other hand, if we restrict our derivation to program statements in a cer
class, then the monotonicity and homomorphism properties that we have identi
for this class of statements permit us to prove stronger properties, which migh
crucial in the derivation. Monotonicity is a good example of this, as it permit
to focus on a component of a statement and refine it in isolation from its conte

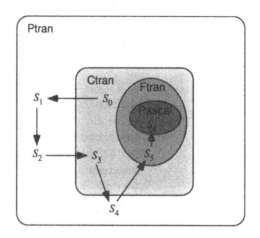

FIGURE 17.1. Program derivation in the refinement calculus

Correctness as Refinement

We have shown that refinement can be described in terms of correctness. We can also describe correctness in terms of refinement. Let predicates p and q be given. Then the statement $\{p\}$; $[\hat{q}]$ is a *pre–post specification statement*, where $\hat{q} = (\lambda\sigma \cdot q)$ is the pointwise extension of the predicate q to a relation. This specification statement establishes postcondition q whenever precondition p holds in the initial state.

An example of a pre–post specification is the statement

$$\{n > 0\} ; [(x^2 \leq n < (x + 1)^2)^{\wedge}] \ .$$

This statement specifies that the final value of program variable x should be the integer number square root of n. Note that this specification allows other program variables to be changed in arbitrary ways. This may not be what we desire, so in practice we prefer to use assignments in specifications, as described later.

The semantics of the pre–post specification is as follows (Exercise 17.4):

$$(\{p\} ; [\hat{q}]).r.\sigma \ \equiv \ p.\sigma \wedge q \subseteq r \ .$$

Lemma 17.4 *Let p and q be predicates and S a monotonic predicate transformer. Then*

$$p \{\!|\, S \,|\!\} q \ \equiv \ \{p\} ; [\hat{q}] \sqsubseteq S \ .$$

Proof

$$S \text{ monotonic}$$
$$\vdash \{p\} ; [\hat{q}] \sqsubseteq S$$
$$\equiv \{\text{semantics of pre–post specification}\}$$
$$(\forall r \ \sigma \cdot p.\sigma \wedge q \subseteq r \Rightarrow S.r.\sigma)$$

$\equiv$ {mutual implication}

- $(\forall r\ \sigma \cdot p.\sigma \land q \subseteq r \Rightarrow S.r.\sigma)$
- $\Rightarrow$ {specialize $r := q$, simplify}
  $(\forall \sigma \cdot p.\sigma \Rightarrow S.q.\sigma)$
- $(\forall r\ \sigma \cdot p.\sigma \land q \subseteq r \Rightarrow \text{`` } S.r.\sigma \text{ ''})$
- $\Leftarrow$ {monotonicity of S, local assumption $q \subseteq r$}
  $(\forall r\ \sigma \cdot p.\sigma \land q \subseteq r \Rightarrow S.q.\sigma)$
  $\equiv$ {quantifier rules}
  $(\exists r \cdot q \subseteq r) \Rightarrow (\forall \sigma \cdot p.\sigma \Rightarrow S.q.\sigma)$
  $\equiv$ {antecedent is trivially true}
  $(\forall \sigma \cdot p.\sigma \Rightarrow S.q.\sigma)$

- $(\forall \sigma \cdot p.\sigma \Rightarrow S.q.\sigma))$

$\equiv$ {pointwise extension}

$p \subseteq S.q$

$\square$

Because correctness can be expressed as refinement, we can start the stepw
refinement from an initial specification statement:

$$\{p\}\ ;\ [\hat{q}] \sqsubseteq S_1 \sqsubseteq S_2 \sqsubseteq \cdots \sqsubseteq S_n\ .$$

From this we see that S_n is correct with respect to the original pre- and postcondi
pair:

$$p \{\!| S_n |\!\} q\ .$$

A refinement step may introduce a new specification statement as a compon
$S_i \sqsubseteq S_{i+1}[X := \{p'\}\ ;\ [\hat{q'}]]$. If we implement the subspecification with a statem
S', so that $\{p'\}\ ;\ [\hat{q'}] \sqsubseteq S'$, then the monotonicity of statements allows u
conclude that $S_{i+1}[X := \{p'\}\ ;\ [\hat{q'}]] \sqsubseteq S_{i+1}[X := S']$. This *top-down* deriva
step thus gives that $S_i \sqsubseteq S_{i+1}[X := S']$. Top-down derivation is an important
of the stepwise refinement paradigm and motivates our choice of monotonicit
a fundamental property of statements.

We can actually treat any statement as a specification. This enlarges the clas
specifications to *abstract statements*. An abstract statement need not be im
mentable, because it is not intended to be executed. It is just intended to serve
high-level description of the kind of behavior that we are interested in achiev
Any refinement of the abstract statement is an implementation of it (the implem
tation may or may not be executable). The notion of abstract statements per
us to treat both implementation of specifications and program transformation
two special cases of the general notion of refining a statement.

General Specification Statements

The specification statement $\{p\}; [\hat{q}]$ establishes the postcondition q independently of what the state is initially, as long as the state satisfies the precondition p. A specification statement that permits us to define the final state as a function of the initial state is of the form $\{p\}; \langle f \rangle$. We refer to this as a *functional specification statement*. The functional update $\langle f \rangle$ is usually given as an assignment statement. An example is the specification of the factorial statement:

$$\{x \geq 0\}; \langle x := \text{factorial}.x \rangle .$$

This requires that the initial state satisfy the condition $x \geq 0$ and that the final state be such that x is set to the factorial of the original x without changing other program variables.

An even more powerful way of specifying what final states are acceptable is to use a relation Q between initial and final states, rather than just a predicate q on the final state. This gives us a specification of the form $\{p\}; [Q]$, which we refer to as a *conjunctive specification statement*. This requires that the precondition p be satisfied and that for any initial state $\sigma \in p$ the final state be in the set $Q.\sigma$. If this set is empty for some σ, then the specification is impossible to satisfy for that specific initial state.

In practice, the precondition is usually a Boolean expression, and the relation is a relational assignment. The specification is then of the form $\{b_1\}; [x := x' \mid b_2]$. This specification shows that only the program variables x are to be changed; all other variables are to keep their old values. An example is the specification that we mentioned in the introduction:

$$\{x \geq 0 \wedge e > 0\}; [x := x' \mid -e < x - x'^2 < e] .$$

This requires that $x \geq 0 \wedge e > 0$ initially and that x be set to the integer square root of its initial value with tolerance e.

The Boolean expression b in a specification $\{p\}; [x := x' \mid b]$ can be very complex. The specification can often be made more readable by dividing the demonic assignment into different cases, giving a *conditional specification*:

$$\{p\}; \text{if } g_1 \rightarrow [x := x' \mid b_1] \text{ [] } \cdots \text{ [] } g_n \rightarrow [x := x' \mid b_n] \text{ fi} .$$

Such a specification can always be reduced to the form with a single demonic assignment (Exercise 17.5):

$$\{p\}; \text{if } g_1 \rightarrow [x := x' \mid b_1] \text{ [] } \cdots \text{ [] } g_n \rightarrow [x := x' \mid b_n] \text{ fi} =$$
$$\{p \wedge (g_1 \vee \cdots \vee g_n)\}; [x := x' \mid (g_1 \wedge b_1) \vee \cdots \vee (g_n \wedge b_n)] .$$

Specification Constants

A *specification constant* is a free variable introduced to name a certain value (
example, the initial value of some variable) in a subsequent derivation. In
section we justify the use of specification constants and show how they mak
possible to work with pre–post specifications $\{p\}$; $[\hat{q}]$ rather than general c
junctive specifications $\{p\}$; $[Q]$ without losing generality. This will be particul
useful in connection with loops, since there is a simple rule for refining a pre–p
specification into a loop (Section 21.6).

A specification constant is introduced as a fresh (free) variable in a statem
Specification constants are not intended to appear in specifications or progra
they are used as a vehicle for performing program derivations.

The following theorem justifies the use of specification constants.

Theorem 17.5   *Let b be a Boolean expression with possible free occurrences of x_0. The follow
rule for handling specification constants is then generally valid:*

$$\frac{\Phi \vdash \{b\} ; S \sqsubseteq S'}{\Phi \vdash \{\exists x_0 \cdot b\} ; S \sqsubseteq S'}$$

- x_0 not free in Φ, S or S'.

Proof We want to derive $\{\exists x_0 \cdot b\}$; $S \sqsubseteq S'$ from $(\forall x_0 \cdot \{b\}$; $S \sqsubseteq S')$. We hav

$$\Phi$$

$$\vdash (\forall x_0 \cdot \{b\} ; S \sqsubseteq S')$$

$$\equiv \{\text{definition of refinement}\}$$

$$(\forall x_0 \, q \, \sigma \cdot b.\sigma \wedge S.q.\sigma \Rightarrow S'.q.\sigma)$$

$$\equiv \{\text{quantifier rules, } x_0 \text{ not free in } S \text{ or } S'\}$$

$$(\forall q \, \sigma \cdot (\exists x_0 \cdot b.\sigma) \wedge S.q.\sigma \Rightarrow S'.q.\sigma)$$

$$\equiv \{\text{pointwise extension}\}$$

$$(\forall q \, \sigma \cdot (\exists x_0 \cdot b).\sigma \wedge S.q.\sigma \Rightarrow S'.q.\sigma)$$

$$\equiv \{\text{definition of refinement}\}$$

$$\{\exists x_0 \cdot b\} ; S \sqsubseteq S'$$

□

The rule is used as follows. If we want to refine the statement $\{\exists x_0 \cdot t\}$; S (wh
x_0 is variable that does not occur free in S), we start a subderivation from $\{t\}$
The assertion can then be used to simplify and refine S. Whenever we rea
statement S' that does not contain x_0 free, we can close the subderivation
deduce $\{\exists x_0 \cdot t\}$; $S \sqsubseteq S'$. Thus the specification constant does not occur fre
the outermost level in the derivation.

The simplest and most common use of specification constants is where x_0 stands for the initial value of some program variable x. Then the predicate t is $x = x_0$, and the assertion $\{\exists x_0 \cdot t\}$ is trivially equal to skip.

Implementing Specifications

Using specification constants, we can derive a rule for reducing a refinement to a correctness condition with program variables.

Theorem 17.6 *Assume that statement S is built from assignments to program variables x and y using statement constructors. The following rule for reducing refinement to correctness is valid:*

$$\frac{(p \wedge x = x_0 \wedge y = y_0) \mathbin{\{\!\!|} S \mathbin{|\!\!\}} (b[x, x' := x_0, x] \wedge y = y_0)}{\{p\}\,;[x := x' \mid b] \sqsubseteq S}.$$

where x_0 and y_0 are fresh variables.

Proof The assumption that S is built from assignments to x and y makes it possible to prove (by induction over the structure of S) the following:

$$p \mathbin{\{\!\!|} S \mathbin{|\!\!\}} q \Rightarrow$$
$$(\lambda \sigma \cdot p.\sigma \wedge \sigma = \sigma_0) \mathbin{\{\!\!|} S \mathbin{|\!\!\}} (\lambda \sigma \cdot q.\sigma \wedge (\exists x' \, y' \cdot \sigma = \mathsf{set}.x.x'.(\mathsf{set}.y.y'.\sigma_0))) .$$

We then have (where b_0 abbreviates $b[x, x' := x_0, x]$)

$$(p \wedge x = x_0 \wedge y = y_0) \mathbin{\{\!\!|} S \mathbin{|\!\!\}} b_0 \wedge y = y_0$$
$\equiv$ {property above}
$$(\lambda \sigma \cdot p.\sigma \wedge \sigma = \sigma_0 \wedge x.\sigma = x_0 \wedge y.\sigma = y_0)$$
$$\mathbin{\{\!\!|} S \mathbin{|\!\!\}}$$
$$(\lambda \sigma \cdot \exists x_1 \, y_1 \cdot b_0.\sigma \wedge \sigma = \mathsf{set}.x.x_1.(\mathsf{set}.y.y_1.\sigma_0) \wedge y.\sigma = y_0)$$
$\equiv$ {use state attribute properties to rewrite}
$$(\lambda \sigma \cdot p.\sigma \wedge \sigma = \sigma_0 \wedge x.\sigma = x_0 \wedge y.\sigma = y_0)$$
$$\mathbin{\{\!\!|} S \mathbin{|\!\!\}}$$
$$(\lambda \sigma \cdot \exists x_1 \cdot b_0.\sigma \wedge \sigma = \mathsf{set}.x.x_1.(\mathsf{set}.y.y_0.\sigma_0) \wedge y.\sigma = y_0)$$
$\equiv$ {Lemma 17.4}
$$\{\lambda \sigma \cdot p.\sigma \wedge \sigma = \sigma_0 \wedge x.\sigma = x_0 \wedge y.\sigma = y_0\}\,;$$
$$[\lambda \sigma \, \sigma' \cdot \exists x_1 \cdot b_0.\sigma' \wedge \sigma' = \mathsf{set}.x.x_1.(\mathsf{set}.y.y_0.\sigma) \wedge y.\sigma' = y_0]$$
$$\sqsubseteq S$$
$\equiv$ {use assertion to rewrite}
$$\{\lambda \sigma \cdot p.\sigma \wedge \sigma = \sigma_0 \wedge x.\sigma = x_0 \wedge y.\sigma = y_0\}\,;$$
$$[\lambda \sigma \, \sigma' \cdot \exists x_1 \cdot b_0.\sigma' \wedge \sigma' = \mathsf{set}.x.x_1.\sigma_0]$$

$$\sqsubseteq S$$

$\Rightarrow$ {subderivation below, transitivity of $\sqsubseteq$}

$$\{\lambda\sigma \bullet p.\sigma \wedge \sigma = \sigma_0 \wedge x.\sigma = x_0 \wedge y.\sigma = y_0\} ;$$
$$[\lambda\sigma \, \sigma' \bullet (\exists x' \bullet \sigma' = \text{set}.x.x'.\sigma \wedge b.\sigma)]$$

$$\sqsubseteq S$$

$\equiv$ {rewrite to assignment notation}

$$\{\lambda\sigma \bullet p.\sigma \wedge \sigma = \sigma_0 \wedge x.\sigma = x_0 \wedge y.\sigma = y_0\} ; [x := x' \mid b] \sqsubseteq S$$

and the result then follows from Theorem 17.5. The subderivation referred to above is as follows:

$$\{\lambda\sigma \bullet p.\sigma \wedge \sigma = \sigma_0 \wedge x.\sigma = x_0 \wedge y.\sigma = y_0\} ;$$
$$[\lambda\sigma \, \sigma' \bullet (\exists x' \bullet \sigma' = \text{set}.x.x'.\sigma \wedge b.\sigma)]$$

$$\sqsubseteq$$

$$\{\lambda\sigma \bullet p.\sigma \wedge \sigma = \sigma_0 \wedge x.\sigma = x_0 \wedge y.\sigma = y_0\} ;$$
$$[\lambda\sigma \, \sigma' \bullet \exists x_1 \bullet b[x, x' := x_0, x].\sigma' \wedge \sigma' = \text{set}.x.x_1.\sigma_0]$$

$\equiv$ {use the rule $\{p\} ; [P] \sqsubseteq \{p\} ; [Q] \equiv |p| ; Q \subseteq P$ (Exercise 17.8)}

$$(\forall\sigma \, \sigma' \, x_1 \bullet p.\sigma \wedge \sigma = \sigma_0 \wedge x.\sigma = x_0 \wedge y.\sigma = y_0 \wedge$$
$$b[x, x' := x_0, x].\sigma' \wedge \sigma' = \text{set}.x.x_1.\sigma_0 \Rightarrow$$
$$(\exists x' \bullet \sigma' = \text{set}.x.x'.\sigma \wedge b.\sigma))$$

$\equiv$ {one-point rule}

$$(\forall\sigma' \, x_1 \bullet p.\sigma_0 \wedge x.\sigma_0 = x_0 \wedge y.\sigma_0 = y_0 \wedge$$
$$b[x, x' := x_0, x].(\text{set}.x.x_1.\sigma_0) \Rightarrow$$
$$(\exists x' \bullet \text{set}.x.x_1.\sigma_0 = \text{set}.x.x'.\sigma_0 \wedge b.\sigma_0))$$

$\equiv$ {use x_1 as existential witness}

$$\mathsf{T}$$

The details of the last step are left as an exercise to the reader. $\square$

This shows that any refinement of the form $\{p\} ; [x := x' \mid b] \sqsubseteq S$ can be proved by proving a corresponding correctness condition. The correctness condition can then be decomposed using the rules given earlier in this chapter, and in the end proving the refinement has been reduced to proving theorems that do not include any programming constructs.

17.3 Refinement Laws

A *refinement law* is an inference rule that allows us to deduce that a certain refinement $S \sqsubseteq S'$ is valid. Since equality is stronger than refinement, any law with a conclusion of the form $S = S'$ can also be used as a refinement law. We use refinement laws to establish that the individual refinement steps are correct in a derivation $S_0 \sqsubseteq S_1 \sqsubseteq \cdots \sqsubseteq S_n$.

We have already encountered numerous refinement laws. Essentially all the monotonicity and homomorphism properties of statements proved in previous chapters can be used as refinement laws. The monotonicity and homomorphism properties that we have established for other entities in the refinement calculus hierarchy (state transformers, state predicates, and state relations) are also very useful in program derivation, because refinement of statements is often reduced to ordering or homomorphism properties at lower levels in the hierarchy. Below we look more closely at some of the basic classes of refinement laws and justify their use in program derivations.

Monotonicity Laws

The monotonicity properties that we have identified in earlier chapters are central to the stepwise refinement paradigm. For example, we can write the monotonicity law for assert as follows:

$$\frac{\Phi \vdash p \subseteq p'}{\Phi \vdash \{p\} \sqsubseteq \{p'\}} \ .$$

This rule tells us that if we prove $\Phi \vdash p \subseteq p'$ (in a subderivation), then we have established $\{p\} \sqsubseteq \{p'\}$, where Φ is the set of current assumptions. In practice, the predicates p and p' are usually Boolean expressions, so proving $p \subseteq p'$ can be further reduced to proving implication between two Boolean terms. In this way, refinement between statements is reduced to implication between Boolean terms, two steps down in the refinement calculus hierarchy. This kind of reduction in the hierarchy is very common. This is the reason why we have put so much emphasis on all domains within the refinement calculus hierarchy.

Similarly, the fact that sequential composition of monotonic predicate transformers is monotonic in both arguments gives us the following rule:

$$\frac{\Phi \vdash S_1 \sqsubseteq S_1' \qquad \Phi \vdash S_2 \sqsubseteq S_2'}{\Phi \vdash S_1 \ ; \ S_2 \sqsubseteq S_1' \ ; \ S_2'} \ .$$

A step according to this rule in a program derivation has two subderivations, one to establish $\Phi \vdash S_1 \sqsubseteq S_1'$ and another to establish $\Phi \vdash S_2 \sqsubseteq S_2'$. In practice, we usually leave one of the two substatements unchanged, and the trivial subderivation (of the form $S \sqsubseteq S$) is then omitted.

The general refinement rule for monotonic statement constructs is just a reformulation of the monotonicity property:

$$\frac{\Phi \vdash t \sqsubseteq t' \qquad \Phi \vdash (\lambda x \cdot S) \text{ is monotonic}}{\Phi \vdash S[x := t] \sqsubseteq S[x := t']} .$$

Here t and t' may be substatements, but they may also be predicates, relations other entities that occur in a monotonic position inside S (with $\sqsubseteq$ replaced b suitable ordering).

Laws for Refining Specification Statements

We will obviously need rules for refining different kinds of specifications. We here consider one important special case: refining a conjunctive specification functional update. A more extensive treatment of refining specification stateme is given in Chapter 27.

We have the following coercion rule (Exercise 17.9) for this purpose:

$$\frac{\Phi \vdash |p| ; |f| \subseteq Q}{\Phi \vdash \{p\} ; [Q] \sqsubseteq \langle f \rangle} .$$

Such a rule is well suited for general reasoning about update statements, bu already noted, in practice we work with the assignment notation. We can formu the above rule for general assignments as follows:

$$\frac{\Phi \vdash b_1 \subseteq b_2[x' := e]}{\Phi \vdash \{b_1\} ; [x := x' \mid b_2] \sqsubseteq \langle x := e \rangle} \qquad \textit{(introduce assignme}$$

- x' not free in Φ or b_1.

To show that this is in fact a special case of the rule given above, we show co spondence between the hypotheses. Assume that p is the Boolean expression f is $(x := e)$, and Q is $(x := x' \mid b_2)$. Then

$|p| ; |f| \subseteq Q$

$\equiv$ {definitions of coercions, composition, and relation order}

$(\forall \sigma \ \sigma'' \cdot (\exists \sigma' \cdot \sigma' = \sigma \wedge p.\sigma \wedge \sigma'' = f.\sigma') \Rightarrow Q.\sigma.\sigma'')$

$\equiv$ {one-point rules}

$(\forall \sigma \cdot p.\sigma \Rightarrow Q.\sigma.(f.\sigma))$

$\equiv$ {assumption about p and f}

$(\forall \sigma \cdot b_1.\sigma \Rightarrow Q.\sigma.(\text{set}.x.(e.\sigma).\sigma))$

$\equiv$ {assumption about Q}

$(\forall \sigma \cdot b_1.\sigma \Rightarrow (\exists x' \cdot \text{`` set}.x.(e.\sigma).\sigma = \text{set}.x.x'.\sigma \text{''} \wedge b_2.\sigma))$

$\equiv$ {state algebra property (Exercise 5.1)}

$(\forall \sigma \cdot b_1.\sigma \Rightarrow (\exists x' \cdot e.\sigma = x' \wedge b_2.\sigma))$

$\equiv$ {one-point rule}

$\qquad (\forall \sigma \cdot b_1.\sigma \Rightarrow b_2[x' := e].\sigma)$

$\equiv$ {pointwise extension}

$\qquad b_1 \subseteq b_2[x' := e]$

As an example of applying this rule, consider the refinement

$$\{x > 0\} ; [x := x' \mid 0 \le x' < x] \;\sqsubseteq\; \langle x := x - 1\rangle \;.$$

The coercion rule says that this refinement holds if

$$(x > 0) \;\subseteq\; (0 \le x - 1 < x) \;.$$

By reduction, this follows from the fact that $x - 1 < x$ and $x > 0 \Rightarrow x - 1 \ge 0$ hold for any natural number x. Hence, the refinement is valid.

Laws for Assignment Statements

We use homomorphism properties to lift properties of state transformers, predicates, and relations to laws for refinement of statements. The properties of assignments proved in Chapter 5 can, e.g., be lifted to properties of assignment statements using the homomorphism of functional update. Thus, Theorem 5.3 gives us the following rule for merging and splitting assignment statements:

$$\langle x := e\rangle ; \langle x := f\rangle \;=\; \langle x := f[x := e]\rangle \qquad \textit{(merge assignments)}$$

(recall that we implicitly assume that var x is satisfied in rules like this). The corollaries of Theorem 5.3 give us additional rules as special cases. The merge/split rule is as follows for assignments to distinct variables x and y:

$$\langle x := e\rangle ; \langle y := f\rangle \;=\; \langle x, y := e, f[x := e]\rangle \;.$$

Furthermore, if y is not free in e, and x is not free in f, then

$$\langle x := e\rangle ; \langle y := f\rangle \;=\; \langle y := f\rangle ; \langle x := e\rangle \;. \qquad \textit{(commute assignments)}$$

Laws for relational assignment statements

The homomorphism properties of relational updates give us similar rules. From Theorem 9.6 we get the following basic rules:

$$[x := x' \mid b] ; [x := x' \mid c] = \qquad\qquad \textit{(demonic merge)}$$
$$\quad [x := x' \mid (\exists x'' \cdot b[x' := x''] \wedge c[x := x''])] \;,$$
$$\{x := x' \mid b\} ; \{x := x' \mid c\} = \qquad\qquad \textit{(angelic merge)}$$
$$\quad \{x := x' \mid (\exists x'' \cdot b[x' := x''] \wedge c[x := x''])\} \;.$$

Special rules then follow from the corollaries of Theorem 9.6. First,

$$[x := x' \mid b] ; [y := y' \mid c[x' := x]] = [x, y := x', y' \mid b \wedge c] .$$

Furthermore, if x and x' do not occur free in c and y and y' do not occur free in
then

$$[x := x' \mid b] ; [y := y' \mid c] = [y := y' \mid c] ; [x := x' \mid b] . \quad (commu$$

The rules for angelic assignments are analogous.

Finally, we have two rules derived from Corollary 9.9. If x' and y' are not free
e, then

$$[x, y := x', y' \mid b[x := e]] = \qquad\qquad (add\ leading\ assignmen$$
$$\langle x := e \rangle ; [x, y := x', y' \mid b] ,$$

and if x' is not free in b and y is not free in e, then

$$[x, y := x', y' \mid b \wedge x' = e] = \qquad\qquad (add\ trailing\ assignmen$$
$$[y := y' \mid b] ; \langle x := e[y' := y] \rangle .$$

The following derivation fragment illustrates adding a trailing assignment:

$$[x, y := x', y' \mid y' \leq y \wedge x' > x]$$
$\sqsubseteq$ {replace subcomponent in antimonotonic context}
$$[x, y := x', y' \mid y' \leq y \wedge x' = x + 1]$$
$\sqsubseteq$ {add trailing assignment}
$$[y := y' \mid y' \leq y] ; \langle x := x + 1 \rangle$$

Introducing and Eliminating Conditional Statements

The monotonicity rules preserve the structure of the statement involved; an as
statement is transformed into another assert statement, or a sequential comp
tion is transformed into another sequential composition. Using various homon
phism rules we can also do derivation steps that change or introduce struct
We have already seen how sequential composition can be introduced by split
assignments (and eliminated by merging assignments). Let us consider sim
introduction/elimination rules for conditional statements.

An intuitively obvious rule for a deterministic conditional is the following:

$$S = \text{if } g \text{ then } S \text{ else } S \text{ fi} . \qquad\qquad (introduce\ condition$$

Since the rule is an equality, it can be used for both introducing and elimina
conditionals. It is formally derived as follows:

$$S$$

$= \{\text{exhaustion, unit}\}$

$$[g \cup \neg g] ; S$$

$= \{\text{homomorphism}\}$

$$([g] \sqcap [\neg g]) ; S$$

$= \{\text{distributivity}\}$

$$[g] ; S \sqcap [\neg g] ; S$$

$= \{\text{characterization of conditional}\}$

$$\text{if } g \text{ then } S \text{ else } S \text{ fi}$$

The generalization of the introduction rule to the guarded conditional statement is

$$S \sqsubseteq [g_1 \cup \cdots \cup g_n] ; \text{if } g_1 \to S \, [\!] \, \cdots \, [\!] \, g_n \to S \text{ fi} .$$

We leave the proof of this rule as an exercise to the reader (Exercise 17.6). Note that the guard statement on the right-hand side is needed, for without it the right-hand side would be aborting in a state where all the guards are false.

The following rule for *eliminating conditionals* is useful when we know that a certain branch of the conditional is enabled:

$$g \subseteq g_i \Rightarrow \qquad\qquad\qquad\qquad (\textit{eliminate conditional})$$
$$\{g\} ; \text{if } g_1 \to S_1 \, [\!] \, \cdots \, [\!] \, g_n \to S_n \text{ fi} \sqsubseteq S_i$$

when $1 \leq i \leq n$.

Introduction and Elimination of Local Variables

A local variable introduction is a refinement of the form begin var $z := e'$; $S \sqsubseteq$ begin var $y, z := e, e'$; S' end, where S and S' are related in some way. We saw in Chapter 5 that such block introductions work on the state transformer level. We shall now show how a corresponding basic principle works on the statement level.

Local variable introduction for statements works in the same way as for state transformers. The general principle can be formulated as follows: if S is a statement built by statement constructors from assignment statements, asserts, and guards only; and y does not appear free in q or S, then

$$\text{begin var } z \mid q ; S \text{ end} \sqsubseteq \qquad\qquad (\textit{introduce local variable})$$
$$\text{begin var } y, z \mid p \wedge q ; S' \text{ end} ,$$

where S' is similar to S, possibly with assignments to y added.

An important special case is the situation where the initial statement has no local variables. Then the rule reduces to block introduction:

$$S \sqsubseteq \text{begin var } y \mid p \text{ ; } S' \text{ end .} \qquad (\textit{introduce bloc}$$

The following derivation outlines how the principle works in the case of bl< introduction when S is a simple demonic assignment, where y does not occur # in b:

$[x := x' \mid b]$

$\sqsubseteq$ {properties of begin and end}

begin var $y \mid p$; skip end ; $[x := x' \mid b]$

$= \{\langle\text{end}\rangle = [y := y' \mid T]$; $\langle\text{end}\rangle$ by state attribute properties}

begin var $y \mid p$; $[y := y' \mid T]$ end ; $[x := x' \mid b]$

$= \{\langle\text{end}\rangle$; $[x := x' \mid b] = [x := x' \mid b]$; $\langle\text{end}\rangle$ by state attribute properti

begin var $y \mid p$; $[y := y' \mid T]$; $[x := x' \mid b]$ end

$= \{\langle\text{end}\rangle = [y := y' \mid T]$; $\langle\text{end}\rangle$ by state attribute properties}

begin var $y \mid p$; $[y := y' \mid T]$; $[x := x' \mid b]$; $[y := y' \mid T]$ end

Now the assignments to y can be made more deterministic and/or merged w other assignment statements. In this case, we can arrive at the following:

$$[x := x' \mid b] \sqsubseteq \text{begin var } y \mid p \text{ ; } [x, y := x', y' \mid b] \text{ end .}$$

For a more complex statement S, the same idea is used, pushing the end of block past all substatements and adding assignments to y. The added variabl is a *ghost variable*; it appears only in assignments to itself. However, once it been introduced, further refinement steps can make it play an active role in computation.

The rule for local variable introduction has refinement rather than equality, beca the initialization and the added assignment to the local variables may introd miracles. Thus it cannot directly be used for block elimination. However, if all assignments to a local (ghost) variable are nonmiraculous, then it can be elimina Thus, if S is a statement built by statement constructors from assignment stateme asserts, and guards only; and y occurs in S only as a ghost variable, and initialization p and all assignments to y are nonmiraculous; and y does not o< free in q, and z does not occur free in p, then

$$\text{begin var } y, z \mid p \wedge q \text{ ; } S \text{ end } = \qquad (\textit{eliminate local variab}$$
$$\text{begin var } z \mid q \text{ ; } S' \text{ end ,}$$

where S' is similar to S, but with all assignments to y removed.

Block Shunting

An alternative to the rules for block introduction and elimination is the following shunting rule for blocks:

Theorem 17.7 *Assume that the block* begin var $y := e$; S end *is well-defined, with global variable(s) x, and that S is constructed by statement constructors from assignment statements, asserts, and guards only. Then*

$$\{p \wedge y = e\} ; [x, y := x', y' \mid b] \sqsubseteq S \equiv$$
$$\{p\} ; [x := x' \mid b] \sqsubseteq \text{begin var } y := e ; S \text{ end} ,$$

provided that y and y' are not free in p or b.

Proof For the forward implication we do not need the assumption about S. An outline of the proof is as follows:

$$\{p \wedge y = e\} ; [x, y := x', y' \mid b] \sqsubseteq S$$
$\Rightarrow$ {monotonicity of the block construct}
   begin var $y := e$; $\{p \wedge y = e\}$; $[x, y := x', y' \mid b]$ end $\sqsubseteq$
      begin var $y := e$; S end
$\equiv$ {drop redundant assertion}
   begin var $y := e$; $\{p\}$; $[x, y := x', y' \mid b]$ end $\sqsubseteq$ begin var $y := e$; S end
$\equiv$ {push ⟨end⟩ leftward, use properties of state attributes}
   ⟨begin⟩ ; ⟨end⟩ ; $\{p\}$; $[x := x' \mid b] \sqsubseteq$ begin var $y := e$; S end
$\equiv$ {homomorphism, begin ; end = id}
   $\{p\}$; $[x := x' \mid b] \sqsubseteq$ begin var $y := e$; S end

The reverse implication in the first step is tricky to prove, since it depends on the fact that the only state changes caused by statement S are changes in the attributes x and y (this can be proved by induction on the structure of statement S). The full proof is long and not very informative, so we omit it. For an indication of the idea used, we refer to the proof of Theorem 17.6. □

4 Refinement in Context

The refinement relation that we have defined for program statements is very restrictive; it requires that a refinement should preserve the correctness of the original statement with respect to any correctness requirements that could be stated for the original statement. This means that a substatement refinement preserves correctness in any monotonic context. In practice this is often too strong, because we are usually interested in refining a subcomponent in a specific context and do not care whether this refinement preserves correctness in other contexts also.

The general problem of *refinement in context* can be described as follows. $C[X := S]$ be a statement with a specific occurrence of substatement S sing出 out. Let us write $C[X := S]$ as $C[S]$ and refer to C as the *context* of S. Sin the statement constructors are monotonic, we can always replace S by ano statement S', where $S \sqsubseteq S'$, and get $C[S] \sqsubseteq C[S']$.

However, it may be possible to replace S with a statement S' that does not refin in isolation, but where $C[S] \sqsubseteq C[S']$ still holds. This can be done systematica in the following way: First find a statement S_0 such that $C[S] = C[S_0]$. Then a refinement S' of S_0. The refinement $C[S] \sqsubseteq C[S']$ then follows by monotonic and transitivity. The less refined we can make S_0 without changing the over effect of $C[S_0]$, the more freedom it gives us in the subsequent refinement.

Consider the simple refinement

$$x := 0 \,;\, y := x + 1 \;\sqsubseteq\; x := 0 \,;\, y := 1 \;.$$

This holds even though $y := 1$ is not a refinement of $y := x + 1$. To pr this refinement, we use the fact that x must have the value 0 right after the assignment. Therefore (and this is easily verified using statement definitions)

$$x := 0 \,;\, y := x + 1 \;=\; x := 0 \,;\, \{x = 0\} \,;\, y := x + 1 \;.$$

Intuitively, this holds because the added assert statement will necessarily act a skip. Next we note that

$$\{x = 0\} \,;\, y := x + 1 \;\sqsubseteq\; y := 1 \;.$$

Transitivity then gives us the required result. The assert statement $\{x = 0\}$ is kno as a *context assertion*, and the refinement $\{x = 0\} \,;\, y := x + 1 \sqsubseteq y := 1$ refinement in context. Intuitively, this says that $y := x + 1$ is refined by $y :=$ when $x = 0$ initially.

We collect information about the context of statement S in a context assertion $\{$ and then refine $\{p\} \,;\, S$. A derivation that takes the context into account thus the following structure:

$$
\begin{aligned}
&C[S] \\
&= \{\text{introduce context assertion}\} \\
&\quad C[\{p\} \,;\, S] \\
&\sqsubseteq \{\text{prove } \{p\} \,;\, S \sqsubseteq S', \text{monotonicity}\} \\
&\quad C[S']
\end{aligned}
$$

Adding Context Information

To make the above method work, we need rules that add context assertions t statement. The most general rule is the following: If S is conjunctive, then

$$(p \cap S.\text{true}) \, \{\!| \, S \, |\!\} \, q \;\Rightarrow\; \{p\} \,;\, S = \{p\} \,;\, S \,;\, \{q\} \,, \qquad (\textit{add assertion})$$

which is proved as follows:

$(p \cap S.\text{true}) \, \{\!| \, S \, |\!\} \, q$, S conjunctive

$\vdash (\{p\} \,;\, S \,;\, \{q\}).r$

$= \{\text{definitions}\}$

$p \cap S.(q \cap r)$

$= \{S \text{ conjunctive}\}$

$p \cap S.q \cap S.r$

$= \{\text{correctness assumption implies } p \cap S.r \subseteq S.q, \text{ lattice property}\}$

$p \cap S.r$

$= \{\text{definitions}\}$

$(\{p\} \,;\, S).r$

If we are faced with a statement S that has no initial assertion, then we can always add the trivial assertion {true} (i.e., skip).

An important special case is where S is a deterministic assignment. In this case we get the rule

$$\{p\} \,;\, \langle x := e \rangle \;=\; \{p\} \,;\, \langle x := e \rangle \,;\, \{\exists x_0 \cdot x = e[x := x_0]\} \,.$$

We can also use guard statements $[p]$ to indicate assumptions about the context of a subcomponent to be refined. The use of such *context assumptions* is dual to the use of context assertions. We will study the rules for adding context assertions and assumptions in much more detail in Chapter 28 and will also study refinement in context for different kinds of statements. Here we have limited ourselves to introducing the basic ideas involved in this refinement technique.

Context Assertions in Conditionals and Blocks

A branch in a conditional statement is chosen depending on the truth of a guard. This means that we can use the information that the guard is true when refining a branch. In particular, we can push assertions into conditionals as follows:

$\{p\} \,;\, \text{if } g \text{ then } S_1 \text{ else } S_2 \text{ fi} =$

    $\text{if } g \text{ then } \{p \cap g\} \,;\, S_1 \text{ else } \{p \cap \neg g\} \,;\, S_2 \text{ fi}$

and

$\{p\} \,;\, \text{if } g_1 \rightarrow S_1 \, [\!] \, \cdots \, [\!] \, g_n \rightarrow S_n \text{ fi} =$

    $\text{if } g_1 \rightarrow \{p \cap g_1\} \,;\, S_1 \, [\!] \, \cdots \, [\!] \, g_n \rightarrow \{p \cap g_n\} \,;\, S_n \text{ fi} \,.$

When a block construct initializes a local variable, the initialization can be used context information when refining the block further. If S is written using progr variable notation (with global variables x) and the block adds local variables, th we can generalize the local variable introduction in a simple way:

$$\text{begin var } z \mid b'\,;\{p\}\,;S \text{ end } \sqsubseteq \text{ begin var } y, z \mid b \wedge b'\,;\{p \wedge b\}\,;S' \text{ end}$$

provided that y does not appear in b' or S. Here S' is similar to S, possibly v assignments to y added. The special case in which there are no local variable start with reduces to the following:

$$\{p\}\,;S \sqsubseteq \text{ begin var } y \mid b\,;\{p \wedge b\}\,;S' \text{ end }.$$

We leave the verification of this rule to the reader as an exercise (Exercise 17.1

Using Context Information

Context information is propagated in order to be used in later refinement ste The most common use of context information is in rewriting an expression ins an assignment statement or a guard of a conditional. We shall here give rules this use of context information; more details and proofs are found in Chapter 2

Context information right in front of an assignment statement can be used rewriting as follows:

$$\frac{\Phi \vdash b \subseteq (e = e')}{\Phi \vdash \{b\}\,;x := e = \{b\}\,;x := e'}\;.$$

For relational assignments, we have that

$$\frac{\Phi \vdash (p \wedge c) \subseteq b}{\Phi \vdash \{p\}\,;[x := x' \mid b] \sqsubseteq \{p\}\,;[x := x' \mid c]}\;,$$

$$\frac{\Phi \vdash (p \wedge b) \subseteq c}{\Phi \vdash \{p\}\,;\{x := x' \mid b\} \sqsubseteq \{p\}\,;\{x := x' \mid c\}}\;.$$

Context information in front of a conditional can be used to modify the guard

$$\frac{\Phi \vdash b \subseteq (g_1 = g_1' \wedge \cdots \wedge g_n = g_n')}{\Phi \vdash \{b\}\,;\text{if } g_1 \rightarrow S_1 \; [] \; \cdots \; [] \; g_n \rightarrow S_n \text{ fi} = \{b\}\,;\text{if } g_1' \rightarrow S_1 \; [] \; \cdots \; [] \; g_n' \rightarrow S_n}$$

Example Derivation

We illustrate these rules by developing a program fragment that computes minimum of two numbers. We do not assume a min operator; instead we start fi a relational assignment.

$$[z := z' \mid (z' = x \wedge x \le y) \vee (z' = y \wedge x \ge y)]$$
$$= \{\text{introduce conditional}\}$$

$$\text{if } x \leq y \rightarrow \{x \leq y\}; [z := z' \mid `` (z' = x \wedge x \leq y) \vee (z' = y \wedge x \geq y) \text{''}]$$
$$[] \; x \geq y \rightarrow \{x \geq y\}; [z := z' \mid (z' = x \wedge x \leq y) \vee (z' = y \wedge x \geq y)]$$
$$\text{fi}$$

$= \{\text{rewrite using context information } x \leq y\}$

$$\text{if } x \leq y \rightarrow \{x \leq y\}; [z := z' \mid z' = x]$$
$$[] \; x \geq y \rightarrow \{x \geq y\}; [z := z' \mid `` (z' = x \wedge x \leq y) \vee (z' = y \wedge x \geq y) \text{''}]$$
$$\text{fi}$$

$= \{\text{rewrite using context information } x \geq y\}$

$$\text{if } x \leq y \rightarrow \{x \leq y\}; [z := z' \mid z' = x]$$
$$[] \; x \geq y \rightarrow \{x > y\}; [z := z' \mid z' = y]$$
$$\text{fi}$$

$= \{\text{rewrite deterministic updates, drop assertions}\}$

$$\text{if } x \leq y \rightarrow z := x \; [] \; x \geq y \rightarrow z := y \text{ fi}$$

.5 Refinement with Procedures

Recall the definition of a (local) procedure:

$$\text{proc } N(\text{var } x, \text{val } y) = S \text{ in} \qquad\qquad (\textit{local procedure})$$
$$\cdots N(u, e) \cdots$$
$$\hat{=}$$
$$\text{let } N = (\lambda x \; y \cdot S) \text{ in}$$
$$\cdots \text{begin var } y' := e \; ; N.u.y' \text{ end} \cdots$$

From the definition of the let construct we have

$$\text{proc } N(\text{var } x, \text{val } y) = S \text{ in}$$
$$\cdots N(u, e) \cdots$$
$$=$$
$$\cdots \text{begin var } y' := e \; ; S[x := u] \text{ end} \cdots$$

This shows that if we prove a refinement $S \sqsubseteq S'$, then we have shown how to refine the whole statement construct including the local procedure declaration, provided that the context indicated by the dots $\cdots$ is monotonic. This justifies the following *rule of procedure refinement*:

$$\frac{S \sqsubseteq S'}{\text{proc } N(\text{var } x, \text{val } y) = S \text{ in } T \sqsubseteq \text{proc } N(\text{var } x, \text{val } y) = S' \text{ in } T} \; .$$

In practice, we assume that T is built from basic statements and procedure calls $N(u, e)$ using monotonic constructors only, so the rule can be applied.

Thus we can identify and introduce a procedure in an early stage of a derivat‖ and then refine the procedure body at a later stage. This makes the derivation m‖ structured and simpler, especially if the program contains many different call‖ the same procedure.

The following simple example illustrates the idea of procedure refinement:

$$\cdots \ [b := b' \mid 0 \leq b' \leq a + c] \cdots$$

$= \{\text{procedure introduction}\}$

proc Between(var y, val x, z) $= \{x \leq z\} ; [y := y' \mid x \leq y' \leq z]$ in
$\quad \cdots$ Between($b, 0, a + c$) $\cdots$

$\sqsubseteq \{\text{make procedure body deterministic}\}$

proc Between(var y, val x, z) $= \langle y := (x + z)/2 \rangle$ in
$\quad \cdots$ Between($b, 0, a + c$) $\cdots$

17.6 Example: Data Refinement

During a program derivation we are often in a situation where we have a block w‖ an abstract (inefficient or unimplementable) local data structure a, and we w‖ to replace it with another, more concrete (efficient, implementable) data struct‖ Such a *data refinement* can be justified using the rules of block introduction ‖ block elimination. The general idea works in three steps:

begin var a ; S_1 end

$\sqsubseteq \{\text{introduce ghost variable } c\}$

begin var a, c ; S_2 end

$\sqsubseteq \{\text{refine the block body so that } a \text{ becomes a ghost variable}\}$

begin var a, c ; S_3 end

$= \{\text{eliminate ghost variable } a\}$

begin var c ; S_4 end

In the first step S_2 is syntactically like S_1, but with assignments to c added (re‖ that c is a ghost variable if it appears only in assignments to c). The added assi‖ ments are chosen such that a certain relationship between c and a (the *abstrac‖ invariant*) always holds. This relationship is then used to refine S_2 into S_3, wh‖ c has taken over the role that a played before and a has become a ghost varia‖ Finally, in the block elimination S_4 is syntactically like S_3 but with all assignme‖ to a removed.

Problem Description: The Least Nonoccurrence

We illustrate the idea of data refinement with an example, developing a program that finds the smallest natural number not occurring in a given array.

We assume that the array B : array Nat of Nat is given and that we want to find the smallest number not occurring in $B[0 \ldots n-1]$. Furthermore, we assume that all elements in $B[0 \ldots n-1]$ are within the range $0 \ldots m-1$. In other words, we assume

$$(\forall i \mid i < n \cdot B[i] < m) .$$

To make specifications easier to read, we introduce notation for when a value occurs as an element in an array segment:

$$\mathsf{elem}.z.a[j \ldots k] \;\hat{=}\; (\exists i \mid j \le i \le k \cdot a[i] = z) .$$

For simplicity, we abbreviate $\mathsf{elem}.z.B[0 \ldots n-1]$ as $\mathsf{elem}.z.B$.

Our specification is then

$$[x := x' \mid \neg\,\mathsf{elem}.x'.B \land (\forall y \cdot \neg\,\mathsf{elem}.y.B \Rightarrow x' \le y)] .$$

First Refinement: A Block Introduction

Our aim is now to develop a program that is reasonably efficient when n is large and m is small. Our idea is first to collect information about what numbers occur in $B[0 \ldots n-1]$ and then find the smallest number that is not among these. To collect this information we add a local variable A : Set of Nat (in variable declarations, we use the notation Set of Σ for $\mathcal{P}(\Sigma)$).

$$[x := x' \mid \neg\,\mathsf{elem}.x'.B \land (\forall y \cdot \neg\,\mathsf{elem}.y.B \Rightarrow x' \le y)]$$

$\sqsubseteq$ {introduce block with initial assignment}

    begin var A : Set of Nat ;

      $[A := A' \mid (\forall y \cdot y \in A' \equiv \mathsf{elem}.y.B)] ; \{\forall y \cdot y \in A \equiv \mathsf{elem}.y.B\} ;$

      $[x := x' \mid \text{``} \neg\,\mathsf{elem}.x'.B \land (\forall y \cdot \neg\,\mathsf{elem}.y.B \Rightarrow x' \le y) \text{''}]$

    end

$\sqsubseteq$ {use assertion to rewrite}

    begin var A : Set of Nat ;

      $[A := A' \mid (\forall y \cdot y \in A' \equiv \mathsf{elem}.y.B)] ;$

      $[x := x' \mid x' \notin A \land (\forall y \cdot y \notin A \Rightarrow x' \le y)]$

    end

Now the problem is divided into two steps: first build the set A and then find the smallest number not in A.

Second Refinement: Change Data Structure

We shall now replace the data structure A (a set) with a more concrete structu
Since we have assumed that the bound m of the numbers in A is reasonably sm
we can implement a set as an array C : array Nat of Bool so that $C[x]$ is true if
only if x is in the set A.

We do this data refinement in the way described above. When adding the l
variable C, we make sure that the abstraction invariant

$$(\forall y \cdot y \in A \equiv y < m \wedge C[y])$$

holds at every point of the block. After that, we make small changes to the prog
text with the aim of making A a ghost variable.

> begin var A : Set of Nat ;
> $\quad [A := A' \mid (\forall y \cdot y \in A' \equiv \text{elem}.y.B)]$;
> $\quad [x := x' \mid x' \notin A \wedge (\forall y \cdot y \notin A \Rightarrow x' \leq y)]$
> end
> $\sqsubseteq$ {introduce local variable with abstraction invariant}
> begin var A : Set of Nat, C : array Nat of Bool ;
> $\quad [A, C := A', C' \mid (\forall y \cdot y \in A' \equiv \text{elem}.y.B) \wedge$
> $\qquad\qquad$ " $(\forall y \cdot y \in A' \equiv y < m \wedge C'[y])$ "] ;
> $\quad \{\forall y \cdot y \in A \equiv y < m \wedge C[y]\}$;
> $\quad [x := x' \mid x' \notin A \wedge (\forall y \cdot y \notin A \Rightarrow x' \leq y)]$
> end
> $=$ {rewrite with local assumption $(\forall y \cdot y \in A' \equiv \text{elem}.y.B)$}
> begin var A : Set of Nat, C : array Nat of Bool ;
> $\quad [A, C := A', C' \mid (\forall y \cdot y \in A' \equiv \text{elem}.y.B) \wedge$
> $\qquad\qquad (\forall y \cdot \text{elem}.y.B \equiv y < m \wedge C'[y])]$;
> $\quad \{\forall y \cdot y \in A \equiv y < m \wedge C[y]\}$;
> $\quad [x := x' \mid " x' \notin A \wedge (\forall y \cdot y \notin A \Rightarrow x' \leq y) "]$
> end
> $=$ {rewrite using context information}
> begin var A : Set of Nat, C : array Nat of Bool ;
> $\quad " [A, C := A', C' \mid (\forall y \cdot y \in A' \equiv \text{elem}.y.B) \wedge$
> $\qquad\qquad (\forall y \cdot \text{elem}.y.B \equiv y < m \wedge C'[y])] "$;
> $\quad [x := x' \mid (x' \geq m \vee \neg C[x']) \wedge (\forall y \cdot y \geq m \vee \neg C[y] \Rightarrow x' \leq$
> end

$\sqsubseteq$ {split assignment}

begin var A : Set of Nat, C : array Nat of Bool ;

$[A := A' \mid (\forall y \cdot y \in A' \equiv \text{elem}.y.B)]$;

$[C := C' \mid (\forall y \cdot \text{elem}.y.B \equiv y < m \wedge C'[y])]$;

$[x := x' \mid (x' \geq m \vee \neg C[x']) \wedge (\forall y \cdot y \geq m \vee \neg C[y] \Rightarrow x' \leq y)]$

end

$\sqsubseteq$ {eliminate local ghost variable A}

begin var C : array Nat of Bool ;

$[C := C' \mid (\forall y \cdot \text{elem}.y.B \equiv y < m \wedge C'[y])]$;

$[x := x' \mid (x' \geq m \vee \neg C[x']) \wedge (\forall y \cdot y \geq m \vee \neg C[y] \Rightarrow x' \leq y)]$

end

Now we have reached a version in which the array C is used to represent the set of numbers that occur in the array B. This version can be implemented in an efficient way using rules for introducing loops (Chapter 21, Exercise 21.9).

7 Summary and Conclusions

We have analyzed the way in which correctness and refinement are related to each other and used this as a basic justification for the stepwise refinement method for program construction. We have also given some practical refinement laws for program derivation. These are proved by using the basic properties of program statements, such as monotonicity and homomorphism properties, together with the basic properties of assignments and assignment statements given in the previous chapter. We will later study other important kinds of refinement laws, concerned with recursion, iteration, specification, and context refinement. Here we wanted only to give a first impression of the kinds of rules that can be proved formally in refinement calculus.

There are many more such refinement rules, most of which can be derived quite easily. Rather than trying to present a long list of more or less ad hoc rules for practical program derivation, we wanted to emphasize the central algebraic structures that underlie the refinement calculus, and have tried to identify the basic definitions and properties that one needs when reasoning in the calculus. The hope is that with this basis it will be simple to prove less common refinement rules on the spot, as they are needed, and only memorize the most important ones.

Early work on correctness and verification of programs was done by Floyd [56]. Hoare gave rules for partial correctness of deterministic programs with while loops [84]. Correctness proofs of programs (both partial and total correctness), in particular for loops, has been treated extensively by, e.g., Dijkstra [53], Gries [64],

John Reynolds [121], and Hehner [75]. An overview of earlier work is given
Krysztof Apt [4].

The notion of refinement as a total correctness-preserving relation between progr
statements and its formulation in terms of predicate transformers was introduced
Back [6, 7]. Back [9] generalized the notion of refinement to preserving arbitr
correctness properties and showed how this notion is related to the denotational
mantic view of approximation of statements, and to the Smyth ordering [119, 1:
He also introduced a notion of refinement that preserves partial correctness
showed that the refinement relation that preserves both partial and total corr
ness is equivalent to the Egli–Milner ordering [35, 118, 123] of (demonica
nondeterministic program statements.

Specification statements as a way of expressing input–output properties directl
a programming language were introduced by Back [6], replacing correctness
soning with a calculus of refinement. Morgan [104] used the pre–post specificat
(with syntax $x : [p, q]$) together with rules for introducing structures rather t
correctness rules.

Specification constants have been a standard method of making postconditi
refer to initial values of program variables. Morgan developed a block wit
"logical constant" (essentially an angelically initialized local variable) to m
specification constants part of the programming notation [106].

Stepwise refinement, essentially in the form of top-down program refinement,
originally introduced as a systematic programming technique by Dijkstra in the
'60s and early '70s [51]. Wirth was also an early proponent of the technique,
he published an influential paper on the practical application of the stepwise ref
ment method to program derivation [141]. Hoare's axiomatic correctness calc
was also inspired by the stepwise and top-down method for program construct
and he illustrated a formal approach to top-down program construction in an e
paper [86]. The formalization of this method based on Dijkstra's weakest prec
dition calculus was the original motivation for developing the refinement calc
[6, 7]. Since then, the refinement calculus has become much broader in scope
aim, but the stepwise refinement method is still one of the main motivations
studying and applying this calculus.

The top-down program derivation method has continued to be one of the n
programming methods taught in programming courses. The basic idea is on
separation of concerns, articulated by Dijkstra in his early work: one should
to separate the issues and design decisions to be made, and attack one prob
at a time. The simple top-down derivation method has also some disadvanta
It tends to lead to large, monolithic, single-purpose programs that are difficu
reuse.

The advantage of the refinement calculus for top-down program constructio
the possibility of using specification statements and the possibility of combi

pure top-down derivations with optimizing program transformations, which do not fit into the standard top-down design method. Such transformations are usually needed, because the top-down method tends to produce independent refinement of specification and duplication of code, which can often be removed by identifying common substructures.

8 Exercises

17.1 Prove the following rules for total correctness:

$$p \: \{\!| \: \{R\} \: |\!\} \: q \quad \equiv \quad \mathrm{ran.}(|p| \: ; R) \cap q \neq \mathrm{false} \: ,$$
$$p \: \{\!| \: [R] \: |\!\} \: q \quad \equiv \quad \mathrm{ran.}(|p| \: ; R) \subseteq q \: .$$

17.2 Prove the correctness rules for the deterministic conditional and for the block construct.

17.3 Use the rules for relational assignments to prove the following correctness assertions:

(a) $x \geq y \: \{\!| \: [x := x' \mid x' > x] \: |\!\} \: x > y$.

(b) $x \leq y \: \{\!| \: \{x := x' \mid x' > x\} \: |\!\} \: x > y$.

17.4 Show that the semantics of the pre–post specification is as follows:

$$(\{p\} \: ; [\hat{r}]).q.\sigma \quad \equiv \quad p.\sigma \: \wedge \: r \subseteq q \: .$$

17.5 Show that a conditional specification can be reduced to the form with a single demonic assignment, as follows:

$$\{p\} \: ; \: \text{if } g_1 \rightarrow [x := x' \mid b_1] \: [\!] \: g_2 \rightarrow [x := x' \mid b_2] \: \text{fi} \: =$$
$$\{p \wedge (g_1 \vee g_2)\} \: ; [x := x' \mid (g_1 \wedge b_1) \vee (g_2 \wedge b_2)] \: .$$

17.6 Prove the rule for introduction of a guarded conditional:

$$S \: \sqsubseteq \: [g_1 \cup \cdots \cup g_n] \: ; \: \text{if } g_1 \rightarrow S \: [\!] \: \cdots \: [\!] \: g_n \rightarrow S \: \text{fi} \: .$$

17.7 Prove the general rule for introduction of a deterministic conditional:

$$\{p\} \: ; \: S \: = \: \text{if } g \: \text{then} \: \{p \cap g\} \: ; \: S \: \text{else} \: \{p \cap \neg g\} \: ; \: S \: \text{fi} \: .$$

17.8 Prove the following rule for refining a specification with another specification:

$$\{p\} \: ; [P] \sqsubseteq \{p\} \: ; [Q] \quad \equiv \quad |p| \: ; Q \subseteq P \: .$$

17.9 Prove the rule for introduction of a functional update:

$$\frac{\Phi \vdash |p| \: ; |f| \subseteq Q}{\Phi \vdash \{p\} \: ; [Q] \sqsubseteq \langle f \rangle} \: .$$

17.10   Use rules for introducing conditionals and assignments to refine the following specification:

$$z := 100 \text{ min } (x \text{ max } y)$$

("set z to the greater of x and y but no greater than 100"). The resulting statement should not use the min and max operators. Hint: either you can modify assignment introduction rule or you can rewrite the specification as a relational assignment.

17.11   Use the rule for adding a leading assignment to derive the following version of minimum calculation:

$$z := x;$$
if $y < z$ then $z := y$ else skip fi .

17.12   Verify the principle of block introduction with context information:

var $x \vdash \{p\}$; $S \sqsubseteq$ begin var $y \mid b$; $\{p \wedge b\}$; S' end ,

where S' is similar to S, provided that y does not appear in S.

17.13   Recall that statement S is finitely conjunctive if $S.(p \cap q) = S.p \cap S.q$ for arbitrary predicates p and q. Define $\mathrm{Corr}(p, q)$ (the *correctness category* for precondition $p : \mathcal{P}(\Sigma)$ and postcondition $q : \mathcal{P}(\Gamma)$) to be the set of all finitely conjunctive statements S satisfying $p \{\! | S |\!\} q$. Show that for any given collection of underlying state spaces, the collection of all $\mathrm{Corr}(p, q)$ is a category.

17.14   Prove the following property of the correctness category:

$$\mathrm{Corr}(p, q) \cap \mathrm{Corr}(p', q') \; \subseteq \; \mathrm{Corr}(p \cup p', q \cup q') .$$

Hint: Show that if S is finitely conjunctive, then

$$(p \{\! | S |\!\} q) \wedge (p' \{\! | S |\!\} q') \; \Rightarrow \; p \cap p' \{\! | S |\!\} q \cap q' .$$

17.15   Show that if $p \subseteq S.\text{true}$, then there is a least (strongest) predicate q that satisfies $p \{\! | S |\!\} q$.

17.16   We define *weak correctness* as follows: statement S is weakly correct with respect to precondition p and postcondition q, written $p \, (\! | S |\!) \, q$, if the following holds

$$p \cap S.\text{true} \; \subseteq \; S.q .$$

Now let $S = \langle x := 0 \rangle \sqcup \langle x := 1 \rangle$ and $T = \{x = 1\}$, with predicates $p = \mathbf{t}$ $q = (x = 0)$, and $r = (x = 0)$. First show that $S ; T = \langle x := 1 \rangle$. Then prove $p \, (\! | S |\!) \, q$ and $q \, (\! | T |\!) \, r$, but not $p \, (\! | S ; T |\!) \, r$.

Part III

Recursion and Iteration

8

Well-founded Sets and Ordinals

So far, we have looked at lattices as a special kind of posets. In this chapter, we focus on another important special kind of posets: *well-founded sets* and *well-ordered sets*. Well-founded sets are partially ordered sets with the additional property that it is possible to use induction to prove that all elements have a given property. Well-ordered sets are simply well-founded sets on which the order is total.

The construction of the natural numbers in higher-order logic provides us with a standard example of a well-ordered set. A more general example of well-ordered sets is given by *ordinals*. The ordinals can be seen as a generalization of the natural numbers. They are useful in arguments in which the set of natural numbers is "too small" to be sufficient. We show how to define primitive recursion on natural numbers and how to extend this notion to ordinal recursion. These notions in turn justify the principle of induction for the natural numbers and ordinal induction (also known as transfinite induction). These will be found very useful, in particular in reasoning about recursion and iteration.

The sections on ordinals contain a considerable amount of material, and to avoid making the chapter too long, many proofs are only sketched or are omitted altogether.

1 Well-Founded Sets and Well-Orders

An element a is *minimal* in a set A if there is no smaller element in the set, i.e., if ($\forall b \in A \cdot b \not\sqsubseteq a$). A partially ordered set $(W, \sqsubseteq)$ is said to be *well-founded* if every nonempty subset of W has a minimal element, i.e., if

$$(\forall A \subseteq W \cdot A \neq \emptyset \Rightarrow (\exists a \in A \cdot \forall b \in A \cdot b \not\sqsubseteq a)) \ .$$

For example, any finite poset is well-founded (strictly speaking, a relation can
well-founded without being a partial order; here we consider only well-foun
partial orders). It is also easy to see that Nat (the natural numbers ordered by
is well-founded. A further example is Nat × Nat with the lexicographical or
(see Exercise 18.1). The natural numbers ordered by $\geq$ are a simple example
partially ordered set that is not well-founded.

An important property of well-founded sets is that any strictly descending seque
must be finite.

Lemma 18.1 *Assume that the set* $(W, \sqsubseteq)$ *is well-founded and that*

$$w_0 \sqsupset w_1 \sqsupset w_2 \sqsupset \cdots$$

is a strictly descending chain in W. *Then the chain must be finite.*

Proof If the chain is not finite, then the set $\{w_n \mid n \in \text{Nat}\}$ does not have a mini
element. □

Well-Founded Induction

In any well-founded set W, the principle of *well-founded induction* is valid.
principle states that in order to prove that a property p holds for all elements in
it is sufficient to prove that p holds for arbitrary w, assuming that p holds fo
$v \in W$ such that $v \sqsubset w$. Thus, if W is well-founded, then

$$(\forall w \in W \cdot (\forall v \in W \cdot v \sqsubset w \Rightarrow p.v) \Rightarrow p.w) \ \Rightarrow \ (\forall w \in W \cdot p.w)$$

for arbitrary p (in fact, the implication can be strengthened to equivalence). In
rule, $(\forall v \in W \cdot v \sqsubset w \Rightarrow p.v)$ is called the *induction assumption*. The princ
of well-founded induction is derived from the definition of well-foundednes
follows:

$$(W, \sqsubseteq) \text{ is well-founded}$$
$$\equiv \ \{\text{definition}\}$$
$$(\forall A \subseteq W \cdot A \neq \emptyset \Rightarrow (\exists a \in A \cdot \forall b \in A \cdot b \not\sqsubseteq a))$$
$$\Rightarrow \ \{\text{specialize } A := \{x \in W \mid \neg p.x\}\}$$
$$(\exists a \in W \cdot \neg p.a) \Rightarrow$$
$$(\exists a \in W \cdot \neg p.a \wedge (\forall b \in W \cdot `` \neg p.b \Rightarrow b \not\sqsubseteq a \text{ ''}))$$
$$\equiv \ \{\text{contrapositive on subterm}\}$$
$$(\exists a \in W \cdot \neg p.a) \Rightarrow$$

$$(\exists a \in W \cdot \neg\, p.a \wedge (\forall b \in W \cdot b \sqsubset a \Rightarrow p.b))$$

$\equiv$ {contrapositive}

$$(\forall a \in W \cdot \text{``}\, p.a \vee \neg\, (\forall b \in W \cdot b \sqsubset a \Rightarrow p.b)\, \text{''}) \Rightarrow (\forall a \in W \cdot p.a)$$

$\equiv$ {rewrite as implication}

$$(\forall a \in W \cdot (\forall b \in W \cdot b \sqsubset a \Rightarrow p.b) \Rightarrow p.a) \Rightarrow (\forall a \in W \cdot p.a)$$

In the special case of the natural numbers, the principle of well-founded induction is called *complete induction*. In fact, this principle can be shown to be equivalent to the ordinary principle of induction on Nat (see Exercise 18.2).

Well-Ordered sets

Recall that a partial order is linear if for arbitrary a and b, either $a \sqsubseteq b$ or $b \sqsubseteq a$ holds. A partial order that is both linear and well-founded is called a *well-order*. Well-orders are central to the foundations of mathematics because of the *well-ordering principle*, which states that every set can be well-ordered. This principle can be shown to be equivalent to the *axiom of choice*, which states that for an arbitrary collection $\mathcal{A}$ of nonempty sets there exists a choice function f that satisfies $f.A \in A$ for all $A \in \mathcal{A}$. Because higher-order logic contains a choice operator, the axiom of choice can be proved as a theorem (see Chapter 7). We return to the well-ordering principle in Section 18.4 below.

The natural numbers is an example of a well-ordered set. Any subset of the natural numbers is also well-ordered. Ordinals, introduced in Section 18.4 below, are also well-ordered.

2 Constructing the Natural Numbers

In Section 10.2, we described how the natural numbers can be defined as a new type that is isomorphic to a subset of the type Ind of *individuals*. We shall now show a different construction that makes Nat isomorphic to a subset of $\mathcal{P}(\text{Ind})$. This type definition acts as an introduction to the definition of ordinals in Section 18.4.

We let every natural number be represented by a subset of Ind. Intuitively speaking, the size of the set shows which natural number is represented, and we get successively larger sets by adding one element at a time (always using the choice operator to select a new element of Ind).

To facilitate this construction, we first define the following constants:

$$\text{rep\_zero} \;\stackrel{\wedge}{=}\; \emptyset\ ,$$
$$\text{rep\_suc}.B \;\stackrel{\wedge}{=}\; B \cup \{\epsilon y : \text{Ind} \cdot y \notin B\}\ .$$

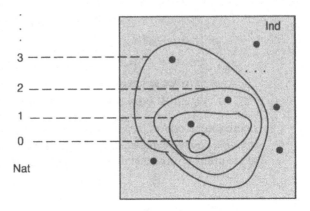

FIGURE 18.1. Constructing the type of natural numbers

We intend rep_zero (the empty set of individuals) to represent zero and rep_s◆ represent the successor function.

We can now describe the set that represents the naturals:

Natset $\stackrel{\wedge}{=}$

$\cap \{\mathcal{B} : \mathcal{P}(\mathcal{P}(\text{Ind})) \mid \text{rep\_zero} \in \mathcal{B} \wedge (\forall B \cdot B \in \mathcal{B} \Rightarrow \text{rep\_suc}.B \in$

This makes Natset the smallest set that contains rep_zero and is closed under rep◆ (Exercise 18.3). We use here the convention that lower-case letters stand fo ements, upper-case letters for sets, and script letters for collections of sets. construction of the natural numbers type is illustrated in Figure 18.1.

We can now prove the following characterization lemma, which shows that N is a suitable set to represent the natural numbers:

Lemma 18.2   *The set* Natset *has the following property:*

$$B \in \text{Natset} \equiv B = \text{rep\_zero} \vee (\exists C \in \text{Natset} \cdot B = \text{rep\_suc}.C) \ .$$

Defining the Type of Natural Numbers

We now have all the pieces needed for the type definition. The set Nats nonempty, since it contains rep_zero, so we introduce the name Nat for the type represented by Natset:

Nat $\cong$ Natset .

As described in Chapter 10, this means that the abstraction and represent◆ functions abs : $\mathcal{P}(\text{Ind}) \rightarrow$ Nat and rep : Nat $\rightarrow \mathcal{P}(\text{Ind})$ satisfy the follo◆ properties:

$$(\forall n \cdot \text{abs.}(\text{rep.}n) = n) \ ,$$
$$(\forall B \cdot B \in \text{Natset} \Rightarrow \text{rep.}(\text{abs.}B) = B) \ .$$

Zero and the successor function now have obvious definitions; they are the abstractions of rep_zero and rep_suc defined earlier:

$$0 \ \stackrel{\wedge}{=} \ \text{abs.rep\_zero} \ ,$$
$$\text{suc.}n \ \stackrel{\wedge}{=} \ \text{abs.}(\text{rep\_suc.}(\text{rep.}n)) \ .$$

Having defined 0 and suc, we really do not want to refer to the functions abs and rep any more when reasoning about the natural numbers. This is made possible by a single theorem that characterizes the natural numbers completely, and which we will describe next.

3   Primitive Recursion

In general, it is desirable to be able to characterize a data type in a single *characterization theorem*. For Nat this is indeed possible; the theorem in question is known as the *primitive recursion theorem*:

heorem 18.3   *For arbitrary type Σ, the following holds:*

$$(\forall g_1 : \Sigma \cdot \forall g_2 : \Sigma \to \text{Nat} \to \Sigma \cdot \exists! f : \text{Nat} \to \Sigma \cdot$$
$$f.0 = g_1 \wedge (\forall n \cdot f.(\text{suc.}n) = g_2.(f.n).n)) \ .$$

A detailed proof of Theorem 18.3 is beyond the scope of this text; it involves proving numerous properties about the set that represents Nat (see Exercise 18.4).

Let us look at the primitive recursion theorem in some detail. It asserts that if we are given an element g_1 of Σ and a function $g_2 : \Sigma \to \text{Nat} \to \Sigma$, then there always exists a uniquely defined function f such that g_1 is the value of f at 0 and such that g_2 gives the value of f at any successor suc.n in terms of n and of the value of f at n. This is a foundation for making *primitive recursive function definitions*. Given g_1 and g_2, the principle of constant definition then permits us to give a name to the function whose existence is guaranteed by the primitive recursion theorem.

As a simple example of function definition by primitive recursion, we show how to define evenness. We give the recursive definition in the form

$$(\text{even.}0 \equiv T) \wedge (\forall n \cdot \text{even.}(\text{suc.}n) \equiv \neg \, \text{even.}n) \ . \tag{$*$}$$

Note that this is *not* a proper definition in higher-order logic, since even is "defined" in terms of itself. In fact, we are here using the primitive recursion theorem with

$g_1 := \mathsf{T}$ and $g_2 := (\lambda b\ m \cdot \neg b)$ to get

$$(\exists! f \cdot (f.0 \equiv \mathsf{T}) \wedge (\forall n \cdot f.(\mathsf{suc}.n) \equiv \neg\ f.n))$$

(the reader is encouraged to verify that this is indeed what we get). We then
the "definition" above by specifying that even is the name of the function wh
existence we have just shown. Formally, we define

$$\mathsf{even} \;\;\hat{=}\;\; (\epsilon f \cdot (f.0 \equiv \mathsf{T}) \wedge (\forall n \cdot f.(\mathsf{suc}.n) \equiv \neg\ f.n))$$

and then use selection introduction to deduce (*) as a theorem.

We can now define other functions in the same way. The following examples sh
how addition and the standard order are defined. In both cases we really def
functions of more than one argument, but the primitive recursion is over exac
one of the arguments.

$$(\forall n \cdot 0 + n = n) \wedge (\forall m\ n \cdot \mathsf{suc}.m + n = \mathsf{suc}.(m + n))\ ,$$

$$(\forall n \cdot 0 \leq n \equiv \mathsf{T}) \wedge (\forall m\ n \cdot \mathsf{suc}.m \leq n \equiv m \leq n \wedge m \neq n)\ .$$

We leave it to the reader to verify that these are in fact valid definitions (comp
this with Exercise 10.6).

Induction

The primitive recursion theorem allows us to deduce that induction over Na
valid. To show this, we let p : Nat $\rightarrow$ Bool be arbitrary and instantiate the type
in the primitive recursion theorem to Bool:

$$(\forall g_1\ g_2 \cdot \exists! f : \mathsf{Nat} \rightarrow \mathsf{Bool} \cdot$$
$$(f.0 \equiv g_1) \wedge (\forall n \cdot f.(\mathsf{suc}.n) \equiv g_2.(f.n).n))$$
$\Rightarrow$ {definition of unique existence}
$$(\forall g_1\ g_2\ f_1,\ f_2 \cdot$$
$$(f_1.0 \equiv g_1) \wedge (\forall n \cdot f_1.(\mathsf{suc}.n) \equiv g_2.(f_1.n).n)\ \wedge$$
$$(f_2.0 \equiv g_1) \wedge (\forall n \cdot f_2.(\mathsf{suc}.n) \equiv g_2.(f_2.n).n)$$
$$\Rightarrow$$
$$f_1 = f_2)$$
$\Rightarrow$ {specialize $f_1 := (\lambda m \cdot \mathsf{T})$ and $f_2 := p$}
$$(\forall g_1\ g_2 \cdot$$
$$g_1\ \wedge\ (\forall n \cdot g_2.\mathsf{T}.n)\ \wedge\ (p.0 \equiv g_1)\ \wedge$$
$$(\forall n \cdot p.(\mathsf{suc}.n) \equiv g_2.(p.n).n)$$
$$\Rightarrow$$
$$(\lambda m \cdot \mathsf{T}) = p)$$

$$\Rightarrow \{\text{specialize } g_1 := \mathsf{T} \text{ and } g_2 := (\lambda b \; m \cdot b \vee p.(\mathsf{suc}.m))\}$$

$$p.0 \wedge (\forall n \cdot p.(\mathsf{suc}.n) \equiv p.n \vee p.(\mathsf{suc}.n)) \;\Rightarrow\; (\lambda m \cdot \mathsf{T}) = p$$

$$\equiv \{\text{rewrite using tautology } (t' \equiv t \vee t') \equiv (t \Rightarrow t')\}$$

$$p.0 \wedge (\forall n \cdot p.n \Rightarrow p.(\mathsf{suc}.n)) \;\Rightarrow\; (\lambda m \cdot \mathsf{T}) = p$$

$$\equiv \{\text{pointwise extension, } \beta \text{ reduction: } ((\lambda m \cdot \mathsf{T}) = p) \equiv (\forall m \cdot p.m)\}$$

$$p.0 \wedge (\forall n \cdot p.n \Rightarrow p.(\mathsf{suc}.n)) \;\Rightarrow\; (\forall m \cdot p.m)$$

Further Properties

It is also possible to prove the other Peano postulates as theorems, by specializing g_1 and g_2 in the primitive recursion theorem in suitable ways. The details are left to the reader as an exercise (Exercise 18.5).

Lemma 18.4   *The following properties hold for* Nat *as constructed above:*

$$(\forall n : \mathsf{Nat} \cdot 0 \neq \mathsf{suc}.n) \;,$$

$$(\forall m \; n : \mathsf{Nat} \cdot \mathsf{suc}.m = \mathsf{suc}.n \Rightarrow m = n) \;.$$

Since the Peano postulates are proved as theorems, we know that our construction of Nat in fact gives us the natural numbers. Thus, the primitive recursion theorem gives an abstract characterization of the natural numbers; no other facts are needed in order to build the whole theory of arithmetic.

Primitive Recursion for Sequences

Sequence types can be characterized with a primitive recursion theorem that is similar to the corresponding theorem for natural numbers:

$$(\forall g_1 : \Gamma \cdot \forall g_2 : \Gamma \to \mathsf{Seq \; of} \; \Sigma \to \Sigma \to \Gamma \cdot \exists! f : \mathsf{Seq \; of} \; \Sigma \to \Gamma \cdot$$

$$(f.\langle \rangle = g_1) \wedge (\forall s \; x \cdot f.(s \& x) = g_2.(f.s).s.x)) \;.$$

From this theorem the axioms given for sequences in Chapter 10 can be derived. Furthermore, the recursion theorem justifies recursive definitions of functions over sequences. A simple example is the length of a sequence, defined as

$$\mathsf{len}.\langle \rangle = 0 \wedge \mathsf{len}.(s \& x) = \mathsf{len}.s + 1 \;.$$

4   Ordinals

All natural numbers are constructed by repeated application of the successor operation, starting from zero. We now generalize this construction process by adding limits. The objects that we construct using repeated application of the successor

and the limit operations are called *ordinals*. It is well known that this charact
zation cannot be realized consistently in set theory; the collection of all ordinal
"too big" to be a set. Thus there is no way of introducing the ordinals as a typ
higher-order logic. However, we introduce the notion of *ordinals over a given* ‹
Σ and show that by choosing Σ in a suitable way, we have access to arbitra
large ordinals.

Construction of Ordinals

Assume that a type Σ is fixed. We shall now show how the type of *ordinals over*
constructed. Exactly as for the natural numbers, we let every ordinal be represe
by a set over Σ. Intuitively speaking, we get successively larger sets by adding
element at a time or by taking the union of all sets constructed so far.

We first make the following constant definitions:

$$\text{rep\_osuc}.B \;\overset{\wedge}{=}\; B \cup \{\epsilon y : \Sigma \cdot y \notin B\} \;,$$
$$\text{rep\_olim}.B \;\overset{\wedge}{=}\; \cup\{B \mid B \in \mathcal{B}\} \;,$$

where the type of $\mathcal{B}$ is $\mathcal{P}(\mathcal{P}(\Sigma))$. The constant rep_olim is intended to represent
operation that produces the limit of a set of ordinals. We do not need to men
an explicit representative for zero; we use the limit of the empty set for this.

Next, we need to describe the set that represents the ordinals over Σ. We cho
the smallest set that is closed under rep_osuc and rep_olim:

$$\text{Ordset} \;\overset{\wedge}{=}\; \cap\{\mathcal{B} \mid (\forall B \cdot B \in \mathcal{B} \Rightarrow \text{rep\_osuc}.B \in \mathcal{B}) \wedge$$
$$(\forall \mathcal{C} \cdot \mathcal{C} \subseteq \mathcal{B} \Rightarrow \text{rep\_olim}.\mathcal{C} \in \mathcal{B})\} \;.$$

Note that this set must be nonempty, since it contains rep_olim.$\emptyset$ (i.e., $\emptyset$).

Exactly as we did for the natural numbers, we can now prove a characteriza
lemma that shows that Ordset is in fact a suitable set to represent the ordinals ‹
Σ (we leave the proof to the reader):

Lemma 18.5 *The set* Ordset *has the following property:*

$$B \in \text{Ordset} \;\equiv\; (\exists C \in \text{Ordset} \cdot B = \text{rep\_osuc}.C) \vee$$
$$(\exists \mathcal{C} \subseteq \text{Ordset} \cdot B = \text{rep\_olim}.\mathcal{C}) \;.$$

Defining a Type of Ordinals

Since Ordset is nonempty, we can introduce the name $\text{Ord}(\Sigma)$ for a new
represented by Ordset (this way, we really introduce a new unary type oper
Ord).

We now define the successor and limit operations for the ordinals, in the obvious way:

$$\text{suc}.a \;\stackrel{\wedge}{=}\; \text{abs}.(\text{rep\_osuc}.(\text{rep}.a)) \;,$$
$$\text{lim}.A \;\stackrel{\wedge}{=}\; \text{abs}.(\text{rep\_olim}.\{\text{rep}.a \mid a \in A\}) \;.$$

Intuitively speaking, these definitions imply that we simply take over the notions of successor and limit from the representing set. We allow binder notation for limits, writing $(\text{lim } a \in A \cdot f.a)$ for $\text{lim}.\{f.a \mid a \in A\}$.

The least and greatest ordinals over Σ can now be defined in terms of the lim operator:

$$0 \;\stackrel{\wedge}{=}\; \text{lim}.\emptyset \;,$$
$$\text{maxord} \;\stackrel{\wedge}{=}\; \text{lim}.\text{Ord} \;.$$

The greatest ordinal maxord has a slight anomaly; it has the undesirable property of being its own successor (Exercise 18.8).

An Order on Ordinals

We define an order on ordinals, corresponding to subset inclusion on the representing set:

$$a \le b \;\stackrel{\wedge}{=}\; \text{rep}.a \subseteq \text{rep}.b \;.$$

In fact, it is possible to prove that this gives a linear order on $\text{Ord}(\Sigma)$. Note that lim is the join operation with respect to this order. As usual, we let $a < b$ stand for $a \le b \wedge a \ne b$.

Next we define an ordinal to be a *limit ordinal* if it is the limit of all ordinals smaller than itself:

$$\text{is\_limit}.a \;\stackrel{\wedge}{=}\; a = \text{lim}.\{b \in \text{Ord}(\Sigma) \mid b < a\} \;.$$

In particular, 0 is a limit ordinal.

The ordinals satisfy the following generalization of the Peano postulate that states that zero is not a successor:

Lemma 18.6   *Every ordinal over Σ except maxord is either a successor ordinal or a limit ordinal (but not both):*

$$a \ne \text{maxord} \;\Rightarrow\; (\text{is\_limit}.a \;\equiv\; (\forall b \cdot a \ne \text{suc}.b)) \;.$$

We have that $\text{Natset} \subseteq \text{Ordset}(\text{Ind})$; i.e., the set that represents the type Nat is a subset of the set that represents the type of ordinals over Ind. Furthermore, $\bigcup\text{Natset}$ represents a nonzero limit ordinal (Exercise 18.7). This ordinal is called

ω ("omega") and is *the first infinite ordinal*. The ordinals thus extend the na
numbers past the first infinite ordinal. The ordinals (over some sufficiently l
type Σ) form a "sequence" of the form

$$0, 1, 2, 3, \ldots, \omega, \omega + 1, \omega + 2, \omega + 3, \ldots, \omega \cdot 2, \omega \cdot 2 + 1, \ldots .$$

18.5   Ordinal Recursion

In analogy with the natural numbers, it is possible to derive an *ordinal recur*
theorem:

Theorem 18.7   *For arbitrary types Σ and Γ, the following holds:*

$$(\forall g_1 : \Sigma \to \mathrm{Ord}(\Gamma) \to \Sigma \cdot \forall g_2 : \mathcal{P}(\Sigma) \to \mathrm{Ord}(\Gamma) \to \Sigma \cdot$$
$$\exists! f : \mathrm{Ord}(\Gamma) \to \Sigma \cdot$$
$$(\forall a \cdot a \neq \mathrm{maxord} \Rightarrow f.(\mathrm{suc}.a) = g_1.(f.a).a) \wedge$$
$$(\forall a \cdot \mathrm{is\_limit}.a \Rightarrow f.a = g_2.\{f.b \mid b < a\}.a)) .$$

This theorem gives a foundation for defining functions by *recursion over th*
dinals. Since 0 is the limit of the empty set of ordinals, we do not need a sep
conjunct for the zero case. In practice, though, functions are usually define
giving three clauses: one for zero, one for successors, and one for (nonzero) li
Note that the successor clause is qualified; this is because maxord is its own
cessor. Since every ordinal (except maxord) is either a successor ordinal or a
ordinal (but not both), the limit clause applies only when the successor clause
not apply.

As an example, we define addition for ordinals. Rather than writing the defir
as one big conjunction, we give the three clauses separately:

$$\begin{aligned} a + 0 &= a , \\ a + (\mathrm{suc}.b) &= \mathrm{suc}.(a + b) , \\ a + b &= \lim\{a + c \mid c < b\} \qquad \text{for nonzero limit ordinals } b. \end{aligned}$$

This makes addition a generalization of addition on Nat. Note that in the se
clause we permit $b = \mathrm{maxord}$, since this makes both sides trivially equal to ma
Ordinal addition has certain surprising properties, such as not being commu
(see Exercise 18.9).

Ordinal Induction and Other Properties

Peano's postulates for the natural numbers tell us that zero is not a successo
that the successor operation always generates new numbers. For the ordinals,
have constructed them here, the situation is not as simple. If the underlying se

finite, then the number of ordinals is also finite and the successor operation cannot generate new ordinals forever. If Σ is infinite, then the limit operator sometimes generates new ordinals but sometimes not. These facts have already shown up when we needed to qualify the clauses in the recursion theorem for ordinals. We shall now show that similar qualifications appear when we prove results that correspond to the Peano postulates for Nat.

From the ordinal recursion theorem, it is possible to derive a principle of *ordinal induction* (also known as *transfinite induction*):

Theorem 18.8   *The following induction principle holds for arbitrary type Σ and arbitrary predicate $p : \mathrm{Ord}(\Sigma) \to \mathrm{Bool}$:*

$$(\forall a \cdot a \neq \mathsf{maxord} \wedge p.a \Rightarrow p.(\mathsf{suc}.a)) \wedge$$
$$(\forall a \cdot \mathsf{is\_limit}.a \wedge (\forall b \cdot b < a \Rightarrow p.b) \Rightarrow p.a)$$
$$\Rightarrow$$
$$(\forall a \cdot p.a) .$$

In practice, we split an inductive proof into three cases; the zero case is considered separately from the nonzero limits.

We can also prove a result corresponding to the second Peano postulate for the natural numbers.

Lemma 18.9   *With the exception of maxord, distinct ordinals have distinct successors:*

$$\mathsf{suc}.a = \mathsf{suc}.b \wedge a \neq \mathsf{maxord} \wedge b \neq \mathsf{maxord} \Rightarrow a = b .$$

In particular, Lemma 18.9 implies that if $a \neq \mathsf{maxord}$, then the successor of a is always distinct from all ordinals up to a.

We know that the natural numbers are well-ordered; i.e., they are linearly ordered and every subset has a least element. The same is also true of ordinals.

Lemma 18.10   *Any type $\mathrm{Ord}(\Sigma)$ of ordinals is well-ordered.*

Proof First, linearity is proved by proving that the subset order on Ordset is linear. Then, well-foundedness is proved by showing that for an arbitrary nonempty set A of ordinals, the ordinal

$$\mathsf{abs}.(\cap a \in A \cdot \mathsf{rep}.a)$$

is the smallest element in A. $\square$

Induction Example

As an example of ordinal induction, we prove the following property of additi·

$$0 + a = a .$$

The proof is by induction on a. The zero case follows directly from the definit
of addition. For the successor case, we have the following derivation:

$$0 + a = a, a \neq \mathsf{maxord}$$
$$\vdash 0 + \mathsf{suc}.a$$
$$= \{\text{definition of addition}\}$$
$$\mathsf{suc}.(0 + a)$$
$$= \{\text{induction assumption}\}$$
$$\mathsf{suc}.a$$

Finally, we have the limit case:

$$\mathsf{is\_limit}.a, a \neq 0, (\forall b \cdot b < a \Rightarrow 0 + b = b)$$
$$\vdash 0 + a$$
$$= \{\text{definition of addition}\}$$
$$\lim.\{0 + b \mid b < a\}$$
$$= \{\text{induction assumption}\}$$
$$\lim.\{b \mid b < a\}$$
$$= \{a \text{ is limit ordinal}\}$$
$$a$$

The ordinal induction principle now asserts that $0 + a = a$ holds for an arbitr
ordinal a.

18.6   How Far Can We Go?

The ordinals over Ind can be seen as an extension of the natural numbers. We s▮
now see that we can in fact construct ordinal types that are 'arbitrarily large' i
very specific sense.

If the underlying type Σ is finite, then the type $\mathsf{Ord}(\Sigma)$ is also finite. In general,
want ordinals for reasoning when the type Nat is not "big enough." The follow▮
result (a version of *Hartog's lemma*) guarantees that we can always find a type
ordinals that is big enough to index any given type Σ.

Lemma 18.11   *Assume that a type Σ is given. Then there exists a type* Ord *of ordinals such t*
there is no injection from Ord *to* Σ.

Proof Choose $\mathcal{P}(\Sigma)$ as the underlying set for the construction of the ordinals. The construction in Exercise 18.11 shows that the cardinality of $\text{Ord}(\Sigma)$ is always at least the same as the cardinality of $\mathcal{P}(\Sigma)$. The result then follows from the fact that for an arbitrary nonempty set A there can be no injection from $\mathcal{P}(A)$ to A. $\square$

We call a set of the form $\{a : \text{Ord}(\Sigma) \mid a < a_0\}$ an *initial segment* of the ordinals over Σ. It is possible to show that for any two types of ordinals, $\text{Ord}(\Sigma)$ and $\text{Ord}(\Gamma)$, one is always order-isomorphic to an initial segment of the other. Thus, whenever we have used two different types of ordinals in some reasoning, we can replace the "smaller" by the "bigger". In fact, one can show that for any two well-ordered sets, one is always order-isomorphic to an initial segment of the other. In particular, we can consider Nat to be an initial segment of the ordinals. Thus, there is really no confusion using the constants 0 and suc for both the natural numbers and the ordinals.

In traditional developments of ordinals, one considers ordinals as *equivalence classes* of well-ordered sets rather than specific instances, as we have done. This allows one to talk about the collection of *all ordinals*, which is sufficient for all set-theoretic reasoning. This collection is not a set, but a proper class, so we cannot construct it inside higher-order logic. However, we can construct arbitrarily large types of ordinals, so once we know what type we want to reason over, we can select a type of ordinals that is sufficient. In subsequent chapters, we talk about "ordinals" without specifying the underlying type. We then assume that the type of ordinals is chosen so large that we do not have to worry about conditions of the form $a \neq \text{maxord}$.

Ordinals as Index Sets

Assume that A is an arbitrary set. Lemma 18.11 then shows that we can find a type Ord of ordinals that cannot be injected into A. In fact, we can find a function $f : \text{Ord} \to A$ and an ordinal $\gamma : \text{Ord}$ such that f maps $\{a : \text{Ord} \mid a < \gamma\}$ bijectively into A. This means that we can *index* A using this set of ordinals. For the construction of this function f, see Exercise 18.11 (in fact, the function f gives a well-ordering of A, so this proves the well-ordering principle).

Using the ordinals as an index set, we can also construct generalized *ordinal-indexed chains*. If $(A, \sqsubseteq)$ is any partially ordered set, an ordinal-indexed chain is a monotonic function $f : \text{Ord} \to A$. Ordinal-indexed chains are typically defined by ordinal recursion, and ordinal induction can be used to reason about them. They are useful for generalized limit arguments, in situations where the natural numbers are not sufficient.

18.7   Summary and Discussion

We have in this chapter defined the notion of well-founded and well-ordered s
and have shown how the induction principle applies to such structures. As an ap
cation, we have given an alternative construction of the type of natural number
higher-order logic. This construction motivates the principle of primitive recursi
which is the main tool for defining functions over natural numbers.

The reason for giving the alternative construction of natural numbers here is t
it generalizes directly to a construction of ordinals (over a given base type Σ),
we showed above how to construct the ordinals in this way. Ordinal recursion v
then defined as a principle for defining functions over all ordinals over a given
and transfinite induction was defined based on ordinal recursion.

The theory of ordinals may seem a little bit esoteric to those who are not fami
with it, but it is surprisingly useful in programming logics. We need ordinals, e
when proving termination of programs that are not necessarily continuous.

For a good introduction to the construction of the ordinals within the type-
framework of Zermelo–Fraenkel set theory, see Johnstone [93]. A theory of w
ordered sets within higher-order logic is described by John Harrison in [73].
and Plotkin [5] give a nice overview of ordinals and some good justification for
use of ordinals in programming language semantics. The main difference betw
ordinals as presented here and the classical theory of ordinals was already poir
out above: we can define only an initial segment of all ordinals, whereas in
classical treatment, it is possible to define the (proper) class of all ordinals
practice, this does not seem to cause any problems, because the initial segment
always be chosen large enough for the problem at hand.

18.8   Exercises

18.1   The lexicographical order $\sqsubseteq$ on Nat $\times$ Nat is defined as follows:

$$(m, n) \sqsubseteq (m', n') \ \triangleq \ m < m' \lor (m = m' \land n \leq n') .$$

Prove that this order is well-founded.

18.2   Show that the two induction principles on natural numbers,

$$(\forall n \in \text{Nat}.(\forall m < n \cdot p.m) \Rightarrow p.n) \ \Rightarrow \ (\forall n \in \text{Nat} \cdot p.n)$$

and

$$p.0 \land (\forall n \in \text{Nat} \cdot p.n \Rightarrow p.(n+1)) \ \Rightarrow \ (\forall n \in \text{Nat} \cdot p.n) ,$$

are equivalent.

18.3   Prove that the set Natset contains rep_zero and is closed under rep_suc, where

Natset =

$$\cap\{B : \text{Ind} \to \text{Bool} \mid \text{rep\_zero} \in B \wedge (\forall x \cdot x \in B \implies \text{rep\_suc}.x \in B)\}$$

Deduce that Natset is the smallest set that contains rep_zero and is closed under rep_suc.

18.4   In the text, we have assumed that the primitive recursion theorem (Theorem 18.3) is proved before any other properties of Nat. Show that it is possible to go the other way, proving the primitive recursion theorem from the Peano postulates.

18.5   Prove the following two Peano postulates from the primitive recursion theorem:

$$(\forall n : \text{Nat} \cdot 0 \neq \text{suc}.n) \,,$$
$$(\forall m\ n : \text{Nat} \cdot \text{suc}.m = \text{suc}.n \implies m = n) \,.$$

Hint: specialize g_1 and g_2 in the primitive recursion theorem to suitable Boolean-valued functions.

18.6   Use list recursion to define the function append : $\text{list}(\Sigma) \to \text{list}(\Sigma) \to \text{list}(\Sigma)$ that appends two lists into a new list.

18.7   Show that Natset $\subseteq$ Ordset(Ind); i.e., the set that represents the type Nat is a subset of the set that represents the type of ordinals over Ind. Furthermore, show that $\cup$ Natset represents a nonzero limit ordinal.

18.8   Prove the following properties of ordinals:

$$a \neq \text{maxord} \implies a < \text{suc}.a \,,$$
$$\text{suc.maxord} = \text{maxord} \,,$$
$$a = \text{lim}.\{b \mid b < a\} \vee a = \text{suc}.(\text{lim}.\{b \mid b < a\}) \,.$$

18.9   Prove the following properties of ordinal addition for any type of ordinals that includes the first infinite ordinal ω (see Exercise 18.7).

$$\omega + 1 = \text{suc}.\omega \,,$$
$$1 + \omega = \omega \,.$$

This shows that addition of ordinals is not commutative.

18.10   Prove that the successor and limit operations on the ordinals are monotonic, in the following sense:

$$a \leq b \implies \text{suc}.a \leq \text{suc}.b \,,$$
$$(\forall a \in A \cdot \exists b \in B \cdot a \leq b) \implies \text{lim}.A \leq \text{lim}.B \,.$$

Furthermore, prove the following property for the order on the ordinals:

$$b \neq \text{maxord} \wedge a < b \implies \text{suc}.a < \text{suc}.b \,.$$

18.11   Let some type Σ be given. Define a function f that maps any ordinal $a \neq$ maxord over Σ to the unique element $b \in \Sigma$ such that $b \notin$ rep.$a \wedge b \in$ rep.(suc.a). Show that the restriction of this function to $B = \{a \mid a \neq$ maxord$\}$ is bijective. Now define the relation $\leq$ on B as follows:

$$b \leq b' \; \stackrel{\Delta}{=} \; f^{-1}.b \leq f^{-1}.b' \; .$$

Show that this gives a well-ordering of Σ.

The statement constructors that we have introduced earlier — sequential composition, join, and meet — are all monotonic with respect to the refinement relation on Mtran. Hence, we can use these constructs to define monotonic functions from the complete lattice of predicate transformers to itself.

From a mathematical point of view, monotonicity of functions over complete lattices is important because it guarantees the existence of (least and greatest) fixed points, which are needed for defining recursion and iteration. In this chapter, we investigate fixed points of functions over complete lattices in general. We also show how ordinals are used to give an alternative characterization of the fixed points of monotonic functions as limits of ordinal-indexed approximation sequences. In the next chapter we apply this theory to recursively defined statements, in particular predicate transformers, and show how fixed points are used to give meaning to recursive definitions.

Fixed Points

Let $f : \Sigma \to \Sigma$ be an arbitrary function. An element $a : \Sigma$ is said to be a *fixed point* of f if $f.a = a$. In general, a function f need not have a fixed point. However, when a complete lattice $A \subseteq \Sigma$ is closed under monotonic f, then the situation is different. The following *Knaster–Tarski theorem* is a central result about fixed points in lattice theory.

eorem 19.1   *Let A be a complete lattice and f a monotonic function on A; i.e., $f \in A \to_m A$. Then f has a least and a greatest fixed point in A.*

Proof We show that f has a least fixed point; the proof for the greatest fixed po
dual. In fact, we show that the least fixed point is given by $(\sqcap x \in A \mid f.x \sqsubseteq x$
We have

$$f.(\sqcap x \in A \mid f.x \sqsubseteq x \cdot x)$$
$$\sqsubseteq \{f \text{ monotonic implies } f.(\sqcap X) \sqsubseteq (\sqcap x \in X \cdot f.x)\}$$
$$(\sqcap x \in A \mid f.x \sqsubseteq x \cdot f.x)$$
$$\sqsubseteq \{\text{replace every element by a larger element}\}$$
$$(\sqcap x \in A \mid f.x \sqsubseteq x \cdot x)$$

and

$$\top$$
$$\Rightarrow \{\text{derivation above}\}$$
$$f.(\sqcap x \in A \mid f.x \sqsubseteq x \cdot x) \sqsubseteq (\sqcap x \in A \mid f.x \sqsubseteq x \cdot x)$$
$$\Rightarrow \{f \text{ monotonic}\}$$
$$f.(f.(\sqcap x \in A \mid f.x \sqsubseteq x \cdot x)) \sqsubseteq f.(\sqcap x \in A \mid f.x \sqsubseteq x \cdot x)$$
$$\equiv \{\text{general rule } p.a \equiv a \in \{b \mid p.b\}\}$$
$$f.(\sqcap x \in A \mid f.x \sqsubseteq x \cdot x) \in \{x \in A \mid f.x \sqsubseteq x\}$$
$$\Rightarrow \{\text{general rule } x \in A \Rightarrow \sqcap A \sqsubseteq x\}$$
$$(\sqcap x \in A \mid f.x \sqsubseteq x \cdot x) \sqsubseteq f.(\sqcap x \in A \mid f.x \sqsubseteq x \cdot x)$$

so $(\sqcap x \in A \mid f.x \sqsubseteq x \cdot x)$ is a fixed point. For arbitrary $y \in A$, we have

$$f.y = y$$
$$\Rightarrow \{a = b \text{ implies } a \sqsubseteq b\}$$
$$f.y \sqsubseteq y$$
$$\equiv \{\text{general rule } p.a \equiv a \in \{b \mid p.b\}\}$$
$$y \in \{x \in A \mid f.x \sqsubseteq x\}$$
$$\Rightarrow \{\text{general rule } x \in A \Rightarrow \sqcap A \sqsubseteq x\}$$
$$(\sqcap x \in A \mid f.x \sqsubseteq x \cdot x) \sqsubseteq y$$

so $(\sqcap x \in A \mid f.x \sqsubseteq x \cdot x)$ is in fact the least fixed point. $\square$

The *least fixed point* of f is denoted by $\mu.f$, while the *greatest fixed po*
by denoted by $\nu.f$. The set A is assumed to be the whole underlying type u
otherwise stated explicitly. If there is danger of confusion, we write $\mu_A.f$ to ind
that we are considering the least fixed point on the set A, and similarly fc
greatest fixed point. The proof of the Knaster–Tarski theorem gives the follc
explicit constructions of the least and greatest fixed points:

$$\mu_A.f = (\sqcap x \in A \mid f.x \sqsubseteq x \cdot x) , \qquad (\mu \text{ characteriza}$$
$$\nu_A.f = (\sqcup x \in A \mid x \sqsubseteq f.x \cdot x) . \qquad (\nu \text{ characteriza}$$

Thus the least fixed point is the meet of all prefixed points (a is a *prefixed point* of f if $f.a \sqsubseteq a$). Dually, the greatest fixed point is the join of all postfixed points (a is a *postfixed point* if $a \sqsubseteq f.a$).

We permit the use of μ and ν as binders. Thus, we can write $(\mu x \cdot t)$ rather than $\mu.(\lambda x \cdot t)$ and $(\nu x \cdot t)$ for $\nu.(\lambda x \cdot t)$. Similarly, we can use index notation $(\mu x \in A \cdot t)$ for $\mu_A.(\lambda x \cdot t)$ and $(\nu.x \in A \cdot t)$ for $\nu_A.(\lambda x \cdot t)$.

The least fixed point of f is characterized by the following two properties (Exercise 19.1):

$$
\begin{array}{ll}
f.(\mu.f) \;=\; \mu.f\,, & \text{(folding least fixed point)} \\
f.x \sqsubseteq x \;\Rightarrow\; \mu.f \sqsubseteq x\,. & \text{(least fixed point induction)}
\end{array}
$$

When we use the folding property as a rewrite rule from left to right, we say that we *fold* the fixed point. Dually, we say that we *unfold* the fixed point when we use it from right to left. The induction property implies that $\mu.f$ is the least (pre)fixed point (this follows from the last derivation in the proof of Theorem 19.1).

The greatest fixed point is characterized by the following dual properties:

$$
\begin{array}{ll}
f(\nu.f) \;=\; \nu.f\,, & \text{(folding greatest fixed point)} \\
x \sqsubseteq f.x \;\Rightarrow\; x \sqsubseteq \nu.f\,. & \text{(greatest fixed point induction)}
\end{array}
$$

Note that least fixed point induction can be used as a μ *elimination* rule, while greatest fixed point induction is a ν *introduction* rule.

Fixed points of a function f are at the same time solutions of the equation $x = f.x$. Thus, $\mu.f$ is the least and $\nu.f$ the greatest solution of this equation. This indicates that fixed points can be used to give meaning to recursively defined statements. We will consider this in more detail after we have studied general properties of fixed points.

Monotonicity of Fixed Points

Monotonicity is sufficient to guarantee the existence of least and greatest fixed points of a function f over a complete lattice. We shall now show that the least and greatest fixed point operators themselves are monotonic (Table 19.1).

Lemma 19.2 *Assume that A is a complete lattice and that the functions $f \in A \to_m A$ and $g \in A \to_m A$ satisfy $(\forall x \in A \cdot f.x \sqsubseteq g.x)$. Then $\mu_A.f \sqsubseteq \mu_A.g$ and $\nu_A.f \sqsubseteq \nu_A.g$.*

Proof

$$
\begin{aligned}
&f \text{ monotonic, } g \text{ monotonic, } f \sqsubseteq g \\
&\vdash \mu.f \sqsubseteq \mu.g \\
&\Leftarrow \{\text{least fixed point induction with } x := \mu.g\}
\end{aligned}
$$

is	$\sqsubseteq$
$(\lambda f \cdot \mu.f)$	yes[1]
$(\lambda f \cdot \nu.f)$	yes[1]

[1] monotonic f

TABLE 19.1. Fixed-point monotonicity

$$f.(\mu.g) \sqsubseteq \mu.g$$
$$\equiv \{\text{unfolding least fixed point}\}$$
$$f.(\mu.g) \sqsubseteq g.(\mu.g)$$
$$\equiv \{\text{assumption } f \sqsubseteq g, \text{ pointwise order}\}$$
$$\top$$

The proof for the greatest fixed point is dual. $\square$

19.2   Fixed points as Limits

In connection with the Knaster–Tarski fixed-point theorem, we showed an exp- construction of the least fixed point $\mu.f$ of a monotonic function f on a comp- lattice. We shall now show that $\mu.f$ has another characterization in terms of a s- cial kind of join (limit) that can be given a computational interpretation. Simila $\nu.f$ has a dual characterization.

Limits and Continuity

In order to define limits and continuity, we first need the notion of a directed se- subset C of a poset $(A, \sqsubseteq)$ is *directed* if every finite subset of C is bounded ab- i.e., if the following condition is satisfied:

$$(\forall a, b \in C \cdot \exists c \in C \cdot a \sqsubseteq c \wedge b \sqsubseteq c) .\qquad (directedne$$

Note that the empty set is directed and that a finite nonempty directed set n- have a greatest element. We refer to the join of a directed set as its *limit*. This - agreement with the notion of limit for ordinals, since a well-ordered set is alw- directed. When we want to show explicitly that an indexed join is a limit, we w- $(\lim i \in I \cdot x_i)$ rather than $(\sqcup i \in I \cdot x_i)$.

We say that the poset $(A, \sqsubseteq)$ is a *complete partial order* (a *cpo*) if $\lim C$ exist- every directed subset C of A. In particular, a cpo A must have a bottom elem- (since the empty set is directed: see Exercise 19.2).

A monotonic function $f : A \rightarrow B$, where A and B are complete partial order- said to be *(join) continuous* if it preserves limits, i.e., if

$$f.(\lim i \in I \cdot x_i) \;=\; (\lim i \in I \cdot f.x_i) \qquad\qquad (f \; continuous)$$

for an arbitrary directed set $\{x_i \mid i \in I\}$. Note that continuity is a weaker property than universal join homomorphism; every universally join homomorphic function is continuous. Furthermore, we note that continuity implies strictness (Exercise 19.2).

Fixed Points as Limits and Colimits

Let f be a monotonic function on a complete lattice, $f \in A \rightarrow_m A$, and define an ordinal-indexed collection of derived functions:

$$\begin{aligned}
f^0.x &= x \;, \\
f^{\alpha+1}.x &= f.(f^\alpha.x) \text{ for arbitrary ordinals } \alpha, \\
f^\alpha.x &= (\lim \beta \mid \beta < \alpha \cdot f^\beta.x) \text{ for nonzero limit ordinals } \alpha.
\end{aligned}$$

We now show that there exists an ordinal γ such that $\mu.f = f^\gamma.\bot$ (each $f^\alpha.\bot$ is called an *approximation* of $\mu.f$).

Theorem 19.3   *Assume that a complete lattice $A \subseteq \Sigma$ is given. Then there exists an ordinal γ such that for any function $f \in A \rightarrow_m A$ the least fixed point of f in A satisfies $\mu.f = f^\gamma.\bot$.*

Proof   The full proof is fairly long, so we only outline it here. First we note that (by induction over ordinals)

$$\alpha \le \beta \;\Rightarrow\; f^\alpha.\bot \sqsubseteq f^\beta.\bot \;. \tag{$*$}$$

Now let γ be an ordinal that cannot be injected into A (such an ordinal exists by Lemma 18.11). Then in the ordinal-indexed chain $\{f^\alpha.\bot \mid \alpha \le \gamma\}$ some element must occur more than once. Thus we can find α and α' where $\alpha < \alpha' \le \gamma$ and $f^{\alpha'}.\bot = f^\alpha.\bot$. Then

$$f^\alpha.\bot$$
$$\sqsubseteq \{(*) \text{ above}\}$$
$$f^{\alpha+1}.\bot$$

and

$$f^{\alpha+1}.\bot$$
$$\sqsubseteq \{\alpha < \alpha', (*) \text{ above}\}$$
$$f^{\alpha'}.\bot$$
$$= \{\text{assumption}\}$$
$$f^\alpha.\bot$$

which shows that $f^\alpha.\bot = f^{\alpha+1}.\bot$, so $f^\alpha.\bot$ is a fixed point. Furthermore, for arbitrary ordinal $\beta \geq \alpha$ we get $f^\beta.\bot = f^\alpha.\bot$. In particular, $f^\gamma.\bot = f^\alpha.\bot$ $f^\gamma.\bot$ is a fixed point.

Now let x be an arbitrary fixed point of f. By ordinal induction one easily she that $f^\alpha.\bot \sqsubseteq x$, for an arbitrary ordinal α. This shows that $f^\gamma.\bot \sqsubseteq x$, and so f^z is in fact the least fixed point. $\square$

Note from the proof of Theorem 19.3 that the ordinal γ can be chosen so that does not depend on the function f, only on the complete lattice A.

In Chapter 22 we show that if the function f is continuous on A, then the natu numbers are sufficient to index the approximations, so we need not go beyond first infinite ordinal ω.

For greatest fixed points, the dual result holds, using *coapproximations*:

Corollary 19.4   *Assume that a complete lattice $A \subseteq \Sigma$ is given. Then there exists an ordina such that for arbitrary $f \in A \to_m A$ the greatest fixed point satisfies $\nu.f = f_\gamma$ where the coapproximations $f_\alpha.x$ are defined as follows:*

$$
\begin{aligned}
f_0.x &= x\ , \\
f_{\alpha+1}.x &= f.(f_\alpha.x) \text{ for arbitrary ordinals } \alpha, \\
f_\alpha.x &= (\sqcap\beta \mid \beta < \alpha \cdot f_\beta.x) \text{ for nonzero limit ordinals } \alpha.
\end{aligned}
$$

19.3   Properties of Fixed Points

The following *fusion theorem* is very useful for proving properties of fixed po Its proof is also a good example of induction over the ordinals.

Theorem 19.5   *Assume that $h : \Sigma \to \Gamma$ is a continuous function and that $f : \Sigma \to \Sigma$ $g : \Gamma \to \Gamma$ are monotonic functions on complete lattices. Then*

$$
h \circ f = g \circ h \implies h.(\mu.f) = \mu.g\ .
$$

The fusion theorem is illustrated in Figure 19.1

Proof   We show that $h.(f^\alpha.\bot) = g^\alpha.\bot$ for an arbitrary ordinal α, under assumption $h \circ f = g \circ h$. The result then follows from Theorem 19.3. The t case $h.\bot = \bot$ follows because h is continuous. The successor case is prove follows:

$$
\begin{aligned}
&h.(f^\alpha.\bot) = g^\alpha.\bot \\
&\vdash h.(f^{\alpha+1}.\bot) \\
&= \{\text{definition of approximation}\}
\end{aligned}
$$

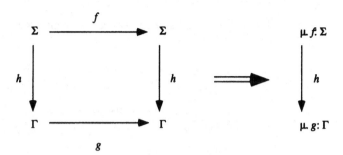

FIGURE 19.1. Fusion theorem

$$h.(f.(f^{\alpha}.\perp))$$
$$= \{\text{assumption } h \circ f = g \circ h\}$$
$$g.(h.(f^{\alpha}.\perp))$$
$$= \{\text{induction assumption}\}$$
$$g.(g^{\alpha}.\perp)$$
$$= \{\text{definition of approximation}\}$$
$$g^{\alpha+1}.\perp$$

Finally, the limit case is as follows, for a nonzero limit ordinal α:

$$(\forall \beta \mid \beta < \alpha \cdot h.(f^{\beta}.\perp) = g^{\beta}.\perp)$$
$$\vdash h.(f^{\alpha}.\perp)$$
$$= \{\text{definition of approximation}\}$$
$$h.(\lim \beta \mid \beta < \alpha \cdot f^{\beta}.\perp)$$
$$= \{\text{assumption } h \text{ continuous}\}$$
$$(\lim \beta \mid \beta < \alpha \cdot h.(f^{\beta}.\perp))$$
$$= \{\text{induction assumption}\}$$
$$(\lim \beta \mid \beta < \alpha \cdot g^{\beta}.\perp)$$
$$= \{\text{definition of approximation}\}$$
$$g^{\alpha}.\perp$$

and the proof is finished. $\square$

We note a special corollary of the fusion theorem.

Corollary 19.6 *Assume that $f : (\Gamma \to \Gamma) \to (\Gamma \to \Gamma)$ and $g : \Gamma \to \Gamma$ are monotonic functions on complete lattices and that $x : \Gamma$ is fixed. Then*

$$(\forall h \cdot f.h.x = g.(h.x)) \;\Rightarrow\; \mu.f.x = \mu.g \;.$$

Proof Since the function $(\lambda k \cdot k.x)$ is continuous (Exercise 19.3), we have

$$\mathsf{T}$$

$\equiv$ {fusion theorem with $h := (\lambda k \cdot k.x)$}

$\quad (\lambda k \cdot k.x) \circ f = g \circ (\lambda k \cdot k.x) \Rightarrow (\lambda k \cdot k.x).(\mu.f) = \mu.g$

$\equiv$ {definition of composition, extensionality}

$\quad (\forall h \cdot (\lambda k \cdot k.x).(f.h) = g.((\lambda k \cdot k.x).h) \Rightarrow (\lambda k \cdot k.x).(\mu.f) = \mu.g$

$\equiv$ {beta reduction}

$\quad (\forall h \cdot f.h.x = g.(h.x) \Rightarrow \mu.f.x = \mu.g)$

$\square$

Fixed Points Preserve Monotonicity

As another example of how the limit characterization of fixed points can be u
in proofs, we show that μ and ν preserve monotonicity (Table 19.2) in the se
that if f is a function that preserves monotonicity and f itself is monotonic, t
$\mu.f$ is a monotonic function.

Lemma 19.7 *Assume that A and B are complete lattices and that $f \in (A \to B) \to_m (A$
$B)$ and f preserves monotonicity. Then $\mu_{A \to B}.f = \mu_{A \to_m B}.f$ and $\nu_{A \to B} f$
$\nu_{A \to_m B} f$.*

Proof We show the proof for least fixed points. The existence of both fixed poin
guaranteed by Tarski's theorem. We show that each approximation f^α of $\mu_{A \to}$
is monotonic. This guarantees that the approximations for $\mu_{A \to B}.f$ and $\mu_{A \to_m}$
are pairwise equal, so the fixed points are also equal. For the base case, we ha

$\quad f^0.\bot$ monotonic

$\equiv$ {definition of approximation}

$\quad \bot_{A \to B}$ monotonic

$\equiv$ {constant function is monotonic}

$\quad \mathsf{T}$

Next, the successor case:

$\quad f^\alpha.\bot$ monotonic

$\vdash\ f^{\alpha+1}.\bot$ monotonic

$\equiv$ {definition of approximation}

$\quad f.(f^\alpha.\bot)$ monotonic

$\equiv$ {f preserves monotonicity by assumption, induction assumption}

$\quad \mathsf{T}$

Finally, the limit case:

$$f^\beta.\bot \text{ monotonic for all } \beta < \alpha$$
$$\vdash \quad f^\alpha.\bot \text{ monotonic}$$
$$\equiv \{\text{definition of approximation}\}$$
$$(\lim \beta \mid \beta < \alpha \cdot f^\beta.\bot) \text{ monotonic}$$
$$\Leftarrow \{\text{all joins preserve monotonicity}\}$$
$$(\forall \beta \mid \beta < \alpha \cdot f^\beta.\bot \text{ monotonic})$$
$$\equiv \{\text{induction assumption}\}$$
$$\top$$

and the proof is finished. $\square$

Generally, we say that μ *preserves property* P if $P.(\mu.f)$ holds whenever the monotonic function f preserves P (and similarly for ν). The above lemma then shows that the fixed-point operators preserve monotonicity.

Homomorphism Preservation for Fixed Point Constructs

In addition to monotonicity, we are also interested in what other homomorphism properties the fixed-point constructors preserve.

Lemma 19.8   *Least fixed points preserve disjunctivity and strictness, while greatest fixed points preserve conjunctivity and termination.*

Proof We consider only least fixed points, as the properties for greatest fixed points are dual. To prove that μ preserves strictness we follow the same idea as in the proof that μ preserves monotonicity (Lemma 19.7); i.e., we show that all approximations f_α of the fixed point $\mu.f$ are disjunctive if f preserves disjunctivity. For the base case we know that abort is disjunctive. For the successor case the assumption that f preserves disjunctivity tells us that $f.(f_\alpha)$ is disjunctive if f_α is disjunctive. Finally, the limit case follows from the fact that joins preserve disjunctivity. Preservation of strictness is proved in the same way as preservation of disjunctivity. $\square$

The following counterexample can be used to show that least fixed points do not preserve conjunctivity. Let the function $f : (\text{Unit} \mapsto \text{Nat}) \to (\text{Unit} \mapsto \text{Nat})$ be defined as follows:

$$f.S = \begin{cases} \text{chaos} & \text{if } S \sqsubseteq \text{chaos,} \\ [\lambda u\ x \cdot x \geq i+1] & \text{if } S \sqsubseteq [\lambda u\ x \cdot x \geq i+1] \text{ and} \\ & \quad S \not\sqsubseteq [\lambda u\ x \cdot x \geq i] \text{ for } i \in \text{Nat,} \\ \text{choose}\,;[\lambda n\ x \cdot x \geq n] & \text{if } S = \text{choose}\,;[\lambda n\ x \cdot x \geq n], \\ \text{magic} & \text{otherwise.} \end{cases}$$

This function is monotonic, so $\mu.f$ exists. From the definition it follows that $\mu.\downharpoonright$ choose; $[\lambda n\, x \cdot x \geq n]$ is the least fixed point (the only other fixed point is ma⊄ However, $\mu.f$ is not conjunctive, even though f preserves conjunctivity (f m⬧ all predicate transformers except $\mu.f$ to conjunctive predicate transformers). see that $\mu.f$ is not conjunctive, consider the collection of predicates $\{p_i \mid i \in \mathbb{N}$ where $p_i.x \equiv x \geq i$. Then $\mu.f$ establishes any p_i but not their meet (false). leave it to the reader to fill in the details of this argument.

In spite of the above counterexample, it is still possible that any least fixed po⬧ $(\lambda\mu\, X \cdot S)$ preserves conjunctivity when S is a statement built from asserts, dem⊄ updates, sequential composition, meet, and the statement variable X. This is ⬧ in the case of tail recursion, since any tail-recursive statement can be written us⬧ iteration statements that preserve conjunctivity (see Chapter 21). We leave general case as an open question; our conjecture is that it is in fact true.

The fixed-point homomorphism properties are summarized in Table 19.2.

19.4 Summary and Discussion

This chapter has given an overview of fixed-point theory, which is central to treatment of recursion. We gave the basic fixed-point theorem by Tarski and sho⬧ that fixed points also can be characterized as limits of directed sets. This charac⬧ ization required the use of ordinals. We then proved a collection of basic proper⬧ about the fixed-point operators that will be very useful later on.

Tarski's influential fixed-point theorem for lattices was originally publishe⬧ [136], but its significance for recursion was discovered by Dana Scott, who u⬧ fixed points to give a semantics for loops and recursive programs, and started⬧ tradition of denotational semantics. The early pioneers in this area were Scott Cristopher Strachey [128] and de Bakker [36]. A good overview of denotati⬧ semantics is given by, e.g., Robert Tennent [137], or David Schmidt [125]. fusion theorem is a classic theorem in fixed-point theory. Its usefulness (in a slig⬧ weaker form requiring universal join homomorphism rather than continuity⬧ demonstrated by Roland Backhouse et al. [34].

preserves	$\sqsubseteq$	$\perp$	$\top$	$\sqcap$	$\sqcup$
μ	yes[1]	yes	no	no	yes
ν	yes[1]	no	yes	yes	no

[1] for monotonicity preserving f

TABLE 19.2. Fixed-point preservation of properties (monotonic arguments)

.5 Exercises

19.1 Show that the least fixed point of a monotonic function f on a complete lattice is characterized by the following two properties:

$$f.(\mu.f) \;=\; \mu.f \;,$$
$$f.x \sqsubseteq x \;\Rightarrow\; \mu.f \sqsubseteq x \;.$$

Furthermore, show that if the equality in the first property is weakened to $\sqsubseteq$, the resulting two properties still characterize the least fixed point.

19.2 Show that the empty set is directed. Then show that every cpo must have a least element. Finally, show that continuity implies strictness.

19.3 Show that the function $(\lambda f \cdot f.x)$ is continuous (in fact, it is a universal join homomorphism).

ecursion

We now apply fixed-point theory to recursively defined statements, interpreting a recursive statement as the least fixed point of a monotonic function on predicate transformers. We show how to construct recursive statements as limits of approximation chains and develop inference rules for introducing recursion as a refinement of a simpler nonrecursive statement. Finally, we show how to define recursive procedures with parameters and give inference rules for working with procedures.

.1 Fixed Points and Predicate Transformers

Let us now consider *recursive contract statements* of the form $(\mu X \cdot S)$, which were briefly described in the introduction. The basic intuitive interpretation of $(\mu X \cdot S)$ is that of *recursive unfoldings*. This means that the contract is carried out (executed) by executing S, and whenever the statement variable X is encountered, it is replaced by the whole statement $(\mu X \cdot S)$ before execution continues. If unfolding can go on infinitely, then the computation is considered to be aborting. As an example, consider the contract statement

$(\mu X \cdot S ; X \sqcap \text{skip})$.

This contract is executed by the demon first choosing either the left- or right-hand side of the meet. If the first alternative is chosen, then S is executed, after which X is replaced by $(\mu X \cdot S; X \sqcap \text{skip})$ and execution continues with this substatement. If the second alternative is chosen, then the skip is executed and execution terminates.

We need to determine the weakest precondition predicate transformer for a rec
sive contract, i.e., define wp.$(\mu X \cdot S)$. In the recursive unfolding interpretation,
find that $(\mu X \cdot S)$ must have the same effect as its recursive unfolding, $S[X$
$(\mu X \cdot S)]$. Hence, we can postulate that wp.$(\mu X \cdot S) = $ wp.$S[X := (\mu X \cdot S)]$.
us extend the definition of wp so that wp.$X = X$, in the sense that the contract st
ment variable X is mapped to a predicate transformer variable X (on the same s
space). Then we have that wp.$S[X := (\mu X \cdot S)] = ($wp.$S)[X := $ wp.$(\mu X \cdot$
because of the way wp is defined as a homomorphism on the contract statem
syntax. In other words, wp.$(\mu X \cdot S)$ is a fixed point of the function $(\lambda X \cdot$ wp.
which maps predicate transformers to predicate transformers.

This narrows the scope of what the weakest precondition of a recursive contr
can be, but does not determine it uniquely, as there may be more than one fi
point for any given function. It is also possible that a function has no fixed po
in which case the definition would not give a weakest precondition interpretat
to all contract statements.

The latter problem is settled by fixed-point theory. The predicate transformer w
is built out of basic predicate transformers and X using sequential compositi
meets, and joins. Hence $T \sqsubseteq T' \Rightarrow (\lambda X \cdot $ wp.$S).T \sqsubseteq (\lambda X \cdot $ wp.$S).T'$, when
and T' are both monotonic predicate transformers (T and T' must be monotoni
that sequential composition is monotonic in both arguments). Thus, $(\lambda X \cdot $ wp
is a monotonic function on the set of monotonic predicate transformers $\Sigma \mapsto_m$
As $\Sigma \mapsto_m \Sigma$ is a complete lattice, the Tarski–Knaster fixed-point theorem sh
that this function has a (least and greatest) fixed point.

The first problem (uniqueness) is settled by the requirement that nonterminat
execution of a recursive contract be identified with breaching the contract.
argument here is that infinitely delaying the satisfaction of a condition require
the contract cannot be considered an acceptable way of satisfying the contrac
contract that never terminates is $(\mu X \cdot X)$, for which we therefore must have
wp.$(\mu X \cdot X) = $ abort. On the other hand, we know that wp.$(\mu X \cdot X)$ must
fixed point of $(\lambda X \cdot $ wp.$X)$, i.e., of $(\lambda X \cdot X)$. Any predicate transformer is a fi
point of this function. Of these predicate transformers, abort is the least one.
take this as a general rule and define the least fixed point of the function $(\lambda X \cdot $ w
as the weakest precondition of the recursive contract statement $(\mu X \cdot S)$:

$$\text{wp.}(\mu X \cdot S) \;\hat{=}\; (\mu X \cdot \text{wp.}S) \;.$$

This means that we can study the satisfaction of recursive contract statement
considering *recursive predicate transformers* $(\mu X \cdot S)$ (standing for $\mu.(\lambda X \cdot$
In this way, the properties of recursive contract statements, as far as satisfac
of contracts goes, is reduced to properties of least fixed points of functions
predicate transformers.

Recursive Statements as Limits

The above argument shows that we should take the least fixed point as the meaning of a recursive contract in the special case of the never terminating contract $(\mu X \cdot X)$. We can give further credibility to the choice of least fixed points by considering the way in which these are determined as limits of approximation sequences.

Assume that f is a monotonic function on predicate transformers. Applying Theorem 19.3, we see that $\mu.f$ can be expressed using approximations

$$
\begin{aligned}
f^0.\text{abort} &= \text{abort}, \\
f^{\alpha+1}.\text{abort} &= f.(f^\alpha.\text{abort}) \text{ for arbitrary ordinals } \alpha, \\
f^\alpha.\text{abort} &= (\lim \beta \mid \beta < \alpha \cdot f^\beta.\text{abort}) \text{ for nonzero limit ordinals } \alpha.
\end{aligned}
$$

Theorem 19.3 then shows that $\mu.f = f^\gamma.\text{abort}$ for some ordinal γ. For $\nu.f$, we have a dual formulation with coapproximations starting from magic.

For a given contract statement $(\mu X \cdot S)$, we can define the approximations $S^\alpha.\{\text{false}\}$ of $(\mu X \cdot S)$ in the same way as for predicate transformers. Each of these approximations denotes a contract statement (remember that we also permit contract statements that are joins over infinitely indexed sets of contract statements).

Assume that the approximation $S^\alpha.\{\text{false}\}$ is executed in an initial state from which execution of $(\mu X \cdot S)$ is guaranteed to terminate. We can then think of a counter initially set at the ordinal α. Each time the recursive definition is unfolded, the counter is decreased. If the ordinal is chosen large enough, then termination occurs before $\alpha = 0$, and the effect of $S^\alpha.\{\text{false}\}$ will be the same as the effect of $(\mu .X \cdot S)$ in this initial state. If the number of unfoldings needed is too large, then the effect of $S^\alpha.\{\text{false}\}$ will be a breach of contract in this state.

As the ordinal α is chosen larger and larger, more and more unfoldings are possible, and for more and more initial states $S^\alpha.\{\text{false}\}$ will have the same effect as $(\mu X \cdot S)$. At γ, we reach the point where all terminating executions are accounted for. For those initial states from which unfolding is infinite, every approximation acts as abort. Hence, the effect of $(\mu X \cdot S)$ will be the same as the effect of $S^\gamma.\{\text{false}\}$, as far as satisfaction of the contract to establish some postcondition goes. Hence wp.$(\mu X \cdot S)$ = wp.$(S^\gamma.\{\text{false}\})$ for some γ. By the definition of weakest preconditions for contract statements, we then have that wp.$(S^\gamma.\{\text{false}\})$ = $(\lambda X \cdot \text{wp}.S)^\gamma.\text{abort}$ = $(\mu X \cdot \text{wp}.S)$. This shows that the weakest precondition of a recursive contract statement should be taken as the least fixed point of the corresponding function on monotonic predicate transformers in the general case also.

This explains why S^α can be seen as an approximation of the recursive contract statement $(\mu X \cdot S)$. In some initial states, the number of unfoldings needed for $(\mu X \cdot S)$ to establish the postcondition may be so small that S^α gives the same result, but in some other states, α may not be sufficiently large, so S^α leads to a breach of contract.

Example

It may not be evident why we need to use ordinals when defining the approxim
tions, i.e., why is it not sufficient to consider only the natural numbers (and th
limit ω). Let us therefore give an example where transfinite ordinals are neede
reach the least fixed point. Consider the statement

$$(\mu X \bullet \{x = 0\} ; [x := x' \mid x' \geq 1] ; X \sqcup$$
$$\{x = 1\} \sqcup$$
$$\{x > 1\} ; x := x - 1 ; X) .$$

The behavior of this statement in initial state $x \neq 0$ is to decrease the value
until $x = 1$, when the execution terminates. In initial state $x = 0$, the progr
variable x is first assigned some arbitrary nonzero natural number, after which
same steps of decreasing x are carried out, eventually leading to termination w
$x = 1$.

Computing successive approximations we get, after some simplifications,

$$S_0 = \text{abort} ,$$
$$S_1 = \{x = 1\} ,$$
$$S_2 = \{1 \leq x \leq 2\} ; x := 1 ,$$

and inductively, for all $n \in$ Nat, we find that $S_n = \{1 \leq x \leq n\} ; x := 1$:

$\quad S_{n+1}$
$= \{\text{definition of approximation}\}$
$\quad \{x = 0\} ; [x := x' \mid x' \geq 1] ; S_n \sqcup \{x = 1\} \sqcup \{x > 1\} ; x := x - 1 ;$
$= \{\text{induction assumption}\}$
$\quad \{x = 0\} ; [x := x' \mid x' \geq 1] ; \{1 \leq x \leq n\} ; x := 1 \sqcup$
$\quad \{x = 1\} \sqcup$
$\quad \{x > 1\} ; x := x - 1 ; \{1 \leq x \leq n\} ; x := 1$
$= \{\text{simplification}\}$
$\quad \text{abort} \sqcup \{x = 1\} \sqcup \{2 \leq x \leq n + 1\} ; x := 1$
$= \{\text{easily verified equality}\}$
$\quad \{1 \leq x \leq n + 1\} ; x := 1$

(for the rules used in the last two steps see Exercises 20.3 and 20.4).

At the first infinite ordinal ω a similar derivation gives us

$$S_\omega = (\sqcup n \in \text{Nat} \bullet S_n) = \{1 \leq x\} ; x := 1 .$$

Note that this statement behaves as abort when $x = 0$. We can still continue
process of computing approximations, getting

$$S_{\omega+1} \;=\; x := 1 \;,$$
$$S_{\omega+2} \;=\; x := 1 \;.$$

(again, we get $S_{\alpha+1}$ by substituting S_α for X in the recursion body). At this point, we have reached the ordinal where no new approximations are produced. This means that the least fixed point is the functional update $x := 1$.

The need for transfinite ordinals does not, of course, not mean that execution of a recursive statement could terminate after an infinite number of recursive calls. Rather, this argument shows that if we want to set a counter at the start so that its value can be decreased at each recursive call, then we have to set the counter to ω (or higher) at the start.

Greatest Fixed Points

We can also introduce $(\nu X \cdot S)$ as an alternative kind of recursively defined statement. In fact, the greatest fixed point is important when we handle different kinds of iterations in Chapter 21.

If we want to understand greatest fixed points in terms of unfoldings, then we cannot use the same argument as for least fixed points. Since the greatest fixed point of a function on predicate transformers is a colimit of a chain of coapproximations starting from magic, this requires that infinite unfolding be treated as miraculous computation. This is not generally the case, but it can be justified in certain cases if a notion of *biased* execution is introduced.

Consider, for example, the recursive definition X:

$$X \;=\; \mathsf{skip} \sqcap S \,;\, X \;.$$

Successive unfolding of this definition leads to a meet of repeated executions of S:

$$\mathsf{skip} \sqcap S \sqcap S \,;\, S \sqcap S \,;\, S \,;\, S \sqcap \cdots \;.$$

(here we have assumed that S is conjunctive, to deduce $S \,;\, (\mathsf{skip} \sqcap S \,;\, X) = S \sqcap S \,;\, S \,;\, X$). If S is not miraculous, we can intuitively think of the demon always choosing one more unfolding, so that an infinite unfolding is possible. This means that $(\mu X \cdot S \,;\, X \sqcap \mathsf{skip})$ is nonterminating. However, our interpretation of $(\nu X \cdot S \,;\, X \sqcap \mathsf{skip})$ is such that the demon must avoid infinite unfolding. Thus the demon will at some point choose the skip alternative, and the whole statement is guaranteed to terminate. This means that there is a bias in the choice; the demon may not neglect the skip alternative forever.

20.2   Recursion Introduction and Elimination

Let $P = \{p_w \mid w \in W\}$ be a collection of predicates that are indexed by well-founded set W, such that $v \sqsubseteq w \Rightarrow p_v \sqsubseteq p_w$. We refer to a predicate in set as a *ranked predicate*. In practice, a ranked predicate p_w is often written as conjunction of an *invariant expression I* and a *variant expression t* (also known a *termination function*):

$$p_w = (\lambda\sigma \cdot I.\sigma \wedge t.\sigma = w)$$

or, with pointwise extension, $p_w = (I \wedge t = w)$. Here w is a fresh variable rang over W.

Assuming a collection of ranked predicates P as above, we define

$$p \overset{\wedge}{=} (\cup w \in W \cdot p_w) ,$$
$$p_{<w} \overset{\wedge}{=} (\cup v \in W \mid v < w \cdot p_v) .$$

Thus, p holds if some ranked predicate holds, while $p_{<w}$ holds if some ran predicate with a "lower rank" than that of p_w holds.

We use ranked predicates to establish that a sequence of nested recursive must eventually terminate. Essentially, the idea is as follows. Assume that the call is made in a state where some ranked predicate is true, i.e., in a state wl p holds. We need to show that each nested call is made in a state that satis a lower-ranked predicate than that which the state of the previous call satis Thus, if a call is made in a state that satisfies the ranked predicate p_w, then nested call should be made in a state that satisfies $p_{<w}$. Because the set of ran predicates is well-founded, there can then be only a finite number of nested c and hence the recursion must terminate.

Recursion Introduction

We shall now derive a rule for *recursion introduction* based on the use of ra predicates. This rule states under what conditions it is possible to refine a state S by a recursive statement $\mu.f$. The rule is based on the following theorem.

Theorem 20.1   *Assume that W is a well-founded set, f a monotonic function on monotonic μ icate transformers, and $\{p_w \mid w \in W\}$ a collection of state predicates indexe W. Then the following holds:*

$$(\forall w \in W \cdot \{p_w\} ; S \sqsubseteq f.(\{p_{<w}\} ; S)) \;\Rightarrow\; \{p\} ; S \sqsubseteq \mu.f .$$

Proof Assume that $\{p_w\} ; S \sqsubseteq f.(\{p_{<w}\} ; S)$ holds for all $w \in W$. First we s that

$$(\forall w \in W \cdot \{p_w\} ; S \sqsubseteq \mu.f)$$

by well-founded induction, as follows. The induction assumption is $(\forall v \cdot v < w \Rightarrow \{p_v\}\,;\, S \sqsubseteq \mu.f)$:

$$\{p_w\}\,;\, S$$

$\sqsubseteq$ {assumption}

$$f.(\{\sqcup\, v \in W \mid v < w \cdot p_v\}\,;\, S)$$

$=$ {homomorphism property of assertion, distributivity}

$$f.(\sqcup\, v \in W \mid v < w \cdot \{p_v\}\,;\, S)$$

$\sqsubseteq$ {induction assumption, monotonicity}

$$f.(\sqcup\, v \in W \mid v < w \cdot \mu.f)$$

$\sqsubseteq$ {empty join gives abort, otherwise $\mu.f$, monotonicity}

$$f.(\mu.f)$$

$=$ {fold fixed point}

$$\mu.f$$

Thus,

$$\{p\}\,;\, S$$

$=$ {definition of p}

$$\{\sqcup\, w \in W \cdot p_w\}\,;\, S$$

$=$ {homomorphism property of assertion, distributivity}

$$(\sqcup\, w \in W \cdot \{p_w\}\,;\, S)$$

$\sqsubseteq$ {(∗) above}

$$\mu.f$$

and the proof is finished. $\square$

From Theorem 20.1 we get the following rule for introducing a recursive statement, when I is a Boolean expression and t an expression that ranges over some well-founded set:

$$\frac{\Phi \vdash \{I \,\wedge\, t = w\}\,;\, S \;\sqsubseteq\; T[X := \{I \,\wedge\, t < w\}\,;\, S]}{\Phi \vdash \{I\}\,;\, S \sqsubseteq (\mu X \cdot T)} \qquad (\mu\ \textit{introduction})$$

• w is a fresh variable.

In practice, this rule of recursion introduction can be used as follows. Viewing a statement S as a specification, we first decide on an invariant I and a variant t ranging over some well-founded set W. We then transform $\{I \,\wedge\, t = w\}\,;\, S$ (where w is a fresh variable), applying refinement rules, until we get as a refinement a term of the form $T[X := \{I \,\wedge\, t < w\}\,;\, S]$. The μ introduction rule then shows that $\{I\}\,;\, S$ is refined by the recursive statement $(\mu X \cdot T)$.

Recursion Elimination

The recursion introduction rule shows how we can introduce recursion in a der‹‐
tion. The opposite, recursion elimination, is also sometimes useful. As alre›
noted, the principle of least fixed point induction is itself a rule for μ eliminat‹
Another rule that can be used is the following:

$$\frac{}{\vdash (\mu X \cdot S) = S} \qquad\qquad (\mu\ eliminati\‐$$

- X not free in S.

In fact, this rule can be used both to introduce and to eliminate a (vacuous) recurs‹

Similarly, the principle of greatest fixed point induction is itself a rule for ν in‐
duction, while a (vacuous) greatest fixed point construct can be eliminated (
introduced) using

$$\frac{}{\vdash (\nu X \cdot S) = S} \qquad\qquad (\nu\ eliminati\‐$$

- X not free in S.

20.3 Recursive Procedures

The definition of a *recursive procedure* is of the following form:

$$\text{rec } N(\text{var } x_1, \ldots, x_m, \text{val } y_1, \ldots, y_n) = S , \qquad (recursive\ procedu\‐$$

where S is a statement that may contain (recursive) calls to N of the form

$$N(z_1, \ldots, z_m, e_1, \ldots, e_n) .$$

Here each z_i is one of the variables $x_1, \ldots, x_m, y_1, \ldots, y_n$ (the *parameters*), ‹
e_j is an expression in the parameters, and the z_i are all distinct. Note that w›
not permit references to "global" program variables in a procedure body.

Intuitively, a call $N(z_1, \ldots, z_m, e_1, \ldots, e_n)$ is executed as a statement

$$\text{begin var } y_1, \ldots, y_n := e_1, \ldots, e_n ; S[x_1, \ldots, x_m := z_1, \ldots, z_m] \text{ end },$$

and calls to N inside S are executed in the same way, recursively. If a formal v‹
parameter y_j has the same name and type as an actual reference parameter,
the local variable y_j has to be renamed. To simplify the presentation, we ass›
that no such name clashes occur.

Note that the intuitive interpretation of recursive calls means that the exec‹
builds up a collection of nested blocks with local variables. The same happen›
recursive call to N inside S is within the scope of a local variable declaration›

Semantics of Recursive Procedures

Even though the intuitive description of a recursive procedure includes a potentially unbounded nesting of blocks, we do not need this construction in order to describe mathematically what a recursive procedure means.

In order to describe what type of predicate transformer such a recursive definition defines, we first consider an example with a single recursive call:

$$\text{rec } N(\text{var } x, y, \text{val } z) \ = \ \cdots N(y, z, x + z) \cdots .$$

We consider this definition as syntactic sugaring, as follows:

$$N.x.y.z \ \overset{\wedge}{=} \ (\mu X \bullet \cdots (\sqcup x_0 \bullet \{x = x_0\} \, ; x, y, z := y, z, x + z;$$
$$X \, ; x, y, z := x_0, x, y) \cdots) .$$

The effect of the angelic choice and the assignments that are wrapped around the recursion variable X is (a) to store and restore the values of the variables (here x) that are not used as reference parameters in the recursive call, and (b) to map the right variables (here y and z) to the reference parameter positions in the call. Using a local variable to get the same effect would lead to a typing problem, since the recursive call would then occur in a different state space.

The combination of angelic choice and asserts keeps the initial value of x in a kind of "suspended animation" during the execution of the nested block; see Exercise 20.5.

Thus we have a method of reducing a recursive procedure definition into a definition where the right-hand side includes a μ-recursion. Furthermore, we consider a call $N(u, v, e)$ to be syntactic sugaring:

$$N(u, v, e) \ = \ \text{begin var } z := e \, ; N.u.v.z \text{ end}$$

(recall that we assume that there is no name clash between z and u or v).

In Section 13.5, we showed that a procedure body can be refined freely, provided that all calls to the procedure are in monotonic positions and that procedure calls preserve the homomorphism properties (strictness, termination, conjunctivity and disjunctivity) of the procedure body. The results obviously remain valid for recursive procedures.

Recursive Procedures with Local Variables

Special care has to be taken when a recursive call occurs within the scope of a block with local variables in the procedure body. We assume that the body is of the form begin var $z := e$; S end where S does not contain blocks with local variables (this is no real restriction because inner blocks can always be pushed to the outermost level in a statement). Then z is handled like a value parameter in the recursive calls. On the outermost level it is a local variable outside the recursion.

The following example should make this clear. Assume the following recursive defined procedure with a single recursive call:

$$\text{rec } N(\text{var } x, \text{val } y) \quad = \quad \text{begin var } z := 0 \, ; \, \cdots N(y, x + z) \cdots \text{ end } .$$

This really defines N as follows:

$$N.x.y$$

$$=$$

begin var $z := 0$;

$$(\mu X \cdot \cdots (\sqcup x_0, z_0 \cdot \{x, z = x_0, z_0\} \, ; \, x, y, z := y, x + z, 0 \, ;$$
$$X \, ; \, x, y, z := x_0, x, z_0) \cdots)$$

end .

Before the recursive call, the old values of x and z are stored, while x plays role of y and y and z are reinitialized. After the call, x and z are restored, and takes back its old role.

Again, we assume for simplicity that if the procedure N is called from a state which a global variable z is used as a reference parameter, then the local variable of the body has been renamed to avoid a name clash.

Procedure Introduction

From the rule for recursion introduction (Section 20.2) we can derive a rule for induction of recursive procedures. For simplicity, we assume only a single recursive call in the body of the procedure definition.

Assume that N is a recursive procedure defined as

$$N(\text{var } x, \text{val } y) \quad \triangleq \quad \text{begin var } z := f \, ; \, S[X := N(\hat{x}, e)] \text{ end } ,$$

where x, y, and z are lists of distinct variables; f is a list of expressions over and y; e is a list of expressions over x, y, and z; and $\hat{x}$ is a list of distinct variable drawn from x, y, and z. Furthermore, assume that $\{p_w \mid w \in W\}$ is a collection ranked predicates over x and y, and that b is a Boolean expression that does contain y' or z free. Then the following rule of *procedure introduction* is valid

$$\frac{\{p_w\} \, ; \, [x, y := x', y' \mid b] \sqsubseteq}{\begin{array}{l} \text{begin var } z := f; \\ \quad S[X := \{p_{<w}[x, y := \hat{x}, e]\} \, ; \, [\hat{x} := x' \mid b[x, y := \hat{x}, e]]] \\ \text{end} \end{array}}{\{p\} \, ; \, [x, y := x', y' \mid b] \sqsubseteq N.x.y} \quad .$$

We show the proof for the special case when $\hat{x} = x$, i.e., when the reference parameters take their own places in the recursive calls. The proof of the general is analogous, except that the assignments immediately surrounding the recursion variable X become more complicated.

$$\{p\} \, ; [x, y := x', y' \mid b] \sqsubseteq N.x.y$$

$\equiv$ {definition of recursive procedure}

$\{p\} \, ; [x, y := x', y' \mid b] \sqsubseteq$

begin var $z := f$;

$\quad (\mu X \cdot S[X := (\sqcup y_0, z_0 \cdot \{y = y_0 \wedge z = z_0\}) \, ; y := e \, ;$

$\quad\quad\quad X \, ; y, z := y_0, z_0)])$ end

$\equiv$ {Theorem 17.7, assume z' not free in b}

$\{p \wedge z = f\} \, ; [x, y, z := x', y', z' \mid b] \sqsubseteq$

$(\mu X \cdot S[X := (\sqcup y_0, z_0 \cdot \{y = y_0 \wedge z = z_0\}) \, ; y := e \, ;$

$\quad\quad\quad X \, ; y, z := y_0, z_0)])$

$\Leftarrow$ {recursion introduction}

$\{p_w \wedge z = f\} \, ; [x, y, z := x', y', z' \mid b] \sqsubseteq$

$S[X := \text{``} (\sqcup y_0, z_0 \cdot \{y = y_0 \wedge z = z_0\}) \, ; y := e \, ;$

$\quad\quad\quad \{p_{<w}\} \, ; [x, y = x', y' \mid b] \, ; y, z := y_0, z_0) \text{''}]$

$\equiv$ {rewrite using context information}

$\cdots (\sqcup y_0, z_0 \cdot \{y = y_0 \wedge z = z_0\}) \, ; y := e \, ;$

$\quad\quad\quad \{p_{<w}[y := e]\} \, ; [x, y = x', y' \mid b[y := e]] \, ; y, z := y_0, z_0) \cdots$

$\equiv$ {remove vacuous assignments}

$\cdots (\sqcup y_0, z_0 \cdot \{y = y_0 \wedge z = z_0\}) \, ;$

$\quad\quad\quad \{p_{<w}[y := e]\} \, ; [x = x' \mid b[y := e]] \, ; y, z := y_0, z_0) \cdots$

$\equiv$ {simplify angelic choice (Exercise 20.6)}

$\cdots \{p_{<w}[y := e]\} \, ; [x = x' \mid b[y := e]] \cdots$

$\equiv$ {substitute back}

$\{p_w \wedge z = f\} \, ; [x, y, z := x', y', z' \mid b] \sqsubseteq$

$S[X := \{p_{<w}[y := e]\} \, ; [x = x' \mid b[y := e]]]$

$\equiv$ {Theorem 17.7}

$\{p_w\} \, ; [x, y := x', y' \mid b] \sqsubseteq$

begin var $z := f$; $S[X := \{p_{<w}[y := e]\} \, ; [x = x' \mid b[y := e]]]$ end

Note the use of ellipsis to hide a context in this proof. We will use this device quite frequently to shorten a derivation and to highlight the places where changes are made in a term. Ellipses are used together with quotation marks: when we quote a subterm in one step, then the ellipses denote the part of the term outside the quotation marks in the next step.

Once the introduction of the recursive procedure N is verified, we can introd
calls to N, using the following rule of *procedure call introduction*:

$$\frac{\{p\} ; [x, y, := x', y' \mid b] \sqsubseteq N.x.y}{\{p[y := e]\} ; [x := x' \mid b[y := e]] \sqsubseteq N(x, e)} \ .$$

Here the hypothesis is that the required refinement holds for the formal proced
parameters x and y, both of which may be lists of program variables. The conclus
then permits us to infer that the required refinement holds for the actual refere
parameters x (a list of distinct program variables) and actual value parameters
list of expressions). The proof is a short derivation:

$$\{p[y := e]\} ; [x := x' \mid b[y := e]] \sqsubseteq N(x, e)$$
$\equiv$ {definition of procedure call}
$$\{p[y := e']\} ; [x := x' \mid b[y := e]] \sqsubseteq \text{begin var } y := e ; N.x.y \text{ end}$$
$\equiv$ {Theorem 17.7}
$$\{p[y := e] \wedge y = e\} ; [x, y := x', y' \mid b[y := e]] \sqsubseteq N.x.y$$
$\equiv$ {use assertion information to simplify}
$$\{p \wedge y = e\} ; [x, y := x', y' \mid b] \sqsubseteq N.x.y$$
$\Leftarrow$ {weaken assertion}
$$\{p\} ; [x, y := x', y' \mid b] \sqsubseteq N.x.y$$

Using the Rule in Practice

In practice, the introduction rules can be used in the following stepwise fashion.
start from a specification $\{p\} ; [x := x' \mid b]$ of the procedure, where x is intende
be a reference parameter and where other free variables y in p and b are inten
to be value parameters. We then develop a recursive procedure N such that

$$\{p\} ; [x, y := x', y' \mid b] \sqsubseteq N.x.y \ .$$

After this, we can replace any specification of the form $\{p[x, y := u, e]\} ; [u
u' \mid b[x, x', y := u, u', e]]$ with a procedure call $N(u, e)$.

As a trivial example, we develop a procedure for calculating whether a numb
even or not, relying only on the following recursive characterization of evenn

$$\text{even.0} \wedge (\forall n \bullet \text{even.}(n + 1) \equiv \neg \text{even.}n) \ .$$

We want the argument n : Nat to be a value parameter and the result to be st
in a reference parameter x : Bool. Thus our specification is

$$x := \text{even.}n$$

or, equivalently, $\{T\}\,;\,[x := x' \mid x' = \mathsf{even}.n]$. As invariant we use true and as variant n. The derivation of the procedure is as follows:

$$\{n = w\}\,;\,[x, n := x', n' \mid x' = \mathsf{even}.n]$$
$\sqsubseteq$ {introduce conditional, simplify if-branch}
  if $n = 0 \rightarrow x := \mathsf{T}$
  $[\!]\ n > 0 \rightarrow$ " $\{n = w \wedge n > 0\}\,;\,[x, n := x', n' \mid x' = \mathsf{even}.n]$ "
  fi
$=$ {characterization of even, context information}
  $\cdots\{n = w \wedge n > 0\}\,;\,[x, n := x', n' \mid x' = \neg\,\mathsf{even}.(n-1)]\cdots$
$=$ {split assignment}
  $\cdots\{n = w \wedge n > 0\}\,;\,[x, n := x', n' \mid x' = \mathsf{even}.(n-1)]\,;\,x := \neg x\cdots$
$\sqsubseteq$ {weaken assertion, make assignment deterministic}
  $\cdots\{n - 1 < w\}\,;\,[x := x' \mid x' = \mathsf{even}.(n-1)]\,;\,x := \neg x\cdots$
$=$ {substitute back}
  if $n = 0 \rightarrow x := \mathsf{T}$
  $[\!]\ n > 0 \rightarrow \{n - 1 < w\}\,;\,[x := x' \mid x' = \mathsf{even}.(n-1)]\,;\,x := \neg x$
  fi

By the rule of procedure introduction (with $p_w := (n = w)$ and $x := x$ and $y := n$ and $b := \mathsf{even}.n$) this derivation proves

$$[x, n := x', n' \mid x' = \mathsf{even}.n] \ \sqsubseteq \ \mathsf{Even}.x.n\ ,$$

where Even is defined as follows:

$\mathsf{Even}(\mathbf{var}\ x, \mathbf{val}\ n)\ =$
  if $n = 0 \rightarrow x := \mathsf{T}\ [\!]\ n > 0 \rightarrow \mathsf{Even}(x, n - 1)\,;\,x := \neg x$ fi .

Furthermore, the rule for introduction of procedure calls allows us to replace statements of the right form with calls to Even. For example, the following replacement is correct:

$$z := \mathsf{even}.(a + b) \ \sqsubseteq \ \mathsf{Even}(z, a + b)\ .$$

Note how the refinement theorem for the procedure itself contains the value parameters as program variables, making the left-hand side look a bit more complicated than we might want (here we must use a demonic assignment rather than a deterministic one). However, the important thing is that we have a rule for deriving a procedure that allows us to replace program statements with procedure calls.

Mutual Recursion

A *mutually recursive definition* is of the form

$$\text{rec } N_1(\text{var } x_1, \text{val } y_1), \ldots, N_m(\text{var } x_1, \text{val } y_1) \;=\; S_1, \ldots, S_m \;.$$

Here the defining expression S_i for each N_i may contain calls to all of the procedu[re]s $N_1, \ldots, N_m$. This kind of definition can easily be handled by considering it to de[fine] a single m-tuple $N.x.y = (N_1.x_1.y_1, \ldots, N_m.x_m.y_m)$. Since the Cartesian prod[uct] of complete lattices is a complete lattice, $N.x.y$ is then a least fixed point in anal[ogy] with the single-recursion case. Now, the definition of $N_1, \ldots, N_m$ above is take[n to] mean that $N_i.x_i.y_i$ is the ith component of this least fixed point, for $i = 1, \ldots$ We will not consider mutual recursion in any more detail here.

20.4 Example: Computing the Square Root

As another example, we derive a recursive procedure for computing the int[eger] square root of a given natural number n, i.e., the (unique) natural number x [sat]isfying $x^2 \le n < (x + 1)^2$. Our plan is to let two variables l and r boun[d an] interval within which the square root of n is guaranteed to be, and to make [the] interval smaller and smaller until $r = l + 1$. This suggests a recursive proce[dure] with one reference parameter (x) and three value parameters $(n, l, \text{and } r)$ and u[se] $l^2 \le n < r^2$ as invariant and $r - l$ as variant. The initial specification is

$$\{l^2 \le n < r^2\} ; [x, n, l, r := x', n', l', r' \mid x'^2 \le n < (x' + 1)^2] \;.$$

We then have the following derivation, where S stands for the statement $[x \mathrel{:=} x' \mid x'^2 \le n < (x' + 1)^2]$:

$$\{l^2 \le n < r^2 \wedge r - l = w\} ; [x, n, l, r := x', n', l', r' \mid x'^2 \le n < (x' + \ldots]$$
$= \{\text{make assignment more deterministic}\}$
$$\{l^2 \le n < r^2 \wedge r - l = w\} ; [x := x' \mid x'^2 \le n < (x' + 1)^2]$$
$= \{\text{introduce conditional, simplify assertions}\}$

$\quad$ if $l + 1 = r \to$ " $\{l^2 \le n < r^2 \wedge r - l = w\} ; S$ "

$\quad$ $[\![\,] l + 1 \ne r \wedge (l + r)^2/4 \le n \to$
$$\{l + 1 < r \wedge (l + r)^2/4 \le n \wedge l^2 \le n < r^2 \wedge r - l = w\} ; S$$

$\quad$ $[\![\,] l + 1 \ne r \wedge (l + r)^2/4 > n \to$
$$\{l + 1 < r \wedge n < (l + r)^2/4 \wedge l^2 \le n < r^2 \wedge r - l = w\} ; S$$

$\quad$ fi

$\sqsubseteq \{\text{introduce assignment}\}$

$\text{if } l+1 = r \rightarrow x := l$

$[\![\ l+1 \neq r \wedge (l+r)^2/4 \leq n \rightarrow$

$\qquad \{l+1 < r \wedge (l+r)^2/4 \leq n \wedge l^2 \leq n < r^2 \wedge r - l = w\} ; S$

$[\![\ l+1 \neq r \wedge (l+r)^2/4 > n \rightarrow$

$\qquad \{l+1 < r \wedge n < (l+r)^2/4 \wedge l^2 \leq n < r^2 \wedge r - l = w\} ; S$

fi

$\sqsubseteq$ {weaken assertions}

$\text{if } l+1 = r \rightarrow x := l$

$[\![\ l+1 \neq r \wedge (l+r)^2/4 \leq n \rightarrow$

$\qquad \{(l+r)^2/4 \leq n < r^2 \wedge r - (l+r)/2 < w\} ; S$

$[\![\ l+1 \neq r \wedge (l+r)^2/4 > n \rightarrow$

$\qquad \{l^2 \leq n < (l+r)^2/4 \wedge (l+r)/2 - l < w\} ; S$

fi

The introduction rule then allows us to define a procedure as follows:

$\text{rec Sqrt}(\text{var } x, \text{val } n, l, r) =$

$\text{if } l+1 = r \rightarrow x := l$

$[\![\ l+1 \neq r \wedge ((l+r)^2/4 \leq n \rightarrow \text{Sqrt}(x, n, (l+r)/2, r)$

$[\![\ l+1 \neq r \wedge ((l+r)^2/4 > n \rightarrow \text{Sqrt}(x, n, l, (l+r)/2)$

fi

and deduce

$\{l^2 \leq n < r^2\} ; [x, n, l, r := x', n', l', r' \mid x'^2 \leq n < (x'+1)^2] \sqsubseteq$
$\text{Sqrt}.x.n.l.r$.

Furthermore, the rule for procedure call introduction tells us that if e is an expression over the program variables, then

$[x := x' \mid x'^2 \leq e < (x'+1)^2] \sqsubseteq \text{Sqrt}(x, e, 0, e+1)$.

To avoid the redundant parameters (0 and $e+1$) we can define an additional procedure with only two parameters (x and e), the body of which consists of only the call $\text{Sqrt}(x, e, 0, e+1)$.

5 Summary and Discussion

This chapter has given an overview of the fixed-point theory of recursion, applied to the framework of predicate transformers and refinement calculus. We have also

shown how recursive procedures with value and reference parameters are deri▮
and used.

Dijkstra's original weakest precondition calculus [53] did not handle recursi▮
it did not use fixed points for defining loops, and it required that loop bo▮
be continuous. The weakest precondition calculus was extended to recursion▮
Hehner in [74]. A predicate transformer semantics for general recursion (includ▮
mutual recursion) is given by Hesselink [78].

Ordinals were first used to describe recursion in terms of limits by Boom [41], ▮
described his results in the framework of constructive mathematics. Dijkstra ▮
van Gasteren used fixed-point reasoning and well-founded induction for loops▮
avoid the restriction to continuity [55]. However, most authors have preferred to ▮
within the realm of bounded nondeterminism (i.e., continuity), where the nat▮
numbers are sufficient. A continuous semantics for unbounded nondeterminism ▮
be given, as shown by Back [8], but such a semantics cannot then be fully abstr▮
i.e., it requires additional information not related to the input–output behavio▮
the program [5].

The original refinement calculus in [7] had only iteration constructs, and no gen▮
recursion. Recursion with noncontinuous statements was added to the refinem▮
calculus by Back [12] using ordinals, essentially following Boom [41]. A fi▮
point version of recursion in the refinement calculus was given by Morris [1▮
The rule for recursion introduction in the refinement calculus was first descri▮
by Back in [11].

Greatest fixed points are used in a partial correctness framework but have ▮
attracted much attention in total correctness formalisms. An exception is David ▮
[114], who used greatest fixed points to describe parallelism and fair terminat▮

Rules for introducing and reasoning about procedures, including recursive ▮
cedures, within the refinement calculus framework were given by Back [▮
Independently, Morgan also derived rules for procedures, but without recur▮
[103].

20.6   Exercises

20.1   Show that the approximation S_ω in the example in Section 20.1 is $\{1 \leq x\}; x :=$▮
while $S_{\omega+1}$ is $x := 1$.

20.2   Assume that each predicate p_w in the ranked collection $\{p_w \mid w \in W\}$ (wher▮
is a well-founded set) is of the form $I \wedge t = w$, where w does not occur free ▮
or t. Show that the predicate $(\cup w \in W \cdot p_w)$ is I.

20.3   Prove the following rules, which were used in Section 20.1:

(a) $(\exists \sigma \cdot q.\sigma \wedge \neg p.\sigma) \Rightarrow [\dot{q}] ; \{p\} = \text{abort}$.

(b) $\langle f \rangle ; \{p\} = \{\lambda \sigma \cdot p.(f.\sigma)\} ; \langle f \rangle$.

(c) $x := e ; x := e' \sqsubseteq x := e'$ if x does not appear in e'.

20.4 Prove the following, which was used in Section 20.1:

$$\{x = 1\} \sqcup \{2 \leq x \leq n + 1\} ; x := 1 = \{1 \leq x \leq n + 1\} ; x := 1 .$$

20.5 Prove the following refinement equality:

$$y := a ; (\sqcup y_0 \mid \{y = y_0\} ; S ; y := y_0) = y := a ; S ; y := a$$

for an arbitrary value a. This shows that the statement $(\sqcup y_0 \mid \{y = y_0\} ; S ; y := y_0)$ manages to execute S but then restore y to its initial value.

20.6 Prove the following result used in the proof of the rule for procedure introduction:

$$(\sqcup y_0 \mid \{y = y_0\} ; \{p\} ; [x := x' \mid b] ; y := y_0) = \{p\} ; [x := x' \mid b] .$$

20.7 Prove the following result used in the proofs of the procedure rules:

$$\{p\} ; x := x' \mid b] \sqsubseteq \text{begin var } y := e ; S \text{ end} \equiv$$
$$\{p \wedge y = e\} ; [x, y := x', y' \mid b] \sqsubseteq S$$

when y and y' do not occur free in p or b.

20.8 Derive a recursive procedure for computing the factorial of a natural number, using the following primitive recursive characterization of fact:

$$(\text{fact}.0 = 1) \wedge (\forall n \cdot \text{fact}.(n + 1) = n \cdot \text{fact}.n) .$$

20.9 Derive a recursive procedure for computing the greatest common factor (also known as the greatest common divisor) for two positive natural numbers, using the following properties of gcf, whenever x and y are positive:

$$\text{gcf}.x.x = x ,$$
$$x \leq y \Rightarrow \text{gcf}.x.y = \text{gcf}.x.(y - x) ,$$
$$\text{gcf}.x.y = \text{gcf}.y.x .$$

A suitable initial specification is

$$\{x > 0 \wedge y > 0\} ; z := \text{gcf}.x.y .$$

20.10 Fill in the missing details in the derivation of the recursive procedure that computes the integer square root, i.e., the details of the derivation steps justified by "introduce assignment" and "weaken assertion."

eration and Loops

The recursive constructs provide powerful programming tools. In the general case, the body S of a recursion $(\mu X \cdot S)$ or $(\nu X \cdot S)$ can be an arbitrary term of predicate transformer type. An important special case of recursion is *iteration*, i.e., the repeated execution of a statement. In this chapter we consider different kinds of iterations.

We introduce two basic iteration constructs, a strong iteration statement given by the least fixed point construct and a weak iteration statement given by the greatest fixed point construction. We study the monotonicity and homomorphism properties of these statements and give rules for reasoning about iteration statements.

We then show how to describe ordinary program constructs such as while loops as derived statements in terms of iterations. In particular, we derive correctness and introduction rules for iteration statements and loops using the corresponding rules for recursive statements.

1   Iteration

Let S be a monotonic predicate transformer. We define two basic iteration constructs over S, *strong iteration* and *weak iteration*, as the following fixed points:

$$S^\omega \;\hat{=}\; (\mu X \cdot S \,;\, X \sqcap \mathsf{skip}) , \qquad\qquad (\textit{strong iteration})$$
$$S^* \;\hat{=}\; (\nu X \cdot S \,;\, X \sqcap \mathsf{skip}) . \qquad\qquad (\textit{weak iteration})$$

Iterations are important building blocks when we introduce and reason about loops. Intuitively speaking, statement S^* is executed so that S is repeated a demonically chosen (finite) number of times. Execution of statement S^ω is similar, but if S ca▪ executed indefinitely, then S^ω is aborting (recall that infinite unfolding correspo▪ to nontermination for least fixed point statements).

Predicate-Level Characterization

The two iterations can also be described using fixed points on the predicate le▪

Lemma 21.1 *Let S be an arbitrary monotonic predicate transformer. Then*

$$S^\omega.q = (\mu x \cdot S.x \cap q) ,$$
$$S^*.q = (\nu x \cdot S.x \cap q)$$

for arbitrary predicate q.

Proof For strong iteration we have for arbitrary predicate q,

$$(\mu X \cdot S ; X \cap \text{skip}).q = (\mu x \cdot S.x \cap q)$$
$$\Leftarrow \{\text{Corollary } 19.6\}$$
$$(\forall T \cdot (\lambda X \cdot S ; X \cap \text{skip}).T.q = (\lambda x \cdot S.x \cap q).(T.q))$$
$$\equiv \{\beta \text{ reduction}\}$$
$$(\forall T \cdot (S ; T \cap \text{skip}).q = S.(T.q) \cap q)$$
$$\equiv \{\text{statement definitions}\}$$
$$\mathsf{T}$$

The proof for S^* is dual. $\square$

As an example of an iteration, consider the weak iteration $(x := x + 1)$▪ increments x a demonically chosen (finite) number of times. Thus it has the s▪ effect as the update $[x := x' \mid x \leq x']$. On the other hand, $(x := x + 1)$▪ nonterminating, since x can be incremented indefinitely, so it has the same e▪ as abort (Exercise 21.4).

Tail Recursion

The choice of skip as the exit alternative (i.e., as the second argument of the ▪ in the body of the recursion) in the definitions of the iterations may seem arbit▪ and in a sense it is. The following lemma shows how we get an iteration wi▪ arbitrary exit alternative T.

Lemma 21.2 *Let S and T be arbitrary monotonic predicate transformers. Then*

$$S^\omega ; T = (\mu X \cdot S ; X \cap T) ,$$
$$S^* ; T = (\nu X \cdot S ; X \cap T) .$$

Proof We have

$$S^\omega ; T = (\mu X \cdot S ; X \sqcap T)$$
$$\equiv \{\text{definitions}\}$$
$$(\mu X \cdot S ; X \sqcap \text{skip}) ; T = (\mu X \cdot S ; X \sqcap T)$$
$$\Leftarrow \{\text{fusion (Theorem 19.5) with } h.X = X ; T\}$$
$$(\forall X \cdot (S ; X \sqcap \text{skip}) ; T = S ; (X ; T) \sqcap T)$$
$$\equiv \{\text{distributivity}\}$$
$$\mathsf{T}$$

which proves (a). The proof for weak iteration is similar. □

Statements of the form $(\mu X \cdot S ; X \sqcap T)$ are important, since they model *tail recursion*, i.e., recursion in which the body of the recursion has no substatement that sequentially follows the recursive call. Thus Lemma 21.2 shows how tail recursion can be written using strong iteration.

Infinite Repetition Statement

We define the *infinite repetition statement* S^∞ as follows:

$$S^\infty \;\hat{=}\; (\mu X \cdot S ; X) \; . \qquad\qquad \textit{(repetition statement)}$$

The following lemma shows what the predicate transformer S^∞ is.

Lemma 21.3 *Assume that S is a monotonic predicate transformer. Then $S^\infty.q = \mu.S$.*

Proof

$$(\mu X \cdot S ; X).q = \mu.S$$
$$\Leftarrow \{\text{Corollary 19.6}\}$$
$$(\forall T \cdot (\lambda X \cdot S ; X).T.q = S.(T.q))$$
$$= \{\beta \text{ reduction, definition of composition}\}$$
$$\mathsf{T}$$

□

Thus, $S^\infty.q = \mu.S$ for an arbitrary postcondition q. Intuitively, this means that the predicate $\mu.S$ characterizes those states from which repeated execution of S eventually terminates miraculously.

Infinite repetition can be expressed using strong iteration (Exercise 21.5):

$$S^\infty \;=\; S^\omega ; \text{magic} \; .$$

This justifies considering the strong and weak iteration statements are more basic that the repetition statement.

21.2   Properties of Iterations

Both iteration statements can be viewed as statement constructors with one statement argument. We now investigate their monotonicity and homomorph properties.

Both iteration statements are monotonic, in a restricted way, as shown by following lemma.

Theorem 21.4   *The iterative constructs S^*, S^ω, and S^∞ are monotonic when restricted to a m tonic argument S. Furthermore, they preserve monotonicity: if S is monote then so are S^*, S^ω, and S^∞.*

Proof   Consider first the monotonicity of the iterative constructs. We have

$$S \sqsubseteq S'$$
$$\Rightarrow \text{\{monotonicity properties of statements\}}$$
$$(\forall X \cdot S ; X \sqcap \text{skip} \sqsubseteq S' ; X \sqcap \text{skip})$$
$$\Rightarrow \text{\{monotonicity of pointwise extension\}}$$
$$(\lambda X \cdot S ; X \sqcap \text{skip}) \sqsubseteq (\lambda X \cdot S' ; X \sqcap \text{skip})$$
$$\Rightarrow \text{\{monotonicity of least fixed point, Lemma 19.2\}}$$
$$(\mu X \cdot S ; X \sqcap \text{skip}) \sqsubseteq (\mu X \cdot S' ; X \sqcap \text{skip})$$
$$\equiv \text{\{definition of strong iteration\}}$$
$$S^\omega \sqsubseteq S'^\omega$$

Monotonicity of S^* is proved with the same argument.

We then also have

$$S^\omega \text{ is monotonic}$$
$$\equiv \text{\{definition of strong iteration\}}$$
$$(\mu X \cdot S ; X \sqcap \text{skip}) \text{ is monotonic}$$
$$\Leftarrow \text{\{Lemma 19.7\}}$$
$$(\lambda X \cdot S ; X \sqcap \text{skip}) \text{ is monotonic } \wedge$$
$$(\lambda X \cdot S ; X \sqcap \text{skip}) \text{ preserves monotonicity}$$
$$\Leftarrow \text{\{basic statements are monotonic and preserve monotonicity\}}$$
$$\mathsf{T}$$

□

These properties are summarized in Tables 21.1 and 21.2.

We next consider which homomorphism properties are preserved by iteration loops.

is	$\sqsubseteq$
$(\lambda S \cdot S^{\omega})$	yes[1]
$(\lambda S \cdot S^*)$	yes[1]
$(\lambda S \cdot S^{\infty})$	yes[1]

[1] monotonic S

TABLE 21.1. Iteration monotonicity

Theorem 21.5 *The iterations S^* and S^{ω} and the infinite repetition S^{∞} have the following properties:*

(a) *Weak and strong iterations are always strict, and infinite repetitions preserve strictness.*

(b) *Weak iterations preserve termination.*

(c) *Weak iterations and infinite repetitions preserve conjunctivity.*

(d) *Infinite repetitions preserve disjunctivity.*

Proof We first show that S^* is strict:

$$S^* .\text{false}$$
$$= \{\text{Lemma } 21.1\}$$
$$(\nu x \cdot S.x \cap \text{false})$$
$$= \{\text{predicate calculus}\}$$
$$(\nu x \cdot \text{false})$$
$$= \{\text{fixed point of constant function}\}$$
$$\text{false}$$

The proof for strong iteration is similar.

Next, Lemma 19.8 is used to show that weak iteration preserves conjunctivity and that infinite repetition preserves disjunctivity. That infinite repetition preserves conjunctivity follows directly from the fact that $S^{\infty}.(\cap i \in I \cdot p_i)$ and $(\cap i \in I \cdot S^{\infty}.p_i)$ are both equal to $\mu.S$ when I is nonempty.

To see that S^* preserves termination, we have the following derivation:

$$S \text{ terminating}$$
$$\vdash S^* .\text{true}$$
$$= \{\text{Lemma } 21.1\}$$
$$(\nu x \cdot S.x \cap \text{true})$$
$$= \{\text{predicate calculus}\}$$
$$(\nu x \cdot S.x)$$

preserves	$\sqsubseteq$	$\perp$	$\top$	$\sqcap$	$\sqcup$
$(\lambda S \cdot S^\omega)$	yes	yes	no	yes	no
$(\lambda S \cdot S^*)$	yes	yes	yes	yes	no
$(\lambda S \cdot S^\infty)$	yes	yes	no	yes	yes

TABLE 21.2. Property preservation for derived
statements

$\quad$ = {assumption S.true = true means true must be greatest fixed point}
$\quad$ true

We leave the proof that infinite repetition preserves strictness as an exercise to
reader (Exercise 21.6). □

In fact, it can be shown that strong iteration also preserves conjunctivity. Howe
the proof of this is most easily done after some further properties of conjunc
statements have been investigated, so we postpone it to Chapter 29 (Theorem 2!

21.3   Correctness of Iterations

Recall the fixed-point properties and the rule of recursion introduction in Cha
20. As an application of these rules, we can derive correctness rules for the
ation statements. Our aim is to show under what conditions the total correct
assertions $p \{\!| S^* |\!\} q$, $p \{\!| S^\omega |\!\} q$, and $p \{\!| S^\infty |\!\} q$ are valid. We start with v
iteration.

Theorem 21.6   *Assume that S is a monotonic predicate transformer.*

$\quad$ (a) *The following correctness rule holds for weak iteration:*

$$r \{\!| S |\!\} r \Rightarrow r \{\!| S^* |\!\} r .$$

$\quad$ (b) *Furthermore, if $\{r_w \mid w \in W\}$ is a collection of ranked predicates, then
$\quad$ following correctness rule holds for strong iterations:*

$$(\forall w \in W \cdot r_w \{\!| S |\!\} r_{<w}) \Rightarrow r \{\!| S^\omega |\!\} r .$$

Proof   Part (a) is really a special case of greatest fixed point induction:

$\quad$ $\top$
$\quad$ ≡ {specialize greatest fixed point induction}
$\quad\quad$ $r \subseteq (\lambda x \cdot S.x \cap r).r \Rightarrow r \subseteq (\nu x \cdot S.x \cap r)$
$\quad$ ≡ {β reduction, Lemma 21.1}
$\quad\quad$ $(r \subseteq S.r \cap r) \Rightarrow r \subseteq S^*.r$

$\equiv$ {lattice property $(x \sqsubseteq y \sqcap x) \equiv (x \sqsubseteq y)$}

$r \subseteq S.r \Rightarrow r \subseteq S^*.r$

and the proof is finished. For (b), recall that $r = (\cup w \in W \bullet r_w)$ and $r_{<w} = (\cup v \in W \mid v < w \bullet r_v)$. The proof is similar to the proof (a), but it relies on the rule for μ-introduction (Theorem 20.1; the details are left to the reader). $\square$

Note the similarities between the two rules in Theorem 21.6. The rule for strong iteration is somewhat more complicated, as it makes use of ranked predicates. The basic idea is that each execution of the statement S has to decrease the rank of the predicate in order to guarantee termination.

Since preconditions can be strengthened and postconditions weakened, we immediately get the following corollary for strong iteration.

Corollary 21.7   *Assume that p and q are predicates and S is a monotonic predicate transformer. Assume that $\{r_w \mid w \in W\}$ is a ranked collection of predicates. Then*

$$p \, \{ \! | \, S^\omega \, | \! \} \, q$$

if

(i) $p \subseteq r$,

(ii) $(\forall w \in W \bullet r_w \, \{ \! | \, S \, | \! \} \, r_{<w})$, *and*

(iii) $r \subseteq q$.

Intuitively, the first condition in Corollary 21.7 means that the invariant r is established by the precondition p. The second condition asserts that each iteration decreases the rank of the invariant. Finally, the third condition states that the postcondition q holds after termination (regardless of which r_w was reached when execution terminated).

4   Loops

We now consider a derivative of the strong iteration S^ω, the *while loop* and its generalizations. The while loop is less general than strong iteration, and its syntax is more restrictive. It models the standard while loop of imperative programming languages.

While Loops

We define the construct while g do S od as follows:

$$\text{while } g \text{ do } S \text{ od } \stackrel{\wedge}{=} (\mu X \bullet \text{if } g \text{ then } S \, ; X \text{ else skip fi}) \, ,$$

where g is a predicate and S a predicate transformer. By unfolding, we see execution of while g do S od consists in repeatedly executing S as long as predicate g holds. Predicate g is called the *guard* and S the *body* of the loop.

While loops can be reduced to iterations. This is useful, since it means that we reduce reasoning about loops to reasoning about iteration.

Lemma 21.8   *Let g be a predicate and S a monotonic predicate transformer. Then*

$$\text{while } g \text{ do } S \text{ od} \ = \ ([g]\,;\,S)^{\omega}\,;\,[\neg g]\ .$$

Proof   The proof is a short calculation:

while g do S od
= {definition}
    $(\mu X \cdot \text{if } g \text{ then } S\,;\,X \text{ else skip fi})$
= {rewrite conditional}
    $(\mu X \cdot [g]\,;\,S\,;\,X \sqcap [\neg g])$
= {Lemma 21.2}
    $([g]\,;\,S)^{\omega}\,;\,[\neg g]$

□

A consequence of Lemma 21.8 is the following predicate-level fixed-point characterization of the while loop:

Lemma 21.9   *Let g and q be predicates and S a monotonic predicate transformer. Then*

$$\text{while } g \text{ do } S \text{ od}.q \ = \ (\mu x \cdot (g \cap S.x) \cup (\neg g \cap q))\ .$$

Proof   We have

while g do S od.q
= {Lemma 21.8, definitions}
    $([g]\,;\,S)^{\omega}.(g \cup q)$
= {Lemma 21.1}
    $(\mu x \cdot ([g]\,;\,S).x \cap (g \cup q))$
= {definitions of sequential composition and guard}
    $(\mu x \cdot (\neg g \cup S.x) \cap (g \cup q))$
= {predicate property}
    $(\mu x \cdot (g \cap S.x) \cup (\neg g \cap q))$

which proves the lemma. □

Guarded Iteration Statements

We have already seen how the guarded conditional generalizes the deterministic conditional by permitting nondeterminism and also more than two alternatives. The *guarded iteration statement* similarly generalizes the while loop. It is defined as

$$\text{do } g_1 \rightarrow S_1 \, [] \, \cdots \, [] \, g_n \rightarrow S_n \text{ od } \stackrel{\wedge}{=}$$
$$\text{while } g_1 \cup \cdots \cup g_n \text{ do } [g_1] \,; S_1 \sqcap \cdots \sqcap [g_n] \,; S_n \text{ od } .$$

This gives the while loop as a special case, when $n = 1$:

$$\text{do } g \rightarrow S \text{ od } = \text{ while } g \text{ do } S \text{ od } .$$

A while loop with a deterministic conditional is easier to understand when rewritten as a guarded conditional:

$$\text{while } g \text{ do if } h \text{ then } S_1 \text{ else } S_2 \text{ fi od } =$$
$$\text{do } g \wedge h \rightarrow S_1 \, [] \, g \wedge \neg h \rightarrow S_2 \text{ od } .$$

This is also true in general; the logic behind a program is often more clearly expressed by the guarded conditional and iteration statements than by their deterministic counterparts. The guarded conditional and iteration statements are also very convenient to use in practical program derivations, as the different cases can be handled more independently of one another.

Properties of Loops

We now investigate the monotonicity and homomorphism properties of loops.

Theorem 21.10 *The while loop and guarded iteration are both monotonic with respect to monotonic predicate transformer arguments. Furthermore, both loop constructs preserve monotonicity.*

Proof For the while loop, both properties follow from Lemma 21.8 and the corresponding properties of strong iteration, the guard statement and sequential composition. The properties for guarded iteration are then easily derived from the properties for while loops and guarded conditionals. □

Monotonicity preservation of guarded iteration means the following:

$$S_1 \sqsubseteq S_1' \wedge \ldots \wedge S_n \sqsubseteq S_n' \Rightarrow$$
$$\text{do } g_1 \rightarrow S_1 \, [] \, \ldots \, [] \, g_n \rightarrow S_n \text{ od } \sqsubseteq \text{ do } g_1 \rightarrow S_1' \, [] \, \ldots \, [] \, g_n \rightarrow S_n' \text{ od}$$

is	$\sqsubseteq$
$(\lambda S \cdot \text{while } g \text{ do } S \text{ od})$	yes[1]
$(\lambda S_1 \cdots S_n \cdot \text{do } g_1 \rightarrow S_1 \, [] \, \cdots \, [] \, g_n \rightarrow S_n \text{ od})$	yes[1]

[1] when restricted to monotonic arguments S

TABLE 21.3. Loop monotonicity

Theorem 21.10 shows that we can extend our syntax of monotonic statements w the while loop and guarded iteration. Thus, whenever S is a monotonic statem while g do S od is then also a monotonic statement, and similarly for do ... Tables 21.3 and 21.4 show the monotonicity properties of loops.

The homomorphism preservation properties of loops are as follows.

Theorem 21.11   *While loops and guarded iterations both preserve strictness. Furthermore, w loops preserve disjunctivity.*

Proof Since guards are conjunctive, sequential composition and strong itera both preserve conjunctivity, and while g do S od $= ([g] ; S)^\omega ; [\neg g]$, it foll that while loops preserve conjunctivity. Next, from Lemma 19.8 it follows while loops preserve disjunctivity. The proof of strictness is left to the reader a exercise. The properties of guarded iterations follow directly from the proper of while loops and guarded conditionals. $\square$

In fact, while loops and guarded iterations also preserve conjunctivity. This be proved in Chapter 29 (Theorem 29.7).

Note that the infinite repetition statement is a special case of the while l (Exercise 21.5):

$$S^\infty = \text{while true do } S \text{ od} .$$

21.5   Loop Correctness

From the correctness rule for strong iteration we can now derive correctness r for loops.

preserves	$\sqsubseteq$	$\perp$	$\top$	$\sqcap$	
$(\lambda S \cdot \text{while } g \text{ do } S \text{ od})$	yes	yes	no	yes	y
$(\lambda S_1 \cdots S_n \cdot \text{do } g_1 \rightarrow S_1 \, [] \, \cdots \, [] \, g_n \rightarrow S_n \text{ od})$	yes	yes	no	yes	

TABLE 21.4. Loop preservation of monotonicity

Theorem 21.12 *Assume that g is a predicate and S a monotonic predicate transformer. Assume that $\{r_w \mid w \in W\}$ is a ranked collection of predicates. Then*

$$(\forall w \in W \cdot r_w \cap g \{ S \} r_{<w}) \implies r \{\text{while } g \text{ do } S \text{ od}\} r \cap \neg g \ .$$

Proof We use the corresponding rule for strong iteration:

$$r \{\text{while } g \text{ do } S \text{ od}\} r \cap \neg g$$

$\equiv$ {Lemma 21.8}

$$r \{ ([g]; S)^{\omega}; [\neg g] \} r \cap \neg g$$

$\equiv$ {definition of correctness}

$$r \subseteq (([g]; S)^{\omega}; [\neg g]).(r \cap \neg g)$$

$\equiv$ {definition of sequential composition and guard}

$$r \subseteq ([g]; S)^{\omega}.(g \cup (r \cap \neg g))$$

$\equiv$ {lattice property}

$$r \subseteq ([g]; S)^{\omega}.(g \cup r)$$

$\Leftarrow$ {monotonicity}

$$r \subseteq ([g]; S)^{\omega}.r$$

$\equiv$ {definition of correctness}

$$r \{ ([g]; S)^{\omega} \} r$$

$\Leftarrow$ {correctness rule for strong iteration (Theorem 21.6)}

$$(\forall w \in W \cdot r_w \{ [g]; S \} r_{<w})$$

$\equiv$ {definitions of guard and correctness}

$$(\forall w \in W \cdot r_w \subseteq \neg g \cup S.r_{<w})$$

$\equiv$ {shunting rule}

$$(\forall w \in W \cdot r_w \cap g \subseteq S.r_{<w})$$

$\equiv$ {definition of correctness}

$$(\forall w \in W \cdot r_w \cap g \{ S \} r_{<w})$$

□

From Theorem 21.12 we get the following general rule for proving correctness of loops:

Theorem 21.13 *Assume that $g_1, \ldots, g_n$, p, and q are predicates and S_i are monotonic statements for $i = 1, \ldots, n$. Furthermore, assume that $\{r_w \mid w \in W\}$ is a ranked collection of predicates. Then*

$$p \{ \text{do } g_1 \rightarrow S_1 \, [] \, \ldots \, [] \, g_n \rightarrow S_n \text{ od} \} q \ ,$$

provided that

(i) $p \subseteq r$,

(ii) $(\forall w \in W \cdot r_w \cap g_i \{\!\| S_i \|\!\} r_{<w})$, for $i = 1, \ldots, n$, and

(iii) $r \cap \neg g \subseteq q$.

where $g = g_1 \vee \cdots \vee g_n$.

The first condition in Theorem 21.13 states that the *loop invariant r* holds initia
the second condition asserts that each iteration of the loop preserves the l
invariant while decreasing the rank of the particular predicate r_w; and the t
condition states that the postcondition q is established upon termination of
loop.

Once we have found a loop invariant, we may use it to modify the loop guard.
have the following general inference rule for this:

$$\frac{\Phi \vdash p \subseteq (g = g')}{\Phi \vdash \{p\} ; \text{while } g \text{ do } S \text{ od} = \{p\} ; \text{while } g' \text{ do } S \text{ od}} \quad,$$

provided that p is preserved by the loop; i.e., $(g \cap p \cap S.\text{true}) \{\!\| S \|\!\} p$.

Example

As a simple example of loop correctness, we consider the following loop:

$$L \;=\; \text{while } y > 0 \text{ do } x, y := x \cdot y, y - 1 \text{ od} \;.$$

It stores the factorial of the initial value of y in x if the condition $x = 1$ h
initially. We show that it satisfies the total correctness assertion

$$\text{var } x, y : \text{Nat} \vdash (x = 1 \wedge y = y_0 \wedge y_0 \geq 0) \{\!\| L \|\!\} x = y_0! \;,$$

where y_0 is a free variable standing for the initial value of y, and $y_0!$ is the fact
of y_0.

We choose $0 \leq y \leq y_0 \wedge x \cdot y! = y_0!$ as the invariant and y as the variant. 1
we have to prove the following conditions:

(i) $x = 1 \wedge y = y_0 \wedge y_0 \geq 0 \Rightarrow 0 \leq y \leq y_0 \wedge x \cdot y! = y_0!$.

(ii) $0 \leq y \leq y_0 \wedge x \cdot y! = y_0! \wedge y_0 > 0 \wedge y = n$
$\{\!\| x, y := x \cdot y, y - 1 \|\!\}$
$0 \leq y \leq Y \wedge x \cdot y! = y_0! \wedge y < n$.

(iii) $0 \leq y \leq y_0 \wedge x \cdot y! = y_0! \wedge \neg (y > 0) \Rightarrow x = y_0!$.

The first and third conditions are straightforward arithmetic truths. The se
condition is reduced using the assignment rule to get the following condition

$$0 \leq y \leq y_0 \wedge x \cdot y! = y_0! \wedge y_0 > 0 \wedge y = n \Rightarrow$$
$$0 \leq y - 1 \leq y_0 \wedge x \cdot y \cdot (y - 1)! = y_0! \wedge y - 1 < n \;.$$

This now follows by standard arithmetic reasoning.

.6   Loop Introduction and Elimination

From the correctness rule we can now derive a simple rule for *while-loop introduction*, where a pre–postcondition specification is refined by a loop:

$$\frac{\Phi \vdash p \subseteq I \qquad \Phi \vdash (I \wedge \neg g) \subseteq b[x' := x]}{\Phi \vdash \{p\}\,;\,[x := x' \mid b] \ \sqsubseteq \ \text{while } g \text{ do } \{g \wedge I\}\,;\,[x := x' \mid I \wedge t[x := x'] < t] \text{ od}}$$

• *x* does not occur free in *b*,

where *t* is a state expression ranging over some well-founded set. This loop introduction rule may seem restrictive, since the original demonic assignment cannot refer to the initial value of the variable *x*. However, by using specification constants (treated in Section 17.2) for the initial values of program variables, we can avoid this restriction.

In some cases we know (or can guess) what the body should be in a loop introduction. In this case we can use a proof rule derived directly from the introduction rule given above:

eorem 21.14   *Assume that g, p, I, and b are Boolean expressions such that x does not occur free in b. Furthermore, assume that state expression t ranges over some well-founded set. Then*

$$\{p\}\,;\,[x := x' \mid b] \ \sqsubseteq \ \text{while } g \text{ do } S \text{ od} ,$$

provided that

(i) $p \subseteq I$,

(ii) $(\forall w \in W \cdot (g \wedge I \wedge t = w)\ \{\!| S |\!\}\ (I \wedge t < w))$, *and*

(iii) $(\neg g \wedge I) \subseteq b[x' := x]$.

For the elimination of loops, the following rule can be used:

$$\frac{}{\{\neg g\}\,;\,\text{while } g \text{ do } S \text{ od} \ \sqsubseteq \ \text{skip}} \ .$$

Example: Exponentiation

As an example of program refinement using loop introduction, we develop a program for computing x^y, where *x* and *y* are program variables that range over natural numbers. We start from the following specification:

$$[x, y, r := x', y', r' \mid r' = x^y] .$$

The idea is to compute the exponentiation step by step, storing intermediate res[...]
in r. Note that the specification allows x and y to be changed arbitrarily. We [...]
make use of this freedom, but first we must introduce specification constant[...]
stand for the initial values of x and y.

We divide the derivation into two parts. The first part introduces specifica[...]
constants and a loop in which y is successively decreased. The loop body [...]
demonic assignment, and in the second part we implement it in an efficient w[...]

$$[x, y, r := x', y', r' \mid r' = x^y]$$
$\sqsubseteq$ {introduce trivially true assertion}
$$\{\exists x_0 \, y_0 \cdot x = x_0 \wedge y = y_0\} \, ; [x, y, r := x', y', r' \mid r' = x^y]$$
$\sqsubseteq$ {introduce leading assignment}
$$r := 1 \, ;$$
$$\{\exists x_0 \, y_0 \cdot x = x_0 \wedge y = y_0 \wedge r = 1\} \, ;$$
$$[x, y, r := x', y', r' \mid r' = x^y]$$
$\sqsubseteq$ {specification-constant rule}
$$\{x = x_0 \wedge y = y_0 \wedge r = 1\};$$
$$[x, y, r := x', y', r' \mid r' = x^y]$$
$\quad \sqsubseteq$ {introduce loop with invariant $r \cdot x^y = x_0^{y_0}$, variant y}
$\quad$ while $y > 0$ do
$$\{y > 0 \wedge r \cdot x^y = x_0^{y_0}\};$$
$$[x, y, r := x', y', r' \mid r' \cdot x'^{y'} = x_0^{y_0} \wedge y' < y]$$
$\quad$ od
$\cdot \ r := 1 \, ;$
while $y > 0$ do
$$\{y > 0 \wedge r \cdot x^y = x_0^{y_0}\} \, ;$$
$$[x, y, r := x', y', r' \mid r' \cdot x'^{y'} = x_0^{y_0} \wedge y' < y]$$
od

In the loop introduction, the entry condition for Theorem 21.14 is

$$x = x_0 \wedge y = y_0 \wedge r = 1 \implies r \cdot x^y = x_0^{y_0} \, ,$$

and the exit condition is

$$\neg (y > 0) \wedge r \cdot x^y = x_0^{y_0} \implies r = x_0^{y_0} \, .$$

These are both easily verified.

We now refine the body of the loop. Rather than decreasing y by 1 all the [...]
(where we would use the property $x^{y+1} = x \cdot x^y$), we use the following prope[...]

$$x^{2 \cdot y} = (x \cdot x)^y$$

to halve y whenever possible. The derivation thus continues as follows (focusing on the loop body):

$$\{y > 0 \wedge r \cdot x^y = x_0^{y_0}\} ;$$
$$[x, y, r := x', y', r' \mid r' \cdot x'^{y'} = x_0^{y_0} \wedge y' < y]$$
$= \{\text{introduce conditional}\}$

if even.y then
$$\{\text{even}.y \wedge y > 0 \wedge r \cdot x^y = x_0^{y_0}\} ;$$
$$[x, y, r := x', y', r' \mid r' \cdot x'^{y'} = x_0^{y_0} \wedge y' < y]$$
else
$$\{\text{odd}.y \wedge y > 0 \wedge r \cdot x^y = x_0^{y_0}\} ;$$
$$[x, y, r := x', y', r' \mid r' \cdot x'^{y'} = x_0^{y_0} \wedge y' < y]$$
fi

$\sqsubseteq \{\text{introduce assignment in both branches}\}$

if even.y then $x, y := x \cdot x, y/2$
else $y, r := y - 1, x \cdot r$
fi

We leave it to the reader to verify that the assignment introductions are correct.

Thus we have reached the following refinement of our initial specification:

$$[x, y, r := x', y', r' \mid r' = x^y]$$
$\sqsubseteq \{\text{above derivations, switch to guarded iteration}\}$

$r := 1 ;$
while $y > 0$ do
 if even.y then $x, y := x \cdot x, y/2$
 else $y, r := y - 1, x \cdot r$ fi
od

Summary and Discussion

The while loop has been part of predicate transformer reasoning since Dijkstra's original work [53]. The weak iteration statement constructor is in many ways similar to the star operation of regular languages, which has been used to describe

imperative programs by Backhouse and Carré [33]. However, in regular langu
the choice operation has no zero element, but for statements we have abort ⊓
abort, so the algebra of regular expressions cannot be applied directly. St
Rönn [124] has also investigated the use of regular language algebra in prog
reasoning.

Weak and strong iteration statements essentially similar to the ones described
were originally introduced in the refinement calculus (as action sequences
Back [15] in connection with a study of refining the atomicity of parallel prog
constructs. They were later studied more carefully by Back [17, 18] and by Mic
Butler and Morgan [44, 46]. The careful study of the homomorphism propertie
weak and strong iteration is believed to be new.

Dijkstra's original definition of the loop semantics (which we will derive in
orem 22.10) attracted a lot of attention, and a number of solutions to the prol
of noncontinuous loops, unbounded nondeterminism, and weak termination v
proposed. These include Back [10] and Boom [41]. The use of implicit fixed pc
and well-founded sets proved a simple and stable solution to the problem, a
Park [114] and Dijkstra and van Gasteren [55]. As an alternative, ordinals v
used by Boom [41], Morris [108], and Back [12]. For a comprehensive stud
the problems connected with lack of continuity (unbounded nondeterminism)
Apt and Plotkin [5].

21.8   Exercises

21.1   Recall that an iteration operation for relations was defined in Chapter 9. Show
the following homomorphism property holds:

$$[R]^* = [R^*] .$$

21.2   Show the following properties for the weak iteration of an arbitrary statemen

$$S ; S^* \sqsubseteq S^* ; S ,$$
$$S^* ; S^* = S^* ,$$
$$(S^*)^* = S^* .$$

21.3   Investigate to what extent the properties of weak iteration in Exercise 21.2 hol
strong iteration also.

21.4   Show that $(x := x + 1)^\omega = $ abort and $(x := x + 1)^* = [x := x' \mid x \le x']$.

21.5   Show that the following characterizations of the infinite repetition statemen
correct:

$$S^\infty = S^\omega ; \text{magic} ,$$
$$S^\infty = \text{while true do } S \text{ od} .$$

21.6 Show that the infinite repetition construct preserves strictness.

21.7 Let predicate g and statement S be arbitrary. Show that

$$\text{while } g \text{ do } S \text{ od } = \text{ while } g \text{ do } S \text{ od} ; \{\neg g\} .$$

21.8 Fill in the details in the proof of Theorem 21.6.

21.9 In Chapter 17 we introduced the problem of finding the smallest natural number not occurring in the array segment $B[0..n-1]$, assuming that all values in this array segment are in the range $0..m-1$. We derived the following:

$$[x := x' \mid \neg \text{elem}.x'.B \wedge (\forall y \cdot \neg \text{elem}.y.B \Rightarrow x' \leq y)]$$

$\sqsubseteq$

begin var C : array Nat of Nat ;
$$[C := C' \mid (\forall y \cdot \text{elem}.y.B \equiv y < m \wedge C'[y])] ;$$
$$[x := x' \mid (x' \geq m \vee \neg C[x']) \wedge (\forall y \cdot y \geq m \vee \neg C[y] \Rightarrow x' \leq y)]$$
end

Continue this derivation until the block body contains three loops: one to set all elements in $C[0..m-1]$ to F, one to make $C[0..m-1]$ represent the set of all elements in $B[0..n-1]$, and finally one to set x to the smallest index such that $x \geq m \vee \neg C[x]$.

21.10 Prove the following rule:

$$p \; \{\!\| \; S^\infty \; \|\!\} \; q \; \equiv \; p \; \{\!\| \; S^\omega \; \|\!\} \; \text{true} .$$

Then use it to prove that $p \; \{\!\| \; S^\infty \; \|\!\} \; q$ holds if

(i) $p \sqsubseteq r$, and

(ii) $(\forall w \in W \cdot r_w \; \{\!\| \; S \; \|\!\} \; r_{<w})$.

2

Continuity and Executable Statements

In Chapter 19, we used ordinals to express fixed points as limits. In practice, the natural numbers are sufficient as long as all statements involved are continuous. In this chapter we will study the notion of continuity more closely and show how fixed points and recursion are handled in the continuous case.

Continuity is a homomorphism property. A predicate transformer is continuous if it preserves limits, and since limits are a special kind of join, continuity is in fact a restricted form of join homomorphism. We consider continuity of statements, identifying which statements are continuous and which constructors preserve continuity.

Continuity is important in computer science because it is connected with the notion of what can be computed in finite time from a finite amount of input information. We use continuity as a guiding principle in defining a subclass of statements that one can consider as executable. The executable statements that we define generalize the traditional guarded commands language to interactive statements, in which the user can carry on a continued dialogue with the computer.

1 Limits and Continuity

We first look at the algebraic notions of complete partial orders and continuity in general. In subsequent sections, we then investigate in more detail continuity properties of predicate transformers.

Recall that a subset C of a poset $(A, \sqsubseteq)$ is *directed* if every finite subset is bounded above and that the poset $(A, \sqsubseteq)$ is a *complete partial order* (a *cpo*) if the limit

$\lim C$ (i.e., $\sqcup C$) exists for every directed subset C of A. A monotonic funct $f : A \rightarrow B$, where A and B are complete partial orders, is *continuous* i preserves limits.

Note that a complete lattice is always a cpo. Any unordered set can be made i a cpo by adding a bottom element (such a cpo is called a *flat cpo*).

We write $A \rightarrow_c B$ for the set of all continuous functions $f \in A \rightarrow B$ from a A to a cpo B. When A is a type Σ, then this set is itself a cpo with the pointw extended order. In general, $A \rightarrow_c B$ need not be a cpo even if A and B are c The reason is the same as for monotonic functions $A \rightarrow_m B$; antisymmetry n not hold.

Lemma 22.1   *Let type Σ and set B be cpos. Then the pointwise extension of B to $\Sigma \rightarrow_c$ also a cpo.*

Since limits preserve continuity (Exercise 22.2), we have the following result.

Lemma 22.2   *The cpo $(\Sigma \rightarrow_c B, \sqsubseteq)$ is a subposet of $(\Sigma \rightarrow_m B, \sqsubseteq)$. Furthermore, limits the same result in $(\Sigma \rightarrow_c B, \sqsubseteq)$ as in $(\Sigma \rightarrow_m B, \sqsubseteq)$.*

Fixed Points and Continuity

For continuous functions $f \in A \rightarrow A$, where A is a cpo, we can give an exp characterization of the least fixed point $\mu.f$ using only natural numbers:

Lemma 22.3   *Assume that f is a continuous function on a cpo A. Then f has a least fi point $\mu.f$. Furthermore, $\mu.f$ can be described as a limit of a countable se approximations:*

$$\mu.f \;=\; (\lim n \in \text{Nat} \cdot f^n . \bot) \;.$$

For a proof of this lemma we refer to standard textbooks on order theory, suc [50].

Lemma 22.3 shows that if f is continuous, then we need not go beyond the infinite ordinal; the least fixed point $\mu.f$ is the limit of a chain of approximati indexed by the natural numbers.

For statements, Lemma 22.3 means that if $(\lambda X \cdot S)$ is a continuous function, the recursive statement $(\mu X \cdot S)$ is the limit $(\lim n \in \text{Nat} \cdot S_n)$, where $S_0 = $ a and $S_{n+1} = S[X := S_n]$.

Colimits and Cocontinuity

The dual notions of directedness and limits are codirectedness and colimits. T C is *codirected* if

$$(\forall a, b \in C \cdot \exists c \in C \cdot c \sqsubseteq a \wedge c \sqsubseteq b) \; , \qquad\qquad (codirectedness)$$

and the meet of a codirected set is called its *colimit*. We write colim.C for the colimit of the set C. A partially ordered set A is a *dual cpo* if every codirected set has a greatest lower bound, i.e., if all colimits exist in A.

A linearly ordered set (such as Nat) is an example of a set that is both directed and codirected.

Using colimits, we can define cocontinuity (the dual notion of continuity). A function $f \in A \rightarrow B$ is *cocontinuous* if it preserves colimits. The properties of cocontinuous functions on dual cpos are in every respect dual to the properties of continuous functions on cpos. Thus the greatest fixed point of a cocontinuous function on a dual cpo is the colimit

$$\nu.f \;=\; (\text{colim}.n \in \text{Nat} \cdot f^n.\top) \; .$$

In particular, a complete lattice is a dual cpo, so this construction can be used for the greatest fixed point of a cocontinuous function on a complete lattice.

2 Continuity of Statements

We shall now investigate which basic statements are continuous and which statement constructors preserve continuity. This allows us to identify statement subclasses that generate continuous statements.

Basic Statements

Since limits are a special kind of join, universally disjunctive predicate transformers are always continuous (note that since the empty set is directed, a continuous predicate transformer is always strict). Hence, we get the following result as an immediate consequence of Theorem 16.1:

Corollary 22.4 *The assert statement, the functional update, and the angelic update are all continuous.*

The demonic update need not be continuous, however. As a counterexample, consider the demonic update

$$[x := x' \mid \top] \; .$$

This *chaotic assignment* assigns an arbitrary natural number to x. Define q_i to be the predicate $x < i$, for $i \in$ Nat. Then $\{q_i \mid i \in \text{Nat}\}$ is an ascending chain.

Consequently, $\{S.q_i \mid i \in \mathrm{Nat}\}$ is also an ascending chain when S is monotonic an ascending chain is also a directed set, we have

$$(\lim i \in \mathrm{Nat} \cdot [x := x' \mid \mathrm{T}].q_i)$$
$$= \{\text{definitions of demonic update and } q_i\}$$
$$(\lim i \in \mathrm{Nat} \cdot (\forall x' \cdot \mathrm{T} \Rightarrow x' < i))$$
$$= \{\text{reduction, order reasoning}\}$$
$$(\lim i \in \mathrm{Nat} \cdot \mathrm{F})$$
$$= \{\text{property of join}\}$$
$$\text{false}$$

However, with $S = [x := x' \mid \mathrm{T}]$,

$$S.(\lim i \in \mathrm{Nat} \cdot q_i)$$
$$= \{\text{definition of } q_i\}$$
$$S.(\lim i \in \mathrm{Nat} \cdot x < i)$$
$$= \{\text{pointwise extension}\}$$
$$S.(\exists i \in \mathrm{Nat} \cdot x < i)$$
$$= \{\text{Nat is upward unbounded}\}$$
$$S.\text{true}$$
$$= \{[x := x' \mid \mathrm{T}] \text{ is terminating}\}$$
$$\text{true}$$

Thus, limits are not preserved, so statement S is not continuous.

We can give the following very general conditions under which the demonic up is continuous. A relation $R : \Sigma \leftrightarrow \Gamma$ is said to be *image-finite* if $\{\gamma \mid R.\sigma$. finite for each $\sigma : \Sigma$.

Theorem 22.5   *The demonic update $[R]$ is continuous if and only if R is total and image-fini*

Proof First assume that R is total and image-finite. Let the directed set $\{q_i \mid i$ and the state σ be arbitrary. If the set is empty, then its limit is false and $[R].\mathrm{fal}$ false holds when R is total (Exercise 22.3). Otherwise, define a new directe $\{p_i \mid i \in I\}$ by

$$p_i = q_i \cap R.\sigma$$

for all $i \in I$. Since R is image-finite, the set $\{p_i \mid i \in I\}$ can contain at most a number of distinct elements, which means that $(\lim i \in I \cdot p_i) = p_n$ for son Then

$$(\lim i \in I \cdot p_i) = p_n$$
$$\vdash [R].(\lim i \in I \cdot q_i).\sigma$$
$$\equiv \{\text{definition of } [R]\}$$

$$(\forall \gamma \cdot R.\sigma.\gamma \Rightarrow (\lim i \in I \cdot q_i).\gamma)$$

$\equiv$ {pointwise extension, predicate properties}

$$(\forall \gamma \cdot R.\sigma.\gamma \Rightarrow (\exists i \in I \cdot q_i.\gamma \wedge R.\sigma.\gamma))$$

$\equiv$ {definition of p_i, pointwise extension}

$$(\forall \gamma \cdot R.\sigma.\gamma \Rightarrow (\lim i \in I \cdot p_i).\gamma)$$

$\equiv$ {assumption}

$$(\forall \gamma \cdot R.\sigma.\gamma \Rightarrow p_n.\gamma)$$

$\equiv$ {definition of p_n}

$$(\forall \gamma \cdot R.\sigma.\gamma \Rightarrow q_n.\gamma \wedge R.\sigma.\gamma)$$

$\equiv$ {predicate calculus}

$$(\forall \gamma \cdot R.\sigma.\gamma \Rightarrow q_n.\gamma)$$

$\equiv$ {definition of $[R]$}

$$[R].q_n.\sigma$$

$\Rightarrow$ {$\exists$ introduction, witness $i := n$}

$$(\exists i \in I \cdot [R].q_i.\sigma)$$

$\equiv$ {pointwise extension}

$$(\lim i \in I \cdot [R].q_i).\sigma$$

which shows that $[R].(\lim i \in I \cdot q_i) \subseteq (\lim i \in I \cdot [R].q_i)$. Since the reverse ordering follows by monotonicity, we have shown that if R is image-finite, then $[R]$ is continuous.

In order to prove the reverse implication, we now assume that R is not image-finite. In particular, let σ be arbitrary but fixed and assume that $R.\sigma.\gamma$ holds exactly for a set of distinct states $\gamma \in \{\gamma_i \mid i \in \text{Nat}\}$. (This argument assumes that $R.\sigma$ is countable; otherwise we have to partition $R.\sigma$ into a countable number of nonempty subsets and change the argument accordingly.) Define the ascending chain $\{q_i \mid i \in \text{Nat}\}$ as follows:

$$q_i = \{\gamma_j \mid j < i\} .$$

Then q_i is a proper subset of $R.\sigma$ for all i. We have

$$(\lim i \in \text{Nat} \cdot [R].q_i).\sigma$$

$\equiv$ {pointwise extension}

$$(\exists i \in \text{Nat} \cdot [R].q_i.\sigma)$$

$\equiv$ {definition of demonic update}

$$(\exists i \in \text{Nat} \cdot R.\sigma \subseteq q_i)$$

$\equiv$ {q_i is a proper subset of $R.\sigma$ for all i}

$$\textsf{F}$$

However,

$$[R].(\lim i \in \text{Nat} \cdot q_i).\sigma$$

$\equiv$ {definition of q_i}

$$[R].(R.\sigma).\sigma$$

$\equiv$ {definition of $[R]$}

$$(\forall \gamma \cdot R.\sigma.\gamma \Rightarrow R.\sigma.\gamma)$$

$\equiv$ {predicate calculus}

$$\mathsf{T}$$

which shows that $[R]$ cannot be continuous. This shows that if $[R]$ is continu
then R must be image-finite. $\square$

A basic constraint that we would expect any computing machine to satisfy is th
should not be able to choose among an infinite number of alternatives in finite t
If the machine attempts to make such a choice, then either the execution migh
terminate, because it has to spend some minimum amount of time on each cas
else it systematically considers only a finite subset of the possible choices. In e
case, the machine would be guaranteed to terminate when executing the dem
update $[R]$ only if R is image-finite. In this way, continuity and executab
are linked, with continuity being a necessary (but not sufficient) condition
executability. A more detailed discussion on executability, or *computabili*
outside the scope of this book.

Statement Constructors

We shall now see that both sequential composition and joins preserve contin
while meets in general do not. However, meets preserve continuity under the s
condition as the demonic update statement does, i.e., when the choice is finit

Theorem 22.6   *Sequential composition and joins of predicate transformers preserve contin
Furthermore, $S_1 \sqcap S_2$ is continuous if both S_1 and S_2 are continuous.*

Proof   For finite meet, assume that S_1 and S_2 are continuous and let $\{q_i \mid i$
be a directed set of predicates. Then

$$(S_1 \sqcap S_2).(\lim i \in I \cdot q_i).\sigma$$

$\equiv$ {definition of meet}

$$S_1.(\lim i \in I \cdot q_i).\sigma \wedge S_2.(\lim j \in I \cdot q_j).\sigma$$

$\equiv$ {continuity, predicate calculus}

$$(\exists i \in I \cdot S_1.q_i.\sigma) \wedge (\exists j \in I \cdot S_2.q_j.\sigma)$$

$\equiv$ {for $\Rightarrow$ choose k with $q_i \subseteq q_k$ and $q_j \subseteq q_k$; for $\Leftarrow$ choose $i = j =$

$$(\exists k \in I \cdot S_1.q_k.\sigma \wedge S_2.q_k.\sigma)$$

is	lim
$\{p\}$	yes
$[p]$	no
$\langle f \rangle$	yes
$\{R\}$	yes
$[R]$	yes[1]

[1] R total, image-finite

preserves	lim
;	yes
$\sqcap$	yes[1]
$\sqcup$	yes
$\neg$	no

[1] meet is finite

TABLE 22.1. Continuity of statements

$\equiv$ {definition of meet}

$$(\lim k \in I \cdot (S_1 \sqcap S_2).q_k).\sigma$$

which shows that $S_1 \sqcap S_2$ is continuous. The proofs for sequential composition and join are left to the reader as exercises (Exercise 22.4). □

Infinite meets do not necessarily preserve continuity. As a counterexample, consider statements $S_i = (x := i)$ for all $i \in$ Nat. Each of these statements is universally disjunctive and hence also continuous. However, their meet is the chaotic assignment $[x := x' \mid T]$, which was already shown to be noncontinuous.

We can summarize our investigation of continuity by adding a column that extends the tables of homomorphism properties given earlier. In Table 22.1 we state which homomorphic properties the constructs have and preserve.

3 Continuity of Derived Statements

We can consider a limit as a new statement constructor. Since limits are a restricted form of joins, we get some homomorphism properties as immediate consequences of Theorem 16.2.

Theorem 22.7 *Limits of predicate transformers preserve monotonicity, strictness, disjunctivity, and continuity.*

Proof The preservation of monotonicity, strictness, and disjunctivity follows directly from Theorem 16.2. For continuity, we leave it as an exercise for the reader to prove the general result that the limit of a set of continuous functions is a continuous function (Exercise 22.2). □

The following counterexample shows that limits do not preserve conjunctivity (it is derived from the counterexample for least fixed points given in Section 19.3). Define a chain $\{S_i : \text{Unit} \mapsto \text{Nat} \mid i \in \text{Nat}\}$ of conjunctive predicate transformers by $S_i = [\lambda u \ x \cdot x \geq i]$. The limit of this chain is the predicate transformer choose ; $[\lambda n \ x \cdot x \geq n]$, which is not conjunctive.

preserves	$\sqsubseteq$	$\bot$	$\top$	$\sqcap$	$\sqcup$	$\neg$	lim
lim	yes	yes	no	no	yes	no	yes

TABLE 22.2. Homomorphic properties preserved by limits

Table 22.2 presents a row for limit that can be added to Table 16.2 of homomorp
properties.

We now consider to what extent conditionals, iterations, and loops preserve
nuity.

Theorem 22.8   *Both the deterministic and the nondeterministic conditional preserve contin*

Proof The result follows immediately by rewriting the conditionals using as
guards, and sequential composition and applying Corollary 22.4 and Theorem
□

Next, consider iterations and loops. Strong iteration, infinite repetition, while l
and guarded iteration can all be defined as least fixed points, and hence as l
Thus they should all preserve continuity.

Theorem 22.9   *Strong iteration, infinite repetition, while loops, and guarded iteration all pre*
continuity.

Proof We outline the proof for strong iteration; the other proofs are similar. As
that S is a continuous predicate transformer. Then S^ω is the limit of an or
indexed sequence of approximations starting from abort. By ordinal inductior
easily shown that every approximation in this sequence is continuous. For the
case, we know that abort is continuous. For the step case, it follows from
results that $S ; X \sqcap$ skip is continuous if S is continuous. Finally, the limi
follows from Theorem 22.7. □

As a counterexample showing that weak iteration does not preserve conti
consider the statement $x := x + 1$. This statement is continuous, but $(x := x$
is $[x := x' \mid x' \geq x]$, which is not continuous. Table 22.3 summarizes con
preservation of derived statements.

Let us finally consider loops in the special case of continuity. Assume that pre
transformer S is continuous. Then the semantics of the loop while g do S od
described using the limit of a countable chain of predicates:

Theorem 22.10   *Define a sequence of functions $\{H_n \mid n \in \text{Nat}\}$ recursively as follows:*

$$H_0.g.S.q = \text{false} ,$$
$$H_{n+1}.g.S.q = (\neg g \cap q) \cup S.(H_n.g.S.q) .$$

Then for continuous predicate transformer S and arbitrary predicates g an

preserves	lim
$(\lambda S_1\, S_2 \cdot \text{if } g \text{ then } S_1 \text{ else } S_2 \text{ fi})$	yes
$(\lambda S_1 \cdots S_n \cdot \text{if } g_1 \to S_1 \,[]\, \cdots \,[]\, g_n \to S_n \text{ fi})$	yes
$(\lambda S \cdot S^\omega)$	yes
$(\lambda S \cdot S^*)$	no
$(\lambda S \cdot S^\infty)$	yes
$(\lambda S \cdot \text{while } g \text{ do } S \text{ od})$	yes
$(\lambda S_1 \cdots S_n \cdot \text{do } g_1 \to S_1 \,[]\, \cdots \,[]\, g_n \to S_n \text{ od})$	yes

TABLE 22.3. Continuity preservation of derived statements

$$(\text{while } g \text{ do } S \text{ od}).q \;=\; (\exists n \cdot H_n.g.S.q) \ .$$

Proof First, we need to show that if S is continuous, then the function

$$(\lambda X \cdot \text{if } g \text{ then } S \,;\, X \text{ else skip fi})$$

is continuous. This follows from the fact that skip is continuous and that sequential and conditional composition both preserve continuity. Next, we use Lemma 22.3 to construct the sequence

$$S_0 \;=\; \text{abort} ,$$
$$S_{n+1} \;=\; \text{if } g \text{ then } S \,;\, S_n \text{ else skip fi} ,$$

for which while g do S od $= (\lim n \in \text{Nat} \cdot S_n)$. It is now possible to show (by induction on n, Exercise 22.8) that $S_n.q = H_n.g.S.q$ for all n and from the definition of limits it follows that $(\lim n \in \text{Nat} \cdot S_n).q.\sigma \equiv (\exists n \cdot H_n.g.S.q.\sigma)$. $\square$

4 Executable Statements

Program derivation can be seen as taking us from an initial specification through a series of intermediate steps to a final program. We have not until now stated what is an acceptable form for the final program, particularly if we assume that it is to be executed by a computer. For execution on a real computer, our final programs have to be written in a real programming language with a real compiler for the computer in question. For our purposes here, this is too demanding. Instead, we will look at how to put together a simple, yet very powerful, programming language from the constructs that we already have defined. The requirements for the statements in this language are that they be continuous and that there be a standard way of executing these statements on a computer.

We will enlarge the notion of execution of a program by considering not only
computer that executes the program but also the user of the program, who exec
the program in order to achieve some specific goals. The user takes on the rol
the angel, while the computer has the role of the demon.

Extended Guarded Commands Language

Dijkstra's guarded commands language forms a suitable basis for our progr
ming language. We define the *basic guarded commands* as statements built by
following syntax.

$$
\begin{aligned}
S \ ::= \ \ & \text{abort} \ , & & \textit{(abortie} \\
| \ \ & \text{skip} \ , & & \textit{(empty stateme} \\
| \ \ & x := e \ , & & \textit{(multiple assignme} \\
| \ \ & S_1 \ ; S_2 \ , & & \textit{(sequential compositi} \\
| \ \ & \text{if } g_1 \rightarrow S_1 \ [] \ \ldots \ [] \ g_n \rightarrow S_n \text{ fi} \ , & & \textit{(conditional compositi} \\
| \ \ & \text{do } g_1 \rightarrow S_1 \ [] \ \ldots \ [] \ g_n \rightarrow S_n \text{ od} \ . & & \textit{(iterative compositi}
\end{aligned}
$$

Here $x = x_1, \ldots, x_m$ is a list of program variables, $e = e_1, \ldots, e_m$ a correspo
ing list of expressions, and $g_1, \ldots, g_n$ Boolean expressions. We assume that
standard types of higher-order logic are available, in particular truth values, nat
numbers, and integers, as well as records and arrays.

Let us extend this simple language by permitting general assert statements, bl
with local variables, and procedure definitions and calls:

$$
\begin{aligned}
S \ ::= \ \ & \ldots \ , & & \\
| \ \ & \{b\} \ , & & \textit{(asse} \\
| \ \ & \text{begin var } x := e \ ; S \text{ end} \ , & & \textit{(blo} \\
| \ \ & \text{proc } P\,(\text{var } x, \text{val } y) = S_1 \text{ in } S_2 \ , & & \textit{(procedu} \\
| \ \ & P(x, e) \ . & & \textit{(procedure c}
\end{aligned}
$$

Here x and y are lists of program variables, and e is a list of expressions.
procedure declaration may be recursive.

The basic statements (abort, the assert statement, skip, and the assignment st
ment) are all conjunctive and continuous predicate transformers (and hence
monotonic and strict). Sequential composition preserves both conjunctivity
continuity, and so do conditional and iterative composition (Exercises 22.7
22.9) and blocks. Procedure calls are conjunctive and continuous if the proce
bodies are.

We consider the extended guarded command language as a small executable
gramming language (assuming that the expressions e in assignments and the gu
g in assertions, conditionals, and iterations can be evaluated). Hence, these st
ments form a suitable goal for a program derivation. The demonic nondetermin

inherent in the conditional and iteration constructs can be understood as under-specification and may in actual computations be implemented by a deterministic choice among the enabled alternatives.

As before, the syntax for the extended guarded commands language is not intended to define a new syntactic category but serves only to identify a certain subclass of statements. Hence, we may mix guarded commands with arbitrary statements, e.g., using demonic updates or joins of guarded commands as subcomponents. These constructs all have a well-defined meaning as monotonic predicate transformers.

Executing Guarded Commands

The extended guarded commands describe a batch-oriented programming language in which the user can initiate a computation but thereafter can only wait to see what will be the result of the computation. The computer will do all the work and make all the choices.

Consider first the execution of the abort statement. We assume that there is no information on how the computer executes this statement. Different computers may execute it in different ways, and the same computer need not execute it in the same way each time. As nothing is known about the execution of this statement, we can also say nothing about the effect that executing it has. In programming language terminology, abort is an undefined statement. It may have some effect, but we do not know what it is and we have no way of finding out what it does. It does not even have to terminate. Hence, there is no postcondition that we can be sure of achieving by executing the abort statement.

The skip and assignment statements are executed by the computer as expected, the first having no effect at all on the present state, the other changing it by updating the state as indicated by the assignment. The sequential composition $S_1 ; S_2$ is also executed as expected, first executing S_1 and then continuing by executing S_2. The conditional statement is executed by first evaluating the guards and then choosing one of the statements for which the guard is true in the present state and executing this statement. If two or more guards are true in the state, then one of these is chosen, but we do not know which one. Different computers may choose in different ways. Thus, if we want to be certain to achieve some postcondition, we have to make certain that the postcondition is achieved no matter how the computer resolves the nondeterministic choice.

The block statement is executed by allocating the local variables on a stack. Thus, the state space is enlarged so that it also supports the new program variables. The local variables are removed from the stack on block exit. The procedure call is also executed in the standard way. In all these cases, it is easy to see that the game interpretation and the standard implementation of these statements on a computer give the same result when one considers whether a certain postcondition can be reached with certainty in finite time.

Consider finally the iteration statement do $g_1 \rightarrow S_1 [] \cdots [] g_n \rightarrow S_n$ od, assum
that the component statements are all continuous and conjunctive. This statem
is equivalent to

$$(\sqcup i \in \mathsf{Nat} \cdot \mathsf{Do}_i)$$

(we write a join rather than a limit here, to emphasize that we have an ang
choice). Here

$$\mathsf{Do}_0 = \mathsf{abort} ,$$
$$\mathsf{Do}_{i+1} = [g_1] ; S_1 ; \mathsf{Do}_i \sqcap \cdots \sqcap [g_n] ; S_n ; \mathsf{Do}_i \sqcap [\neg (g_1 \cup \cdots \cup g_n)] .$$

In the game semantics, the angelic choice is executed by the angel. If there i
$i \geq 0$ such that Do_i.true holds in the current state, then we have that $\mathsf{Do}_m = \mathsf{Do}_i$
each $m \geq i$. The angel chooses an alternative Do_i for which Do_i.true holds in
current state. By the equivalence, it does not matter which alternative satisfying
condition is chosen, as all have the same effect. If there is no alternative for wh
this condition holds, then the angel has to choose one alternative nonetheless,
will lose the game eventually because the demon can play the game so that
abort statement inside the chosen Do_i is eventually reached. After the choice,
game continues with playing the selected Do_i.

The notion of iteration in the execution of the iteration statement arises f
the way in which we suppose that the computer simulates the angel in choo
the right alternative. We assume that the computer scans through the alterna
$\mathsf{Do}_0, \mathsf{Do}_1, \mathsf{Do}_2, \ldots$ in this order, until it finds a statement Do_n that satisfies
required condition. If such a statement is found, then execution continues wit
If, however, there is no such statement, then the scanning of the alternatives n
terminates, because there are infinitely many of these. Hence, we get an infi
execution. The angel, on the other hand, can with infinite foresight immediately
the right number of iterations and so chooses the right approximation directly.
different ways in which the computer and the angel execute a loop are illustr
in Figure 22.1.

The computer execution of iteration is closely related to the game interpretat
The computation can be infinite (nonterminating), but it is always finitely wid
continuous statements (i.e., there is never a choice of more than a finite nur
of alternatives). In the game interpretation, there are no infinite computations
there may be infinitely wide choices. If these choices are scanned in some o
one at a time, then the infinitely wide choice point becomes a possible inf
computation.

Even though the user plays the role of the angel and in principle should choos
right number of iterations, this is not necessary, because there is at most one
choice. If there is a number of iterations n that is sufficient for termination, the
computer can choose the right alternative Do_n by scanning through the alternat
and thus do the job of the user. If no n is sufficiently large, then the computer

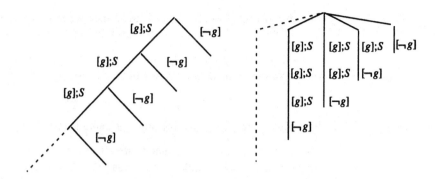

FIGURE 22.1. Iteration versus infinite angelic choice

be stuck in an infinite loop. The result is then the same; i.e., no postcondition is established.

5   Interactive Guarded Commands

The extended guarded commands defined above are essentially batch oriented, as there is no real place for user interaction. By adding angelic statements to the language, we can make it into an interactive programming language. Let us extend the language as follows:

$$
\begin{aligned}
S \ ::= \ & \ldots \ , \\
 | \ & \{x := x' \mid b\} \ , & \textit{(input statement)} \\
 | \ & \text{if } g_1 :: S_1 \ [] \ \cdots \ [] \ g_n :: S_n \ \text{fi} \ , & \textit{(conditional choice)} \\
 | \ & \text{do } g_1 :: S_1 \ [] \ \cdots \ [] \ g_n :: S_n \ \text{od} \ . & \textit{(iterative choice)}
\end{aligned}
$$

The *input statement* is the angelic assignment statement. We interpret $\{x := x' \mid b\}$ as a request to the user to supply a new value x' for the program variable x. This new value must satisfy the condition b in the current state.

The *conditional choice* construct was already mentioned in the introduction:

$$
\begin{aligned}
&\text{if } g_1 :: S_1 \ [] \ \cdots \ [] \ g_n :: S_n \ \text{fi} \ \stackrel{\wedge}{=} \\
&\quad \{g_1\} \ ; S_1 \sqcup \cdots \sqcup \{g_n\} \ ; S_n \ .
\end{aligned}
$$

The effect of the conditional choice is to let the user choose one of the alternatives S_i for which the enabledness condition g_i is true in the current state.

The *iterative choice* was also mentioned in the introduction, as describing an event loop:

$$
\begin{aligned}
&\text{do } g_1 :: S_1 \ [] \ \cdots \ [] \ g_n :: S_n \ \text{od} \ \stackrel{\wedge}{=} \\
&\quad (\mu X \cdot \{g_1\} \ ; S_1 \ ; X \sqcup \cdots \sqcup \{g_n\} \ ; S_n \ ; X \sqcup \text{skip}) \ .
\end{aligned}
$$

The effect of the iterative choice is to let the user repeatedly choose an alterna
that is enabled and have it executed until the user decides to stop.

Using distributivity, the iterative choice can be written in the form $(\mu X \cdot S; X \sqcup s$
(note that this is the dual construct of weak iteration). We have

$$(\mu X \cdot S; X \sqcup \text{skip}).q = (\mu x \cdot S.x \cup q)$$

by a similar argument as in the proof of Lemma 21.1.

The interactive guarded commands are all continuous, but they need not be
junctive. Interactive guarded commands extend the guarded commands langu
further, so that ongoing interaction between the user and the computer ca
described. The user may, for instance, give the input data as needed but no
at once as a batch-oriented execution requires. The user may determine the
input based on the decisions the computer has taken before. Also, the user may
alternative commands as menu choices, picking the alternatives that will fur
the goals that he or she is presently pursuing. In particular, this means tha
same interactive guarded command can be used for different purposes on diffe
occasions.

The following example illustrates the interactive iterative choice:

$$S = \text{do } z \geq 2 :: z := z - 2 \ [] \ z \geq 5 :: z := z - 5 \text{ od} .$$

Intuitively, this is executed as follows. On every iteration, the user can choo
decrease z by 2 or 5, if possible, or to stop. The predicate $S.(z = 0)$ holds in t
states from which it is possible to make a sequence of choices such that z
holds when we choose to stop. An intuitive argument indicates that we shoul

$$S.(z = 0) = (z = 0 \vee z = 2 \vee z \geq 4) .$$

We have

$$S.(z = 0) =$$
$$(\mu x \cdot (\{z \geq 2\} ; z := z - 2 \sqcup \{z \geq 5\} ; z := z - 5).x \vee (z = 0))$$

When we compute approximations p_i for this least fixed point, we find

$$
\begin{aligned}
p_0 &= \text{false} , \\
p_1 &= (z = 0) , \\
p_2 &= (z = 0 \vee z = 2 \vee z = 5) , \\
p_3 &= (z = 0 \vee z = 2 \vee z = 4 \vee z = 5 \vee z = 7 \vee z = 10) , \\
p_3 &= (z = 0 \vee z = 2 \vee 4 \leq z \leq 7 \vee z = 9 \vee z = 10 \vee z = 12 \vee z = 1
\end{aligned}
$$

and so on. Every approximation p_n holds in those states from which it is pos
to reach $z = 0$ in fewer than n steps by making suitable choices. We sho
calculation of p_2:

p_2

= {definition of approximation}

$(\{z \geq 2\} ; z := z - 2 \sqcup \{z \geq 5\} ; z := z - 5).p_1 \vee (z = 0)$

= {assumption $p_1 = (z = 0)$, statement definitions}

$(z \geq 2 \wedge z - 2 = 0) \vee (z \geq 5 \wedge z - 5 = 0) \vee (z = 0)$

= {arithmetic}

$z = 2 \vee z = 5 \vee z = 0$

Every new approximation p_{n+1} adds disjuncts $z = z_0 + 2$ and $z = z_0 + 5$ if $z = z_0$ is a disjunct of p_n. By induction and by computing limits, we find that $(\sqcup i : \text{Nat} \cdot p_i) = (z = 0 \vee z = 2 \vee z \geq 4)$. This can be seen as a (computational) proof of the fact that any natural number greater than or equal to 4 can be written in the form $2x + 5y$ for suitable natural numbers x and y.

General Specification Language

The extensions to the language of guarded commands that we have defined above essentially include all statement constructs we have defined earlier, except magic and guard statements, demonic assignment, and arbitrary indexed meets and joins. We could even add finite meets and arbitrary indexed joins, and the language would still be continuous. For practical purposes, the role of the former is handled by conditional composition and the role of the latter by recursion and iterative choice. Furthermore, arbitrary joins are not finitary, so we prefer not to consider them as executable statements. We could also include finite demonic assignment, but the problem there is that it may not be possible to decide whether an assignment is finite or not. This justifies excluding demonic assignments from the class of executable statements.

Guards, magic, and demonic assignments may be used in specification statements in program derivations. Let us extend our programming language with these constructs to get a *specification language*:

$$
\begin{array}{llr}
S ::= & \dots \; , & \\
 & | \quad \text{magic} \; , & (\textit{magic}) \\
 & | \quad [b] \; , & (\textit{guard statement}) \\
 & | \quad [x := x' \mid b] \; . & (\textit{demonic assignment})
\end{array}
$$

Statements in the specification language are not necessarily continuous, but they are monotonic. Hence, we are free to replace any component statement with its refinement, preserving correctness of the whole statement. We have shown earlier how to use specification statements in program derivations making essential use of this monotonicity property. We will analyze specification statements in more

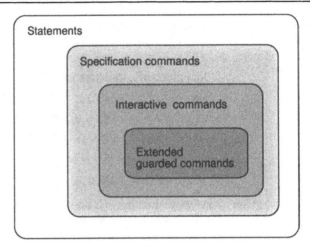

FIGURE 22.2. Guarded commands extensions

detail in Chapter 27. The languages defined here form a hierarchy as show
Figure 22.2.

Note that specifying programs by pre- and postconditions is not sufficient any
for interactive guarded commands. For extended guarded commands they are
ficient, as will be shown in Chapter 26 when we study normal forms for diff
classes of statements. However, when the programs may involve nontrivial
interaction, then we need more expressive specifications for programs.

22.6 Summary and Discussion

In this chapter we have studied continuous statements more carefully. We
noted the central role that finiteness plays for continuity. We have also iden
the homomorphism properties of continuous statements.

Continuity as a general property of cpos and lattices is described in more det
Davey and Priestley [50]. The connection between continuity and fixed poi
countable limits has a long tradition in denotational semantics. Models of prog
have often restricted attention to continuous semantics. Continuity has been
to model implementability; noncontinuous constructs can generally not be i
mented on a computer. Continuity is also a requirement for the solution of recu
domain equations, which appear in most theories of denotational semantics
Stoy [134] or Schmidt [125]).

In Dijkstra's original weakest precondition calculus, continuity was identifi
one of the "healthiness conditions" that all programs were assumed to satisfy
This made it possible to define the semantics of iteration using limits of c
indexed by the natural numbers. Back introduced a noncontinuous nondetermi

assignment [6] and used infinitary logic to reason about programs [10]. A number of other authors also challenged Dijkstra's definition of the semantics of loops; they used either abstract fixed-point properties (Hehner [74]) or limits of ordinal-indexed chains (Boom [41]).

In general, one could argue that continuity is much overrated as a semantic restriction. Most arguments go through quite easily without the continuity assumption. In general, our view is that complete lattices with monotonic functions provide a much better foundation (both easier and more intuitive) for programming language semantics than cpos with continuous functions. It is interesting to note that Scott's original formulation of the fixed-point theory for program semantics did use complete lattices (and continuous functions). The complete lattices were dropped, because a cpo was a weaker structure that was sufficient for the theory, and the miraculous top element was difficult to justify in the context of a semantics that essentially was concerned only with partial functional statements. In the more general framework of the refinement calculus, the complete lattices are well justified, and the mathematical framework is simpler and more regular. Continuity can be assumed whenever needed, as this chapter has tried to show, but there is no point in restricting the mathematical treatment to only continuous statements.

We have looked at the mathematical properties of continuous statements and have also defined a simple yet very expressive programming language that can be considered as executable. The extended guarded commands add some features to the traditional guarded commands, like blocks with local variables and procedures. The interactive guarded commands are a real strengthening of the expressive power of the language. They allow us to describe permitted user interaction with a computer and also to analyze what the user can achieve through this interaction. The interactive guarded commands are continuous but not conjunctive, and can be seen as executable if a wider interpretation of this term is used. The analogue here is computability with an oracle that is studied in computability theory.

7   Exercises

22.1   Show that if f is a monotonic function and K is a directed set, then im. $f.K$ is also directed.

22.2   Show that limits preserve continuity; i.e., if F is a directed set of continuous functions on a cpo, then $(\sqcup f \in F \cdot f)$ is continuous.

22.3   Show that if the relation R is total, then $[R].\mathsf{false} = \mathsf{false}$.

22.4   Complete the proof of Theorem 22.6.

22.5   Continuity of a function f from a cpo $(A, \sqsubseteq)$ to a cpo $(B, \sqsubseteq)$ is sometimes defined using chains indexed by natural numbers (ω-chains) rather than directed sets. We say that f is ω-continuous if it preserves limits of ω-chains, i.e., if

$$f.(\sqcup n \in \mathsf{Nat} \cdot x_n) \;=\; (\sqcup n \in \mathsf{Nat} \cdot f.x_n)$$

whenever $x_1 \sqsubseteq x_2 \sqsubseteq \cdots$. Show that

(a) If f is continuous then it is ω-continuous.

(b) If f is strict and ω-continuous and A and B are countable sets, then continuous.

Hint: a set A is countable if there exists a bijection (a function that is one-to and onto) from Nat to A.

22.6   Let f be the function on predicates over Nat defined by

$$f.q \;=\; (\lambda x : \mathsf{Nat} \cdot x = 0 \vee q.(x - 1)) \;.$$

Show that f is continuous and compute $\mu.f$. Furthermore, show that f is co tinuous (in fact, f preserves arbitrary meets) and compute $\nu.f$.

22.7   Show that nondeterministic conditional composition preserves continuity.

22.8   Fill in the details of Theorem 22.10.

22.9   Show that if S is continuous, then S^ω and while g do S od are continuous.

3

Working with Arrays

In this chapter we look at how to construct programs that work on more advanced data structures, concentrating in particular on arrays. No new theory needs to be introduced for this purpose, as all the tools needed have already been built. We illustrate array manipulation techniques by constructing some searching and sorting algorithms. The case studies in this chapter also give us the opportunity to show how to structure somewhat larger program derivations.

1 Resetting an Array

Let us start with a very simple problem: how to set all elements in an array A : array Nat of Nat to zero in the range $m..n$ (recall that $m..n$ is an abbreviation for the set $\{j \mid m \le j \le n\}$). This is done in the obvious way, by scanning through the elements in A from m to n and setting each element to zero. We assume that $m \le n$, so that the range in question is nonempty. We show how to derive this solution in full detail. The other algorithms will use the same pattern of reasoning, so it is good to look at this first one in a very simple context.

Let us define

$$\text{allreset}.A.m.n \;\triangleq\; (\forall i \mid m \le i \le n \cdot A[i] = 0) \;.$$

Our task is to find an implementation for the specification

$$[A := A' \mid \text{allreset}.A'.m.n] \;.$$

Note that if $n < m$ then this specification is equivalent to $[A := A' \mid \text{T}]$, since allreset$.A'.m.n$ is then trivially satisfied.

Introduce Loop

We start by introducing a new local variable that we will use as a loop counter

$[A := A' \mid \text{allreset}.A'.m.n]$;

$\sqsubseteq$ {introduce local variable j}

begin var j : Nat ; $j := m$;

" $\{j = m\}$; $[A, j := A', j' \mid \text{allreset}.A'.m.n]$ "

end

Next, we introduce the loop itself. The loop invariant is in this case very simpl
states that the initial part of the array, up to $j - 1$, has already been set to zer
addition, it must state that the termination function is bounded from below (in
case by zero). We choose $n + 1 - j$ as the termination function. Let us introe
an abbreviation for the invariant:

$$\text{resetbelow}.A.j.m.n \; \overset{\wedge}{=} \; (\forall i \mid m \le i < j \cdot A[i] = 0) \wedge j \le n + 1 \; .$$

We have that

$\{j = m\}$; $[A, j := A', j' \mid \text{allreset}.A'.m.n]$

$\sqsubseteq$ {introduce loop, choose $n + 1 - j$ as termination function}

while $j \le n$ do

" $\{\text{resetbelow}.A.j.m.n \wedge j \le n\}$;

$[A, j := A', j' \mid \text{resetbelow}.A'.j'.m.n \wedge$

$n + 1 - j' < n + 1 - j]$ "

od

We need to check that the conditions for loop introduction are satisfied:

(i) $j = m \Rightarrow \text{resetbelow}.A.j.m.n$,

(ii) $\text{resetbelow}.A.j.m.n \wedge j > n \Rightarrow \text{allreset}.A.m.n$.

The initialization condition holds, because

$j = m$

$\vdash (\forall i \mid m \le i < j \cdot A[i] = 0) \wedge j \le n + 1$

$\equiv$ {assumption}

$(\forall i \mid m \le i < m \cdot A[i] = 0) \wedge m \le n + 1$

$\equiv$ {empty range, $m \le n$}

T

The exit condition again holds, because

$$(\forall i \mid m \le i < j \cdot A[i] = 0) \land j \le n + 1 \land j > n$$
$$\vdash (\forall i \mid m \le i \le n \cdot A[i] = 0)$$
$$\equiv \{\text{assumption implies } j = n + 1\}$$
$$(\forall i \mid m \le i < j \cdot A[i] = 0)$$
$$\equiv \{\text{assumption}\}$$
$$\mathsf{T}$$

Introduce Assignment

We then implement the loop body. This is now done with a single assignment statement, as follows:

$$\{\text{resetbelow}.A.j.m.n \land j \le n\} ;$$
$$[A, j := A', j' \mid \text{resetbelow}.A'.j'.m.n \land n + 1 - j' < n + 1 - j]$$
$$\sqsubseteq \{\text{introduce assignment statement}\}$$
$$A[j], j := 0, j + 1$$

We have to show that the assignment introduction is correctly done:

$$\text{resetbelow}.A.j.m.n \land j \le n \Rightarrow$$
$$\text{resetbelow}.A'.j'.m.n \land n + 1 - j' \le n + 1 - j ,$$

where

$$A' = A(j \leftarrow 0) ,$$
$$j' = j + 1 .$$

We have

$$(\forall i \mid m \le i < j \cdot A[i] = 0) \land j \le n + 1 \land j \le n$$
$$\vdash (\forall i \mid m \le i < j + 1 \cdot A(j \leftarrow 0)[i] = 0) \land$$
$$j + 1 \le n + 1 \land n + 1 - (j + 1) < n + 1 - j$$
$$\equiv \{\text{assumption } j \le n\}$$
$$(\forall i \mid m \le i < j + 1 \cdot A(j \leftarrow 0)[i] = 0) \land \mathsf{T} \land \mathsf{T}$$
$$\equiv \{\text{range split}\}$$
$$(\forall i \mid m \le i < j \cdot A(j \leftarrow 0)[i] = 0) \land A(j \leftarrow 0)[j] = 0$$
$$\equiv \{\text{array indexing}\}$$
$$(\forall i \mid m \le i < j \cdot A[i] = 0) \land 0 = 0$$
$$\equiv \{\text{assumption}\}$$
$$\mathsf{T}$$

Note how the array property is proved by splitting the range of the universal quantifier into two parts, one for the index being changed (here j) and the other for the other index values, which are not changed by the array assignment.

Final Implementation

Let us define the procedure

proc Reset(var A, val m, n) =
begin var j : Nat ; $j := m$;
    while $j \leq n$ do $A[j], j := 0, j + 1$ od
end

This procedure is the solution to our programming problem. We have that

$$[A := A' \mid allreset.A'.m.n] \sqsubseteq Reset(A, m, n)$$

for any program variable A and any natural number expressions m and n.

23.2   Linear Search

Assume that we want to find an index i pointing to the smallest element in array segment $A[m..n]$, where $m \leq n$ (so the segment is nonempty). We do this with a linear search where i is initially equal to m and updated whenever a value smaller than $A[i]$ is found.

We consider A : array Nat of Nat and m, n : Nat to be constants with $m \leq n$, i : Nat is a global program variable. The local variable k is used to index values during the search.

We define minat.$i.A.m.n$ to hold when the minimum value in $A[m..n]$ is found in $A[i]$:

$$minat.i.A.m.n \;\hat{=}\; m \leq i \leq n \wedge (\forall j \mid m \leq j \leq n \cdot A[i] \leq A[j]) .$$

Then

$\{m \leq n\} ; [i := i' \mid minat.i'.A.m.n]$
$\sqsubseteq$ {introduce local variable k}
    begin var $k := m + 1$;
    " $\{m \leq n \wedge k = m + 1\} ; [i, k := i', k' \mid minat.i'.A.m.n]$ "
    end
$\sqsubseteq$ {add initial assignment, use assumption $m \leq n$}

$\cdots i := m$; " $\{i = m \wedge k = i + 1 \wedge i \le n\}$;

$\quad [i, k := i', k' \mid \text{minat}.i'.A.m.n]$ " $\cdots$

$\sqsubseteq$ {introduce loop}

$\cdots$ while $k \le n$ do

$\quad$ " $\{k \le n \wedge k \le n + 1 \wedge \text{minat}.i.A.m.k\}$;

$\qquad [i, k := i', k' \mid k' \le n + 1 \wedge \text{minat}.i'.A.m.k' \wedge$

$\qquad\qquad n + 1 - k' < n + 1 - k]$ "

$\quad$ od $\cdots$

$\sqsubseteq$ {simplify condition in assertion}

$\cdots \{k \le n \wedge \text{minat}.i.A.m.k\}$;

$\quad [i, k := i', k' \mid k' \le n + 1 \wedge \text{minat}.i'.A.m.k' \wedge$

$\qquad n + 1 - k' < n + 1 - k] \cdots$

$\sqsubseteq$ {introduce conditional}

$\quad$ if $k \le n \wedge A[k] < A[i] \rightarrow$

$\qquad \{A[k] < A[i] \wedge k \le n \wedge \text{minat}.i.A.m.k\}$;

$\qquad [i, k := i', k' \mid k' \le n + 1 \wedge \text{minat}.i'.A.m.k' \wedge$

$\qquad\qquad n + 1 - k' < n + 1 - k]$

$\quad [\!] \ k \le n \wedge A[k] \ge A[i] \rightarrow$

$\qquad \{A[k] \ge A[i] \wedge k \le n \wedge \text{minat}.i.A.m.k\}$;

$\qquad [i, k := i', k' \mid k' \le n + 1 \wedge \text{minat}.i'.A.m.k' \wedge$

$\qquad\qquad n + 1 - k' < n + 1 - k]$

$\quad$ fi

$\sqsubseteq$ {introduce assignments}

$\quad$ if $k \le n \wedge A[k] < A[i] \rightarrow i, k := k, k + 1$

$\quad [\!] \ k \le n \wedge A[k] \ge A[i] \rightarrow k := k + 1$

$\quad$ fi

$=$ {substitute back, switch to guarded iteration}

$\quad$ begin var $k := m + 1$; $i := m$;

$\qquad$ do $k \le n \wedge A[k] < A[i] \rightarrow i, k := k, k + 1$

$\qquad [\!] \ k \le n \wedge A[k] \ge A[i] \rightarrow k := k + 1$

$\qquad$ od

$\quad$ end

We leave the details of the loop introduction and assignment introduction steps to the reader. The invariant and variant of the introduced loop are seen from the

body of the loop; the invariant is $k \leq n + 1 \wedge \text{minat}.i.A.m.k$, while the varia̶
$n + 1 - k$.

We summarize the result of our derivation in a procedure definition. We defin̶

```
proc FindMin(var i, val A, m, n) =
begin var k := m + 1 ; i := m ;
  do k ≤ n ∧ A[k] < A[i] → i, k := k, k + 1
  [] k ≤ n ∧ A[k] ≥ A[i] → k := k + 1
  od
end
```

Then we know that

$$\{m \leq n\} \, ; \, [i := i' \mid \text{minat}.i'.A.m.n] \ \sqsubseteq \ \text{FindMin}(i, A, m, n)$$

for arbitrary program variable i and expressions A, m, and n of appropriate ty̶

23.3　Selection Sort

We now derive a sorting program for the array $A[0..n-1]$, where we assume n
The idea of the algorithm is to let i go from 0 to $n - 1$, so that $A[0..i - 1]$ cont̶
the i smallest elements sorted, while the rest of the elements are in $A[i..n - 1$
each step, we find the least element in $A[i..n - 1]$ and swap this with $A[i]$ be̶
incrementing i. This method is known as *selection sort*.

We introduce abbreviations as follows:

$$
\begin{aligned}
\text{perm}.A.B.n \ &\overset{\wedge}{=} \ \text{permutation}.A.(0..n - 1).B.(0..n - 1) \ , \\
\text{sort}.A.n \ &\overset{\wedge}{=} \ \text{sorted}.A.(0..n - 1) \ , \\
\text{part}.A.i.n \ &\overset{\wedge}{=} \ \text{sorted}.A.(0..i - 1) \wedge \\
& \qquad (\forall h \ k \mid 0 \leq h \leq i < k < n \cdot A[h] \leq A[k]) \ ,
\end{aligned}
$$

Thus $\text{perm}.A.B.n$ means that $B[0..n - 1]$ is a permutation of $A[0..n - 1]$, sort̶
means that $A[0..n - 1]$ is sorted and $\text{part}.A.i.n$ means that A is partitioned
so that $A[0..i - 1]$ is sorted and all its elements are smaller than all elemen̶
$A[i..n - 1]$. The specification that we want to implement is expressed in ter̶
these notions as

$$[A := A' \mid \text{sort}.A'.n \wedge \text{perm}.A.A'.n] \ .$$

The derivation uses a specification constant A_0 to stand for the initial value o̶
array A. A program implementing the given specification is derived as follow̶

$\{A = A_0\} \, ; [A := A' \mid \text{sort}.A'.n \wedge \text{perm}.A.A'.n]$

$\sqsubseteq$ {introduce local variable i}

   begin var $i := 0$;

      " $\{i = 0 \wedge A = A_0\} \, ; [A, i := A', i' \mid \text{sort}.A'.n \wedge \text{perm}.A.A'.n]$ "

   end

$=$ {rewrite using context assertion}

$\cdots \{i = 0 \wedge A = A_0\} \, ; [A, i := A', i' \mid \text{sort}.A'.n \wedge \text{perm}.A_0.A'.n] \cdots$

$\sqsubseteq$ {introduce loop}

$\cdots$ **while** $i < n - 1$ **do**

    " $\{i < n - 1 \wedge 0 \le i < n \wedge \text{perm}.A_0.A.n \wedge \text{part}.A.i.n\}$;

       $[A, i := A', i' \mid 0 \le i' < n \wedge \text{perm}.A_0.A'.n \wedge \text{part}.A'.i'.n \wedge$

            $n - i' < n - i]$ "

   od $\cdots$

$\sqsubseteq$ {make assignment more deterministic, use assertion}

$\cdots \{0 \le i < n - 1 \wedge \text{perm}.A_0.A.n \wedge \text{part}.A.i.n\}$;

  " $[A, i := A', i' \mid i' = i + 1 \wedge \text{perm}.A_0.A'.n \wedge \text{part}.A'.(i + 1).n]$ " $\cdots$

$\sqsubseteq$ {add trailing assignment}

$\cdots [A := A' \mid \text{perm}.A_0.A'.n \wedge \text{part}.A'.(i + 1).n] \, ; i := i + 1 \cdots$

$=$ {substitute back}

  begin var $i := 0$;

    while $i < n - 1$ **do**

      $\{0 \le i < n - 1 \wedge \text{perm}.A_0.A.n \wedge \text{part}.A.i.n\}$;

      $[A := A' \mid \text{perm}.A_0.A'.n \wedge \text{part}.A'.(i + 1).n] \, ; i := i + 1$

    od

  end

$\sqsubseteq$ {introduce local variable j}

  begin var $i, j := 0, 0$;

    while $i < n - 1$ **do**

      $[j := j' \mid \text{minat}.j'.A.i.n]$;

      " $\{\text{minat}.j.A.i.n \wedge 0 \le i < n - 1 \wedge \text{perm}.A_0.A.n \wedge$

         $\text{part}.A.i.n\}$;

      $[A := A' \mid \text{perm}.A_0.A'.n \wedge \text{part}.A'.(i + 1).n]$; "

      $i := i + 1$

    od

```
            end
         ⊑ {introduce assignment}
            begin var i, j := 0, 0 ;
               while i < n − 1 do
                  [j := j' | minat. j'.A.i.n] ;
                  A := swap.i. j.A ;
                  i := i + 1
               od
            end
         ⊑ {procedure call rule}
            begin var i, j := 0, 0 ;
               while i < n − 1 do
                  FindMin( j, A, i, n − 1) ;
                  A := swap.i. j.A ;
                  i := i + 1
               od
            end
```

We need to prove that the conditions for introducing the loop and introducing assignment in the next-to-last step are satisfied. For the assignment introduc the proof obligation is

$$\text{minat.} j.A.i.n \wedge 0 \le i < n − 1 \wedge \text{perm.} A_0.A.n \wedge \text{part.} A.i.n \Rightarrow$$
$$\text{perm.} A_0.A'.n \wedge \text{part.} A'.(i + 1).n \ ,$$

where

$$A' = \text{swap.} i. j.A \ .$$

The first conjunct of the conclusion follows by the results of Exercise 10.11. rest of this proof obligation and the proof for the loop introduction are left exercise (Exercise 23.2).

23.4 Counting Sort

We consider next another approach to sorting, which gives a sorting time th linear in the number of items to be sorted and the range of the sorted values need to know beforehand that all values are integers within a given range. price to be paid for the efficiency in sorting time is that space efficiency is r poor: the algorithm needs additional space for sorting that is linear in the leng the integer range.

The Sorting Problem

We assume that m, n, l, and k are given natural numbers. The purpose of the program is to sort the elements in the array segment $A[m..n]$, where

A : array Nat of Nat .

We assume that the array range is not empty and that the values in A are all in the range $l..k$:

$$m \leq n \wedge (\forall i \mid m \leq i \leq n \cdot l \leq A[i] \leq k) .$$

The array A will not be changed by the program. Instead, we assume that the sorted array is constructed in another array segment $B[m..n]$:

B : array Nat of Nat .

We define a few abbreviations before we formulate the sorting problem in more precise terms. Assume that A is an array with the natural numbers as index set. A subarray of A is determined by an index range $m..n$. We describe the subarray as a triple (A, m, n). We will write such a triple more suggestively as $A[m..n]$.

We write sort.$X[a..b]$ for sorted.$X.(a..b)$ and just sort.X for sorted.$X[m..n]$. This indicates that the index range $m..n$ is the one we are chiefly interested in. Similarly, we write occur.$i.X[a..b]$ for occurrence.$i.X.(a..b)$ (the number of occurrences of i in $X[a..b]$) and just occur.$i.X$ for occur.$i.X[m..n]$. Finally, we write perm.$X.Y$ for permutation.$X.(m..n).Y.(m..n)$.

With these abbreviations, we are ready to give the specification of the problem: Construct an array B that is sorted and whose values form a permutation of the values in A, i.e.,

$$[B := B' \mid \text{sort}.B' \wedge \text{perm}.A.B'] .$$

Here, A, m, n, k, and l are constants (meaning that we can take the restrictions on them as global assumptions rather than initial assertions), while B is the only global program variable.

A First Solution

The basic solution idea is the following. We introduce an auxiliary array

C : array Nat of Nat;

that contains an entry for each value in the range $l..k$. Thus we only use the array segment $C[k..l]$, which is what makes the space complexity of the algorithm linear in the length of the range. We then record in $C[i]$ the number of times the value i occurs in the array A. This step will establish the condition

$$\text{countedocc}.C \; \stackrel{\triangle}{=} \; (\forall i \mid l \leq i \leq k \cdot C[i] = \text{occur}.i.A[m..n]) .$$

From this we can compute the sorted array B. One possible way is to scan thro
the value range $i = l, l + 1, \ldots, k - 1, k$, and successively insert the number C
of values i into B for each i. However, this would make our algorithm linea
the value range, which usually would be much larger than the size of the arra
itself. We will therefore derive another method below, which will be linear in
size of the array A.

Based on these considerations, we derive an initial solution to the programm
problem:

$[B := B' \mid \mathsf{sort}.B' \wedge \mathsf{perm}.A.B']$

$\sqsubseteq$ {introduce local variable C}

  begin var C : array Nat of Nat ;

    " $[B, C := B', C' \mid \mathsf{sort}.B' \wedge \mathsf{perm}.A.B']$ " ;

  end

$\sqsubseteq$ {introduce sequential composition}

  begin var C : array Nat of Nat ;

    " $[C := C' \mid \mathsf{countedocc}.C']$ " ;

    {countedocc.C} ;

    $[B, C := B', C' \mid \mathsf{sort}.B' \wedge \mathsf{perm}.A.B']$

  end

Let us next consider how to implement the first step, counting the occurrence
the different values in array A. We decide to first reset the array elements in
zero before starting the actual counting:

$[C := C' \mid \mathsf{countedocc}.C']$

$\sqsubseteq$ {introduce sequential composition}

  Reset(C, l, k) ;

  {allreset.$C.l.k$} ;

  $[C := C' \mid \mathsf{countedocc}.C']$

Here the first step establishes the condition allreset.$C.l.k$ which then can be assu
by the second step.

Thus, we arrive at the following first implementation of our specification:

$[B := B' \mid \mathsf{sort}.B' \wedge \mathsf{perm}.A.B']$

$\sqsubseteq$ {above derivation}

  begin var C : array Nat of Nat ;

    Reset(C, l, k) ;

    {allreset.$C.l.k$} ;

$[C := C' \mid \text{countedocc}.C']$;

$\{\text{countedocc}.C\}$;

$[B, C := B', C' \mid \text{sort}.B' \wedge \text{perm}.A.B']$;

end

This reduces our task to implementing the following two steps: counting the value occurrences and then constructing the final sorted array.

Counting Occurrences

Our next task is to count the occurrences of the different values in A. This is simply done by scanning through the array A and updating the appropriate counter in C each time. We give the derivation first and then show that the individual steps are indeed correct.

$\{\text{allreset}.C.l.k\}$;

$[C := C' \mid \text{countedocc}.C']$;

$\sqsubseteq$ {introduce local variable j}

begin var j : Nat ; $j := m$;

" $\{\text{allreset}.C.l.k \wedge j = m\}$;

$[C, j := C', j' \mid \text{countedocc}.C']$ " ;

end

$\sqsubseteq$ {introduce loop, choose $n + 1 - j$ as termination function}

$\cdots$ while $j \leq n$ do

" $\{\text{countedbelow}.C.j \wedge j \leq n\}$;

$[C, j := C', j' \mid \text{countedbelow}.C'.j' \wedge n + 1 - j' < n + 1 - j]$ "

od $\cdots$

$\sqsubseteq$ {introduce assignment statement}

$\cdots C[A[j]], j := C[A[j]] + 1, j + 1 \cdots$

$\sqsubseteq$ {substitute back}

begin var j : Nat ; $j := m$;

while $j \leq n$ do $C[A[j]], j := C[A[j]] + 1, j + 1$ od

end

Here we have used the abbreviation countedbelow, defined as follows:

$\text{countedbelow}.C.j \overset{\wedge}{=}$

$(\forall i \mid l \leq i \leq k \cdot C[i] = \text{occur}.i.A[m..j-1]) \wedge j \leq n + 1$.

Loop Introduction Conditions

The derivation again leaves us with two conditions to be proved: loop introduc[tion]
and assignment introduction. Consider first the loop introduction. We have to [show]
that

(i) allreset.$C.l.k \wedge j = m \Rightarrow$ countedbelow.$C.j$,

(ii) countedbelow.$C.j \wedge j > n \Rightarrow$ countedocc.C .

The invariant here states that the elements in the initial part of the array, up to
have already been counted.

The initialization condition holds, because

$$(\forall i \mid l \le i < j \cdot C[i] = 0) \wedge j = m$$
$$\vdash (\forall i \mid l \le i \le k \cdot C[i] = \text{occur}.i.A[m..j-1]) \wedge j \le n+1$$
$$\equiv \{\text{assumption } j = m\}$$
$$(\forall i \mid l \le i \le k \cdot C[i] = \text{occur}.i.A[m..m-1]) \wedge m \le n+1$$
$$\equiv \{\text{array has empty range, } m \le n\}$$
$$(\forall i \mid l \le i \le k \cdot C[i] = 0) \wedge \mathsf{T}$$
$$\equiv \{\text{assumption}\}$$
$$\mathsf{T}$$

The exit condition again holds, because

$$(\forall i \mid l \le i \le k \cdot C[i] = \text{occur}.i.A[m..j-1]) \wedge j \le n+1 \wedge j >$$
$$\vdash (\forall i \mid l \le i \le k \cdot C[i] = \text{occur}.i.A[m..n])$$
$$\equiv \{\text{assumption implies } j = n+1\}$$
$$(\forall i \mid l \le i \le k \cdot C[i] = \text{occur}.i.A[m..j-1])$$
$$\equiv \{\text{assumption}\}$$
$$\mathsf{T}$$

Assignment Introduction Conditions

Finally, we have to show that the assignment introduction is correctly done[.]
means that we have to show that

$$\text{countedbelow}.C.j \wedge j \le n \Rightarrow$$
$$\text{countedbelow}.C'.j' \wedge n+1-j' < n+1-j ,$$

where

$$C' = C(A[j] \leftarrow C[A[j]]+1) ,$$
$$j' = j+1 .$$

We have

$$(\forall i \mid l \le i \le k \cdot C[i] = \text{occur}.i.A[m..j-1]) \land$$
$$j \le n+1 \land j \le n$$
$$\vdash (\forall i \mid l \le i \le k \cdot C(A[j] \leftarrow C[A[j]] + 1)[i] = \text{occur}.i.A[m..j]) \land$$
$$j+1 \le n+1 \land n+1-(j+1) < n+1-j$$
$$\equiv \{\text{assumption } j \le n\}$$
$$(\forall i \mid l \le i \le k \cdot C(A[j] \leftarrow C[A[j]] + 1)[i] = \text{occur}.i.A[m..j])$$
$$\equiv \{\text{range split}\}$$
$$(\forall i \mid l \le i \le k \land i \ne A[j] \cdot$$
$$\quad C(A[j] \leftarrow C[A[j]] + 1)[i] = \text{occur}.i.A[m..j]) \land$$
$$\text{`` } (\forall i \mid l \le i \le k \land i = A[j] \cdot$$
$$\quad C(A[j] \leftarrow C[A[j]] + 1)[i] = \text{occur}.i.A[m..j]) \text{ ''}$$
$$\equiv \{\text{one point rule}\}$$
$$\cdots C(A[j] \leftarrow C[A[j]] + 1)[A[j]] = \text{occur}.A[j].A[m..j] \cdots$$
$$\equiv \{\text{array indexing rule, arithmetic}\}$$
$$\cdots C[A[j]] + 1 =$$
$$\quad \text{occur}.A[j].A[m..j-1] + \text{occur}.A[j].A[j..j] \cdots$$
$$\equiv \{\text{arithmetic, occur}.A[j].A[j..j] = 1\}$$
$$\cdots C[A[j]] + 1 = \text{occur}.A[j].A[m..j-1] + 1 \cdots$$
$$\equiv \{\text{arithmetic}\}$$
$$\cdots C[A[j]] = \text{occur}.A[j].(A[m..j-1]) \cdots$$
$$\equiv \{\text{substitute back}\}$$
$$(\forall i \mid l \le i \le k \land i \ne A[j] \cdot$$
$$\quad \text{`` } C(A[j] \leftarrow C[A[j]] + 1)[i] = \text{occur}.i.A[m..j] \text{ ''}) \land$$
$$(\forall i \mid l \le i \le k \land i = A[j] \cdot C[i] = \text{occur}.i.A[m..j-1])$$
$$\equiv \{\text{array indexing rule, assume } i \ne A[j]\}$$
$$\cdots C[i] = \text{occur}.i.A[m..j] \cdots$$
$$\equiv \{\text{arithmetic, assume } i \ne A[j]\}$$
$$\cdots C[i] = \text{occur}.i.A[m..j-1] \cdots$$
$$\equiv \{\text{substitute back}\}$$
$$(\forall i \mid l \le i \le k \land i \ne A[j] \cdot C[i] = \text{occur}.i.A[m..j-1]) \land$$
$$(\forall i \mid l \le i \le k \land i = A[j] \cdot C[i] = \text{occur}.i.A[m..j-1])$$
$$\equiv \{\text{merge ranges}\}$$
$$(\forall i \mid l \le i \le k \cdot C[i] = \text{occur}.i.A[m..j-1])$$

$\equiv$ {assumption }

T

The range split method thus works well also in the more general case where have an array index that itself is an array access. In this way, we can work indirect references in an array without any further complications.

Computing Cumulative Occurrences

Let us finally construct the sorted array B from the counter array C. The met we will use is as follows. Making use of the fact that $C[i]$ records the numbe occurrences of i in array A, we first change C so that $C[i]$ records the numbe occurrences of values less than or equal to i in A. Let us for this purpose defi

$$\text{cumsum}.i.X[a..b] \;\hat{=}\; (\#j \mid a \le j \le b \cdot X[j] \le i) \;.$$

We write cumsum.$i.X$ for cumsum.$i.X[m..n]$.

The first step will thus be to establish the condition

$$\text{countedcum}.C \;\hat{=}\; (\forall i \mid l \le i \le k \cdot C[i] = \text{cumsum}.i.A) \;.$$

After this step, we know what the index of each element $A[j] = i$ should be in sorted array B. There are $C[i]$ values in A that are less than or equal to i. If is only one element $i = A[j]$ in A, then this element should obviously be pl in position $C[i]$ in array B. If there are more elements with value i in A, then other elements should be placed immediately below $C[i]$ in array B.

These considerations lead to the following derivation:

{countedocc.C} ;
$[B, C := B', C' \mid \text{sort}.B' \land \text{perm}.A.B']$;
$\sqsubseteq$ {introduce sequential composition}
" {countedocc.C} ;
$[C := C' \mid \text{countedcum}.C']$ " ;
{countedcum.C} ;
$[B, C := B', C' \mid \text{sort}.B' \land \text{perm}.A.B']$

The implementation of the first step is as follows:

{countedocc.C} ;
$[C := C' \mid \text{countedcum}.C']$

⊑ {exercise}
 begin var j : Nat ; $j := l + 1$;
  while $j \leq k$ do $C[j], j := C[j] + C[j-1], j+1$ od
 end

We leave this step as an exercise for the reader, and concentrate on the final, most difficult step in the last section.

Constructing the Sorted Array

We will here first give the derivation of the final step and then justify the steps in more detail. We have

{countedcum.C} ;
 [$B, C := B', C'$ | sort.$B' \wedge$ perm.$A.B'$] ;
⊑ {introduce local variable}
 begin var j : Nat ; $j := n$;
  " {countedcum.$C \wedge j = n$} ;
   [$B, C, j := B', C', j'$ | sort.$B' \wedge$ perm.$A.B'$] "
 end
⊑ {introduce loop}
 $\cdots$while $j \geq m$ do
  " {movedpart.$j.B.C \wedge j \geq m$} ;
   [$B, C, j := B', C', j'$ | movedpart.$j'.B'.C' \wedge j' < j$] "
 od $\cdots$
⊑ {introduce assignment}
 $\cdots B[C[A[j]]], C[A[j]], j := A[j], C[A[j]] - 1, j - 1 \cdots$
⊑ {substitute back}
 begin var j : Nat ; $j := n$;
  while $j \geq m$ do
   $B[C[A[j]]], C[A[j]], j := A[j], C[A[j]] - 1, j - 1$
  od
 end

Justifying the Loop Introduction

The invariant for the loop introduction describes the fact that the elements $A[j + 1..n]$ have already been moved to B and that the counters in C have been adjusted appropriately, so that $C[i]$ now counts the number of values smaller or equal to i in the remaining array $A[m..j]$:

$$\text{movedpart}.j.B.C \;\triangleq$$
$$(\forall i \mid l \le i \le k \cdot \text{occur}.i.A[m..j] = C[i] - \text{cumsum}.(i - 1).A) \;\wedge$$
$$(\forall i\ r \mid l \le i \le k \wedge C[i] < r \le \text{cumsum}.i.A \cdot B[r] = i) \;\wedge$$
$$m - 1 \le j \le n$$

The termination function is simply j.

As usual, we have to show that the invariant holds initially and that the exit condition holds when the loop is terminated. For the entry condition, we have to show that

$$\text{countedcum}.C \wedge j = n \;\Rightarrow\; \text{movedpart}.j.B.C \;.$$

We have

$$(\forall i \mid l \le i \le k \cdot C[i] = \text{cumsum}.i.A) \wedge j = n$$
$$\vdash (\forall i \mid l \le i \le k \cdot \text{occur}.i.A[m..j] = C[i] - \text{cumsum}.(i - 1).A) \;\wedge$$
$$(\forall i\ r \mid l \le i \le k \wedge C[i] < r \le \text{cumsum}.i.A \cdot B[r] = i) \;\wedge$$
$$m - 1 \le j \le n$$
$$\equiv \{\text{assumption } j = n\}$$
$$(\forall i \mid l \le i \le k \cdot \text{occur}.i.A[m..n] = C[i] - \text{cumsum}.(i - 1).A) \;\wedge$$
$$(\forall i\ r \mid l \le i \le k \wedge C[i] < r \le \text{cumsum}.i.A \cdot B[r] = i) \wedge \mathsf{T}$$
$$\equiv \{\text{assumption, abbreviation } A \text{ for } A[m..n]\}$$
$$(\forall i \mid l \le i \le k \cdot \text{occur}.i.A = \text{cumsum}.i.A - \text{cumsum}.(i - 1).A) \;\wedge$$
$$(\forall i\ r \mid l \le i \le k \wedge \text{cumsum}.i.A < r \le \text{cumsum}.i.A \cdot B[r] = i) \wedge \mathsf{T}$$
$$\equiv \{\text{definition of cumsum, empty range}\}$$
$$\mathsf{T}$$

For the exit condition, we have to show that

$$\text{movedpart}.j.B.C \wedge j < m \;\Rightarrow\; \text{sort}.B \wedge \text{perm}.A.B \;.$$

This is shown as follows:

$$(\forall i \mid l \le i \le k \cdot \text{occur}.i.A[m..j] = C[i] - \text{cumsum}.(i - 1).A) \;\wedge$$
$$(\forall i\ r \mid l \le i \le k \wedge C[i] < r \le \text{cumsum}.i.A \cdot B[r] = i) \;\wedge$$
$$m - 1 \le j \le n \wedge j < m$$
$$\vdash \mathsf{T}$$

$\Rightarrow$ {assumptions, $j = m - 1$}

$(\forall i \mid l \le i \le k \cdot \text{occur}.i.A[m..m-1] = C[i] - \text{cumsum}.(i-1).A) \wedge$

$(\forall i\, r \mid l \le i \le k \wedge C[i] < r \le \text{cumsum}.i.A \cdot B[r] = i)$

$\Rightarrow$ {occur.$i.A[m..m-1] = 0$}

$(\forall i \mid l \le i \le k \cdot C[i] = \text{cumsum}.(i-1).A) \wedge$

$(\forall i\, r \mid l \le i \le k \wedge \text{cumsum}.(i-1).A < r \le \text{cumsum}.i.A \cdot B[r] = i)$

$\Rightarrow$ {cumsum.$l.A \le$ cumsum.$(l+1).A \le \cdots \le$ cumsum.$k.A$}

$(\forall j\, r \mid m \le j \le r \le n \cdot B[j] \le B[r]) \wedge$

$(\forall i \mid l \le i \le k \cdot \text{occur}.i.B = \text{cumsum}.i.A - \text{cumsum}.(i-1).A)$

$\equiv$ {definition of sorted and cumsum}

sort.$B \wedge (\forall i \mid l \le i \le k \cdot \text{occur}.i.B = \text{occur}.i.A)$

$\equiv$ {definition of perm}

sort.$B \wedge$ perm.$A.B$

Justifying the Assignment Statement

Finally, we need to justify the assignment introduction. We need to show that

$$\text{movedpart}.j.B.C \wedge j \ge m \;\Rightarrow\; \text{movedpart}.j'.B'.C' \wedge j' < j\ ,$$

where

$$
\begin{aligned}
j' &= j - 1\ ,\\
h &= A[j]\ ,\\
C' &= C(h \leftarrow C[h] - 1)\ ,\\
B' &= B(C[h] \leftarrow h)\ .
\end{aligned}
$$

The proof is as follows:

$(\forall i \mid l \le i \le k \cdot \text{occur}.i.A[m..j] = C[i] - \text{cumsum}.(i-1).A) \wedge$

$(\forall i\, r \mid l \le i \le k \wedge C[i] < r \le \text{cumsum}.i.A \cdot B[r] = i) \wedge$

$m - 1 \le j \le n \wedge j \ge m$

$\vdash (\forall i \mid l \le i \le k \cdot \text{occur}.i.A[m..j-1] = C'[i] - \text{cumsum}.(i-1).A) \wedge$

$(\forall i\, r \mid l \le i \le k \wedge C'[i] < r \le \text{cumsum}.i.A \cdot B'[r] = i) \wedge$

$m - 1 \le j - 1 \le n \wedge j - 1 < j$

$\equiv$ {assumption $m \le j$}

" $(\forall i \mid l \le i \le k \cdot \text{occur}.i.A[m..j-1] = C'[i] - \text{cumsum}.(i-1).A)$ " $\wedge$

$(\forall i\, r \mid l \le i \le k \wedge C'[i] < r \le \text{cumsum}.i.A \cdot B'[r] = i) \wedge \top \wedge \top$

$\equiv$ {range split}

$\cdots (\forall i \mid l \le i \le k \wedge i \ne h \cdot$

$\qquad \text{occur}.i.A[m..j-1] = C'[i] - \text{cumsum}.(i-1).A) \wedge$

$$\text{occur}.h.A[m..j-1] = C'[h] - \text{cumsum}.(h-1).A) \cdots$$

$\equiv$ {definition of C'}

$$\cdots(\forall i \mid l \leq i \leq k \wedge i \neq h \cdot$$
$$\text{occur}.i.A[m..j-1] = C[i] - \text{cumsum}.(i-1).A) \wedge$$
$$\text{occur}.h.A[m..j-1] = C[h] - 1 - \text{cumsum}.(h-1).A) \cdots$$

$\equiv$ { $h = A[j]$}

$$\cdots(\forall i \mid l \leq i \leq k \wedge i \neq h \cdot$$
$$\text{occur}.i.A[m..j] = C[i] - \text{cumsum}.(i-1).A) \wedge$$
$$\text{occur}.h.A[m..j] = C[h] - \text{cumsum}.(h-1).A \cdots$$

$\equiv$ {merge ranges}

$$(\forall i \mid l \leq i \leq k \cdot \text{occur}.i.A[m..j] = C[i] - \text{cumsum}.(i-1).A) \wedge$$
$$(\forall i\, r \mid l \leq i \leq k \wedge C'[i] < r \leq \text{cumsum}.i.A \cdot B'[r] = i)$$

$\equiv$ {assumption}

$$\mathsf{T} \wedge (\forall i\, r \mid l \leq i \leq k \wedge C'[i] < r \leq \text{cumsum}.i.A \cdot B'[r] = i)$$

$\equiv$ {range split}

$$(\forall i\, r \mid l \leq i \leq k \wedge C'[i] < r \leq \text{cumsum}.i.A \wedge i \neq h \cdot B'[r] = i) \wedge$$
$$(\forall r \mid C'[h] < r \leq \text{cumsum}.h.A \cdot B'[r] = h)$$

$\equiv$ {definition of B' and C'}

$$(\forall i\, r \mid l \leq i \leq k \wedge C[i] < r \leq \text{cumsum}.i.A \wedge i \neq h \cdot$$
$$B(C[h] \leftarrow h)[r] = i) \wedge$$
$$(\forall r \mid C[h] - 1 < r \leq \text{cumsum}.h.A \cdot B(C[h] \leftarrow h)[r] = h)$$

$\equiv$ {array indexing}

$$(\forall i\, r \mid l \leq i \leq k \wedge C[i] < r \leq \text{cumsum}.i.A \wedge i \neq h \cdot B[r] = i) \wedge$$
$$(\forall r \mid C[h] < r \leq \text{cumsum}.h.A \cdot B[r] = h)$$

$\equiv$ {merge ranges}

$$(\forall i\, r \mid l \leq i \leq k \wedge C[i] < r \leq \text{cumsum}.i.A \cdot B[r] = i)$$

$\equiv$ {assumption }

$$\mathsf{T}$$

Final Result

Combining the separate refinements, we get the following theorem:

$$[B := B' \mid \text{sort}.B' \wedge \text{perm}.A.B']$$

$\sqsubseteq$ {above derivation}

```
begin var C : array Nat of Nat ;
   begin var j : Nat ; j := l ;
      while j ≤ k do C[j], j := 0, j + 1 od ;
   end ;
   begin var j : Nat ; j := m ;
      while j ≤ n do C[A[j]], j := C[A[j]] + 1, j + 1 od
   end ;
   begin var j : Nat ; j := m + 1 ;
      while j ≤ k do C[j], j := C[j] + C[j − 1], j + 1 od
   end ;
   begin var j : Nat ; j := n ;
      while j ≥ m do
            B[C[A[j]]], C[A[j]], j := A[j], C[A[j]] − 1, j − 1
      od
   end
end
```

Finally, we move the local variable j to the outermost level (we leave the proof of this to the reader as an exercise) and get the following final version of the program:

$$[B := B' \mid \text{sort}.B' \wedge \text{perm}.A.B']$$

⊑ {merge blocks (Exercise 23.5)}

```
begin var C : array Nat of Nat, j : Nat ;
   j := l ;
   while j ≤ k do C[j], j := 0, j + 1 od ;
   j := m ;
   while j ≤ n do C[A[j]], j := C[A[j]] + 1, j + 1 od ;
   j := m + 1 ;
   while j ≤ k do C[j], j := C[j] + C[j − 1], j + 1 od ;
   j := n ;
   while j ≥ m do
         B[C[A[j]]], C[A[j]], j := A[j], C[A[j]] − 1, j − 1
   od
end
```

23.5   Summary and Discussion

We have shown in this chapter how to build programs that manipulate arr
looking in particular at searching and sorting. The counting sort example sh
that the methods introduced earlier can also handle quite tricky array manipulati
The importance of having a good program derivation environment also beco
much more evident in looking at a larger derivation. The ratio of invention to
copying of text and checking that inference rules are correctly applied beco
quite small. Hence, there is a strong need for computer-supported tools for carr
out program refinements.

The programming problems treated above are all classical, and we do not clai
contribute anything new to the algorithmic solution of these. A classical refere
to sorting and searching algorithms is the book written by Donald Knuth [96]

23.6   Exercises

23.1   Prove that the conditions for introducing a loop and for introducing an assignm
are satisfied in the derivation of the linear search algorithm.

23.2   Prove that the conditions for introducing a loop and for introducing an assignm
are satisfied in the derivation of the selection sort algorithm.

23.3   In the derivation of the selection sort program we assumed that $n > 0$. Show
the final program in fact gives the right result also when $n = 0$. In a situation
this, the following rule can be useful:

$$\frac{\{p\}\, ;\, S \sqsubseteq S' \qquad \{q\}\, ;\, S \sqsubseteq S'}{\{p \cup q\}\, ;\, S \sqsubseteq S'} .$$

Derive this rule.

23.4   Complete the derivation in the counting-sort case study by showing how to de
the computation of cumulative occurrences of values.

23.5   Prove the following rule for merging blocks:

begin var $y := e_1$; S_1 end ; begin var $y := e_2$; S_2 end $=$

begin var $y := e_1$; S_1 ; $y := e_2$; S_2 end ,

provided that y does not occur free in e_2.

4

The N-Queens Problem

The *n-queens problem* is to place n queens (where $n > 0$) on an n-by-n chessboard so that no queen is threatened by another one. According to the rules of chess, this is equivalent to the requirement that no two queens be on the same row or the same column or on a common diagonal. For some values of n this is possible but for some values (for example, for $n = 2$) there is no solution. In this chapter we show how one solution for a particular value of n is found with a depth-first search. The program derivation illustrates both recursion and loop introduction in a nontrivial setting. It also illustrates how to handle data structures like sequences in a program derivation.

1 Analyzing the Problem

Let us start by analyzing the problem domain in somewhat more detail and finding out some basic facts. The number of queens (and the size of the board) is n : Nat. We think of the board as a matrix with rows and columns numbered $0, \ldots, n-1$. A pair of numbers (r, c) represents a position on the board, with r and c in $0, \ldots, n - 1$. It is obvious that in a solution there must be one queen in each row. Thus we can represent a solution as a sequence of numbers $c_0, \ldots, c_{n-1}$, where c_i is the column number of the queen in row i.

We allow sequences to be indexed; $s[i]$ stands for the ith element in s (for $i = 0, \ldots, \text{len}.s - 1$, where $\text{len}.s$ is the length of sequence s). However, indexing is not considered implementable, so it must not appear in the final program.

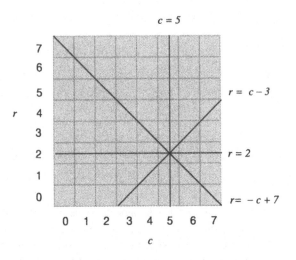

FIGURE 24.1. Queen threat on a board

First let us define what it means for two queens in positions (i, x) and (j, y) n
threaten each other:

$$nothreat.(i, x).(j, y) \triangleq$$
$$i \neq j \wedge x \neq y \wedge i + x \neq j + y \wedge i + y \neq j + x \ .$$

These four conditions are illustrated in Figure 24.1. They guarantee that the
queens are not on the same row, the same column, the same downward diago
or the same upward diagonal.

Next, we define safecon.$s.n$ to mean that the sequence s represents legally pla
queens on an n-by-n board that do not threaten each other:

$$safecon.s.n \triangleq$$
$$(\forall i \mid i < len.s \cdot s[i] < n) \wedge$$
$$(\forall i \ j \mid i < j < len.s \cdot nothreat.(i, s[i]).(j, s[j])) \ .$$

We can then define when a sequence q is a solution to the n-queens problem:

$$solution.q.n \triangleq len.q = n \wedge safecon.q.n \ .$$

Our idea is to solve the problem as follows. We start from an empty board. T
queens are added, one by one. If at some point it is impossible to place a qu

then we recursively backtrack to the previous queen and try a new place for this queen.

Before starting the derivation, we define the following functions:

$$s \ll s' \triangleq \text{len}.s \leq \text{len}.s' \wedge (\forall i \mid i < \text{len}.s \cdot s[i] = s'[i]) \ ,$$
$$\text{safeadd}.s.x \triangleq (\forall i \mid i < \text{len}.s \cdot \text{nothreat}.(i, s[i]).(\text{len}.s, x)) \ ,$$
$$\text{qinit}.s.n \triangleq (\exists q \cdot \text{solution}.q.n \wedge s \ll q) \ .$$

Thus $s \ll s'$ holds if s is a *prefix* of s'. Furthermore, safeadd.$s.x$ means that if we place a queen in position (len.s, x), then it is not threatened by any queen in s. Finally, qinit.$s.n$ means that the queens in s form the initial part of a solution. In particular, qinit.$\langle \rangle.n$ holds if and only if there is a solution for an n-by-n board.

The following properties that will be used in the derivation can be proved from the definitions given above (Exercise 24.1):

$$\text{safecon}.s.n \wedge x < n \wedge \text{safeadd}.s.x \equiv \text{safecon}.(s\&x).n \ , \qquad (*)$$
$$\text{qinit}.s.n \wedge \text{len}.s < n \Rightarrow (\exists x \mid x < n \cdot \text{qinit}.(s\&x).n) \ , \qquad (**)$$
$$\neg\, \text{safeadd}.s.x \Rightarrow \neg\, \text{qinit}.(s\&x).n \ , \qquad (***)$$
$$\text{safecon}.s.n \wedge \text{len}.s = n \Rightarrow \text{qinit}.s.n \ . \qquad (****)$$

The n-queens problem can now be specified as follows:

$\{n > 0 \wedge q = \langle\rangle\}$;
if qinit.$\langle\rangle.n \rightarrow [q := q' \mid \text{solution}.q'.n]$
$[\!]\, \neg\, \text{qinit}.\langle\rangle.n \rightarrow \text{skip}$
fi .

Thus the sequence q is assumed to be empty initially. At the end, q contains a solution, or, if no solution exists, q is still empty.

We aim at a recursive procedure Queens(var q, val s, n). The reference parameter q will receive the result sequence, and the value parameter s is used to collect and pass on partial solutions. The value parameter n is the number of queens (the size of the board); it is always passed on unchanged. Thus the procedure will explicitly change the value only of q (and the value of s at the calls), and at every recursive call, $n > 0 \wedge \text{len}.s \leq n \wedge q = \langle\rangle \wedge \text{safecon}.s.n$ should hold. For every call we want one queen to be added to the board (i.e., s to be extended with one value), so the variant is $n - \text{len}.s$. Thus the starting point of our derivation of the recursive procedure is the following:

$\{n > 0 \wedge \text{len}.s \leq n \wedge q = \langle\rangle \wedge \text{safecon}.s.n \wedge n - \text{len}.s = w\}$;
if qinit.$s.n \rightarrow [q := q' \mid s \ll q' \wedge \text{solution}.q'.n]$
$[\!]\, \neg\, \text{qinit}.s.n \rightarrow \text{skip}$
fi

(note that if $s = \langle \rangle$, then this reduces to the original specification of the proble
By rewriting the conditional specification as a basic one (Exercise 17.5) and u
the initial assertion, we find that the specification can be rewritten as

$$\{n > 0 \wedge \text{len}.s \leq n \wedge q = \langle \rangle \wedge \text{safecon}.s.n \wedge n - \text{len}.s = w\} \,;$$
$$[q := q' \mid \text{if qinit}.s.n \text{ then } s \ll q' \wedge \text{solution}.q'.n \text{ else } q' = \langle \rangle \text{ fi}] \,.$$

Although this form may be harder to read, it is easier to use in formal manipulati
For brevity, we introduce the abbreviation $S.s.q.n$ for the demonic assignmer
this specification statement.

24.2 First Step: The Terminating Case

We begin by separating the recursive case from the terminating case. In the
minating case the solution has been collected in s, so we have only to move
q.

$$\{n > 0 \wedge \text{len}.s \leq n \wedge q = \langle \rangle \wedge \text{safecon}.s.n \wedge n - \text{len}.s = w\} \,;$$
$$S.s.q.n$$

$= \{\text{introduce conditional, unfold abbreviation}\}$

if $\text{len}.s = n \rightarrow$

" $\{n > 0 \wedge \text{len}.s = n \wedge q = \langle \rangle \wedge \text{safecon}.s.n \wedge n - \text{len}.s = w\} \,;$

$[q := q' \mid \text{if qinit}.s.n \text{ then } s \ll q' \wedge \text{solution}.q'.n \text{ else } q' = \langle \rangle \text{ fi}]$ "

[] $\text{len}.s < n \rightarrow$

$\{n > 0 \wedge \text{len}.s < n \wedge q = \langle \rangle \wedge \text{safecon}.s.n \wedge n - \text{len}.s = w\} \,;$

$S.s.q.n$

fi

$\sqsubseteq \{\text{use (****) and assertion}\}$

if $\text{len}.s = n \rightarrow$

" $\{n > 0 \wedge \text{len}.s = n \wedge q = \langle \rangle \wedge \text{safecon}.s.n \wedge n - \text{len}.s = w\} \,;$

$[q := q' \mid s \ll q' \wedge \text{solution}.q'.n]$ "

[] $\text{len}.s < n \rightarrow$

$\{n > 0 \wedge \text{len}.s < n \wedge q = \langle \rangle \wedge \text{safecon}.s.n \wedge n - \text{len}.s = w\} \,;$

$S.s.q.n$

fi

$\sqsubseteq \{\text{use definition of solution to make assignment deterministic}\}$

if len.$s = n \rightarrow q := s$

[] len.$s < n \rightarrow$

$\quad \{n > 0 \wedge \text{len}.s < n \wedge q = \langle\,\rangle \wedge \text{safecon}.s.n \wedge n - \text{len}.s = w\}\,;$

$\quad S.s.q.n$

fi

3 Second Step: Extending a Partial Solution

Now we find out how to extend the partial solution s in the recursive case. The idea is that if there is a solution, then we can extend s with one of the values in $0, \ldots, n - 1$. We can try them in order, one by one. We continue from the last version by unfolding the abbreviation:

$=$ {unfold abbreviation}

   if len.$s = n \rightarrow q := s$

   [] len.$s < n \rightarrow$

     " $\{n > 0 \wedge \text{len}.s < n \wedge q = \langle\,\rangle \wedge \text{safecon}.s.n \wedge n - \text{len}.s = w\}\,;$

      $[q := q' \mid$ if qinit.$s.n$ then $s \ll q' \wedge \text{solution}.q'.n$ else $q' = \langle\,\rangle$ fi] "

   fi

$\sqsubseteq$ {introduce local variable x with assignments}

$\cdots$begin var $x := 0$;

     " $\{x = 0 \wedge n > 0 \wedge \text{len}.s < n \wedge q = \langle\,\rangle \wedge \text{safecon}.s.n \wedge n - \text{len}.s = w\}\,;$

      $[q, x := q', x' \mid$ if qinit.$s.n$ then $s \ll q' \wedge \text{solution}.q'.n$ else $q' = \langle\,\rangle$ fi] "

   end$\cdots$

$\sqsubseteq$ {introduce loop}

$\cdots$while $x < n \wedge q = \langle\,\rangle$ do

     " $\{x < n \wedge \text{len}.s < n \wedge q = \langle\,\rangle \wedge \text{safecon}.s.n \wedge n - \text{len}.s = w\}\,;$

      $[q := q' \mid$ if qinit.$(s\&x).n$ then $(s\&x) \ll q' \wedge \text{solution}.q'.n$

           else $q' = \langle\,\rangle$ fi] " ;

     $x := x + 1$

   od$\cdots$

$=$ {fold abbreviation}

$\cdots\{x < n \wedge \text{len}.s < n \wedge q = \langle\,\rangle \wedge \text{safecon}.s.n \wedge n - \text{len}.s = w\}\,;$

   $S.(s\&x).q.n\cdots$

Loop Introduction

We now show the proof of the loop introduction in the derivation above, us
Theorem 21.14. The idea of the loop introduction is to find a suitable placeme
of the next queen. We let x count from 0 and stop when either $qinit.(s\&x).n$ h
(meaning that a suitable position is found) or when $x = n \land q = \langle\rangle$ (meaning
no suitable position exists).

The invariant (let us call it J) is

$$x \le n \land len.s < n \land safecon.s.n \land n - len.s = w \ \land$$
$$((q = \langle\rangle \land (\forall y \mid y < x \cdot \neg qinit.(s\&y).n)) \ \lor$$
$$(x > 0 \land qinit.(s\&(x-1)).n \land (s\&(x-1))\lll q \land solution.q.n))$$

(in the second half of this invariant, the first disjunct holds when a position has
yet been found for the next queen, and the second disjunct holds when a posi
has been found). The variant is simply $n - x$.

To prove that the invariant holds initially, we have to prove

$$x = 0 \land n > 0 \land len.s < n \land q = \langle\rangle \land safecon.s.n \land n - len.s = w$$
$$\Rightarrow J ,$$

which is not hard (select the first disjunct in J).

Next, we must show that the loop body preserves the invariant and decreases
variant. Since x is increased by the loop body, the variant is obviously decrea
For the invariant, we must prove

$$x < n \land q = \langle\rangle \land J \land qinit.(s\&x).n \land (s\&x)\lll q' \land solution.q'.n \Rightarrow$$
$$J[q, x := q', x+1]$$

and

$$x < n \land q = \langle\rangle \land J \land \neg qinit.(s\&x).n \land q' = \langle\rangle \Rightarrow$$
$$J[q, x := q', x+1] .$$

Both conditions can be proved using the properties of sequences given earlie

Finally, to show that the postcondition holds on termination, we show

$$(x \ge n \lor q \ne \langle\rangle) \land J \land qinit.s.n \Rightarrow s\lll q \land solution.q.n$$

and

$$(x \ge n \lor q \ne \langle\rangle) \land J \land \neg qinit.s.n \Rightarrow q = \langle\rangle .$$

All these conditions are most easily proved by case analysis on $q = \langle\rangle$.

4   Third Step: Completing for Recursion Introduction

The body of the loop now contains almost what we need for recursion introduction; the only problem is that the assertion should contain safecon.$(s\&x).n$ instead of safecon.$s.n$ in order for the variant to decrease. To get this, we need to introduce a conditional, based on whether safeadd.$s.x$ holds or not. We continue the derivation as follows:

$=$ {introduce conditional, unfold abbreviation}

$\cdots$ if safeadd.$s.x \rightarrow$

   {safeadd.$s.x \wedge x < n \wedge$ len.$s < n \wedge q = \langle \rangle \wedge$

   safecon.$s.n \wedge n -$ len.$s = w$} ;

   $S.(s\&x).q.n$

[] $\neg$ safeadd.$s.x \rightarrow$

   {$\neg$ safeadd.$s.x \wedge x < n \wedge$ len.$s < n \wedge q = \langle \rangle \wedge$

   safecon.$s.n \wedge n -$ len.$s = w$} ;

   [$q := q'$ | if qinit.$(s\&x).n$ then $(s\&x) \ll q' \wedge$ solution.$q'.n$

                     else $q' = \langle \rangle$ fi]

   fi$\cdots$

$\sqsubseteq$ {use (∗∗∗) and assertion to simplify}

$\cdots$ if safeadd.$s.x \rightarrow$

   " {safeadd.$s.x \wedge x < n \wedge$ len.$s < n \wedge q = \langle \rangle \wedge$

   safecon.$s.n \wedge n -$ len.$s = w$} " ;

   $S.(s\&x).q.n$

[] $\neg$ safeadd.$s.x \rightarrow$ skip

   fi$\cdots$

$\sqsubseteq$ {weaken assertion, use (∗)}

$\cdots${$n > 0 \wedge$ len.$(s\&x) \leq n \wedge q = \langle \rangle \wedge$

   safecon.$(s\&x).n \wedge n -$ len.$(s\&x) < w$}$\cdots$

$= \{\text{substitute back}\}$
   if len.$s = n \rightarrow q := s$
   [] len.$s < n \rightarrow$
     begin var $x := 0$;
       while $x < n \wedge q = \langle\,\rangle$ do
         if safeadd.$s.x \rightarrow$
           $\{n > 0 \wedge \text{len}.(s\&x) \leq n \wedge q = \langle\,\rangle \wedge$
              safecon.$(s\&x).n \wedge n - \text{len}.(s\&x) < w\}$;
           $S.(s\&x).q.n$
         [] $\neg$ safeadd.$s.x \rightarrow$ skip
         fi ;
         $x := x + 1$
       od
     end
   fi
$= \{\text{move block to outermost level}\}$
   begin var $x := 0$;
     if len.$s = n \rightarrow q := s$
     [] len.$s < n \rightarrow$
       while $x < n \wedge q = \langle\,\rangle$ do
         if safeadd.$s.x \rightarrow$
           $\{n > 0 \wedge \text{len}.(s\&x) \leq n \wedge q = \langle\,\rangle \wedge$
            safecon.$(s\&x).n \wedge n - \text{len}.(s\&x) < w\}$;
          $S.(s\&x).q.n$
         [] $\neg$ safeadd.$s.x \rightarrow$ skip
         fi ;
         $x := x + 1$
       od
     fi
   end

5   Final Result

We now use the rule for procedure introduction and define

Queens(var q, val s, n)

$\stackrel{\wedge}{=}$

begin var $x := 0$;
  if len.$s = n \rightarrow q := s$
  [] len.$s < n \rightarrow$
    while $x < n \wedge q = \langle\,\rangle$ do
      if safeadd.$s.x \rightarrow$ Queens(q, $s\&x$, n)
      [] $\neg$ safeadd.$s.x \rightarrow$ skip
      fi ;
      $x := x + 1$
    od
  fi
end

The preceding derivations then allow us to conclude the following:

$\{n > 0 \wedge q = \langle\,\rangle\}$;
if $(\exists q \cdot \text{solution}.q.n) \rightarrow [q := q' \mid \text{solution}.q'.n]$
[] $\neg (\exists q \cdot \text{solution}.q.n) \rightarrow$ skip
fi
$\sqsubseteq$
  Queens(q, $\langle\,\rangle$, n)

so the procedure Queens indeed gives us a solution to the n-queens problem.

6   Summary and Discussion

This chapter has shown how to derive a somewhat more complicated recursive algorithm, using both recursion introduction and loop introduction. The solution illustrates the need for analyzing the problem domain carefully before starting the derivation, in order to capture the essential aspects of the problem and to find good data representations for the information that needs to be manipulated. The n-queens problem is a classical exercise in program derivation and has been treated systematically by Wirth, e.g., as an example of stepwise refinement [141].

24.7 Exercises

24.1   Derive properties (*)–(****) for sequences given in the text.

24.2   Complete the details of the proof for the loop introduction in the derivation o
Queens procedure.

oops and Two-Person Games

We have looked at recursion and iteration in general in the preceding chapters. In this chapter, we will show that the refinement calculus framework is usable beyond its original area of application, by showing how to model and analyze two-person games in the calculus. We show how to use total correctness reasoning to show the existence of winning strategies for such games. Furthermore, we show how one can derive a program that actually plays a game against an opponent. We choose the game of nim as an example and study it within the refinement calculus framework.

1 Modeling Two-Person Games

A typical two-person game (such as chess, checkers, tic-tac-toe or nim) involves two players taking turns in making moves. In order to model such games as statements, we first note that the game board can be represented as a state space. A move is an action that changes the board, i.e., a nondeterministic statement whose nondeterminism is determined by the possible legal alternatives in the current situation. We call one contestant Player and the other Opponent; then Player's moves are represented as angelic updates, while Opponent's moves are demonic updates.

A typical game can then be represented by an ordinary iteration:

while g do S od .

An execution of this iteration corresponds to a *run* (a play) of the game. If the body S aborts at some point (i.e., Player is not able to move), then Player has lost the game. Dually, if S is miraculous at some point (i.e., Opponent is not able to move), then Player has won the game. The game is a draw if the loop terminates nonmiraculously (i.e., if $\neg g$ holds after a normally terminating execution of body). The game is also considered to be a draw if the execution is nonterminat (the game continues indefinitely).

In terms of the game semantics for statements, this means that we are only in ested in a game where the postcondition is false. In this case, normal terminat nontermination, and abortion all imply that Player has lost, and only miracu termination is a win for Player.

As a simple example, consider the repetition

while true do $[x := x' \mid x' < x] ; \{x := x' \mid x' > x\}$ od

assuming program variable x : Nat. In this game, Opponent always decre the value of x while Player always increases it. Opponent begins, and the contestants alternate making moves (i.e., changing the value of x). It is easily that if the initial value of x is 0, then Player wins. This is because Opponent no possible opening move (the demonic choice is empty). In any other initial s the game goes on forever. Note that the guard true indicates that the game n ends in a draw in finite time.

Example Game: Nim

As a more interesting example, we consider a simple version of the game of in which the contestants alternate removing one or two matches from a pile. Pl is the first to move, and the one who removes the last match loses.

The state has only one attribute, x, the number of matches, ranging over the na numbers. Thus, we can consider the state space to be the type Nat.

We introduce the abbreviation Move for the state relation $(x := x' \mid x - 2 \leq x)$ (since we are talking about natural numbers, we follow the convention $m - n = 0$ when $m \leq n$). Then the game can be expressed in the following si form:

while true do $[x \neq 0] ; \{Move\} ; \{x \neq 0\} ; [Move]$ od .

The game can be explained as follows. The loop guard true shows that the never ends in a draw in finite time. The body shows the sequence of moves th repeated until the game ends (or indefinitely). First, the guard statement $[x$ is a check to see whether Player has already won (Opponent has lost if the p matches is empty when it is Player's move). If there are matches left ($x \neq 0$), Player moves according to the relation Move, i.e., removes one or two ma (decreases x by 1 or 2). Now the dual situation arises. The assert statement $\{x$ is a check to see whether Player has lost. If there are matches left, then Opp moves according to the relation Move, i.e., removes one or two matches.

Other two-person games can be represented by similar kinds of iterations. Typically, the iteration body contains guard and assert statements that detect situations in which either Player or Opponent has lost, and angelic and demonic updates that describe the permitted moves.

2 Winning Strategies

We have shown how games can be represented as iterations. The obvious question is now, what can we prove about a game?

Assume that the loop while g do S od represents a game and that the initial board is described by the predicate p. If the loop establishes postcondition false from precondition p, then from the semantics of statements we know that Player can make choices in the angelic updates in such a way as to be guaranteed to win, regardless of what choices Opponent makes in the demonic updates. Thus there exists a winning strategy for Player under precondition p if the following total correctness assertion holds:

$p \, \{\!| \, \text{while } g \text{ do } S \text{ od} \, |\!\} \, \text{false}$.

By instantiating in the correctness rule for loops, we get the following rule for proving the existence of winning strategies in two-person games.

Corollary 25.1 *Player has a winning strategy for game* while g do S od *under precondition* p, *provided that the following three conditions hold for some ranked collection of predicates* $\{r_w \mid w \in W\}$:

(i) $p \subseteq r$,

(ii) $(\forall w \in W \cdot r_w \, \{\!| \, S \, |\!\} \, r_{<w})$, *and*

(iii) $r \subseteq g$.

Proof By specializing q to false in Theorem 21.13 we get the following three conditions:

(i) $p \subseteq r$,
(ii) $(\forall w \in W \cdot g \cap r_w \, \{\!| \, S \, |\!\} \, r_{<w})$, and
(iii) $\neg g \cap r \subseteq$ false.

Straightforward simplification now shows that the third of these conditions is equivalent to $r \subseteq g$ and also to $(\forall w \in W \cdot r_w \subseteq g)$. This can then be used to simplify the second condition. $\square$

As before, the ranked predicate r_w is usually described as a conjunction of invariant I and a variant t, so that r_w is $I \wedge t = w$. Note that in the case $g = $ true, the third condition in Corollary 25.1 is trivially satisfied.

Winning Strategy for Nim

We now return to the example game of nim. For Player to be assured of winning this game, it is necessary that he always make the number x of matches remain satisfy the condition $x \bmod 3 = 1$. The strategy consists in always removing number of matches such that $x \bmod 3 = 1$ holds.

Assume that the precondition p is $x \bmod 3 \neq 1$ (since Player moves first, it necessary to guarantee that Player can actually establish $x \bmod 3 = 1$ in the move). The invariant I is simply p, and the variant t is x.

Since the guard of the iteration that represents nim was true, the third condition of Corollary 25.1 is trivially satisfied. Furthermore, the choice of invariant is that the first condition is also trivially satisfied. Thus, it remains only to prove second condition, i.e., that

$$x \bmod 3 \neq 1 \wedge x = n \; \{\!\{ S \}\!\} \; x \bmod 3 \neq 1 \wedge x < n$$

holds for an arbitrary natural number n, where $S = [x > 0] \; ; \{\text{Move}\} \; ;$ $0\} \; ; [\text{Move}].$

We prove $(*)$ by calculating $S.(x \bmod 3 \neq 1 \wedge x < n)$ in two parts. First, we the intermediate condition:

$$(\{x > 0\} \; ; [\text{Move}]).(x \bmod 3 \neq 1 \wedge x < n)$$
$$= \{\text{definitions}\}$$
$$x > 0 \wedge (\forall x' \cdot x - 2 \leq x' < x \Rightarrow x' \bmod 3 \neq 1 \wedge x' < n)$$
$$= \{\text{reduction, arithmetic}\}$$
$$x \bmod 3 = 1 \wedge x \leq n$$

This is the condition that Player should establish on every move.

Continuing, we find the precondition

$$([x > 0] \; ; \{\text{Move}\}).(x \bmod 3 = 1 \wedge x \leq n)$$
$$= \{\text{definitions}\}$$
$$x = 0 \vee (\exists x' \cdot x - 2 \leq x' < x \wedge x' \bmod 3 = 1 \wedge x' \leq n)$$
$$\supseteq \{\text{reduction, arithmetic}\}$$
$$x \bmod 3 \neq 1 \wedge x = n$$

Thus we have shown that $(*)$ holds, i.e., that the game has a winning strategy.

3 Extracting Winning Strategies

We have shown how to use loop reasoning with invariants to show that Player has a winning strategy in a two-person game. We shall now show how to extract a strategy for Player in the form of a nonangelic program statement (i.e., a program that plays the game, with the role of Player). The result of this operation is a new loop that still describes the same game as the old one, but with a more restricted set of alternatives for Player. We also consider refinements that improve Opponent's strategy; this is done by removing "bad" alternatives from the demonic nondeterminism that describes Opponent's moves.

First consider the simple case of the form while g do $\{Q\}$; $[R]$ od in which every round consists of a move by Player followed by a move by Opponent. Furthermore, assume that we have proved that there exists a winning strategy for this game with respect to precondition p, i.e., that the following total correctness assertion holds:

$$p \; \{\!| \; \text{while } g \text{ do } \{Q\} \, ; \, [R] \text{ od } |\!\} \; \text{false} \; .$$

If the role of Player was performed by an angel, then the game would always be won. However, if the role of Player is played by a human being (or a computer program), then the mere *existence* of a winning strategy is not enough, since the angelic update $\{Q\}$ does not tell us which alternative should be taken in order to win the game. Thus, we would want to replace $\{Q\}$ with a new angelic update $\{Q'\}$ such that Q' only gives alternatives that are guaranteed to lead eventually to a win for Player. This replacement is *not* a refinement of the original game, since it means replacing Q with a Q' such that $Q' \subseteq Q$ (and the angelic update is monotonic, not antimonotonic). However, we can still give a formal argument for the replacement.

Lemma 25.2   *Assume that the three conditions of Corollary 25.1 hold for the game* while g do $\{Q\}$; $[R]$ od *with precondition p and ranked predicates $\{r_w \mid w \in W\}$. Furthermore, assume that relation Q' satisfies the following three conditions:*

(i) $Q' \subseteq Q$,

(ii) $(\forall \sigma \cdot r.\sigma \;\Rightarrow\; Q'.\sigma \neq \emptyset)$, *and*

(iii) $(\forall w \in W \cdot r_w \subseteq ([Q'] \,;\, [R]).r_{<w})$.

Then the existence of a winning strategy for the game while g do $\{Q'\}$; $[R]$ od *with respect to precondition p can be proved using the same ranked predicates r_w.*

Proof   If we can show that $(\forall w \in W \cdot r_w \subseteq ([Q'] \,;\, [R]).(\bigcup v \in W \mid v < w \cdot r_v))$ holds, then all three conditions of Corollary 25.1 are satisfied, and we have proved the lemma. We first note that the third condition can be rewritten as

$$r_w.\sigma \;\Rightarrow\; (\forall \gamma \cdot Q'.\sigma.\gamma \;\Rightarrow\; [R].(\bigcup v \in W \mid v < w \cdot r_v).\gamma) \; . \qquad (*)$$

We have for arbitrary $w \in W$ and for arbitrary σ that

$$r_w.\sigma$$

$\Rightarrow$ {second assumption and (∗)}

$$Q'.\sigma \neq \emptyset \wedge (\forall \gamma \cdot Q'.\sigma.\gamma \Rightarrow [R].(\cup v \in W \mid v < w \cdot r_v).\gamma)$$

$\Rightarrow$ {simplify}

$$(\exists \gamma \cdot Q'.\sigma.\gamma \wedge [R].(\cup v \in W \mid v < w \cdot r_v).\gamma)$$

$\equiv$ {definitions}

$$(\{Q'\};[R]).(\cup v \in W \mid v < w \cdot r_v).\sigma$$

and the desired result follows by pointwise extension. □

The three conditions in Lemma 25.2 can be interpreted as follows. The first dition implies that the new game while g do $\{Q'\}$; $[R]$ od is compatible with old one, in the sense that the only difference is that Player has fewer alterna to choose from. In other words, Opponent is not disadvantaged if we replac by Q' in the game. The second condition tells us that under Q', Player always a move available. Thus, there is a proof of a winning strategy for the new ga Finally, the third condition implies that Q' only offers alternatives that pres the invariant, i.e., Q' offers only winning alternatives.

Whenever the conditions of Lemma 25.2 hold, we say that $\{r\};[Q']$ is a specific for a program that plays the role of Player in the game. The justification for is that whenever a ranked predicate r_w holds (and the setup is such that a ra predicate in fact always holds when Player is to move), any move permitte the relation Q' takes Player closer to a win. Later, in Section 25.4, we con the question of what Player should do in situations in which the invariant doe hold.

A Program for Nim

In order to apply the ideas above to the game of nim, we need a slight generaliza Consider the more general game while g do S od where the body S has the $[q]$; $\{Q\}$; S' for some statement S' containing only demonic updates and as This means we allow a check of whether Player has won before Player moves we also allow Opponent's move to be mixed with checks of whether Playe lost. The idea of Lemma 25.2 can be used in this situation also. The specific for Player's move is then $\{r \cap q\}$; $[Q']$, where the conditions on the new rel Q' are

(i) $Q' \subseteq Q$,

(ii) $(\forall \sigma \cdot r.\sigma \wedge q.\sigma \Rightarrow Q'.\sigma \neq \emptyset)$, and

(iii) $(\forall w \in W \cdot r_w \cap q \subseteq ([Q'];S').r_{<w})$

(the proof of this follows the proof of Lemma 25.2 exactly).

In the case of nim, we first compute the three conditions with Q as Move, q as $x > 0$, r_n as $x \bmod 3 \neq 1 \wedge x = n$, and S' as $\{x > 0\}$; [Move]. After some simplifications, we get

(i) $(\forall x\ x' \cdot Q'.x.x' \Rightarrow x - 2 \leq x' < x)$,

(ii) $(\forall x \cdot x \bmod 3 \neq 1 \wedge x > 0 \Rightarrow (\exists x' \cdot Q'.x.x'))$, and

(iii) $(\forall x\ x' \cdot x \bmod 3 \neq 1 \wedge x > 0 \wedge Q'.x.x' \Rightarrow x' > 0 \wedge x' \bmod 3 = 1)$.

The third condition was arrived at as follows:

$$(\forall n \cdot r_n \cap q \subseteq ([Q']\,;\,S').(\cup m \mid m < n \cdot r_m))$$

$\equiv$ {fill in current instances, pointwise extension}

$$(\forall n\ x \cdot x \bmod 3 \neq 1 \wedge x = n \wedge x > 0 \Rightarrow$$
$$([Q']\,;\,S').(x \bmod 3 \neq 1 \wedge x < n)$$

$\equiv$ {fill in current S', definitions}

$$(\forall n\ x \cdot x \bmod 3 \neq 1 \wedge x = n \wedge x > 0 \Rightarrow$$
$$(\forall x' \cdot Q'.x.x' \Rightarrow x' > 0 \wedge$$
$$(\forall x'' \cdot x' - 2 \leq x'' < x' \Rightarrow x'' \bmod 3 \neq 1 \wedge x'' < n)))$$

$\equiv$ {one-point rule, quantifier rules}

$$(\forall x\ x' \cdot x \bmod 3 \neq 1 \wedge x > 0 \wedge Q'.x.x' \Rightarrow x' > 0) \wedge$$
$$(\forall x\ x'\ x'' \cdot x \bmod 3 \neq 1 \wedge x > 0 \wedge Q'.x.x' \wedge x' - 2 \leq x'' < x' \Rightarrow$$
$$x'' \bmod 3 \neq 1 \wedge x'' < x)$$

$\equiv$ {simplify second conjunct}

$$(\forall x\ x' \cdot x \bmod 3 \neq 1 \wedge x > 0 \wedge Q'.x.x' \Rightarrow x' > 0) \wedge$$
$$(\forall x\ x' \cdot x \bmod 3 \neq 1 \wedge x > 0 \wedge Q'.x.x' \Rightarrow x' \bmod 3 = 1)$$

The easiest way to find a relation that satisfies these three conditions is to use the first and third conditions to find a candidate,

$$Q'.x.x' \equiv x - 2 \leq x' < x \wedge x' > 0 \wedge x' \bmod 3 = 1 ,$$

and to check that the second condition is satisfied:

$$x \bmod 3 \neq 1 \wedge x > 0 \Rightarrow$$
$$(\exists x' \cdot x - 2 \leq x' < x \wedge x' > 0 \wedge x' \bmod 3 = 1)$$

$\equiv$ {property of $\bmod$, predicate calculus}

$$(x \bmod 3 = 0 \wedge x > 0 \Rightarrow$$
$$(\exists x' \cdot x - 2 \leq x' < x \wedge x' > 0 \wedge x' \bmod 3 = 1)) \wedge$$
$$(x \bmod 3 = 2 \wedge x > 0 \Rightarrow$$
$$(\exists x' \cdot x - 2 \leq x' < x \wedge x' > 0 \wedge x' \bmod 3 = 1))$$
$$\equiv \{\text{quantifier rules}\}$$
$$(\exists x' \cdot x \bmod 3 = 0 \wedge x > 0 \Rightarrow$$
$$x - 2 \leq x' < x \wedge x' > 0 \wedge x' \bmod 3 = 1) \wedge$$
$$(\exists x' \cdot x \bmod 3 = 2 \wedge x > 0 \Rightarrow$$
$$x - 2 \leq x' < x \wedge x' > 0 \wedge x' \bmod 3 = 1)$$
$$\Leftarrow \{\text{use } x - 2 \text{ and } x - 1 \text{ as existential witnesses}\}$$
$$(x \bmod 3 = 0 \wedge x > 0 \Rightarrow$$
$$x - 2 < x \leq x \wedge x - 2 > 0 \wedge (x - 2) \bmod 3 = 1) \wedge$$
$$(x \bmod 3 = 2 \wedge x > 0 \Rightarrow$$
$$x - 1 < x \leq x + 1 \wedge x - 1 > 0 \wedge (x - 1) \bmod 3 = 1)$$
$$\equiv \{\text{arithmetic simplification}\}$$
$$\mathsf{T}$$

Thus we have shown that a specification for a Player program is the following:

$$\{x > 0 \wedge x \bmod 3 \neq 1\};$$
$$[x := x' \mid x - 2 \leq x' < x \wedge x' > 0 \wedge x' \bmod 3 = 1] \ .$$

We can develop this further (Exercise 25.1) by refining it into a conditional:

$$\text{if } x > 0 \wedge x \bmod 3 = 0 \to x := x - 2$$
$$[] \ x \bmod 3 = 2 \to x := x - 1$$
$$[] \ x \bmod 3 = 1 \to \text{abort}$$
$$\text{fi} \ .$$

This describes Player's winning strategy as follows: if $x \bmod 3$ is zero, then remove two matches; if it is 2, then remove one match. If $x \bmod 3 = 1$, then the strategy says simply to give up (since the statement aborts in this case). Giving up in this way is reasonable when playing against a perfect opponent, but in practice not a very useful strategy. Instead, we would want a strategy that might work if an imperfect opponent makes a mistake. Below, we shall see how refinement and heuristics together can be used to improve the strategies of both contestants in such a way.

4   Strategy Improvement

So far, we have considered two-person games as they would be played perfectly. We shall now consider how the notion of winning strategy and invariant can be used to describe strategy improvements that increase a contestant's chances of winning against an imperfect strategy. We first consider Player and then Opponent. To make the argument simple, we assume that the game has the simple form while g do $\{Q\}$; $[R]$ od, with precondition p and ranked predicates $\{r_w \mid w \in W\}$.

Improving Player's Strategy

Assume that we have found a specification $\{r\}$; $[Q']$ of Player's winning strategy, where $r = (\cup w \in W \cdot r_w)$. The initial assertion $\{r\}$ indicates that unless the invariant holds (which is a requirement for the strategy to work against a perfect opponent), Player may as well give up. It is now straightforward to show that an equally good strategy is specified by

if r then $[Q']$ else $[Q]$ fi

(by choosing Q as the specification in the case when the invariant does not hold, we permit any legal move). We can now continue refining this strategy, making the else branch more deterministic. In particular, we may try to find permitted moves that could give an imperfect opponent a chance to establish the invariant by mistake.

In the example of nim, a first improvement to Player's strategy gives us

if $x > 0 \land x \bmod 3 = 0 \rightarrow x := x - 2$
$[]\ x \bmod 3 = 2 \rightarrow x := x - 1$
$[]\ x \bmod 3 = 1 \rightarrow [x := x' \mid x - 2 \leq x' < x]$
fi .

Next, we note that Player cannot force Opponent to establish the invariant $x \bmod 3 \neq 1$ unless it holds when Player is to move. Thus, we cannot essentially improve Player's strategy further. It could be argued that the best way of implementing the nondeterministic choice in the third branch of the conditional is by randomly choosing to remove either one or two matches, since this makes it hard for an opponent to figure out what strategy is used.

Improving Opponent's Strategy

Opponent's strategy can be analyzed in the same way as Player's. The demonic update $[R]$ is a specification, and by making it more deterministic, Opponent can discard bad choices. In particular, Opponent should try to avoid establishing the invariant p, if possible. Thus, it is desirable to find a total relation $R' \subseteq R$ such

that $r \subseteq [R'].(\neg p)$ for as weak a predicate r as possible. This guarantees tha
Player makes a move that establishes r, then Opponent can break the invariar
least temporarily.

In the example of nim, this idea is used as follows. The invariant p is $x \bmod 3$
and the specification for Opponent's move is $[x := x' \mid x - 2 \leq x' < x]$. This
be made more deterministic by changing it to $x := x - 1$ (provided that $x > 0$
$x := x - 2$ (provided that $x > 1$). The assignment $x := x - 1$ establishes $\neg$
$x \bmod 3 = 2$, and the assignment $x := x - 2$ establishes $\neg p$ if $x \bmod 3 = 0$. 1
an improved strategy for Opponent is

> if $x > 0 \wedge x \bmod 3 = 0 \to x := x - 2$
> $[] \; x \bmod 3 = 2 \to x := x - 1$
> $[] \; x \bmod 3 = 1 \to [x := x' \mid x - 2 \leq x' < x]$
> fi .

It turns out that we get exactly the same strategy as for Player. This is not surpris
since nim is a symmetric game; the rules are the same for both contestants.

25.5   Summary and Discussion

We have shown how to formalize two-person games as statements in the refiner
calculus and how to use standard correctness-proof techniques, with invariants
termination functions, to prove the existence of a winning strategy in the ga
Furthermore, we have shown how to use refinement techniques to derive an a
game-playing program from an original abstract description of the game.

The idea of using predicate-transformer semantics for describing two-person ga
was introduced by Back and von Wright in [32]. The correspondence between
correctness reasoning and winning strategy extends the applicability of the p
cate transformer and refinement calculus framework quite far outside its ori
area of application.

25.6   Exercises

25.1   Prove the refinement equivalence

> $\{x > 0 \wedge x \bmod 3 \neq 1\};$
> $[x := x' \mid x - 2 \leq x' < x \wedge x' > 0 \wedge x' \bmod 3 = 1]$

$$=$$
if $x > 0 \wedge x \bmod 3 = 0 \rightarrow x := x - 2$
[] $x \bmod 3 = 2 \rightarrow x := x - 1$
[] $x \bmod 3 = 1 \rightarrow$ abort
fi .

25.2   There is a dual version of nim in which the winner is the one who takes the last match. Describe this game using the statement notation (when Player can move first) and investigate under what precondition there is a winning strategy.

25.3   Tick-tack-toe (or noughts and crosses) on a 3×3 board can be represented using three sets A, B, and C of natural numbers $1, \ldots, 9$. The squares on the board are numbered so that every line-of-three adds up to 15 (i.e., as in a magic square). The set A contains the numbers of the empty squares, B contains the numbers of the squares where Player has placed a marker, and C contains the numbers of the squares where Opponent has placed a marker. A move consists in removing one number from A and adding it to B (Player's move) or C (Opponent's move). The game ends when either A is empty (a draw) or when either B or C contains three numbers that add up to 15. Describe this game using statement syntax and outline a proof that if Player starts by placing a cross in the center square and Opponent then places one in a corner square, then Player has a winning strategy.

Part IV

Statement Subclasses

In Chapter 16, we showed how the homomorphism properties give rise to a number of subcategories of statements. In this chapter, we study the most interesting of these subcategories in more detail and show how they can be expressed with a subset of the statement constructors. We concentrate on universally conjunctive and conjunctive statements, on disjunctive statements, on (partial and total) functional statements, and on continuous statements.

For each of these subcategories, we also give a normal form for statements. We will later see that these normal forms correspond to specification statements in the different statement subclasses. Because they are normal forms, any requirement can be expressed as a specification statement of this kind. On the other hand, these normal forms contain a minimum of information about how the statement would actually be implemented.

Universally Conjunctive Predicate Transformers

The general structure of $\text{Ctran}^\top$, the universally conjunctive predicate transformers, is summarized in the following lemma, which we state without proof (the proof is straightforward).

eorem 26.1 *For arbitrary Σ and Γ, $\text{Ctran}^\top(\Sigma, \Gamma)$ is a complete lattice. Meets in $\text{Ctran}^\top(\Sigma, \Gamma)$ give the same result as in $\text{Mtran}(\Sigma, \Gamma)$, but joins generally do not. The top element of $\text{Ctran}^\top(\Sigma, \Gamma)$ is* magic, *and the bottom element is the arbitrary demonic update* chaos = [True].

From Theorems 16.1 and 16.2 we see that guards, functional updates, and dem
updates are always universally conjunctive and that furthermore, sequential
position and meets preserve universal conjunctivity. This means that if we res
ourselves to these constructs, then we only generate predicate transformers tha
universally conjunctive. Hence, any statement generated by the following sy
is universally conjunctive:

$$S ::= [g] \mid \langle f \rangle \mid [R] \mid S_1 ; S_2 \mid (\sqcap i \in I \cdot S_i) .$$

Of the derived constructs, the deterministic conditional, ν-recursion, and ν
iteration also preserve universal conjunctivity, so they can also be used in a synt
universally conjunctive statements. As the normal form theorem below shows
universally conjunctive predicate transformer that can be expressed in higher-
logic can be expressed as a universally conjunctive statement.

Normal Form

The normal form theorem for Mtran (Theorem 13.10) showed that every mono
predicate transformer can be written as a sequential composition of an angelic
a demonic update. This result has a counterpart in Ctran$^\top$:

Theorem 26.2 *Let S be an arbitrary universally conjunctive predicate transformer. Then
exists a unique relation R such that*

$$S = [R] .$$

Proof We first note that for universally conjunctive S, the following holds f
predicates q and all states σ:

$$S.q.\sigma \equiv (\sqcap p \mid S.p.\sigma \cdot p) \subseteq q .$$

The proof of this is left to the reader as an exercise (Exercise 26.2).

Now set $R.\sigma = (\sqcap p \mid S.p.\sigma \cdot p)$. Then

$\quad [R].q.\sigma$
$\equiv$ {definition}
$\quad (\forall \sigma' \cdot (\sqcap p \mid S.p.\sigma \cdot p).\sigma' \Rightarrow q.\sigma')$
$\equiv$ {pointwise extension}
$\quad (\sqcap p \mid S.p.\sigma \cdot p) \subseteq q$
$\equiv$ {($*$) above}
$\quad S.q.\sigma$

which shows that $[R] = S$. For uniqueness we have

$$[R] = [R']$$
$$\equiv \{\text{antisymmetry}\}$$
$$[R] \sqsubseteq [R'] \wedge [R] \sqsupseteq [R']$$
$$\equiv \{\text{order embedding}\}$$
$$R \supseteq R' \wedge R \subseteq R'$$
$$\equiv \{\text{antisymmetry}\}$$
$$R = R'$$

□

Theorem 26.2 shows that if we want to prove some general property about universally conjunctive predicate transformers, it is sufficient that we prove it for predicate transformers of the form $[R]$, where R is an arbitrary relation. From the homomorphism properties of the demonic choice constructor, we see that the relation space is in fact embedded inside the predicate transformer space as universally conjunctive predicate transformers.

2   Conjunctive Predicate Transformers

By adding the possibility of nontermination, we move from universally conjunctive predicate transformers to conjunctive ones. We shall now investigate the conjunctive predicate transformers Ctran, which form a framework for demonically nondeterministic statements that can be both miraculous and nonterminating.

Theorem 26.3   *For arbitrary Σ and Γ, Ctran(Σ, Γ) is a complete lattice. Meets in* Ctran(Σ, Γ) *give the same result as in* Mtran(Σ, Γ), *but joins generally do not. The top element of* Ctran(Σ, Γ) *is* magic, *and the bottom element is* abort.

The assert, guard, functional update, and demonic update are conjunctive. Furthermore, sequential composition and meet preserve conjunctivity. Only angelic update and join break this property. The *conjunctive basic statements* are generated by the following syntax:

$$S \quad ::= \quad \{g\} \mid [g] \mid \langle f \rangle \mid [R] \mid S_1 \,;\, S_2 \mid (\sqcap i \in I \cdot S_i) \ .$$

Compared with the universally conjunctive statements, the only addition is the assert statement. Again, the normal form theorem below states that any conjunctive predicate transformer that can be expressed in higher-order logic can also be expressed as a conjunctive statement.

Of the derived statements, conditionals, fixed points, iterations and loops all preserve conjunctivity. This means that we can use a very broad range of predicate

transformer constructors and still stay within the realm of conjunctive predi
transformers.

Normal Form

The normal form theorem for universally conjunctive predicate transformers
be generalized to Ctran:

Theorem 26.4 *Let S be an arbitrary conjunctive predicate transformer. Then there exists a uni*
predicate p and a relation R such that

$$S = \{p\} ; [R] .$$

Proof Recall that the termination guard of S is $t.S = S.\text{true}$. It is easily seen
we must choose $p = t.S$:

$$S = \{p\} ; [R]$$
$\Rightarrow$ {congruence, definitions}
$$S.\text{true} = p \cap [R].\text{true}$$
$\equiv$ {demonic update is terminating}
$$S.\text{true} = p \cap \text{true}$$
$\equiv$ {predicate calculus, definition of $t.S$}
$$t.S = p$$

Then $[t.S] ; S$ is universally conjunctive (Exercise 26.1), and we know from
proof of Theorem 26.2 that $[t.S] ; S = [R]$ where $R.\sigma = (\cap p \mid ([t.S] ; S).p.\sigma$
Then

$$(\{t.S\} ; [R]).q$$
$=$ {definition}
$$(\{t.S\} ; [t.S] ; S).q$$
$=$ {definitions}
$$t.S \cap (\neg t.S \cup S.q)$$
$=$ {general lattice property}
$$t.S \cap S.q$$
$=$ {definition of $t.S$}
$$S.\text{true} \cap S.q$$
$=$ {S monotonic}
$$S.q$$

and the proof is finished. $\square$

Theorem 26.4 can in fact be strengthened somewhat; it is possible to prove that if we require that dom.$R \subseteq p$, then R is uniquely determined by S. Similarly, R is uniquely defined if we require that $(\forall \sigma \ \gamma \cdot \neg p.\sigma \Rightarrow R.\sigma.\gamma)$. In the first case, the condition means that the relation R must be undefined outside the domain of termination for S, while the second case implies that R must map any state outside the domain of termination for S to all possible final states.

Theorem 26.4 shows that if we want to prove some general property about conjunctive predicate transformers, it is sufficient that we prove it for predicate transformers of the form $\{p\} ; [R]$, where p and R are arbitrary. We showed earlier that normal forms like this can be taken as basic *specification statements* in a systematic program refinement technique.

3   Disjunctive Predicate Transformers

Since disjunctivity is dual to conjunctivity, and universal disjunctivity is dual to universal conjunctivity, we can transform the above results immediately to corresponding results about disjunctive and universally disjunctive predicate transformers. Let us first consider Dtran$^\perp$, the universally disjunctive predicate transformers. Duality and Theorem 26.1 then give the following result.

Corollary 26.5   *For arbitrary Σ and Γ, Dtran$^\perp(\Sigma, \Gamma)$ is a complete lattice. Joins in Dtran$^\perp(\Sigma, \Gamma)$ give the same result as in Mtran(Σ, Γ), but meets generally do not. The bottom element of Dtran$^\perp(\Sigma, \Gamma)$ is abort, and the top element is the arbitrary angelic update choose $= \{$True$\}$.*

The previous results show that assert, functional update, and angelic update are universally disjunctive, and that sequential composition and joins preserve universal disjunctivity. The *basic universally disjunctive statements* are thus defined by the following syntax:

$$S \ ::= \ \{g\} \mid \langle f \rangle \mid \{R\} \mid S_1 ; S_2 \mid (\sqcup i \in I \cdot S_i) \ .$$

In addition to this, the deterministic conditional, (μ-) recursion, and while loops preserve universal disjunctivity, so they can also be used to construct universally disjunctive statements.

The normal form theorem for universally disjunctive predicate transformers is dual to the one for universally conjunctive predicate transformers. It shows that the universally disjunctive statements are sufficient to express the universally disjunctive predicate transformers.

Corollary 26.6   *Let S be an arbitrary universally disjunctive predicate transformer. Then there is a unique relation R such that*

$$S \ = \ \{R\} \ .$$

This shows that the angelic update is a normal form for universally disjun~~c~~ predicate transformers and that the relation space is embedded inside the predi~~c~~ transformer space as universally disjunctive predicate transformers.

Exactly as for conjunctivity, relaxing universal disjunctivity to plain disjuncti~~v~~ means we get a slightly larger collection of predicate transformers, Dtran, w~~.~~ has properties dual to those of Ctran.

Corollary 26.7   *For arbitrary Σ and Γ,* Dtran(Σ, Γ) *is a complete lattice. Joins in* Dtran(Σ, Γ) *the same result as in* Mtran(Σ, Γ), *but meets generally do not. The bottom ele~~ment~~ of* Dtran(Σ, Γ) *is* abort, *and the top element is* magic.

Next, Theorem 26.4 immediately has the following dual:

Corollary 26.8   *Let S be an arbitrary disjunctive predicate transformer. Then there exists a un~~ique~~ predicate p and a relation R such that*

$$S = [p];\{R\} \ .$$

Thus, the form $[p];\{R\}$ is a *normal form for disjunctive predicate transformers.* disjunctive statements are defined in the obvious way, by adding guard statem~~ents~~ to the syntax of universally disjunctive statements.

26.4   Functional Predicate Transformers

Recall that a predicate transformer that is both conjunctive and disjunctive is c~~alled~~ *functional* (it could also be called *deterministic*, since the normal form theor~~ems~~ below show that if such a statement terminates normally when executed in s~~ome~~ initial state, then it has a uniquely defined final state). We shall now briefly con~~sider~~ different kinds of functional predicate transformers.

Total Functional Predicate Transformers

Predicate transformers that are both universally conjunctive and universally ~~dis~~junctive are called *total functional*. We call these TFtran $=$ Ftran$_{\perp\top}$. The refine~~ment~~ ordering for TFtran reduces to equality.

Lemma 26.9   *For arbitrary Σ and Γ,* TFtran(Σ, Γ) *is discretely ordered.*

The fact that $S \sqsubseteq S'$ holds if and only if $S = S'$ when S and S' are elemen~~ts of~~ TFtran is a direct consequence of the following normal form theorem. It jus~~tifies~~ calling the predicate transformers in TFtran "total functional."

Theorem 26.10   *If the predicate transformer S is both universally conjunctive and univer~~sally~~ disjunctive, then there is a unique state transformer f such that $S = \langle f \rangle$.*

We do not prove this lemma separately; it is a consequence of Theorem 26.14 below. Note that Theorem 26.10 shows that the functional update is a normal form for total functional predicate transformers.

Of the basic predicate transformer constructs, only functional update and sequential composition give us both universal conjunctivity and universal disjunctivity. In addition to this, conditional composition also preserves both universal conjunctivity and universal disjunctivity. Thus the following syntax generates a language of *functional statements*:

$$S \ ::= \ \langle f \rangle \mid S_1 \ ; S_2 \mid \text{if } g \text{ then } S_1 \text{ else } S_2 \text{ fi} \ .$$

Partial Functional Predicate Transformers

The collection TFtran is a very restricted class of predicate transformers. It permits no recursive or iterative construct. This is remedied by moving to a slightly larger class of predicate transformers. A predicate transformer that is conjunctive and universally disjunctive is called *partial functional*. We use the name PFtran for the collection of all partial functional predicate transformers (so PFtran = Ftran$^{\perp}$).

Theorem 26.11   *For arbitrary Σ and Γ, PFtran(Σ, Γ) is a complete meet semilattice with bottom element* abort.

Exactly as for the classes of predicate transformers treated earlier, we can give a normal form for the partial functional case.

Theorem 26.12   *If the predicate transformer S is conjunctive and universally disjunctive, then there is a unique predicate p and a state function f such that $S = \{p\} \ ; \langle f \rangle$.*

We do not prove this lemma separately, since it is a consequence of Theorem 26.14 below. Theorem 26.12 shows that $\{p\} \ ; \langle f \rangle$ is a *normal form for partial functional predicate transformers*. From the homomorphism properties we see that partial functional predicate transformers are generated by asserts, functional updates, and sequential composition. In addition to this, deterministic conditionals and while loops also preserve conjunctivity and universal disjunctivity and can thus be used to build partial functional statements. Thus a language of *partial functional statements* is generated by the following syntax:

$$S \ ::= \ \{g\} \mid \langle f \rangle \mid S_1 \ ; S_2 \mid \text{if } g \text{ then } S_1 \text{ else } S_2 \text{ fi} \mid \text{while } g \text{ do } S \text{ od} \ .$$

Functional Predicate Transformers

We now consider Ftran, the collection of all conjunctive and disjunctive predicate transformers. As noted above, such predicate transformers are called *functional*.

Theorem 26.13   *For arbitrary Σ and Γ, Ftran(Σ, Γ) is a complete lattice, but neither meets nor joins generally give the same result as in* Mtran. *The bottom element of* Ftran(Σ, Γ) *is* abort, *and the top element is* magic.

The normal form for Ftran uses asserts, guards, and functional updates. This juscalling these predicate transformers functional; they can be expressed without wnondeterministic constructs such as relational updates, meets, and joins.

Theorem 26.14   *Assume that S is a functional predicate transformer. Then there are predica*
and q and a state transformer f such that

$$S = [q] ; \{p\} ; \langle f \rangle .$$

Proof   Assume that S is both conjunctive and disjunctive. By earlier normal
theorems, we know that S can be written in the form $\{p\} ; [P]$ but also in the
$[q] ; \{Q\}$, for predicates p and q and relations P and Q such that

$$(\forall \sigma \; \gamma \cdot Q.\sigma.\gamma \Rightarrow q.\sigma)$$

(i.e., dom.$Q \subseteq q$). The equality $\{p\} ; [P] = [q] ; \{Q\}$ can be written as follow

$$(\forall r \; \sigma \cdot p.\sigma \wedge P.\sigma \subseteq r \equiv \neg q.\sigma \vee (Q.\sigma \cap r \neq \emptyset)) .$$

We first show that Q must be deterministic:

$$Q.\sigma.\gamma \wedge Q.\sigma.\gamma'$$
$\Rightarrow$ {assumption $(*)$}
$$q.\sigma \wedge Q.\sigma.\gamma \wedge Q.\sigma.\gamma'$$
$\Rightarrow$ {assumption $(**)$}
$$q.\sigma \wedge p.\sigma \wedge P.\sigma \subseteq \{\gamma\} \wedge P.\sigma \subseteq \{\gamma'\}$$
$\Rightarrow$ {set theory}
$$q.\sigma \wedge p.\sigma \wedge (P.\sigma = \emptyset \vee \gamma = \gamma')$$
$\Rightarrow$ {$q.\sigma \wedge p.\sigma \wedge P.\sigma = \emptyset$ would contradict $(**)$ with $r := \emptyset$}
$$q.\sigma \wedge p.\sigma \wedge \gamma = \gamma'$$

One can now show that the determinism of Q implies that $\{Q\} = \{\lambda \sigma \cdot Q$
$\emptyset\} ; \langle \lambda \sigma \cdot \varepsilon \gamma \cdot Q.\sigma.\gamma \rangle$ (Exercise 26.5). Thus S can be rewritten in the desired f
□

It should be noted that the normal form in Theorem 26.14 is not the only pos
one. We could as well use $\{p\} ; [q] ; \langle f \rangle$ as the normal form (this follows e
from the general rule for reversing the order of a guard and an assert: $[q] ; \{$
$\{\neg q \cup p\} ; [q]$).

Note also that in the normal form $[q] ; \{p\} ; \langle f \rangle$, the predicate q is unique,
$\neg S.$false, while p and f are not. However, they are restricted so that $S.$tu
$\neg S.$false $\subseteq p \subseteq S.$true and so that f is uniquely defined on $S.$true $\cap \neg S.$fals

This completes our investigation of the statement subclasses characterized b
four basic lattice-theoretic homomorphism properties.

5 Continuous Predicate Transformers

Let us finally consider the subclass of monotonic predicate transformers that is formed by the continuity restriction. Continuity is also a kind of homomorphism property, as it requires that limits of directed sets be preserved by the predicate transformer.

We let $\Sigma \mapsto_c \Gamma$ as before stand for the continuous predicate transformers in $\Sigma \mapsto \Gamma$. Let CNtran$_X$ denote the category with types in X as objects and the continuous predicate transformers as morphisms, i.e., CNtran$(\Sigma, \Gamma) = \Sigma \to_c \Gamma$. Basic properties of CNtran are collected in the following lemma:

Theorem 26.15 CNtran *is a category; it is a subcategory of* Mtran. *For each pair of state spaces* Σ *and* Γ, CNtran(Σ, Γ) *is a complete lattice, but meets in* CNtran(Σ, Γ) *generally do not give the same results as in* Mtran(Σ, Γ). CNtran(Σ, Γ) *has bottom element* abort *and top element* magic.

The normal form theorem for monotonic predicate transformers has a counterpart in CNtran, in the situation where the underlying state spaces are countable.

Theorem 26.16 *Let* $S : \Sigma \mapsto \Gamma$ *be an arbitrary continuous predicate transformer, where* Σ *and* Γ *are countable state spaces. Then there exists a relation* P *and a total and image-finite relation* Q *such that* $S = \{P\} ; [Q]$.

Proof The proof rests on the fact that a continuous function $f : \mathcal{P}(A) \to \mathcal{P}(B)$ (where A and B are countable) is uniquely defined by its behavior on the finite subsets of A (the proof of this fact is beyond the scope of this book).

Assume that a continuous $S \in$ Ptran(Σ, Γ) is given. The construction is then almost as in the normal form theorem for monotonic predicate transformers (Theorem 13.10). However, now we consider an intermediate state space consisting of all finite nonempty subsets of Γ (to be really precise, we would have to construct a new type that is isomorphic to this set of subsets, but that is a complication without real significance). One can then define P and Q exactly as in the proof of Theorem 13.10 and show that $S = \{P\} ; [Q]$ (see also the proof of Theorem 26.18 below). □

Thus $\{P\} ; [Q]$, where Q is total and image-finite, is a *normal form for continuous predicate transformers*. Furthermore, for $S : \Sigma \mapsto \Sigma$ with Σ countably infinite it can be shown that both P and Q can be chosen to be relations over Σ (this is because the finite subsets of a countably infinite set can be mapped bijectively into the set itself).

Combining Continuity and Conjunctivity

In addition to the continuous predicate transformers, we can consider subalgebras that satisfy a combination of continuity and some other homomorphism property.

A combination that is particularly useful is that of conjunctivity and contin
We let CCNtran stand for the collection of all conjunctive and continuous pred
transformers.

Lemma 26.17   CCNtran *is a category; it is a subcategory of* Mtran. *For each pair of state sp*
Σ *and* Γ, CCNtran(Σ, Γ) *is a meet semilattice, and it has bottom element ab*
In fact, any continuous and conjunctive predicate transformers can be written
sequential composition of an assert and a continuous demonic update:

Theorem 26.18   *Let* $S : \Sigma \mapsto \Gamma$ *be an arbitrary continuous conjunctive predicate transfor*
where Σ *and* Γ *are countable state spaces. Then there exists a unique predic*
and a total and image-finite relation R *such that* $S = \{p\} ; [R]$.

Proof   Assume that predicate transformer S is continuous and conjunctive.
construction is almost as in the normal form theorem for conjunctive pred
transformers (Theorem 26.4). We set $p = t.S$ and

$$R.\sigma = \begin{cases} (\cap q \mid S.q.\sigma \cdot q) & \text{if } t.S.\sigma, \\ \{\epsilon\gamma \cdot T\} & \text{otherwise} \end{cases}$$

(the set $\{\epsilon\gamma \cdot T\}$ is a singleton containing some unspecified state $\gamma \in \Gamma$). The
argument as in the proof of Theorem 26.4 now shows that $S = \{t.S\} ; [R]$. Thu
have only to show that $R.\sigma$ is nonempty and finite. This is obviously true if $\neg$ t
since $R.\sigma$ in that case is a singleton. Now assume t.$S.\sigma$. Then $S.\text{true}.\sigma \equiv T$, s
set $\{p \mid S.p.\sigma\}$ is nonempty. Furthermore, we get

$\quad S.(R.\sigma).\sigma$

$\equiv \{S$ conjunctive, definition of $R\}$

$\quad (\forall q \mid S.q.\sigma \cdot S.q.\sigma)$

$\equiv \{$trivial quantification$\}$

$\quad$ T

Since continuity implies $S.\text{false} = \text{false}$, this shows that $R.\sigma$ must be nonem

Finally, we prove that $R.\sigma$ is finite by contradiction. Let C be the collecti
all finite subsets (predicates) of $R.\sigma$. Note that C, ordered by set inclusion
directed set. Assume that $R.\sigma$ is infinite. Then

$\quad (\lim q \in C \cdot S.q).\sigma$

$\equiv \{$pointwise extension$\}$

$\quad (\exists q \in C \cdot S.q.\sigma)$

$\equiv \{R.\sigma$ infinite implies $S.q.\sigma \equiv F$ for all $q \in C\}$

$\quad$ F

However, we have

$$S.(\lim q \in C \cdot q).\sigma$$
$$\equiv \{\text{the limit of } C \text{ is } R.\sigma, \text{ because of countability}\}$$
$$S.(R.\sigma).\sigma$$
$$\equiv \{\text{above}\}$$
$$\top$$

which contradicts continuity of S. Thus $R.\sigma$ must be finite. $\square$

This theorem shows that $\{p\}$; $[R]$ (where R is total and image-finite) is a normal form for conjunctive continuous predicate transformers.

5 Homomorphic Choice Semantics

The choice semantics for statements that we described earlier showed how predicate transformers can be identified with generalized state transformers that map initial states to sets of postconditions. We shall now consider how the homomorphism properties of predicate transformers translate into properties of state transformers. Each homomorphism property of a basic predicate transformer construct can be translated into a property of the corresponding generalized state transformer. Thus to every subclass of statements corresponds a subclass of generalized state transformers.

Our aim here is to show how traditional denotational semantics of subclasses of statements can be extracted from the choice semantics in a simple way, using the state transformer characterizations of homomorphism properties. In this way, we get a unification of programming logics, including both backward predicate transformer semantics and forward state transformer and relational semantics, and in which the more traditional semantics can be identified as special cases.

Homomorphism Properties

Recall the function that maps any predicate transformer $S : \Sigma \mapsto \Gamma$ to a generalized state transformer $\overline{S} : \Sigma \to \mathcal{P}(\mathcal{P}(\Gamma))$, defined by

$$\overline{S}.\sigma = \{q \mid S.q.\sigma\} .$$

Thus $\overline{S}$ maps initial state σ to the set of all postconditions that S is guaranteed to establish. We shall now consider how homomorphism properties translate into generalized state transformer equivalents. We have already noted in Chapter 14 that monotonicity of S corresponds to upward closedness of $\hat{S}$.

We first consider strictness and termination.

Theorem 26.19   *Let S be an arbitrary statement. Then*

(a) *S strict* $\equiv (\forall \sigma \cdot \emptyset \notin \overline{S}.\sigma)$.

(b) *S terminating* $\equiv (\forall \sigma \cdot \overline{S}.\sigma \neq \emptyset)$.

Proof   We show the proof of part (b), which is the more difficult part. Let arbitrary. We have

$$S \text{ terminating}$$
$$\equiv \{\text{definition of termination}\}$$
$$(\forall \sigma \cdot S.\text{true}.\sigma)$$
$$\equiv \{\text{definition of } \overline{S}\}$$
$$(\forall \sigma \cdot \text{true} \in \overline{S}.\sigma)$$
$$\equiv \{\Rightarrow \text{ is trivial}; \Leftarrow \text{ since } \overline{S}.\sigma \text{ is upward closed}\}$$
$$(\forall \sigma \cdot \overline{S}.\sigma \neq \emptyset)$$

and the proof is finished. $\square$

Note how the three basic cases for initial state σ (abortion, normal termina miracle) are reflected in the choice semantics. Statement S aborts if $\overline{S}.\sigma = \emptyset$ miraculous if $\emptyset \in \overline{S}.\sigma$, and it terminates normally otherwise.

We next show that conjunctivity corresponds to intersection closedness. Du then gives a characterization of disjunctivity.

Theorem 26.20   *Predicate transformer S is conjunctive if and only if*

$$(\forall i \in I \cdot p_i \in \overline{S}.\sigma) \equiv (\cap i \in I \cdot p_i) \in \overline{S}.\sigma$$

holds for an arbitrary nonempty collection $\{p_i \mid i \in I\}$ *of predicates and fo states* σ. *Dually, S is disjunctive if and only if*

$$(\exists i \in I \cdot p_i \in \overline{S}.\sigma) \equiv (\cup i \in I \cdot p_i) \in \overline{S}.\sigma$$

holds for an arbitrary nonempty collection $\{p_i \mid i \in I\}$ *of predicates and fo states* σ.

Proof   First assume that S is conjunctive and let the state σ and a none collection $\{p_i \mid i \in I\}$ of predicates be given. Then

$$S \text{ conjunctive}, I \neq \emptyset$$
$$\vdash (\cap i \in I \cdot p_i) \in \overline{S}.\sigma$$
$$\equiv \{\text{definition of } \overline{S}\}$$
$$S.(\cap i \in I \cdot p_i).\sigma$$
$$\equiv \{S \text{ conjunctive, pointwise extension}\}$$
$$(\forall i \in I \cdot S.p_i.\sigma)$$

$\equiv$ {definition of $\overline{S}$}

$\quad (\forall i \in I \cdot p_i \in \overline{S}.\sigma)$

Now assume that $(\cap i \in I \cdot p_i) \in \overline{S}.\sigma \equiv (\forall i \in I \cdot p_i \in \overline{S}.\sigma)$ holds for an arbitrary state σ and an arbitrary nonempty collection $\{p_i \mid i \in I\}$ of predicates. Then, for $I \neq \emptyset$,

$\quad S.(\cap i \in I \cdot p_i).\sigma$

$\equiv$ {definition of $\overline{S}$}

$\quad (\cap i \in I \cdot p_i) \in \overline{S}.\sigma$

$\equiv$ {assumption}

$\quad (\forall i \in I \cdot p_i \in \overline{S}.\sigma)$

$\equiv$ {definition of $\overline{S}$}

$\quad (\forall i \in I \cdot S.p_i.\sigma)$

$\equiv$ {pointwise extension}

$\quad (\cap i \in I \cdot S.p_i).\sigma$

so S is conjunctive. The proof for disjunctivity is dual. $\square$

Choice Semantics for Universally Conjunctive Statements

The choice semantics maps statement S into the rich structure Stran(Σ, Γ). We will now show that for subclasses of Mtran it is possible to map S to an alternative $\widetilde{S}$ so that intuition behind the choice semantics is preserved but the structure that S is mapped into is simpler.

If $S \in$ Mtran(Σ, Γ) is universally conjunctive, then for an arbitrary state σ the set $(\cap p \mid S.p.\sigma \cdot p)$ is the unique smallest element in $\overline{S}.\sigma$ (Theorem 26.19). Furthermore, upward closure guarantees that the intersection is nonempty, and Theorem 26.20 guarantees that it is an element of $\overline{S}.\sigma$. Thus $\overline{S}.\sigma$ is completely characterized by this element. For a conjunctive statement S we define

$$\widetilde{S}.\sigma \triangleq (\cap p \mid S.p.\sigma \cdot p) .$$

This makes $\widetilde{S}$ a function in $\Sigma \to \mathcal{P}(\Gamma)$. Note that this interprets universally conjunctive statements directly as relations; setting $S = [R]$ we immediately have

$$\gamma \in [\widetilde{R}].\sigma \equiv R.\sigma.\gamma .$$

Exactly as for the general choice semantics, we have operators corresponding to the different operators on predicate transformers. For example, demonic choice on Ctran$^\top$ corresponds to pointwise union, while refinement corresponds to pointwise reverse subset inclusion:

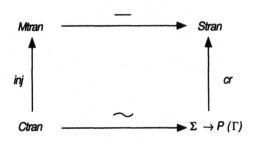

FIGURE 26.1. Semantics for universally
conjunctive statements

$$S_1 \widetilde{\sqcap} S_2.\sigma = \widetilde{S}_1.\sigma \cup \widetilde{S}_2.\sigma ,$$
$$S \sqsubseteq S' \equiv (\forall \sigma \cdot \widetilde{S}'.\sigma \subseteq \widetilde{S}.\sigma) .$$

The relationship between the semantic functions and the four domains invo
(Mtran, Ctran$^\top$, Stran, and $\Sigma \to \mathcal{P}(\Gamma)$) can be described nicely if we first de
the function cr that recovers $\overline{S}$ from $\widetilde{S}$:

$$\text{cr}.T.\sigma = \{q \mid T.\sigma \subseteq q\}$$

for $T : \Sigma \to \mathcal{P}(\Gamma)$, so that $\text{cr}.(\widetilde{S}) = \overline{S}$. The commuting diagram in Figure 26.1
shows the situation, where inj is the injection function that maps any $S \in$ Ct
to the same predicate transformer in Mtran.

The functions involved are also homomorphic. For example, for arbitrary S_1
S_2 in Ctran$^\top$ we have

$$\text{cr}.(\lambda\sigma \cdot \widetilde{S}_1.\sigma \cup \widetilde{S}_2.\sigma) = (\lambda\sigma \cdot \overline{\text{inj}.S_1.\sigma} \cap \overline{\text{inj}.S_2.\sigma})$$

(recall that $\overline{S_1 \sqcap S_2} = (\lambda\sigma \cdot \overline{S}_1.\sigma \cap \overline{S}_2.\sigma)$). Similar results can be shown for e
operators; this is pursued in Exercise 26.7.

Conjunctivity

If S is conjunctive but possibly nonterminating, we have only to define $\widetilde{S}$ sli
differently, compared with the universally conjunctive case. Now $\widetilde{S}$ is a fun
in $\Sigma \to \{\bot\} + \mathcal{P}(\Gamma)$ (thus we have added an artificial bottom element $\bot$ t
state space), and

$$\widetilde{S}.\sigma \overset{\wedge}{=} \begin{cases} \bot & \text{if } \overline{S}.\sigma = \emptyset, \\ (\sqcap p \mid S.p.\sigma \cdot p) & \text{otherwise.} \end{cases}$$

In fact, $\overline{S}$ then gives the relational interpretation often used to justify weakest precondition semantics. Again, $\overline{S}$ can immediately be recovered from $\widetilde{S}$, and the refinement relation has the following characterization:

$$S \sqsubseteq S' \;\equiv\; (\forall \sigma \cdot \widetilde{S}.\sigma = \bot \lor \widetilde{S'}.\sigma \subseteq \widetilde{S}.\sigma) \;.$$

This is the *Smyth powerdomain ordering* on $\{\bot\} + \mathcal{P}(\Sigma)$. Exercise 26.8 elaborates further on the alternative choice semantics for conjunctive statements.

Disjunctivity

For disjunctive predicate transformers, the results are dual to those for the conjunctive case, so we outline only the universally disjunctive case here. From Theorems 26.20 and 26.19 it follows that $\overline{S}.\sigma$ is uniquely determined by its singleton elements, so we define $\widetilde{S}.\sigma$ to contain all members of singleton elements of $\overline{S}.\sigma$:

$$\widetilde{S}.\sigma \;\triangleq\; \{\sigma' \mid \{\sigma'\} \in \overline{S}.\sigma\} \;.$$

This makes $\widetilde{S}$ a function in $\Sigma \to \mathcal{P}(\Gamma)$. Nontermination here corresponds to $\widetilde{S}.\sigma$ being empty, and refinement corresponds to pointwise subset inclusion:

$$S \sqsubseteq S' \;\equiv\; (\forall \sigma \cdot \widetilde{S}.\sigma \subseteq \widetilde{S'}.\sigma) \;.$$

Determinism

Determinism means that the final state of a normally terminating computation is always uniquely determined for a given initial state. For deterministic predicate transformers, we thus want to simplify the state transformer interpretation so that $\widetilde{S}.\sigma$ is the final state that is reached when S is executed in initial state σ.

We first consider the special case $S \in$ TFtran, when predicate transformer S is deterministic (i.e., both conjunctive and disjunctive) and also terminating and nonmiraculous. In this case, Theorem 26.10 shows that $S = \langle f \rangle$ for the state function f defined by

$$f.\sigma \;=\; (\epsilon \gamma \cdot (\forall p \mid S.p.\sigma \cdot p.\gamma)) \;,$$

and from Chapter 14 we know that

$$\overline{S}.\sigma \;=\; \{p \mid f.\sigma \in p\} \;.$$

In other words, $\overline{S}.\sigma$ contains all those predicates that contain $f.\sigma$. Thus we lose no information if we give the simpler semantics

$$\widetilde{S} \;\triangleq\; f$$

that identifies S with a function $\widetilde{S} : \Sigma \to \Gamma$. Since TFtran is discretely ordered, refinement reduces to equality.

If S is partial functional, i.e., conjunctive, disjunctive, and strict, it follows from the above that given a state σ, either there is a unique state σ' such that $\overline{S}.\sigma = \{q \mid \sigma' \in q\}$, or $\overline{S}.\sigma = \emptyset$. Using the additional element $\perp$ (standing for abortion) we can define a simpler state transformer semantics without losing information:

$$\widetilde{S}.\sigma \;\triangleq\; \begin{cases} \perp & \text{if } \overline{S}.\sigma = \emptyset, \\ (\varepsilon\,\sigma' \cdot \overline{S}.\sigma = \{q \mid \sigma' \in q\}) & \text{otherwise.} \end{cases}$$

This definition makes $\widetilde{S}$ a function in $\Sigma \to \{\perp\} + \Gamma$. In this way, we recover traditional denotational semantics for partial functions, where $\perp$ is the undefined state.

In order to characterize refinement, we recall that the default ordering on a sum $A + B$ is defined such that the orderings inside A and B are preserved but all elements of A are smaller than all elements of B. Refinement then corresponds to the pointwise extension of this ordering on $\{\perp\} + \Gamma$:

$$S \sqsubseteq S' \;\equiv\; (\forall \sigma \cdot \widetilde{S}.\sigma = \perp \lor \widetilde{S}.\sigma = \widetilde{S}'.\sigma) \ .$$

The case when S is deterministic (i.e., conjunctive and disjunctive) is handled in a similar way, but the range of $\widetilde{S}$ is $\Sigma \to \{\perp\} + \Gamma + \{\top\}$, where $\top$ stands for miraculous termination.

Finite Conjunctivity and Disjunctivity

In predicate transformer semantics, it is often assumed that (executable, implementable) programs are represented by predicate transformers that are finitely conjunctive and nonmiraculous. Recall that S is finitely conjunctive if $S(p \cap q) = S.p \cap S.q$ for arbitrary predicates p and q. Finite conjunctivity is slightly weaker than positive conjunctivity, but all examples of predicate transformers that are finitely conjunctive but not conjunctive that we have found are pathological and far removed from ordinary program specifications (see Exercise 26.9).

It is interesting to note that S is a finitely conjunctive, strict statement if and only if for all states σ the following three conditions hold:

(a) $\emptyset \notin \overline{S}.\sigma$,

(b) $p \in \overline{S}.\sigma \land q \in \overline{S}.\sigma \;\Rightarrow\; p \cap q \in \overline{S}.\sigma$, and

(c) $p \in \overline{S}.\sigma \land p \subseteq q \;\Rightarrow\; q \in \overline{S}.\sigma$;

i.e., $\overline{S}.\sigma$ is either empty or (in topological terminology) a *filter*.

Furthermore, if we strengthen the conjunctivity condition, requiring S to be universally conjunctive and strict, then $\overline{S}.\sigma$ is a *principal filter*, i.e., a filter generated by a specific set of states.

7   Summary and Discussion

In this chapter we have studied the main subclasses of monotonic predicate transformers, identified by the homomorphism properties they satisfy. For each subclass, we have identified the normal form for predicate transformers in this class and also identified the collection of basic statement constructs that generate this subclass.

Subclasses of predicate transformers have been investigated by Back and von Wright [27, 29]. Distributivity and homomorphism properties of conjunctive predicate transformers are the basis for Hesselink's command algebras [80, 81].

Universally conjunctive predicate transformers are not very expressive for reasoning about programs, because they cannot express nontermination. However, it should be noted that if a language (with demonic nondeterminism) is given a weakest liberal precondition semantics, then its statements denote universally conjunctive predicate transformers. Thus $Ctran^\top$ is suitable for reasoning about partial correctness of demonically nondeterministic programs.

The special cases of the general choice semantics described in this chapter yield semantics that have been used earlier for various programming languages and paradigms. The choice semantics for universally conjunctive statements corresponds to traditional relational semantics. For conjunctive statements, we have a version of the Smyth powerdomain ordering without the restriction to continuity [130]. These correspondences were noted already in [9].

The choice semantics for deterministic statements (with artificial bottom and top elements added to the state space) correspond to the ideas of Scott [126] that treat data types as lattices. Later mainstream denotational semantics worked with cpos and omitted the top element; see, e.g., [125]. This corresponds to our semantics for partial functional statements.

The way in which we have identified statement subclasses should be seen as an alternative to the traditional approach in programming logics, where a particularly interesting class of program statements is singled out, and characterized by its properties. Statements in this class are given a syntax and a semantic meaning, and properties of statements are then studied within this framework. This approach is actually quite restrictive. First of all, it introduces an unnecessary element into the discussion, the choice of statement syntax. This is an area where people have strong preferences, and it usually only confuses the issue. Secondly, the analysis is then locked into the fixed framework, and comparison with alternative statement classes becomes difficult and can be carried out only on a semantic level.

Our formalization of programming languages in higher-order logic avoids these problems, because we stay within a single very general framework, that of higher-order logic. We do not introduce a specific programming language syntax for our statement subclasses, but concentrate instead on the collection of operations that generate this subclass. This allows us to freely mix components from different

statement classes and derive properties for such new mixtures. Of course,
framework is also restricted, in the sense that we interpret our programs as predi
transformers, so we are essentially considering only the input–output behavic
programs.

26.8 Exercises

26.1   Show that if S is conjunctive, then $[t.S]$; S is universally conjunctive.

26.2   Show that if S is universally conjunctive, then the following holds for all predic
q and all states σ:

$$S.q.\sigma \;\equiv\; (\cap p \mid S.p.\sigma \cdot p) \subseteq q \;.$$

Hint: First show that $(\wedge x \mid B.x \cdot B.x) = \top$ for arbitrary B.

26.3   Show that the demonic update chaos $= [\text{True}]$ is the bottom element of Ctr
i.e., the least universally conjunctive predicate transformer.

26.4   Prove Theorem 26.11.

26.5   Show that if the relation Q is deterministic, then

$$\{Q\} \;=\; \{\lambda\sigma \cdot Q.\sigma \neq \emptyset\} ; \langle \lambda\sigma \cdot \varepsilon\gamma \cdot Q.\sigma.\gamma \rangle \;.$$

26.6   In this chapter, we defined the various homomorphic choice semantics by apply
suitable transformation to the original choice semantics. Another possibility w
be to define the homomorphic choice semantics recursively over the syntax fo
corresponding subclass of contract statements and then show that the two cl
semantics are related as stated in the text. For the universally conjunctive cas
define

$$
\begin{aligned}
\text{ch}'.[R].\sigma &\equiv R.\sigma \;, \\
\text{ch}'.(S_1 ; S_2).\sigma &\equiv \text{im } (\text{ch}'.S_2).(\text{ch}'.S_1.\sigma) \;, \\
\text{ch}'.(\cap i \in I \cdot S_i).\sigma &\equiv (\cup i \in I \cdot \text{ch}'.S_i.\sigma), \; I \neq \emptyset \;.
\end{aligned}
$$

Show that with this definition,

$$\text{ch}.S.\sigma \;\equiv\; \{q \mid \text{ch}'.S.\sigma \subseteq q\}$$

for $S \in \text{Ctran}^\top$.

26.7   Recall the definitions of $\widetilde{S}$ and $\text{cr}.\widetilde{S}$ for universally conjunctive S given in the
Prove that the diagram in Figure 26.1 commutes and then prove the follo
homomorphism property for demonic choice:

$$\text{cr}.(\lambda\sigma \cdot \widetilde{S}_1.\sigma \cup \widetilde{S}_2.\sigma) \;=\; (\lambda\sigma \cdot \overline{\text{inj}.S_1.\sigma} \cap \overline{\text{inj}.S_2.\sigma}) \;.$$

Then formulate the corresponding homomorphism property for sequential composition and prove it.

26.8 For the conjunctive case we define the function ch′ recursively over the syntax of a subset of contract statements as follows:

$$
\begin{aligned}
\mathrm{ch}'.\{p\}.\sigma &= \begin{cases} \{\sigma\} & \text{if } p.\sigma, \\ \bot & \text{otherwise;} \end{cases} \\
\mathrm{ch}'.[R].\sigma &= R.\sigma \ ; \\
\mathrm{ch}'.(S_1\,;\,S_2).\sigma &= \begin{cases} \bot, & \text{if } \mathrm{ch}'.S_1.\sigma = \bot, \\ \bot, & \text{if } \mathrm{ch}'.S_1.\sigma \ne \bot \wedge \\ & \quad (\exists \gamma \in \mathrm{ch}'.S_1.\sigma \cdot \mathrm{ch}'.S_2.\gamma = \bot), \\ \mathrm{im}.(\mathrm{ch}'.S_2).(\mathrm{ch}'.S_1.\sigma), & \text{otherwise;} \end{cases} \\
\mathrm{ch}'.(\sqcap i \in I \cdot S_i).\sigma &= \begin{cases} \bot, & \text{if } (\exists i \in I \cdot \mathrm{ch}'.S_i.\sigma = \bot), \\ (\cap i \in I \cdot \mathrm{ch}'.S_i.\sigma), & \text{otherwise.} \end{cases}
\end{aligned}
$$

(when $I \ne \emptyset$). Show that this semantics is related to the original choice semantics as follows:

$$
\mathrm{ch}'.S.\sigma = \begin{cases} \bot & \text{if } \mathrm{ch}.S.\sigma = \emptyset, \\ \cap \mathrm{ch}.S.\sigma & \text{otherwise.} \end{cases}
$$

26.9 A set is said to be *cofinite* if its complement is finite. Since predicates are sets of states, it makes sense to talk abut cofinite predicates also. Let S be the predicate transformer in Mtran(Nat, Nat) defined as follows:

$$S.q.\sigma \equiv q \text{ is cofinite.}$$

Show that S is finitely conjunctive, i.e., that $S.(p \cap q) = S.p \cap S.q$ for arbitrary predicates p and q. S is not conjunctive, however. Show this by exhibiting a set of predicates $\{q_i \mid i \in \mathrm{Nat}\}$ such that $S.(\cap i \in \mathrm{Nat} \cdot q_i) \ne (\cap i \in \mathrm{Nat} \cdot S.q_i)$. Hint: a set of natural numbers A is cofinite if and only if there is $n \in \mathrm{Nat}$ such that A contains all numbers that are greater than or equal to n.

ecification Statements

In this chapter we describe in more detail how to model program specifications as program statements. We give an exact characterization of what a *specification statement* is, and we study refinement of specification statements by other specification statements. We also look at methods for combining two or more (conjunctive) specifications into a single specification that retains the same information.

A stepwise refinement of a specification statement embodies some design decision as to how the specification is to be implemented. The term *top-down program development* is often used to describe this classical technique for program development. One starts with an abstract specification statement that describes the intended behavior of the program and refines this step by step. At each step, a specification statement is replaced with some compound statement, possibly containing new specification statements as subcomponents.

We concentrate on refinement of conjunctive statements. We give the basic rules for refining conjunctive specification statements by a sequential composition or meet of other specification statements, and illustrate the top-down development method with a small example. We choose the Guarded commands language by Dijkstra to represent the programming language that we are programming into. We describe this language first, in particular to determine its homomorphism properties, which can then be used in program derivations.

We finally consider the problem of refining a specification statement by an arbitrary statement. We consider two kinds of specification statements: conjunctive specifications and universally disjunctive specifications. In both cases, we show how to reduce a refinement to a correctness assertion, which then can be proved using correctness rules from earlier chapters.

27.1   Specifications

In preceding chapters we have shown that subclasses of statements can be •
acterized by normal forms for statements. We shall now show that these no
forms really correspond to specifications of program behaviors. By a *specifice*
we mean a statement that indicates in a simple way *what* is to be computed wit
saying *how* it is computed. For example, the statement

x := factorial.x

specifies that the output value of x should be the factorial of the input value. I
programming language used has an explicit factorial operator, then this would
be an executable statement. By a sequence of refinement steps (a derivation), w•
refine this to an implementation that, e.g., uses only multiplications and addit
We will not address here the question of what operations are implemented, a:
differs from programming language to programming language. A programm
language implementation of a statement is a refinement of the statement th
directly expressible in the chosen programming language and hence executab•
the chosen computer.

We have shown in Chapter 13 that every monotonic predicate transformer
can be written in statement form $\{P\} ; [Q]$. We consider a predicate transfo
of this form to be a *general monotonic specification*. Intuitively, such a spec:
tion describes a two-step game in which the angel chooses an intermediate •
according to relation P, after which the demon chooses a final value accordi
Q. In a similar way, we also consider the other normal forms from Chapter
be specifications.

Conjunctive Specifications

A *conjunctive specification* is a predicate transformer of the form $\{p\} ; [Q]$.
is a normal form for conjunctive predicate transformers; i.e., every conjun
predicate transformer term can be written in this form. Furthermore, it descri
computation in a concise form: the relation Q shows how the final state is rela
the initial state, while the predicate p (the *precondition*) characterizes those i
states that we are interested in. An implementation of the specification $\{p\}$
must behave as permitted by Q whenever p holds in the initial state. Arb•
behavior (even nontermination) is acceptable in states where p does not hol•

In practice, we usually write the relation Q as a relational assignment. For exa
$$\{x > 2\} ; [y := y' \mid 1 < y' < x \land (\exists a \cdot a \cdot y' = x)]$$

is a specification for a program that stores some proper factor of x in y i•
initially greater than 2.

If the precondition is the predicate true, then the specification is in fact a *universally conjunctive specification*. We do not consider universally conjunctive specifications separately; we simply treat them as special cases of conjunctive ones. An example (with $x, y :$ Nat) is

$$[y := y' \mid y'^2 \leq x < (y' + 1)^2] \ ,$$

which assigns to y the (natural number) square root of x. Note that even though the square root is uniquely defined for arbitrary x, it would be much more complicated to specify it as a function of x. This is a strong argument in favor of conjunctive specifications even when specifying a deterministic computation: we can specify by giving constraints rather than by giving an explicit function.

Other Specifications

Dually to the conjunctive specification, the statement $[p] ; \{Q\}$ is a *disjunctive specification* and $\{Q\}$ is a *universally disjunctive specification*. Similarly, $\{p\} ; \langle f \rangle$ is a *partial function specification*. An example of a universally disjunctive specification is

$$\{x, e := x', e' \mid 0 < e' < x'\} \ .$$

This specifies setting x and e to any (angelically chosen) nonnegative values with $0 < e < x$.

An example of a partial functional specification is

$$\{x > 0\} ; z := y/x \ ,$$

which specifies that z is assigned the result of the division y/x, with precondition $x > 0$. If $x \leq 0$, then any behavior, even nontermination, is acceptable.

The partial functional specification is easily seen to be a special case of the conjunctive specification, since any functional update can be rewritten as a demonic update. Even though the partial functional specification predicate transformer is sufficient to specify arbitrary partial functions, the natural number square root example above shows that it can be more convenient to specify a function using the more general conjunctive specifications.

Refining Specifications by Specifications

Specifications are canonical ways of expressing statements. It is therefore useful to know when one specification refines another one. Refinement between specifications corresponds to refining the requirements of the program statement to be built, without going into the details of how the statement is to be constructed in terms of sequential composition, conditionals, and loops.

Refinement Between Similar Specifications

The rules for refinement between similar specifications generalize the homo*
phism properties given earlier. We consider seven basic forms of specificati*
monotonic $\{P\} ; [Q]$, conjunctive $\{p\} ; [Q]$, universally conjunctive $[Q]$, disj*
tive $[p] ; \{Q\}$, universally disjunctive $\{Q\}$, partial functional $\{p\} ; \langle f \rangle$, and *
functional $\langle f \rangle$.

Theorem 27.1   *The following rules hold for arbitrary predicates p, p'; arbitrary state transform*
f, f'; and arbitrary relations $P, P', Q,$ and Q'.

    (a) $\{P\} ; [Q] \sqsubseteq \{P'\} ; [Q'] \Leftarrow P \subseteq P' \wedge Q' \subseteq Q$,
    (b) $\{p\} ; [Q] \sqsubseteq \{p'\} ; [Q'] \equiv p \subseteq p' \wedge |p| ; Q' \subseteq Q$,
    (c) $[Q] \sqsubseteq [Q'] \equiv Q' \subseteq Q$,
    (d) $[p] ; \{Q\} \sqsubseteq [p'] ; \{Q'\} \equiv p' \subseteq p \wedge Q \subseteq |p'| ; Q'$,
    (e) $\{Q\} \sqsubseteq \{Q'\} \equiv Q \subseteq Q'$,
    (f) $\{p\} ; \langle f \rangle \sqsubseteq \{p'\} ; \langle f' \rangle \equiv p \subseteq p' \wedge |p| ; |f| \subseteq |f'|$,
    (g) $\langle f \rangle \sqsubseteq \langle f' \rangle \equiv f = f'$.

Proof We first note that (a) holds by homomorphism and monotonicity proper*
To prove (b) we have

$$\{p\} ; [Q] \sqsubseteq \{p'\} ; [Q']$$

$\equiv$ {definitions}

$$(\forall \sigma\, r \cdot p.\sigma \wedge Q.\sigma \subseteq r \Rightarrow p'.\sigma \wedge Q'.\sigma \subseteq r)$$

$\equiv$ {$\Rightarrow$ by specialization $(r := Q.\sigma)$, $\Leftarrow$ by transitivity of $\subseteq$}

$$(\forall \sigma \cdot p.\sigma \Rightarrow p'.\sigma \wedge Q'.\sigma \subseteq Q.\sigma)$$

$\equiv$ {calculus, definition}

$$(\forall \sigma \cdot p.\sigma \Rightarrow p'.\sigma) \wedge (\forall \sigma\, \sigma' \cdot p.\sigma \wedge Q'.\sigma.\sigma' \Rightarrow Q.\sigma.\sigma')$$

$\equiv$ {definitions}

$$p \subseteq p' \wedge |p| ; Q' \subseteq Q$$

This proves (b). Now (c) follows as a special case of (b) when p and p' are *
true. The rule for disjunctive specifications (d) follows from (b) by dual reaso*
(Exercise 27.1). Finally, (e) is a special case of (d), (f) is a special case of (b),*
(g) is a special case of (f). $\square$

Note that rules (b)–(g) in Theorem 27.1 are all equivalences, so they can be *
for refinements in both directions. All the rules in Theorem 27.1 give condi*
for refinement in terms of predicates, functions, and relations. This is impor*
it allows us to *reduce* refinement of statements to properties on lower levels i*
predicate transformer hierarchy: to properties of functions, relations, and p*
cates. When the rules are applied to a concrete specification, the conditions*

easily be reduced further to first-order formulas. For example, the second conjunct on the right-hand side in (f) can be rewritten as

$$(\forall \sigma \cdot p.\sigma \;\Rightarrow\; f.\sigma = f'.\sigma) \;.$$

Theorem 27.1 may seem like an unnecessarily long list. In fact, as noted in the proof, three of the cases (c, e, and g) are direct special cases of the others. From now on, we will not consider these specifications (universally conjunctive, universally disjunctive, and total functional) separately.

Refinement Between Different Specifications

In many cases, it is possible to refine a specification of one form into a specification of another form. We concentrate on those situations in which a specification is refined by a more restricted kind of specification (where $\{P\};[Q]$ is the most general and $\langle f \rangle$ the most restricted form). Furthermore, we concentrate on four basic forms of specifications: general, conjunctive, disjunctive, and partial functional.

Theorem 27.2   *The following holds for arbitrary predicates* p, p'; *arbitrary state transformer* f; *and arbitrary relations* $P, P',$ *and* Q.

$$
\begin{aligned}
&\text{(a)} \quad \{P\};[Q] \sqsubseteq \{p'\};[Q'] \;\equiv\; \text{dom}.P \subseteq p' \wedge P^{-1};Q' \subseteq Q \;, \\
&\text{(b)} \quad \{p\};[Q] \sqsubseteq \{p'\};\langle f' \rangle \;\equiv\; p \subseteq p' \wedge |p|;|f'| \subseteq Q \;, \\
&\text{(c)} \quad \{P\};[Q] \sqsubseteq [p'];\{Q'\} \;\equiv\; |p'|;P \subseteq Q';Q^{-1} \;, \\
&\text{(d)} \quad \{Q\} \sqsubseteq \{p'\};\langle f' \rangle \;\equiv\; \text{dom}.Q \subseteq p' \wedge Q \subseteq |f'| \;.
\end{aligned}
$$

Proof   We first prove (a). We have

$\qquad \{P\};[Q] \sqsubseteq \{p'\};[Q']$

$\equiv$ {definitions}

$\qquad (\forall \sigma\, r \cdot (\exists \gamma \cdot P.\sigma.\gamma \wedge Q.\gamma \subseteq r) \;\Rightarrow\; p'.\sigma \wedge Q'.\sigma \subseteq r)$

$\equiv$ {quantifier rules}

$\qquad (\forall \sigma\, \gamma\, r \cdot P.\sigma.\gamma \wedge Q.\gamma \subseteq r \;\Rightarrow\; p'.\sigma \wedge Q'.\sigma \subseteq r)$

$\equiv$ {$\Rightarrow$ by specialization ($r := Q.\gamma$), $\Leftarrow$ by transitivity of $\subseteq$}

$\qquad (\forall \sigma\, \gamma \cdot P.\sigma.\gamma \;\Rightarrow\; p'.\sigma \wedge Q'.\sigma \subseteq Q.\gamma)$

$\equiv$ {predicate calculus}

$\qquad (\forall \sigma\, \gamma \cdot P.\sigma.\gamma \Rightarrow p'.\sigma) \wedge (\forall \sigma\, \gamma\, \delta \cdot P.\sigma.\gamma \wedge Q'.\sigma.\delta \;\Rightarrow\; Q.\gamma.\delta)$

$\equiv$ {quantifier rules}

$\qquad (\forall \sigma \cdot (\exists \gamma \cdot P.\sigma.\gamma) \Rightarrow p'.\sigma) \wedge (\forall \gamma\, \delta \cdot (\exists \sigma \cdot P.\sigma.\gamma \wedge Q'.\sigma.\delta) \;\Rightarrow\; Q.\gamma.\delta)$

$\equiv$ {definitions}

$\qquad \text{dom}.P \subseteq p' \wedge P^{-1};Q' \subseteq Q$

Next, we find that (b) is in fact a special case of Theorem 27.1 (b), specializing to $|f'|$. For (c) we have a derivation similar to the one for (a). Finally, (d) foll as a special case of (a) with $P := Q$, $Q := \text{Id}$, and $Q' := |f'|$, together wi small derivation to show $Q^{-1} ; |f'| \subseteq \text{Id} \equiv Q \subseteq |f'|$. $\Box$

In the rule in Theorem 27.2 (d) it is sufficient to have the universally disjund specification $\{Q\}$ on the left-hand side rather than the disjunctive specifica $[p] ; \{Q\}$ because the refinement

$$[p] ; \{Q\} \sqsubseteq \{p'\} ; \langle f' \rangle$$

is possible only if $p = \text{true}$ (Exercise 27.2).

In some situations, we may also be interested in refining a specification into of a more general form. Since the less general form can always be rewritten the more general one, the problem here reduces to refinement between sir specifications. For example, the refinement

$$\{p\} ; \langle f \rangle \sqsubseteq \{p'\} ; [Q']$$

is equivalent to

$$\{p\} ; [\,|f|\,] \sqsubseteq \{p'\} ; [Q']$$

and can be handled by the rule in Theorem 27.1 (b). Another similar example be found in Exercise 27.3.

Example

As an example, we consider refining the conjunctive specification $\{x > 0\} ; [$ $x' \mid x' < x]$. We propose to refine this by replacing the demonic assignment a functional one. Theorem 27.2 (b) gives us a rule for proving the refinement

$$\{x > 0\} ; [x := x' \mid x' < x] \sqsubseteq \{x > 0\} ; x := x - 1 .$$

Since both specifications have the same precondition, the proof obligation simplified. We have

$$\{x > 0\} ; [x := x' \mid x' < x] \sqsubseteq \{x > 0\} ; x := x - 1$$
$$\equiv \quad \{\text{Theorem 27.2 (b)}\}$$
$$\qquad |x > 0| ; |x := x - 1| \subseteq (x := x' \mid x' < x)$$
$$\Leftarrow \quad \{\text{reduction to Boolean terms}\}$$
$$\qquad (\forall x\, x' \cdot x > 0 \wedge x' = x - 1 \Rightarrow x' < x)$$
$$\equiv \quad \{\text{arithmetic}\}$$
$$\qquad \mathsf{T}$$

3   Combining Specifications

There are many cases in which we do not start with a single specification, but rather with a collection of requirements that our program has to satisfy. Before starting a derivation, we first need to combine these different requirements into a single specification. We shall now give basic rules for this.

We assume that the requirements are themselves given as specifications, and we concentrate on conjunctive statements. We first show that if S_1 and S_2 are conjunctive specifications, then S_1 ; S_2 and $S_1 \sqcap S_2$ can also be expressed as conjunctive specifications. The join $S_1 \sqcup S_2$ is the least common refinement of the two specifications, but it need not be conjunctive, since joins introduce angelic nondeterminism. But since the conjunctive predicate transformers Ctran(Σ, Γ) form a complete lattice, any set of conjunctive predicate transformers must also have a unique least conjunctive upper bound. We will show below how to derive this.

Sequential Composition and Meet

Sequential composition and meet preserve conjunctivity. Hence, composing two conjunctive specifications with these operators gives us conjunctive statements. These can again be expressed as a conjunctive specification, as shown by the following result.

Theorem 27.3   *Let predicates p and q and relations P and Q be arbitrary. Then*

(a) $\{p\} ; [P] ; \{q\} ; [Q] = \{p \cap [P].q\} ; [P ; Q]$.

(b) $\{p\} ; [P] \sqcap \{q\} ; [Q] = \{p \cap q\} ; [P \cup Q]$.

Proof   We use the following *assertion propagation* rule for conjunctive S, which the reader can easily verify (Exercise 27.4):

$$S ; \{p\} = \{S.p\} ; S .$$

For (a), we have

$\qquad \{p\} ; [P] ; \{q\} ; [Q]$

$\equiv$ {assertion propagation}

$\qquad \{p\} ; \{[P].q\} ; [P] ; [Q]$

$\equiv$ {homomorphisms}

$\qquad \{p \cap [P].q\} ; [P ; Q]$

and for (b),

$\qquad (\{p\} ; [P] \sqcap \{q\} ; [Q]).r.\sigma$

$\equiv$ {definitions}

$$p.\sigma \wedge (\forall \gamma \cdot P.\sigma.\gamma \Rightarrow r.\gamma) \wedge q.\sigma \wedge (\forall \gamma \cdot Q.\sigma.\gamma \Rightarrow r.\gamma)$$
$$\equiv \{\text{predicate calculus}\}$$
$$p.\sigma \wedge q.\sigma \wedge (\forall \gamma \cdot P.\sigma.\gamma \vee Q.\sigma.\gamma \Rightarrow r.\gamma)$$
$$\equiv \{\text{definitions}\}$$
$$(\{p \cap q\} ; [P \cup Q]).r.\sigma$$

which finishes the proof. □

Least Conjunctive Refinement

Theorem 27.3 states that the meet (greatest lower bound) of specifications $\{p\}$; and $\{q\}$; $[Q]$ is $\{p \cap q\}$; $[P \cup Q]$. Intuitively, it may seem that the rule for a conjunctive upper bound should be dual. However, we cannot simply take disjunction of the preconditions and the conjunction of the next-state relations Exercise 27.5).

We will here need the *relational quotient* operator, defined as follows:

$$P \backslash Q \;\; \hat{=} \;\; (\lambda \sigma \; \delta \cdot \forall \gamma \cdot P.\sigma.\gamma \Rightarrow Q.\gamma.\delta) \; . \qquad \textit{(relation quotie}$$

Intuitively, $(P \backslash Q).\sigma.\delta$ means that whenever P relates σ to some γ, then Q relate this γ to δ (the quotient can be seen as a dual to composition of relations) assume that the quotient operator binds more tightly than meet but more we than composition.

The following properties of this quotient operator show that it is related to con sition similarly to how implication is related to meet.

Lemma 27.4   *Assume that P, Q, and R are relations. Then*

(a) $P \backslash Q \; = \; \neg (P ; \neg Q)$,

(b) $P \backslash (Q \backslash R) \; = \; (P ; Q) \backslash R$,

(c) $P \subseteq Q \backslash R \; \equiv \; Q^{-1} ; P \subseteq R$,

(d) $(P \backslash Q)^{-1} \; = \; (\neg Q^{-1}) \backslash (\neg P^{-1})$,

(e) $\text{Id} \backslash R \; = \; R$.

The proof is left as an exercise to the reader (Exercise 27.7).

Lemma 27.4 (c) shows that the quotient can be given the following intuitio we want to divide relation R into relations Q and P so that $Q ; P \subseteq R$, and given, then for P we can take $Q^{-1} \backslash R$.

The relational quotient can be used to give a simple characterization of conjunctive upper bounds.

Theorem 27.5 *The least conjunctive upper bound of two conjunctive specifications $\{p\} ; [P]$ and $\{q\} ; [Q]$ is given by*

$$\{p \cup q\} ; [|p|\backslash P \cap |q|\backslash Q] .$$

Proof We develop the proof by finding what characterizes a specification $(\{r\};[R])$ that refines both $\{p\} ; [P]$ and $\{q\} ; [Q]$.

$$\{p\};[P] \sqsubseteq \{r\};[R] \ \wedge \ \{q\};[Q] \sqsubseteq \{r\};[R]$$

$\equiv \ \{$Theorem 27.1 (d)$\}$

$$p \subseteq r \wedge |p|;R \subseteq P \wedge q \subseteq r \wedge |q|;R \subseteq Q$$

$\equiv \ \{$Lemma 27.4 (c), $|p|^{-1} = |p|\}$

$$p \subseteq r \wedge q \subseteq r \wedge R \subseteq |p|\backslash P \wedge R \subseteq |q|\backslash Q$$

$\equiv \ \{$lattice properties$\}$

$$(p \cup q) \subseteq r \wedge R \subseteq |p|\backslash P \ \cap \ |q|\backslash Q$$

This shows that the least conjunctive upper bound is $\{p \cup q\} ; [|p|\backslash P \cap |q|\backslash Q].$ $\square$

We call the least conjunctive upper bound of S_1 and S_2 the *least conjunctive refinement*, written $S_1 \mathbin{\hat{\sqcup}} S_2$. The expression for $S_1 \mathbin{\hat{\sqcup}} S_2$ given in Theorem 27.5 is fairly complicated. However, if the conjunctive specification $\{p\} ; [P]$ is normalized so that relation P is full wherever p does not hold (i.e., $(\forall \sigma \cdot \neg p.\sigma \Rightarrow (\forall \gamma \cdot P.\sigma.\gamma)))$, and similarly for $\{q\};[Q]$, then the expression for the least conjunctive upper bound reduces to the simpler form

$$\{p \cup q\} ; [P \cap Q] .$$

Showing this is left to the reader as an exercise (Exercise 27.9).

In the special case in which the two preconditions are the same, the least conjunctive refinement can also be simplified.

Theorem 27.6 *Let p be a predicate and P and Q relations. Then*

$$\{p\} ; [P] \mathbin{\hat{\sqcup}} \{p\} ; [Q] \ = \ \{p\} ; [P \cap Q] .$$

Proof

$$\{p\} ; [P] \mathbin{\hat{\sqcup}} \{p\} ; [Q]$$

$= \ \{$Theorem 27.5$\}$

$$\{p\} ; [|p|\backslash P \cap |p|\backslash Q]$$

$= \ \{$definitions$\}$

$$\{p\} ; [\lambda \sigma \ \gamma \cdot (p.\sigma \Rightarrow P.\sigma.\gamma) \wedge (p.\sigma \Rightarrow Q.\sigma.\gamma)]$$

$= \ \{$use assertion (Exercise 27.8$\}$

$$\{p\} ; [\lambda \sigma \ \gamma \cdot p.\sigma \wedge (p.\sigma \Rightarrow P.\sigma.\gamma) \wedge (p.\sigma \Rightarrow Q.\sigma.\gamma)]$$

$= $ {predicate calculus}

$\{p\} ; [\lambda \sigma \; \gamma \cdot p.\sigma \wedge P.\sigma.\gamma \wedge Q.\sigma.\gamma]$

$= $ {use assertion (Exercise 27.8}

$\{p\} ; [\lambda \sigma \; \gamma \cdot P.\sigma.\gamma \wedge Q.\sigma.\gamma]$

$= $ {definitions}

$\{p\} ; [P \cap Q]$

$\square$

The least conjunctive upper bound can be seen as a way of combining specificati⊲ If we specify different aspects of a program separately, we want the implementa⊤ to satisfy (refine) each of the component specifications. Theorem 27.5 gives ⊩ rule for computing the combined specification. Since the result is the *least* u⊅ bound, we do not lose any refinement potential when combining the compo⊁ specifications if we have decided that the refinement must be conjunctive.

Example: Merging Arrays

As an example, we specify a merging algorithm, intended to merge two sorted ar⧈ A and B into an array C. We assume that only the array segments $A[0..m -$ $B[0..n - 1]$, and $C[0..m + n - 1]$ are used. Thus we use the abbreviation sorte⊲ for sorted.$A.(\lambda i \cdot i < n)$ and occur.$A.x$ for occur.$A.(\lambda i \cdot i < n).x$ (and simi⊩ for B and C). We require that the input and the output be sorted:

$$S_1 \;\; = \;\; \{\text{sorted}.A \wedge \text{sorted}.B\} ; [C := C' \mid \text{sorted}.C'] \; .$$

Furthermore, we require that all input elements occur in the output list:

$$S_2 \;\; = \;\; \{\text{sorted}.A \wedge \text{sorted}.B\};$$
$$[C := C' \mid (\forall i \cdot \text{occur}.C'.i = \text{occur}.A.i + \text{occur}.B.i)] \; .$$

The result of combining the two specifications S_1 and S_2 is, by Theorem 27.6

$\{\text{sorted}.A \wedge \text{sorted}.B\} ;$

$[(C := C' \mid \text{sorted}.C') \cap$

$\qquad (C := C' \mid (\forall i \cdot \text{occur}.C'.i = \text{occur}.A.i + \text{occur}.i))]$

$= $ {combine relations}

$\{\text{sorted}.A \wedge \text{sorted}.B\} ;$

$[(C := C' \mid \text{sorted}.C' \wedge (\forall i \cdot \text{occur}.C'.i = \text{occur}.A.i + \text{occur}.B.i))]$

Note that although both component specifications were nondeterministic, the re⊲ of combining them is deterministic.

It is not necessary to go directly to the least conjunctive refinement of the two statements, because the ordinary join of the two statements is also an acceptable refinement. If we take the join as the basis for further refinement, where the angelic choice is removed at one stage or another (or maybe left in the program as a user interaction point), then there is no reason why we should avoid the join.

4 Refining Conjunctive Specifications

Now consider the problem of finding rules that state exactly when a refinement of the form $S \sqsubseteq S_1 ; S_2$ (and similarly for meet and join) is valid, where S, S_1, and S_2 are all specifications of the same form. Given such rules, we can later derive corresponding rules for other composition operations, such as conditionals and loops.

We concentrate on conjunctive specifications. This means that we take sequential composition and meet as basic constructors. However, similar rules can be derived for other classes of specifications. For example, every rule for conjunctive specifications gives rules for universally conjunctive and partial functional specifications as special cases. We do not state all these special cases explicitly. Instead, a number of additional rules are given in the exercises.

Refining Specifications by Composed Specifications

We give two basic rules that show how sequential composition and meet can be introduced in conjunctive specifications.

Theorem 27.7 *Let predicates p and q and relations P, Q, and R be arbitrary. Then*

(a) *Refinement of a conjunctive specification with a sequential composition satisfies*

$$\{p\} ; [P] \sqsubseteq \{p\} ; [Q] ; \{q\} ; [R] \equiv p \subseteq [Q].q \wedge |p| ; Q ; R \subseteq P .$$

(b) *Refinement of a conjunctive specification with a demonic choice satisfies*

$$\{p\} ; [P] \sqsubseteq \{p\} ; [Q] \sqcap \{p\} ; [R] \equiv |p| ; Q \subseteq P \wedge |p| ; R \subseteq P .$$

Proof For (a), we have

$$\{p\} ; [P] \sqsubseteq \{p\} ; [Q] ; \{q\} ; [R]$$
$$\equiv \{\text{Theorem 27.3 (a)}\}$$
$$\{p\} ; [P] \sqsubseteq \{p \cap [Q].q\} ; [Q ; R]$$
$$\equiv \{\text{Theorem 27.1 (b)}\}$$

$$p \subseteq p \cap [Q].q \wedge |p| \; ; \; Q \; ; \; R \subseteq P$$
$$\equiv \{\text{property of meet}\}$$
$$p \subseteq [Q].q \wedge |p| \; ; \; Q \; ; \; R \subseteq P$$

The rule in (b) follows from Theorems 27.3 (b) and 27.1 (b). We leave it t[o] reader to verify this. $\square$

In a similar way it is possible to derive rules for introducing sequential compos[ition] and join of disjunctive specifications.

Note that the rule for *adding a leading assignment* given in Chapter 17 is a sp[ecial] case of the rule in Theorem 27.7 (a). The following derivation shows this fo[r] case that b is a Boolean expression in which y does not occur free and e i[s] expression in which neither y nor y' occurs free.

$$[x, y := x', y' \mid b]$$
$$\sqsubseteq \{\text{refine specification with composition}\}$$

- true $\subseteq [y := y' \mid y' = e](y = e)$
  $\equiv \{\text{rule for demonic assignment}\}$
  true $\subseteq (\forall y' \cdot y' = e \Rightarrow (y = e)[y := y'])$
  $\equiv \{\text{one-point rule, } y' \text{ not free in } e \}$
  true $\subseteq ((y = e)[y := e])$
  $\equiv \{\text{reduction, } y \text{ not free in } e \}$
  T

- $(y := y' \mid y' = e) \; ; \; (x, y := x', y' \mid b) \subseteq (x, y := x', y' \mid b)$
  $\equiv \{\text{composition of assignments}\}$
  $(x, y := x', y' \mid (\exists x'' \, y'' \cdot x'' = x \wedge y'' = e \wedge b[x, y := x'', y]$
  $\quad \subseteq (x, y := x', y' \mid b)$
  $\equiv \{\text{one-point rule}\}$
  $(x, y := x', y' \mid b[y := e]) \subseteq (x, y := x', y' \mid b)$
  $\equiv \{y \text{ not free in } b\}$
  T

$\cdot \; [y := y' \mid y' = e] \; ; \; \{y = e\} \; ; \; [x, y := x', y' \mid b]$
$\sqsubseteq \{\text{rewrite demonic assignment (coercion), drop assertion}\}$
$y := e \; ; \; [x, y := x', y' \mid b]$

27.5 General Refinement of Specifications

We now consider the situation in which a specification is refined by an arbi[trary] statement. The rules that we get are very general, but their verification condi[tions] are more complicated than what we get in the more specific rules given above[.]

first consider refinements of the form $\{p\} ; [Q] \sqsubseteq S$, where $\{p\} ; [Q]$ is a given conjunctive specification. This expresses Theorem 17.6 in a more general form.

Theorem 27.8   *Assume that p and q are predicates, Q a relation, and S a monotonic predicate transformer. Then*

$$\{p\} ; [Q] \sqsubseteq S \;\equiv\; (\forall \sigma \cdot p.\sigma \Rightarrow S.(Q.\sigma).\sigma) \;.$$

Proof   We have

$$\{p\} ; [Q] \sqsubseteq S$$

$\equiv$ {definitions}

$$(\forall q\, \sigma \cdot p.\sigma \wedge Q.\sigma \subseteq q \Rightarrow S.q.\sigma)$$

$\equiv$ {mutual implication; subderivations}

- $(\forall q\, \sigma \cdot p.\sigma \wedge Q.\sigma \subseteq q \Rightarrow S.q.\sigma)$
- $\Rightarrow$ {specialization $q := Q.\sigma$; simplification}

  $(\forall \sigma \cdot p.\sigma \Rightarrow S.(Q.\sigma).\sigma)$
- $(\forall q\, \sigma \cdot p.\sigma \wedge Q.\sigma \subseteq q \Rightarrow S.q.\sigma)$
- $\Leftarrow$ {S monotonic}

  $(\forall \sigma \cdot p.\sigma \Rightarrow S.(Q.\sigma).\sigma)$
- $(\forall \sigma \cdot p.\sigma \Rightarrow S.(Q.\sigma).\sigma)$

□

Note that Lemma 17.4 follows as a special case of this, by choosing $Q := (\lambda \sigma \cdot q)$. The reader can verify that Theorem 27.8 can be reformulated as follows:

$$\{p\} ; [Q] \sqsubseteq S \;\equiv\; (\forall \sigma_0 \cdot (\lambda \sigma \cdot \sigma = \sigma_0) \cap p \; \{ S \} \; Q.\sigma_0) \;.$$

This shows the similarity with Theorem 17.6 that was given in terms of program variables.

We now derive a rule for refining a disjunctive specification. The rule is not dual to the rule for conjunctive specifications, since a dual rule would use the reverse refinement relation.

Theorem 27.9   *Let S be a monotonic predicate transformer and Q a relation. Then*

$$\{Q\} \sqsubseteq S \;\equiv\; (\forall \sigma_0.\sigma_1 \cdot Q.\sigma_0.\sigma_1 \Rightarrow (\lambda \sigma \cdot \sigma = \sigma_0) \; \{ S \} \; (\lambda \sigma \cdot \sigma = \sigma_1)) \;.$$

Proof

$\quad S$ monotonic

$\vdash \{Q\} \sqsubseteq S$

$\equiv$ {definitions, rewriting implication}

$\quad (\forall q\, \sigma \cdot (\exists \sigma' \cdot Q.\sigma.\sigma' \wedge q.\sigma') \Rightarrow S.q.\sigma)$

$\equiv$ {properties of $\Rightarrow$, quantifiers}

$\quad (\forall \sigma\ \sigma'.q \cdot q.\sigma' \Rightarrow (Q.\sigma.\sigma' \Rightarrow S.q.\sigma))$

$\equiv$ {$\Rightarrow$ by specialization $(q := (\lambda\sigma \cdot \sigma = \sigma')),$ }

$\quad \Leftarrow$ by monotonicity $(q.\sigma' \Rightarrow (\lambda\sigma \cdot \sigma = \sigma') \subseteq q)$

$\quad (\forall \sigma\ \sigma' \cdot Q.\sigma.\sigma' \Rightarrow S.(\lambda\sigma \cdot \sigma = \sigma').\sigma)$

$\equiv$ {one-point rule}

$\quad (\forall \sigma\ \sigma'\ \sigma_0 \cdot (\sigma = \sigma_0) \Rightarrow (Q.\sigma_0.\sigma' \Rightarrow S.(\lambda\sigma \cdot \sigma = \sigma').\sigma))$

$\equiv$ {properties of $\Rightarrow$, quantifiers}

$\quad (\forall \sigma'\ \sigma_0 \cdot Q.\sigma_0.\sigma' \Rightarrow (\forall \sigma \cdot (\sigma = \sigma_0) \Rightarrow S.(\lambda\sigma \cdot \sigma = \sigma').\sigma))$

$\equiv$ {pointwise order, α-renaming}

$\quad (\forall \sigma_0\ \sigma_1 \cdot Q.\sigma_0.\sigma_1 \Rightarrow (\lambda\sigma \cdot \sigma = \sigma_0) \{\!| S |\!\} (\lambda\sigma \cdot \sigma = \sigma_1))$

$\square$

Intuitively speaking, Theorem 27.9 shows that S refines the disjunctive speci‐
tion $\{Q\}$ if and only if S can choose (angelically) every computation path betv
states related by Q.

27.6 Summary and Discussion

This chapter has identified specification statements with the normal form
statement subclasses that we gave previously. We have studied the refineme
specification statements by other specifications in detail and have given a colle
of useful inference rules for this. We have also studied the problem of comb
specification statements using the basic statement constructors: sequential
position, meets, and joins. We have in particular looked at the least conjun
refinement of conjunctive specification statements.

Specification statements were originally introduced in a predicate transfo
framework as a way of expressing general input–output specifications wit
programming language by Back [6], who called the specification statement a
deterministic assignment. Morgan later introduced a variant of this, which he c
a *specification statement* [104]. Back's specification statement uses a single
tion, while Morgan's specification is a pre- and postcondition pair. However,
express specifications for conjunctive predicate transformers only. This chapte
shown how to generalize the notion of specification statements to other state
subclasses.

The least conjunctive refinement is a good example of a case in which some
that is quite simple on the relational level becomes much harder in the ge
case of predicate transformers. On the relational level, the least upper bou

two demonic updates is just the demonic update for conjunction of the relations involved: $[P] \sqcup [Q] = [P \cap Q]$. This has sometimes been taken as an argument for why a relational semantics for programs is superior to a predicate transformer approach [76, 89]. As we have tried to show here, this argument is not really valid, because relational semantics forms a subclass of predicate transformer semantics. Hence, we do not lose anything by choosing predicate transformer semantics, but rather we gain expressibility. A relational specification can be built, combined and analyzed within the relational domain, and once the different requirements have been combined into a good specification, refinement can continue on the statement/predicate transformer level. The problem of conjunctive upper bounds and ways of finding the least one has been studied by a number of authors, including Morgan [107] and Back and Butler [19].

The quotient operator on relations is very close to the *weakest prespecification* operator that Hoare and He use as a basis for a method of stepwise refinement [91] within a relational framework.

We also gave a general rule for refining any (conjunctive or universally disjunctive) specification statement with an arbitrary statement. This shows that refinement between programs can always be reduced to a correctness formula in the weakest precondition calculus, and thus refinement provides a bridge in the other direction between refinement calculus and weakest precondition calculus for total correctness (the other direction being the definition of the refinement relation itself). This characterization of refinement was originally given by Back [7] in terms of strongest postconditions. A similar characterization was also given by Morgan [104].

7 Exercises

27.1 Show that Theorem 27.1 (d) follows from (b) by duality.

27.2 Show that the refinement

$$[p] ; \{P\} \sqsubseteq \{q\} ; \langle f \rangle$$

is possible only if $p = \text{true}$.

27.3 Show that the following rule for refinement between different specifications is valid:

$$\{p\} ; \langle f \rangle \sqsubseteq [q] ; \{Q\} \equiv (\forall \sigma \cdot p.\sigma \wedge q.\sigma \Rightarrow Q.\sigma.(f.\sigma)) .$$

27.4 Show that the following equality always holds when S is a conjunctive predicate transformer:

$$S ; \{p\} = \{S.p\} ; S .$$

27.5   Show that $\{p \cup q\}; [P \cap Q]$ is always a refinement of both $\{p\}; [P]$ and $\{q\};$ ▮
       This means that $\{p \cup q\}; [P \cap Q]$ is an upper bound of $\{p\}; [P]$ and $\{q\}; [Q]$. ⊂
       a counterexample showing that $\{p \cup q\}; [P \cap Q]$ need not be the least conjunc
       upper bound.

27.6   Prove that the following equivalence holds:

$$\{p\}; [Q] \sqsubseteq \langle f \rangle \;\equiv\; (\forall \sigma \cdot p.\sigma \Rightarrow Q.\sigma.(f.\sigma)) \ .$$

27.7   Prove Lemma 27.4.

27.8   Show the following:

$$\{p\}; [Q] \;=\; \{p\}; [\lambda \sigma\, \gamma \cdot p.\sigma \wedge Q.\sigma.\gamma] \ .$$

27.9   Show that $(\forall \sigma \cdot \neg\, p.\sigma \Rightarrow (\forall \gamma \cdot P.\sigma.\gamma))$ implies $|p|\backslash P = P$.

27.10 Use Theorem 27.8 to derive necessary and sufficient conditions for when
       refinement

$$\{p\}; [P] \sqsubseteq \{q\}; [Q]$$

holds.

27.11 Use the rules for top-down program development to refine the specification

$$[x := x' \mid x'^2 \le y < (x' + 1)^2]$$

to

```
x := 0 ;
while (x + 1)² < y do
    x := x + 1
od .
```

efinement in Context

The refinement relation is very restrictive, as it requires that the refining statement preserve the correctness of the original statement no matter what pre- and post-conditions are assumed for the original statement. In practice, we are interested mostly in refining a statement that occurs as a component of a larger statement. This context will then restrict the pre- and postconditions that need to be preserved for the whole statement to be refined.

We described in Section 17.4 how to carry out such refinements in context. In this chapter, we will look at this technique in more detail, in particular on the methods for propagating context information inside a program statement. We consider only conjunctive commands here, though a dual theory can be built up for disjunctive commands (see the exercises).

1 Taking the Context into Account

Let us first recall the method for using context information in a refinement as it was described in Section 17.4. We assume that C is a statement built from conjunctive components and with possible occurrences of a statement variable X. Then $C[S]$ (i.e., $C[X := S]$) is a conjunctive statement with a specific occurrence of substatement S singled out. We refer to C as the *context* of S. Since the statement constructors are monotonic, we have that $S \sqsubseteq S' \Rightarrow C[S] \sqsubseteq C[S']$. We are thus permitted to replace S by a refinement S' in C, getting as the result a refinement $C[S']$ of the original statement $C[S]$.

In many situations, the requirement that $S \sqsubseteq S'$ is, however, too strong, so the question is whether we might replace S by some statement S' for which $S \sqsubseteq S'$

does not hold, but for which $C[S] \sqsubseteq C[S']$ would still hold. In other words, replacement of S by S' preserves the correctness of the whole statement.

This can indeed be done in a systematic way, as follows: First find a statement S_0 such that $C[S] = C[S_0]$. Then find a refinement S' of S_0. The refinement $C[S] \sqsubseteq C[S']$ then follows by monotonicity and transitivity. The less refined is, the more freedom it gives us in the subsequent refinement.

Kernel Equivalence

Refinement in context can be described in terms of kernel equivalence. Given arbitrary function $f : \Sigma \to \Gamma$, we define $=_f$, the *kernel equivalence* of f, by

$$x =_f y \ \hat{=} \ f.x = f.y \qquad\qquad \textit{(kernel equivalence)}$$

(when applying kernel equivalence to context refinement, the function $(\lambda X \cdot$ corresponds to f in this definition). It is easily seen that $=_f$ is an equivalence relation.

Lemma 28.1   *Assume that Σ and Γ are complete lattices and that the function $f : \Sigma \to \Gamma$ is homomorphic. Furthermore, let $x : \Sigma$ be arbitrary. Then the set $\{y : \Sigma \mid x = \ \ \}$ has a smallest element.*

Proof   It suffices to show that $\{y : \Sigma \mid y =_f x\}$ (i.e., the equivalence class under $=_f$) is nonempty and closed under nonempty meets. First, we always know $x =_f x$, so the set is nonempty. For an arbitrary set $\{x_i : \Sigma \mid i \in I\}$ we have

$$(\forall i \in I \cdot x_i =_f x), \ f : \Sigma \to \Gamma \text{ meet homomorphic}, I \text{ nonempty}$$
$$\vdash f.(\sqcap i \in I \cdot x_i)$$
$$= \{\text{meet homomorphism}\}$$
$$(\sqcap i \in I \cdot f.x_i)$$
$$= \{\text{kernel equivalence}\}$$
$$(\sqcap i \in I \cdot f.x)$$
$$= \{I \text{ nonempty}\}$$
$$f.x$$

$\square$

We can now show that the smallest element shown to exist in Lemma 28.1 desirable property.

Lemma 28.2   *Assume that Σ and Γ are complete lattices and that the function $f : \Sigma \to$ meet homomorphic. Then the following holds, for arbitrary $x, y : \Sigma$:*

$$(\sqcap z \mid x =_f z \cdot z) \sqsubseteq y \ \Rightarrow \ f.x \sqsubseteq f.y \ .$$

Proof

$$(\sqcap z \mid z =_f x \cdot z) \sqsubseteq y$$

$$\vdash f.y$$

$$\sqsupseteq \{\text{assumption, } \sqcap\text{-homomorphism implies monotonicity}\}$$

$$f.(\sqcap z \mid z =_f x \cdot z)$$

$$= \{\sqcap\text{-homomorphism}\}$$

$$(\sqcap z \mid z =_f x \cdot f.z)$$

$$= \{\text{kernel equivalence}\}$$

$$(\sqcap z \mid z =_f x \cdot f.x)$$

$$= \{\text{meet of singleton set}\}$$

$$f.x$$

□

For predicate transformers, the two lemmas above show the following. Consider a statement $C[S]$ where $C[\cdot]$ is a meet homomorphic context. Then there always exists a smallest predicate transformer S_0 such that $C[S] = C[S_0]$, and furthermore, a refinement $C[S_0] \sqsubseteq C[S']$ holds whenever $S_0 \sqsubseteq S'$ holds. We can build meet homomorphic contexts by using guards, asserts, demonic updates, sequential composition, meets, least and greatest fixed points, iterations, and all other constructs that are conjunctive or preserve conjunctivity.

Context Assertions

Assume that $C[S]$ is given, with S a predicate transformer and $C[\cdot]$ a meet homomorphic context. It may not be feasible to find the least predicate transformer S_0 such that $C[S] = C[S_0]$. In practice, we can make considerable progress by finding a (reasonably strong) predicate p (a *context assertion*) such that $C[S] = C[\{p\}; S]$. When we then refine $\{p\}; S$, we are really refining S under the (contextual) knowledge that the predicate p can be assumed to hold in any initial state from which S is executed.

For this to work we need rules for *propagating* context assertions. We can start with outermost assertions {true} (i.e., skip) and then propagate these inwards until the assertions meet at the subcomponent that we want to refine. The structure of the derivation is then

$$C[S]$$

$$= \{\text{skip} = \{\text{true}\}\}$$

$$\{\text{true}\} ; C[S] ; \{\text{true}\}$$

$$\sqsubseteq \{\text{propagate context assertions}\}$$

$$C[\{p\}\,;\{q\}\,;S]$$
$$= \{\text{merge assertions, } \{p\}\,;\{q\} = \{p \cap q\}\}$$
$$C[\{p \cap q\}\,;S]$$
$$\sqsubseteq \{\text{prove } \{p \cap q\}\,;S \sqsubseteq S', \text{monotonicity}\}$$
$$C[S']$$

Note that we here have generalized the method for propagating context asserti⬤
as compared to Section 17.4, by permitting both forward and backward propaga⬤
of assertions. In practice, forward propagation seems to be the most useful met⬤

A restricted refinement puts weaker constraints on the refining statement:

$$\{p\}\,;S \sqsubseteq S' \;\equiv\; (\forall\sigma \cdot p.\sigma \Rightarrow (\forall q \cdot S.q.\sigma \Rightarrow S'.q.\sigma))\ .$$

Thus, we have to prove refinement between S and S' only for those initial stat⬤
that satisfy the condition p. This is weaker than $S \sqsubseteq S'$, which requires refinen⬤
between S and S' for every initial state. We have that $S \sqsubseteq S' \Rightarrow \{p\}\,;S \sqsubseteq S'$,
the converse need not hold.

Example

Consider, as an example, the following statement, where x and y are assume⬤
be program variables ranging over the natural numbers:

$$x := x+1\,;\,y := x+2\,;\,\text{if } y \le 3 \text{ then skip else abort fi}\ .$$

Let us simplify this statement. The rules for assertion propagation to be g⬤
below permit us to construct the following derivation:

$$x := x+1\,;\,y := x+2\,;\,\text{if } y \le 3 \text{ then skip else abort fi}$$
$$= \{\text{add initial and final trivial assertions}\}$$
$$\{\text{true}\}\,;\,x := x+1\,;\,y := x+2\,;\,\text{if } y \le 3 \text{ then skip else abort fi}\,;\,\{\text{true}\}$$
$$\sqsubseteq \{\text{propagate assertion forward}\}$$
$$x := x+1\,;\,\{x \ge 1\}\,;\,y := x+2\,;\,\text{if } y \le 3 \text{ then skip else abort fi}\,;\,\{\text{tru}⬤$$
$$\sqsubseteq \{\text{propagate assertion backwards}\}$$
$$x := x+1\,;\,\{x \ge 1\}\,;\,y := x+2\,;\,\{y \le 3\}\,;\,\text{if } y \le 3 \text{ then skip else ab}⬤$$
$$= \{\text{propagate assertion backwards}\}$$
$$x := x+1\,;\,\{x \ge 1\}\,;\,\{x \le 1\}\,;\,y := x+2\,;\,\text{if } y \le 3 \text{ then skip else ab}⬤$$
$$= \{\text{merge assertions}\}$$
$$x := x+1\,;\,\{x = 1\}\,;\,y := x+2\,;\,\text{if } y \le 3 \text{ then skip else abort fi}$$
$$= \{\text{refinement in context}\}$$
$$x := x+1\,;\,y := 3\,;\,\text{if } y \le 3 \text{ then skip else abort fi}$$

This derivation illustrates the way in which statements preceding the component to be replaced, as well as statements following this component, can contribute to the context assertion that we can assume when refining the component.

Guards as Context Assumptions

Context assertions allow us to transport information from one place in a program text to another. The amount of information that is available in assertions is often huge. Of course, we can always weaken an assertion (since $p \subseteq q \Rightarrow \{p\} \sqsubseteq \{q\}$), but it can be difficult to decide what information to discard. By using guard statements in addition to asserts, we can avoid this problem.

Since any guard statement $[p]$ refines skip, we can always introduce guards in a program text. Intuitively, introducing a guard means that we introduce a hypothetical assumption that will later need to be discharged (otherwise we are left with a miraculous component in our program).

We propose the following method for working with context assumptions. Assume that we want to refine a subcomponent S of a statement $C[S]$. Furthermore, assume that we feel confident that it would be possible to propagate information that establishes an assertion $\{p\}$ at S, and that this assertion would be useful in subsequent refinements. We can then introduce a guard–assert pair using the following general rule (which is straightforward to verify):

$$S \sqsubseteq [p] ; \{p\} ; S .$$

Now we can refine S in context $\{p\}$. Furthermore, we need rules by which we can show that $C[[p] ; \{p\} ; S] = C[\{p\} ; S]$; i.e., the context assumption $[p]$ can be discharged. The rules for propagating the guard $[p]$ backwards in order to discard are described below. If we have chosen the context assumption correctly, then the propagated guard statement is eventually reduced to skip and can then be removed. This will then establish that $C[S] = C[\{p\} ; S]$, from which we then continue with a refinement in context as before.

Restricted refinement can also be expressed in terms of context assumptions. From Lemma 13.12 we know that $\{p\} ; S \sqsubseteq S' \equiv S \sqsubseteq [p] ; S'$, so we could first carry out refinements that add context assumptions, $C[S] = C[[p] ; S']$, and then show that the guard statement can actually be removed.

2 Rules for Propagating Context Assertions

Assume that a conjunctive statement is given. The two basic constructors used in conjunctive statements are sequential composition and meet. For sequential composition, we need rules that propagate assertions *forward* and *backwards* through a

statement. For meet, we need a rule that to one conjunct adds assertions induce⋯
the other conjuncts (we refer to this as *sideways propagation*). Intuitively speak⋯
forward propagation carries information about the results of previous computati⋯
while backward and sideways propagation carries information about what st⋯
can be treated arbitrarily, since they would lead to nontermination in the subseq⋯
computation.

Rules for Sequential Composition and Meet

The basic rules in the following theorem determine how assertions can be pr⋯
gated forward, backwards and sideways.

Theorem 28.3 *Let S and S' be arbitrary conjunctive predicate transformers and p and q pr⋯
cates. Then*

(a) $\{p\} ; S = \{p\} ; S ; \{q\}$ if and only if $p \cap S.\text{true} \subseteq S.q$;

(b) $S ; \{q\} = \{p\} ; S ; \{q\}$ if and only if $S.q \subseteq p$;

(c) $S \sqcap S' = \{p\} ; S \sqcap S'$ if and only if $S.\text{true} \cap S'.\text{true} \subseteq p$.

Proof Assume that S and S' are conjunctive. Since dropping an assertion is alw⋯
a valid refinement, we need only consider left-to-right refinement in the proof.⋯
(a), we have

$$\{p\} ; S \sqsubseteq \{p\} ; S ; \{q\}$$
$$\equiv \{\text{definitions}\}$$
$$(\forall r \cdot p \cap S.r \subseteq p \cap S.(q \cap r))$$
$$\equiv \{S \text{ conjunctive}\}$$
$$(\forall r \cdot p \cap S.r \subseteq p \cap S.q \cap S.r)$$
$$\equiv \{\text{lattice property } x \sqsubseteq x \sqcap y \equiv x \sqsubseteq y\}$$
$$(\forall r \cdot p \cap S.r \subseteq S.q)$$
$$\equiv \{\Rightarrow \text{ by specialization } (r := \text{true}), \Leftarrow \text{ by monotonicity } (r \subseteq \text{true})\}$$
$$p \cap S.\text{true} \subseteq S.q$$

The proofs of (b) and (c) are similar. □

In general we are interested in adding the strongest (i.e., least with respect t⋯
refinement ordering) assertions possible, since a stronger assertion carries ⋯
information than a weaker one. Theorem 28.3 (b) and (c) immediately give us ⋯
for finding the strongest possible assertion to be added. In (a), we do not gi⋯
closed expression for the strongest forward-propagated assertion. However,⋯
can show that such an assertion always exists:

Lemma 28.4 *Let conjunctive predicate transformer* $S : \Sigma \mapsto \Gamma$ *and predicate p over* Σ *be given. Then the strongest predicate q such that* $\{p\} ; S = \{p\} ; S ; \{q\}$ *is the following:*

$$(\cap q \mid p \cap S.\text{true} \subseteq S.q \cdot q) \ .$$

Proof We give the predicate $(\cap q \mid p \cap S.\text{true} \subseteq S.q \cdot q)$ the name q_0. First we show that q_0 satisfies the desired condition:

$$\{p\} ; S = \{p\} ; S ; \{q_0\}$$
$$\equiv \{\text{Theorem 28.3 (a), definition of } q_0\}$$
$$p \cap S.\text{true} \subseteq S.(\cap q \mid p \cap S.\text{true} \subseteq S.q \cdot q)$$
$$\equiv \{S \text{ conjunctive}\}$$
$$p \cap S.\text{true} \subseteq (\cap q \mid p \cap S.\text{true} \subseteq S.q \cdot S.q)$$
$$\equiv \{\text{general rule } (\forall x \in A \cdot y \sqsubseteq x) \equiv y \sqsubseteq \cap A\}$$
$$\top$$

We then show that q_0 is in fact the strongest of all predicates satisfying the condition in question:

$$\{p\} ; S = \{p\} ; S ; \{q\}$$
$$\equiv \{\text{Theorem 28.3 (a)}\}$$
$$p \cap S.\text{true} \subseteq S.q$$
$$\equiv \{\text{rewrite}\}$$
$$q \in \{q \mid p \cap S.\text{true} \subseteq S.q\}$$
$$\Rightarrow \{\text{general rule } x \in A \Rightarrow \cap A \sqsubseteq x\}$$
$$(\cap q \mid p \cap S.\text{true} \subseteq S.q \cdot q) \subseteq q$$
$$\equiv \{\text{definition of } q_0\}$$
$$q_0 \subseteq q$$

This finishes the proof. □

Propagation of context assertions is closely linked to correctness of statements. The following is a direct consequence of Theorem 28.3.

Corollary 28.5 *Assume that predicates p and q are given and that S is a conjunctive predicate transformer. Then*

(a) $p \cap S.\text{true} \{\!\mid S \mid\!\} q \equiv \{p\} ; S \sqsubseteq S ; \{q\}$.

(b) $p \{\!\mid S \mid\!\} q \Rightarrow \{p\} ; S \sqsubseteq S ; \{q\}$.

This shows that correctness assuming termination, or *weak correctness*, is equivalent to forward propagation of context assertions and that ordinary correctness is a sufficient condition for propagation.

Propagation Rules for Basic Statements

The forward propagation rule of Theorem 28.3 is not as such very useful, s
it does not give us a way of calculating the propagated assertion. Below, we
individual rules for forward propagation through different constructs. The pr
of these rules are left to the reader as an exercise (Exercise 28.1).

$$\{p\};\{q\} = \{p\};\{q\};\{p \cap q\} ,$$
$$\{p\};[q] = \{p\};[q];\{p \cap q\} ,$$
$$\{p\};\langle f \rangle = \{p\};\langle f \rangle;\{\text{im}.f.p\} ,$$
$$\{p\};[Q] = \{p\};[Q];\{\text{im}.Q.p\} .$$

Recall here that $\text{im}.f.p = \{\gamma \mid (\exists \sigma \cdot p.\sigma \wedge \gamma = f.\sigma)\}$ (the image of p under
while $\text{im}.Q.p = \{\gamma \mid (\exists \sigma \cdot p.\sigma \wedge Q.\sigma.\gamma)\}$ (the image of p under relation Q).

For backward propagation, we immediately get the following rules for basic st
ments:

$$\{q\};\{p\} = \{p \cap q\};\{q\};\{p\} ,$$
$$[q];\{p\} = \{\neg q \cup p\};[q];\{p\} ,$$
$$\langle f \rangle;\{p\} = \{f^{-1}.p\};\langle f \rangle;\{p\} ,$$
$$[Q];\{p\} = \{\lambda \sigma \cdot Q.\sigma \subseteq p\};[Q];\{p\} .$$

Example Derivation

The following derivation illustrates how one works with assertions. We start f
the following statement over program variables x, y : Nat:

$$x := x + 1 ; (y := x + 1 \sqcap \{x < 2\} ; y := x) .$$

The main aim is to refine the substatements $y := x + 1$ and $y := x$.

$$x := x + 1 ; (y := x + 1 \sqcap \{x < 2\} ; y := x)$$
$= \{\text{add vacuous assertion}\}$
$$\{true\} ; x := x + 1 ; (y := x + 1 \sqcap \{x < 2\} ; y := x)$$
$= \{\text{forward propagation for functional update, simplify}\}$
$$x := x + 1 ; \{x > 0\} ; (y := x + 1 \sqcap \{x < 2\} ; y := x)$$
$= \{\text{sideways propagation (Exercise 28.2)}\}$
$$x := x + 1 ; \{x > 0\} ; (\{x < 2\} ; y := x + 1 \sqcap \{x < 2\} ; y := x)$$
$= \{\text{distributivity, merge assertions (homomorphism property)}\}$
$$x := x + 1 ; (\{x = 1\} ; y := x + 1 \sqcap \{x = 1\} ; y := x)$$

Now we can focus inside the assignment $y := x + 1$. Our derivation continue
follows:

$$x := x + 1 ; (\{x = 1\} ; y := \text{``} x + 1 \text{''}) \sqcap \{x = 1\} ; y := x)$$

$= \{$arithmetic, use local assumption $x = 1\}$

$\quad x := x + 1 \,;\, (\{x = 1\} \,;\, y := 2 \sqcap \{x = 1\} \,;\, y := \text{``} x \text{''})$

$= \{$substitute, use local assumption $x = 1\}$

$\quad x := x + 1 \,;\, (\{x = 1\} \,;\, y := 2 \sqcap \{x = 1\} \,;\, y := 1)$

$\sqsubseteq \{$drop assertions$\}$

$\quad x := x + 1 \,;\, (y := 2 \sqcap y := 1)$

The final step here was to drop all assertions, in order to make the final statement easier to read. We could also leave the assertions in the code, since they convey information that might be used if the result is to be refined further.

3 Propagation in Derived Statements

We have shown how to propagate context assertions into statements built out of basic statements using only sequential composition, meets, and joins. Below, we use these basic rules to derive propagation rules for derived statements. These are more useful in practical program development.

Conditionals

The rules for sequential composition and meet can be used to derive rules for other constructors. For the deterministic conditional, we have the following rule:

Theorem 28.6 *Assertions are propagated into and out of a deterministic conditional as follows:*

(a) $\{p\}\,;\,$ if g then S else S' fi $\,;\, \{q\} =$
$\quad \{p\}\,;\,$ if g then $\{p \cap g\}\,;\, S\,;\, \{q\}$ else $\{p \cap \neg g\}\,;\, S'\,;\, \{q\}$ fi $\,;\, \{q\}$.

(b) if g then $\{p\}\,;\, S\,;\, \{q\}$ else $\{p'\}\,;\, S'\,;\, \{q'\}$ fi $=$
$\quad \{(g \cap p) \cup (\neg g \cap p')\}\,;\,$ if g then $\{p\}\,;\, S\,;\, \{q\}$ else $\{p'\}\,;\, S'\,;\, \{q'\}$ fi $\,;\, \{q \cup q'\}$.

Proof We apply the rules for assertion propagation given above.

$\quad \{p\}\,;\,$ if g then S else S' fi $\,;\, \{q\}$

$= \{$definition of deterministic conditional$\}$

$\quad \{p\}\,;\, ([g]\,;\, S \sqcap [\neg g]\,;\, S')\,;\, \{q\}$

$= \{$distributivity$\}$

$\quad \{p\}\,;\, [g]\,;\, S\,;\, \{q\} \sqcap \{p\}\,;\, [\neg g]\,;\, S'\,;\, \{q\}$

$= \{$forward propagation$\}$

$\quad \{p\}\,;\, [g]\,;\, \{p \cap g\}\,;\, S\,;\, \{q\} \sqcap \{p\}\,;\, [\neg g]\,;\, \{p \cap \neg g\}\,;\, S'\,;\, \{q\}$

$= \{$homomorphism property, $q \cap q = q\}$

$$\{p\} ; [g] ; \{p \cap g\} ; S ; \{q\} ; \{q\} \sqcap \{p\} ; [\neg g] ; \{p \cap \neg g\} ; S' ; \{q\} ; \{$$
$$= \{\text{distributivity}\}$$
$$\{p\} ; ([g] ; \{p \cap g\} ; S ; \{q\} \sqcap [\neg g] ; \{p \cap \neg g\} ; S' ; \{q\}) ; \{q\}$$
$$= \{\text{definition of deterministic conditional}\}$$
$$\{p\} ; \text{if } g \text{ then } \{p \cap g\} ; S ; \{q\} \text{ else } \{p \cap \neg g\} ; S' ; \{q\} \text{ fi} ; \{q\}$$

The proof of (b) is similar. $\square$

The generalization of Theorem 28.6 to guarded conditionals is straightforw
Thus, for example, the rule for propagation into a guarded conditional is

$$\{p\} ; \text{if } g_1 \rightarrow S_1 \ [] \ \cdots \ [] \ g_n \rightarrow S_n \text{ fi} ; \{q\} =$$
$$\{p\} ; \text{if } g_1 \rightarrow \{p \cap g_1\} ; S_1 ; \{q\} \ [] \ \cdots \ [] \ g_n \rightarrow \{p \cap g_n\} ; S_n ; \{q\} \text{ fi} ; \{$$

Loops

For loops, we derive a rule for adding an invariant as a context assertion. In add
to the invariant, the guard of the loop gives information; it always holds whe
body is executed, and it cannot hold after the loop has terminated.

Theorem 28.7 *Assume that the following condition holds:*

$$g \cap p \cap S.\text{true} \subseteq S.p .$$

Then context assertions can be added to a while loop as follows:

$$\{p\} ; \text{while } g \text{ do } S \text{ od} = \{p\} ; \text{while } g \text{ do } \{p \cap g\} ; S ; \{p\} \text{ od} ; \{\neg g \cap $$

Proof We first note that the condition is equivalent to the condition

$$\{g \cap p\} ; S = \{g \cap p\} ; S ; \{p\}$$

(use Corollary 28.5). Now define functions f and h by

$$f.X = \text{if } g \text{ then } S ; X \text{ else skip fi} ,$$
$$h.X = \text{if } g \text{ then } \{g \cap p\} ; S ; \{p\} ; X \text{ else skip fi} .$$

We show by ordinal induction that for an arbitrary ordinal α,

$$\{p\} ; (f^\alpha.\text{abort}) = \{p\} ; (h^\alpha.\text{abort}) ; \{\neg g \cap p\} .$$

The base case ($\alpha = 0$) is

$$\{p\} ; \text{abort} = \{p\} ; \text{abort} ; \{\neg g \cap p\} ,$$

which is obviously true. For the successor case, we assume that (∗) holds for α.
Then

$\qquad \{p\} \, ; (f^{\alpha+1}.\text{abort})$

$= \{\text{definition of } f\}$

$\qquad \{p\} \, ; \text{if } g \text{ then } S \, ; (f^{\alpha}.\text{abort}) \text{ else skip fi}$

$= \{\text{assertion propagation rule, skip} = \{\text{true}\}\}$

$\qquad \{p\} \, ; \text{if } g \text{ then } \{g \cap p\} \, ; S \, ; (f^{\alpha}.\text{abort}) \text{ else } \{\neg g \cap p\} \text{ fi}$

$= \{\text{assumption of the lemma}\}$

$\qquad \{p\} \, ; \text{if } g \text{ then } \{g \cap p\} \, ; S \, ; \{p\} \, ; (f^{\alpha}.\text{abort}) \text{ else } \{\neg g \cap p\} \text{ fi}$

$= \{\text{induction assumption}\}$

$\qquad \{p\} \, ; \text{if } g \text{ then } \{g \cap p\} \, ; S \, ; \{p\} \, ; (h^{\alpha}.\text{abort}) \, ; \{\neg g \cap p\} \text{ else } \{\neg g \cap p\} \text{ fi}$

$= \{\text{assertion propagation rule}\}$

$\qquad \{p\} \, ; \text{if } g \text{ then } \{g \cap p\} \, ; S \, ; \{p\} \, ; (h^{\alpha}.\text{abort}) \text{ else skip fi} \, ; \{\neg g \cap p\}$

$= \{\text{definition of } h^{\alpha+1}\}$

$\qquad \{p\} \, ; (h^{\alpha+1}.\text{abort}) \, ; \{\neg g \cap p\}$

Finally, we have the limit case, assuming that (∗) holds for all ordinals $\beta < \alpha$:

$\qquad \{p\} \, ; (f^{\alpha}.\text{abort})$

$= \{\text{definition of } f^{\alpha}\}$

$\qquad \{p\} \, ; (\sqcup \beta \mid \beta < \alpha \cdot f^{\beta}.\text{abort})$

$= \{\text{distributivity (assert is disjunctive)}\}$

$\qquad (\sqcup \beta \mid \beta < \alpha \cdot \{p\} \, ; (f^{\beta}.\text{abort}))$

$= \{\text{induction assumption}\}$

$\qquad (\sqcup \beta \mid \beta < \alpha \cdot \{p\} \, ; (h^{\beta}.\text{abort}) \, ; \{\neg g \cap p\})$

$= \{\text{distributivity}\}$

$\qquad \{p\} \, ; (\sqcup \beta \mid \beta < \alpha \cdot h^{\beta}.\text{abort}) \, ; \{\neg g \cap p\}$

$= \{\text{definition of } h^{\alpha}\}$

$\qquad \{p\} \, ; (h^{\alpha}.\text{abort}) \, ; \{\neg g \cap p\}$

Thus (∗) holds for an arbitrary ordinal, and the proof is finished. □

Note that the predicate p in Theorem 28.7 is a *weak invariant*: the body S has to preserve p only if S terminates. This is different from the *strong invariant* used in total correctness proofs of loops. Propagation of assertions in the loop does not require the loop to terminate.

The generalization of Theorem 28.7 to guarded iteration is straightforward: if $g_i \cap p \cap S_i.\text{true} \subseteq S_i.p$ for $i = 1, \ldots, n$, then

$$\{p\} ; \mathbf{do}\ g_1 \rightarrow S_1 \mathbin{[\!]} \cdots \mathbin{[\!]} g_n \rightarrow S_n\ \mathbf{od}\ =$$
$$\{p\} ; \mathbf{do}\ g_1 \rightarrow S_1' \mathbin{[\!]} \cdots \mathbin{[\!]} g_n \rightarrow S_n'\ \mathbf{od} ; \{\neg g \cap p\} ,$$

where $S_i' = \{p \cap g_i\} ; S_i ; \{p\}$ and $g = g_1 \cup \cdots \cup g_n$.

Blocks

For blocks we need two rules: one for propagating an assertion into the b
from the left and one to propagate an assertion out from the block on the r
For simplicity, we use the general demonic (nondeterministically initialized) b
construct in the rule, since the other block constructs are special cases of this

Theorem 28.8   *Assume that p, q, and r are Boolean expressions such that y does not occur
in p or q. Furthermore, assume that p and p' are similar, and that r and r
similar. Then*

(a) $\{p\} ; \mathbf{begin\ var}\ y \mid q ; S\ \mathbf{end}\ =$
$\{p\} ; \mathbf{begin\ var}\ y \mid q ; \{p' \cap q\} ; S\ \mathbf{end}$.

(b) $\mathbf{begin\ var}\ y \mid q ; S ; \{r\}\ \mathbf{end}\ =$
$\mathbf{begin\ var}\ y \mid q ; S ; \{r\}\ \mathbf{end} ; \{\exists y \cdot r'\}$.

Proof Both proofs are straightforward, using the definition of the block. We s
the crucial derivation for the second part. We have

$$\{r\} ; \langle \mathbf{end} \rangle \sqsubseteq \langle \mathbf{end} \rangle ; \{\exists y \cdot r\}$$
$$\equiv \{\text{definitions}\}$$
$$\{\lambda \gamma\ \sigma \cdot r.\gamma \wedge \sigma = \mathrm{end}.\gamma\} \sqsubseteq \{\lambda \gamma\ \sigma \cdot \sigma = \mathrm{end}.\gamma \wedge (\exists y \cdot r).\sigma\}$$
$$\Leftarrow \{\text{homomorphism}\}$$
$$(\forall \gamma\ \sigma \cdot r.\gamma \wedge \sigma = \mathrm{end}.\gamma \Rightarrow \sigma = \mathrm{end}.\gamma \wedge (\exists y \cdot r).\sigma)$$
$$\equiv \{\text{one-point rule}\}$$
$$(\forall \gamma \cdot r.\gamma \Rightarrow (\exists y \cdot r).(\mathrm{end}.\gamma))$$
$$\equiv \{\text{pointwise extension}\}$$
$$(\forall \gamma \cdot r.\gamma \Rightarrow (\exists y \cdot r.(\mathrm{end}.\gamma)))$$
$$\equiv \{\text{use } y.\gamma \text{ as existential witness}\}$$
$$\mathsf{T}$$

and the rule now follows from the definition of the block. $\square$

Similar rules can also be derived for propagating assertions backwards int
out of blocks (Exercise 28.4).

4   Context Assumptions

The rules for backward propagation of context assumptions (guards) are in many ways dual to those for forward propagation of asserts. We start with a general rule.

Theorem 28.9 *Guard statements can be propagated backwards according to the following rule whenever S is conjunctive:*

$$S ; [q] \ \sqsubseteq \ [S.q] ; S \ .$$

Proof

$$S ; [q] \sqsubseteq [S.q] ; S$$
$$\equiv \{\text{Lemma 13.12}\}$$
$$\{S.q\} ; S \sqsubseteq S ; \{q\}$$
$$\equiv \{\text{Theorem 28.3 (b)}\}$$
$$\mathsf{T}$$

$\square$

We can now state rules for individual program constructs that can be used in practical program derivations. Most of the rules follow directly from Theorem 28.9.

Theorem 28.10 *The following rules are available for basic statements:*

(a) $[\mathsf{true}] \ = \ \mathsf{skip}$.

(b) $\{p\} ; [q] \ = \ [\neg p \cup q] ; \{p\}$.

(c) $[p] ; [q] \ = \ [p \cap q]$.

(d) $\langle f \rangle ; [q] \ \sqsubseteq \ [\mathsf{preim}.f.q] ; \langle f \rangle$.

(e) $[Q] ; [q] \ \sqsubseteq \ [\lambda \sigma \cdot Q.\sigma \subseteq q] ; [Q]$.

(f) $(S_1 \sqcap S_2) ; [q] \ \sqsubseteq \ S_1 ; [q] \sqcap S_1 ; [q]$.

(g) $[q_1] ; S_1 \sqcap [q_2] ; S_2 \ \sqsubseteq \ [q_1 \cap q_2] ; (S_1 \sqcap S_2)$.

The lemma can be then be used as a basis for proving the corresponding propagation rules for our derived constructs.

Theorem 28.11 *The following rules are available for derived statements:*

(a) if g then S else S' fi ; $[q]$ $=$ if g then S ; $[q]$ else S' ; $[q]$ fi .

(b) if g then $[q]$; S else $[q']$; S' fi $=$ $[(g \cap q) \cup (\neg g \cap q')]$; if g then S else S' fi .

(c) begin var $y \mid p$; S end ; $[q]$ = begin var $y \mid p$; S ; $[q]$ end *provided th* *does not occur free in q.*

(d) begin var $y \mid p$; $[q]$; S end = $[\forall y \cdot p \Rightarrow q]$; begin var $y \mid p$; S end .

Proof The rules for conditional and block are proved in the same way as corresponding rules for propagating assertions. $\square$

The idea behind guard propagation is that we want to eliminate guards from program. By propagating guards backwards we hope to weaken the predicate i the guard statement, so that it eventually reduces to true and the whole g statement can be removed. Note that there is no rule for loops; we assume whenever a loop is introduced, sufficient information about the loop is added assertion after the loop.

As an example, we show how context assumptions are used to refine a si sequential composition. Here we introduce the pair $[x = 0]$; $\{x = 0\}$ at a in the program where we (by looking at the preceding assignment) feel confi that $x = 0$ must hold.

$x, z := 0, z \cdot z$; $y := x + 1$

$\sqsubseteq$ {add context assumption pair; skip $\sqsubseteq$ $[p]$; $\{p\}$}

$\quad x, z := 0, z \cdot z$; $[x = 0]$; $\{x = 0\}$; $y := \text{“ } x + 1 \text{ ”}$

$=$ {use assertion for refinement in context}

$\quad x, z := 0, z \cdot z$; $[x = 0]$; $y := 1$

$=$ {propagate guard statement}

$\quad [\text{true}]$; $x, z := 0, z \cdot z$; $y := 1$

$=$ {$[\text{true}]$ = skip }

$\quad x, z := 0, z \cdot z$; $y := 1$

To show that the context assumption approach allows propagating smaller am of information, we also show an alternative derivation using context asse propagation only:

$x, z := 0, z \cdot z$; $y := x + 1$

$=$ {add initial assertion; skip = {true}}

$\quad \{\text{true}\}$; $x, z := 0, z \cdot z$; $y := x + 1$

$=$ {propagate assert}

$\quad x, z := 0, z \cdot z$; $\{x = 0 \wedge (\exists z_0 \cdot z_0 \cdot z_0 = z)\}$; $y := x + 1$

$=$ {use assertion for refinement in context}

$\quad x, z := 0, z \cdot z$; $\{x = 0 \wedge (\exists z_0 \cdot z_0 \cdot z_0 = z)\}$; $y := 1$

$\sqsubseteq$ {drop assert}

$$x, z := 0, z \cdot z \,;\, y := 1$$

These two examples also show the duality between the two approaches; the justifications in the first derivation are very similar to those in the second derivation, but in reverse order.

Correctness and Propagation

Propagation of context assumptions is also closely linked to correctness of statements, in a way similar to propagation of context assertions.

eorem 28.12 *Assume that predicates p and q are given and that S is a conjunctive predicate transformer. Then*

(a) $p \cap S.\text{true} \{\!\{ S \}\!\} q \;\equiv\; S\,;[q] \sqsubseteq [p]\,;S$.

(b) $p \{\!\{ S \}\!\} q \;\Rightarrow\; S\,;[q] \sqsubseteq [p]\,;S$.

Proof The result follows directly from Corollary 28.5 and Lemma 13.12. $\square$

Exactly as in the case of the corresponding result for assertions (Corollary 28.5), this result can be useful when we assume a certain correctness condition and want to use it in an algebraic manipulation of statements.

5 Summary and Discussion

The idea of using state assertions as part of the statement language was introduced in Back's original formulation of the refinement calculus [6, 7]. The basic rules for propagating context assertions into subcomponents were also given there. The present treatment generalizes this considerably and also takes into account the dual notion of context assumptions (guard statements). This dual way of handling context information was introduced by Morgan [105].

The propagation rules for context assertions and context assumptions are also interesting in their own right. They give a general paradigm for transporting information relevant for total correctness around in a program statement. Although one might expect otherwise, these rules are not the same as one would get by considering a proof system for partial correctness. There are a number of places where the context assertions and assumptions propagate in a different way than partial correctness assertions, which essentially express reachability of states.

28.6   Exercises

28.1   Prove the following rules for forward propagation of context assertions throu different statements:

$$\{p\} ; \{q\} \ = \ \{p\} ; \{q\} ; \{p \cap q\} ,$$
$$\{p\} ; [q] \ = \ \{p\} ; [q] ; \{p \cap q\} ,$$
$$\{p\} ; \langle f \rangle \ = \ \{p\} ; \langle f \rangle ; \{\text{im}. f.p\} ,$$
$$\{p\} ; [Q] \ = \ \{p\} ; [Q] ; \{\text{im}.Q.p\} .$$

28.2   Show that the following rule follows from Theorem 28.3 (c):

$$S \cap \{p\} ; T \ = \ \{p\} ; S \cap \{p\} ; T .$$

28.3   Give an example of a statement $\{p\} ; S$ for which there is no predicate q satisfy

$$\{p\} ; S \ = \ S ; \{q\} .$$

Conclude that it is impossible to give a rule for forward propagation of asser without loss of information.

28.4   Derive rules for propagating assertions backwards into and out of blocks.

28.5   In a language of disjunctive statements, assertions can also be used to indic context information. In the disjunctive case, assertions have to be interpre differently. For example, the assertion introduction

$$S \ = \ S ; \{p\}$$

now means that for all initial states there is a possible execution of S such tha holds in the final state. However, the principle of restricted refinement can stil used. Derive rules for introducing assertions before and after the angelic upd command. Is there a rule for adding an assertion to one element of a join?

28.6   Complete the proof of Theorem 28.10.

28.7   Complete the proof of Corollary 28.5 (a); i.e., prove that

$$p \cap S.\text{true} \subseteq S.q \ \equiv \ \{p\} ; S \sqsubseteq S ; \{q\}$$

for conjunctive S.

28.8   Prove the following refinement with a detailed derivation:

$$x := \max(x, y) \ \sqsubseteq \ \text{if } x < y \text{ then } x := y \text{ else skip fi} .$$

eration of Conjunctive Statements

In our preceding treatment of iteration, we have considered the situation where the body of the iteration is either monotonic or continuous. In this chapter, we look at some of the additional properties that iterative statements have when the bodies are conjunctive. We show how weak and strong iteration are related in this case. We also prove two important properties that hold for iterations of conjunctive predicate transformers: the *decomposition* property, which shows how iteration of a meet can be rewritten in terms of iteration and sequential composition only, and the *leapfrog* property. The chapter also gives examples of program transformations that are used to modify the control structure of program statements.

1 Properties of Fixed Points

Before going in more detail into properties of conjunctive iterations, we need to establish a few technical results about fixed points. The first shows how to treat fixed points in multiple variables, while the second describes how to distribute function application into a fixed-point expression.

Fixed-Point Diagonalization

The following *diagonalization lemma* gives a way of moving between fixed points over one variable and fixed points over multiple variables. Exactly as for λ-abstraction, the notation $(\mu\, x\, y \cdot t)$ abbreviates $(\mu\, x \cdot (\mu\, y \cdot t))$.

Lemma 29.1   *Assume that the type Σ is a complete lattice and that the function $f : \Sigma \to \Sigma \to \Sigma$ is monotonic in both its arguments, Then*

$$(\mu\, x\, y \cdot f.x.y) \;=\; (\mu\, x \cdot f.x.x) \;.$$

Proof We prove mutual ordering. First:

$(\mu\, x\, y \cdot f.x.y) \sqsubseteq (\mu\, x \cdot f.x.x)$

$\Leftarrow$ {least fixed point induction with $f := (\lambda x\, y \cdot f.x.y)$}

$(\mu\, y \cdot f.(\mu\, x \cdot f.x.x).y) \sqsubseteq (\mu\, x \cdot f.x.x)$

$\Leftarrow$ {least fixed point induction with $f := (\lambda y \cdot f.(\mu\, x \cdot f.x.x).y)$}

$f.(\mu\, x \cdot f.x.x).(\mu\, x \cdot f.x.x) \sqsubseteq (\mu\, x \cdot f.x.x)$

$\equiv$ {unfold least fixed point}

$f.(\mu\, x \cdot f.x.x).(\mu\, x \cdot f.x.x) \sqsubseteq f.(\mu\, x \cdot f.x.x).(\mu\, x \cdot f.x.x)$

$\equiv$ {reflexivity}

$\top$

Then

$(\mu\, x \cdot f.x.x) \sqsubseteq (\mu\, x\, y \cdot f.x.y)$

$\Leftarrow$ {least fixed point induction with $f := (\lambda x \cdot f.x.x)$}

$f.(\mu\, x\, y \cdot f.x.y).(\mu\, x\, y \cdot f.x.y) \sqsubseteq (\mu\, x\, y \cdot f.x.y)$

$\equiv$ {unfold least fixed point with $f := (\lambda x \cdot (\mu\, y \cdot f.x.y))$}

$f.(\mu\, x\, y \cdot f.x.y).(\mu\, x\, y \cdot f.x.y) \sqsubseteq (\mu\, y \cdot f.(\mu\, x\, y \cdot f.x.y).y)$

$\equiv$ {unfold least fixed point with $f := (\lambda y \cdot f.(\mu\, x\, y \cdot f.x.y).y)$}

$f.(\mu\, x\, y \cdot f.x.y).(\mu\, x\, y \cdot f.x.y) \sqsubseteq$
    $f.(\mu\, x\, y \cdot f.x.y).(\mu\, y \cdot f.(\mu\, x\, y \cdot f.x.y).y)$

$\equiv$ {fold least fixed point with $f := (\lambda x \cdot (\mu\, y \cdot f.x.y))$}

$f.(\mu\, x\, y \cdot f.x.y).(\mu\, x\, y \cdot f.x.y) \sqsubseteq f.(\mu\, x\, y \cdot f.x.y).(\mu\, x\, y \cdot f.x.y)$

$\equiv$ {reflexivity}

$\top$

□

Distributivity into a Fixed Point

Many proofs in the rest of this chapter rest on the following important lemma distributing function application into a fixed-point expression, also known as rolling rule.

Lemma 29.2 *Assume that f and g are monotonic functions on a complete lattice. Then*

$$f.(\mu.(g \circ f)) \;=\; \mu.(f \circ g) \;,$$
$$f.(\nu.(g \circ f)) \;=\; \nu.(f \circ g) \;.$$

Proof We prove the first part; the proof for the greatest fixed point is similar. We first note that $f \circ g$ and $g \circ f$ are both monotonic, so the fixed points are well-defined. Now we prove mutual ordering:

$\quad \mu.(f \circ g) \sqsubseteq f.(\mu.(g \circ f))$

$\equiv$ {definition of composition, change to binder notation for μ}

$\quad (\mu\, x \cdot f.(g.x)) \sqsubseteq f.(\mu\, x \cdot g.(f.x))$

$\Leftarrow$ {least fixed point induction}

$\quad f.(g.(f.(\mu\, x \cdot g.(f.x)))) \sqsubseteq f.(\mu\, x \cdot g.(f.x))$

$\equiv$ {fold least fixed point}

$\quad f.(\mu\, x \cdot g.(f.x)) \sqsubseteq f.(\mu\, x \cdot g.(f.x))$

$\equiv$ {reflexivity}

$\quad \mathsf{T}$

and

$\quad f.(\mu.(g \circ f)) \sqsubseteq \mu.(f \circ g)$

$\equiv$ {definition of composition, change to binder notation for μ}

$\quad f.(\mu\, x \cdot g.(f.x)) \sqsubseteq (\mu\, x \cdot f.(g.x))$

$\equiv$ {unfold least fixed point}

$\quad f.(\mu\, x \cdot g.(f.x)) \sqsubseteq f.(g.(\mu\, x \cdot f.(g.x)))$

$\Leftarrow$ {f monotonic}

$\quad (\mu\, x \cdot g.(f.x)) \sqsubseteq g.(\mu\, x \cdot f.(g.x))$

$\Leftarrow$ {least fixed point induction}

$\quad g.(f.(g.(\mu\, x \cdot f.(g.x)))) \sqsubseteq g.(\mu\, x \cdot f.(g.x))$

$\equiv$ {fold least fixed point}

$\quad g.(\mu\, x \cdot f.(g.x)) \sqsubseteq g.(\mu\, x \cdot f.(g.x))$

$\equiv$ {reflexivity}

$\quad \mathsf{T}$

$\square$

We immediately have two important consequences of this result.

Theorem 29.3 *Assume that h is a monotonic function on predicate transformers and S is a monotonic predicate transformer. Then $(\lambda X \cdot h.(S \, ; X))$ and $(\lambda X \cdot S \, ; h.X)$ are*
monotonic functions, and

$$S \, ; (\mu X \cdot h.(S \, ; X)) \;=\; (\mu X \cdot S \, ; h.X) \, ,$$
$$S \, ; (\nu X \cdot h.(S \, ; X)) \;=\; (\nu X \cdot S \, ; h.X) \, .$$

Proof Use Lemma 29.2 with $f := (\lambda X \cdot S \, ; X)$ and $g := h. \; \square$

The other consequence is the following *rolling property* for least fixed points
sequential composition:

Corollary 29.4 *For arbitrary monotonic predicate transformers S and T,*

$$\mu.(S \, ; T) \;=\; S.(\mu.(T \, ; S)) \, .$$

Proof Use Lemma 29.2 with $f := S$ and $g := T. \; \square$

29.2 Relating the Iteration Statements

In the conjunctive case, the weak and strong iterations are related as follows.

Lemma 29.5 *Let S be an arbitrary conjunctive predicate transformer. Then*

(a) $S^{\omega} = \{\mu.S\} \, ; S^{*}$.

(b) $S^{\omega} = S^{*} \, ; \{\mu.S\}$.

Proof The first part is proved as follows:

$\qquad$ S conjunctive
$\qquad$ $\vdash \{\mu.S\} \, ; S^{*} = S^{\omega}$
$\qquad$ $\equiv$ {definitions, β reduction}
$\qquad\qquad$ $(\lambda p \cdot \{p\} \, ; S^{*}).(\mu.S) = (\mu X \cdot S \, ; X \sqcap \text{skip})$
$\qquad$ $\Leftarrow$ {fusion theorem (Theorem 19.5)}
$\qquad\qquad$ $(\lambda p \cdot \{p\} \, ; S^{*}) \circ S = (\lambda X \cdot S \, ; X \sqcap \text{skip}) \circ (\lambda p \cdot \{p\} \, ; S^{*})$
$\qquad$ $\equiv$ {definition of composition, pointwise extension, β reduction}
$\qquad\qquad$ $(\forall p \cdot \{S.p\} \, ; S^{*} = S \, ; \{p\} \, ; S^{*} \sqcap \text{skip})$
$\qquad$ $\equiv$ {unfold least fixed point}
$\qquad\qquad$ $(\forall p \cdot \{S.p\} \, ; (S \, ; S^{*} \sqcap \text{skip}) = S \, ; \{p\} \, ; S^{*} \sqcap \text{skip})$
$\qquad$ $\equiv$ {pointwise extension, statement definitions}

$$(\forall p \; q \cdot S.p \cap S.(S^*.q) \cap q \;=\; S.(p \cap S^*.q) \cap q)$$
$$\equiv \{S \text{ conjunctive}\}$$
$$\top$$

We leave it to the reader to show that $(\lambda q \cdot \{q\} \,;\, S)$ is continuous for arbitrary monotonic S (this guarantees that the second step of the derivation is valid). The second part of the lemma can be proved in a similar way, showing $\{\mu.S\} \,;\, S^* = S^* \,;\, \{\mu.S\}$ using the dual of fusion (with greatest fixed points) and relying on the fact that the function $(\lambda S \cdot \{q\} \,;\, S)$ is cocontinuous (Exercise 29.2). $\square$

Recall that $\mu.S$ characterizes those states from which repeated execution of S is guaranteed to terminate. Thus Lemma 29.5 shows how the strong iteration S^ω can be divided into two parts; the assertion checks for possible nontermination, and the weak iteration performs the repeated execution of S. This is reminiscent of the traditional decomposition of total correctness into termination and partial correctness. The same correspondence can also be expressed using infinite repetition:

Theorem 29.6   *Assume that S is a conjunctive predicate transformer. Then*

$$S^\omega \;=\; S^* \cap S^\infty .$$

Proof   For arbitrary q, we have

$$S^\omega.q$$
$$= \{\text{Lemma 29.5}\}$$
$$(\{\mu.S\} \,;\, S^*).q$$
$$= \{\text{definitions}\}$$
$$\mu.S \cap S^*.q$$
$$= \{S^\infty.q = \mu.S \text{ for arbitrary } q \text{ (Lemma 21.3)}\}$$
$$S^\infty.q \cap S^*.q$$
$$= \{\text{pointwise extension}\}$$
$$(S^\infty \cap S^*).q$$

which proves the lemma. $\square$

Now we can prove the result that was announced in Chapter 21.

Theorem 29.7   *Strong iterations, while loops, and guarded iterations preserve conjunctivity.*

Proof   We have the following derivation:

$$S \text{ conjunctive}, I \text{ nonempty}$$
$$\vdash S^\omega.(\cap i \in I \cdot p_i)$$
$$= \{\text{Theorem 29.6}\}$$

$$S^*.(\cap i \in I \cdot p_i) \sqcap S^\infty.(\cap i \in I \cdot p_i)$$
$= \{\text{weak iteration preserves conjunctivity}\}$
$$(\cap i \in I \cdot S^*.p_i) \sqcap S^\infty.(\cap i \in I \cdot p_i)$$
$= \{S^\infty.q = \mu.S \text{ for arbitrary } q\}$
$$(\cap i \in I \cdot S^*.p_i) \sqcap (\cap i \in I \cdot S^\infty.p_i)$$
$= \{\text{distributivity}\}$
$$(\cap i \in I \cdot S^*.p_i \sqcap S^\infty.p_i)$$
$= \{\text{Theorem 29.6}\}$
$$(\cap i \in I \cdot S^\omega.p_i)$$

The results for while loops and guarded iterations now follow directly, since ⬛ can be rewritten using strong iteration. □

29.3   Iteration of Meets

We shall now prove a number of results for weak and strong iterations. Th results show clearly the usefulness of algebraic reasoning in general and fix point reasoning in particular. Although the general results are for weak and str iteration only, they can be used for deriving properties of while loops as well shown later in this chapter.

Leapfrog Properties

The following lemma states that conjunctive iterations have what is someti called the *leapfrog property*.

Lemma 29.8   *Assume that predicate transformer S is conjunctive and T monotonic. Then*

$$S ; (T ; S)^\omega = (S ; T)^\omega ; S ,$$
$$S ; (T ; S)^* = (S ; T)^* ; S .$$

Proof   The second part of the lemma is proved as follows:

S conjunctive, T monotonic
$\vdash S ; (T ; S)^*$
$= \{\text{definition}\}$
$\qquad S ; (\nu X \cdot T ; S ; X \sqcap \text{skip})$
$= \{\text{Theorem 29.3 with } h := (\lambda X \cdot T ; S ; X \sqcap \text{skip})\}$
$\qquad (\nu X \cdot S ; (T ; X \sqcap \text{skip}))$

$$= \{S \text{ conjunctive}\}$$
$$(\nu X \cdot S ; T ; X \sqcap S)$$
$$= \{\text{Lemma } 21.2\}$$
$$(S ; T)^* ; S$$

The proof of the first part is similar. □

The proof of Lemma 29.8 rests heavily on the conjunctivity of S. If S is not assumed to be conjunctive, it is possible to show the following (Exercise 29.3):

$$S ; (T ; S)^* \sqsubseteq (S ; T)^* ; S .$$

The leapfrog property can now be used to prove a rule for manipulating while loops.

Lemma 29.9   *Assume that S and T are conjunctive and that g and g' are predicates such that $g \{\!| S |\!\} g'$ and $\neg g \{\!| S |\!\} \neg g'$. Then the following refinement holds:*

$$S ; \text{while } g \text{ do } T ; S \text{ od} \sqsubseteq \text{ while } g' \text{ do } S ; T \text{ od} ; S .$$

Proof   The proof is a short derivation:

$$S ; \text{while } g \text{ do } T ; S \text{ od}$$
$$= \{\text{Lemma } 21.8\}$$
$$S ; ([g] ; T ; S)^\omega ; [\neg g]$$
$$= \{\text{leapfrog property for strong iteration}\}$$
$$(S ; [g] ; T)^\omega ; S ; [\neg g]$$
$$\sqsubseteq \{\text{assumptions, Theorem } 28.12\}$$
$$([g'] ; S ; T)^\omega ; [\neg g'] ; S$$
$$= \{\text{Lemma } 21.8\}$$
$$\text{while } g' \text{ do } S ; T \text{ od} ; S$$

□

Decomposition Properties

The following *iteration decomposition* lemma shows that it is possible to rewrite iterations of meets in a form that contains only sequential composition and iteration:

Lemma 29.10   *Assume that predicate transformer S is conjunctive and T monotonic. Then*

$$(S \sqcap T)^* = S^* ; (T ; S^*)^* ,$$
$$(S \sqcap T)^\omega = S^\omega ; (T ; S^\omega)^\omega .$$

Proof We show the proof for strong iteration (the proof for weak iteration similar).

> S conjunctive, T monotonic
>
> $\vdash (S \sqcap T)^{\omega}$
>
> $= \{\text{definition}\}$
>
> $\quad (\mu X \cdot (S \sqcap T) ; X \sqcap \text{skip})$
>
> $= \{\text{distributivity}\}$
>
> $\quad (\mu X \cdot S ; X \sqcap T ; X \sqcap \text{skip})$
>
> $= \{\text{diagonalization (Lemma 29.1)}\}$
>
> $\quad (\mu X \cdot \mu Y \cdot S ; Y \sqcap T ; X \sqcap \text{skip})$
>
> $= \{\text{Lemma 21.2}\}$
>
> $\quad (\mu X \cdot S^{\omega} ; (T ; X \sqcap \text{skip}))$
>
> $= \{\text{Theorem 29.3}\}$
>
> $\quad S^{\omega} ; (\mu X \cdot T ; S^{\omega} ; X \sqcap \text{skip})$
>
> $= \{\text{definition of strong iteration}\}$
>
> $\quad S^{\omega} ; (T ; S^{\omega})^{\omega}$

$\square$

Combining Lemma 29.10 with the leapfrog properties in Lemma 29.8 we immediately get the following corollary:

Corollary 29.11 *Assume that predicate transformer S is conjunctive and T monotonic. Then*

$$(S \sqcap T)^{*} = (S^{*} ; T)^{*} ; S^{*} ,$$
$$(S \sqcap T)^{\omega} = (S^{\omega} ; T)^{\omega} ; S^{\omega} .$$

29.4 Loop Decomposition

The decomposition rule for iterations can be used to prove a decomposition for while loops. It can be seen as a basic rule, useful for deriving more specific rules.

Theorem 29.12 *Assume that statements S and T are conjunctive. Then*

> while $g \cup h$ do if g then S else T fi od $=$
>
> $\quad$ while g do S od ; while h do T ; (while g do S od) od

for arbitrary predicates g and h.

Proof

while $g \cup h$ do if g then S else T fi do

$=$ {rewrite loop using iteration}

$([g \cup h] ; \text{if } g \text{ then } S \text{ else } T \text{ fi})^{\omega} ; [\neg(g \cup h)]$

$=$ {rewrite conditional}

$([g \cup h] ; ([g] ; S \sqcap [\neg g] ; T))^{\omega} ; [\neg(g \cup h)]$

$=$ {distributivity, homomorphism, lattice properties}

$([g] ; S \sqcap [\neg g \cap h] ; T)^{\omega} ; [\neg g \cap \neg h)]$

$=$ {decomposition (Lemma 29.10)}

$(([g] ; S)^{\omega} ; [\neg g \cap h] ; T)^{\omega} ; ([g] ; S)^{\omega} ; [\neg g \cap \neg h)]$

$=$ {homomorphism}

$(([g] ; S)^{\omega} ; [\neg g] ; [h] ; T)^{\omega} ; ([g] ; S)^{\omega} ; [\neg g] ; [\neg h]$

$=$ {leapfrog (Lemma 29.8)}

$([g] ; S)^{\omega} ; [\neg g] ; ([h] ; T ; ([g] ; S)^{\omega} ; [\neg g])^{\omega} ; [\neg h]$

$=$ {rewrite iterations into loops}

while g do S od ; while h do T ; (while g do S od) od

□

Theorem 29.12 may not seem very useful at first sight, but if the inner loop on the right-hand side can be refined by a simple statement, then the right-hand side may be a more efficient loop than that on the left-hand side (it may involve a smaller number of repetitions).

5 Other Loop Transformations

By setting $T = S$ in Theorem 29.12 we immediate get the following rule:

Corollary 29.13 *Assume that statement S is conjunctive. Then*

while $g \cup h$ do S od $=$
  while h do S od ; while g do S ; (while h do S od) od

for arbitrary predicates g and h.

Next, we consider a rule that allows us to remove (or add) a redundant loop:

Theorem 29.14 *Assume that S is monotonic. Then*

while g do S od ; while g do S od $=$ while g do S od .

Furthermore, if S is conjunctive, then

$$\text{while } g \text{ do } S \text{ od} \; = \; \text{while } g \cap h \text{ do } S \text{ od} \,;\, \text{while } g \text{ do } S \text{ od} \,.$$

Proof We have

while g do S od ; while g do S od
= {rewrite loop using iteration}
$([g]\,;\,S)^{\omega}\,;\,[\neg g]\,;\,([g]\,;\,S)^{\omega}\,;\,[\neg g]$
= {unfold iteration}
$([g]\,;\,S)^{\omega}\,;\,[\neg g]\,;\,([g]\,;\,S\,;\,([g]\,;\,S)^{\omega} \sqcap \text{skip})\,;\,[\neg g]$
= {distributivity}
$([g]\,;\,S)^{\omega}\,;\,([\neg g]\,;\,[g]\,;\,S\,;\,([g]\,;\,S)^{\omega} \sqcap [\neg g]\,;\,\text{skip})\,;\,[\neg g]$
= {skip is unit, guard homomorphism}
$([g]\,;\,S)^{\omega}\,;\,([\neg g \cap g]\,;\,S\,;\,([g]\,;\,S)^{\omega} \sqcap [\neg g])\,;\,[\neg g]\,;$
= {guard property}
$([g]\,;\,S)^{\omega}\,;\,(\text{magic}\,;\,S\,;\,([g]\,;\,S)^{\omega} \sqcap [\neg g])\,;\,[\neg g]$
= {magic properties}
$([g]\,;\,S)^{\omega}\,;\,[\neg g]\,;\,[\neg g]$
= {guard property}
$([g]\,;\,S)^{\omega}\,;\,[\neg g]$
= {rewrite into loop}
while g do S od

For the second half, we then have

while g do S od
= {Theorem 29.12 with $h := g \cap h$}
while $g \cap h$ do S od ; while $g \cap h$ do S ; (while $g \cap h$ do S od) od
= {first part of theorem}
while $g \cap h$ do S od ; while $g \cap h$ do S od ;
while g do S ; (while $g \cap h$ do S od) od
= {Theorem 29.12}
while $g \cap h$ do S od ; while g do S od

□

.6 Example: Finding the Period

We finish the chapter with a small case study, developing a program that finds the period of function iteration. Iterating a function f at a value x means constructing a sequence

$$x, \ f.x, \ f^2.x, \ \ldots$$

(recall that $f^0.x = x$ and $f^{n+1}.x = f.(f^n.x)$).

When constructing the iterated sequence, two things can happen. Either the iteration generates new values forever, or else at some point $f^{k+n}.x = f^k.x$ for some k and some $n > 0$. In the latter case the sequence has a *period*.

Now assume that $f : \text{Nat} \to \Sigma$ is a function such that iteration of f from 0 has a period, i.e., assume

$$(\exists k \ n \cdot n > 0 \wedge f^{k+n}.0 = f^k.0) \ . \tag{$*$}$$

The problem is to find the minimal period p and a value x in the period. Using the definition

$$\text{minper}.f.p.x \ \stackrel{\wedge}{=} \ p > 0 \wedge f^p.x = x \wedge (\exists m \cdot x = f^m.0) \wedge$$
$$(\forall n \cdot n > 0 \wedge f^n.x = x \Rightarrow p \leq n)$$

we can specify the problem as the following relational assignment:

$$[x, p := x', p' \mid \text{minper}.f.p'.x'] \ .$$

First Solution

Let us give the name k_0 to the smallest number of iterations that takes us into the period of f:

$$k_0 \ \stackrel{\wedge}{=} \ \min.\{k \mid \exists n \cdot n > 0 \wedge f^{k+n}.0 = f^k.0\} \ .$$

The assumption $(*)$ guarantees that the set is nonempty, so it has a well-defined smallest element (because the natural numbers are well-ordered).

A simple way of finding the period would be to compute the iteration sequence (by executing $x := f.x$ repeatedly, starting from $x = 0$) and at every step compare the new value with all the previous values. When the first repetition is found, we have reached the point where $x = f^{k_0}.0$ and $f^p.x = x$, and we know both the period and a value in the period. However, this solution consumes too much of both time and space, so we want to find a more efficient solution.

We still want to use the idea of executing $x := f.x$ repeatedly, starting with $x = 0$, but without having to store the values generated so far. One way of doing this is to introduce an extra variable y and repeatedly execute $x, y := f.x, f.(f.y)$, starting from $x = 0 \wedge y = f.0$. An informal argument for this is as follows:

(i) When $x = f^{k_0}.0$, we know that y must also be a value inside the period, s y races ahead of x (and since both are then inside the period, y is also be x).

(ii) When we continue, we know that y moves inside the period one step cl to x every time $x, y := f.x, f.(f.y)$ is executed.

This means that when $y = x$, we can be sure that x is inside the period. After we can find the length of the period separately.

The idea described above is the basis for dividing the problem into subproble

$$[x, p := x', p' \mid \text{minper}.f.p'.x']$$
$\sqsubseteq$ {introduce sequential composition}
$$[x := x' \mid (\exists n \cdot \text{minper}.f.n.x')] \,;$$
$$\{\exists n \cdot \text{minper}.f.n.x\} \,;$$
$$[p := p' \mid \text{minper}.f.p'.x]$$
$\sqsubseteq$ {introduce block with local variable}
begin var y : Nat ;
" $[x, y := x', y' \mid (\exists n \cdot \text{minper}.f.n.x')]$ " ;
$\{\exists n \cdot \text{minper}.f.n.x\} \,;$
$[p, y := p', y' \mid \text{minper}.f.p'.x]$
end
$\sqsubseteq$ {introduce sequential composition}
begin var y : Nat ;
$[x, y := x', y' \mid x' = f^{k_0}.0 \wedge (\exists m \mid m > 0 \cdot y' = f^m.x')] \,;$
$\{\text{" } x = f^{k_0}.0 \wedge (\exists m \mid m > 0 \cdot y = f^m.x) \text{ "}\} \,;$
$[x, y := x', y' \mid (\exists n \cdot \text{minper}.f.n.x')] \,;$
$\{\exists n \cdot \text{minper}.f.n.x\} \,;$
$[p, y := p', y' \mid \text{minper}.f.p'.x]$
end
$\sqsubseteq$ {rewrite assertion (Exercise 29.9)}
begin var y : Nat ;
$[x, y := x', y' \mid x' = f^{k_0}.0 \wedge (\exists m \mid m > 0 \cdot y' = f^m.x')] \,;$
$\{x = f^{k_0}.0 \wedge (\exists m \mid m > 0 \cdot y = f^m.x) \wedge (\exists n \cdot x = f^n.y)\} \,;$
$[x, y := x', y' \mid (\exists n \cdot \text{minper}.f.n.x')] \,;$
$\{\exists n \cdot \text{minper}.f.n.x\} \,;$
$[p, y := p', y' \mid \text{minper}.f.p'.x]$
end

Here the first step divides the derivation into two parts: first we find a value x in the period, and then we find the length p of the period. The second step adds the local variable y, and the third step divides finding the right value for x into two parts (in accordance with the argument above): first we make x equal to $f^{k_0}.0$, and then we continue until we can detect that x is in fact within the period. The last step rewrites the assertion from stating that y is ahead of x to stating that y is both ahead of and behind x. This information will be crucial in later loop introductions.

The verification of the two sequential composition introductions and the block introduction is straightforward, so we leave them to the reader.

Introducing Loops

We are now in a position to introduce the repeated assignments to x and y that were announced earlier. We start from the first demonic assignment:

$$[x, y := x', y' \mid x' = f^{k_0}.0 \wedge (\exists m \mid m > 0 \cdot y' = f^m.x')]$$

$\sqsubseteq$ {add initial assignment}

$$x, y := 0, f.0 \,; \{x = 0 \wedge y = f.0\} \,;$$
$$[x, y := x', y' \mid x' = f^{k_0}.0 \wedge (\exists m \mid m > 0 \cdot y' = f^m.x')]$$

$\sqsubseteq$ {introduce loop}

$$x, y := 0, f.0 \,;$$
$$\textbf{while } x \neq f^{k_0}.0 \textbf{ do}$$
$$\qquad [x, y := x', y' \mid x' = f.x \wedge (\exists m \mid m > 0 \cdot y' = f^m.x')]$$
$$\textbf{od}$$

The loop invariant here is $(\exists k \cdot k \leq k_0 \wedge x = f^k.0) \wedge (\exists m \mid m > 0 \cdot y = f^m.x)$, "$x$ has not passed $f^{k_0}.0$, and y is ahead of x". The variant is $k_0 - \min.\{k \mid x = f^k.0\}$, "the number of iterations remaining" (the minimum operator min is discussed in Exercise 29.11). Note that by initializing y to $f.0$ we make sure that y is initially ahead of x. The nondeterminism in the loop body allows y to be updated freely on every iteration, as long as it is "ahead of" x.

Next we can introduce a loop for the second part (an assertion plus a demonic assignment):

$$\{x = f^{k_0}.0 \wedge (\exists m \mid m > 0 \cdot y = f^m.x) \wedge (\exists n \cdot x = f^n.y)\} \,;$$
$$[x, y := x', y' \mid (\exists n \cdot \text{minper}.f.n.x')] \,;$$

$\sqsubseteq$ {introduce loop}

$$\textbf{while } x \neq y \textbf{ do } x, y := f.x, f^2.y \textbf{ od}$$

In this case the loop invariant is $(\exists m \mid m > 0 \cdot y = f^m.x) \wedge (\exists n \cdot x = f^n.y)$, "$y$ is both ahead of and behind x". The variant is $\min.\{m \mid x = f^m.y\}$, the number of iterations remaining.

Finally, we introduce a loop for finding the period once x has its correct value
final combination of an assertion and a demonic assignment):

$\{\exists n \cdot \text{minper}. f.n.x\}$;
$[p, y := p', y' \mid \text{minper}. f.p'.x]$
$\sqsubseteq$ {add initial assignment}
$\quad p, y := 1, f.x$; " $\{p = 1 \land y = f.x \land (\exists n \cdot \text{minper}. f.n.x)\}$;
$\quad [p, y := p', y' \mid \text{minper}. f.p'.x]$ "
$\sqsubseteq$ {introduce loop}
$\cdots$ while $x \neq y$ do $p, y := p + 1, f.y$ od $\cdots$

Here the loop invariant is $(\exists n \cdot \text{minper}. f.n.x \land 0 < p \leq n \land y = f^p.x)$, "$p$
not passed the value of the period". The variant is $\min.\{n \mid n > 0 \land f^n.x = x\}$
the number of iterations remaining.

Loop Introduction Proofs

The second loop introduction is the most interesting one, so we show its proof
some detail. To show that the invariant holds initially, we need to prove

$$x = f^{k_0}.0 \land x \neq y \land (\exists m \mid m > 0 \cdot y = f^m.x) \land (\exists n \cdot x = f^n.y) \Rightarrow$$
$$(\exists m \mid m > 0 \cdot y = f^m.x) \land (\exists n \cdot x = f^n.y) ,$$

which is trivially true. We then show invariance and termination separately.
loop body must preserve the invariant:

$$x \neq y \land (\exists m \mid m > 0 \cdot y = f^m.x) \land (\exists n \cdot x = f^n.y) \Rightarrow$$
$$(\exists m \mid m > 0 \cdot f^2.y = f^{m+1}.x) \land (\exists n \cdot f.x = f^{n+2}.y)$$
$$\equiv \{\text{quantifier rules}\}$$
$$(\forall m\, n \cdot x \neq y \land m > 0 \land y = f^m.x \land x = f^n.y \Rightarrow$$
$$(\exists m \mid m > 0 \cdot f^2.y = f^{m+1}.x) \land (\exists n \cdot f.x = f^{n+2}.y))$$

This is not hard; we choose $m + 1$ and $n - 1$ as existential witnesses (from x
it follows that $n > 0$).

Next, the loop body must decrease the variant:

$$(\forall w \cdot x \neq y \land (\exists m \mid m > 0 \cdot y = f^m.x) \land (\exists n \cdot x = f^n.y) \land$$
$$\min.\{m \mid x = f^m.y\} = w \Rightarrow$$
$$\min.\{m \mid f.x = f^{m+2}.y\} < w)$$
$$\equiv \{\text{quantifier rules}\}$$
$$(\forall m\, n \cdot x \neq y \land m > 0 \land y = f^m.x \land x = f^n.y \Rightarrow$$
$$\min.\{m \mid f.x = f^{m+2}.y\} < \min.\{m \mid x = f^m.y\})$$

Here the argument is that for every element m in $\{m \mid x = f^m.y\}$, the number $m - 1$ must be in $\{m \mid f.x = f^{m+2}.y\}$ (the antecedent implies that 0 is not in $\{m \mid x = f^m.y\}$ and that the sets are nonempty). The full formal proof requires some properties of the min operator (see Exercise 29.11).

Finally, the postcondition must hold on exit:

$$x = y \wedge (\exists m \mid m > 0 \cdot y = f^m.x) \wedge (\exists n \cdot x = f^n.y) \Rightarrow$$
$$(\exists n \cdot \text{minper}.f.n.x) \ .$$

This follows because $(\exists m \mid m > 0 \cdot x = f^m.x)$ implies $(\exists n \cdot \text{minper}.f.n.x)$ (the natural numbers are well-ordered, so the nonempty set of periods at x has a smallest element).

Final Refinements

Collecting the loop introductions, we get the following version of the program:

```
begin var y : Nat ;
    x, y := 0, f.0 ;
    " while x ≠ f^{k₀}.0 do
          [x, y := x', y' | x' = f.x ∧ x' ≠ y' ∧ (∃m · y' = f^m.x')]
      od ;
      while x ≠ y do x, y := f.x, f².y od " ;
      p, y := 1, f.x ;
      while x ≠ y do p, y := p + 1, f.y od
end .
```

There is still a loop guard that mentions the unknown value k_0. However, if the body of that loop can be made the same as the body of the following loop, then we can try to merge the two loops. To do that, we first make the first loop body more deterministic and then use the loop invariant of the first loop to rewrite the guard:

```
while x ≠ f^{k₀}.0 do
    " [x, y := x', y' | x' = f.x ∧ (∃m | m > 0 · y' = f^m.x')] "
od ;
while x ≠ y do x, y := f.x, f².y od
= {make loop body more deterministic}
    while " x ≠ f^{k₀}.0 " do x, y := f.x, f².y od ;
    while x ≠ y do x, y := f.x, f².y od
= {use loop invariant to rewrite guard}
    while x ≠ y ∧ x ≠ f^{k₀}.0 do x, y := f.x, f².y od ;
```

while $x \neq y$ do $x, y := f.x, f^2.y$ od
$= \{$Theorem 29.14$\}$
while $x \neq y$ do $x, y := f.x, f^2.y$ od

When rewriting the guard of the first loop we used the following fact:

$(\exists k \cdot k \leq k_0 \wedge x = f^k.0) \wedge (\exists m \mid m > 0 \cdot y = f^m.x) \wedge x \neq f^{k_0}.0 \Rightarrow x \neq$

i.e., "if x is not yet in the period and y is ahead of x, then $x \neq y$" (Exercise 29.

Thus we have reached the final version of the program; if the sequence $f.0, \; f.1,$ has a period, then

$[x := x' \mid (\exists n \cdot \mathrm{minper}.f.n.x')]$

$\sqsubseteq$

begin var y : Nat ;
$\quad x, y := 0, f.0 ;$
$\quad$ while $x \neq y$ do $x, y := f.x, f^2.y$ od ;
$\quad p, y := 1, f.x ;$
$\quad$ while $x \neq y$ do $p, y := p + 1, f.y$ od
end .

29.7 Summary and Discussion

The properties of conjunctive iterations, as described here, are motivated by sin
efforts by other researchers to handle the leapfrog properties and other related n
The diagonalization lemma and the rolling lemma are "folk theorems'.' The
composition and leapfrog properties have been proved using a fixed-point calc
by Backhouse et al. [34]. Both the decomposition and the leapfrog properties
for regular languages and are essential in applying the algebra of regular langu
to reasoning about programs [124]. Leapfrog rules for loops have been discu
in unpublished notes by Nelson and van de Snepscheut. The problem of findin;
period for the iteration of a function was used as an example of a "nice algorit
by van de Snepscheut [132].

29.8 Exercises

29.1   Prove that if predicate transformer S is conjunctive, then the following holds

$S ; S^* \;=\; S^* ; S .$

Compare this with Exercise 21.2.

29.2 The dual of the fusion theorem guarantees that if h is universally meet homomorphic, then

$$h \circ f = g \circ h \ \Rightarrow \ h.(v.f) = v.g \ .$$

First show that the function $(\lambda S \cdot \{q\} ; S)$ is universally meet homomorphic for an arbitrary predicate q. Then prove $\{\mu.S\} ; S^* = S^* ; \{\mu.S\}$ for conjunctive S (begin by writing the right-hand side as $(v\,X \cdot S ; X \sqcap \{\mu.S\})$).

29.3 Prove that if predicate transformers S and T are monotonic, then the following holds:

$$S ; (T ; S)^* \ \sqsubseteq \ (S ; T)^* ; S \ .$$

29.4 Investigate whether it is possible to use the leapfrog rule for strong iteration to get a refinement rule for loops in the opposite direction from that in Lemma 29.9, i.e., a rule of the form

while g do $S ; T$ od $; S \ \sqsubseteq \ S ;$ while g' do $T ; S$ od $.$

29.5 Show the following rule for an arbitrary monotonic predicate transformer S:

$$S^\omega ; S^\omega \ = \ S^\omega \ .$$

29.6 Prove the following loop elimination rule:

$\{\neg g\} ;$ while g do S od $\ \sqsubseteq \ $ skip $.$

29.7 Prove the following variation on the loop decomposition rule, for conjunctive S and T:

while g do if h then S else T fi od $=$
    while $g \cap h$ do S od $;$ while g do $\{\neg h\} ; T ;$ (while $g \cap h$ do S od) od

(the assertion can be useful in subsequent refinement steps).

29.8 Prove the following general facts about periodicity of function iteration:

$$f^{k+p}.x = f^k.x \ \Rightarrow \ f^{k+2p}.x = f^k.x \ ,$$
$$f^{k+p}.x = f^k.x \ \Rightarrow \ f^{k+m+p}.x = f^{k+m}.x \ .$$

29.9 Prove the following, under assumption $(*)$ and the definition of k_0 given in the text.

$$x = f^{k_0}.0 \wedge (\exists m \mid m > 0 \cdot y = f^m.x) \ \Rightarrow \ (\exists n \cdot x = f^n.y) \ .$$

29.10 Prove the following, under assumption $(*)$ and the definition of k_0 given in the text.

$$(\exists k \cdot k \leq k_0 \wedge x = f^k.0) \wedge (\exists m \mid m > 0 \cdot y = f^m.x) \wedge x \neq f^{k_0}.0 \ \Rightarrow$$
$$x \neq y \ .$$

29.11 Define the minimum operator for sets of natural numbers as follows:

$$\text{min}.A \ \hat{=} \ (\varepsilon n \in A \cdot (\forall m \in A \cdot n \leq m)) \ .$$

Prove the following properties:

$$A \neq \emptyset \Rightarrow (\forall m \in A \cdot \min.A \leq m) \ ,$$
$$A \neq \emptyset \wedge (\forall m \in A \cdot (\exists n \in B \cdot n < m)) \Rightarrow \min.B < \min.A \ .$$

Appendix

Association and Precedence

The association rules for operators are as follows:

- Postfix operators associate to the left, so $S^{\circ\circ}$ means $(S^\circ)^\circ$
- Function application associates to the left, so $f.x.y$ means $(f.x).y$
- Prefix operators associate to the right, so $\neg\neg t$ means $\neg(\neg t)$
- Infix operators associate to the left, so $a - b - c$ means $(a - b) - c$

Generally, the precedences are as follows (where 1 is highest):

1. Postfix operators (written as subscript or superscript)
2. Function application
3. Prefix operators
4. Infix operators (for details, see below)
5. Mixfix operators and binders (scope is indicated by a pair of delimiters)

Infix operators have precedences as follows (where 1 is highest):

1. $\cdot$ / div mod $\times$
2. $+$ $-$ $\rightarrow$
3. $\leq$ $<$ $\geq$ $>$
4. ; $\bullet$ $\circ$ \
5. $\sqcap$ $\cap$

6. ⊔ ∪ ⊔̂

7. :=

8. ⊑ ⊏ ⊆ ⊂

9. = ∈

10. ∧

11. ∨

12. ⇒ ⇐

13. ... ⦃ ... ⦄ ...   ... ⦅ ... ⦆ ...

14. ≡

Negated operators have the same precedence as the original operator.

B: Homomorphism Tables

In these tables we use the following abbreviations for statement constructors:

IfThen $= (\lambda S, S' \cdot$ if g then S else S' fi$)$

If $= (\lambda S_1, \ldots, S_n \cdot$ if $g_1 \to S_1 \;[]\; \cdots \;[]\; g_n \to S_n$ fi$)$

While $= (\lambda S \cdot$ while g do S od$)$

Do $= (\lambda S_1, \ldots, S_n \cdot$ do $g_1 \to S_1 \;[]\; \cdots \;[]\; g_n \to S_n$ od$)$

preserves	⊑	⊥	⊤	⊓	⊔	lim	¬
;	yes	yes	yes	yes	yes	yes	yes
⊓	yes	no	yes	yes	no	yes[1]	no
⊔	yes	yes	no	no	yes	yes	no
lim	yes	yes	no	no	yes	yes	no
IfThen	yes	yes	yes	yes	yes	yes	no
If	yes	yes	no	yes	no	yes	no
μ	yes[2]	yes[2]	no	no	yes[2]	yes[2]	no
ν	yes[2]	no	yes[2]	yes[2]	no	no	no
$(\lambda S \cdot S^\omega)$	yes	yes	no	yes	no	yes	no
$(\lambda S \cdot S^*)$	yes	yes	yes	yes	no	no	no
$(\lambda S \cdot S^\infty)$	yes	yes	no	yes	yes	yes	no
While	yes	yes	no	yes	yes	yes	no
Do	yes	yes	no	yes	no	yes	no

[1] if the meet is finite
[2] when argument is in Mtran$(\Sigma, \Gamma) \to_m$ Mtran(Σ, Γ)

TABLE 29.1. Preservation of homomorphic properties

is	⊑	⊥	⊤	⊓	⊔	lim	¬
$\{p\}$	yes	yes	no	yes	yes	yes	no
$[p]$	yes	no	yes	yes	yes	no	no
$\langle f \rangle$	yes	yes	yes	yes	yes	yes	yes
$\{R\}$	yes	yes	no	no	yes	yes	no
$[R]$	yes	no	yes	yes	no	yes[1]	no

[1]if R is total and image-finite

TABLE 29.2. Homomorphic properties of basic statements

is	⊑	⊥	⊤	⊓	⊔	lim	¬	1	;
$(\lambda p \cdot \{p\})$	yes	yes	no	yes[1]	yes	yes	no	yes	yes
$(\lambda p \cdot [p])$	yes°	yes°	no	yes°[1]	yes°	yes°	no	yes	yes
$(\lambda f \cdot \langle f \rangle)$	yes	-	-	-	-	-	-	yes	yes
$(\lambda R \cdot \{R\})$	yes	yes	no	no	yes	yes	no	yes	yes
$(\lambda R \cdot [R])$	yes°	yes°	no	no	yes°	yes°	no	yes	yes
$(\lambda S \cdot S ; T)$	yes	yes	yes	yes	yes	yes	yes	no	no
$(\lambda T \cdot S ; T)$	yes	yes[2]	yes[3]	yes[4]	yes[5]	yes[6]	yes[7]	no	no
$(\lambda S, T \cdot S ; T)$	yes	yes	yes	no	no	no	no	no	no
$(\lambda S \cdot S \sqcap T)$	yes	yes	no	yes	yes	yes	no	no	no
$(\lambda S, T \cdot S \sqcap T)$	yes	yes	yes	yes	no	no	no	no	yes°
$(\lambda S \cdot S \sqcup T)$	yes	no	yes	yes	yes	yes	no	no	no
$(\lambda S, T \cdot S \sqcup T)$	yes	yes	yes	no	yes	yes	no	no	yes°
$(\lambda S \cdot \neg S)$	yes°	yes°	yes°	yes°	yes°	yes°	yes	no	no
$(\lambda S \cdot S°)$	yes°	yes°	yes°	yes°	yes°	yes°	yes	yes	yes
$(\lambda S \cdot S^*)$	yes	yes	no	no	no	no	no	yes	no
$(\lambda S \cdot S^\omega)$	yes	yes	no	no	no	no	no	no	no
$(\lambda S \cdot S^\infty)$	yes	yes	no	no	no	no	no	no	no
IfThen	yes	yes	yes	no	no	no	no	no	no
If	yes	yes	no	no	no	no	no	no	no
While	yes	no	no	no	no	no	no	no	no
Do	yes	no	no	no	no	no	no	no	no

[1]when the meet is taken over nonempty sets   [2]if S is strict   [3]if S is terminating
[4]if S is conjunctive   [5]if S is disjunctive   [6]if S is continuous   [7]if S is ¬-homomorphic

TABLE 29.3. Homomorphic properties of predicate transformers

For each operation on the left, the entry indicates whether the construct preserves (or has) the homomorphism property indicated in the column: ⊑ (monotonicity); ⊥ (bottom), ⊤ (top), ⊓ (meet), ⊔ (join), and ¬ (negation). Duality (yes°) indicates that the property holds for the dual lattice.

eferences

[1]M. Abadi, L. Lamport, and P. Wolper. Realizable and unrealizable specifications of reactive systems. In G. Ausiello et al., editor, *Proc. 16th ICALP*, 1–17, Stresa, Italy, 1989. Springer-Verlag.

[2]P. Aczel. Quantifiers, games and inductive definitions. In *Proc. 3rd Scandinavian Logic Symposium*. North-Holland, 1975.

[3]P.B. Andrews. *An Introduction to Mathematical Logic and Type Theory: To Truth through Proof*. Academic Press, 1986.

[4]K.R. Apt. Ten years of Hoare's logic: A survey — part 1. *ACM Transactions on Programming Languages and Systems*, 3:431–483, 1981.

[5]K.R. Apt and G.D. Plotkin. Countable nondeterminism and random assignment. *Journal of the ACM*, 33(4):724–767, October 1986.

[6]R.J. Back. On the correctness of refinement in program development. Ph.D. thesis, Report A-1978-4, Department of Computer Science, University of Helsinki, 1978.

[7]R.J. Back. *Correctness Preserving Program Refinements: Proof Theory and Applications*, volume 131 of *Mathematical Centre Tracts*. Mathematical Centre, Amsterdam, 1980.

[8]R.J. Back. Semantics of unbounded non-determinism. *Proc. 7th Colloqium on Automata, Languages and Programming (ICALP)*, volume 85 of *Lecture Notes in Computer Science*, 51–63. Springer-Verlag, 1980.

[9]R.J. Back. On correct refinement of programs. *Journal of Computer and Systems Sciences*, 23(1):49–68, August 1981.

[10]R.J. Back. Proving total correctness of nondeterministic programs in infinitary logic. *Acta Informatica*, 15:233–250, 1981.

[11]R.J. Back. Procedural abstraction in the refinement calculus. Reports on computer science and mathematics 55, Åbo Akademi, 1987.

[12]R.J. Back. A calculus of refinements for program derivations. *Acta Informatica*, 25:593–624, 1988.

[13]R.J. Back. Changing data representation in the refinement calculus. In *21st Ha* *International Conference on System Sciences*, January 1989.

[14]R.J. Back. Refinement calculus, part II: Parallel and reactive programs. In *REX W* *shop for Refinement of Distributed Systems*, volume 430 of *Lecture Notes in Comp* *Science*, Nijmegen, the Netherlands, 1989. Springer-Verlag.

[15]R.J. Back. Refining atomicity in parallel algorithms. In *PARLE Conference on* *allel Architectures and Languages Europe*, Eindhoven, the Netherlands, June 1 Springer-Verlag.

[16]R.J. Back. Refinement diagrams. In J.M. Morris and R.C.F. Shaw, editors, *F* *4th Refinement Workshop*, Workshops in Computer Science, 125–137, Cambri England, 9–11 Jan. 1991. Springer-Verlag.

[17]R.J. Back. Atomicity refinement in a refinement calculus framework. Report computer science and mathematics 141, Åbo Akademi, 1992.

[18]R.J. Back. Refinement calculus, lattices and higher order logic. Technical re Marktoberdorf Summer School on Programming Logics, 1992.

[19]R.J. Back and M.J. Butler. Exploring summation and product operations in the re ment calculus. In *Mathematics of Program Construction*, volume 947 of *Lecture N* *in Computer Science*, 128–158, Kloster Irsee, Germany, July 1995. Springer-Ve

[20]R.J. Back and R. Kurki-Suonio. Distributed co-operation with action systems. *A* *Transactions on Programming Languages and Systems*, 10:513–554, October 1

[21]R.J. Back, A. Martin, and K. Sere. Specifying the Caltech asynchronous micro cessor. *Science of Computer Programming*, 26:79–97, 1996.

[22]R.J. Back and K. Sere. Stepwise refinement of action systems. In *Mathematics of* *gram Construction*, volume 375 of *Lecture Notes in Computer Science*, Gronin the Netherlands, June 1989. Springer-Verlag.

[23]R.J. Back and K. Sere. Stepwise refinement of parallel algorithms. *Scienc* *Computer Programming*, 13:133–180, 1990.

[24]R.J. Back and K. Sere. Stepwise refinement of action systems. *Struct* *Programming*, 12:17–30, 1991.

[25]R.J. Back and J. von Wright. Duality in specification languages: a lattice-theore approach. Reports on computer science and mathematics 77, Åbo Akademi, 19

[26]R.J. Back and J. von Wright. A lattice-theoretical basis for a specification langu In *Mathematics of Program Construction*, volume 375 of *Lecture Notes in Comp* *Science*, Groningen, the Netherlands, June 1989. Springer-Verlag.

[27]R.J. Back and J. von Wright. Duality in specification languages: a lattice-theore approach. *Acta Informatica*, 27:583–625, 1990.

[28]R.J. Back and J. von Wright. Refinement concepts formalised in higher-order l *Formal Aspects of Computing*, 2:247–272, 1990.

[29]R.J. Back and J. von Wright. Combining angels, demons and miracles in pro specifications. *Theoretical Computer Science*, 100:365–383, 1992.

[30]R.J. Back and J. von Wright. Predicate transformers and higher order logic. In J.V Bakker, W-P. de Roever, and G. Rozenberg, editors, *REX Workshop on Semar* *Foundations and Applications*, *LNCS 666*, 1–20, Beekbergen, the Netherlands, 1992. Springer-Verlag.

[31]R.J. Back and J. von Wright. Trace refinement of action systems. In B. Jonsson and J. Parrow, editors, *Proc. CONCUR-94*, Volume 836 of *Lecture Notes in Computer Science*, Uppsala, Sweden, 1994. Springer-Verlag.

[32]R.J. Back and J. von Wright. Games and winning strategies. *Information Processing Letters*, 53(3):165–172, February 1995.

[33]R. Backhouse and B. Carré. Regular algebra applied to path finding problems. *J. Inst. Math. Appl.*, 15:161–186, 1975.

[34]R. Backhouse et al. Fixpoint calculus. *Information Processing Letters*, 53(3), February 1995.

[35]J.W. de Bakker. Semantics and termination of nondeterministic programs. In S. Michaelson and R. Milner, editors, *Proc. 3th International Colloqium on Automata, Languages and of Programming*, 435–477, Edinburgh, Scotland, July 1976. Edinburgh University Press.

[36]J.W. de Bakker. *Mathematical Theory of Program Correctness*. Prentice-Hall, 1980.

[37]H. Barendregt. *The Lambda calculus: Its Syntax and Semantics*. North-Holland, 1984.

[38]M. Barr and C. Wells. *Category Theory for Computing Science*. Prentice-Hall, 1990.

[39]E. Best. Notes on predicate transformers and concurrent programs. Technical Report 145, University of Newcastle Computing Laboratory, 1980.

[40]G. Birkhoff. *Lattice Theory*. American Mathematical Society, Providence, 1961.

[41]H.J. Boom. A weaker precondition for loops. *ACM Transactions on Programming Languages and Systems*, 4(4):668–677, October 1982.

[42]M. Broy. A theory for nondeterminism, parallellism, communications and concurrency. *Theoretical Computer Science*, 46:1–61, 1986.

[43]R.M. Burstall and J. Darlington. Some transformations for developing recursive programs. *Journal of the ACM*, 24(1):44–67, 1977.

[44]M.J. Butler. *A CSP Approach to Action Systems*. Ph.D. thesis, Oxford University, Oxford, England, 1992.

[45]M.J. Butler, J. Grundy, T. Långbacka, R. Rukšėnas, and J. von Wright. The Refinement Calculator: Proof support for Program refinement. *Proc. Formal Methods Pacific (FMP'97)*, Wellington, New Zealand. Springer Series in Discrete Mathematics and Theoretical Computer Science, 1997.

[46]M.J. Butler and C.C. Morgan. Action systems, unbounded nondeterminism and infinite traces. *Formal Aspects of Computing*, 7(1):37–53, 1995.

[47]D. Carrington, I.J. Hayes, R. Nickson, G. Watson, and J. Welsh. Refinement in Ergo. Technical Report 94-44, Department of Computer Science, University of Queensland, QLD 4072, Australia, Dec. 1994.

[48]A. Church. A formulation of the simple theory of types. *Journal of Symbolic Logic*, 5:56–68, 1940.

[49]T. Coquand and G. Huet. The Calculus of Constructions. *Information and Computation*, 76:95–120, 1988.

[50]B.A. Davey and H.A. Priestley. *Introduction to Lattices and Order*. Cambridge University Press, 1990.

[51]E.W. Dijkstra. Notes on structured programming. In O. Dahl, E.W. Dijkstra, and C.A.R. Hoare, editors, *Structured Programming*. Academic Press, 1971.

[52]E.W. Dijkstra. Guarded commands, nondeterminacy and the formal derivation of programs. *Communications of the ACM*, 18:453–457, 1975.

[53]E.W. Dijkstra. *A Discipline of Programming*. Prentice-Hall International, 1976.

[54]E.W. Dijkstra and C.S. Scholten. *Predicate Calculus and Program Seman* Springer-Verlag, 1990.

[55]E.W. Dijkstra and A.J.M. van Gasteren. A simple fixpoint argument without restriction to continuity. *Acta Informatica*, 23:1–7, 1986.

[56]R. Floyd. Assigning meanings to programs. *Proc. 19th ACM Symp. on App Mathematics*, 19–32, 1967.

[57]P.H. Gardiner and O. de Moer. An algebraic construction of predicate transform In *Mathematics of Program Construction*, volume 669 of *Lecture Notes in Comp Science*. Springer-Verlag, 1992.

[58]P.H. Gardiner, C. Martin, and O. de Moer. An algebraic construction of predi transformers. *Science of Computer Programming*, 22:21–44, 1994.

[59]P.H. Gardiner and C.C. Morgan. Data refinement of predicate transform *Theoretical Computer Science*, 87(1):143–162, 1991.

[60]A.J.M. van Gasteren. *On the Shape of Mathematical Arguments*. Volume 44 Lecture Notes in Computer Science. Springer-Verlag, Berlin, 1990.

[61]S.L. Gerhart. Correctness preserving program transformations. *Proc. 2nd A Conference on Principles of Programming Languages*, 1975.

[62]M.J.C. Gordon and T.F. Melham. *Introduction to HOL*. Cambridge University P New York, 1993.

[63]G. Grätzer. *General Lattice Theory*. Birkhäuser Verlag, Basel, 1978.

[64]D. Gries. *The Science of Programming*. Springer-Verlag, New York, 1981.

[65]D. Gries and D. Levin. Assignment and procedure call proof rules. *ACM Transac on Programming Languages and Systems*, 2(4):564–579, 1980.

[66]D. Gries and F. Schneider. *A Logical Introduction to Discrete Mathematics*. Sprir Verlag, 1993.

[67]L. Groves and R. Nickson. A tactic driven refinement tool. In C.B. Jones et al., ed *Proc. 5th Refinement Workshop*, London, Jan. 1992. Springer-Verlag.

[68]J. Grundy. A window inference tool for refinement. In C.B. Jones et al., editors, *5th Refinement Workshop*, London, Jan. 1992. Springer-Verlag.

[69]J. Grundy. Transformational Hierarchical Reasoning. *The Computer Jou 39(4):291–302, 1996.

[70]J. Grundy and T. Långbacka. Recording HOL proofs in a structured browsable fo Technical Report 7, Turku Center for Computer Science, 1996.

[71]P. Guerreiro. Another characterization of weakest preconditions. In volume 1. *Lecture Notes in Computer Science*. Springer-Verlag, 1982.

[72]D. Harel. And/or programs: A new approach to structured programming. *Transactions on Programming Languages and Systems*, 2(1):1–17, 1980.

[73]J. Harrison. Inductive definitions: automation and application. In P. Windley, T. S bert, and J. Alves-Foss, editors, *Higher Order Logic Theorem Proving and Its A cations: Proc. 8th International Workshop*, volume 971 of *Lecture Notes in Com Science*, 200–213, Aspen Grove, Utah, USA, September 1995. Springer-Verlag

[74]E. Hehner. **do** considered **od**: A contribution to the programming calculus. *Informatica*, 11:287–304, 1979.

[75]E. Hehner. *The Logic of Programming*. Prentice-Hall, 1984.

[76]E. Hehner. Predicative programming, part I. *Communications of the ACM*, 27(2):134–143, 1984.

[77]W.H. Hesselink. An algebraic calculus of commands. Report CS 8808, Department of Mathematics and Computer Science, University of Groningen, 1988.

[78]W.H. Hesselink. Interpretations of recursion under unbounded nondeterminacy. *Theoretical Computer Science*, 59:211–234, 1988.

[79]W.H. Hesselink. Predicate-transformer semantics of general recursion. *Acta Informatica*, 26:309–332, 1989.

[80]W.H. Hesselink. Command algebras, recursion and program transformation. *Formal Aspects of Computing*, 2:60–104, 1990.

[81]W.H. Hesselink. *Programs, Recursion and Unbounded Choice*. Cambridge University Press, 1992.

[82]W.H. Hesselink. Nondeterminism and recursion via stacks and games. *Theoretical Computer Science*, 124:273–295, 1994.

[83]J. Hintikka. *Language Games and information*. Clarendon, London, 1972.

[84]C.A.R. Hoare. An axiomatic basis for computer programming. *Communications of the ACM*, 12(10):576–583, 1969.

[85]C.A.R. Hoare. Procedures and parameters: An axiomatic approach. In E. Engeler, editor, *Symposium on Semantics of Algorithmic Languages*, volume 188 of *Lecture Notes in Mathematics*, 102–116. Springer-Verlag, 1971.

[86]C.A.R. Hoare. Proof of a program: Find. *Communications of the ACM*, 14:39–45, 1971.

[87]C.A.R. Hoare. Proofs of correctness of data representation. *Acta Informatica*, 1(4):271–281, 1972.

[88]C.A.R. Hoare. *Communicating Sequential Processes*. Prentice-Hall, 1985.

[89]C.A.R. Hoare. Programs are predicates. In C.A.R. Hoare and J. Shepherdson, editors, *Mathematical Logic and Programming Languages*, 141–155. Prentice-Hall, 1985.

[90]C.A.R. Hoare, I.J. Hayes, J. He, C.C. Morgan, A.W. Roscoe, J.W. Sanders, I.H. Sorensen, J.M. Spivey, and A. Sufrin. Laws of programming. *Communications of the ACM*, 30(8):672–686, August 1987.

[91]C.A.R. Hoare and J. He. The weakest prespecification. *Information Processing Letters*, 24:127–132, 1987.

[92]D. Jacobs and D. Gries. General correctness: A unification of partial and total correctness. *Acta Informatica*, 22:67–83, 1985.

[93]P.T. Johnstone. *Notes on logic and set theory*. Cambridge University Press, 1987.

[94]C.B. Jones. *Systematic Software Development Using VDM*. Prentice–Hall International, 1986.

[95]C.R. Karp. *Languages with Expressions of Infinite Length*. North-Holland, 1964.

[96]D. Knuth. *The Art of Computer Programming: Fundamental Algorithms*. Addison-Wesley, 1973.

[97]T. Långbacka, R. Rukšėnas, and J. von Wright. TkWinHOL: A tool for doing window inference in HOL. *Proc. 1995 International Workshop on Higher Order Logic Theorem Proving and its Applications*, Salt Lake City, Utah, USA. Volume 971 of *Lecture Notes in Computer Science*, Springer-Verlag, 1995.

[98]C.E. Martin. *Preordered Categories and Predicate Transformers*. Ph.D. the Oxford University, 1991.

[99]P. Martin-Löf. A theory of types. Techn. Rep. 71-3, University of Stockholm, 1!

[100]R. Milner. The Standard ML core language. Internal Report CSR-168-84, Univer of Edinburgh, 1984.

[101]R. Milner. *Communication and Concurrency*. Prentice-Hall, 1989.

[102]C.C. Morgan. Data refinement by miracles. *Information Processing Letters*, 26:2 246, January 1988.

[103]C.C. Morgan. Procedures, parameters and abstraction: separate concerns. *Scienc Computer Programming*, 11:27, 1988.

[104]C.C. Morgan. The specification statement. *ACM Transactions on Programm Languages and Systems*, 10(3):403–419, July 1988.

[105]C.C. Morgan. Types and invariants in the refinement calculus. In *Mathematics of I gram Construction*, volume 375 of *Lecture Notes in Computer Science*, Gronin; the Netherlands, June 1989. Springer-Verlag.

[106]C.C. Morgan. *Programming from Specifications*. Prentice-Hall, 1990.

[107]C.C. Morgan. The cuppest capjunctive capping. In A.W. Roscoe, editor, *A Class Mind: Essays in Honour of C.A.R. Hoare*. Prentice-Hall, 1994.

[108]J.M. Morris. A theoretical basis for stepwise refinement and the programm calculus. *Science of Computer Programming*, 9:287–306, 1987.

[109]Y.N. Moschovakis. The game quantifier. *Proceedings of the American Mathema Society*, 31(1):245–250, January 1972.

[110]Y.N. Moschovakis. A model of concurrency with fair merge and full recurs *Information and Computation*, 114–171, 1991.

[111]D.A. Naumann. Predicate transformer semantics of an Oberon-like language. Ir R. Olderog, editor, *Programming Concepts, Methods and Calculi*, 460–480, Miniato, Italy, 1994. IFIP.

[112]D.A. Naumann. *Two-Categories and Program Structure: Data Types, Refiner Calculi and Predicate Transformers*. Ph.D. thesis, University of Texas at Au 1992.

[113]G. Nelson. A generalization of Dijkstra's calculus. *ACM Transactions on Progr ming Languages and Systems*, 11(4):517–562, October 1989.

[114]D. Park. On the semantics of fair parallelism. In volume 86 of *Lecture Note Computer Science*, 504–526, Berlin, 1980. Springer-Verlag.

[115]L.C. Paulson. *Logic and Computation*. Cambridge University Press, 1987.

[116]B.C. Pierce. *Basic Category Theory for Computer Scientists*. MIT Press, 1991.

[117]J. Plosila and K. Sere. Action systems in pipelined processor design. In *Proc International Symposium on Advanced Research in Asynchronous Circuits and tems (Async97)*, Eindhoven, the Netherlands, April 1997. IEEE Computer So Press.

[118]G.D. Plotkin. A power-domain construction. *SIAM Journal of Computing*, 5(3):- 487, 1976.

[119]G.D. Plotkin. Dijkstra's weakest preconditions and Smyth's powerdomains. In stract Software Specifications, volume 86 of *Lecture Notes in Computer Sci* Springer-Verlag, June 1979.

[120]G.D. Plotkin. A structural approach to operational semantics. DAIMI FN 19, Computer Science Dept., Aarhus University, April 1981.

[121]J.C. Reynolds. *The Craft of Programming*. Prentice-Hall, 1981.

[122]P.J. Robinson and J. Staples. Formalising a hierarchical structure of practical mathematical reasoning. *Journal of Logic and Computation*, 3(1):47–61, 1993.

[123]W.-P. de Roever. Dijkstra's predicate transformer, non-determinism, recursion and termination. In *Mathematical Foundations of Computer Science*, volume 45 of *Lecture Notes in Computer Science*, 472–481. Springer-Verlag, 1976.

[124]S. Rönn. *On the Regularity Calculus and its Role in Distributed Programming*. Ph.D. thesis, Helsinki University of technology, Helsinki, Finland, 1992.

[125]D. Schmidt. *Denotational Semantics: Methodology for Language Development*. Allyn and Bacon, 1986.

[126]D.S. Scott. Data types as lattices. *SIAM Journal of Computing*, 5:522–587, 1976.

[127]D.S. Scott. Logic with denumerably long formulas and finite strings of quantifiers. In *Symp. on the Theory of Models*, 329–341. North-Holland, 1965.

[128]D.S. Scott and C. Strachey. Towards a mathematical semantics for computer languages. Tech. monograph PRG-6, Programming Research Group, University of Oxford, 1971.

[129]E. Sekerinski. A type-theoretic basis for an object-oriented refinement calculus. In S. Goldsack and S. Kent, editors, *Formal Methods and Object Technology*. Springer-Verlag, 1996.

[130]M.B. Smyth. Powerdomains. *Journal of Computer and Systems Sciences*, 16:23–36, 1978.

[131]J.L.A. van de Snepscheut. Proxac: An editor for program transformation. Technical Report CS-TR-93-33, Caltech, Pasadena, California, USA, 1993.

[132]J.L.A. van de Snepscheut. *What Computing is All About*. Springer-Verlag, 1994.

[133]J.M. Spivey. *The Z Notation*. Prentice-Hall International, 1989.

[134]J. Stoy. *Denotational Semantics*. Prentice-Hall International, 1976.

[135]A. Tarski. On the calculus of relations. *J. Symbolic Logic*, 6:73–89, 1941.

[136]A. Tarski. A lattice theoretical fixed point theorem and its applications. *Pacific J. Mathematics*, 5:285–309, 1955.

[137]R.D. Tennent. The denotational semantics of programming languages. *Communications of the ACM*, 19:437–452, 1976.

[138]M. Utting and K. Robinson. Modular reasoning in an object-oriented refinement calculus. In R. Bird, C.C. Morgan, and J. Woodcock, editors, *Mathematics of Program Construction*, volume 669 of *Lecture Notes in Computer Science*, 344–367. Springer-Verlag, 1993.

[139]N. Ward and I.J. Hayes. Applications of angelic nondeterminism. In P.A.C. Bailes, editor, *Proc. 6th Australian Software Engineering Conference*, 391–404, Sydney, Australia, 1991.

[140]A. Whitehead and B. Russell. *Principia Mathematica*. Cambridge University Press, 1927.

[141]N. Wirth. Program development by stepwise refinement. *Communications of the ACM*, 14:221–227, 1971.

[142] J. von Wright. Program inversion in the refinement calculus. *Information Proces Letters*, 37(2):95–100, January 1991.

[143] J. von Wright. The lattice of data refinement. *Acta Informatica*, 31:105–135, 19

[144] J. von Wright. Program refinement by theorem prover. In *Proc. 6th Refinen Workshop*, London, January 1994. Springer-Verlag.